Business Int[...] Model

# Applied Microsoft SQL Server 2012 Analysis Services

## Tabular Modeling

**Teo Lachev**

**Prologika Press**

# Applied Microsoft SQL Server 2012 Analysis Services
## Tabular Modeling

Published by:
**Prologika Press**
*info@prologika.com*
*http://www.prologika.com*



Printed in the United States of America

| | |
|---|---|
| ISBN 13, print edition | 978-0-9766353-5-2 |
| ISBN 10, print edition | 0-9766353-5-6 |
| First printing | 2012 |

| | |
|---|---|
| Author: | Teo Lachev |
| Editor: | Edward Price |
| Technical Reviewers: | Burzin Mehernosh Daruwalla |
| | Greg Galloway |
| | Jen Underwood |
| | Norma O'Harra |
| Cover Designer: | Zamir Creations |

---

The manuscript of this book was prepared using Microsoft Word 2010. Screenshots were captured using TechSmith SnagIt 10.0. The video demos were captured using TechSmith Camtasia Studio 7.1.

# contents

# preface

At SQL Pass 2010 in November 2010, Microsoft announced that in the forthcoming release of SQL Server, PowerPivot has been extended with features for organizational BI under a new name – Business Intelligence Semantic Model (BISM). This news took many BI professionals, including your humble correspondent, by surprise. Prior to PASS, Microsoft disclosed that organizational business intelligence (BI) would be a major focus in Denali, which I interpreted to mean that they'd add enhancements to multidimensional cubes, only to find out that all the buzz was about PowerPivot and BISM.

I have to admit that I was disappointed at first. I felt that Microsoft was shifting their focus in the wrong direction. Not surprisingly, there was a plenty of negativity from influencers and the community. Some pronounced UDM dead. Others sneered at BISM as a toy. To its credit, Microsoft was quick to cover the collateral damage and to clarify the BISM positioning. They made it clear that BISM doesn't intend to replace OLAP and multidimensional cubes. Later, at TechEd North America 2011 in Atlanta, Microsoft rebranded BISM as an umbrella name for both the multidimensional (Multidimensional) and tabular (Tabular) paths to further reinforce this message.

So, how did I convert from a Tabular critic to its aficionado and decided to write a book about it? During the year after PASS, I've exchanged plenty of e-mails with the product groups and Microsoft was patient enough to listen to me and address my concerns. Their answers helped me to "get it" and see the big picture through more optimistic lenses. Tabular is essentially a fresh start for Microsoft in the BI space. It has a great potential because it aims to simplify OLAP, and it makes BI even more accessible – "to the masses, by the masses", as the popular Microsoft slogan goes. Its elegancy and versatility open new opportunities outside the core OLAP model, especially in the area of personal BI and team BI.

At the same time, however, I think that Microsoft got overexcited with Tabular and tilted too fast toward. They were missing the required balance at the expense of Multidimensional. Multidimensional has a very large install base, and it's still the preferred choice for data warehousing and OLAP. I personally believe that the Tabular journey will be evolutionary and that the market will decide the adoption pace.

This book attempts to restore that balance. I worked closely with Microsoft's Analysis Services team to provide an authoritative (yet independent) view of this technology to help you understand where and how to use it. Over the past two years, I've gathered plenty of real-life experience from BI solutions that used PowerPivot in one form or another. I've taught private and public classes and presented Tabular at conferences and local community chapters.

I decided to write this book to share with you the knowledge I harvested from my work with Tabular and to help you use it appropriately and efficiently. As its name suggests, the main objective of *Applied Microsoft SQL Server 2012 Analysis Services (Tabular Modeling)* it so to teach you the practical skills to implement Tabular-centric solutions for personal, team, and organizational BI.

Although this book is designed as a comprehensive guide to this technology, it's likely that you might have further questions or comments. As with my previous books, I am committed to help my readers with book-related questions via the book discussion forums on my company's web site, www.prologika.com. Happy modeling with Tabular!

*Teo Lachev*
*Atlanta, GA*

# *acknowledgements*

Another SQL Server release and yet another book! Writing this one has been a lot of fun and a lot of work. It would not have been a reality without the help of many people to whom I am thankful. First and foremost, I'd like to thank my family for their ongoing support. They had to tolerate my long absence and put up with more than they had to. To my family I owe my greatest thanks.

Here is how my 8-year old son, Martin, and 11-year old daughter, Maya, portrait their absent father during his book writing project.

As an MVP, I've been privileged to enjoy close relationships with the SQL Server product groups. If it wasn't for their support, this book wouldn't have been a reality. Not only did they not mind my constant pestering and nagging, but they were even more eager to help me understand the "dark side" of Tabular! Akshai Mirchandani, Amir Netz, Ashvini Sharma, Cathy Dumas, Dave Wickert, Denny Lee, Edward Melomed, Jeffrey Wang, Julie Strauss, Kasper de Jonge, Marius Dumitru, Thomas Keiser, and T.K. Anand have contributed plenty of their time to educate me. The "insiders" lists rock! Special thanks to Akshai Mirchandani, Cathy Dumas, and Nickolai Medveditskov, for reviewing parts of the book and for helping ensure that it's technically accurate.

Writing a technical book while the product is still in development is like trying to hit a moving target because the product is constantly changing. Kudos to my technical reviewers, Burzin Mehernosh Daruwalla, Greg Galloway, Jen Underwood, and Norma O'Harra, for meticulously reviewing the manuscript and for proving feedback on how to improve it.

Thanks to my editor, Ed Price, from the SQL Server User Education team, for not losing faith that my incoherent readings could turn into something readable. Thank you for taking an extra mile and going beyond just checking the grammar. Your commitment and work was outstanding!

Finally, thank *you* for purchasing this book! I sincerely hope that you'll find it as enjoyable to read as it has been for me to write!

# about the book

The book doesn't assume any prior experience with Microsoft Analysis Services or PowerPivot. It's designed as an easy-to-follow guide for navigating the personal-team-organizational BI continuum with Tabular. It starts by introducing you to the Microsoft BI platform and to the Business Intelligence Semantic Model (BISM). You need to know that each chapter builds upon the previous ones, to introduce new concepts and to extend the sample Adventure Works model that you'll implement in the exercises. Therefore, I'd recommend you read the chapters and do the exercises in the order they appear in the book.

Part 1, *Personal Business Intelligence*, teaches business users how to implement personal BI models with PowerPivot. Chapter 2, *Personal BI Basics*, lays out the foundation of personal BI, and it provides the necessary technical background to understand PowerPivot models. In Chapter 3, *Importing the Data*, you'll witness the impressive data acquisition capabilities of PowerPivot. In Chapter 4, *Refining the Model*, you'll explore and enhance the raw model to make it suitable for reporting. Chapter 5, *Analyzing Data*, shows you how to build interactive Excel pivot reports to gain data insights. And, in Chapter 6, *Implementing Calculations*, you'll further extend the model with useful business calculations.

Part 2, *Team Business Intelligence*, teaches business users and IT professionals how to take advantage of the SharePoint document management and collaboration features to share PowerPivot models with other team members. Chapter 7, *Team BI Basics*, introduces you to the SharePoint Products and Technologies and teaches you how to install and configure PowerPivot for SharePoint. Written for business users, Chapter 8, *SharePoint Insights*, walks you through the steps for authoring interactive and operational reports. In Chapter 9, *Managing PowerPivot for SharePoint*, IT administrators will learn how to manage published models, configure data refresh, secure user access, and monitor the server utilization and PowerPivot activity.

Part 3, *Organizational Business Intelligence*, shows BI pros how to bring tabular models to the enterprise. Chapter 10, *Organizational BI Basics*, introduces you to organizational BI and shows you different ways to implement tabular models. In Chapter 11, *Designing Storage and Security*, you'll learn how to extend your models with scalability, security, and low-latency features. In Chapter 12, *Managing Tabular Models*, you'll wear administrator hats and learn how to manage deployed models and how to perform common management tasks, including backing up databases, scripting objects, deploying changes, automating and programming management jobs.

# source code

*Applied Microsoft SQL Server 2012 Analysis Services* demonstrates the full capabilities of Tabular for implementing personal, team, and organizational BI models. This requires installing and configuring various software products and technologies. **Table 1** lists the main software that you need for all the exercises in the book. Depending on your computer setup, you might need to download and install other components, as I explain throughout the book.

**Table 1 The complete software requirements for practices and code samples in the book**

| Software | Required | Purpose | Chapters |
|---|---|---|---|
| Excel 2010 with PowerPivot for Excel | Yes | Implementing personal BI models. | 2, 3, 4, 5, 6 |
| SharePoint Server 2010 Enterprise with Reporting Services and PowerPivot for SharePoint | Yes | Implementing team BI models | 7, 8, 9 |
| Analysis Services Tabular with SQL Server Developer Tools Developer, Business Intelligence, or Enterprise edition | Yes | Implementing organizational BI models | 10, 11, 12 |
| SQL Server Database Engine Developer, Standard, or Enterprise 2008 R2 or later with the AdventureWorksDW2008R2 database | Yes | Importing and processing data | All |
| Analysis Services Multidimensional Developer, Standard, or Enterprise 2008 or later with the Adventure Works DW 2008 cube | No | Importing multidimensional data | 3 |
| Reporting Services Developer, Standard, or Enterprise 2008 R2 or later | No | Importing report feeds | 3 |
| Visual Studio 2010 Professional | No | Implement C# console application | 12 |

Although the list is long, don't despair! The book includes step-by-step instructions for installing the first three software prerequisites, PowerPivot for Excel, PowerPivot for SharePoint, and Analysis Services in Tabular mode, in Chapters 2, 7, and 10 respectively. The book also provides alternative steps to complete the exercises if you don't install Analysis Services and Reporting Services.

You can download the book source code from the book page at http://bit.ly/thebismbook. After downloading the zip file, extract it to any folder of your hard drive. Once this is done, you'll see a folder for each chapter that contains the source code for that chapter. The source code in each folder includes the changes you need to make in the exercises in the corresponding chapter, plus any supporting files required for the exercises. For example, the Adventure Works.xlsx workbook in the Ch03 folder includes the changes that you'll make during the Chapter 3 practices and includes additional files for importing data. Save your files under different names or in different folders in order to avoid overwriting the files that are included in the source code.

The source code was tested with the Release Candidate 0 (RC0) build of SQL Server 2012 which was released in November 2011. Microsoft announced that this is a production-ready and feature-complete build.

**NOTE** The data source settings of the sample models in this book have connection strings to databases and text files. If you decide to test the finished samples, you need to update all the data sources to reflect your specific setup. To do so, open the Adventure Works workbook in Excel, click the PowerPivot ribbon tab (you must have PowerPivot for Excel installed first), and then click the PowerPivot Window button. In the PowerPivot window (Design tab), click the Existing Connections button. Click each connection, and then click Edit. In the Edit Connection dialog box, change the connection settings as needed.

***Installing the Adventure Works databases***

Most of the code samples use the AdventureWorksDW2008R2 database. This is the R2 build of a Microsoft-provided sample database that simulates a data warehouse. The Product Catalog 2008 report in Chapter 3 also uses the AdventureWorks2008R2 database. However, if you don't have the AdventureWorks2008R2 database or Reporting Services, you can still follow this book because I provide alternative steps to import the required data from the data warehouse database (AdventureWorksDW2008R2). Microsoft has bundled all the Adventure Works databases into a single download.

**NOTE** Microsoft is working on an updated version of the Adventure Works databases for SQL Server 2012. The SQL Server 2012 versions are expected to include incremental changes from the R2 releases. They haven't been tested with this book's code samples. If you decide to install the SQL Server 2012 version of the sample databases, you might find that the practice steps differ somewhat from your setup and that the reports might show different data.

Follow these steps to download the Adventure Works databases:

1. Open the Microsoft SQL Server Product Samples Database webpage on Codeplex (http://www.codeplex.com/MSFTDBProdSamples).
2. Click the SQL Server 2008R2 link. The link URL as of the time of this writing is http://bit.ly/adventureworksR2. Click the AdventureWorks2008R2_SR1.exe link.
3. When Internet Explorer prompts you, click Run to download and execute the setup program.
4. The setup program includes all the Adventure Works databases. In the Adventure Works Community Sample Databases step of the setup, make sure that the "AdventureWorks OLTP 2008R2" and "AdventureWorks Data Warehouse 2008R2" are selected. If you plan to deploy the Adventure Works cube, select also the "AdventureWorks OLAP Standard 2008R2" database if you have SQL Server 2008 (or above) Standard edition. Or, check the "AdventureWorks OLAP Enterprise 2008R2" database if you have SQL Server Developer, Enterprise, or Business Intelligence edition. The setup installs only the project files and it doesn't deploy the cube (the cube deployment steps are provided in the "Installing the Adventure Works cube" section.
5. To verify that the relational databases are installed, open SQL Server Management Studio (SSMS), and then connect to the SQL Server instance that hosts the Adventure Works databases.
6. Expand the Databases folder. You should see the AdventureWorks2008R2 and AdventureWorksDW2008R2 databases.

***Installing the Adventure Works cube***

In Chapter 3, you import data from the AdventureWorks Analysis Services cube, but I include alternative import steps if installing the cube is not an option. If you decide to import from the cube, install the Analysis Services AdventureWorks solution as follows:

1. Open the AdventureWorks Analysis Services solution (Adventure Works.sln) in Business Intelligence Development Studio (if you have SQL Server 2008 R2) or SQL Server Data Tools (if you have SQL Server 2012). Here is default folder where the Analysis Services solution is located:

```
\Program Files\Microsoft SQL Server\100\Tools\Samples\AdventureWorks 2008 Analysis Services Project
```

2. In the Solution Explorer, right-click the project node, and then click Properties.
3. In the Property Pages dialog box, click the Deployment tab. In the Server field, type the Analysis Services instance to which the cube will be deployed, such as *localhost* if you've installed Analysis Services on the default instance on your local server. Click OK.
4. In Solution Explorer, right-click the project node, and then click Deploy to deploy the project.
5. In SQL Server Management Studio, connect to the Analysis Services instance (see Step 3).
6. Expand the Databases folder. You should see the Adventure Works DW 2008 database.

***Watching the video demos***

Designing a tabular model is a click-intensive process. I captured video demos to help you stay on track when a picture is worth more than a thousand words (sometimes you just have to see it to understand). The video demos are bonus material to the book. The play symbol (▶) next to a section title indicates that there is a video demo for this section. Video demos are provided for a subset of the practical exercises and are not intended to exactly match the steps included in the book. The book web page (http://bit.ly/thebismbook) provides a link to the video demos that you can watch online.

***Reporting errors***

This book has no bugs! Well, that's the goal, anyway. We both know that this statement is over-ambitious to say the least. Please submit bug reports to the book discussion list on http://prologika.com/cs/forums/default.aspx. Confirmed bugs and inaccuracies will be published to the book errata document. A link to the errata document is provided in the book web page.

The book includes links to web resources for further study. Due to the transient nature of the Internet, some links might be no longer valid or might be broken. Searching for the document title is usually sufficient to recover the new link.

Your purchase of APPLIED MICROSOFT SQL SERVER 2012 ANALYSIS SERVICES (Tabular Modeling) includes free access to a web forum sponsored by the author, where you can make comments about the book, ask technical questions, and receive help from the author and the community. The author is not committed to a specific amount of participation or successful resolution of the question and his participation remains voluntary. You can subscribe to the forum from the author's personal website http://prologika.com/cs/forums/default.aspx.

# *about the author*

Teo Lachev (MVP, MCSD, MCT, MCITP) is a consultant, author, and mentor, with a focus on Microsoft Business Intelligence. His Atlanta-based company "Prologika" helps organizations make sense of data by effectively applying Microsoft BI technologies. Teo has authored and co-authored several BI books, including Applied Microsoft Analysis Services 2005 and Applied SQL Server 2008 Reporting Services, and he has co-authored the Microsoft SQL Server Business Intelligence Implementation and Maintenance Training Kit. He speaks frequently at industry conferences and leads the Microsoft Business Intelligence Group in Atlanta, GA.

## Chapter 1

# Introducing Business Intelligence Semantic Model



In the digital and fast-paced world of today, technologies undergo monumental shifts to help organizations streamline their processes and transact business in more efficient ways. Information technology, for example, has witnessed these changes with the Internet boom, cloud computing, and mobile devices. In the business intelligence (BI) space, the arrival of Microsoft Business Intelligence Semantic Model (BISM) in Microsoft SQL Server 2012 is a paradigm shift because it allows you to implement a new class of applications for personal, team, and organizational business intelligence (BI) solutions. BISM makes BI pervasive and accessible to both business users and BI professionals. If you're a business user, you can use BISM to import massive amounts of data and to build personal BI solutions without relying too much on your IT department. And, if you're a BI professional, you'll find that BISM empowers you to implement both relational and multidimensional solutions on a single platform.

This guide discusses the tabular capabilities of BISM, and this chapter is the most important chapter of the book. I'll start by introducing you to BISM, explaining how it fits into the Microsoft BI stack and when to use it. If you're familiar with Analysis Services cubes, you'll learn how the Multidimensional and Tabular paths compare with each other. Then, I'll take you on a tour of the BISM features and tools. I'll help you understand the product architecture and programming interfaces so that you have the necessary technical background to tackle more advanced topics later on in this book.

## 1.1 What is Business Intelligence Semantic Model?

Before I explain what Business Intelligence Semantic Model (BISM) is, I'll clarify what business intelligence (BI) is. You'll probably be surprised to learn that even BI professionals disagree about its definition. In fact, Forester Research offers two definitions (see http://bit.ly/foresterbi).

**DEFINITION** Broadly defined, BI is a set of methodologies, processes, architectures, and technologies that transform raw data into meaningful and useful information that's used to enable more effective strategic, tactical, and operational insights and decision-making. A narrower definition of BI might refer to just the top layers of the BI architectural stack, such as reporting, analytics, and dashboards.

In the world of Microsoft BI, BISM represents a semantic layer at the top of the BI architectural stack. In general, semantics relates to discovering the meaning of the message behind the words. In the context of data and BI, semantics represents the user's perspective of data: how the end user views the data to derive knowledge from it. As a modeler, your job is to translate the machine-friendly database structures and terminology into a user-friendly semantic layer that describes the business problems to be solved. To address this need, you create a Business Intelligence Semantic Model (BISM).

Microsoft BISM is a unifying name for both multidimensional (OLAP) and tabular (relational) features in the Microsoft SQL Server 2012 release of Analysis Services. Since its first release in 1998, Analysis Services has provided Online Analytical Processing (OLAP) capabilities so that IT professionals can implement multidimensional OLAP cubes for slicing and dicing data. The OLAP side of Analysis Services is now referred to as *Multidimensional*. SQL Server 2012 expands the Analysis Services capabilities by adding a new path for implementing analytical models where entities are represented as relational constructs, such as two-dimensional tables, columns, and relationships. I'll refer to this new path as *Tabular*.

**DEFINITION** Analysis Services is a unified platform for implementing data analytical models for personal, team, and organizational BI solutions. BISM is a semantic layer that supports two paths for implementing analytical models: Multidimensional for OLAP cubes and Tabular for relational-like models.

Several terms in this definition might be unfamiliar to you, so let's take a closer look. To start with, Analysis Services is a platform that uses BISM as the metadata definition and semantic layer. Analysis Services provides tools to help you develop custom BI solutions for the full spectrum of BI needs:

- Personal BI (or self-service BI) – Personal BI enables business users to offload effort from IT pros and to build BI models for self-service data exploration and reporting. Suppose that Maya from the sales department wants to analyze some sales data that's stored in a Microsoft Access database or in an Excel workbook. With a few clicks Maya can import the data into a PowerPivot model, build pivot reports, and gain valuable insights.
- Team BI – Business users can share the reports and dashboards they've implemented with other team members without requiring them to install modeling or reporting tools. Suppose that Maya would like to share her sales analysis application with her coworker, Martin. Once Maya has uploaded the PowerPivot model to SharePoint, Martin can view online the pivot reports Maya has created, or he can author his own reports that connect to Maya's model.
- Organizational BI (or corporate BI) – BI professionals can enhance the tabular models developed by business users and deploy them to a dedicated server for added performance and security. Or, BI professionals can implement multidimensional cubes for data warehousing and OLAP. Continuing the previous example, suppose that over time the sales database has grown to millions of rows. Moreover, Maya's sales model has grown in popularity, and more coworkers are requesting access to it. Maya can now hand over the model to Bob, who is a BI pro. Bob can upgrade the model to a scalable and secure model that coexists with the multidimensional cubes that Bob has created for historical and trend analysis.

As you could imagine, Analysis Services is a versatile BI platform that enables different groups of users to implement a wide range of BI solutions. Writing a single book that covers in detail both the multidimensional and tabular aspects of BISM would be an impossible task. I discussed the OLAP capabilities of Analysis Services in my book *Applied Analysis Services 2005* (Prologika Press, 2005). This book covers Tabular only. However, if you're familiar with OLAP cubes, then you'll find plenty of information in this chapter and later chapters in order to understand Tabular from an OLAP point of view. Then you can decide which path is a better choice for the task at hand.

## 1.1.1 Understanding Analysis Services History

BISM is a component of Microsoft SQL Server Analysis Services. Before we get into the BISM technical details and capabilities, let's step back for a moment and review the Analysis Services history to understand its genesis and evolution. **Figure 1.1** shows the major product releases.

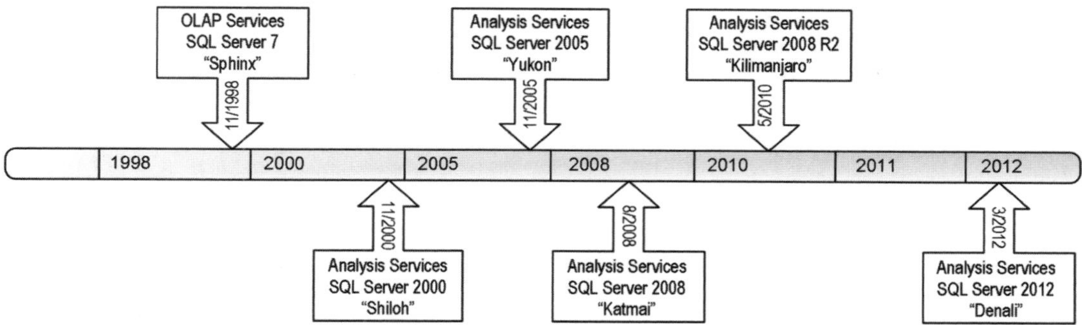


**Figure 1.1** The SQL Server Analysis Services history at a glance.

After acquiring the OLAP software technology from an Israeli-based company, Panorama Software, Microsoft bundled the first release with SQL Server 7 in 1998 under the name "OLAP Services". The product provided tools to building OLAP cubes and supported Multidimensional Expressions (MDX) as a query language. In 2000, the name changed to "Analysis Services" due to inclusion of data mining capabilities for trend discovery and data mining.

***About UDM***

In SQL Server 2005, Microsoft completely redesigned Analysis Services and introduced the next generation of OLAP and data mining technologies under the name Unified Dimensional Model (UDM). UDM departed from the classic OLAP space and provided more flexibility for modeling multidimensional cubes, as explained in the "Introduction to the Unified Dimensional Model (UDM)" article by Paul Sanders at http://bit.ly/udmintro. For example, instead of limiting data exploration across predefined hierarchies, such as Category ⇨ Subcategory ⇨ Product, UDM allows you to slice and dice data by each column (attribute), such as Color, Size, Price, and so on. UDM became very successful over time, and it made Analysis Services an industry-leading BI platform and the most popular OLAP engine according to the Gartner's Magic Quadrant for Business Intelligence Platforms (http://bit.ly/gartnerquadrant).

**NOTE** The terms "UDM" and "cube" are often used interchangeably. Although initially positioned as a unification of dimensional and relational reporting, UDM is an OLAP-based model with additional features that aren't found in classic OLAP, such as attribute hierarchies, relationships, key performance indicators (KPIs), perspectives, and so on. The physical manifestation of UDM is the Analysis Services cube. As a term, UDM is no longer used in SQL Server 2012, and it's succeeded by BISM.

SQL Server 2008 brought incremental changes to Analysis Services in the areas of performance and manageability. For example, a block computation mode was introduced to eliminate unnecessary aggregation calculations and to improve the performance of queries.

***About BISM***

SQL Server 2008 R2 added a new technology for personal and team BI called PowerPivot, whose data engine later became the foundation of Tabular. If you were going to compare PowerPivot to the world of database development, then PowerPivot is to Analysis Services as Microsoft Access is to SQL Server. Extending the Excel capabilities, PowerPivot enabled business users to create their own BI applications. At PASS Summit 2010, Microsoft announced its BI roadmap for SQL Server 2012 and introduced BISM as a continuum of personal, team, and organizational BI on a single platform, as explained in the "Analysis Services – Roadmap for SQL Server "Denali" and Beyond" blog post by T.K. Anand (http://bit.ly/bismatpass). The plans for BISM were to extend the Power-Pivot capabilities so BI professionals can build relational-like tabular models for organizational BI solutions.

Later at TechEd North America 2011, Microsoft rebranded BISM as an umbrella name for both multidimensional and tabular models. The TechEd presentation, "What's New in Microsoft SQL Server Code-Named "Denali" for SQL Server Analysis Services and PowerPivot" by T.K. Anand and Ashvini Sharma, unveiled the new positioning, followed by the blog post "Analysis Services – Vision & Roadmap Update" (http://bit.ly/bismatteched). The article states "By bringing the two data models together, we will provide a powerful yet flexible platform that can tackle the diverse needs of BI applications – needs such as advanced analytics, sophisticated business logic, professional developer tools, choice of end user tools, performance, scalability, ease of use, and time to solution."

One of the prevailing themes of SQL Server 2012 is breakthrough insights. SQL Server 2012 adds new BI capabilities for pervasive data discovery and analysis across the organization. And, BISM is the analytical layer that powers BI.

## 1.1.2 Understanding the Microsoft BI Platform

Analysis Services is not the only BI product that Microsoft provides. It is an integral part of the Microsoft BI platform that was initiated in early 2004 with the powerful promise to bring "BI to the masses." Microsoft subsequently extended the message to "BI to the masses, by the masses" to emphasize its commitment to make BI broadly accessible. Indeed, a few years after Microsoft got into the BI space, the BI landscape changed dramatically. Once a domain of cost-prohibitive and highly specialized tools, BI is now within the reach of every user and organization.

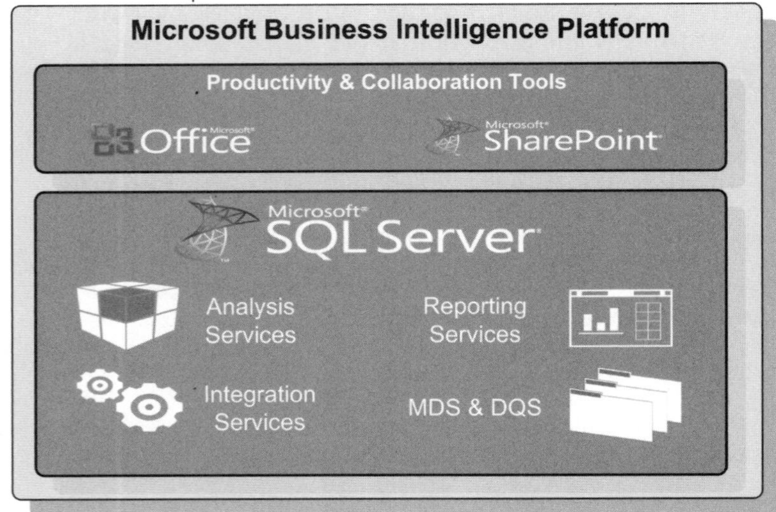


**Figure 1.2** The Microsoft BI Platform provides services and tools that address various data analytics and management needs.

**DEFINITION** The Microsoft Business Intelligence Platform is a multi-product offering that addresses the most pressing data analytics and management needs that many organizations encounter every day.

Given Forester Research's broad definition of BI that I mentioned above, the Microsoft BI Platform includes tools that address the entire spectrum of BI needs. **Figure 1.2** illustrates the building blocks of the Microsoft BI Platform. Microsoft SQL Server forms the foundation of the Microsoft BI Platform and bundles services for structural data storage, data integration, reporting, and analysis.

***Analysis Services***

As I mentioned, Analysis Services provides OLAP and data mining services. Traditionally, organizations have used the OLAP capabilities of Analysis Services to implement multidimensional cubes on top of a data warehouse or data mart for trend and historical reporting. An Analysis Services cube can help business users analyze numeric data (measures) from different subject areas (dimensions). Coupled with a "smart" OLAP browser, such as Microsoft Excel, an Analysis Services cube could be a dream come true for every manager or decision maker. That's because analytical needs have been traditionally addressed by authoring operational reports, such as Sales by Product, Sales by Country, Sales by Year, and so on. Please don't misunderstand me. Operational reports do have their purpose. However, a multidimensional cube allows power users to author their own interactive reports without relying on IT pros.

**REAL WORLD** How much effort does your company spend on canned reports? One of our clients had an IT department with some 30 BI pros whose main responsibility was authoring operational reports from stored procedures. There was a significant schema overlap between the datasets returned by the stored procedures. Report results were inconsistent because business metrics were not shared between reports. Performance was an issue due to the extensive data crunching that the reports had to perform to aggregate large datasets from the company's data warehouse database. We addressed these challenges by implementing a multidimensional cube. While operational reports were still required to address external reporting needs, their number was significantly reduced, as well as the effort to prepare and verify the data.

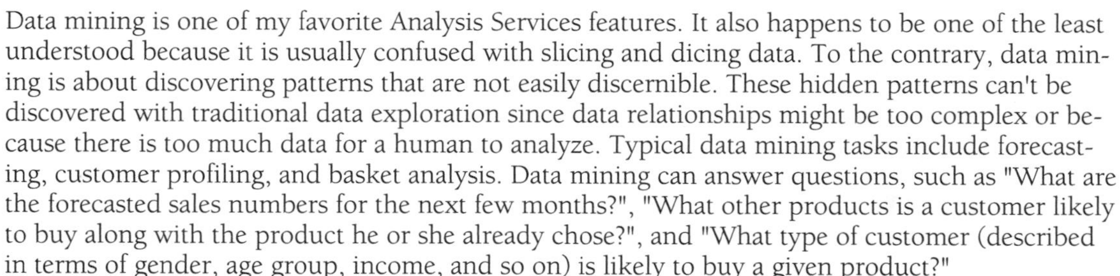

Data mining is one of my favorite Analysis Services features. It also happens to be one of the least understood because it is usually confused with slicing and dicing data. To the contrary, data mining is about discovering patterns that are not easily discernible. These hidden patterns can't be discovered with traditional data exploration since data relationships might be too complex or because there is too much data for a human to analyze. Typical data mining tasks include forecasting, customer profiling, and basket analysis. Data mining can answer questions, such as "What are the forecasted sales numbers for the next few months?", "What other products is a customer likely to buy along with the product he or she already chose?", and "What type of customer (described in terms of gender, age group, income, and so on) is likely to buy a given product?"

**REAL WORLD** I conducted a BI training class once for a well-known online recruitment company. At the end of the training, the BI manager mentioned that he had a project to better understand their customers and the customers' buying behavior. I showed him how to build an Analysis Services data mining model for customer profiling. This company was using multidimensional cubes, but the BI manager didn't know about the Analysis Services data mining capabilities. He said that my mining model demo was "the icing on the cake."

In SQL Server 2012, Analysis Services adds the Tabular model, which is the subject of this book. If you're a BI pro and you implement OLAP cubes, SQL Server 2012 adds incremental features to Multidimensional, including dimension stores that are larger than 4GB to accommodate string-based attributes with millions of members, support for SQL Server Extended Events (XEvents), Analysis Management Objects (AMO) for PowerShell, and improved support for Non-Uniform Memory Access (NUMA) memory architectures.

### *Integration Services*

Today's enterprise IT shop is often required to maintain an assortment of data sources and technologies. These include desktop databases, legacy mainframe systems (that no one dares to touch), relational database management systems (RDBMS), and so on. For example, order tracking data could reside in a SQL Server database, and HR data could be stored in an Oracle database, while the manufacturing data could be located in a mainframe database. Integrating disparate and heterogeneous data sources presents a major challenge for many organizations. Integration Services helps you address this challenge. It's typically used for extracting, transforming, and loading (ETL) processes.

Integration Services complements BISM very well because BISM doesn't have capabilities to transform and clean data. You would typically use Integration Services to extract data from the source systems, cleanse it, and then load it to a database, such as your company data warehouse.

New features in the 2012 release include usability, developer productivity, and manageability improvements, as discussed in the "What's New in Microsoft SQL Server Code-Named "Denali" for SQL Server Integration Services" video presentation by Matt Masson (http://bit.ly/ssis2012).

### *Reporting Services*

Reporting is an essential feature of every BI application. With Reporting Services, you can create standard and ad hoc reports from various data sources, including BISM models. Since the 2005 release, Reporting Services includes a graphical query designer that auto-generates cube and data mining queries. To create basic queries, you can simply drag the required measures and dimensions to the query results area and then filter the results in the filter area. As a result, BI professionals can create standard reports and power users can author ad hoc reports. You can also implement reports that leverage Analysis Services data mining capabilities to display prediction results, such as forecasted sales, as I discussed in my article, "Implementing Smart Reports with the Microsoft Business Intelligence Platform" at http://bit.ly/smartreports. Once you've authored the report, you can publish it to the report server or to a SharePoint site and then make it available to other users.

The major focus for the SQL Server 2012 release was a new SharePoint 2010-integrated tool, named Power View, for authoring ad-hoc reports for data visualization and exploration. Similar to Report Builder, Power View targets business users, but it doesn't require report authoring experience. Suppose that Maya has uploaded her PowerPivot model to SharePoint. Now Maya (or anyone else who has access to the model) can quickly build a great-looking tabular or chart report in 20 minutes that visualizes data from the PowerPivot model.

Unlike Report Builder, Power View is highly interactive and presentation-ready, meaning that it doesn't require switching between report layout and preview modes. **Figure 1.3** illustrates a Power View report that shows the correlation between a sales persons' actual sales and their sales quota. You can click the play button on the CalendarYear play axis to see an animated video that shows how the performance changes over time.

Another welcome end-user oriented feature in this release is data alerts. Data alerts allow report users to subscribe to alerts when the report data changes. For example, suppose that your IT department has implemented and deployed an operational report that shows sales by countries. You want to be notified when the United States sales exceed one million. Once you set up a data alert, the report server will send you an e-mail when the condition is met. For more information about data alerts, read my blog post, "Reporting Services Data Alerts", at http://bit.ly/rsdataalerts. For more information about the Reporting Services enhancements in SQL Server 2012, see the video, "What's New in Microsoft SQL Server Code-Named "Denali" for Reporting Services" by Carolyn Chao (http://bit.ly/ssrs2012). You might find my book, *Applied SQL Server 2008 Reporting Services* (http://amzn.to/appliedssrs), useful for an in-depth knowledge of Reporting Services.

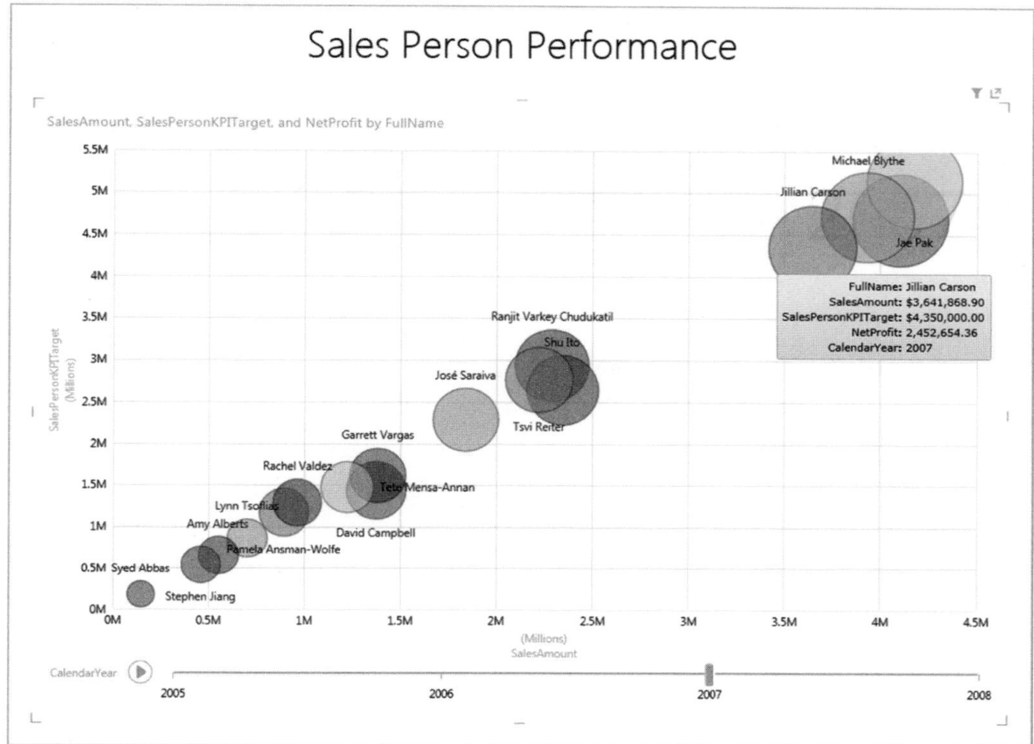


**Figure 1.3** Business users can use Power View to create interactive reports.

***Master Data Services and Data Quality Services***

There are other SQL Server components that you might find more or less relevant to your BI projects. As you would probably agree, data quality and stewardship is an issue with many mid-size and large organizations. Chances are that your organization would like to maintain a centralized list of important entities, such as products, customers, vendors, and so on. In SQL Server 2008 R2, Microsoft introduced Master Data Services (MDS) to help enterprises centrally manage and standardize master data. The 2012 release adds the ability to use Microsoft Excel as a front-end tool to manage master data, as demonstrated in the video, "Managing Master Data with MDS and Microsoft Excel" by John McAllister (http://bit.ly/mds2012).

SQL Server 2012 introduces Data Quality Services (DQS) to enable organizations to create a knowledge base and to specify domain rules in order to perform data cleansing. For example, you can use DQS to standardize customer data, such as to change "St." to "Street" and to enrich data by filling in missing elements, such as to change "1 Microsoft way Redmond 98006" to "1 Microsoft Way, Redmond, WA 98006". Integration Services includes a new DQS Cleansing task that BI professionals can use to automate the DQS processes. For more information, see the video, "Using Knowledge to Cleanse Data with Data Quality Services" by Elad Ziklik (http://bit.ly/dqs2012).

***Productivity and collaboration tools***

Data by itself is useless if there is no way to make it available to the people who need it. Besides disseminating data via Reporting Services reports, the Microsoft BI platform supports other data presentation channels, such as Microsoft Office and Microsoft SharePoint.

Microsoft significantly broadened the BI features in the Microsoft Office suite of products. First, Microsoft positioned the ubiquitous Microsoft Excel as a premium client for Analysis Services. For example, business users can use Excel to connect to a tabular or multidimensional model and build interactive PivotTable reports to slice the cube data. To help end users perform data mining tasks in Excel, Microsoft released a Data Mining add-in for Microsoft Office. Unfortunately, the BI trend somewhat ebbed away and Microsoft Excel 2010 added only incremental BI features, such as slicers and the ability to search dimension members. Let's hope that a future version will add modern Power View-like data visualization features to supplement the venerable PivotTable and PivotChart reports.

Whether you like SharePoint or not, Microsoft continues adding BI features to SharePoint. Organizations can use SharePoint to build BI portals and dashboards that contain Reporting Services reports and Excel reports that are connected to BISM models. To simplify setup, the SQL Server 2012 version of Reporting Services now integrates natively with SharePoint 2010 via the SharePoint service application architecture. As a result, you don't need to install a standalone report server for SharePoint integration mode. With the Excel Services components of SharePoint 2010 Enterprise, you can deploy and process Excel spreadsheets on the server and then view them in HTML via a web browser. With PerformancePoint Services, you can implement scorecards and management dashboards, such as a scorecard that displays key performance indicators (KPIs) defined in a multidimensional or tabular model. Finally, as I pointed out, Power View augments the SharePoint 2010 BI ecosystem with ad hoc reporting from predefined BISM models.

You might have heard about the Azure Services Platform, which is a Microsoft cloud offering for hosting and scaling applications and databases through Microsoft datacenters. Microsoft Azure gives you the ability to focus on your application and to outsource infrastructure maintenance to Microsoft. IT trends indicate that cloud computing will be the next frontier for software development. As of the time of this writing, however, Analysis Services isn't available on Azure. As a result, you can't deploy multidimensional and tabular models to the cloud. However, a tabular model can import data from the cloud, and more cloud-based BI features are anticipated in future releases.

**Table 1.1** summarizes the products in the Microsoft BI Platform listed in the order discussed.

**Table 1.1 The Microsoft BI Platform addresses the most pressing data analysis and management needs.**

| Product | Acronym | Purpose |
|---|---|---|
| SQL Server Analysis Services | SSAS | Provides analytical and data mining services. You can use the analytical services to implement OLAP multidimensional cubes and Tabular relational-like models. |
| SQL Server Integration Services | SSIS | Allows BI professionals to implement extraction, transformation, and loading (ETL) processes, such as to load data from text files into a data warehouse database. |
| SQL Server Reporting Services | SSRS | Empowers business users and BI professionals to create standard and ad hoc reports from a variety of data sources. |
| SQL Server Master Data Services | MDS | Allows organizations to manage non-transactional entities, such as customer, product, and vendor, with the goal of compiling master lists. |
| SQL Server Data Quality Services | DQS | Provides tools to set up a knowledge base to perform a variety of data quality tasks, including correction, enrichment, standardization, and de-duplication of your data. |
| Microsoft Excel | Excel | Includes BI client features, such as browsing multidimensional cubes, implementing personal PowerPivot models, and performing data mining tasks. |
| SharePoint Products and Technologies | SharePoint | Hosts reports, PowerPivot models, and dashboards. |

## 1.1.3 Understanding the BISM Components

Now that I've introduced you to BISM and the Microsoft BI Platform, let's take a look at its logical architecture. This will help you understand at a high-level its building blocks and how multidimensional and tabular paths fit in the BISM ecosystem. Don't worry if you don't immediately understand some of the acronyms and technologies. I'll clarify them throughout the rest of the chapter.

Vertically, BISM can be visualized as a three-tier model consisting of data access, business logic, and data model layers (see **Figure 1.4**). Horizontally, it has two implementation paths: Multidimensional and Tabular. I'll be quick to point out that although there is a significant feature overlap between these two paths, they're very different from an implementation standpoint. If you take the multidimensional path, you'll end up with an OLAP cube(s), as with prior versions of Analysis Services.

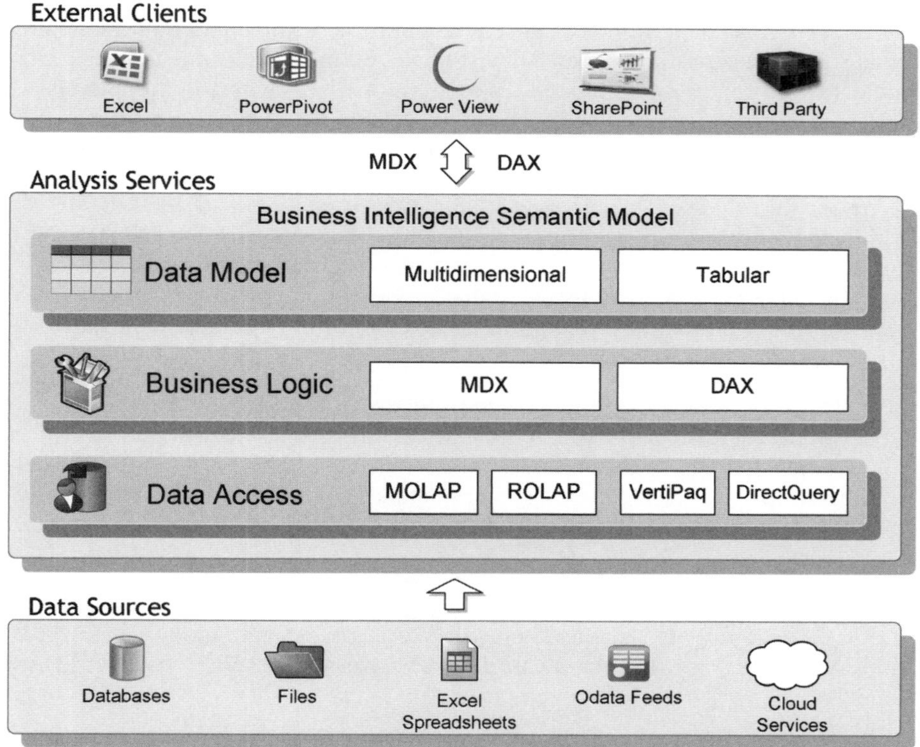


**Figure 1.4** BISM has two implementation paths: Multidimensional and Tabular.

By contrast, the Tabular path leads to, you've guessed it, a tabular model. In SQL Server 2012, Microsoft doesn't provide a migration option between Multidimensional and Tabular. Therefore, it's important to carefully consider both options and then make an appropriate choice based on your requirements. Later in this chapter, Section 1.4 provides a detailed feature comparison between Multidimensional and Tabular.

***Logical components***
Next, I'll explain the BISM logical components.

- Data Model layer – This is the conceptual model layer that's exposed to external clients. Again, Multidimensional equates OLAP cubes. Tabular is a new model that's more relational in nature and represents data as tables and columns.
- Business Logic layer – This layer allows the modeler to define business logic, such as variances, time calculations, and key performance indicators (KPIs). Multidimensional empowers the modeler to implement this layer using Multidimensional Expressions (MDX) artifacts, such as calculated members, named sets, and scope assignments. Tabular embraces a new Excel-like expression language called Data Analysis Expressions (DAX). DAX was first introduced in PowerPivot 1.0, which was released with SQL Server 2008 R2. SQL Server 2012 adds additional formulas and extends DAX to organizational models. This release also adds a DAX-based query language so that Power View reports can query tabular models natively.
- Data Access layer – This layer interfaces with external data sources. By default, both Multidimensional and Tabular import data from the data sources and cache the dataset on the server for best performance. The default multidimensional storage option is Multidimensional OLAP (MOLAP), where data is stored in a compressed disk-based format. The default Tabular storage option is VertiPaq, which was first introduced in PowerPivot. VertiPaq is an in-memory columnar database that compresses and stores data in the computer main memory. Both Multidimensional and Tabular support real-time data access by providing a Relational OLAP (ROLAP) storage mode for Multidimensional and a DirectQuery storage mode for Tabular (organization BI models only). When a multidimensional cube is configured for ROLAP, Analysis Services doesn't process and cache data on the server. Instead, it auto-generates and sends queries to the database. Similarly, when a tabular model is configured for DirectQuery, Analysis Services doesn't keep data in VertiPaq but sends queries directly to the data source.

***Data sources***
Although Multidimensional and Tabular can import data from any data source that provides standard connectivity options, there are some differences. Multidimensional works best with a single database, such as a data warehouse database. By contrast, Tabular can connect and import data equally well from heterogeneous data sources, such as databases, text files, and even data feeds, such as a Reporting Services report or a SharePoint list.

***External clients***
BISM provides two interfaces to the outside world for querying Multidimensional and Tabular models: MDX and DAX. OLAP browsers, such as Microsoft Excel, can see both models as OLAP cubes and can send MDX queries. And, Tabular-aware clients, such as Power View, can send DAX queries to tabular models.

**NOTE** As of now, the only Microsoft client that generates DAX queries is Power View. As it stands, Power View auto-generates DAX queries to tabular models only. Microsoft is working on extending BISM with DAX support for multidimensional cubes so that Power View can use them as data sources. The rest of the Microsoft-provided reporting tools, such as Reporting Services designers and Excel, can connect to a tabular model as a cube and send MDX queries to it.

**Table 1.2** shows the most commonly used Microsoft-provided clients and the query options they support for integrating with BISM.

***Understanding BISM unification***
Outside query and management interfaces, there aren't many commonalities between Multidimensional and Tabular in SQL Server 2012. As you'll see in Section 1.4.1, which compares Multi-

dimensional and Tabular side by side, there is a significant functionality overlap, but each model implements features on its own, and the models are not compatible with each other. For example, you can't get a hierarchy definition from Multidimensional and add it to Tabular or use MDX to define calculations in Tabular. So, why are we implying unification here? Let's think of BISM as a prediction of the future. In time, Tabular might "borrow" OLAP features, such as MDX calculations, and Multidimensional might get Tabular artifacts, such as in-memory data storage. Thus, the difference between the two paths is likely to blur to a point where Tabular is as feature-rich as Multidimensional.

**Table 1.2 Microsoft-provided clients and query options.**

| Tool | Multidimensional | Tabular | Business Intelligence Need |
|---|---|---|---|
| Excel | MDX | MDX | Personal and organizational BI |
| Excel PowerPivot | MDX | MDX | Personal and team BI |
| Power View | N/A | DAX | Personal, team, and organizational BI |
| PerformancePoint | MDX | MDX | Organizational BI |
| SSRS report designers | MDX | MDX | Personal and Organizational BI |

Taking this further, I'd like to indulge myself and think that one day, I hope in the not-so-distant future, BISM will evolve to become a true single model that delivers on the unification promise and that combines the best of Multidimensional and Tabular. Then, we would be able to pick and mix features from both paths, such as in-memory storage with MDX calculations, and we could use the best technology for the task at hand. Until then, we will have to choose between the multidimensional and tabular paths. The next section provides the necessary technical information to help you make this choice.

# 1.2 Understanding Tabular

Let's now take a more detailed look at Tabular. I'll start by explaining why we need it. Next, I'll discuss when to use it and scenarios where it might not be a good fit. Finally, I'll provide a feature comparison between Tabular and Multidimensional, and between Tabular and Report Builder models.

## 1.2.1 Why We Need Tabular

The short answer is to have a simple and efficient BI model that promotes rapid BI development and is well suited for both personal and organizational BI projects. Next, I'll review the main events that led to the development of Tabular.

***Advances in computer hardware***

When OLAP systems came to existence and the first version of Analysis Services was released, the computer landscape was quite different. Back then, one gigabyte was a lot of data. Nowadays, terabyte-sized databases are not uncommon. You can buy an inexpensive laptop for home use that's equipped with a 64-bit multi-core processor, 4GB of RAM, and one terabyte of disk space for less than $1,000. A typical enterprise database server has four physical processors and at least 64GB of RAM. That's a lot of raw power!

**REAL WORLD** I recall working as a consultant in 2000 on a data warehouse project and I wondered where to store a few gigabytes of call center data. To get us out of this predicament, the customer eventually shipped a very expensive server that could handle the "massive" data volumes.

These advances in desktop and server hardware led to the rise of the in-memory databases (IMDBs). Unlike the traditional database management systems (DBMS), which employ a disk-storage mechanism, an in-memory database stores data in the computer main memory (RAM) because RAM is still the fastest storage medium. IMDBs have actually been around since the 1970s, but high-capacity RAM has only recently become an affordable option to store large volumes of data, such as millions or even billions of rows.

***Demand for self-service business intelligence***

On the software side of things, in recent years there has been a need for personal (self-service) BI tools, such as to allow a business user to import and analyze some data without reliance on IT pros. However, OLAP and multidimensional cubes were never intended for personal BI. In a typical OLAP project, BI professionals would develop and deploy a cube to a dedicated server, and end users would run standard or interactive reports that source data from the cube. Although the data is clean and trusted, it's restricted to what's in the cube and how often the cube is refreshed.

The BI competitive landscape has also changed. New vendors and products are emerging every day, including QlikView, Tableau, SiSense Prism, Spotfire, and BusinessObjects to name a few. The main selling point of these BI vendors is that organizational BI is too complex and cost-prohibitive. They promise a faster BI track. In reality, however, you should view organizational BI and personal BI as completing and not competing technologies because both might be required for companies to meet their analytical needs. For example, many companies require extract, transform, and load (ETL) processes, a data warehouse, and an OLAP layer. At the same time, there are cases where power users can do data analysis and reporting without reliance on IT pros. And, in many cases there is a demand for both.

**REAL WORLD** You should doubt any statements where someone says that organizational BI or OLAP are not needed or are obsolete. I've seen cases where BI vendors swear by self-service BI, but they build demos directly on top of a data warehouse where data is neatly organized and stored in a set of dimensions and fact tables. However, you should know that the effort required for extracting, cleaning, and loading data usually takes about 60-80% of the development effort for implementing a BI solution. Once this is done, building analytical layers is a straightforward process. A major hospital once decided they didn't need organizational BI and purchased a popular self-service BI tool. In less than a year, they went back to data warehousing and OLAP. As with most things in life, if something sounds too good to be true, it probably is.

## 1.2.2 Understanding Tabular Design Goals

The Analysis Services architects were looking for ways to capitalize on the modern hardware advances and to provide tools for personal BI. They envisioned a model that's simple to use and yet performs well. They had a dilemma — should they continue building on the OLAP foundation or go back to the drawing board. Microsoft realized that, although it's very successful and widely adopted, the Multidimensional internal architecture and storage model have become increasingly complex over the years, thus barring major changes and growth. Instead of continuing to build on the past, they've decided to architect a new model – Tabular.

***Striving for simplicity***

Simplicity was the main design goal for Tabular. A self-service BI tool that targets business users shouldn't assume expert technical knowledge or skills. A lot of effort went into simplifying Tabular in all directions. As its name suggests, Tabular embraces a more intuitive entity representation, using relational constructs such as tables and relationships, as opposed to multidimensional artifacts, such as cubes and dimensions. Moving to the business logic layer, Data Analysis Expressions (DAX) uses the standard Excel formula syntax. There are millions of Microsoft Excel users who are familiar with using Excel formulas to perform calculations. DAX continues this trend by extending Excel formulas so that users can define business logic in Tabular that ranges from simple calculated columns, such as a column that concatenates the customer's first and last name, to more advanced aggregations, such as YTD and QTD calculations.

**NOTE** It's easy to get started with DAX, to create basic expression-based columns, and to implement simple calculated measures, such as distinct count, time calculations, and so on. However, I'll be quick to point out that DAX can get complicated. If your goal in moving to Tabular is to avoid MDX, you might be disappointed. While a future release might be easier to learn, for now, after you moved beyond the basics, be prepared to struggle and invest time to learn DAX.

Furthermore, the Tabular data access layer makes it really easy to import data from virtually any data source without requiring scripting or query knowledge. Finally, data analysis and reporting can be performed with the familiar Excel PivotTable and PivotChart or with Power View, all without requiring prior report authoring experience. These are just a few examples of how Microsoft designed Tabular with simplicity in mind.

Of course, a simple model probably won't go very far if it lacks essential features. Although in its first release (or second if you count PowerPivot), you might find Tabular surprisingly feature-rich, depending on your reference point. For example, you'll probably find Tabular more advanced and powerful than other in-memory offerings on the market. However, if you compare it with multidimensional cubes, you'll undoubtedly find missing features. This isn't surprising because Multidimensional sets a very high bar.

***Striving for performance***

Next to simplicity and ease of use, the second tenet of the Tabular design is performance. Tabular is designed to give you high performance by default without requiring special tuning. To provide the best storage performance, Microsoft implemented a proprietary in-memory store called VertiPaq. VertiPaq is an in-memory database, which means it loads data in the computer main memory. As its name suggests, it stores and compresses data vertically by columns to pack as much data as possible in order to minimize the storage footprint. Column-based storage fits BI like a glove because data is typically analyzed by columns. And, the lower the data cardinality (that's the more repeating values a column has), the higher its compression rate is. **Figure 1.5** shows a hypothetical table containing some sales data.

Two distinct values
Seven distinct values
Five distinct values
Two distinct values
Five distinct values

| Date | ProductName | Product Subcategory | ProductCategory | SalesAmount |
|---|---|---|---|---|
| 1/1/2011 | Hitch Rack - 4-Bike | Bike Racks | Accessories | 44.88 |
| 1/1/2011 | Bike Wash - Dissolver | Cleaners | Accessories | 2.9733 |
| 1/1/2011 | Mountain-400-W Silver, 38 | Mountain Bikes | Bikes | 419.7784 |
| 1/2/2011 | Mountain-400-W Silver, 40 | Mountain Bikes | Bikes | 419.7784 |
| 1/2/2011 | Road-250 Red, 44 | Road Bikes | Bikes | 1518.7864 |
| 1/2/2011 | Road-250 Red, 48 | Road Bikes | Bikes | 1518.7864 |
| 1/2/2011 | Sport-100 Helmet, Red | Helmets | Accessories | 12.0278 |

**Figure 1.5** VertiPaq compresses well columns with many repeating values.

After reviewing the column data, we realize that across all rows the Date column has only two unique values, the ProductName column has seven, the ProductSubcategory has five, ProductCategory two, and Sales Amount has five. Consequently, the Product Category and Date columns will compress the most since they have the most repeating values, while the ProductName column won't compress so well. Since it's common to have columns with many repeating values in large datasets, expect a high data compression ratio (five times or higher).

Another performance-related effort went into DAX. Specifically, Microsoft optimized DAX for modern multi-core processors. For readers experienced in Analysis Services and MDX, all DAX formulas operate in a block computation mode and should give you performance at par with optimized MDX queries.

## 1.2.3 Understanding Tabular and VertiPaq Implementations

Having reviewed the Tabular logical architecture and genesis, let's discuss its physical realization. As it turns out, SQL Server 2012 includes more than one implementation of both Tabular and VertiPaq, as shown in **Figure 1.6**.

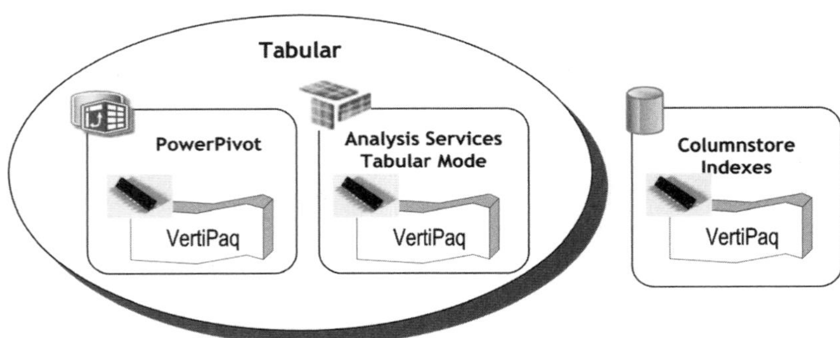


**Figure 1.6** In SQL Server 2012, Tabular is delivered as PowerPivot and Analysis Services in Tabular mode.

***Tabular implementations***

In SQL Server 2012, Tabular is delivered in two ways:

- PowerPivot (for Excel and SharePoint) – PowerPivot is an implementation of Tabular for personal and team BI. When the model is loaded, data resides in the in-memory VertiPaq store.
- Analysis Services in Tabular mode – Analysis Services in Tabular mode is an implementation of Tabular for organizational BI. By default, Analysis Services in Tabular mode caches data in the VertiPaq store, but it can be configured to generate and pass queries to a SQL Server database.

Both PowerPivot and Analysis Services in Tabular mode include modeling environments for implementing tabular solutions, and therefore, they are Tabular.

***VertiPaq implementations***

Microsoft provides three VertiPaq hosting implementations:

- PowerPivot (Excel and SharePoint) – When an end-user creates a PowerPivot model in Excel, behind the scenes PowerPivot stores the imported data in an in-process VertiPaq store. Similarly, if the user deploys the model to SharePoint, an Analysis Services server running in a SharePoint integration mode extracts the model data and caches it in a VertiPaq engine that's hosted by an Analysis Services instance configured in SharePoint integration mode.

- Analysis Services in Tabular mode – SQL Server 2012 allows you to install a stand-alone instance of Analysis Services in Tabular mode that uses the VertiPaq engine by default for storage without requiring SharePoint. Because of this, you can deploy a tabular model to a dedicated server just like you could deploy a cube. One caveat is that you can't deploy both Tabular and Multidimensional models to the same Analysis Services instance. However, you can install multiple Analysis Services instances, such as one instance for Multidimensional and another Tabular, on the same server.
- Columnstore indexes – Another interesting VertiPaq implementation that debuts in SQL Server 2012 is creating a new type of index on a database table, such as a fact table in a data warehouse database. A columnstore index might dramatically improve performance of queries that aggregate data from that table, such as an operational report that sources and aggregates data directly from a data warehouse database. Behind the scenes, a columnstore index is powered by VertiPaq running inside the SQL Server Database Engine. For more information about columnstore indexes, see the video, "Columnstore Indexes Unveiled" by Eric Hanson (http://bit.ly/colulmnstoreindex). Columnstore indexes are not an implementation of Tabular because they don't provide a modeling environment.

At this point, you should have a good high-level understanding of Tabular and what factors led to its invention. Let's now turn our focus to its usage scenarios.

## 1.3 When to Use Tabular

You can use Tabular to implement BI solutions that can address various personal, team, and organizational BI needs on a single platform, as shown in **Figure 1.7**. Before explaining each scenario, let me emphasize the flexibility that the platform offers. As the diagram suggests, a business user can start the BI journey with a small, personal model that she implements in Excel. Then, she might decide to share it with co-workers by deploying the Excel workbook to SharePoint. At the other end of the spectrum, BI pros can upgrade the model for organizational use when it exceeds Excel capabilities. But you don't necessarily have to follow this continuum story. For example, a BI professional can develop a PowerPivot model and then deploy it to SharePoint if business requirements call for online and offline Excel-based reporting. Or, the BI pro can jump straight into organizational BI and implement a tabular model from scratch on top of an existing database. There are many possibilities that depend on your requirements.

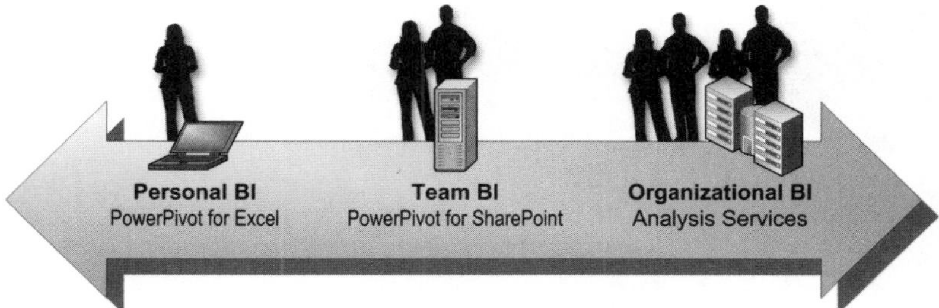


**Figure 1.7** You can use Tabular to implement personal, team, and organizational BI solutions.

In general, Tabular is specifically suited for personal BI (PowerPivot for Excel) and team BI (PowerPivot for SharePoint) projects. Organizational BI projects that seek to implement a centralized analytical layer, such as a layer on top of a data warehouse database for trend or historical analysis, will require careful evaluation of Multidimensional and Tabular in order to choose the best technology for the task at hand. The following sections clarify how you might use Tabular usage.

## 1.3.1 Personal Business Intelligence

Remember that personal BI is about empowering business users to build ad hoc BI models and to analyze data on their own. The natural choice for a personal BI tool would be the most popular application, which is used by millions of users – Microsoft Excel. A special Excel add-in, called PowerPivot for Excel, allows you to import data from virtually any data source, and you use the familiar Excel PivotTable and PivotChart to analyze the data.

**NOTE** Personal BI requires only Microsoft Excel 2010 and the free PowerPivot for Excel add-in. You don't need SharePoint, SQL Server, or any other software if you don't plan to share your PowerPivot models with other users.

***Understanding personal BI components***

Personal BI deployment is simple (see **Figure 1.8**). The PowerPivot for Excel add-in extends Microsoft Excel's capabilities and enables you to import tables of data, set up relationships, and define calculations. The imported data is saved inside the Excel 2010 workbook file, but it's loaded into the in-memory VertiPaq engine when you work with and query the model.

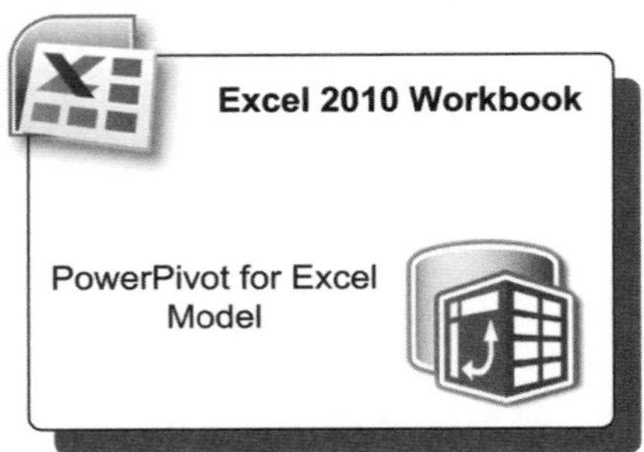


**Figure 1.8** PowerPivot for Excel saves the model data inside the Excel 2010 workbook file.

For reporting, PowerPivot for Excel falls back on the Excel PivotTable and PivotChart. **Figure 1.9** shows a sample PowerPivot for Excel dashboard, which you'll design in Chapter 5.

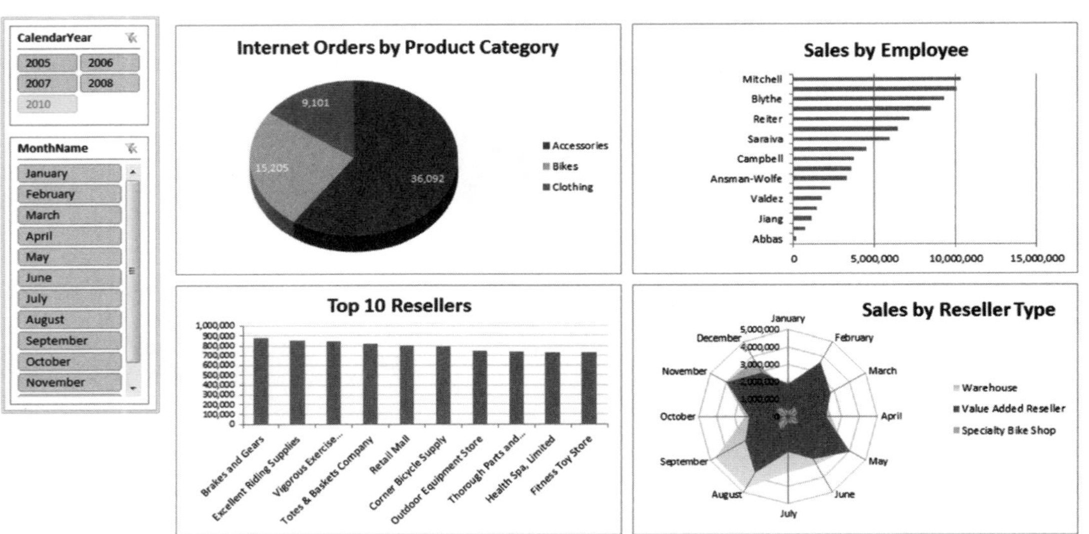


**Figure 1.9** Use PowerPivot for Excel to create dashboards consisting of PivotTable and PivotChart reports.

PowerPivot for Excel lifts the Excel data restrictions and lets business users import more than a million rows from external data sources, if needed. However, because SharePoint is limited to two gigabytes of maximum file upload size, PowerPivot for Excel limits the Excel workbook file to that size. Although this may sound limiting, recall that the data is saved in a highly compressed state. Therefore, a gigabyte of compressed data might contain millions of rows. If the file size becomes a limiting factor, consider upgrading the PowerPivot model to an organizational model that's deployed to a dedicated Analysis Services server, as I'll discuss later in Section 1.3.3.

***New features in PowerPivot for Excel***

Microsoft introduced PowerPivot for Excel in May 2010. PowerPivot version 2 coincides with the SQL Server 2012 release and adds features that extend PowerPivot capabilities and that make business users more productive. For example, one of the most requested features was the ability to visualize the model schema and relationships graphically. PowerPivot 2.0 responds to this need by introducing Diagram View, as shown in **Figure 1.10**.

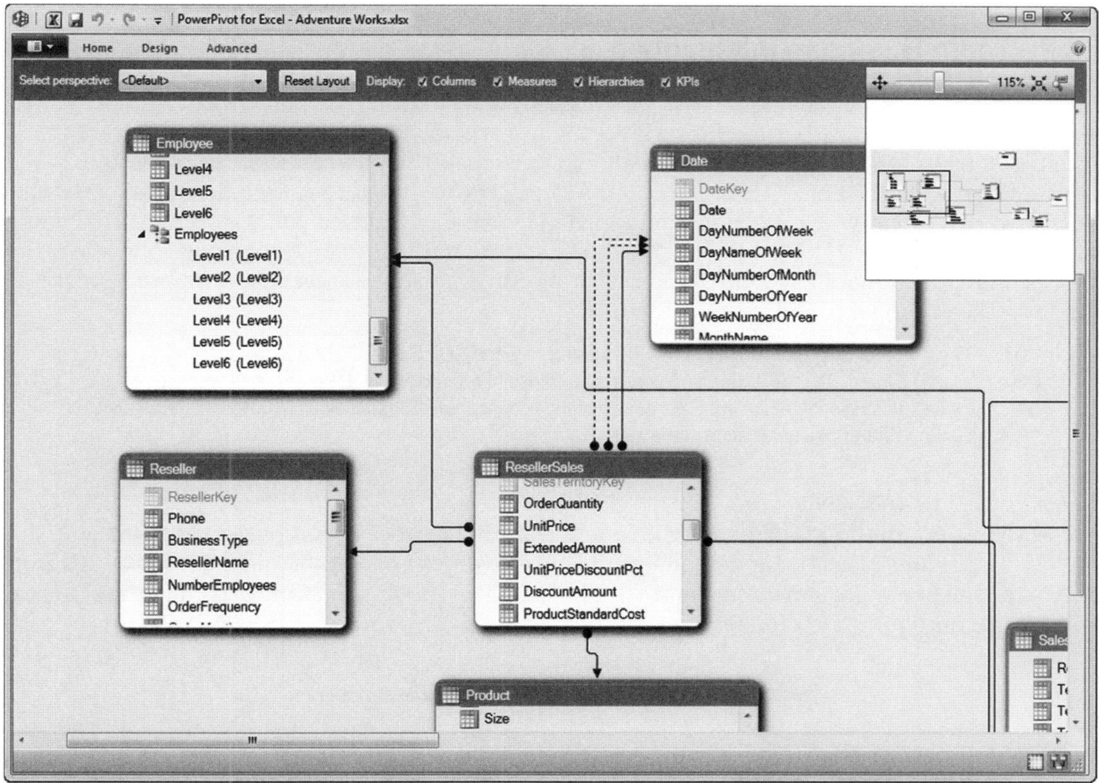


**Figure 1.10** PowerPivot for Excel adds Diagram View to visualize tables and relationships.

PowerPivot 2.0 introduces new modeling features to make the model more intuitive for analysis and reporting. You can now create hierarchies to provide useful navigation, such as a product hierarchy where you drill into data by product category, subcategory, and product levels. With key performance indicators (KPIs), you can track the company's performance against a predefined goal. And, perspectives define logical views that reduce the perceived complexity of the model.

PowerPivot now automatically supports drillthrough actions in Excel so you could see the level of detail behind a cell.

Microsoft improved the metadata presentation, including sorting column values by another column, applying model data types and formats to pivot reports, sorting object names alphabetically, formatting calculated measures, and providing descriptions for tables and measures. PowerPivot now supports dates better and allows you to mark a table as a Date table to enable date filters in Excel reports. A set of reporting properties was introduced to support Power View reports. For example, PowerPivot now supports importing images so you can display them on a Power View report, such as to allow the user to filter the report data by clicking a product image.

Finally, this release adds new DAX functions for implementing advanced business calculations. DAX has been extended with new ranking, statistical functions, information functions, and functions to handle parent-child hierarchies, such as an organizational chart. DAX now supports a query language to allow report clients, such as Power View, to query models deployed to SharePoint and Analysis Services servers.

## 1.3.2 Team Business Intelligence

Team BI enables business users to share the BI artifacts they create. Microsoft SharePoint 2010 has been extended to support hosting PowerPivot models and to allow business users to create reports from them. If you've used Multidimensional, you've probably deployed Excel and Reporting Services reports to SharePoint so team BI is nothing new to you. If you've started down the personal BI road with Tabular, you'll probably find e-mailing large Excel files to your coworkers impractical. Instead, consider deploying PowerPivot models to SharePoint to take advantage of features, such as online viewing of Excel pivot reports, authoring interactive Power View reports, and setting PowerPivot models to refresh on schedule.

**NOTE** Team BI requires SharePoint Server 2010 Enterprise and SQL Server 2012 Business Intelligence or Enterprise Edition. To learn about SQL Server editions and licensing, refer to the SQL Server 2012 website at http://bit.ly/sql2012editions. An Analysis Services instance configured in SharePoint integrated mode needs to be installed on the SharePoint application server.

***Understanding team BI components***

Due to the nature of the SharePoint architecture, team BI has a more complicated deployment model that requires installing and configuring PowerPivot for SharePoint and SQL Server 2012 on the SharePoint server, as shown in **Figure 1.11**. This diagram illustrates only the high-level logical components and hides their interactions.

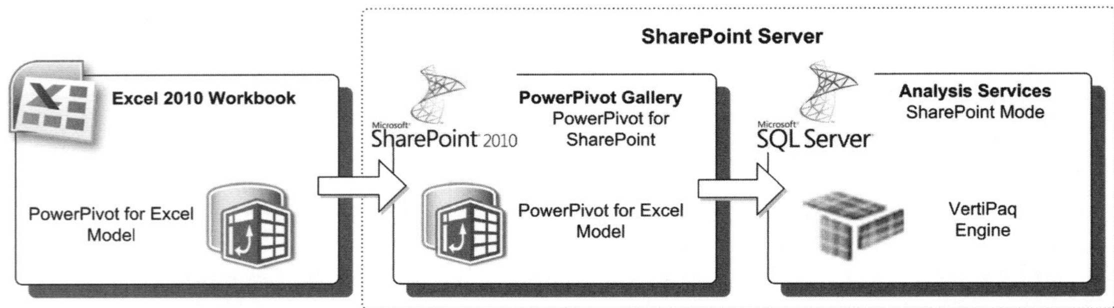


**Figure 1.11** Team BI requires SharePoint Server, SQL Server, and PowerPivot for SharePoint.

The PowerPivot for SharePoint add-in extends SharePoint's capabilities to support deploying and querying PowerPivot models. End users can upload the Excel workbooks to a special SharePoint PowerPivot Gallery document library, which is specifically designed to support PowerPivot models and Power View reports. When a user clicks on the workbook link, SharePoint renders the workbook in a thin-client HTML format inside the web browser. Consequently, Excel 2010 doesn't need to be installed on the desktop for the sole purpose of viewing reports only. This is no different than rendering Excel pivot reports that are connected to multidimensional cubes and deployed to SharePoint.

Excel web reports support limited interactivity when filtering and sorting data on the report. However, the end user can't change the report layout. For example, the user can't add or remove fields and can't switch between a pivot report to a chart report. When the user attempts an interactive feature, Excel forwards the request to an Analysis Services instance configured in SharePoint integrated mode. Analysis Services extracts the model data, restores it on the Analysis Services instance, and services report queries from that instance. In this way, the PowerPivot model can scale up to many simultaneous users. PowerPivot for SharePoint also adds the ability to refresh the model data on a set schedule, such as once every month.

As you would probably agree, personal BI is great, but "managed" personal BI is even better. PowerPivot for SharePoint provides a management dashboard for IT pros to gain insights about the server and model utilization and to take actions. For example, after analyzing the server workload and activity, the IT department might want to upgrade a frequently used PowerPivot model to an organizational tabular model to make it more scalable or to apply row-level security.

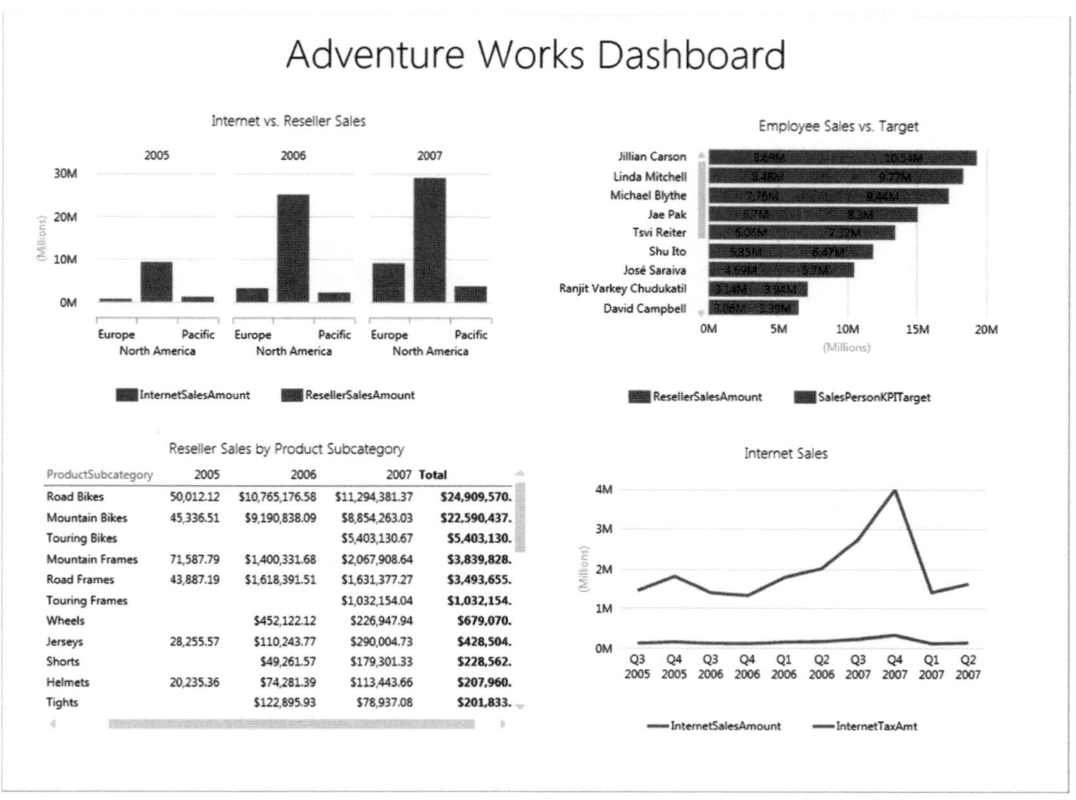


| ProductSubcategory | 2005 | 2006 | 2007 | Total |
|---|---|---|---|---|
| Road Bikes | 50,012.12 | $10,765,176.58 | $11,294,381.37 | **$24,909,570.** |
| Mountain Bikes | 45,336.51 | $9,190,838.09 | $8,854,263.03 | **$22,590,437.** |
| Touring Bikes | | | $5,403,130.67 | **$5,403,130.** |
| Mountain Frames | 71,587.79 | $1,400,331.68 | $2,067,908.64 | **$3,839,828.** |
| Road Frames | 43,887.19 | $1,618,391.51 | $1,631,377.27 | **$3,493,655.** |
| Touring Frames | | | $1,032,154.04 | **$1,032,154.** |
| Wheels | | $452,122.12 | $226,947.94 | **$679,070.** |
| Jerseys | 28,255.57 | $110,243.77 | $290,004.73 | **$428,504.** |
| Shorts | | $49,261.57 | $179,301.33 | **$228,562.** |
| Helmets | 20,235.36 | $74,281.39 | $113,443.66 | **$207,960.** |
| Tights | | $122,895.93 | $78,937.08 | **$201,833.** |

**Figure 1.12** Business users can author interactive reports with Power View.

***New features for team BI***

SQL Server 2012 adds new features to team BI, including:

- Power View reporting – With a click of a button, you can launch Power View and create an interactive report that's using a PowerPivot model or an organizational model as a data source. And, you can quickly assemble interactive reports that consolidate and aggregate information to analyze important metrics at a glance, such as the report shown in **Figure 1.12**.
- Easier setup – SQL Server setup has been refactored to exclude the PowerPivot for SharePoint installation tasks in order to simplify configuration and troubleshooting. Microsoft has provided the new PowerPivot Configuration Tool for configuring, repairing, and uninstalling PowerPivot for SharePoint.

## 1.3.3 Organizational Business Intelligence

Personal and team BI scenarios with PowerPivot have been possible since its first release in May 2010. However, using the VertiPaq technology to implement organizational analytical models is new with SQL Server 2012. Organizational BI is powered by an Analysis Services instance configured in Tabular mode. For a lack of a better term, I'll refer to organizational BI with Tabular as *Analysis Services Tabular*. Consider Analysis Services Tabular when:

- You've outgrown the PowerPivot capabilities. For example, a business user might have started with a PowerPivot model but have exceeded the Excel file size limit. Or, you might require row-level security to the model – a feature that PowerPivot doesn't support.
- You start from scratch, and all you need is a simple model for slicing and dicing data that wraps an existing database. Be careful here because many projects start simple but grow in complexity over time. For this reason, I personally favor Multidimensional as an analytical layer for data warehousing projects because it's more mature and feature-rich. I'll provide a detailed feature comparison between Tabular and Multidimensional in the next section to help you make an educated choice.

**NOTE** Organizational BI requires SQL Server 2012 Business Intelligence or Enterprise Edition. A dedicated Analysis Services instance configured in Tabular mode is required to deploy tabular models. You can't deploy tabular models to an Analysis Services instance that's configured in SharePoint mode or to an Analysis Services instance that's configured in Multidimensional mode.

***Understanding Analysis Services Tabular components***

As a BI pro, you would use a professional toolset to model organizational models, as shown in **Figure 1.13**.

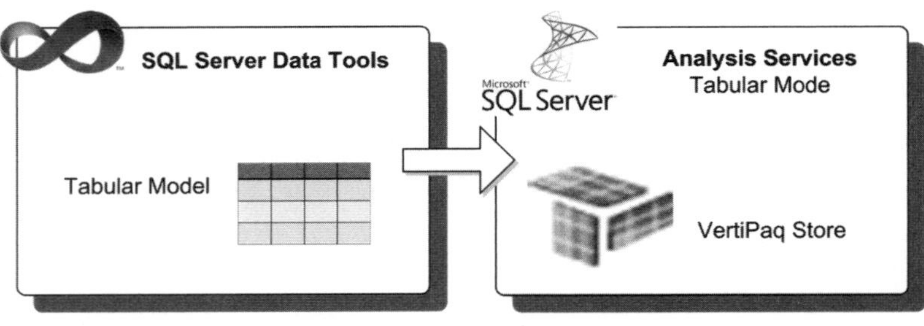


**Figure 1.13** Professionals can use SQL Server Data Tools to design models for organizational BI and deploy them to Analysis Services configured in Tabular mode.

This release introduces SQL Server Data Tools, which provides an integrated environment for database and BI developers to design for SQL Server (both on and off premise) within the Visual Studio 2010 IDE. SQL Server Data Tools (SSDT) succeeds Business Intelligence Development Studio (BIDS) and extends its capabilities to support SQL Server development (hence the name change). As far as tabular modeling goes, the design experience is very similar to PowerPivot. However, SSDT adds new features that aren't available in PowerPivot, such as source code control and project deployment. Similar to implementing multidimensional cubes, once the model is ready it can be deployed to a standalone Analysis Services instance. The difference is that this instance must run in Tabular mode, which is new to this release of Analysis Services.

***Understanding organizational BI features***

Analysis Services Tabular adds two main features for organizational use that are not found in PowerPivot. First, the modeler can define row-level security by using row filters and DAX formulas to restrict access to data. Also, the row filters can use the Windows identity of the user to implement dynamic data security, such as to restrict a manager to see data for his subordinates only. As with Multidimensional, Analysis Services Tabular supports only Windows-based security where the user is authenticated and authorized, based on her Windows logon account.

Analysis Services Tabular also adds the ability to partition large tables in order to manage them more efficiently, such as to refresh only new data instead of reimporting all the data. VertiPaq is the default storage of Analysis Services Tabular. Consequently, the compressed data resides in memory. This works great when all the data fits in a computer's main memory. When it doesn't, Analysis Services Tabular starts paging data to disk in order to reduce the memory consumption at the expense of query performance. Interestingly, Analysis Services Tabular supports a second storage mode where the server auto-generates and passes through queries to the SQL Server database that's used as a data source. This storage option, called DirectQuery, could be useful when data doesn't fit in memory or when you need real-time data access. The name "DirectQuery" reflects the main characteristics of this storage mode, which is to directly query the database.

## 1.3.4 Comparing Tabular Features

To summarize, Tabular supports personal BI (PowerPivot), team BI (PowerPivot for SharePoint), and organizational BI (Analysis Services Tabular) deployment scenarios. Let's take a moment to recap features and to compare these three deployment scenarios. This will help you understand their commonalities and differences. **Table 1.3** compares PowerPivot for Excel, PowerPivot for SharePoint, and Analysis Services Tabular features.

***Data model differences***

To start with, only PowerPivot for Excel and Analysis Services Tabular (with SQL Server Data Tools) provide modeling capabilities. You can use PowerPivot for SharePoint to publish PowerPivot models and to report from published models or external Analysis Services Tabular models. Only SQL Server Data Tools (SSDT), which is used to develop organizational models deployed to Analysis Services Tabular, provides source control. Although PowerPivot for SharePoint doesn't support source control, SharePoint can be configured to maintain document versions and checking out/in documents. Each time you check in a PowerPivot workbook, a new version is created.

Only Analysis Services Tabular models support row-level security. PowerPivot for Excel models are saved as Excel files and can't be accessed and queried by external clients without SharePoint. By contrast, team BI models deployed to SharePoint and organizational BI models deployed to Analysis Services Tabular can be used as data sources and queried by report clients.

Table 1.3 Understanding Tabular features for personal, team, and organizational BI

| Layer | Feature | PowerPivot for Excel<br>Personal BI | PowerPivot for SharePoint<br>Team BI | Analysis Services Tabular<br>Organizational BI |
|---|---|---|---|---|
| Data Model | Modeling environment | Yes | No | Yes |
| | Source control | No | No | Yes |
| | Row-level security | No | No | Yes |
| | Externally accessible | No | Yes | Yes |
| Data Access | Dataset size | 2GB | 2GB | Unlimited |
| | Partitions | No | No | Yes |
| | DirectQuery | No | No | Yes |
| | Auto-refresh | No | Yes | Yes |

***Data access differences***

PowerPivot models are limited to 2GB of compressed data. By contrast, organizational models don't have this restriction. Only Analysis Services Tabular models can have partitions and paging. This makes sense, considering they can store large volumes of data. Partitions can help the administrator refresh data selectively, such as to import only the most recent data.

DirectQuery facilitates real-time data access by passing queries directly to the database instead of caching data in the model. DirectQuery is supported for organizational BI models only. Finally, PowerPivot for Excel doesn't support refreshing data automatically. Both PowerPivot for SharePoint and Analysis Services provide options to schedule automatic data refreshes.

## 1.4 Comparing Tabular with Other Models

As you've seen, Tabular is an excellent choice for personal and team BI. That's because Multidimensional was never meant to fulfill these needs. But which path should BI professionals take for organizational BI solutions? This is where things get trickier because you need to weigh the different model capabilities and make a choice. This section is meant for readers who have experience with multidimensional cubes or Report Builder models. First, I'll compare Tabular and Multidimensional followed by an evaluation of Tabular and Report Builder models.

### 1.4.1 Comparing Tabular and Multidimensional

**Table 1.4** provides a side-by-side feature comparison of Tabular and Multidimensional. You'll find that Tabular is somewhat lacking in features in comparison with Multidimensional. That shouldn't surprise you, considering that Microsoft OLAP has been around for 15 years and has had many releases of features and improvements.

**Table 1.4 Comparing Tabular and Multidimensional**

| Layer | Feature | Tabular | Multidimensional |
|---|---|---|---|
| Data Model | Schema | Relational (tables, columns) | Multidimensional (cubes, dimensions, attributes, measures) |
| | Declarative relationships | Regular, role-playing (with DAX only) | Regular, parent-child, many-to-many, referenced, role-playing, data mining |
| | End-user model | KPIs, perspectives, default drillthrough action | KPIs, perspectives, translations, actions |
| | Aggregation functions | Sum, Count, Min, Max, Average, DistinctCount | Sum, Count, Min, Max, DistinctCount, semi-additive functions |
| Business Logic | Expression language | DAX | MDX |
| | Constructs | Calculated columns, calculated measures | Calculated members, named sets, scope assignments |
| | Extensibility | No | .NET stored procedures |
| Data Access | Primary storage | Memory | Disk |
| | Partitions | Processed serially | Processed in parallel |
| | Aggregations | N/A | Yes |
| | Data sources | Relational, multidimensional, flat files, OData, SSRS reports | Relational (single database best) |
| | Storage modes | VertiPaq, DirectQuery | MOLAP, ROLAP, HOLAP, proactive caching |

Let's discuss these results in more detail, starting with the data model layer.

***Data model***

The Tabular schema is expressed in relational constructs, such as tables and columns. Therefore, novice users might find Tabular easier to start with and more suitable for simple models. By contrast, Multidimensional has deep roots in OLAP and its artifacts: cubes, dimensions, and measures. Multidimensional is a more sophisticated and mature model, and it presents a higher learning curve. There are more knobs to turn, many of which don't have Tabular equivalents, such as default members, custom rollup, discretized attributes, unary operators, attribute types, and controlling the visibility of hierarchy levels.

**REAL WORLD** I worked once for a provider of solutions for the finance industry, and I implemented OLAP cubes for accounting and profitability management. Finance applications tend to be rather complex. Some of the Multidimensional features mentioned above proved very useful to meet our requirements, such as custom rollup and unary operators to aggregate a chart of accounts, as well as scope assignments to implement custom aggregation. The point I am trying to make is that although Tabular is simple, it's also lacking features. The more complex the requirements are, the more you should gravitate toward Multidimensional.

Declarative relationships help you define entity relationships when you're designing the model (design time), without using programming constructs. Tabular supports only regular and role-playing declarative relationships with the limitation that only one role-playing relationship can be configured as active. By contrast, Multidimensional supports more flexible relationship types. The most useful types are parent-child relationships that represent recursive hierarchies and many-to-many relationships. An example of a parent-child relationship is an organizational chart where a manager can have subordinates.

A classic example for a many-to-many relationship is a joint bank account that's shared by two or more individuals. With Tabular, you can use DAX formulas to handle parent-child relationships and many-to-many relationships but there are some pitfalls. For example, you need to "naturalize" a parent-child hierarchy by using DAX functions that expand levels into columns. To handle many-to-many relationships, you need to define calculated measures for each numeric column that needs to be aggregated. This increases the model complexity and might present usability and maintenance challenges.

By end-user features, I mean additional features that can be added to the model to further enrich it and make it more intuitive and useful for end users. With Tabular, you can define key performance indicators (KPIs), which are essentially "super" measures with goal and target expressions. You can use perspectives to define logical metadata views to reduce the perceived complexity of models with many tables. In addition, Tabular supports default drillthrough actions that show the detail rows and all the table columns behind an aggregated cell value. Tabular doesn't support other action types, such as report actions that launch a web page or a Reporting Services report.

**NOTE** The BIDS Helper project (http://bidshelper.codeplex.com) allows you to customize columns returned by drillthrough actions in tabular models. It also supports report, URL, and rowset actions.

Tabular doesn't support translations to localize the metadata and data for international users. Display folders and member properties are not supported in Tabular. Multidimensional supports semi-additive functions, such as to support account and inventory balances. Tabular requires DAX calculations to support semi-additive measures.

***Business logic***

Now we are moving to the business logic layer. Data Analysis Expressions (DAX) is the expression language for Tabular. You can use DAX to define calculated columns that store (materialize) the expression results. The closest Multidimensional equivalent of DAX calculated columns are named calculations in the Data Source View (DSV). You can also define calculated measures whose aggregation behavior is evaluated dynamically, depending on the execution context, that is, how the user slices and dices data. Calculated measures are to the MDX regular calculated members.

Tabular doesn't support named sets (pre-defined sets of members, such as top ten products), dimension calculated members, and scope assignments. The most important of these are scope assignments that let you write to the multidimensional cube space. Since scope assignments are not supported in Tabular, you have no other choice but to create a calculated measure for each column that needs a custom aggregation, such as Sales Amount YTD, Order Quantity YTD, and so on. Again, this might present maintenance and usability challenges. Finally, Multidimensional can be extended with external .NET code in the form of Analysis Services stored procedures. This option isn't available with Tabular.

Tabular doesn't include a business intelligence wizard and it doesn't support pre-defined analytical features, such as currency conversion, time intelligence, unary operators, custom member formulas, and account intelligence. Since Tabular doesn't support writeback, you can't use Excel what-if analysis.

***Data access***

The default storage mode for Tabular is memory while Multidimensional keeps data on the disk. With the exception of distinct count calculations, you shouldn't expect a substantial performance improvement by just migrating from Multidimensional to Tabular. That's because Multidimensional caches query results in memory too. Moreover, the Windows operating system maintains its own cache and keeps raw file data in memory. Consequently, chances are that the more memory you have on the server and the more end users query the cube, the more of its data will end up in memory. Aggregations, which are pre-calculated summaries of data in multidimensional cubes, can improve dramatically the performance of multidimensional cubes. Aggregations are not supported in Tabular. However, you might find better out-of-the-box performance with Tabular compared to a cube that isn't optimized. That's because VertiPaq has been specifically designed for retrieving data fast from in-memory data structures, which is not the case for cubes.

Both Multidimensional and Tabular support partitioning large tables to improve manageability. However, Tabular processes partitions within a table sequentially. As a result, processing large tables will take much longer with Tabular. Multidimensional has a strict division between dimensions and measures groups. When configuring incremental processing, the administrator must account for object dependencies. For example, fully processing a dimension invalidates the cube referencing the dimension. Processing dimensions with Process Update, drops indexes and aggregations for that dimension on related partitions so you have to restore them with Process Index. Processing is simplified in Tabular where all tables are treated the same. And, processing a table doesn't impact other tables.

VertiPaq compresses data by columns while Multidimensional OLAP (MOLAP) compresses data by rows. The typical VertiPaq compression ratio is five to ten times while the typical MOLAP compression ratio is about three times. However, the actual VertiPaq compression ratio depends on the data cardinality. For example, typically 99% of data in a data warehouse database is stored in the fact tables. Suppose you need to import most of the fact table columns, such as for end users to drill down to details. Chances are that will import high cardinality columns with many unique values, such as order number, transaction identifier, and so on. As I explained, high-cardinality columns will reduce the VertiPaq compression ratio, and you might not get a substantially better data footprint than Multidimensional.

The data acquisition capabilities of Tabular are impressive. It can import data from a variety of data sources, including relational databases, cubes, flat files, Excel files, Reporting Services R2 or later reports, and any application that exposes data as an Open Data Protocol (OData) feed, such as a SharePoint list. By contrast, Multidimensional is designed and works best when it sources data from a single database, such as a data warehouse database. Each model imports and caches unless the modeler configures the model in a pass-through (DirectQuery) mode for Tabular or Relational OLAP (ROLAP) for Multidimensional.

In cached mode (default), both models have to be explicitly processed to refresh the contained data. Tabular works best when all the data fits into memory. When estimating the Tabular memory requirements, you should account for at least twice the size of the disk footprint because additional memory is needed for refreshing data. Tabular models deployed to a dedicated Analysis Services server support basic paging, where the server pages memory to disk under memory pressure. Multidimensional has extensive paging support, and it's designed to scale to terabytes of data.

#### *Choosing between Tabular and Multidimensional*

To summarize, consider Tabular for simple analytical models where all or most of data fits into the server memory. Consider Multidimensional for more complex and enterprise-wide projects that can scale up to large data volumes. Here are a few examples to help you decide between Tabular and Multidimensional:

- Upgrading personal BI models – Suppose a business user has implemented a PowerPivot model and the model has been gaining popularity. You need to accommodate larger data volumes and secure its data. Tabular is a natural choice for this scenario. By deploying the model to Analysis Services in Tabular mode, you gain scalability and data security.

- Rapid development -- The marketing department has a new advertising effort that is scheduled for next week. They require some custom product categorizations, new dimensions that don't exist in the data warehouse and new attributes to existing dimensions, such as a custom hierarchy. The marketing department is testing three different kinds of advertising options. They'd like to compare data and analyze which of the three campaigns sold the best by grouping results by product. There is no time to develop ETL processes and enhance multidimensional cubes, especially given that this will be one-time analysis. This scenario is also a good candidate for Tabular thanks to its rapid development capabilities.
- Financial models – Suppose that you're tasked to implement an analytical layer for financial reporting. The requirements call for fairly complex business rules and aggregations, such as weighted averages and currency conversion. I recommend you use Multidimensional because it supports features specifically suited for such requirements, such as custom operators, scope assignments, and semi-additive functions.
- Data warehousing – A data warehouse database requires an analytical layer for historical and trend reporting. My preference is Multidimensional due to its maturity, richness, and ability to scale to terabytes of data.

## 1.4.2 Comparing Tabular and Report Builder Models

If you've used Reporting Services Report Builder models, then you might wonder how they compare with Tabular. Microsoft introduced the Report Builder technology in SQL Server 2005 as a feature of Reporting Services for business users to author ad hoc reports from pre-defined models. Report Builder consists of two components: a Report Builder model that is layered on top of a database and a Report Builder client that information workers can use for report authoring.

In SQL Server 2012, Report Builder models are deprecated and superseded by Tabular models. Report Model projects are no longer supported. Therefore, you can't create new Report Model projects or open existing Report Model projects in SQL Server Data Tools. Microsoft doesn't provide a migration path from Report Builder to Tabular. If you don't plan to upgrade Report Builder models, you need to keep Business Intelligence Development Studio (BIDS) from prior releases of SQL Server. **Table 1.5** provides a side-by-side feature comparison of Tabular and Report Builder models.

**NOTE** Microsoft deprecated the Report Builder models only. The Report Builder client is not deprecated and supports both tabular and multidimensional models. End users can use the Report Builder client to author ad hoc reports from Tabular just like they can do so from multidimensional cubes.

***Data model***

Unlike Tabular, Report Builder embraces the Object Role Modeling (ORM) methodology and represents database artifacts as entities, fields, and roles. One interesting feature that the Report Builder client supports is role navigation, where you can select only related entities in the report. Power View has a similar feature that inspects the table relationships defined in the model and that prevents the user from selecting columns from unrelated tables.

In general, the Report Builder supports only regular relationships where tables are directly related to each other. It also supports more advanced relationship features that don't have Tabular equivalents, including entity inheritance (for example, a sales person is an employee), role expansion (adding fields from the Contact entity to the Employee entity to expand employees with contact details), and lookup entities (bringing entities from another lookup table, such as adding (denormalizing) a product category from the Product Category entity to the Product entity).

Another Report Builder-specific feature is infinite clickthrough, which gives the modeler the ability to define drillthrough paths in the model. Then, the end user can click any clickthrough-enabled fields to see the details of the related entity. The closest Tabular equivalent of this feature is the default drillthrough action, although it's isolated to a single table only.

**Table 1.5 Comparing Tabular and Report Builder models**

| Layer | Feature | Tabular Model | Report Builder Model |
|---|---|---|---|
| Data Model | Schema | Relational (tables and columns) | Semantic (entities, fields, roles) |
| | Declarative relationships | Regular, role-playing | Regular, entity inhertiance, role expansion, lookup entities |
| | End-user model | KPIs, perspectives, actions (drillthrough) | Clickthrough (requires Enterprise edition) |
| | Aggregation functions | Sum, Count, Min, Max, Average, DistinctCount | Sum, Count, Min, Max, Average, DistinctCount |
| Business Logic | Expression language | DAX | Visual Basic functions |
| | Constructs | Calculated columns, calculated measures | Named calculations |
| Data Access | Storage type | In-memory cache and basic passthrough | Passthrough |
| | Data sources | Relational, multidimensional, flat files, OData, SSRS reports | SQL Server, Oracle, Analysis Services, Teradata |
| | Storage modes | VertiPaq, DirectQuery | Pass-through queries |

***Business logic***

The business logic capabilities of Report Builder are limited to a subset of Visual Basic functions that can be used to define custom expressions, such as aggregate functions. DAX is a more powerful query language. The Report Builder business logic constructs are limited to defining calculations in the data source view. This works in the same way as it does with Multidimensional.

***Data access***

The most important difference between the two models in terms of data access is that Report Builder doesn't cache data. Instead, it auto-generates queries to the source database in a pass-through mode. I mentioned that, by default, Tabular caches data for the best possible performance. Since data is cached, you need to explicitly process the model to synchronize the data changes. On the upside, Tabular performs much better when aggregating larger data volumes.

Report Builder supports SQL Server, Analysis Services, Oracle, and Teradata databases only. By contrast, as long as data is accessible, Tabular can retrieve data from virtually anywhere. Finally, Report Builder doesn't store data. It simply receives the report from the client and auto-generates queries to the supported data sources. By contrast, Tabular caches data by default.

In summary, if you decide to replace your Report Builder models with tabular models, you'll undoubtedly find that Tabular is a richer and more efficient model. Unfortunately, migrating to Tabular will require a complete rewrite. If this isn't an option, you can still continue using your Report Builder models with SQL Server 2012. Although you must use Business Intelligence Development Studio (BIDS) to make changes to the model, you can deploy the model to SQL Server 2012 Reporting Services.

## 1.5 Summary

This chapter has been a whirlwind tour of the innovative Business Intelligence Semantic Model (BISM) and its features. By now, you should view BISM as a flexible platform that meets a variety of BI requirements. A component of SQL Server 2012 Analysis Services, BISM is a collective name of Multidimensional and Tabular models. You've learned about the history of Analysis Services and how it fits into the Microsoft BI stack. We took a close look at the BISM logical architecture and its data model, business logic, and data access layers.

Next, this chapter focused on Tabular. I explained the events that led to the arrival of Tabular and its design objectives to help you create BI solutions that are simpler to implement and that perform well. These solutions can span the entire spectrum of personal, team, and organizational BI.

Readers familiar with multidimensional cubes saw how Tabular and Multidimensional compare and how to choose between them. This chapter also provided a feature comparison between Tabular and Report Builder models.

Having laid the foundation, we are ready to put our knowledge to use. Let's continue our journey by exploring personal BI with PowerPivot.

# PART 

# *Personal Business Intelligence*

If you are new to Microsoft personal BI, welcome! This part of the book provides the essential fundamentals to introduce you to personal BI with PowerPivot, and help you understand its capabilities. While specifically targeting business users, it will benefit BI practitioners new to Tabular too because PowerPivot is just one of the two flavors of Tabular. Remember from Chapter 1 that both PowerPivot and Analysis Services Tabular share the same modeling framework allowing you to easily transition personal BI models to organizational models.

The Microsoft BI tool for personal BI is PowerPivot. Now in its second release, PowerPivot has evolved into a feature-rich BI tool without sacrificing its end-user focus and simplicity. Business users will favor PowerPivot for implementing a plethora of BI solutions, ranging from single-table models for slicing and dicing data to more complex models that mash up data from a variety of data sources and further enrich it with business calculations.

If you're already a PowerPivot user, you'll find that its second release brings appealing features that can makes the tool more intuitive and powerful. A brand new Diagram View helps you visualize the model schema at a glance. Hierarchies allow you to implement common navigational paths for data exploration. Perspectives define logical metadata views to expose a subset of the model metadata to end users in order to reduce the perceived complexity of large models. This version removes annoying limitations by introducing metadata-oriented features, such as custom sorting, persisted data types and format settings. It also adds support for images, key performance indicators (KPIs), and new DAX functions.

PowerPivot is a free add-on to Microsoft Excel 2010. This part of the book starts with providing the necessary background to understand and install PowerPivot. Then, it walks you through the steps for implementing a personal model for sales analysis and reporting.

Chapter 2

# Personal BI Basics



In the previous chapter I explained how the Tabular side of the business intelligence semantic model (BISM) can help you implement solutions for a wide spectrum of data analysis and reporting needs. These solutions range from simple models for personal business intelligence (BI) to more complex and highly scalable models for organizational BI. Personal BI (also known as self-service BI) empowers businesses to offload effort from IT pros and build their own models for self-service data exploration and reporting.

This chapter lays out the foundation of personal BI. First, I'll help you understand when personal BI is a good choice. I'll introduce you to PowerPivot for Excel and show you how to install it. Next, this chapter provides the necessary technical background to understand PowerPivot models. Finally, the chapter walks you through a hands-on lab that demonstrates how PowerPivot can help you implement an analytical model for reporting and data analysis.

## 2.1 Introducing Personal Business Intelligence

Remember that Personal BI enables business users (information workers, like business managers or marketing managers, and power users) to offload effort from IT pros and build BI models for self-service data exploration and reporting. And, team BI allows the same users to share their reports with other team members without requiring them to install modeling or reporting tools. The Tabular manifestation for personal and team BI is a technology called PowerPivot. PowerPivot allows you to import data from various data sources, analyze it in the familiar Excel environment, and share PowerPivot reports by deploying them to Microsoft SharePoint Server 2010.

PowerPivot is freely available and consists of two components – PowerPivot for Excel (an Excel add-in) and PowerPivot for SharePoint. As a business domain expert, you can use PowerPivot for Excel to create PowerPivot models in Excel and to analyze data in pivot reports. Once the model is ready, you can deploy the Excel workbook (containing the model and pivot reports) to SharePoint to make it immediately available to other users. Your teammates can view your pivot reports online even if they don't have Excel 2010 installed. And, they can create their own interactive and operational reports that query your model.

## 2.1.1 About Organizational BI

To understand PowerPivot and personal BI better, let's compare it with organizational BI, which you might already be familiar with. This will help you view personal BI not as a competing technology but as a completing technology to organizational BI. In other words, personal BI and organizational BI are both necessary for most businesses, and they complement each other.

***Classic solution for organizational BI***

Organizational BI defines a set of technologies and processes for implementing an end-to-end BI solution where the implementation effort is shifted to IT professionals (as opposed to information workers and people who use Excel as part of their job). Its main objective is to provide accurate and trusted analysis and reporting. **Figure 2.1** shows a classic organizational BI implementation.

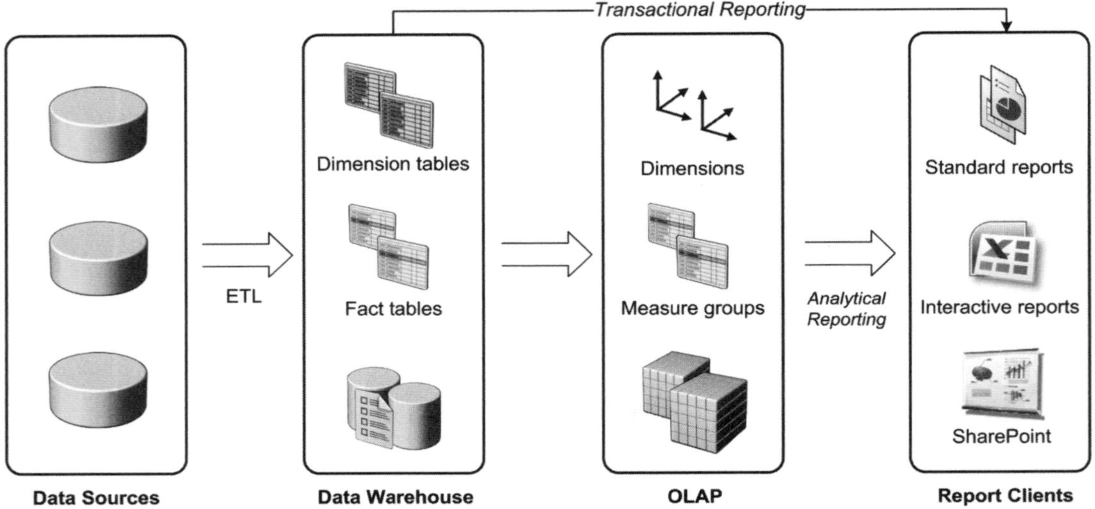


**Figure 2.1** Organizational BI typically includes ETL processes, data warehousing, and OLAP.

In a typical corporate environment, data is scattered in a variety of data sources, and consolidating it presents a major challenge. Extraction, transformation, and loading (ETL) processes extract data from the original data sources, clean it, and then load the trusted data in a data warehouse or data mart. The data warehouse organizes data in a set of dimensions and fact tables. Data denormalization is used to reduce the number of tables and to facilitate reporting processes. For example, an operational database might be highly normalized and have Product, Subcategory, and Category tables. However, when designing a data warehouse, the modeler might decide to have a single Product table that includes columns from the Subcategory and Category tables. So, instead of three tables, the data warehouse now has only one table and end users don't need to join multiple tables.

While end users could run transactional reports directly from the data warehouse, many organizations also implement an Online Analytical Processing (OLAP) layer in the form of one or more Analysis Services multidimensional cubes for analytical reporting. As an information worker, you can use Excel (or another OLAP browser) to connect to the cube in order to slice and dice data, such as to see how the product sales are doing over time. And, IT pros can create operational reports from the cube. Having such an OLAP layer is valuable for the following reasons:

- Implicit relationships – In the process of designing a cube, the modeler defines relationships between dimensions and measure groups. As a result, end users don't need to join tables explicitly because the relationships have already been established at design time. For example, you don't have to know how to join the Product table to the Sales table. You simply add the fields you need on the report, and then the model knows how to relate them.
- Interactive data analysis – From an end-user perspective, OLAP data analysis is a matter of dragging and dropping attributes on the report to slice and dice data. A "smart" OLAP-capable client, such as Excel, could auto-generate the report queries, and the server takes care of aggregating data, such as to summarize sales at the year level.
- Great performance – Analysis Services cubes are optimized to aggregate data very fast. Most queries are answered within seconds even when aggregating huge datasets. Organizational BI solutions can scale to terabytes of data.
- Business calculations – Business logic can be centralized in the OLAP layer. Because of this, report developers and end users don't need to redefine important metrics from one report to another.

**REAL WORLD** The MIS department of a retail company included some 20 report developers on staff whose sole responsibility was creating operational reports from SQL stored procedures. Over time, stored procedures have grown in complexity and developers have defined important business metrics differently. Needless to say, operational reports didn't tally. Although the term "a single version of the truth" is somewhat overloaded, a centralized OLAP layer can get pretty close to it.

- Data security – Data can be secured based on the user's Windows identity, such as to allow Bob to see data only for the partners he is authorized to access.
- Client support – There are many reporting tools (such as Excel and Report Builder) that support Analysis Services cubes and address various reporting needs, including standard reports, interactive reports, and performance dashboards.

***Understanding organizational BI challenges***

Although well-defined and established, organizational BI might face a few challenges, including the following:

- Significant implementation effort – Implementing an organizational BI solution isn't a simple undertaking. Business users and IT pros must work together to derive requirements. Most of the implementation effort goes into data logistics processes to clean, verify, and load data. For example, Susan and Jeff from the IT department are tasked to implement an organizational BI solution. First, they need to meet with business users to obtain the necessary business knowledge and gather requirements (business requirements might be hard to come by). Then, they have to identify where data resides and how to extract, clean, and transform the data. Then, Susan and Jeff must implement ETL processes, cubes, and reports. QA must test the solution. And, IT pros must configure the hardware and software, as well as deploy and maintain the solution. Security and huge datasets bring additional challenges.
- Highly specialized skillset – Organizational BI require specialized skills, such as ETL developers, Analysis Services developers, and report developers. Given the increasing popularity of SharePoint as a BI platform, SharePoint expertise might be needed as well. System engineers and developers must work together to plan security, which sometimes might be more complicated than the actual BI solution.
- Less flexibility – Organization BI might not be flexible enough to react quickly to new or changing business requirements. For example, Alice from the Accounting department might

be tasked to analyze expense reports that are not in the data warehouse. Alice might need to wait for a few months before data is imported and validated.

The good news is that personal BI can complement organizational BI quite well to address these challenges. Given the above example, while waiting for the pros to enhance the organization BI solution, Alice can use PowerPivot for Excel to import and analyze expenses. She already has the domain knowledge. However, she needs to learn PowerPivot for Excel and modeling concepts. At the beginning, she'll probably struggle and she'll need a lot of guidance from IT pros, such as to get access to and import data, how to build a personal BI model, how to create calculations, and so on. She also needs to take *responsibility* that her model is correct and can be trusted. But, isn't personal BI better than waiting?

## 2.1.2 Understanding Personal BI

Personal BI empowers business users to implement their own BI models with guidance from their IT department. For companies that don't have organizational BI or can't afford it, personal BI presents an opportunity for building customized ad-hoc solutions to gain data insights outside the capabilities of organizational BI solutions and line-of-business applications. On the other hand, organizations that have invested in organizational BI might find that personal BI opens additional options for valuable data exploration and analysis.

**REAL WORLD** I led a PowerPivot training class for a large company that has invested heavily in organizational BI. They have implemented a data warehouse and OLAP cubes. Only a subset of data in the data warehouse was loaded in the cubes. Their business analysts were looking for a tool that would let them join and analyze data from the cubes and the data warehouse. In another case, an educational institution had to analyze expense report data that wasn't stored in a data warehouse. Such scenarios can benefit greatly from personal BI and PowerPivot.

***Personal BI benefits***

Microsoft personal BI with PowerPivot offers important benefits. First, it makes BI pervasive and accessible to practically everyone. Anyone can implement BI applications if they have access to and understand the data. Users can import data from virtually any data source, ranging from flat files to cloud applications. Then they can mash it up and gain insights. Once data is imported, the users can build their own reports. For example, Alice understands Excel but she doesn't know SQL or relational databases. Fortunately, PowerPivot for Excel doesn't require any technical skills. Alice could import and join data from her Excel files with corporate data from a data warehouse, and build consolidated reports.

Microsoft personal BI is Excel-centric. There are millions of users who use Excel day in and day out. These users would appreciate the ability to model and analyze data right in Excel (the application they're already using). PowerPivot for Excel extends the Excel capabilities and allows you to analyze large data volumes without performance degradation. Data modeling is intuitive without requiring data to be shaped to conform to Excel pivot requirements, and it doesn't require VLOOKUPs to join data. And the price is right too (PowerPivot is free)!

***Personal BI considerations***

Any personal BI rollout requires careful evaluation. Here are some considerations you should keep in mind before deciding in its favor:

- Know your business users – What kind of business users do you have? Are they power users who have the time, desire, and patience to learn a new technology and to design models?

- Data access – How will the end users access data? Should they connect directly to the data source or should they get data extracts, such as flat files? If users are given direct access to the data source, how does importing and data refreshing data impact the system?
- Security – What subset of data should the users have access to?
- IT involvement – Personal BI might be good, but managed personal BI (personal BI under the supervision of IT pros) is even better and sometimes a must. Therefore, the IT group must budget time and resources to help end users when needed, such as to give users access to data, to help with data integrity and more complex business calculations, and to troubleshoot issues when things go wrong.
- "Spreadmarts" – I left the most important consideration for last. If your IT department has spent a lot of effort to avoid using Excel for data management, should we allow the data to end up in spreadsheets again? Whose model and calculations do we trust?

Now that you understand the personal BI pros and cons, let's dive into PowerPivot for Excel.

## 2.2 Understanding PowerPivot for Excel

In Chapter 1, I introduced you to Tabular. I explained that in SQL Server 2012, Tabular is available in two flavors: PowerPivot and Analysis Services configured in Tabular mode. Microsoft's PowerPivot is the company's premium tool for personal and team BI. It enables business users to import data from various data sources, analyze it with Excel pivot reports, and then share the PowerPivot models with other users by deploying the models to SharePoint.

### 2.2.1 Installing PowerPivot for Excel

Since this part of the book is about personal BI, we will focus on PowerPivot for Excel. This section walks you through the installation of PowerPivot and introduces you to the PowerPivot modeling environment.

***Understanding system requirements***

PowerPivot for Excel requires Excel 2010. Because the imported data is embedded inside the Excel workbook file, Microsoft introduced changes to the Excel 2010 storage format and new application programming interfaces (APIs) that are not available in previous versions of Excel.

**NOTE** Although PowerPivot requires Excel 2010, Excel 2007 users can open Excel 2010 workbooks that contain PowerPivot models and view the included pivot reports. However, users won't be able to interact with the reports because any interactive action results in a query to PowerPivot, which Excel 2007 doesn't support. In addition, Excel 2010-specific features, such as slicers, are not available.

PowerPivot isn't available for the Macintosh release of Excel. Currently, PowerPivot is a Windows-only product. You can't install PowerPivot with Excel Starter Edition, which you might get if you've purchased a new computer. You won't get PowerPivot with Excel Web Applications or with Office 365.

***Deciding between Excel 32 bit or 64 bit***

Modern computers ship with 64-bit CPUs and 64-bit Windows installations. 32-bit applications are limited to 2GB of memory. 64-bit computing enables applications to address more than 2GB of memory which is especially useful for in-memory databases, such as VertiPaq, which as you might remember is the storage engine of Tabular. In general, if you have a 64-bit version of Windows, you should install the 64-bit version of any software if a 64-bit version is available. Unlike prior releases, Excel 2010 comes in 32-bit and 64-bit versions.

**TIP** Microsoft Knowledge Base article 827218 (http://support.microsoft.com/kb/827218) describes how to check if you have a 32-bit or 64-bit version of Windows. If you have Excel 2010 installed, click File ⇨ Help, and then examine the version number on the right side of the Help page. If Excel is a 32-bit version, you'll see something like this: "Version 14.0.5128.5000 (32-bit)".

Unfortunately, with Microsoft Office 2010, the choice of whether you should install a 32-bit or a 64-bit version isn't so straightforward. The issue is that many Excel add-ins haven't been upgraded to Excel 2010 or are available in 32-bit versions only, such as the Adobe Acrobat add-ins for Microsoft Office. As a result, these add-ins (as well as 32-bit ActiveX controls) won't work with a 64-bit version of Excel 2010. To make things worse, you can't run the 32-bit and 64-bit versions of Excel 2010 side by side.

If you have 32-bit legacy add-ins, you should consider the 32-bit version of Excel, which is the default installation option if you install it from the Microsoft Office 2010 setup disk. If you decide to install the 64-bit version, uninstall the 32-bit version of Excel, and then run the setup from the x64 folder on the disk. The default setup options should install everything PowerPivot needs. If you decide to customize the setup, make sure you leave the Microsoft Office Shared Features option selected. If you don't have the Office Shared Features installed, you'll get the following message when you attempt to install PowerPivot: "The add-in requires that the Office Shared Features component of Microsoft Office 2010 is installed."

**NOTE** Don't despair if the IT department has already installed the 32-bit version of Excel on your computer. Thanks to the VertiPaq's efficient data compression, you'll still be able to import and work with large datasets (in the range of millions).

### *Installing PowerPivot for Excel*

PowerPivot for Excel is implemented as an Excel add-in, and it doesn't ship with Excel. Once you figure out whether to use a 32-bit or 64-bit version of Excel, the PowerPivot installation story is simple. You can download and install the free PowerPivot for Excel add-in from http://www.powerpivot.com. Remember to choose the correct version (32-bit or 64-bit) to match the Excel version installed. Once you install it, the next time you launch Excel, it will ask you if you want to register the PowerPivot for Excel add-in. Follow these steps to verify if the PowerPivot add-in is installed and functional:

1. Open Excel 2010 and go to File ⇨ Options. In the Excel Options window, click Add-Ins.
2. In the "View and Manage Microsoft Office Add-ins" dialog box, expand the Manage drop-down list at the bottom, select COM Add-Ins, and then click Go.
3. In the COM Add-Ins dialog box, make sure that PowerPivot for Excel is listed and checked.

To uninstall PowerPivot completely, close Excel, and go to Programs and Features in the Windows Control Panel. Then, uninstall Microsoft SQL Server 2012 PowerPivot for Excel.

### *Upgrading from previous versions*

The PowerPivot for Excel upgrade story is also simple. In fact, it's automatic! PowerPivot simply asks you to upgrade. Suppose you have a PowerPivot model that you've created with version 1 of PowerPivot for Excel (released in May 2010) or version 1.5 (released a few months later to support importing data from Microsoft Azure Marketplace). Once you click the PowerPivot button, PowerPivot for Excel automatically detects an older version and then prompts you to upgrade to version 2. If you decide to upgrade, PowerPivot for Excel automatically upgrades your model.

Note that PowerPivot for Excel doesn't have an option to downgrade models to previous versions. In other words, once you decide to upgrade, you commit yourself and other users to using version 2 of PowerPivot for Excel and SharePoint. Users who have the older version will be able to open the workbook and see pivot reports. However, they won't be able to interact with reports or access the PowerPivot model.

Before you decide to upgrade, you might want to evaluate the new features. The most significant new features in PowerPivot for Excel 2.0 include:

- Diagram View – Provides a graphical representation of the model schema so you can see the entire model schema at a glance. You can easily create relationships by dragging and dropping columns.
- Hierarchies – You can now create useful navigational paths by combining columns in a hierarchy, such as a Product by Category hierarchy where you can drill down data by product category, subcategory, and product levels. For example, Alice typically analyzes sales data by year, quarter, and month. Instead of adding three fields separately in an Excel pivot report, she could implement a Calendar Dates hierarchy, and then she can drag it on the report.
- Key Performance Indicators (KPIs) – A KPI is an enhanced measure that tracks an important metric, such as company's revenue, against a predefined goal. For example, management might request a Return on Investment (ROI) KPI to measure it against a predefined goal
- Perspectives – Similar to multidimensional cubes, you can create perspectives to define logical views and reduce the perceived complexity of the model. For example, Alice might have imported 20 tables to analyze direct sales to consumers and reseller sales. Since some tables are only relevant to a given subject area, she can create Internet Sales and Reseller Sales perspectives. When she builds a report, she can select the appropriate perspective to see a subset of the model metadata, such as to view only tables and measures that apply to direct sales.
- Calculation Area – With the Calculation Area, you can view measures in a grid pattern, so you can easily create, edit, and manage measures and KPIs within the model.
- Metadata improvements – Microsoft improved the presentation of the model metadata. You can now sort column values by another column, apply model data types and formats to pivot reports, format calculated measures, and provide descriptions for tables and measures.
- Image data type support – Now PowerPivot supports importing images and then displaying them in Power View reports.
- Reporting properties – Microsoft added advanced properties to support better Power View reports, such as the ability to group values based on a table identifier, to add table details, and to set a representative column and image URL.
- New DAX functions – DAX is extended with new statistical and ranking functions (DISTINCTCOUNT, RANKX, TOPN, STDEV, VAR, and so on), information functions (LOOKUPVALUE, FILTERS), functions to handle parent-child hierarchies (PATH, PATHCONTAINS, and so on), and filter functions (CONTAINS, ALLSELECTED, ISFILTERED, and so on). For example, suppose that a table includes an organizational parent-child hierarchy that models a manager-subordinate recursive relationship (a manager can have subordinates which in turn can have employees reporting to them). With the parent-child functions, you can add a column for each level so that you can drill down the hierarchy.

## 2.2.2 Getting to Know PowerPivot for Excel

Once PowerPivot for Excel is installed, it extends the Excel ribbon and adds new menu items, dialog boxes, and the PowerPivot window. Let's spend some time to understand these changes and to get familiar with the PowerPivot environment.

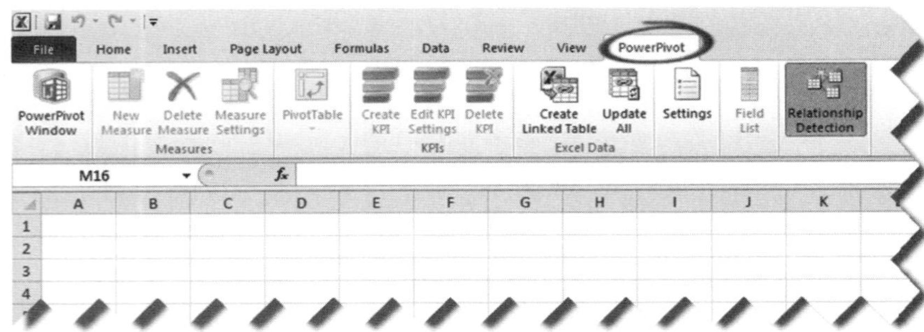


**Figure 2.2** PowerPivot extends the Excel ribbon and adds new menu items and buttons.

***Understanding the PowerPivot ribbon***

PowerPivot adds a new PowerPivot tab to the end of the Excel ribbon, as shown in **Figure 2.2**. Here is a brief description of the ribbon groups of the PowerPivot tab:

- PowerPivot window – Opens a new window that represents the PowerPivot modeling environment.
- Measures – Allows you to create and edit calculated measures to implement business logic.
- PivotTable – Adds one or more PivotTable or PivotChart reports to analyze the model data.
- KPIs – Create and edit key performance indicators (KPIs).
- Excel Data – The easiest way to import Excel data from the same workbook, where the PowerPivot model is saved, is to link the data by clicking the Create Linked Table button. Once the data is linked, you can make changes to it in Excel and PowerPivot will automatically pick up the changes.
- Settings – Opens the PowerPivot Options & Diagnostics dialog box. You can use this dialog box to check the PowerPivot version, to enable logging of MDX queries that Excel sends to PowerPivot, to set the language, and to enroll into a customer experience program that sends feedback to Microsoft.

**TIP** Excel connects to the embedded PowerPivot model as a multidimensional cube and sends MDX queries to it when you create reports. Besides PowerPivot logging, another way to see the actual MDX queries is to install the excellent OLAP PivotTable Extensions add-in (http://olappivottableextend.codeplex.com/) by Greg Galloway. Once you install it, you can simply right-click a pivot report, click OLAP PivotTable Extensions, and then select the MDX tab to view the MDX query. When connected to a multidimensional cube, the add-in offers other goodies, such as defining calculated members and a search feature that exceeds the Excel 2010 search capabilities.

- Field List – Shows/hides the PowerPivot Field List that displays the model metadata. You can use the Power Field List to add fields to a pivot report and build custom calculations.
- Relationship Detection – Enables/disables automatic relationship discovery among tables. By default, the relationship detection feature is on and PowerPivot attempts to discover table relationships if they don't exist in the model.

***Understanding the PowerPivot window***

Excel 2010 has a limitation of 1,048,576 rows per worksheet. Since it's likely that you might work with larger datasets, PowerPivot bypasses Excel and provides its own modeling environment, the PowerPivot window. One confusing aspect is that this window pops up outside Excel, so when you work with PowerPivot, you have at least two Excel windows in the Windows taskbar: the Excel window and the PowerPivot window.

A second potential confusion is that if you click Help in the Excel window and then click Help in the PowerPivot window, you get two different Help experiences that address the different interfaces (this could be confusing because the two windows look very similar). Remember that modeling is done exclusively in the PowerPivot window, while data analysis is performed in Excel. **Figure 2.3** shows the PowerPivot window. It's empty because no data has been loaded yet.

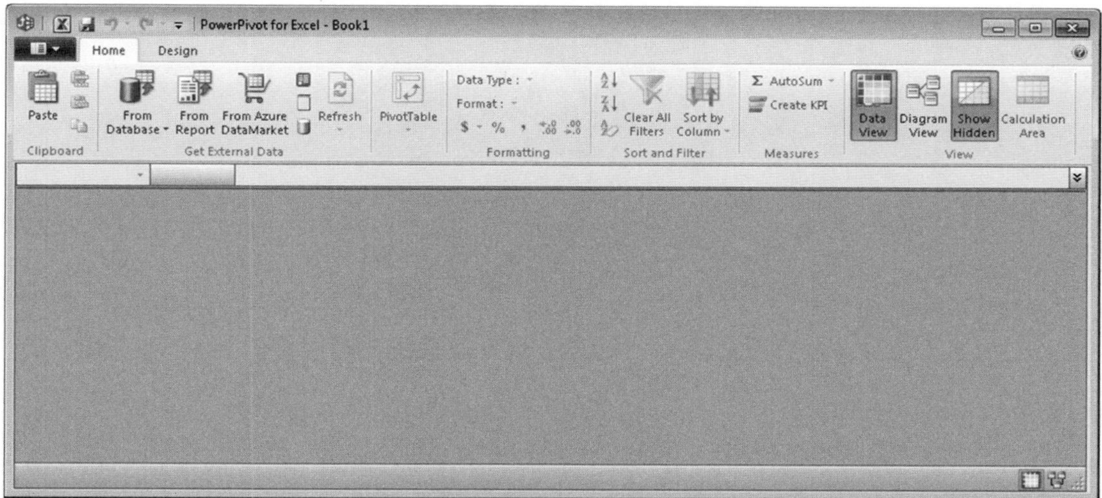


**Figure 2.3** The PowerPivot window represents the PowerPivot modeling environment.

The PowerPivot window has its own ribbon, consisting of the Home and Design tabs. Each tab has ribbon groups that group logically related buttons. I'll briefly describe these ribbon groups.

***Home***

The Home tab gives you access to data import, formatting, and sorting options.

- Clipboard – Pastes data from the Windows Clipboard.
- Get External Data – Imports and refreshes data from external data sources. For example, you can use the From Database button if you want to import data from relational and multidimensional databases.
- PivotTable – Adds a PivotTable or PivotChart report(s). It's the same as the PivotTable button in the Excel PowerPivot ribbon.
- Formatting – Changes the data type of table columns and it formats data in columns, such as to format a column as a decimal number with a thousand separator and two decimal digits.
- Sort and Filter – Sorts and filters the column values.
- Measures – This is a new group in this release that allows you to create key performance indicators (KPIs) and calculations with predefined aggregation functions, such as Sum.

- View – Toggles between Data View and Diagram View. The features include controlling the visibility of hidden columns and a Calculation pane that can be used to test custom calculations, similar to how you enter formulas to aggregate data in Excel.

***Design***

The Design tab (**Figure 2.4**) gives you the ability to enhance the model with calculated columns and relationships. It has the following ribbon groups:

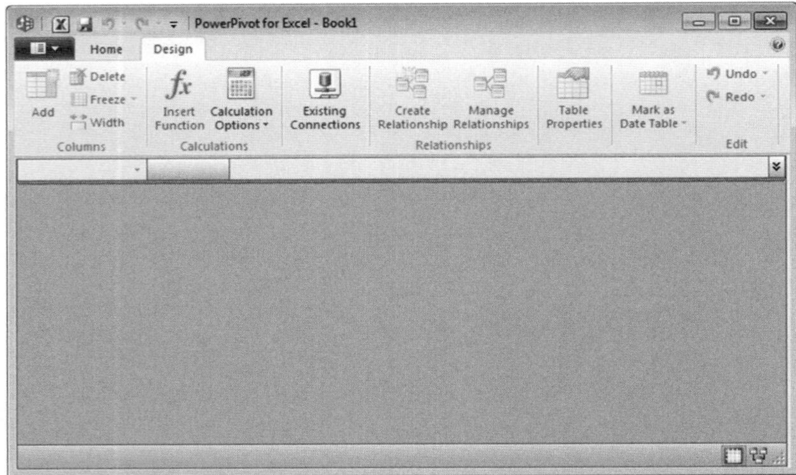


**Figure 2.4** The Design tab of the PowerPivot window.

- Columns – Adds or deletes a calculated column that uses a DAX formula, such as to concatenate the employee's first and last name. It also includes features that control the column appearance, such as the column width.
- Calculations – The Insert Function button opens a dialog box that shows the available DAX functions and their arguments to help you create calculated columns. The Calculations Options button switches between automatic and manual calculation mode for calculated columns. By default, PowerPivot automatic detects data changes and recalculates formulas in calculated columns. For example, any changes to data in the model that could cause the formula results to change will trigger recalculation of the entire calculated column. However, you can choose to forego the automatic behavior and only update calculated columns manually, especially if your model has complex formulas or very large datasets and you want to control when to update the column formulas.
- Existing Connections – Allows you to review data source connections and to refresh data.
- Relationships – Creates and manages relationships between tables. For example, your model might have a Date table (with Day, Quarter, and Year columns), and a Sales table (with Day, SalesAmount, and other columns) that stores sales for each day. However, before you can analyze sales by quarters and years, you must join the Sales table to the Date table.
- Table Properties – Opens the table definition to edit table, column, and filter mappings. For example, you might have imported a Sales table but might have missed a column. You can click the Table Properties button to add that column and reimport the data.
- Mark as Date Table – Marks a table that contains dates as a Date table. Some report clients, such as Excel, enable additional features for date tables, such as relative dates (Yesterday, Last

Week, Next Quarter, and so on). In addition, DAX time calculations require a Date table, such as to compute inventory balances or year-to-date calculations.

- Edit – Performs undo and redo operations.

***Understanding the Quick Access Toolbar***

Similar to Excel, the PowerPivot window features a Quick Access Toolbar, as shown in **Figure 2.5**. The Switch to Workbook button takes you to the Excel window. The Save button saves the model changes in the Excel workbook.

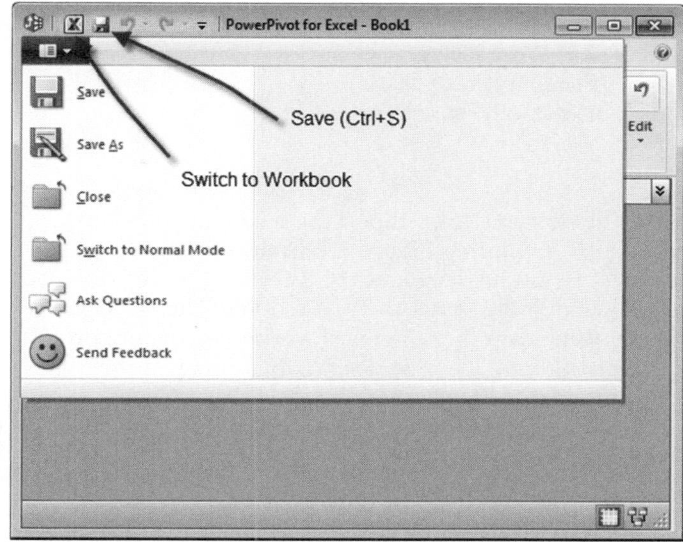


**Figure 2.5** With the Quick Access Toolbar, you can save the workbook or switch to Excel.

The drop-down menu offers similar options to what the Excel File menu has. You can save the Excel workbook or close the PowerPivot window. The "Switch to Advanced Mode" option adds the Advanced tab to the Power Window ribbon, which enables additional features, such as perspectives. The Ask Questions menu item navigates you to the PowerPivot public discussion forum where you can post questions. Finally, Send Feedback takes you to http://connect.microsoft.com, where you can log bugs or suggestions to improve PowerPivot.

**TIP** If the PowerPivot ribbon buttons get in the way, you can right-click the menu area and then click "Minimize the Ribbon". This will collapse the ribbon button area, although the buttons will still be accessible when you click the menu tabs. To restore the ribbon, right-click the menu again and toggle the "Minimize the Ribbon" menu item. Or, you can click the up and down button in the upper-right corner (to the left of the Excel help icon) to collapse and expand the ribbon.

## 2.2.3 Understanding PowerPivot Models

Although PowerPivot for Excel is implemented as an Excel add-in and it's integrated with Excel, it is not Excel. You can't create PowerPivot reports directly from data in Excel worksheets as you can do with Excel pivot reports. Before you can analyze data, you must create a PowerPivot model and import the data. Don't despair though, if this sounds complicated. PowerPivot includes wizards that walk you through the import process. But before I show you how easy this is, let's see first how PowerPivot stores the data that you import from external data sources. **Figure 2.6** helps you visualize a PowerPivot model.

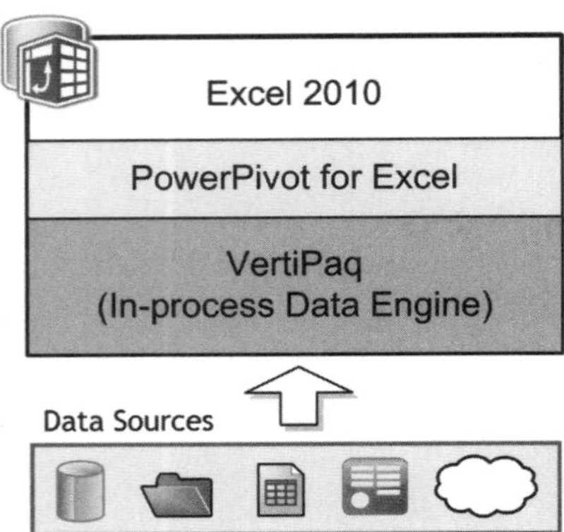


**Figure 2.6** When you query the model, PowerPivot loads data in the in-process VertiPaq engine.

***Understanding how PowerPivot stores data***

As a first step of implementing a PowerPivot model, you must import the data that you need to analyze even if that data is in an Excel workbook. Exploring **Figure 2.6** from the bottom up, you can import data from a variety of data sources, including databases (SQL Server, Oracle, multidimensional cubes, and so on), text files, Excel workbooks, and other data sources (Reporting Services reports, cloud applications, data feeds). When you save the Excel workbook, the imported data is saved in the Excel workbook file. The workbook file provides durable storage. When you save the Excel workbook file, the PowerPivot model and its data are saved to disk. When you reopen the Excel file, PowerPivot tells VertiPaq to load data from disk into the computer main memory.

**NOTE** If you're curious where Excel saves the PowerPivot data, rename the Excel file to include a zip extension, such as Ch02.xlsx.zip, and then double-click the file to open it with your archival program, such as WinZip or 7-Zip. Since an Excel file is really a ZIP compressed archive, it contains a folder structure. The PowerPivot data is kept in a compressed format inside the \xl\customData folder. The storage format is the Analysis Services ABF backup file format: the one you'll get when you back up a multidimensional cube.

The Excel bit-ness (32-bit vs. 64-bit) impacts how much memory is allocated to Excel and how much data PowerPivot can import, as shown in **Table 2.1**.

**Table 2.1 How much data you can import with Excel 32-bit and 64-bit**

| Feature | Excel 32-bit | Excel 64-bit |
|---|---|---|
| Maximum Excel memory | 2 GB | Constrained by physical memory only |
| Maximum memory for data | About 1 GB | About 4 GB |
| Maximum Excel file size | 500-700 MB | About 2 GB |

If you install 32-bit Excel, Excel will be limited to a maximum of 2 GB of memory, even if you have more memory on your computer. Given that the Excel itself, add-ins, and VertiPaq consume plenty of memory, you have about one gigabyte of memory left for the data that you'll import and analyze. Since the typical VertiPaq memory-to-disk compression is about 2:1, the maximum file size of your PowerPivot workbook is around 500-700 MB. However, data is stored in a highly compressed format with a typical compression ratio of ten times and more. Therefore, you can still pack millions of rows into 500 MB of storage. The exact number depends on several factors, including the number of the columns you're importing, the density of the columns (number of unique values in a column), and the column data types.

**NOTE** Check my blog post, "Estimating Data Compression" (http://bit.ly/powerpivotcompression), to learn how to determine the PowerPivot compression ratio. I used a helpful script that was developed by a SQL Server MVP, Vidas Matelis. The script examines the PowerPivot storage and then reports how much space each table is using in the PowerPivot workbook.

If you try to import more data that exceeds the available memory, you'll get the following error, and there is no workaround for it:

Memory error: Allocation failure : Not enough storage is available to process the command. The Operation has been cancelled.

By contrast, 64-bit Excel doesn't have memory limits, and PowerPivot can import more data with the 64-bit installations of Excel and PowerPivot. However, because SharePoint is limited to a maximum upload file size of two gigabytes, the PowerPivot for Excel add-in watches its memory utilization and limits the Excel workbook file to that size. Because of this, PowerPivot won't allow you to save the workbook if the VertiPaq memory utilization exceeds about four gigabytes. In general, aim for much smaller files than two gigabytes, because Excel becomes somewhat unwieldy and slows down with larger files. For example, you might find that it takes a while to open and save a 500 MB file. Therefore, keep the file size below a half of gigabyte.

When you open the model in the PowerPivot window or create a report that queries the model, PowerPivot extracts data from the workbook and loads in the in-memory VertiPaq engine. The VertiPaq engine runs in process, which means that it's loaded in the Excel memory space. Data analysis and reporting is always done in memory. Besides the model initialization at startup, data is never read from the disk. Once data is imported in PowerPivot, data is always read only. Consequently, if you need to change data, you must do so in the original data source and reimport the data because you won't be able to make changes in the PowerPivot window.

***Implementing PowerPivot models***

Implementing a PowerPivot model and analyzing data consists of the following high-level steps:

1. Switch from Excel to the PowerPivot window.
2. Import data from one or more data sources.
3. If you import multiple tables (or files), join tables by creating relationships.
4. Define DAX calculations to implement the business logic.
5. Switch to Excel, and then create pivot reports to analyze data.

## 2.2.4 Comparing Excel Reporting Options

PowerPivot isn't the only way to import and analyze data in Excel. For more than a decade, Excel has been supporting pivot reports and ways to import and analyze data from external data sources.

**NOTE** Excel includes a Microsoft Query tool (Data ⇨ From Other Data Sources ⇨ From Microsoft Query) that allows you import data from Open Database Connectivity (ODBC)-compliant databases. Similar to PowerPivot, Excel saves the data inside the workbook and shows the data in an Excel list formatted as a table. Once data is in an Excel list, you can create a pivot report from the Insert ⇨ PivotTable menu to analyze the data. For a lack of a better term, I'll refer to a pivot report connected to an Excel list as a "native" pivot report.

Choosing between two pivot report options can be confusing, and you might wonder how PowerPivot reports compare with native pivot reports. **Table 2.2** summarizes the main differences.

**Table 2.2 Comparing PowerPivot with Excel Pivot Reports**

| Feature | PowerPivot for Excel | Native Pivot Reports |
|---|---|---|
| Data sources | Databases, flat files, OData feeds, reports, and so on | ODBC-compliant data sources |
| Data volumes | Up to 2 GB of compressed data | Up to one million rows in a worksheet |
| Data modeling | Tables and relationships | VLOOKUP |
| Business logic | DAX formulas for calculated columns and measures | Excel formulas and calculated fields |
| Performance | Better performance with aggregating large datasets | Better performance with detail-level reporting |

***Understanding PowerPivot benefits***

In general, you should view PowerPivot as a next-generation Excel reporting tool that supersedes the Excel native pivot reports (but don't be surprised if PowerPivot becomes more integrated with Excel in the future). To start with, PowerPivot has a much broader data reach and can import data from any accessible data source, while Microsoft Query is limited to ODBC-compliant data sources only. PowerPivot lifts the Excel limitation of one million rows and can import massive datasets. Native pivot reports are subject to a number of other limitations, as discussed in Microsoft Knowledge Base article 820742 (http://support.microsoft.com/kb/820742). PowerPivot also gives you better compression and performance with larger data volumes.

As far as data modeling goes, PowerPivot is the clear winner. It organizes data in tables that be joined with relationships. This is much more intuitive and efficient than using the Excel VLOOKUP function to reference data scattered across various worksheets.

Have you tried implementing calculations, such as distinct count or time calculations (YTD, QTD, and so on) with Excel native pivot reports? If so, you'll appreciate how easy and efficient DAX expressions are for implementing business logic in PowerPivot.

PowerPivot offers additional benefits that might be relevant to your reporting requirements, such as the ability to convert PivotTables to formulas, to define named sets to build asymmetric report layouts, and to use slicers for cross-report filtering, which is useful with dashboard pages that consist of several report views.

***Understanding PowerPivot report limitations***

At the same time, analyzing PowerPivot models in Excel has certain limitations when you compare them to native pivot reports. One annoying limitation is that PowerPivot pivot reports ignore the column data types. For example, a Customer table might have a BirthDate column of a DateTime date type. However, when you add it to an Excel report, you'll find that it's treated as a text column. Because of this, the report sorts dates alphanumerically, and you can't use date filtering and relative dates, such as to show dates for the last quarter. Only columns in a table(s) marked as a Date table preserve their data types. As a workaround, if you need to report on dates in other tables, format the date column so years come first, such as YYYY-MM-DD.

While we are on the subject of data types, data type limitations apply to numeric columns as well. For example, if you filter the Weight column in the Product table for products whose weight is greater than 100, you'll get 2, 3, and so on, because the numbers are treated as text. Please note that this is a limitation of PowerPivot reports in Excel. Power View, which you can use to create SharePoint-based interactive reports, preserves the column data types. I've written more about this limitation in my blog post, "Handling Dates in BISM Tabular" at http://bit.ly/bismdates.

Another limitation specific to Excel PowerPivot reports is that while PowerPivot is very efficient when aggregating large data volumes, you might get inadequate performance with detail-level reporting. For example, you might need to report on customers and accounts. Unfortunately, you'll find the more columns you add to the report, the slower it gets, especially when you start filtering data. This stems from the fact that Excel sends MDX queries to the model, and these queries are not optimized for detail-level reporting.

**REAL WORLD** This performance-related limitation bit me really bad with the first release of PowerPivot. I had to implement a financial PowerPivot model with a few detail-level reports. Reports would show all bank customers and accounts and have many columns, such as customer name, rating, account number, balance, and so on, and allow the user to filter customers and accounts. As it turned out, the report performance would degrade quickly with larger datasets exceeding a few thousands rows. I posted this issue at http://bit.ly/ppdetailreports. The slowdown is caused by the subselects that Excel adds to the MDX query when you use slicers or column filters. Specifically, when the query requests calculations, the server applies Autoexists before doing NON EMPTY, which could be rather expensive over a large space. Filtering on a field added to the Report Filter zone is very fast because the query uses a WHERE clause. To make a long story short, you should carefully test performance with detail-level reports if you plan to use Excel pivot reports. If you find performance inadequate, consider Power View for such reports.

You can use Visual Basic for Applications (VBA) and macros to automate Excel PivotTable and PivotChart reports that get data from a PowerPivot model. However, PowerPivot doesn't have an object model. Because of this, you won't be able to automate any data modeling task, such as model creation or data import.

Unlike native pivot reporting, PowerPivot data is read-only. To make changes, you have to do so in the original data source and reimport the data. Going through the list of the PowerPivot limitations, you'll lose also the Undo feature because PowerPivot is an external add-in. The Excel what-if analysis feature, which allows you to use several different sets of values in one or more formulas to explore various outcomes, doesn't work with PowerPivot reports.

## 2.3 Applied PowerPivot

Now that I've introduced you to PowerPivot for Excel, let's see how a power user can use it to implement a personal BI model. The short hands-on lab that follows will give you a taste of personal BI with PowerPivot. Before we start, let's introduce an imaginary company called Adventure Works Cycles. Adventure Works Cycles is a large, multinational company that manufactures and sells bicycles to individuals and resellers in the North American, European, and Asian commercial markets.

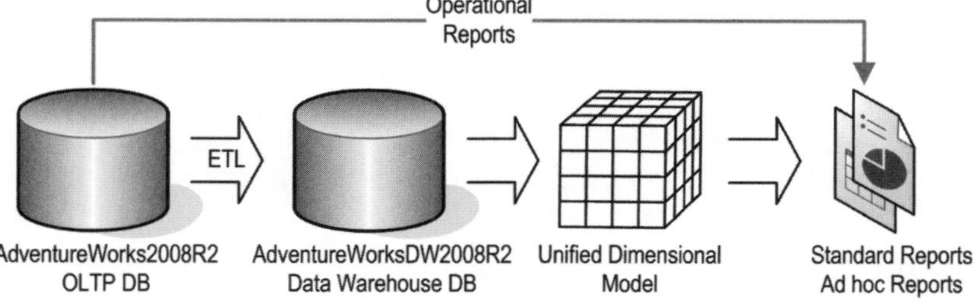


**Figure 2.7** Adventure Works has implemented BI processes for organizational BI.

## 2.3.1 Introducing Adventure Works Organizational BI

Adventure Works has already implemented BI processes for operational reporting and multidimensional analysis, as shown in **Figure 2.7**.

***Analyzing the current system***

Sales representatives use an intranet application to capture orders placed through the resale channel. Individual customers purchase Adventure Works products online through the Adventure Works web site. In both cases, the sales ordering data is captured in a SQL Server 2008 online transaction processing (OLTP) database called AdventureWorks2008R2.

**NOTE** The SQL Server 2008 R2 samples include two databases. AdventureWorks2008R2 simulates an OLTP sales order database, and AdventureWorksDW2008R2 demonstrates a data warehouse database. With the exception of the Product Catalog 2008 report, which Chapter 3 uses to demonstrate importing from reports, the practice exercises in this book require the AdventureWorksDW2008R2 database only. The book front matter provides instructions about how to download and install the Adventure Works sample databases.

Adventure Works has also built a data warehouse that archives the sales data. Integration Services data flow tasks periodically extract, transform, and load the data from various sources into the data warehouse database, which is physically implemented as a SQL Server database called AdventureWorksDW2008R2. A set of standard reports have been implemented to report on the transactional data stored in the data warehouse. Adventure Works has also implemented a Multidimensional layer on top of the data warehouse database for analytical reporting. This layer is realized as the Adventure Works multidimensional cube.

***Understanding personal BI needs***

Meet Alice, who works as a business analyst at Adventure Works. Alice often analyzes reseller sales order data that isn't imported in the data warehouse. The Adventure Works IT department provides this data to Alice as an Excel workbook file at the end of each month. Usually, Alice would rely on Excel PivotTable and PivotChart reports to analyze data. Since she needs to perform an analysis by several subject areas, such as Reseller and Date, she needs to transform data in a format that Excel native pivot reports understand. Bob from the IT department helps Alice get data in a pivot-compliant format and then teaches her how to use the Excel VLOOKUP function to perform lookups. This requires quite a few steps that Alice promptly forgets until the next month's data arrives. And, Bob comes to rescue again.

Alice has heard of PowerPivot and believes that it can help her avoid the data preparation chores so she can spend more time analyzing data. She decides to give personal BI and PowerPivot a try.

## 2.3.2 Implementing a PowerPivot Model ▶

Next, you'll implement a simple PowerPivot model to analyze reseller sales. The PowerPivot model includes three tables: a Sales table that contains the actual sales, a Reseller table that includes the list of the Adventure Works resellers, and the Date table that contains date columns, such as month, quarter and year. The Ch02.xlsx file includes the changes from all practices in this chapter.

**NOTE** Remember that the play symbol (▶) next to the section title indicates that the exercise that follows is accompanied with a video presentation. See the book front matter for instructions about where to find and how to watch the book video tutorials.

*Understanding the source data*

Let's take a moment to get familiar with the reseller sales source data that Alice receives from the IT department on a monthly basis.

1. Open Windows Explorer, and then navigate to the folder containing the Chapter 2 source code (\Source\ch02 folder).
2. Double-click the "Reseller Sales Source.xlsx" file to open it. **Figure 2.8** shows the source data.

| | A | B | C | D | E | F | G | H | I |
|---|---|---|---|---|---|---|---|---|---|
| 1 | OrderDate | ResellerID | SalesOrderNumber | SalesOrderLineNumber | RevisionNumber | OrderQuantity | UnitPrice | ExtendedAmount | UnitPriceDiscountP |
| 2 | 1/1/2008 | AW00000676 | SO61173 | 1 | 1 | 3 | 323.994 | 971.982 | |
| 3 | 1/1/2008 | AW00000676 | SO61173 | 2 | 1 | 2 | 323.994 | 647.988 | |
| 4 | 1/1/2008 | AW00000676 | SO61173 | 3 | 1 | 2 | 338.994 | 677.988 | |
| 5 | 1/1/2008 | AW00000676 | SO61173 | 4 | 1 | 1 | 338.994 | 338.994 | |
| 6 | 1/1/2008 | AW00000676 | SO61173 | 5 | 1 | 1 | 338.994 | 338.994 | |
| 7 | 1/1/2008 | AW00000676 | SO61173 | 6 | 1 | 1 | 461.694 | 461.694 | |
| 8 | 1/1/2008 | AW00000676 | SO61173 | 7 | 1 | 2 | 1376.994 | 2753.988 | |
| 9 | 1/1/2008 | AW00000676 | SO61173 | 8 | 1 | 4 | 1376.994 | 5507.976 | |
| 10 | 1/1/2008 | AW00000676 | SO61173 | 9 | 1 | 1 | 1391.994 | 1391.994 | |
| 11 | 1/1/2008 | AW00000676 | SO61173 | 10 | 1 | 2 | 37.152 | 74.304 | |
| 12 | 1/1/2008 | AW00000676 | SO61173 | 11 | 1 | 2 | 158.43 | 316.86 | |
| 13 | 1/1/2008 | AW00000676 | SO61173 | 12 | 1 | 2 | 218.454 | 436.908 | |
| 14 | 1/1/2008 | AW00000676 | SO61173 | 13 | 1 | 5 | 32.394 | 161.97 | |
| 15 | 1/1/2008 | AW00000676 | SO61173 | 14 | 1 | 5 | 41.994 | 209.97 | |
| 16 | 1/1/2008 | AW00000676 | SO61173 | 15 | 1 | 2 | 38.1 | 76.2 | |
| 17 | 1/1/2008 | AW00000676 | SO61173 | 16 | 1 | 2 | 5.394 | 10.788 | |

**Figure 2.8** The source dataset that contains reseller sales.

As you can see in **Figure 2.8**, this is a plain-looking dataset (no formatting, no titles, and so on). When you import data in Tabular, all you need is tabular datasets that contain the data only.

**TIP** In order to successfully import all the data from an Excel worksheet, you should be able to format the source data as a table (click the "Format as a Table" button found in the Excel ribbon's Home tab, or press Ctrl+T). Also, if your source data is pivoted, such as by month on columns, you should "unpivot" it because pre-aggregated data can't be easily joined to other tables. Kasper de Jonge, Microsoft PM, provides a tip about how to unpivot Excel data in his blog post, "How to unpivot using Excel and load it into PowerPivot" (http://bit.ly/unpivotExcel).

In our case, the dataset contains the daily sales order information and includes the typical columns, such as order date (Order Date), reseller identifier (Reseller ID), sales order number (SalesOrderNumber), order quantity (Order Quantity), and so on.

3. Close the "Reseller Sales Source.xlsx" file.

*Importing source data*

Before analyzing data with PowerPivot, you need to import it. Follow these steps to create a PowerPivot model that imports data from the "Reseller Sales Source.xlsx" file:

1. Open the "Ch02 Start.xlsx" file from the \Source\Ch02 folder. This file represents the starting point for this exercise and contains additional data that you'll later need. For now, ignore the data in the Reseller and Date tabs. Save the file as *Ch02.xlsx* in another folder on your disk so you don't overwrite the existing "Ch02.xlsx" file in the \Source\Ch02 folder.
2. In Excel, click the PowerPivot tab in the ribbon. If you don't see the PowerPivot tab, you don't have PowerPivot for Excel installed. Please read the installation instructions in Section 2.2.1.
3. In the PowerPivot ribbon, click the PowerPivot Window button. After a few seconds of delay, Excel launches the PowerPivot window that opens in addition to the Excel main window.
4. One of PowerPivot's strengths is that it provides a wizard to import data without requiring programming experience and scripting. In the PowerPivot window, click the From Other Sources

button (in the Home tab of the PowerPivot ribbon) to launch the Table Import Wizard, as shown in **Figure 2.9**.

**Figure 2.9** Click "From Other Sources" to import data from Excel files.

5. In the "Connect to a Data Source" step of the Table Import Wizard, scroll down the list until you see the Text Files section, and then select the Excel File option. Click Next.
6. In the "Connect to a Microsoft Excel File" step, type *Sales* as a friendly connection name to help you identify this connection if you need to change it later on. Click the Browse button, and then select the "Reseller Sales Source.xlsx" file found in the \Source\ch02 folder. Check the "Use first row as column headers" option (see **Figure 2.10**) because the first row in the Excel sheet contains the column names. Click Test Connection to test the connectivity. Click OK to close the dialog box, and then click Next.

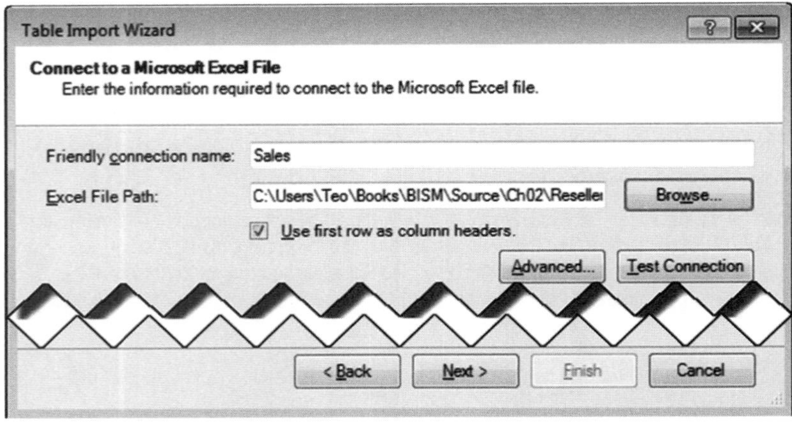


**Figure 2.10** Specify the location of the Excel file, the connection name, and column headers.

7. In the "Select Tables and Views" step (see **Figure 2.11**), check Sheet1$ because the reseller data you need to import is located in first worksheet.
8. Type *Sales* in the Friendly Name column next to Sheet1$. As a result, PowerPivot will name the imported table "Sales". Optionally, click Preview & Filter to preview the data, and then close the Preview Selected Table dialog box. Click Finish.
9. The Importing dialog box should inform that the import operation is successful. Click Close. PowerPivot imports data into a new table called Sales, and it shows the data in the read-only PowerPivot window, as shown in **Figure 2.12**. I depressed the Calculation Area button in the View group of the Home ribbon to hide the Calculations pane at the lower part of the PowerPivot window because you don't need it for this practice.

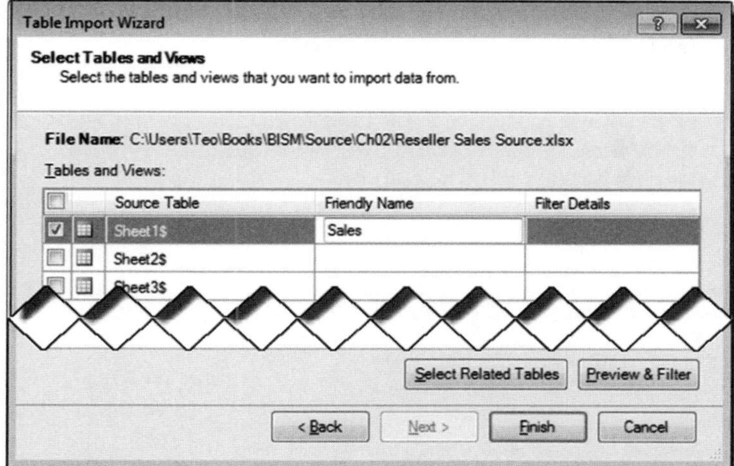

**Figure 2.11** Specify which Excel sheets you want to import and friendly names for the tables.

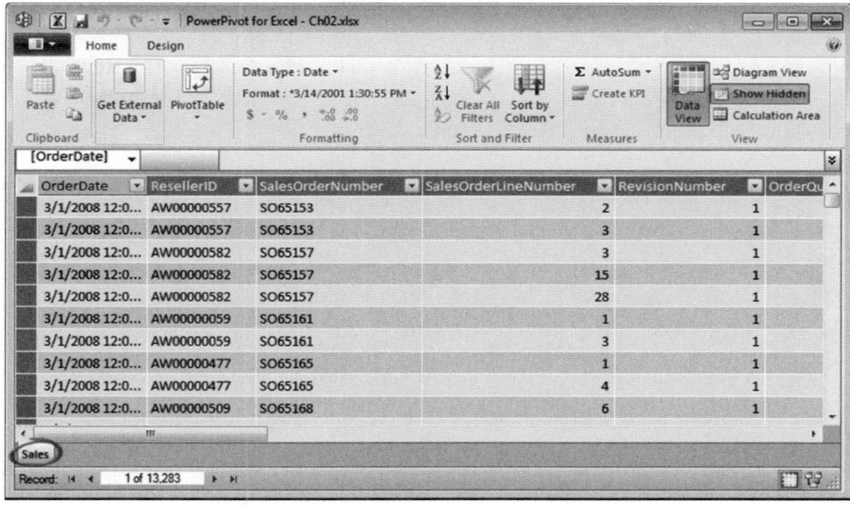

**Figure 2.12** The PowerPivot window shows data in a read-only view.

10. Click Ctrl+S (or click the Save button in the Quick Access toolbar) to save the Excel workbook and PowerPivot model. This action brings you back to the Excel window. You can then press Alt+Tab to switch to the PowerPivot window.

***Understanding reference data***

Alice would like to analyze the reseller sales by common time periods, such as month, quarter, and year, but there are no such columns in the Sales table that we've just imported. There aren't any reseller-related columns either, such as the reseller name, reseller type, and so on. Alice could have asked her IT department to provide additional files so she could import the Date and Reseller tables, and that would work just fine. However, let's suppose that this information isn't readily available. Alice has no choice but to maintain the Reseller and Date tables herself, by entering it directly in Excel and then importing it in the PowerPivot model.

1. Assuming the PowerPivot window is active, click the Switch to Workbook button (the one with the Excel icon) in the PowerPivot window to switch to the Excel window (with the Ch02.xlsx file open). Or, you can press Alt + Tab to switch to the Excel window.
2. Notice that the Ch02.xlsx workbook has Reseller and Date tabs. Click the Reseller tab to navigate to the first worksheet in the workbook, as shown in **Figure 2.13**. Notice that the Reseller worksheet has a row for each reseller. Once you import this table in PowerPivot and relate it to the Sales table, you'll be able to analyze the data by each of these columns.

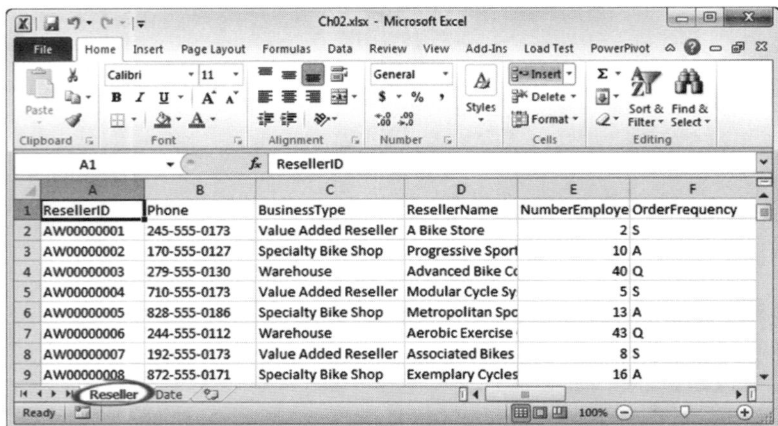


**Figure 2.13** The Reseller worksheet includes a list of resellers.

3. Click the Date worksheet tab on the bottom, which is shown in **Figure 2.14**. Notice that the Date list contains Date, Month, Quarter, and Year columns, which allow Alice to aggregate data by the day, month, quarter, and year levels respectively. The worksheet includes dates in the range of 1/1/2008 - 6/1/2009. If Alice imports reseller sales for later dates, she can simply append the new dates to the end of the worksheet. Notice that I used Excel formulas to derive the Month, Quarter, and Year columns from the Date column to show you that you don't have to enter them manually.

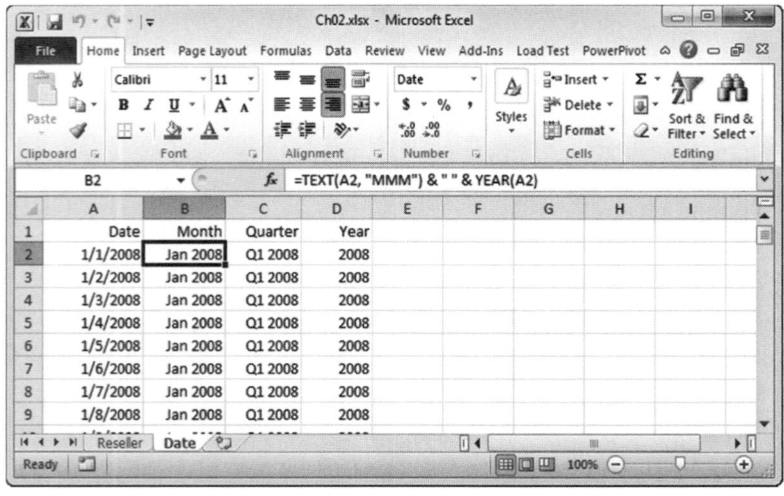


**Figure 2.14** The Date worksheet includes the dates required for analysis, as well as derived columns for months, quarters, and years.

***Linking data***

Since the Reseller and Date worksheets are in the same workbook where Alice created the PowerPivot model, she can simply import her data into PowerPivot by linking the Excel tables. This allows her to make changes to the referenced data, such as to add new resellers or to change existing resellers, and then the model will automatically pick up the changes.

1. Click the Reseller worksheet tab on the bottom, and then click the PowerPivot tab on the Excel ribbon. Don't click the PowerPivot Window button yet.
2. Click the "Create Linked Table" ribbon button. Excel selects all the data in the Reseller worksheet and pops up a Create Table dialog box to confirm the table selection. If the dialog box has the "My Table Has Headers" checkbox unchecked, check it, and then click OK.
3. Excel converts the worksheet data into an Excel table, opens the PowerPivot window, and then adds a new table named Table1 to the PowerPivot model. The link icon in the PowerPivot tab indicates that this table is linked to an Excel worksheet. Right-click the Table1 tab at the bottom, and then click Rename. Type *Reseller*, and then press Enter to rename the table to Reseller.
4. Click the "Switch to Workbook" button to go back to the Excel window. Click the Date tab and follow the same steps to create a new linked table. Rename the new table to *Date*.
5. Back in the PowerPivot window, compare your results with **Figure 2.15**. The PowerPivot model should have three tables: Sales, Reseller, and Date.

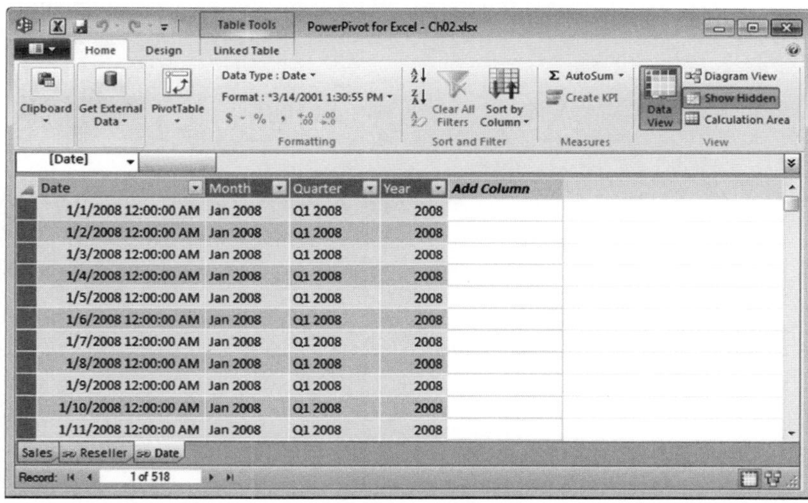


**Figure 2.15** The PowerPivot model consists of Sales, Reseller, and Date tables.

***Creating table relationships***

If your real-life projects require you to import only one table, then you can start creating reports once data is loaded in PowerPivot. However, before you can analyze data across multiple tables, you need to tell PowerPivot how the tables are related to each other so that it can aggregate data correctly. I'll explain table relationships in more detail in Chapter 4 but for now let's create two relationships, between Sales and Date tables and Sales and Reseller tables.

1. In the PowerPivot window, click the Sales tab.
2. Right-click the column header of the OrderDate column, and then click Create Relationship.
3. In the Create Relationship dialog box that follows, expand the Related Lookup Table drop-down list, and then select the Date table, as shown in **Figure 2.16**.

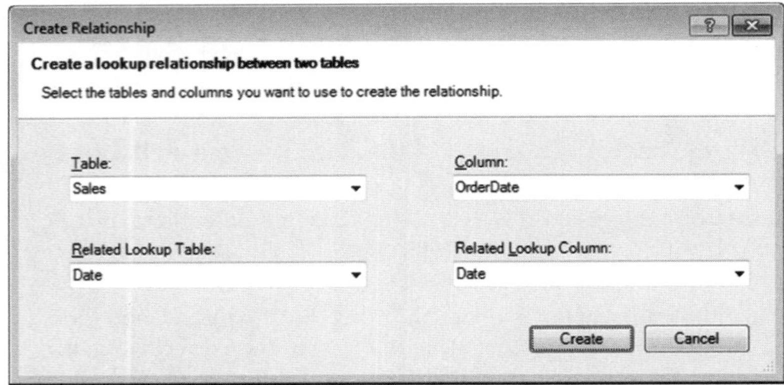


**Figure 2.16** Joining two tables requires matching columns.

4. Expand the "Related Lookup Column" drop-down list, and then select the Date column. Click Create to create a new relationship between the OrderDate column from the Sales table and the Date column from the Date table. This tells PowerPivot that when you analyze data by the columns in the Date table, such as Month, Quarter, and Year, it needs to follow this relationship to find the matching rows in the Sales table.
5. Follow similar steps to create a relationship between the ResellerID column of the Sales table and the ResellerID column in the Reseller table. This relationship allows you to analyze sales data by the columns in the Reseller table.
6. To verify that the correct relationships are created, click the Design tab in the PowerPivot ribbon, and then click the Manage Relationships button. Compare your results with **Figure 2.17**.

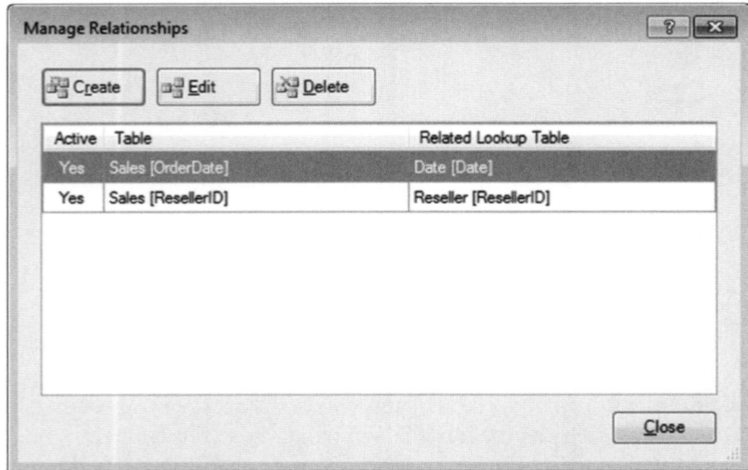


**Figure 2.17** The PowerPivot model has two relationships: between the Sales and Date tables and between the Sales and Reseller tables.

If your results don't match, delete the relationship by clicking the Delete button and re-create the relationship between the correct columns.

7. Click the Close button to close the Manage Relationships dialog box. Press Ctrl+S to save the Excel workbook. This operation switches you to the Excel window. Press Alt+Tab to switch back to the PowerPivot window. Don't close Excel yet.

That's it! With a few mouse clicks, Alice has implemented a tabular model with PowerPivot, which consists of three tables. She's now ready to analyze the data.

## 2.3.3 Analyzing Data ▶

Once the model is in place, Alice is ready to analyze her data right in Excel. For analysis, she would rely on the familiar Excel PivotTable and PivotChart to create interactive reports for slicing and dicing data. Next, I'll walk you through the steps to implement a pivot report that uses the PowerPivot model that we've just built. This crosstab report displays the reseller sales for the top ten resellers, as shown in **Figure 2.18**.

BusinessType
Specialty Bike Shop
Value Added Reseller
Warehouse

ProductLine
Mountain
Road
Touring

| Sum of SalesAmount | Column Labels | | | | | | |
|---|---|---|---|---|---|---|---|
| Row Labels | Jan 2008 | Feb 2008 | Mar 2008 | Apr 2008 | May 2008 | Jun 2008 | Grand Total |
| Roadway Bicycle Supply | | 108,184 | | | 112,313 | | 220,497 |
| Westside Plaza | 94,494 | | | 116,154 | | | 210,647 |
| Thorough Parts and Repair Services | | 81,697 | | | 106,268 | | 187,965 |
| Field Trip Store | | 104,325 | | | 82,062 | | 186,388 |
| Brakes and Gears | | 86,975 | | | 92,941 | | 179,916 |
| Perfect Toys | | 66,376 | | | 108,983 | | 175,358 |
| Rally Master Company Inc | 70,731 | | | 101,438 | | | 172,169 |
| Action Bicycle Specialists | | | 67,831 | | | 89,869 | 157,701 |
| Global Bike Retailers | | 73,017 | | | 83,968 | | 156,985 |
| Rural Cycle Emporium | | | 68,748 | | | 83,077 | 151,825 |
| Grand Total | 165,225 | 520,573 | 136,580 | 217,592 | 586,535 | 172,946 | 1,799,451 |

**Figure 2.18** This PivotTable report shows sales for the top ten resellers.

The report also includes two Excel slicers (BusinessType and ProductLine), so Alice can filter data interactively. Slicers were introduced in Microsoft Excel 2010 and can be used with native and PowerPivot reports.

***Creating a PivotTable report***

The easiest way to get you started with a PivotTable report is to initiate the report authoring process directly from PowerPivot.

1. With the PowerPivot window open, make sure that the Home ribbon tab is active. Click the PivotTable button in the ribbon (or expand it, and then click PivotTable), as shown in **Figure 2.19**.

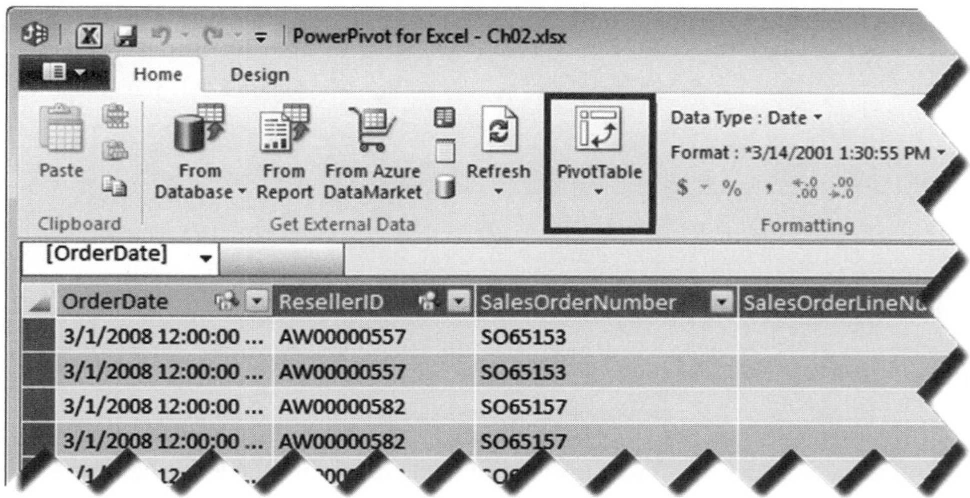


**Figure 2.19** Click the PivotTable ribbon button to create a new pivot report.

2. In the Create PivotTable dialog box, select the Existing Worksheet option, and then type *'Sheet3'!$B$2* in the Location field, as shown in **Figure 2.20**, and the click OK. This tells Excel to place the upper-left corner of the report in cell B2 on the third worksheet. Or, you can click the Selector button, navigate to the Excel worksheet, and then click the cell where you want to place the report.

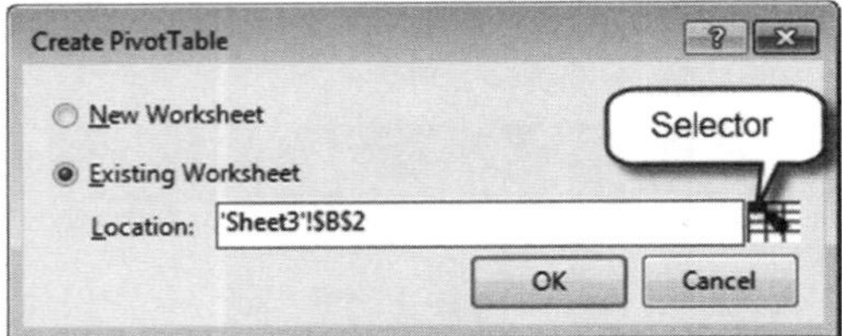


**Figure 2.20** Use the Create PivotTable dialog box to specify the location of the PivotTable report.

Excel creates an empty PivotTable report and shows the PowerPivot Field List pane on the right, as shown in **Figure 2.21**.

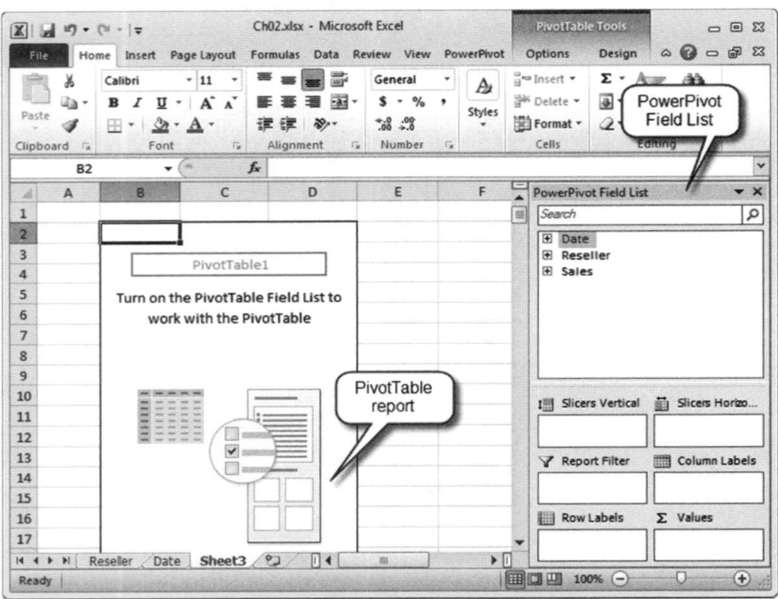


**Figure 2.21** The PowerPivot Field List pane shows the tables and fields defined in the model.

The PowerPivot Field List shows the model metadata. The top nodes correspond to the three tables you imported in the model. If you expand a table, such as Sales, you'll see the columns (fields) in that table that you can use in the report. At the lower part of the PowerPivot Field List pane, you'll find six areas that control the report layout. For example, if you place a field in the Row Labels area, the PivotTable will group the report data by that field on rows.

3. Expand the Sales table and check the SalesAmount field. Because this field is numeric, PowerPivot assumes that it needs to be aggregated and adds it to the Values area of the PowerPivot Field List. By default, Excel uses the Sum aggregation function. This explains the results in the PivotTable report (see **Figure 2.22**). The report has a single cell that shows the grand total sales amount. Adventure Works has made over $16 million across all resellers and all dates.

| Sum of SalesAmount |
|---|
| 16038062.6 |

Figure 2.22 The report shows the grand total SalesAmount value.

4. In the PowerPivot Field List, expand the Reseller table, and then check the ResellerName field. Since this field contains text values, PowerPivot adds it to the Row Labels area. Excel updates the report to show sales grouped by resellers on rows, as shown in **Figure 2.23**. At the end of the report, Excel automatically generates a grand total row (not shown in the figure) that shows the reseller grand total sales amount.

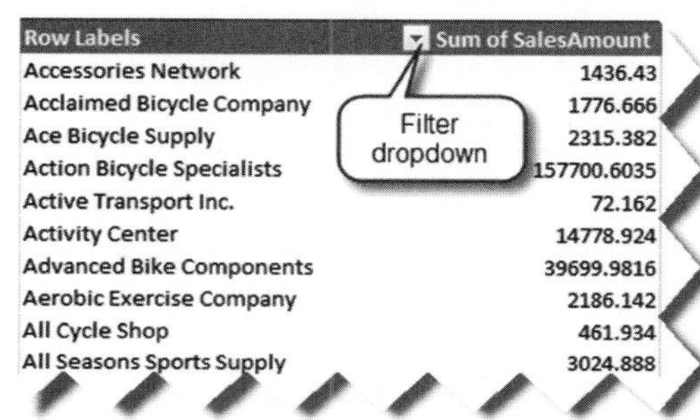


| Row Labels | Sum of SalesAmount |
|---|---|
| Accessories Network | 1436.43 |
| Acclaimed Bicycle Company | 1776.666 |
| Ace Bicycle Supply | 2315.382 |
| Action Bicycle Specialists | 157700.6035 |
| Active Transport Inc. | 72.162 |
| Activity Center | 14778.924 |
| Advanced Bike Components | 39699.9816 |
| Aerobic Exercise Company | 2186.142 |
| All Cycle Shop | 461.934 |
| All Seasons Sports Supply | 3024.888 |

Figure 2.23 This report shows sales grouped by resellers on rows.

5. In the PowerPivot Field List, expand the Date table. Drag the Month field to the Column Labels area to pivot SalesAmount by months on columns. If you just check the Month field, Excel will add it to the Row Labels area. To fix this, you could drag the field from the Row Labels area and drop it in the Column Labels area.
6. To filter only the top ten resellers, expand the filter drop-down list in the Row Labels column header of the PivotTable report (see **Figure 2.23**). Click Value Filters ⇨ Top 10. In the Top 10 Filter dialog box that follows, click OK to accept the defaults.

***Custom sorting***

You might notice that report can be improved to sort months in their natural order (Jan, Feb, March, and so on) instead of an alphabetical order. Fortunately, PowerPivot 2.0 supports custom sorting. As a prerequisite, you need to add a calculated column to the Date table that defines the correct order so you can sort the months by that column.

1. Switch to the PowerPivot window and then click the Date tab to select the Date table.
2. Click the Design tab in the ribbon, and then click the Add button. This operation highlights the last column, whose column header is Add Column, and puts the cursor in the formula bar to allow you to type in a formula for the calculated column. In the formula bar, enter the following expression (see **Figure 2.24**):

```
=[Year] * 100 + MONTH([Date])
```

This expression returns an integer for each row in the Date table in the format YYYYMM, such as 200801, 200802, 200803, and so on.

3. Right-click the calculated column, and then click Rename Column. Change the column caption to *MonthSort*, and then press Enter.
4. Click the column header of the Month column to select the entire column.

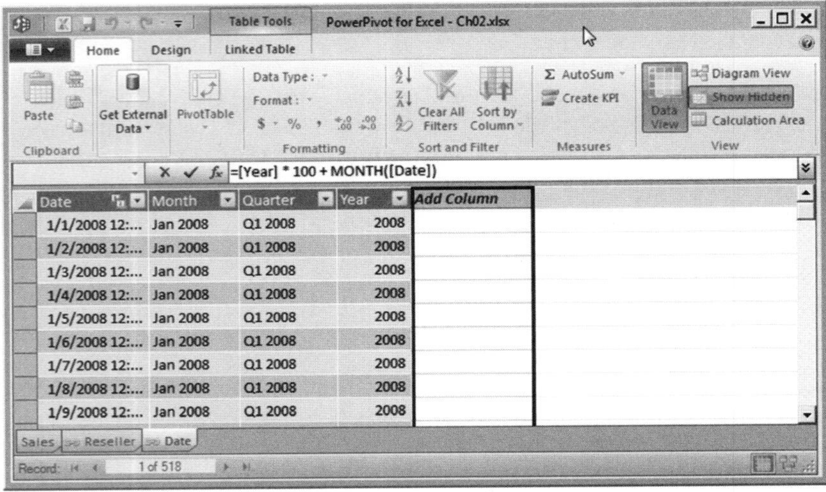


**Figure 2.24** Create a calculated column to define custom sorting for months.

5. In the Home tab of the ribbon, click the "Sort by Column" drop-down toolbar button. In the "Sort by Column" dialog box, expand the second drop-down, and then select the MonthSort column, as shown in **Figure 2.25**. This tells PowerPivot to sort months by the MonthSort column. Since the MonthSort column is a numeric column, months will be sorted as numbers and not alphabetically. Click OK to close the Sort by Column dialog box.

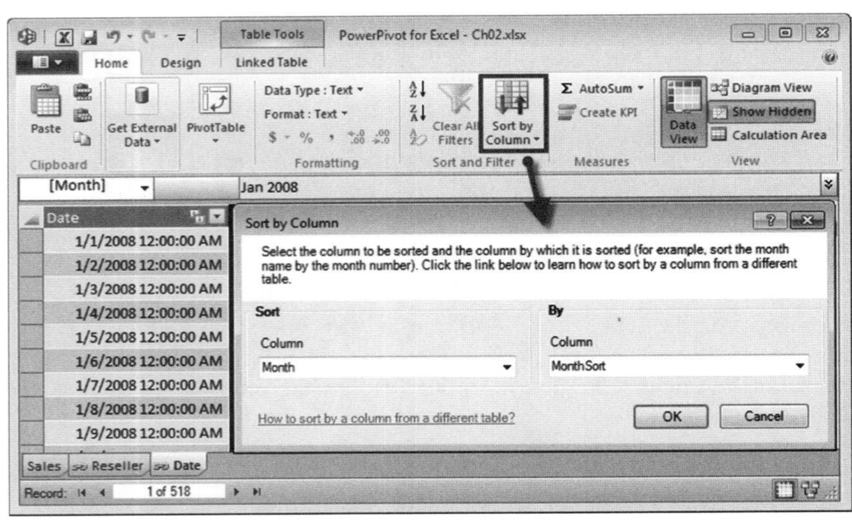


**Figure 2.25** Use the "Sort by Column" ribbon button to set up custom sorting.

6. Switch back to Excel. The PowerPivot Field List should have detected the model changes and displayed a warning message. Click the Refresh button in the PowerPivot Field List to apply the changes. Months should now sort in their natural order.
7. You can format fields in the model or on the report. It's preferable to apply formatting to the model so all reports can pick up the format settings. Switch to the PowerPivot window, and then

click the Sales tab. Click any cell in the SalesAmount column, and then use the Formatting group in the Home tab of the ribbon to format the column with zero decimal places and a thousands separator (,).

8. Click the "Switch to Workbook" button in the top-left area of the PowerPivot window to return to the Excel report. Excel should have detected the change and you should see the same warning message in the PowerPivot Field List. Click the Refresh button. Notice that the report now shows numbers without decimal places. If you don't see the warning message, click the Refresh All button in Excel's Data ribbon tab.
9. To sort resellers in descending order by their sales, right-click any cell in the Grand Total column of the pivot report, and then click Sort ⇨ Sort Largest to Smallest. Notice that the Roadway Bicycle Supply reseller has made the most sales overall, followed by Westside Plaza, and so on.

***Using slicers***

Excel slicers are visual filters that enable you to filter data interactively on the report. Suppose that Alice frequently analyzes data by the reseller business type and product line.

1. In the PowerPivot Field List, expand the Reseller table. Right-click the BusinessType field, and then click "Add to Slicers Vertical". Excel adds a rectangle to the left of the report and inserts a slicer in it.

   Now Alice can click any of the reseller's business types (Specialty Bike Shop, Value Added Reseller, and Warehouse) to filter the report. Or, she can hold the Ctrl key and select multiple reseller types. Notice that when you apply a filter selection, Excel updates the PivotTable report accordingly. For example, if you select the Specialty Bike Shop reseller type, the report shows the top ten resellers that are specialty bike shops. To clear the filter selection, click the Clear Filter button found in the upper-right area of each slicer or press Alt+C with the slicer selected. To select a slicer, make sure to click the slicer itself and not the enclosing rectangle.
2. In the PowerPivot Field List, drag the ProductLine field from the Reseller table to the Slicers Vertical area to filter by product lines.
3. Press Ctrl+S to save the Excel workbook file.

   That's it! With a few mouse clicks, you've created an interactive report and gained valuable insights about the Adventure Works sales performance. You might wonder what Alice needs to do the next month when she receives updated files and she wants to synchronize the PowerPivot model data. All that's required is a couple of mouse clicks to refresh the data, as follows:
4. Switch to the PowerPivot window.
5. Expand the Refresh drop-down button found in the ribbon's Home tab, and then click Refresh All (see **Figure 2.26**). This action reloads all the data from the data sources and then refreshes the report.

To recap what we've learned, PowerPivot modeling doesn't require any special data massaging or VLOOKUPs. You import data as tables and join the tables with relationships. Once the model is in place, data is easy to refresh and analyze.

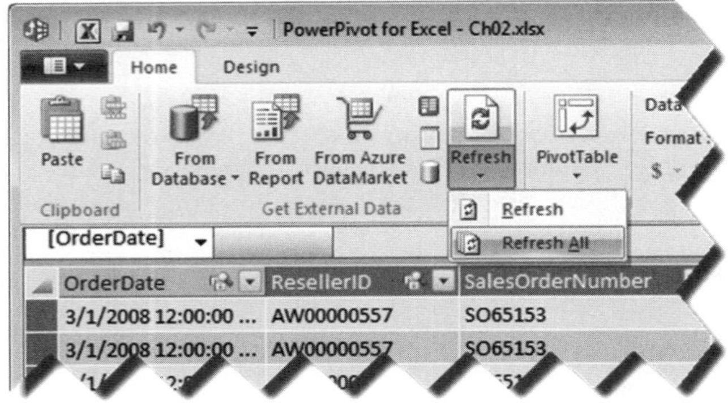


**Figure 2.26** Click the Refresh All button to reimport the data in all the tables contained in the model.

## 2.4 Summary

Personal BI broadens the reach of BI and enables business users to create their own solutions for data analysis and reporting. By now you should view personal BI not as a competing technology but as a completing technology to organizational BI.

Microsoft's PowerPivot is the company's premium tool for personal and team BI. PowerPivot enables business users to import data from various data sources, analyze it in the familiar Excel environment, and then share PowerPivot reports by deploying them to SharePoint.

PowerPivot for Excel is implemented as an add-in that extends the Microsoft Excel 2010 capabilities. The PowerPivot window provides a modeling environment that represents the PowerPivot model. The data is stored in a highly compressed state inside the Excel workbook. You import data as tables and create relationships to join tables. Then, you use PivotTable and PivotChart reports to analyze the data.

This chapter walked you through a practice that demonstrated how PowerPivot can help a business user implement a personal BI solution for sales analysis. The next chapter focuses on the PowerPivot data-import capabilities and teaches you how to import data from virtually any data source.

## Chapter 3

# Importing Data



As a first step to building a PowerPivot model, you need to acquire the data that you'll analyze and report on. PowerPivot makes it easy to access data directly from a variety of data sources, ranging from relational databases, such as a SQL Server database, to text files, such as a comma-delimited file extracted from a mainframe system. The most common way of bringing data into PowerPivot is by importing it from a relational database. When the data isn't in a database, PowerPivot supports other data acquisition methods, including text files, cubes, published PowerPivot workbooks, data feeds, linked Excel tables, and Windows Clipboard.

In this chapter, you'll begin the process of implementing a PowerPivot model to analyze the Adventure Works sales. You'll practice several data import options to load data from the Adventure Works data warehouse database, a multidimensional cube, an Excel workbook, a comma-delimited file, copy and paste, and even from a Reporting Services report.

## 3.1 Data Modeling Concepts

PowerPivot allows you to import data from virtually anywhere with a few mouse clicks. While importing data is easy, relating data in your model requires some planning on your side in order to avoid inconsistent or even incorrect results. For example, you might have imported a Customer table and a Sales table but if there isn't a way to relate the data in these tables, you'll get the same sales amount repeated for each customer. Therefore, before you run the Data Import Wizard, you should have some basic understanding about the PowerPivot data modeling requirements and limitations. And, since PowerPivot is a scaled-down version of Tabular, you'll find that the same considerations that apply to PowerPivot also apply to organizational tabular models.

### 3.1.1 Understanding Schema Types

I previously wrote that PowerPivot imports data in tables. If all the data is provided to you as just one table, then you could congratulate yourself and skip this Data Modeling Concepts section altogether. Chances are, however, that you might not be that lucky, and you might need to import multiple tables. This requires learning some basic database and schema concepts. The term "schema" here is used to describe the table definitions and how tables relate to each other. I'll keep the discussion light on purpose to get you started with PowerPivot modeling as fast as possible. I'll revisit table relationships in Chapter 4.

**NOTE** Importing a large dataset as one table doesn't require modeling but it isn't a best practice. A large table might strain your computer resources as it will require more time to import and more memory to store data. It's also difficult to maintain. At the same time, a fully normalized schema, such as modeling a product entity with Product, Subcategory, and Category tables, is also not desirable because you'll end up with many tables and the model might become difficult to understand and navigate. When modeling the input data, it's important to find a good balance and that balance is the star schema.

***Understanding star schemas***

For a lack of better terms, I'll use the dimensional modeling terminology to explain schema elements. **Figure 3.1** shows two schema types. Similar to Online Analytical Processing (OLAP), PowerPivot works best with *star* schemas (see http://en.wikipedia.org/wiki/Star_schema). The left diagram illustrates a star schema where the ResellerSales table is in the center. This table stores the history of the Adventure Works reseller sales and each row records a sale, including the sales amount, tax amount, discount, and other numeric fields. Dimensional modeling refers to these tables as *fact* tables. As you can imagine the ResellerSales table can be very long if it keeps several years of sales data.

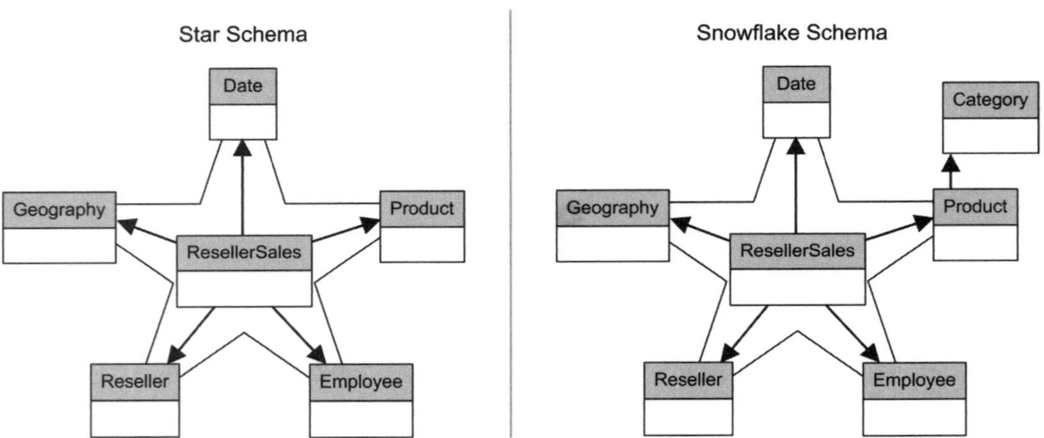


**Figure 3.1** PowerPivot supports both star and snowflake schema types.

The ResellerSales table is related to other tables, called *dimension* tables in dimensional modeling or *lookup* tables in PowerPivot. These tables provide contextual information to each sales row stored in the ResellerSales table. For example, the Date table might have a Date, Quarter, and Year columns to allow you to aggregate data at day, quarter, and year levels. The Product table might include ProductName, Color, and Size attributes, and so on.

The reason why the data source might have these columns in separate tables is that, for the most part, their content doesn't need a historical record. For example, if the product name changes, this would be an in-place change. If you were to continue adding columns to the ResellerSales table, you might end up with performance and maintenance issues. If you need to make a change, you might have to update millions of rows of data as opposed to updating a single row. Similarly, if you were to add a new column to the Date table, such as FiscalYear, you'll have to update all the rows in the ResellerSales table.

Are you limited to only one fact table for aggregating data in PowerPivot? Absolutely not. For example, you could have an InternetSales fact table that stores direct sales to individuals. In the case of multiple fact tables, ideally you would want fact tables that share some common dimension tables so that you could match and consolidate data for cross-reporting purposes, such as to show reseller and Internet sales side by side and grouped by year and product.

***Understanding snowflake schemas***

A *snowflake* schema is where some dimension tables relate to other dimension tables and not directly to the fact table. Going back to **Figure 3.1**, you can see that for whatever reason, the product categories are kept in a Category table that relates to the Product table and not directly to the ResellerSales table.

Tabular supports snowflake schemas just fine. However, if you have a choice, you should minimize snowflaking for two important reasons. First, snowflaking increases the number of tables in the model, making it more difficult to comprehend the model schema. Second, if the intermediate lookup table (the Product table in our example) is a large table with more than one million rows, snowflaking might lead to performance degradation when aggregating sales by product category.

If you import data from a database, you can minimize snowflaking by merging snowflaked tables. For example, you can use a SQL query that joins the Product and Category tables. But, if you import text files, you won't have that option because you can't use SQL. However, you can add calculated columns that use DAX expressions to accomplish the same goal, such as by adding a column to the Product table to look up the product category from the Category table. Then, you can hide the Category table.

## 3.1.2 Introducing Table Relationships

Once you import multiple tables, you need a way to relate them. If two tables are not related, PowerPivot won't aggregate data in one table by columns from another table. To understand how to relate tables, you need to learn about relationships and keys.

***Relationships and keys***

In order to relate two tables, there must be schema and data commonalities between the two tables. For example, you won't be able to analyze sales by product if there isn't a common column between the ResellerSales and Date tables that ties a date to a sale (see **Figure 3.2**).

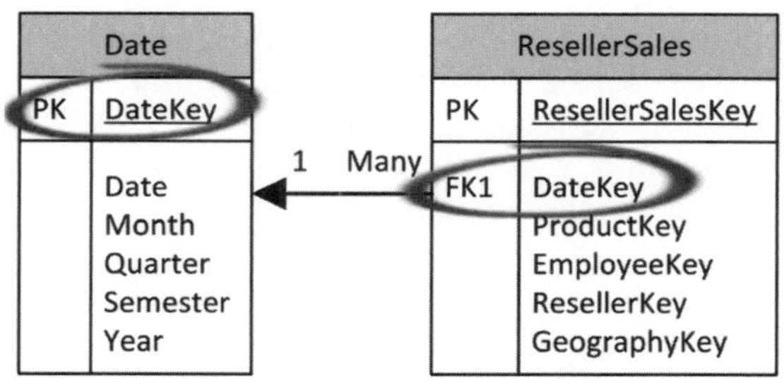


**Figure 3.2** The DateKey column (primary key) in the Date table is related to the matching DateKey column (foreign key) in the ResellerSales table.

Common columns in each pair of tables are called *keys*. A *primary key* is a column that uniquely identifies each row in a table. A primary key column can't have duplicate values. For example, the DateKey column uniquely identifies each row in the Date table and no other row has the same value. An employee identifier or an e-mail address can be used as a primary key in an Employee table. To join Date to ResellerSales, in the ResellerSales table we must have a matching column, which is called a *foreign key*. For example, the DateKey column in the ResellerSales table is a foreign key. Typically, a fact table has several foreign keys, so it can be related to the dimension tables.

For performance reasons it's advisable to use shorter data types for primary and foreign keys, such as Integer. For example, the DateKey column could be a date column of a Date data type. Or, if you importing from a data warehouse database, it might be of an Integer data type with the values 20110101 for January 1st, 2011, 20110102 for January 2nd, 2011, and so on.

***About relationship types***

Notice that the relationship arrow points out from the ResellerSales table to denote that this relationship is one-to-many. For example, one date in the Date table has one or more recorded sales in ResellerSales, one product in the Product table corresponds to one or more sales in ResellerSales, and so on. To relate two tables, PowerPivot insists that the dimension (lookup) table has a primary key that uniquely identifies each row. You might find that other self-service BI tools on the market are more relaxed, and they allow you to join any pair of tables if they have matching columns. However, the caveat is that data might be duplicated, and the subtotals could be wrong. By contrast, PowerPivot and Tabular require a primary key in each lookup table, and there is no exception.

And, here is the most important part. In order for PowerPivot to aggregate data correctly between tables, the columns to be aggregated must be on the "many" side of the relationship, which is typically the fact table (the ResellerSales table in the diagram). PowerPivot produces wrong results if you try to aggregate a hypothetical Cost column in the Product table by any column in any other table that doesn't have a one-to-many relationship with the Product table. As a workaround, you can write DAX calculated measures to overwrite the default aggregation behavior if you have valid reasons. For example, this will be the case of a many-to-many relationship that represents a joint account that's owned by two or more individuals. This scenario requires DAX calculations to produce correct results, as I'll demonstrate in Chapter 6.

**NOTE** We can say that Tabular is somewhat more flexible than OLAP and Multidimensional when it comes to schemas. In Multidimensional, there is a strict division between fact and dimension tables. As a result, Multidimensional aggregates only numeric columns in the fact tables and doesn't allow you to aggregate columns in dimension tables. By contrast, Tabular doesn't have this limitation. For example, you can aggregate a Cost column in the Product table, such as to find the total cost across all products. However, trying to aggregate the product cost by any columns in a Date table produces wrong results if there isn't a direct or indirect one-to-many relationship between the Date and Product tables.

The same rule applies to snowflake schemas. As long as there is a one-to-many path from a lookup table, such as the Category table or the Product table, all the way to the ResellerSales table, you can aggregate the ResellerSales column just fine. Let's consider another example. Suppose you have OrderHeader and OrderDetails tables. If there is a one-to-many relationship between the Date and OrderHeader tables and a one-to-many relationship between the OrderHeader and OrderDetails tables, you can slice data in both OrderHeader and OrderDetails by date.

That's all you need to know about data modeling for now. The next section (Section 3.2) introduce you the PowerPivot data import options. In Section 3.3, you'll practice many of these options to import data from a variety of data sources.

## 3.2 Understanding Data Access Options

Now we're going back to Alice, who you've met in Chapter 2, and the Adventure Works personal BI needs. Suppose that Alice needs to consolidate data from multiple data sources, including data residing in the data warehouse, multidimensional cube, flat files, and so on. As a first step, Alice needs to import data from these data sources in PowerPivot. Luckily, PowerPivot includes the

Table Import Wizard that will walk Alice through a series of steps to import data from all these data sources.

It's important to understand that the data import capabilities of PowerPivot are limited to extracting data only. With the exception of being able to write custom queries to import data from relational databases, PowerPivot doesn't have data transformation capabilities. Since you can't update the model data either, your only option to customize and modify data is to create calculated columns with DAX expressions. Therefore, before you start the import process or after the data is imported in PowerPivot, explore the data. In case of missing or cryptic data, ask your IT department to address the issues at the data source.

## 3.2.1 Introducing the Table Import Wizard

PowerPivot includes the handy Table Import Wizard that can import data from a plethora of data sources with a few clicks and without requiring any scripting or programming skills. You can launch this wizard by clicking any button in the Get External Data group in the PowerPivot window ribbon, as shown in **Figure 3.3**. Naturally, the ribbon drop-down buttons provide shortcuts to Microsoft-provided data sources. When discussing the data source capabilities of PowerPivot, I'll deviate somewhat from the way the buttons are ordered in the ribbon, so I can emphasize their commonalities by the data source type, such as relational databases, multidimensional databases, and so on.

**Figure 3.3** Launch the Table Import Wizard from the PowerPivot window ribbon.

**Table 3.1** shows the types of data sources that PowerPivot supports. The Custom Query column indicates whether the data source type allows custom queries, which is in case you need more control over the data import process. The Filter Options column indicates if the data source type supports interactive filtering by rows and columns in the Table Import Wizard.

**Table 3.1 The Table Import Wizard supports various data sources.**

| Data Source Type | Data Sources | Custom Query | Filter Options |
|---|---|---|---|
| Relational databases | SQL Server, Access, Microsoft Parallel Data Warehouse, SQL Azure, Oracle, Teradata, Sybase, Infiormix, IBM DB2, OLE DB/ODBC-compilant | Yes | Row and Column |
| Multidimensional databases | Analysis Services (Multidimensional and Tabular), PowerPivot workbooks deployed to SharePoint | Yes | Query Filter |
| Text files | Flat files, Excel workbooks | No | Row and Column |
| Data feeds | Reporting Services reports (R2 or above), Azure Marketplace, OData feeds | No | Column only |

**NOTE** Although PowerPivot doesn't natively support custom queries and filtering for all data sources, the data source itself might support custom filtering. For example, a Reporting Services report might have parameters or a data feed might support query parameters to restrict data. Research the data source capabilities to understand query and filtering options.

Let's explain the data source types in more detail. You'll find step-by-step instructions to practice the data import process in the exercise that follows.

## 3.2.2 Importing from Relational Databases

Nowadays, most corporate data resides in relational databases, such as SQL Server and Oracle databases. Microsoft tested PowerPivot with a subset of the most popular databases on the market. To see the full list, click the "From Other Sources" button in the Home tab of the PowerPivot window, and then examine the Relational Databases section in the Connect to a Data Source step of the wizard, as shown in **Figure 3.4**. The "Data Sources Supported in PowerPivot Workbooks" topic in Books Online (http://bit.ly/ppdatasources) describes these relational databases, lists the supported versions, and lists the required providers.

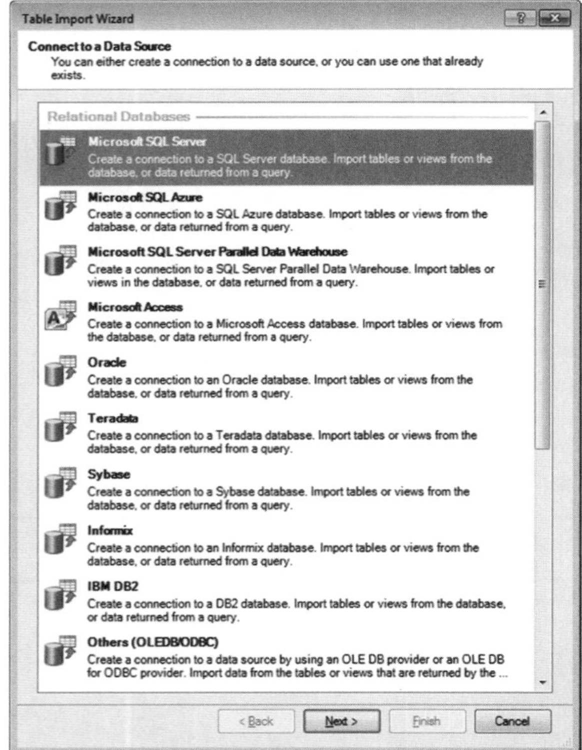


**Figure 3.4** PowerPivot supports the most popular relational databases on the market. If you need to connect to a database that isn't listed, use the Other (OLEDB/ODBC) option.

***Understanding supported data sources***

To successfully connect to a database, PowerPivot for Excel needs connectivity software called a *data provider* or driver to be installed locally on your computer. With the exception of the Microsoft SQL Server provider and ACE provider (imports Access, Excel, and text files), which are installed by the Excel setup program, PowerPivot doesn't come with any other data providers. The

Table Import Wizard doesn't validate connectivity or hide data sources with missing providers. What happens if you don't have the required data provider installed? Once you enter the connection details in the Connect to a Database step and attempt to continue, you'll see the following error message:

Failed to connect to the server. Reason: The '<provider>' provider is not registered on the local machine.

Therefore, you must install the required connectivity software for the data source that you want to access. How do you know which data providers are supported by PowerPivot? Click the Advanced button in the "Connect to a Database" step. In the Set Advanced Properties dialog box that follows, expand the Providers drop-down list (see **Figure 3.5**). When PowerPivot supports multiple providers, it uses the first one installed in the order listed in the drop-down list. You can use the Set Advanced Properties dialog box to specify additional parameters that you can pass to the provider if needed.

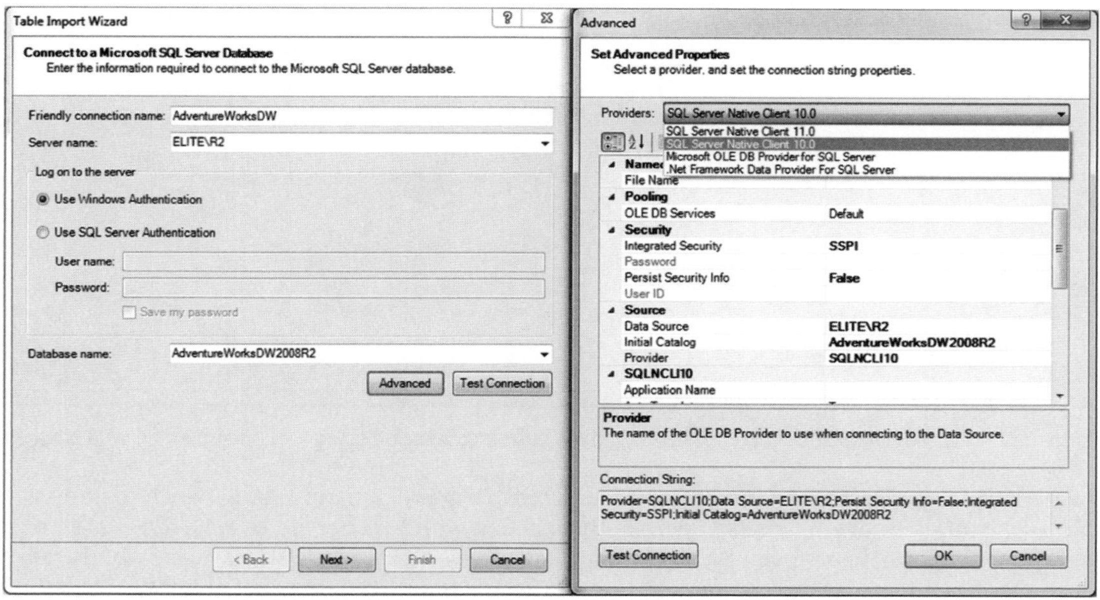


**Figure 3.5** Use the Providers drop-down list to see the data providers supported for a given database.

What if you need to connect to a data source that isn't among the supported data sources in **Figure 3.4**, such as MySQL? First, you need to obtain and install an object linking and embedding database (OLE DB) or open database connectivity (ODBC) data provider for that database on your machine. Next, select the "Others (OLEDB/ODBC)" option in the "Connect to a Data Source" page of Table Import Wizard. This will bring up the "Specify a Connection String" dialog box, where you can type in a connection string, as shown in **Figure 3.6**. Or, you can click the Build button to open the Data Link Properties dialog box and specify connection specifics for PowerPivot to autogenerate the connection string. Use the Provider tab in Data Link Properties to select an OLE DB provider. If you don't have an OLE DB provider and you're connecting to an ODBC-compliant data source, try the generic Microsoft OLE DB Provider for the ODBC Drivers provider.

***Understanding authentication options***

As a part of establishing connectivity, you need to specify the server name and a friendly connection name to help you identify this connection later on. In addition, you need to tell the data provider how you'll log into the database. **Figure 3.5** shows the authentication options that you get when you connect to SQL Server. The default is the Use Windows Authentication option, which will attempt to log you into the database using your Windows credentials. As a prerequisite, the database administrator (DBA) must grant your Windows login account at least read rights to the required tables or/and views in the database.

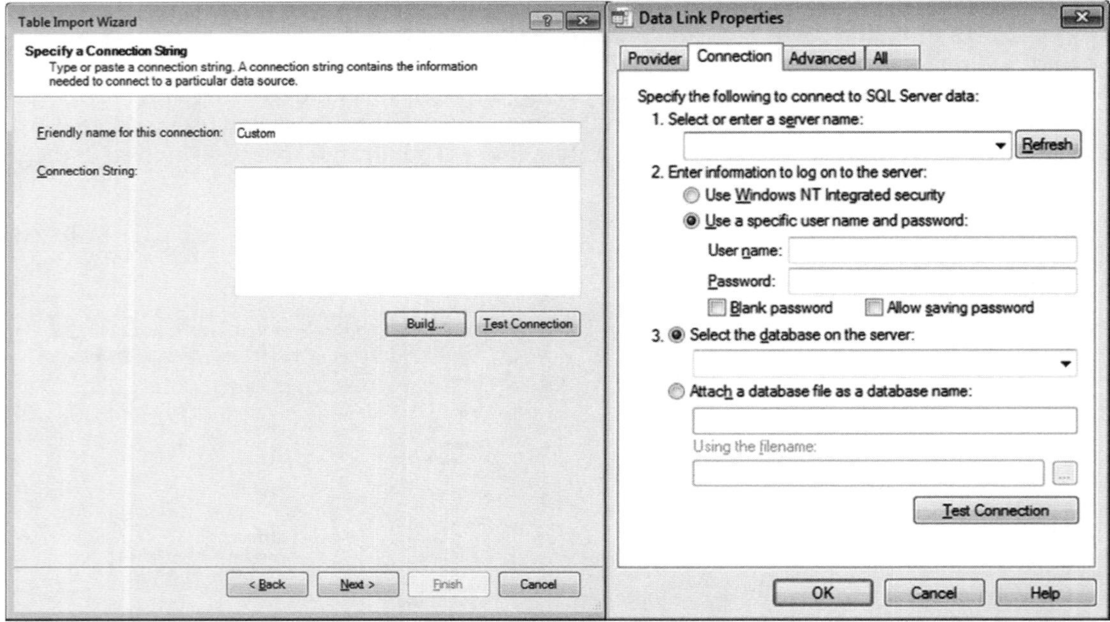


**Figure 3.6** Use the "Data Link Properties" dialog box to build a connection string for non-supported data sources.

Most relational databases on the market supports only standard authentication, which requires a user login and password. To use standard authentication with SQL Server, select Use SQL Server Authentication, and then type in the login name and password that the DBA gave you. Optionally, check the "Save my password" option (or "Allow saving password" in the "Data Link Properties" dialog box) to save the password so that PowerPivot doesn't ask you to retype the password each time you close and reopen the Excel file, and then refresh the model data.

**NOTE** If you check the "Save my password" checkbox, PowerPivot saves the password inside the Excel workbook in an encrypted format. The saved password is used by the VertiPaq engine when refreshing the model data. The PowerPivot user interface doesn't use the stored password. However, it does cache it in memory until you close the workbook. If you reopen the workbook and go back to the connection definition, such as to import new tables, you'll be asked to enter the password again. This behavior prevents another user from connecting to the data source and fetching more data. If you're BI pro working with an Analysis Services Tabular project in SQL Server Data Tools, note that the password is always saved on the server even if the "Save my password" checkbox isn't checked in order for the model to process successfully on the server.

After you specify the login information, expand the Database Name drop-down list. If the database server authenticates you successfully, you'll see all the databases you have rights to access. Select a database, and then click the Test Connection button to test connectivity. If all is well, PowerPivot will display a "The connection succeeded" confirmation message.

*Importing tables*

Once you have tested connectivity, click Next to advance to the "Choose How to Import Data" step. Here, you'll be given two options to retrieve data, as shown in **Figure 3.7**. The first (default) option gives you the ability to import data from the tables and/or SQL views that are defined in the source database.

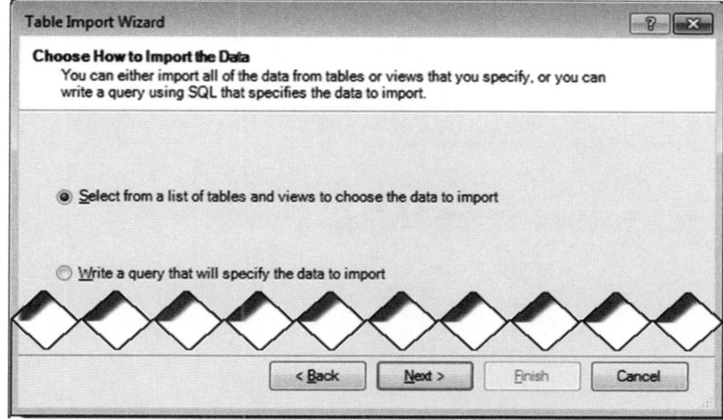


**Figure 3.7** You can import entire tables or write a custom query to select data.

When you click Next, the "Select Tables and Views" step examines the database schema and shows the tables and views, as shown in **Figure 3.8**.

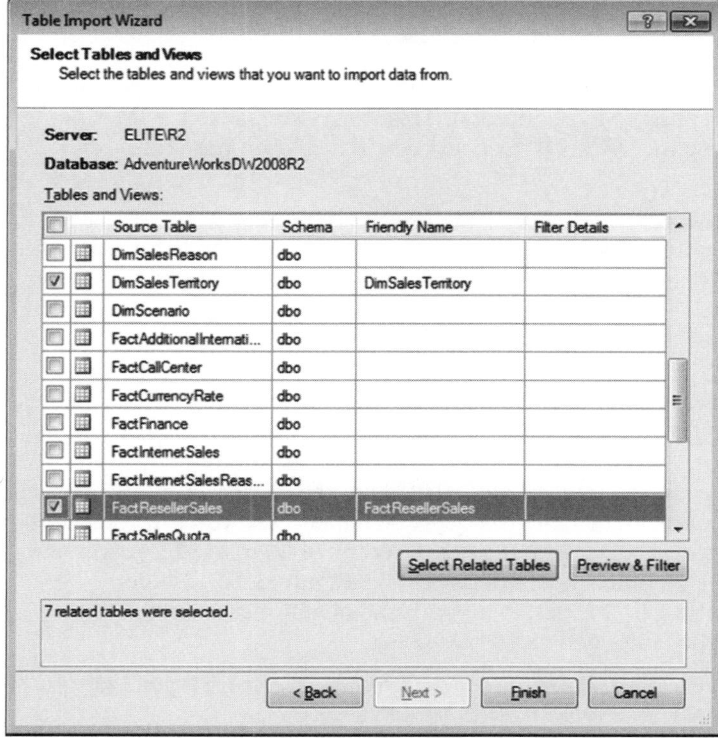


**Figure 3.8** Use the "Select Tables and Views" step to select related tables.

If the relational database has table joins (referential integrity) defined, you can select a table and then click the "Show Related Tables" button for PowerPivot to examine these relationships and select the related tables. In this case, I've selected FactResellerSales, and I clicked the "Select Related Tables" button to import additional seven tables that are related to this table.

***Filtering data***

You can click the "Preview & Filter" button on the "Select Tables and Views" step to import a subset of data by specifying filters. PowerPivot supports different filtering options based on the column data type. **Figure 3.9** shows the options available for numeric columns.

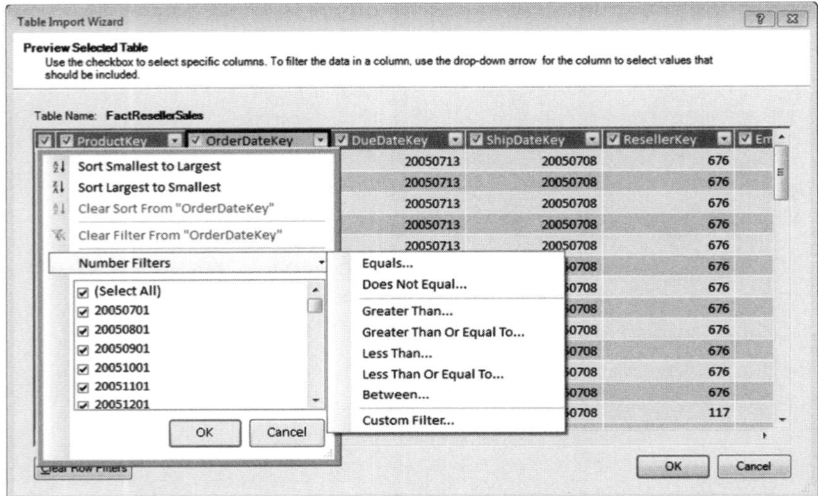


**Figure 3.9** Specify column and row filters to filter data horizontally and vertically.

You can filter specific values by checking the checkbox next to the value. Or, you can expand the Number Filters drop-down list and specify a filter criterion. This is very similar to the filtering options available in an Excel pivot report. Uncheck the checkbox in a column header to exclude the entire column from importing.

**NOTE** Chances are that you'll be given access to large tables or SQL views containing many columns. To improve performance and reduce storage, one of the easiest and most effective things you can do right off the bat is to limit the amount of data you import in your PowerPivot model. You can use row and column filters to do that without requiring SQL query skills.

***Using a custom query***

The second option to import data from a relational database (again see **Figure 3.7**) is to write a custom query to select data. This could be useful when you need to join tables, such as to avoid snowflaking, or when you want to perform simple data transformation tasks. Once you select "Write the query that will specify the data to import" and click Next, the wizard shows the "Specify a SQL Query" step. Here, you can type in or paste the query statement. Or, you can click the Design button, and then use a query designer to test the query. When you target SQL Server as a data source, PowerPivot opens a nice graphical query designer (see **Figure 3.10**), which PowerPivot "borrowed" from Reporting Services. This designer is capable of auto-generating SQL SELECT statements that are based on the tables and views you select.

**NOTE** The query designer might open by default in text mode and your screen might not match **Figure 3.10**. If this happens, depress the Edit As Text button in the upper-left corner of the query designer.

In this example, I've checked the FactResellerSales and DimReselellerSales tables because I want to import their data. If the database has table joins (referential integrity) defined, the designer automatically detects these table relationship and then displays them in the Relationships area (click the drop-down arrows to expand it). For example, a table relationship exists between the FactResellerSales and DimReseller tables. You can disable the auto detect feature by depressing the Auto Detect button, and then manually define table relationships. You can also use the Applied Filters area to set up basic filter options, such as to return rows where UnitPrice is more than 1,000. The filter clause generates a WHERE clause in the SQL SELECT statement. Ignore the Parameter checkbox because it applies to Reporting Services only. You can click the Run Query button in the toolbar to execute the query and view the results in the "Query results" grid.

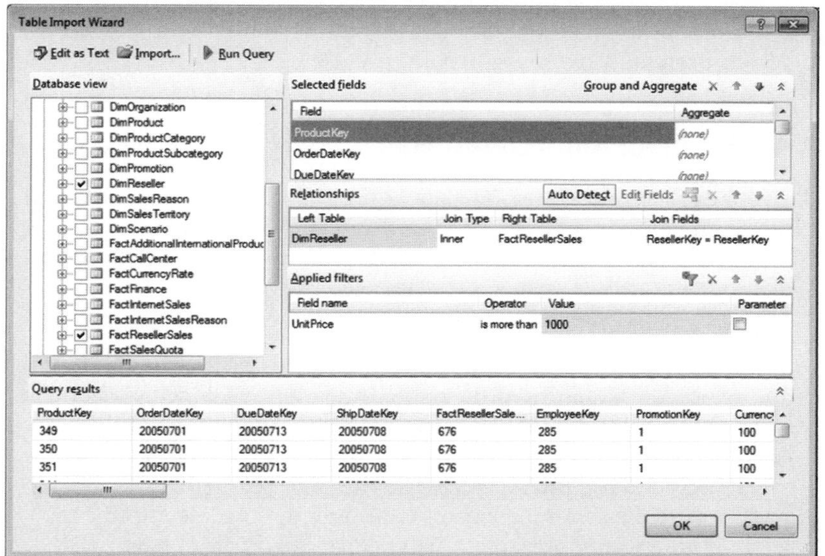

**Figure 3.10** Use the graphical SQL query designer to auto-generate SQL queries or enter a custom query.

The "Edit as Text" button switches to a generic query designer, which is shown in **Figure 3.11**.

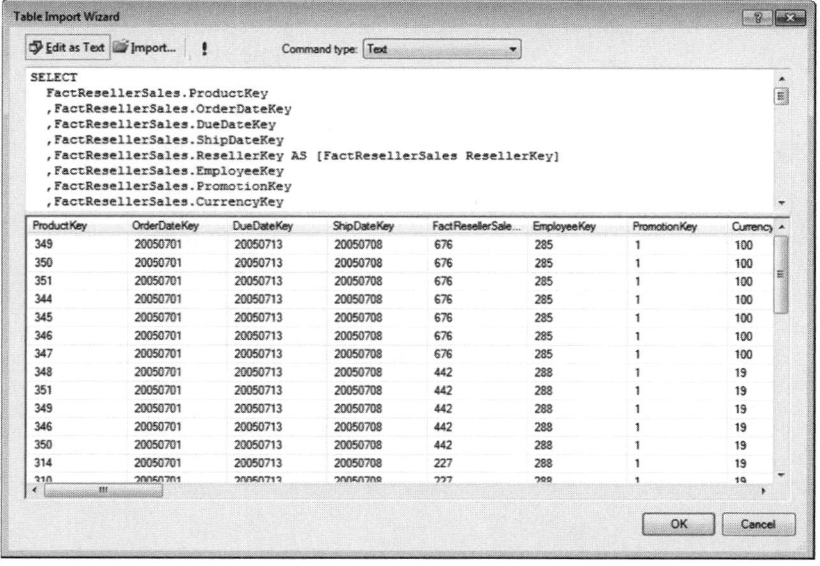

**Figure 3.11** Use the generic query designer to type or import a SQL SELECT statement.

This is the only query designer you'll get when you target a relational database other than SQL Server. It provides a basic user interface that allows you to type in the query text and execute the query. However, be careful when you target SQL Server because if you switch to the generic designer and make changes, then you won't be able to switch back to the graphical query designer without losing your changes. Finally, if you need help with writing SQL queries, you can always ask your database administrator (DBA) to send you the query as a file. Then click the Import button to import the query text. The generic query designer also supports stored procedure. If you're given access to a stored procedure, type in the stored procedure name and any parameters it takes, as instructed by your DBA.

Based on your requirements, you might need to import data from other relational databases. Once you install the required data providers, the import process should be straightforward. If you have a database hosted on SQL Azure, please read the blog post, "Getting Started with PowerPivot and SQL Azure", by Wayne Walter Berry at http://bit.ly/ppazure.

## 3.2.3 Importing from Multidimensional Databases

You can import data from Analysis Services databases. This includes multidimensional cubes and PowerPivot models deployed to SharePoint or Analysis Services Tabular. I bundled both types under the "multidimensional" umbrella because PowerPivot sees Tabular models as multidimensional cubes.

***Importing from Multidimensional***

Although PowerPivot is a component of Analysis Services, you can't use PowerPivot as an OLAP browser that auto-generates and sends MDX queries to the cube. Instead, just like with other data sources, you must import data from the cube as a tabular dataset. To start the import process, in the PowerPivot window, expand the From Database drop-down in the Home tab of the ribbon, and then select the "From Analysis Services or PowerPivot" option.

When you use a multidimensional cube as a data source, your only option is to specify an MDX query, and you won't get an option to import tables. Don't worry if you don't have MDX experience though. PowerPivot includes a graphical MDX query designer (the same one that is included in Reporting Services) that's capable of auto-generating MDX queries, as shown in **Figure 3.12**.

The Metadata pane displays the cube metadata. The MDX query designer supports two modes that you can toggle by clicking the Design Mode toolbar button: design mode and query mode. In design mode, the MDX query designer auto-generates the MDX query statement when you drag and drop objects from the Metadata pane to the Data pane. You can drag attribute and user-defined hierarchies, hierarchy levels, measures, calculated members, and key performance indicator (KPI) properties (such as Value, Goal, Target, and Status).

In some cases, you'll need to fine-tune the MDX query statement to support more advanced analytical needs, such as when you need to return a list of top ten products. The query mode allows you to view the raw MDX query and make changes to it. However, be aware that your changes will be lost if you switch back to design mode. You can filter the query results by dragging objects from the Metadata pane to the Filter pane, such as to filter the query results for a given year. You can drag attribute and user-defined hierarchies, individual members, hierarchy levels, and named sets.

**DEFINITION** A named set is a pre-defined set of dimension members that's assigned an alias. For example, the Reseller dimension in the Adventure Works cube includes a Large Resellers set that returns resellers with a number of employees between 81 and 100.

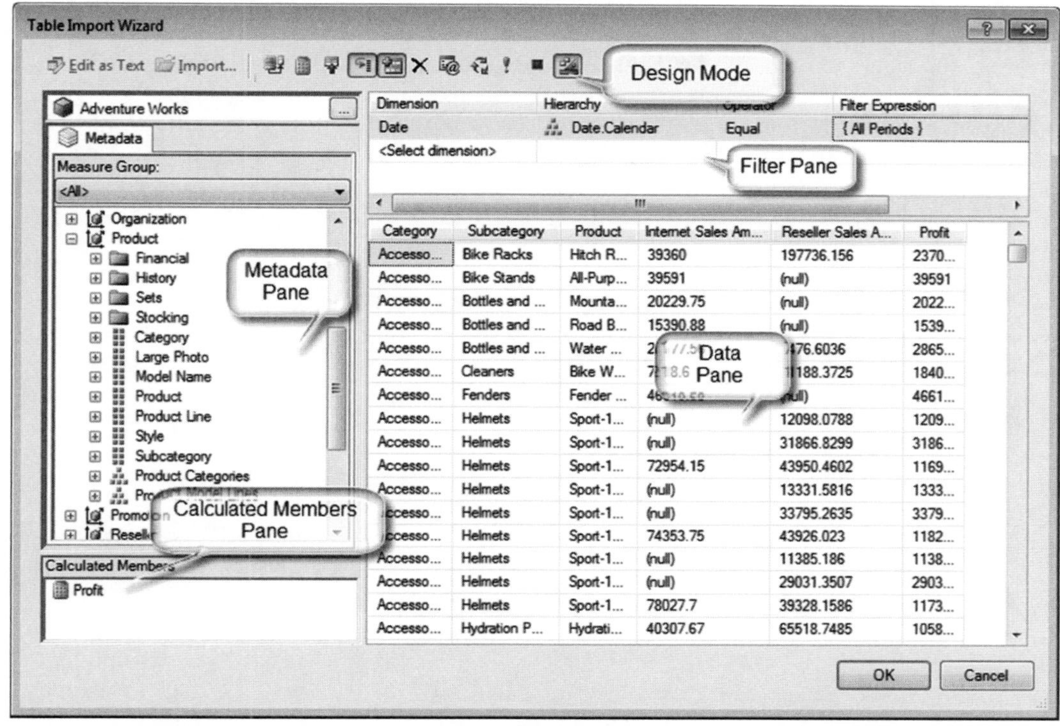


**Figure 3.12** The MDX query designer auto-generates the MDX query as you drag and drop objects.

Finally, the Calculated Members pane lets you define expression-based members that can be used on the report. For example, you can define a Profit calculated member that uses the following MDX expression to subtract the Total Product Cost measure from the Sales Amount measure:

```
[Measures].[Sales Amount] - [Measures].[Total Product Cost]
```

Once the calculated member is defined, you can drag it to the Data pane just like you can do with regular measures.

***Importing from Tabular***

You can also import data from Tabular models, including:

- PowerPivot workbooks published to SharePoint
- Organizational Tabular models deployed to an Analysis Services instance in Tabular mode

You can't import data or query external PowerPivot workbooks that are saved to disk; they must be deployed to SharePoint or restored to an Analysis Services instance in Tabular mode. To initiate the import process, expand the From Database button, and then click "From Analysis Services or PowerPivot", just like you did when connecting to a multidimensional cube. If you target an organizational Tabular model deployed to an Analysis Services instance in Tabular mode, enter the server name and database name. Or, if you want to connect to a PowerPivot workbook deployed to SharePoint, in the "Connect to Microsoft SQL Server Analysis Services" step, enter the URL address of the workbook in the following format:

```
http://<SharePoint Site>/<Document Library>/<Workbook File Name>
```

Suppose that someone has deployed a PowerPivot workbook named "Reseller Sales.xlsx" to the PowerPivot Gallery document library in a SharePoint site hosted on a server ELITEX. Assuming you have security rights to open the file, you can configure the connection (see **Figure 3.13**). PowerPivot recognizes that you're connecting to a PowerPivot workbook and disables the SQL Server Authentication option because Analysis Services supports only Windows security. PowerPivot also disables the Database dropdown list, which applies when you connect to Analysis Services databases (Tabular or Multidimensional) only. Next, the Table Import Wizard opens the same MDX query designer that you'll get when importing from multidimensional cubes.

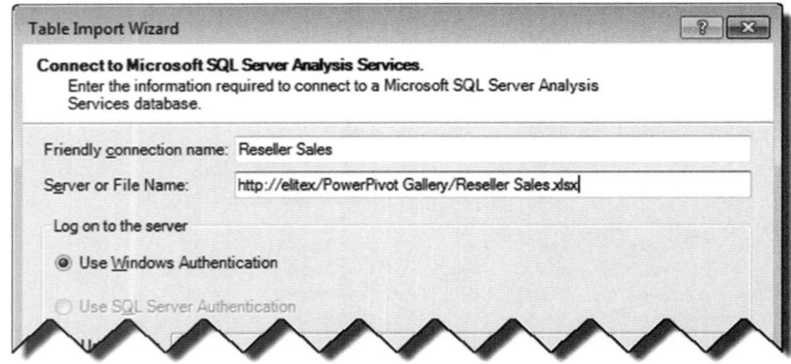


**Figure 3.13** When connecting to a published workbook, enter its full SharePoint URL address.

***Understanding metadata improvements***

Microsoft improved the integration with multidimensional databases. Previously, all measures were imported as text. In this release, the measure data type is inferred as follows:

- Multidimensional regular measures – Regular measures are measures that map directly to columns in the fact tables. They inherit the data type of the underlying column.
- Multidimensional calculated members – Calculated members are defined in the cube script or in the MDX query. If the calculated member is formatted as Currency or Percent, the import process will use the corresponding Tabular data type. Otherwise, the calculated member will be imported as text.
- Data Analysis Expressions (DAX) measures – When importing from tabular models (PowerPivot workbooks deployed to SharePoint or organizational models), PowerPivot will inherit the data type of the measure.

Sometimes the import process might be unable to infer the type of a Multidimensional measure, such as when a scope assignment overwrites the measure. In such cases, the Table Import Wizard will fail. To avoid this, check the "Import Measures as Text" checkbox in the Specify a MDX Query step. After you do this, the import process will bypass inferring the data types and import all the measures as text.

## 3.2.4 Importing from Text Files

The next most popular data source type you'll encounter is text files. This might be the case when your IT department doesn't give you direct access to the database or when the data is provided to you as extracts from another database. PowerPivot can import data from flat files and from Excel workbooks.

**NOTE** The Microsoft ACE OLE DB data provider is required to import from text files, Excel files, and Microsoft Access databases. This provider is included in Microsoft Office. If you get an error that the ACE provider isn't registered, you can download and install it from the Microsoft Download Center at http://bit.ly/accessredistr. For more information about additional deployment requirements for the ACE provider, read the blog post, "Working With The 2010 Office ACE Provider" by Dave Wickert (http://bit.ly/aceproviderpp) and the blog post, "Working With The ACE Provider In The Tabular Designer" by Cathy Dumas (http://bit.ly/aceprovidertab).

### *Importing from flat files*

The most common flat file format is comma-delimited and this is the default format supported by PowerPivot. To initiate the import process, click the From Text button in the PowerPivot Get External Data ribbon group. This will bring you to the Connect to Flat File dialog box, as shown in **Figure 3.14**.

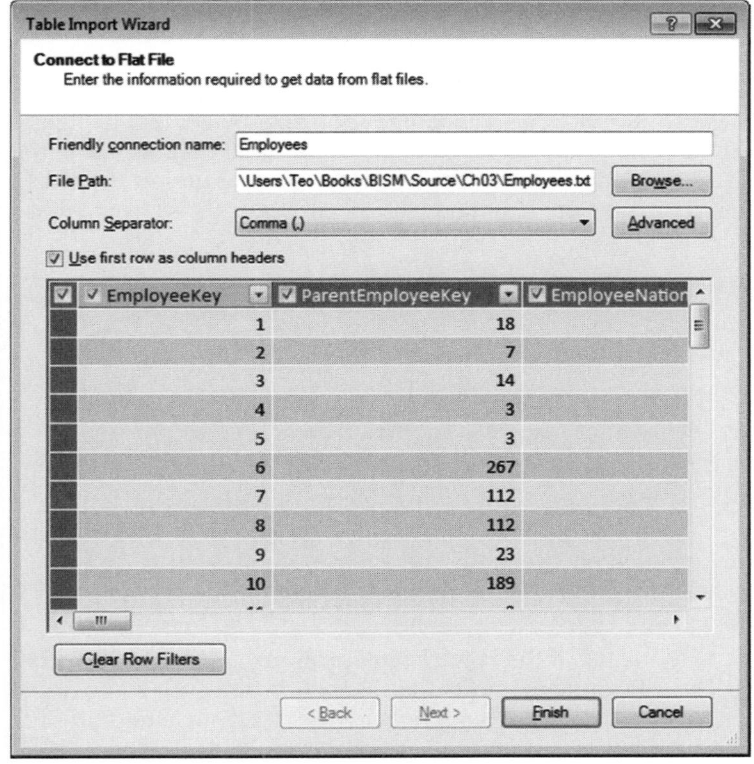


**Figure 3.14** PowerPivot supports various options to import data from flat files.

Here, you specify the file path and column separator. Besides a comma (,) column separator, PowerPivot supports other pre-defined separators including tab (t), semicolon (;), space ( ), colon (:), and vertical bar (|). If the file includes column headers, check the "Use first row as column headers" checkbox. Click the Advanced button to specify additional settings, including the encoding and locale. PowerPivot will then show you a preview of the file data. As with relational databases, set up row and column filters if you want to import a subset of the data in the file.

What if you need to import a fixed-length file or a file that uses some other delimiter? You can prepare a special schema.ini file that describes the file format, and then save that file in the same folder where the flat file is located. For example, suppose you're given a file with the following data:

```
EmployeeID    FirstName   LastName     Title
14417807      Guy         Gilbert      Production Technician
253022876     Kevin       Brown        Marketing Assistant
509647174     Roberto     Tamburello   Engineering Manager
112457891     Rob         Walters      Senior Tool Designer
```

This is an example of a file with a fixed-length column schema. You'll find this file saved as Employee2.txt in the Ch03 source folder. To import this file, you need to create the following schema.ini file and you must save the file in the same folder where the source file is located.

```
[Employees2.txt]
Format=FixedLength
Col1=EmployeeID Long Width 12
Col2=FirstName Text width 11
Col3=LastName Text Width 14
Col4=Title Text Width 50
```

The first line specifies the name of the source file. The second line tells the provider that the file has a fixed-length format. The next four lines describe the columns in the order they appear in the file, including the column name, date type, and width. When you run the Table Import Wizard and enter the file path in the "Connect to Flat File" step, PowerPivot will detect the schema.ini file and display the following informational message in the bottom of the dialog box.

A Schema.ini file has been detected in the current import folder "<file path>". Settings from this file will override your current import settings.

For more information about the schema.ini file specification, see the "Schema.ini File (Text File Driver)" document at http://bit.ly/schemaini.

***Importing from Excel workbooks***

There are probably myriads of Excel files with valuable data scattered around your company. PowerPivot supports three ways of getting data from Excel: linked tables, copy and paste, and importing Excel files. Importing data from Excel files has some benefits in comparison with linking and pasting, as follows:

- The Excel workbook file could be placed on a centrally accessible location, such as on a network share. People can share and work on this file, or they can refresh the file periodically with a new extract from the data source.
- PowerPivot stores the connection to the file. If the PowerPivot user wants to update the model data, he can simply refresh the PowerPivot model to get the changes. In addition, if you deploy the PowerPivot workbook to SharePoint, you can schedule PowerPivot to connect to the source file and refresh data automatically.
- You're not limited to importing only Excel tables. This gives you more flexibility with the subset of data that you want to bring into PowerPivot. For example, you can define a range of cells to import. However, importing entire worksheets might be beneficial because PowerPivot automatically picks up new rows.

Importing an Excel file takes a few mouse clicks. The following steps describe the import process (the actual exercise is provided in Section 3.3).

1. Before you start the import process, close the source Excel file if it's open in Excel.
2. Click the "From Other Sources" button in the Get External Data ribbon group.

3. In the "Connect to a Data Source" dialog box, scroll to the bottom and select the Excel File option found in the Text File section.
4. In the "Connect to a Microsoft Excel File" step, specify the path to the Excel file you want to import. Similarly to importing flat files, check the "Use first row as column headers" checkbox if the first row of the source data includes the column headers. Click Next.
5. In the "Select Tables and Views" step (see **Figure 3.15**), check the Excel worksheets and ranges that you want to import. Optionally, specify a friendly name for each table. Click Finish.

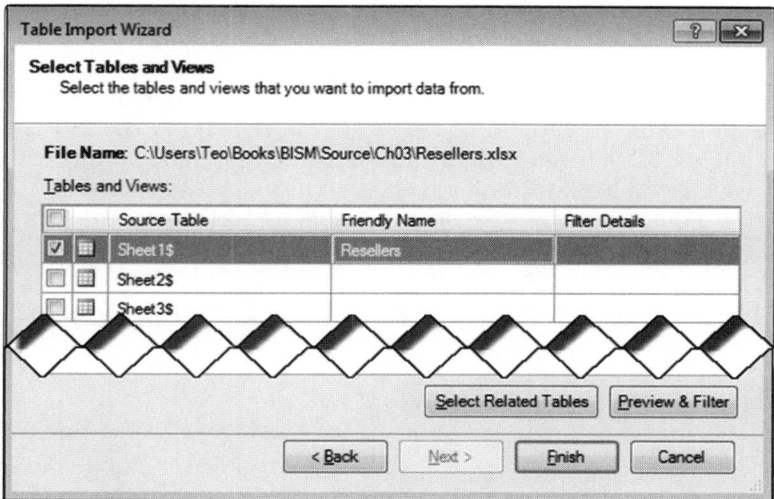


**Figure 3.15** In the "Select Tables and Views" step, select the Excel worksheets and ranges that you want to import.

Note that PowerPivot will import only text data from Excel. It won't import objects, such as charts and slicers.

## 3.2.5 Importing from Data Feeds

Open Data Protocol (OData) is a standard web protocol for querying and updating data. The protocol allows a client application (consumer), such as PowerPivot, to query a service (provider) over the HTTP protocol and then get the result back in popular data formats, such as Atom Syndication Format (ATOM), JavaScript Object Notation (JSON), or Plain Old XML (POX) formats. PowerPivot can integrate with any OData-compliant provider, including SQL Server Reporting Services reports, Azure Marketplace, SharePoint 2010, and cloud applications. This makes it possible to acquire data from virtually any application and platform provided that developers have implemented an OData API, such as a .NET Windows Communication Foundation (WCF) layer. For more information about OData, see http://odata.org.

***Importing from reports***

Many organizations have invested in implementing operational Reporting Services reports. Starting with SQL Server 2008 R2, Reporting Services reports are accessible as ATOM data feeds to allow external applications to subscribe to and import data (see the "Generating Data Feeds from Reports" MSDN article at http://bit.ly/rsdatafeeds). There are two ways to initiate the PowerPivot import process: from Reporting Services and from within PowerPivot.

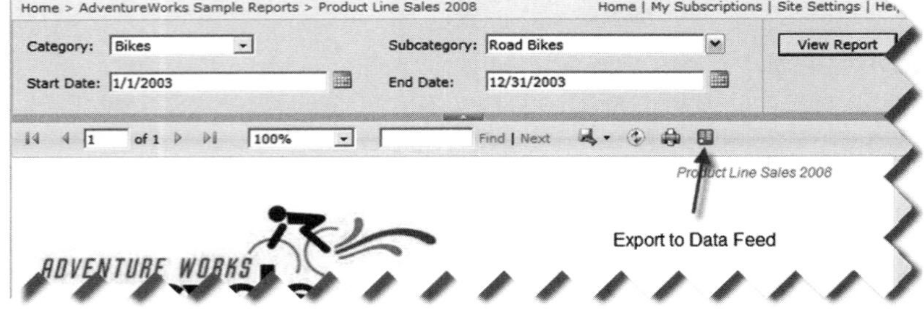


**Figure 3.16** Click the "Export to Data Feed" button to export report data to PowerPivot.

You can navigate to the Report Manager (or to SharePoint if Reporting Services is configured for SharePoint integrated mode), and then run a report. In the report toolbar, click the "Export to Data Feed" button, as shown in **Figure 3.16**. If you have an Excel workbook open, Reporting Services will ask you to specify which workbook you want to import data to, or if you want to create a new workbook. If Excel isn't open, Reporting Services will launch Excel, open the PowerPivot Window, and then launch the Table Import Wizard.

The second option is to click the From Report button in the PowerPivot Get External Data ribbon group. This brings you to the "Connect to a Microsoft SQL Server Reporting Services Report" step (see **Figure 3.17**).

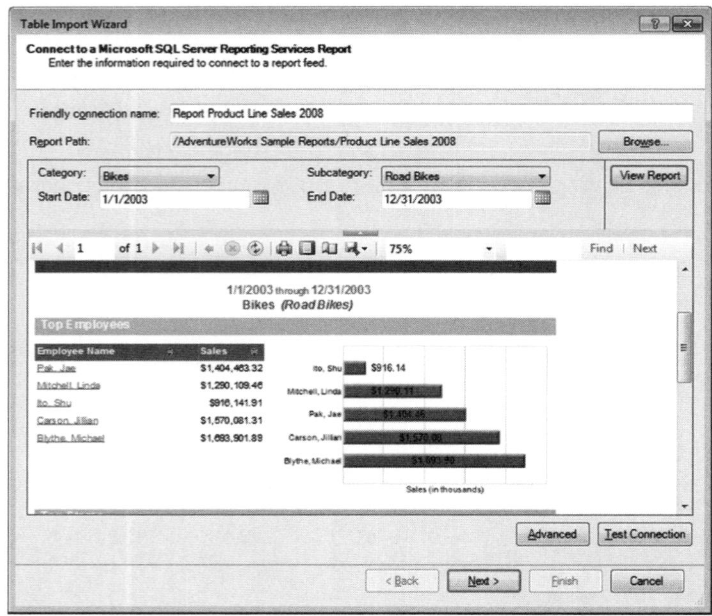


**Figure 3.17** Use this step to browse a report and to optionally specify report parameters that filter that data you want to import.

Click the Browse button to connect to a SQL Server 2008 R2 (or above) report server, and then select a report. The Table Import Wizard shows a report preview. If the report has parameters, you can specify the parameter values to filter the report data. Next, the Select Tables and Views step (see **Figure 3.18**) shows all the report sections (data regions) that can be imported, including data visualization regions, such as charts and gauges.

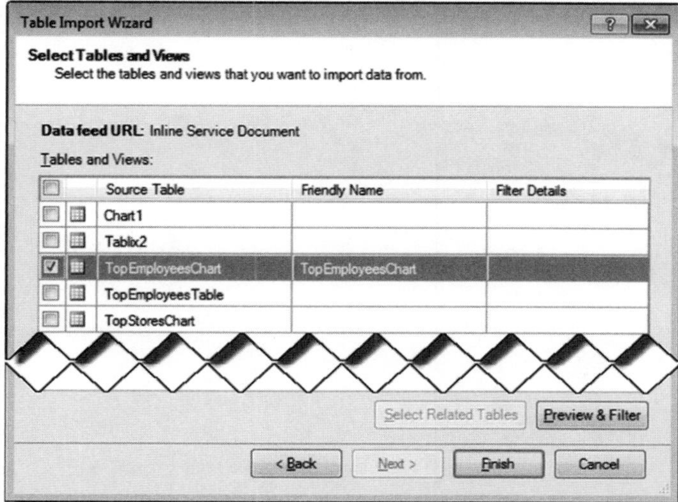


**Figure 3.18** You can import data from any section on the report, including charts and gauges.

***Importing from Azure Marketplace***

Windows Azure Marketplace (https://datamarket.azure.com) is a cloud service that provides a wide range of content from authoritative commercial and public sources in a central place. Marketplace makes it easier to find and purchase the external data you need to power your applications and analytics. To get started, you need to register on Azure Marketplace using your Windows Live ID so you can log in to the site. Then, you can browse the service categories and search for the available datasets to view their details, such as description, pricing, visualizations, and terms of use, and to understand which one can meet your need. The My Data section enables you to create an account key that PowerPivot and other applications need to access your Marketplace subscriptions. You can use some of the free services, such as WeatherBug Historical Observations and DATA.GOV 2006 - 2008 Crime in the United States, to test how PowerPivot integrates with Azure Marketplace.

1. In the PowerPivot window, click the "From Azure DataMarket" button in the Home ribbon tab.
2. In the "Connect to an Azure DataMarket Dataset" step (see **Figure 3.19**), specify the dataset URL. You can click the hyperlink to browse the Azure Marketplace site and to search for a dataset. Use the Browse button to load a feed file (Atom service document or Atom Feed), if you have one saved locally.
3. Enter the Marketplace account key or click the Find button to navigate to the Marketplace site, and then copy the key from the Account Keys section.
4. Click Next to get to the familiar "Select Tables and Views" step, where you can select which tables to import and can specify column filters.

**TIP** Another useful cloud service is the Open Government Data Initiative project (http://ogdisdk.cloudapp.net). It provides many useful and freely available OData feeds for importing a wide variety of public data from government agencies.

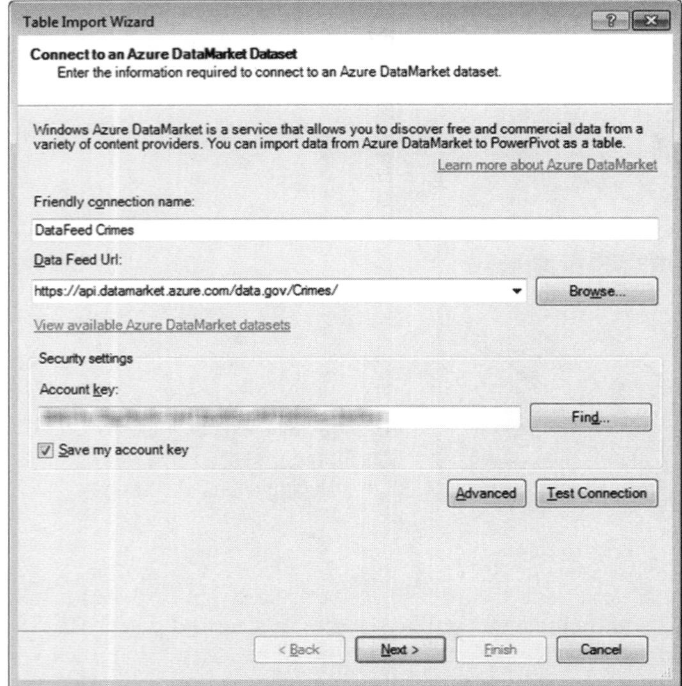


**Figure 3.19** To consume an Azure Marketplace service, specify the dataset URL and account key.

***Importing data from SharePoint***

Many organizations use SharePoint for document management and collaboration. Beginning with SharePoint 2010, you can import content from SharePoint using the OData protocol. As a prerequisite, you need to install Windows Communication Foundation (WCF) Data Services (http://msdn.microsoft.com/en-us/data/ee720179) on the SharePoint server. Once this is done, import SharePoint data in PowerPivot with the following steps:

1. Click the "From Data Feeds" button in the Get External Data ribbon group.

   In the Data Feed Url field, enter http://<site>/_vti_bin/listdata.svc/, as shown in **Figure 3.20**. Replace <site> with the name of your SharePoint site.

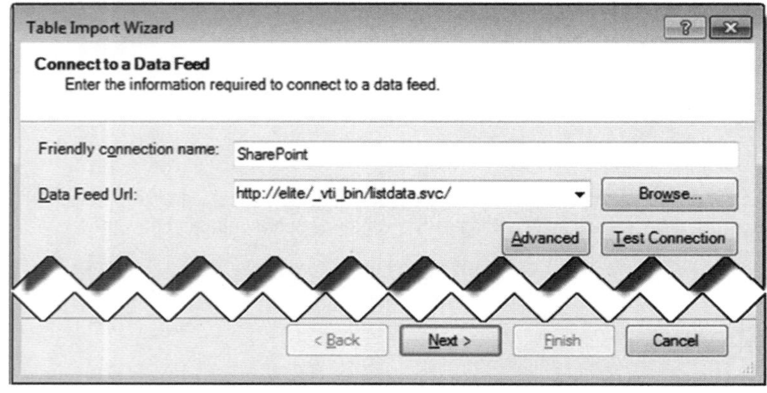


**Figure 3.20** PowerPivot can subscribe and import SharePoint content as data feeds.

When you click Next, the Select Tables and Views step shows all the SharePoint lists that you have access to. Select one or more lists, and then click Finish to import the data.

## 3.2.6 Other Import Options

So far, all the import options that I discussed used the Table Import Wizard and assumed that can connect to a data source. There two more options for bringing data into PowerPivot that I'll explain next: linked Excel tables and Windows Clipboard.

***Linking Excel tables***

Besides importing from an external Excel file, you can link Excel tables to PowerPivot. You can only link Excel tables in the same workbook where the PowerPivot model is saved. Linked tables could be useful if you need to maintain the source data manually inside the Excel workbook and you want to create the PowerPivot model in the same workbook where the source data is. For example, in Chapter 2, I showed you how Alice can maintain her own Excel list of resellers and link it to PowerPivot.

Irrespective of the fact that you're "linking" an Excel table, PowerPivot imports the source data just like it does with any other data source. Moreover, PowerPivot maintains a connection to the linked table. As a result, PowerPivot for Excel synchronizes the data changes automatically. If you change the data in the Excel table, the next time the PowerPivot Window has focus on the data, PowerPivot will synchronize the changes. A linked table adds its own Linked Table tab to the PowerPivot ribbon. Follow these steps to understand the PowerPivot user interface when you work with linked tables:

1. Open Ch02.xlsx from the Ch02 folder, and then click the PowerPivot tab in the Excel ribbon.
2. In the PowerPivot window, observe that the Reseller and Date table tabs (on the bottom, like Excel worksheet tabs) have a special link icon to indicate that they're linked to Excel tables. Click the Reseller table tab. PowerPivot adds the contextual Linked Table tab to the ribbon, as shown in **Figure 3.21**. The tab is only there when the linked table is active.

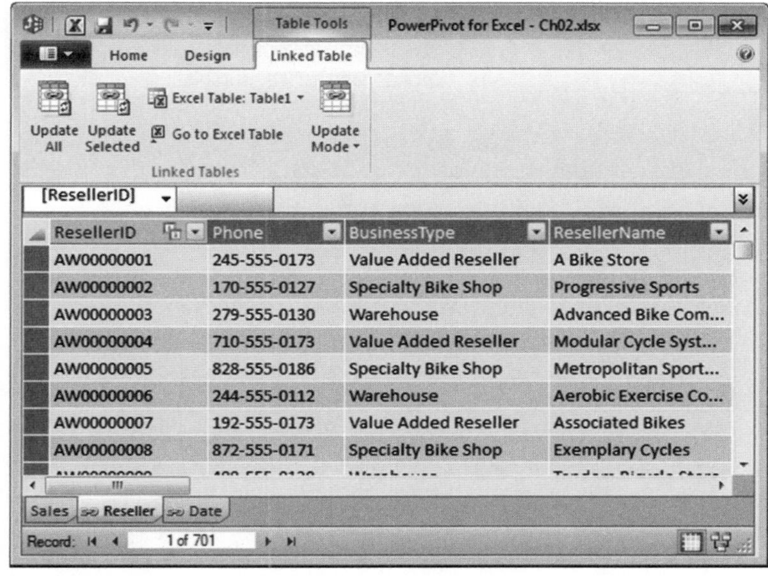


**Figure 3.21** PowerPivot adds the Linked Table tab to the ribbon.

You can use the Update Mode button to set the update mode to automatic (default) or manual. In the case of the manual update mode, you can click the Update All button to synchronize your changes to all linked tables. In Excel's PowerPivot ribbon tab, there is an Update All button that performs the same task. The Update Selected button updates the currently active table only. The Excel Table drop-down button allows you to link the active PowerPivot table to another Excel table. Finally, the "Go to Excel Table" button navigates you to the linked Excel table.

Suppose you delete or rename the linked Excel table, which you can do when you click the Excel Design ribbon tab. The next time PowerPivot attempts to synchronize data, it will detect the issue and display the error message shown in **Figure 3.22**. If you click the Options button, you'll find several options: do nothing, change the source table to another table, remove the link, or delete the PowerPivot table.

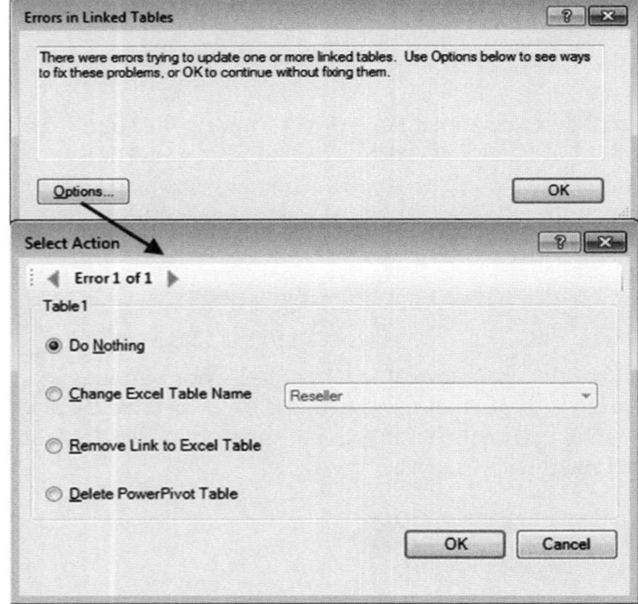


**Figure 3.22** PowerPivot gives you several options to handle broken links to linked tables.

Before you decide on using linked tables, consider the following tradeoffs.

- You can't link data from external Excel workbooks. In other words, you can only link to Excel data in the same workbook that contains the PowerPivot model.
- If you publish the PowerPivot model to SharePoint, you can't set up an automatic refresh for linked tables. Therefore, consider using linked tables when your data changes infrequently. The only option to update the linked table is to open the Excel workbook and then make the changes manually.
- If you're a BI pro, note that linked tables are not supported in organizational models that are deployed to Analysis Services Tabular. When you import a PowerPivot workbook in an Analysis Services Project, the import process automatically converts all linked tables to internal data sources.

3. Close the Ch02.xlsx file in Excel.

***Copying and pasting data***
Finally, if the previously discussed import options don't work for you, you can always just copy and paste your data. This option uses the Windows Clipboard and requires the source data to be in an HTML tabular format, such as data that's copied from Microsoft Word or Excel. Consider copying and pasting data when you can't connect to the data source, such as when you need to import data from an application screen or from a web page.

**Figure 3.23** PowerPivot detects that tabular data is copied in the Windows Clipboard and activates the Paste button.

When the data in the Windows Clipboard has the required format, PowerPivot enables the Paste button in the Clipboard ribbon group on Home tab, as shown in **Figure 3.23**. When you click the Paste button, you'll see a dialog box that shows you a preview of the data to be pasted. Once you click OK, PowerPivot creates a new table. There are two ways to update the data in the table:

- Paste Append – appends the new data at end of the table.
- Paste Replace – replaces the entire table with the new data.

It's important to note that pasted tables can't be configured for an automatic refresh in SharePoint. Therefore, consider this option as a last resort and when your data changes infrequently.

## 3.3 Importing Adventure Works Data

This section starts you on the process for implementing a PowerPivot model for analyzing the Adventure Works sales. You'll practice different options for importing data from a variety of data sources, including relational and multidimensional databases, text files, and data feeds.

### 3.3.1 Importing from a Data Warehouse Database ▶

In this exercise, you'll import the main dataset for analyzing the Adventure Works reseller sales from the FactResellerSales table in the AdventureWorksDW2008R2 database. FactResellerSales represents a fact table and it keeps a historical record of numeric values (facts), such as Sales Amount and Order Quantity. You'll also import the DimDate table from the same database so that you can aggregate data by date periods, such as month, quarter, year, and so on.

***Connecting to the database***
Follow these steps to import data from the FactResellerSales table:

1. Open Excel 2010, and then save the empty workbook as *Adventure Works.xlsx* in a folder on your local hard drive.
2. Click the PowerPivot ribbon tab in Excel, and then click the PowerPivot Window button.
3. In the Home tab of the PowerPivot window, expand the From Database toolbar drop-down in the Get External Sources ribbon group, and then select From SQL Server. This opens the Table Import Wizard.

4. In the Connect to a Microsoft SQL Server Database step, enter *AdventureWorksDW* in the "Friendly Connection Name" field. In the Server Name field, enter the SQL Server instance, such as *ELITE* if SQL Server is installed on a server called ELITE, or *ELITE\R2* if the SQL Server is running on a named instance R2 on a server called ELITE.

> **TIP** Even if the database is installed on your local computer, enter the computer name in the Server Name field instead of (local) or localhost. This will avoid connectivity issues that will require you to change the connection string if you decide to deploy the model to SharePoint or move the workbook to another computer.

5. Assuming that you have access to the AdventureWorksDW2008R2 database via Windows security, leave the Use Windows Authentication option selected. Or, if the database administrator (DBA) has created a login for you, select the "Use SQL Server Authentication" option, and then enter the login credentials.
6. Expand the Database Name drop-down list. If SQL Server authenticates you successfully, you should see a list of databases that you have access to. Select the AdventureWorksDW2008R2 database.
7. Click Test Connection to test the connectivity, and then click Next.

***Importing and filtering data***

Next, you'll import two tables from the Adventure Works data warehouse database.

1. In the "Choose How to Import the Data" step, leave the default option "Select from a list of tables and views" preselected, and then click Next.
2. In the "Select Tables and Views" step, check the DimDate and FactResellerSales tables.
3. You can use the Preview Selected Table step to set up row and column filters. This will limit the data you're importing. With the FactResellerSales table selected, click the Preview & Filter button to preview the data in the table.
4. Suppose that you don't need the RevisionNumber column for analysis. Scroll all the way to the right, and then clear the checkbox in the column header of the RevisionNumber column.
5. (Optional) Expand the drop-down indicator in any column header. Notice that you can use various options to filter the values in this column based on the column data type. This will result in a row filter that limits the number of rows imported. For example, if you want to import only rows where SalesAmount > 1,000, you can click the column header of the SalesAmount column, and then use the Number Filters option. Click OK to return to the "Select Tables and Views" step.
6. Notice that the Filter Details column shows "Applied filters" next to the FactResellerSales table to inform you that this table has a filter. Click the Applied Filters link. The Filter Details dialog box opens and tells you which columns will be imported. Click OK to close the Filter Details dialog box. Also, you can click the "Select Related Tables" button if you want to preselect tables that are related to FactResellerSales in the AdventureWorksDW2008R2 database.
7. Select the DimDate table, and then click the Preview & Filter button. Uncheck all the columns whose names start with "French" or "Spanish", and then click OK.
8. Click Finish. The Importing dialog box shows the progress of the import operation, as shown in **Figure 3.24**. Notice that the last row says Data Preparation and shows a Details link in the Message column. Click on the Details link.

A Details window opens to inform you that PowerPivot has detected several referential integrity relationships between the DimDate and FactResellerSales tables in the AdventureWorksDW2008R2 database and PowerPivot applied these relationships to the model. Specifically, DimDate is joined three times to the FactResellerSales table via the ShipDateKey, DueDateKey, and OrderDateKey columns. Such relationships are called role-playing relationships and are discussed in more details in Chapter 4.

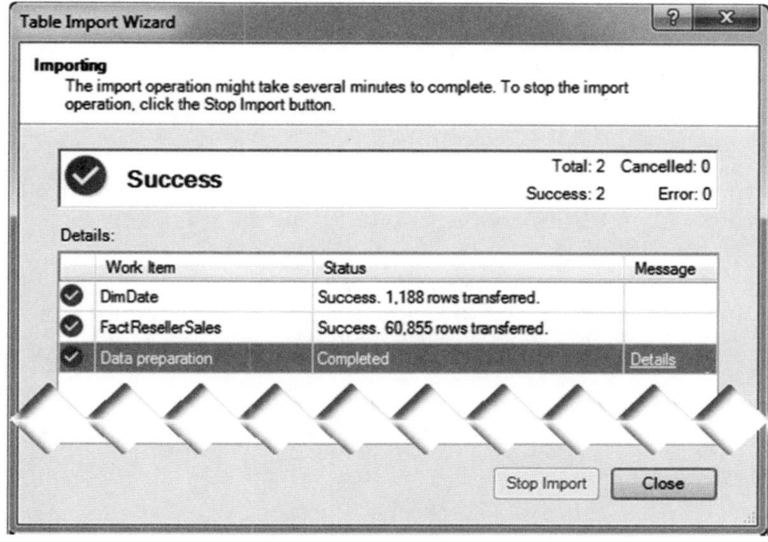


**Figure 3.24** The Importing step informs you about the status of the import process.

9. Click OK to close the Details dialog box. Click Close to go back to the PowerPivot window. PowerPivot adds the FactResellerSales and DimDate tables to the model.

## 3.3.2 Importing from a Multidimensional Cube ▶

If your organization has multidimensional cubes, you can use PowerPivot to import data from these cubes. You can use similar steps to import data from PowerPivot workbooks that are deployed to SharePoint or tabular models deployed to an Analysis Services instance configured in Tabular mode. Next, you'll import the Sales Territory dimension data and a (key performance indicator) KPI from the Adventure Works cube. The book front matter includes steps for installing the Adventure Works cube.

**IMPORTANT** If you don't have an Analysis Services instance with the Adventure Works cube, you can import the DimSalesTerritory table from the AdventureWorksDW2008R2 database to complete this practice. To do so, on the PowerPivot Design ribbon tab, click the Existing Connections button, select the AdventureWorksDW connection, and then click Open. In the "Choose How to Import Data" step, accept the default option to select from a list of tables and click Next. In the Select Tables and Views step, check the DimSalesTerritory table, and then enter *SalesTerritories* in the Friendly Name column. Importing DimSalesTerritory won't import the Revenue KPI because it's only defined in the cube. When going through subsequent exercises, ignore steps that reference the Revenue KPI.

***Connecting to Multidimensional***

Start by connecting to the Adventure Works cube as follows:

1. In the PowerPivot window, click the Home ribbon tab.
2. Expand the From Database drop-down list and click "From Analysis Services or PowerPivot".
3. In the "Connect to Microsoft SQL Server Analysis Services" step of the Table Import Wizard, enter *AdventureWorksAS* as a connection name. In the "Server Name or File Name" field, enter the name of the server where Analysis Services is installed, such as *ELITE* if Multidimensional is installed on

a server called ELITE. Expand the Database Name drop-down list and select the "Adventure Works DW 2008R2 Analysis Services" database.

4. Click Test Connection to check your connectivity, and then click the Next button.
5. In the "Specify a MDX Query" step, enter *SalesTerritories* as a friendly query name.

***Using the MDX query designer***

PowerPivot includes the same MDX query designer that's found in Reporting Services.

1. Instead of typing the MDX query manually, click the Design button.
2. In the Metadata pane, scroll down until you see the Sales Territory dimension. Expand the dimension, and then drag the Sales Territory Group, Sales Territory Country, and Sales Territory Region attributes to the right pane.
3. In the Metadata pane, expand the KPIs folder, and then expand Revenue KPI. Drag the Value element and drop it into the right pane. At this point, your results should resemble **Figure 3.25**.

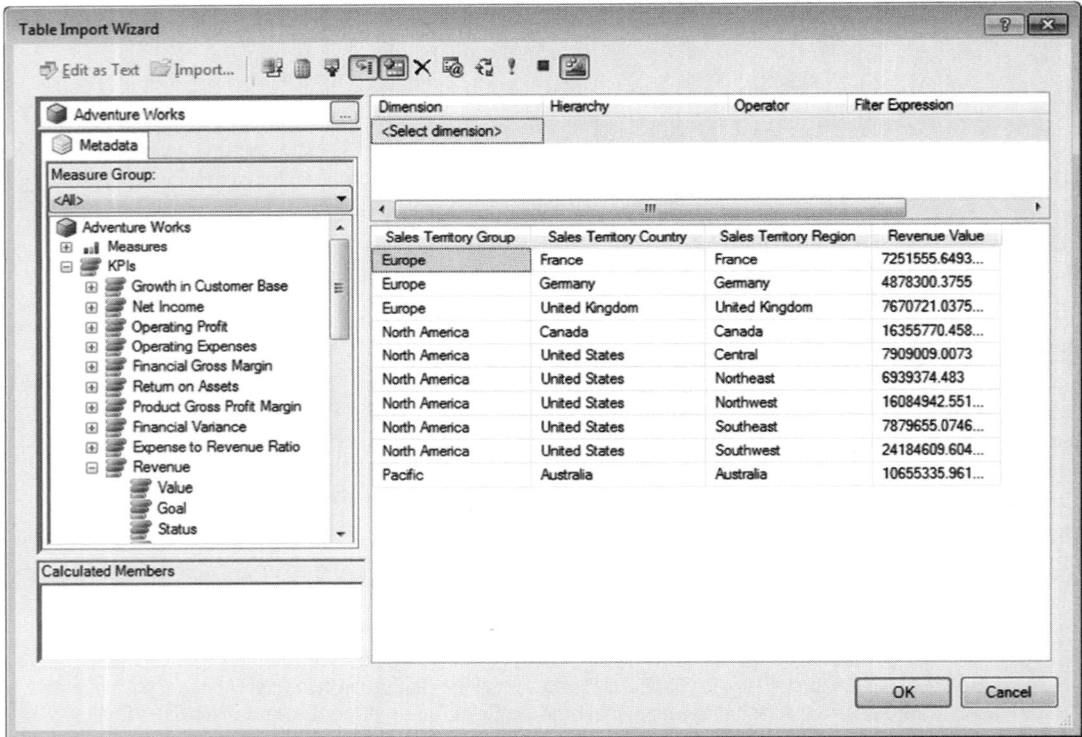


**Figure 3.25** Use the MDX query designer to create queries by dragging and dropping objects.

4. Click OK to return to the Table Import Wizard. The MDX statement field has this query:

```
SELECT { KPIValue("Revenue") } ON COLUMNS,
{ ([Sales Territory].[Sales Territory Group].[Sales Territory Group].ALLMEMBERS * [Sales Territory].[Sales Territory Country].[Sales Territory Country].ALLMEMBERS * [Sales Territory].[Sales Territory Region].[Sales Territory Region].ALLMEMBERS ) } DIMENSION PROPERTIES MEMBER_CAPTION, MEMBER_UNIQUE_NAME ON ROWS
FROM [Adventure Works] CELL PROPERTIES VALUE, BACK_COLOR, FORE_COLOR, FORMATTED_VALUE, FORMAT_STRING, FONT_NAME, FONT_SIZE, FONT_FLAGS
```

5. Click Finish. PowerPivot imports the data and adds a new SalesTerritories table.

## 3.3.3 Importing From Files ▶

Besides databases, PowerPivot could import data stored in text files. Next, you'll import data from text files, including flat files and Excel workbooks.

***Importing data from flat files***

Security and operational requirements might prevent you from connecting directly to a database. In such cases, data could be provided to you as text files. Suppose that Adventure Works keeps the employee information in an HR mainframe database. Instead of having direct access to the database, you're given an extract as a comma-separated values (CSV) file. Follow these steps to import this file:

1. In the Home ribbon tab of the PowerPivot window, click the From Text button.
2. In the "Connect to Flat File" step of the Table Import Wizard, enter *Employees* as the friendly connection name.
3. Click the Browse button, and then select the Employees.txt file found in the Ch03 folder. The Table Import Wizard parses the file and then shows its content in the preview grid.

   With PowerPivot, you can specify various options to customize the import process from flat files. Notice that by default PowerPivot includes the first row, which contains the column headers in this case, in the imported data.
4. Check the "Use first row as column headers" checkbox. Compare your results with **Figure 3.26**.

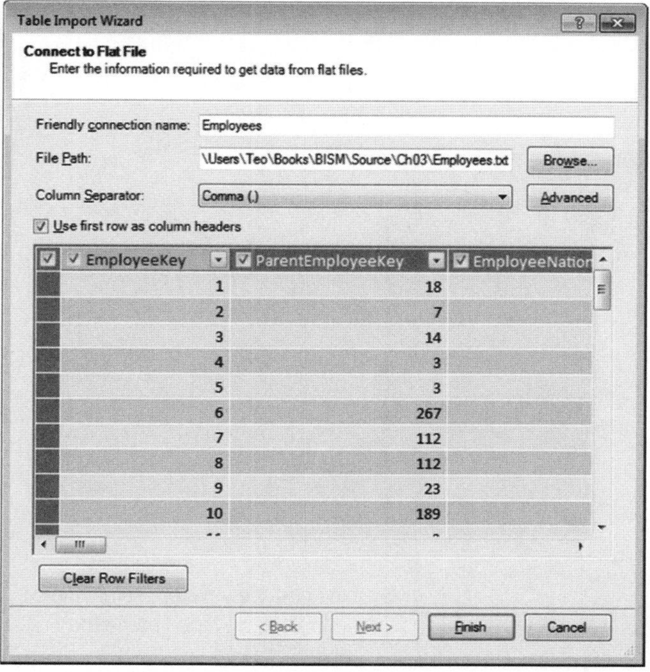


**Figure 3.26** Importing from a flat file requires specifying the file path and column separator.

5. Notice that the EmployeeKey column header includes some special characters. To fix this issue, you need to change the encoding option. Click the Advanced button, and then change the Encoding drop-down list to UTF-8. Click OK.

6. Back in the "Connect to Flat File" step, click Finish to import the data and create the Employees table.
7. Sometimes, you might need to exclude columns that you don't need for analysis after data is already imported. Instead of deleting the PowerPivot table and then reimporting data again, you can go to the table properties and make the desired changes. With the Employees tab selected in the PowerPivot window, click the Design ribbon tab, and then click the Table Properties button.
8. Exclude the EmployeeNationalIDAlternateKey, ParentNationalIDAlternateKeyEmployeeKey, StartDate, EndDate, and Status columns by unchecking the checkboxes in the column headers.
9. Click the Save button. PowerPivot connects to the flat file and then reimports the data without the column you selected.

***Importing from Excel workbooks***

Suppose that you're given a list of resellers as an Excel file. You want to import this list in PowerPivot.

1. In the Home ribbon tab of the PowerPivot window, click the From Other Data Sources button.
2. In the "Connect to a Data Source" step of the Table Import Wizard, scroll all the way down, and then select the Excel File option found in the Text Files section. Click Next.
3. In the "Connect to a Microsoft Excel File" step, enter *Resellers* as a friendly connection name. Click the Browse button, and then select the Resellers.xlsx file found in the Ch03 folder. Check the "Use first row as column headers" checkbox.
4. Click Test Connection to test the connectivity, and then click Next.

When you import data from Excel workbooks, PowerPivot considers each worksheet to be a separate table. In our case, only the first worksheet contains the data you need to import.

6. In the "Select Tables and Views" step, check the checkbox in the Sheet 1$ row.
7. Enter *Resellers* in the Friendly Name column, as shown in **Figure 3.27**.

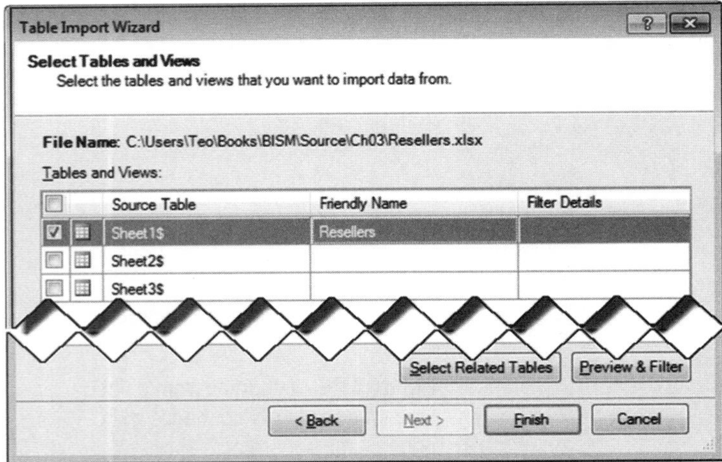


**Figure 3.27** In the "Select Tables and Views" step, select the first sheet, and then name the table Resellers.

8. Click the "Preview & Filter" button.
9. In the "Preview Selected Table" dialog box, uncheck the GeographyKey and ResellerAlternateKey columns because you won't need these columns for analysis.
10. Click Finish. PowerPivot adds a new Resellers table to the Adventure Works model.

## 3.3.4 Importing from Reporting Services Reports ▶

PowerPivot is capable of importing data feeds that are compatible with the Open Data (OData) protocol. Starting with the R2 release, Reporting Services allows you to expose reports as feeds. In the steps that follow, you'll import the product information from the Product Catalog 2008 report. The Product Catalog 2008 report is one of the Reporting Services sample reports that ship with SQL Server. This report must be deployed to a Reporting Services server. If you have Reporting Services R2 or later installed, upload the Product Catalog 2008.rdl from the Ch03 folder to your report server. Please note that the report data source uses the AdventureWorks2008R2 database (see the book front matter for setup instructions) and you probably need to change the connection string in the report data source to reflect your specific setup.

**IMPORTANT** If configuring Reporting Services isn't an option, you can import the required data from the AdventureWorksDW2008R2 database. To do so, in the PowerPivot Design ribbon tab, click the Existing Connections button, select the AdventureWorksDW connection, and then click Open. In the "Choose How to Import Data" step, select the "Write a query that will specify the data to import" option. In the Specify a SQL Query step, enter *Products* as a friendly name for the table. Then to import data from the DimProduct table, paste the query I provided in the Products.sql file (Ch03 folder). The query doesn't return exactly the same results as the Product Catalog report and that's OK.

***Testing the Product Catalog 2008 report***

Follow these steps to test the Product Catalog 2008 report and to make sure that it is functional.

1. Open the Report Manager by navigating to its URL in your web browser.
2. Navigate to the "Adventure Works Sample Reports" folder. Click the Product Catalog 2008 report to run the report. The report should run with no errors.

***Importing the Product Catalog 2008 report***

Once you verified that the report is functional, follow these steps to import it:

1. In the PowerPivot window, click the Home ribbon tab, and then click the From Report button.
2. In the "Connect to Microsoft SQL Server Reporting Services Report" step, enter *Reporting Services* as a friendly connection name.
3. Click the Browse button. In the Open Report dialog box that follows, enter the report server URL in the Name field, and then press Enter. Navigate to the Adventure Works Sample Reports folder, and then select the Product Catalog 2008 report, as shown in **Figure 3.28**. Click Open.
4. PowerPivot shows a preview of the report. Click Next.
5. In the "Select Tables and Views" step, you can select which report section you want to import data from. A Reporting Services report can have multiple sections (data regions) and each data region is available as a data feed. The Product Catalog 2008 report has only one section. Check the checkbox next to the Tablix1 section, and then enter *Products* in the Friendly Name column next to it (see **Figure 3.29**).
6. (Optional) Click the "Preview & Filter" button to preview the report data.
7. Click Finish to import the data from the report and to create a new table named Products.

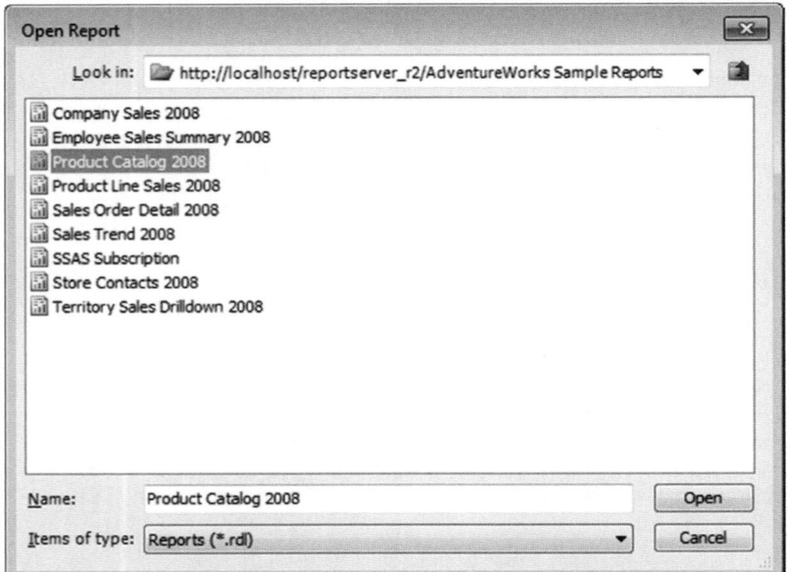


**Figure 3.28** Use the Open Report dialog box to browse the report catalog, and then select the Product Catalog 2008 report.

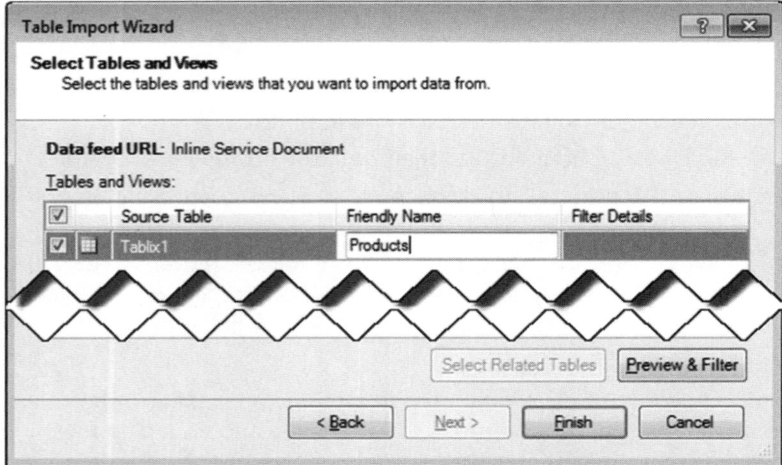


**Figure 3.29** Each section on the Reporting Services report is available as a data feed.

## 3.3.5 Copying and Pasting Data ▶

Copying and pasting data is another option to import data that can't be obtained by connecting to a data source. For example, you might need to bring data from an HTML table on a web page. Since you can't connect, you can copy the HTML table and paste it into PowerPivot.

***Copying data***

Adventure Works captures sales in the original currency of the country where the sale was made. Suppose that you want to analyze data by the regional currency, and suppose that Adventure Works maintains a web page of the world currencies. Follow these steps to copy the currencies and to paste them into the PowerPivot model:

1. Open Windows Explorer, navigate to the Ch03 folder, and then double-click the Currencies.html page. This opens the Currencies.html file in your web browser. This process simulates navigating to an actual web page on the Internet.
2. Press Ctrl+A to select the entire HTML table, and then press Ctrl+C to copy the data.

***Pasting data***

If the content of the clipboard is in a tabular format that PowerPivot recognizes, you'll be able to paste the data into your PowerPivot model.

1. Back in the PowerPivot window, click the Home tab. Notice that the Paste button is now active.
2. Click the Paste button. This opens the Paste Preview dialog box, which shows a preview of the data that you've copied to the Windows Clipboard.
3. Enter *Currencies* as the table name, as shown in **Figure 3.30**.

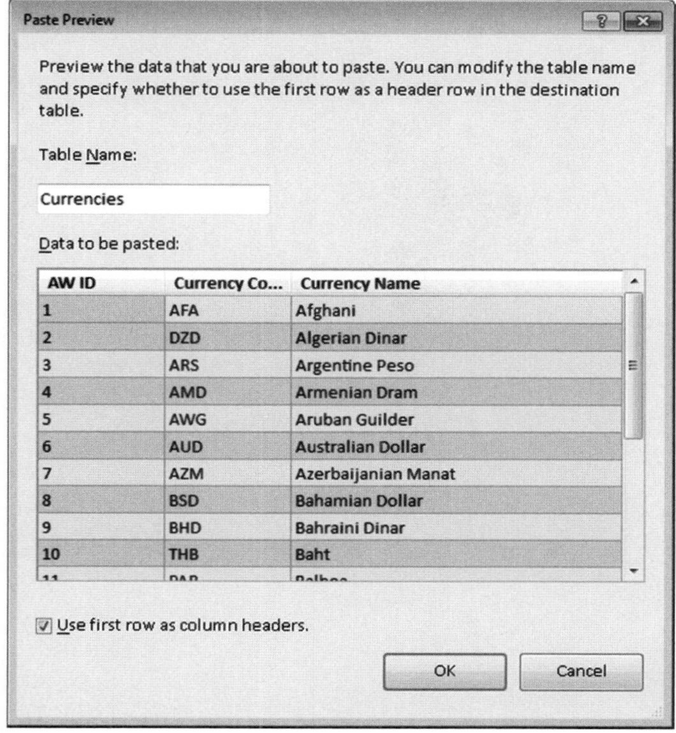


**Figure 3.30** Use the Paste Preview dialog box to preview the data pasted from the Windows Clipboard.

4. Click OK to create the Currencies table.

This completes the import process of the initial set of tables you need to analyze the Adventure Works reseller sales. At this point, the PowerPivot window should have seven tabs that represent the tables you imported: FactResellerSales, DimDate, SalesTerritories, Resellers, Employees, Currencies, and Products.

## 3.4 Summary

Tabular is a relational-like model and represents data as tables and columns. This chapter started by laying out fundamental data modeling concepts (such as table schemas, relationships, and keys) that you need to understand before you import data.

Next, the chapter explained the data import capabilities of PowerPivot. As you've seen, PowerPivot can acquire data from a wide variety of data sources, including databases, text files, data feeds, Excel linked tables, and pasting data. The main way to import data into PowerPivot is to use the Table Import Wizard, which doesn't require database query or scripting knowledge.

Finally, you've started the process for implementing a PowerPivot model for analyzing the Adventure Works sales. Specifically, you loaded data from the Adventure Works data warehouse, from a multidimensional cube, a comma-delimited file, an Excel workbook, a Reporting Services report, and from Windows Clipboard. Next, you'll learn how to explore the imported data and how to refine the model.

# Chapter 4

# Refining the Model



In Chapter 3, you learned how to import data from various data sources. The next step is to explore and refine the model before analyzing its data. Typical tasks in this phase include rearranging and renaming columns, sorting and filtering data, and changing the column type and formatting options. You also need to set up table relationships if you import multiple tables.

In this chapter, you'll practice common tasks to enhance the Adventure Works PowerPivot model. First, you'll learn how to explore your data and to refine the model metadata. Next, I'll show you how to manage schema and data changes, including managing connections and tables, and refreshing the model data to synchronize it with changes in the data sources. Finally, I'll walk you through the steps needed to set up table relationships.

## 4.1 Understanding Tables and Columns

PowerPivot stores imported data in tables. Although the data might originate from heterogeneous data sources, once it enters the model it's treated the same irrespective of its origin. Similar to a relational database, a table consists of columns and rows. You can use the PowerPivot window to explore the table schema and data.

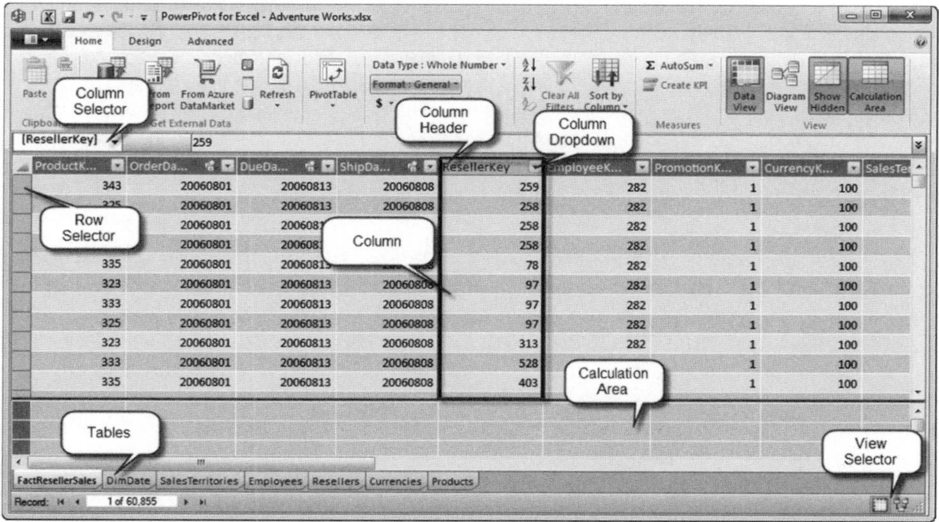


**Figure 4.1** In Data View, you can browse the model schema and data.

## 4.1.1 Understanding the Data View

I previously mentioned that the PowerPivot window represents the PowerPivot modeling environment and the model itself. To launch PowerPivot, click the PowerPivot Window button found in the PowerPivot tab in the Excel ribbon. The PowerPivot window always opens as a new window that is separate from the Excel window. The PowerPivot window supports two views: Data View and Diagram View. As its name suggests, Data View allows you to browse the model data. By contrast, Diagram View shows a graphical representation of the model schema only.

By default, the PowerPivot window opens in Data View (the Data View button in the Home ribbon tab is depressed). **Figure 4.1** shows the Adventure Works model open in Data View. You can toggle the view by using the buttons in the Home ribbon's View group or by using the View Selector buttons in the bottom-right corner of the PowerPivot window.

***Understanding tables***

The table tabs that appear at the bottom of Data View represent the tables in the model (similar to the worksheet tabs at the bottom the Excel window). As it stands, the Adventure Works model has seven tables. The table tabs are sorted in the order that the tables were imported in the model. However, you can change that order by dragging a tab to a new position. Or, you can right-click a tab, and then click Move. This will pop up a Move Table dialog box where you specify before which table you want to move the selected table. In this release, the table order is for the modeler's convenience only and doesn't affect how the metadata is presented to client tools.

The table name is significant because it's included in the model metadata and it's shown to the end user. In addition, when you create calculated columns and measures, the Data Analysis Expressions (DAX) formulas reference the table and column names. Therefore, spend some time to choose suitable names and to rename objects accordingly. You can also enter helpful descriptions by right-clicking on an object, such as a table, column, or measure, and the clicking Description. It's up to the client tool to support the metadata descriptions. Excel pivot reports, for example, will display the description in a tooltip when the user points to the metadata object in the PowerPivot Field List pane.

**TIP** When it comes to naming conventions, I like to keep table and column names short. I prefer camel casing where the first letter of each word is capitalized. I also prefer to use a plural case for fact tables, such as ResellerSales, and a singular case for lookup (dimension) tables, such as Reseller. You don't have to follow this convention, but it's important to have one and to stick to it. While we are on this subject, unlike Multidimensional, Tabular supports identical column names across fact tables, such as SalesAmount in the ResellerSales table and SalesAmount in the InternetSales table. However, some reporting tools, such as Power View, don't support renaming fields on the report, and you won't be able to tell the two fields apart in a consolidated report that shows both fields. Therefore, consider renaming the columns and adding a prefix to have unique column names across tables, such as ResellerSalesAmount and InternetSalesAmount. Or, you can create explicit measures with unique names and then hide the original columns.

The horizontal bands with alternating background colors represent rows of the table. The Record field in the status bar indicates which row is currently selected and the total number of rows in the table. For example, if you type in *10000* in the Record field, PowerPivot will navigate to the 10,000$^{nd}$ row in the ResellerSales table.

***Understanding columns***

The vertical bands represent table columns. Click any cell to activate the row and column where the cell is located and to highlight the row and column header. The Formatting ribbon group in the Home tab shows the data type of the active column. The Column Selector (see **Figure 4.1** again) shows the name of the active column, and the grayed out formula bar next to it shows the first column value. You can expand the Column Selector and select another column to navigate to that column.

As you can see, Data View resembles the Excel user interface. The big difference is that it's read-only. You can't change the data–not even a single cell. If you find a data error that requires a correction, you must change the source data in the data source and then reimport the table.

## 4.1.2 Exploring Data

If there were data modeling commandments, the first one would be "Know thy data". Realizing the common need to explore the raw data, the Analysis Services team has added features to Data View to sort and filter the model data. You'll probably find that these features are very similar to Excel PivotTable sorting and filtering, so I won't spend much time discussing them. You can use the buttons in the Sort and Filter group in the Home ribbon (see **Figure 4.2**) to sort and filter the data respectively.

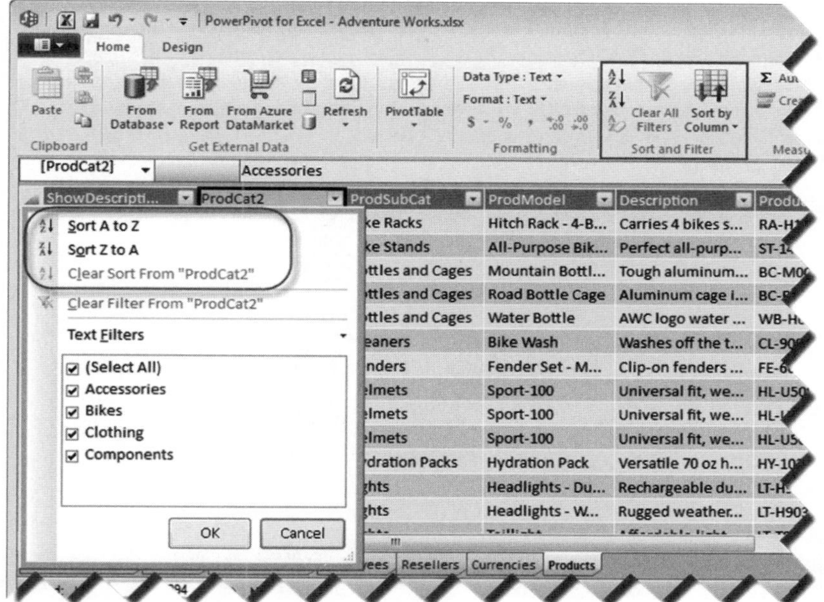


**Figure 4.2** You can sort the column content in ascending or descending order.

***Sorting data***

PowerPivot doesn't sort data by default. As a result, Data View shows the imported data as it's loaded from the source. PowerPivot supports two column sorting options:

- Sorting in Data View – You can sort the content of a column in an ascending or descending order. This type of sorting is for the benefit of the modeler as it allows you to get familiar with the imported data, such as to see what's the minimum or maximum value in a column. PowerPivot doesn't save the sorting changes in the model. For example, you might sort the ProductCategory column in Data View in a descending order. However, when you create a pivot report that uses the ProductCategory column, Excel ignores the Data View sorting changes and sorts the product categories in an ascending order.
- Custom Sorting – You can click the Sort by Column button to sort a column by another column. Custom sorting doesn't change the way the data is displayed in Data View, but it affects

how the data is presented in reports. For example, in Section 2.3.3, I showed you how to use custom sorting to sort months in their natural order as opposed to an alphabetical order.

Sorting a column in Data View, such as to see which products belong to the Accessories product category, takes two mouse clicks:

1. Click the column header to select the column.
2. In the Home ribbon tab, click the "Sort A to Z" button in the "Sort and Filter" group to sort the column values in an ascending order, or click the "Sort Z to A" button to sort in a descending order. Or you can expand the column drop-down menu and use the same options.

When a column is sorted, you'll see an up or down arrow in the column drop-down button that indicates the sort order. You can sort the table data by only one column at a time. To clear sorting and to revert to the data source sort order, select the column, and then click the Clear Sort button in the "Sort and Filter" ribbon group or the "Clear Sort From <Column>" option in the column drop-down menu (see **Figure 4.2**).

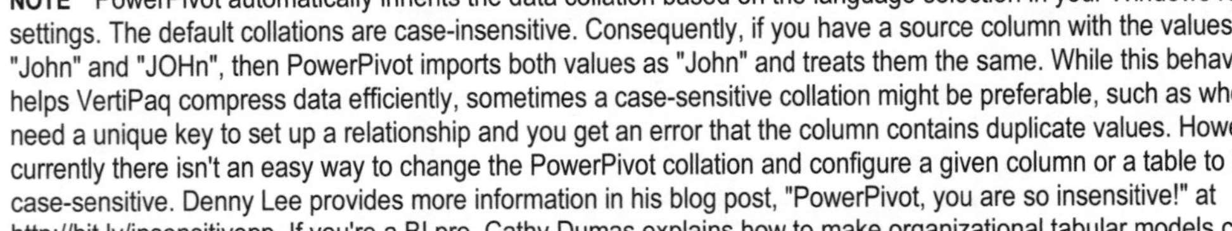

**NOTE** PowerPivot automatically inherits the data collation based on the language selection in your Windows regional settings. The default collations are case-insensitive. Consequently, if you have a source column with the values "John" and "JOHn", then PowerPivot imports both values as "John" and treats them the same. While this behavior helps VertiPaq compress data efficiently, sometimes a case-sensitive collation might be preferable, such as when you need a unique key to set up a relationship and you get an error that the column contains duplicate values. However, currently there isn't an easy way to change the PowerPivot collation and configure a given column or a table to be case-sensitive. Denny Lee provides more information in his blog post, "PowerPivot, you are so insensitive!" at http://bit.ly/insensitivepp. If you're a BI pro, Cathy Dumas explains how to make organizational tabular models case-sensitive in the blog post, "Making tabular models more sensitive" (http://bit.ly/insensitivetabular).

***Filtering data***

You can use the column drop-down to filter the column content, such as to find which resellers have more than 100,000 in annual sales. You'll get the same filtering options as with row filtering during data import from relational data sources and text files. Similar to sorting a column in Data View, filtering is for the benefit of the data modeler only. For example, you might filter the Product table in the PowerPivot window to show only bikes. However, when the user queries the model, he will see all the products.

**NOTE** Readers familiar with the Multidimensional data exploration capabilities will probably find that sorting and filtering in Data View is similar to the DSV Explore Data feature.

PowerPivot supports different filtering options based on the column data type. You can apply a simple filter by unchecking the column values in the list (again see **Figure 4.2**). You can filter by multiple columns. PowerPivot applies each filter condition as an AND filter, such as resellers with annual sales greater than 100,000 and the year opened is equal to 2000. Once you apply a filter, you'll see a special funnel icon in the column drop-down menu. To clear a column filter, click Filter ⇨ "Clear Filter from <Column>" in the column drop-down menu. To remove all filters from the active table and to see all the data, click the Clear All Filters button in the "Sort and Filter" ribbon group.

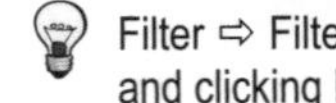

**TIP** Another way to filter on a particular value is to right-click the cell containing the value, and then click Filter ⇨ Filter by Selected Cell Value. You can remove a column filter on a particular column by right-clicking the column and clicking Filter ⇨ Remove Filter From <Column Name> option.

## 4.1.3 Understanding Column Data Types

A PowerPivot table column has a data type associated with it. PowerPivot can import data from a variety of data sources and each data source supports its own data types. When PowerPivot imports data, it attempts to infer the column data type from the data provider and maps it to one of the data types it supports.

**Table 4.1 PowerPivot supports the following column data types.**

| Data Type | Representation | Description |
|---|---|---|
| Text | String | A Unicode character string with a max length of 268,435,456 characters |
| Decimal Number | A 64 bit (eight-bytes) real number | Numbers with decimal places |
| Whole Number | A 64 bit (eight-bytes) integer value | Numbers with no decimal places |
| Currency | Currency | Currency data type with four decimal places of fixed precision |
| Date | Date/Time | Dates and times after March 1st, 1900 |
| TRUE/FALSE | Boolean | True or False value |
| Binary | Binary data type | An image or blob |

***Supported data types***

PowerPivot supports the data types shown in **Table 4.1**. PowerPivot might perform a widening data conversion on import. For example, if the underlying SQL Server data type is tinyint (one byte), PowerPivot will map it to the Whole Number data type because that's the only data type that PowerPivot supports for whole numbers. PowerPivot won't import data types it doesn't understand and won't import the corresponding columns. For example, PowerPivot won't import a SQL Server column of a geography data type that stores geodetic spatial data. A new feature in this release is the ability to import images. Importing images is useful for creating banded Power View reports, such as to allow you to click a product image and filter data for that product.

If the data source doesn't provide schema information, PowerPivot imports data as text and use the Text data type for all columns. In such cases, you should overwrite the data types after import when it makes sense.

***Changing the column data type***

As I mentioned, the Formatting ribbon group indicates the data type of the active column. You should review and change the column type when needed for the following reasons:

- Data aggregation – You can sum or average only numeric columns.
- Data validation – Suppose you're given a text file with a SalesAmount column that stores decimal data. What happens if an 'NA' value sneaks into the next month's import? If you set the data type of the SalesAmount column in the PowerPivot model to Decimal, PowerPivot will replace the 'N/A' value with a blank value. You can examine the model data after import and detect such issues. This won't happen if the column data type is Text.

**NOTE** What really happens in the case of a data type mismatch depends on the underlying data provider. The text data provider (Microsoft ACE OLE DB provider) replaces mismatched data values with blank values. But in the case of a linked Excel table, you'll get an error message upon refresh.

- Better performance – Smaller data types have more efficient storage and query performance. For example, a whole number is more efficient than text because it occupies only eight bytes irrespective of the number of digits.

You can change the column data type by expanding the Data Type drop-down list in the Formatting ribbon group and then select another type. PowerPivot shows only a list of the data types applicable for conversion. For example, if the original data type is Currency, you can use PowerPivot to convert the data type to Text, Decimal Number, and Whole Number (see **Figure 4.3**).

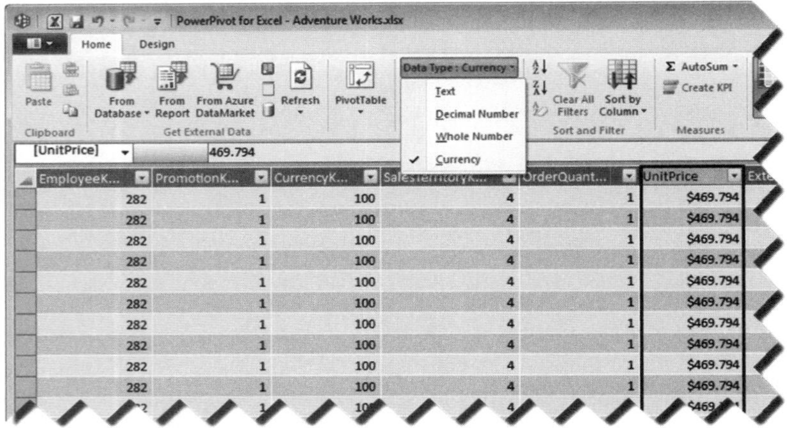

**Figure 4.3** PowerPivot allows you to convert the column data type to a subset of data types.

If the column is of a Text data type, the Data Type drop-down list would show all data types. However, you'll get a type mismatch error if the conversion fails, such as when trying to convert a non-numeric text value to a number. Converting to a smaller data type, such as Decimal to Whole Number, might result in a loss of precision. When PowerPivot detects this, it displays a warning message to warn you about potential loss of data.

**NOTE** If the source column contains blank (NULL) values, PowerPivot will import them as blank values. Readers with Multidimensional experience know that Multidimensional converts NULL values to zeros by default, but it has an option to preserve NULLs. Tabular always preserves blank values, and it doesn't support an automatic replacement option. The reason for this change is that tables in tabular models can be built on "dirty" data. By contrast, cubes are typically built on top of data warehouses that have clean data and NULLs in fact tables are quite uncommon.

***Understanding column formatting***

Each column has a default format based on its data type and Windows regional settings. For example, my default format for Date columns is MM/dd/yyyy hh:mm:ss tt because my computer is configured for English US regional settings (such as 12/24/2011 13:55:20 PM). However, if a European user opens my PowerPivot model, he would probably see a different date format based on his regional settings, and that's the expected behavior. The only special case to watch for is Currency columns because the default format includes the currency symbol, and no automatic currency conversion is applied.

**TIP** If you plan to send your PowerPivot model to international users, consider changing the format of Currency columns to Decimal Number to avoid unexpected results and confusion.

Use the Formatting ribbon group to change the column format settings, as shown in **Figure 4.4**.

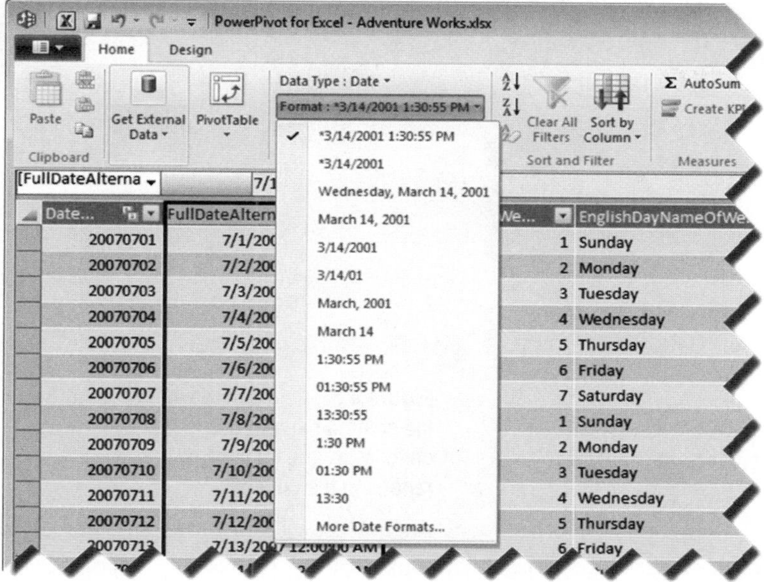


**Figure 4.4** Use the Formatting ribbon group to change the column format.

You can use the format buttons in the Formatting ribbon group to apply changes interactively, such as to add a thousand separator or to increase the number of decimal places.

**NOTE** A welcome addition as a result of the metadata improvements in PowerPivot 2.0 is that format settings now carry over to Excel pivot reports. Previously, the format settings would apply only to Data View. The end user had to reapply the same format settings using the Excel format capabilities.

If the column width is too narrow to show the formatted values, you can the column width by dragging the right column border. Or, you can right-click the column header and then click Column Width to enter a precise width in pixels. Changing the column width in Data View has no effect on reports.

## 4.1.4 Understanding Column Operations

You can perform various column-related tasks to explore data and improve the metadata visual appearance. These tasks include renaming columns, changing the column order, removing and hiding columns, and so on.

***Renaming columns***

Table columns inherit their names from the underlying data source during the initial import process. These names might be somewhat cryptic, such as TRANS_AMT. The column name becomes a part of the model metadata that end users interact with. You can make the column name more descriptive and intuitive by renaming the column. To do so, double-click the column header to enter edit mode, and then type in the new name. Or, right-click the column, and then click Rename Column, as shown in **Figure 4.5**.

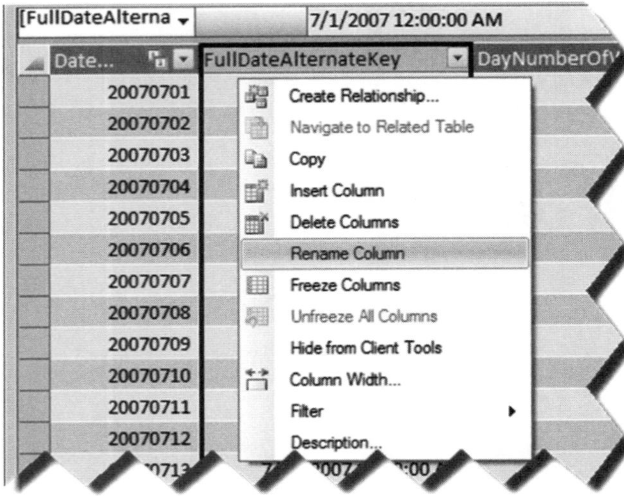


**Figure 4.5** You can make the column name more descriptive and intuitive by renaming the column.

The context menu includes a Description option. This opens the Column Description dialog box where you can enter some text that describes the column content.

*Moving columns*

The initial column order is based on the positional order of the columns in the imported dataset. One reason to change the default order is to locate columns faster in Data View, such as to move a key column in front of all the columns or to analyze related columns.

**NOTE** In the previous PowerPivot versions, the metadata column order was fixed at import and Excel pivot reports would show the columns sorted in the same way. The only way to customize the column order was to change it in the data source, and then to drop and re-import the table. In this version, Excel reports sort column names in ascending order. Changing the column order in the PowerPivot window has no effect on the model metadata in pivot reports. As it stands, Tabular doesn't have the Multidimensional equivalent of display folders to group related columns into folders, such as Demographics to group all demographics-related columns of a hypothetical Customer table.

To move a column, select the column by clicking its header. You must click the column and wait for the cursor to change to a cross. Then, drag the column to its new location. If you attempt to select and drag a column in one step while the mouse cursor is a down arrow, you won't be able to move the column. Instead, you'll select multiple columns and expand the current selection.

In case you moved the column to a wrong location, press Ctrl+Z to undo the change. Or you can click the Undo button found in the Design ribbon tab or in the Quick Access toolbar at the top-left of the PowerPivot window. By the way, you can undo and redo some model changes, such as renaming and formatting columns. Other changes can't be undone, such as deleting a column or importing a new column.

Similar to Excel, you can freeze one or more columns to keep them visible when scrolling wide tables to the right. To freeze a column, right-click the column header, and then click Freeze Columns. Or you can use the Freeze drop-down in the Home ribbon tab. Freezing a column(s) moves the column to become the first column in the table. You must unfreeze the column(s) if you want to move them to a new position. To unfreeze a column, right-click the column, and then click Unfreeze Columns (or use the Freeze drop-down button in the Columns group of the Design ribbon tab). Unlike Excel, you can't freeze rows, although the header row remains fixed when scrolling rows.

The Insert Column menu (again see **Figure 4.5**) adds an empty calculated column before the currently selected column. Previously, you could only add a calculated column at the end of the table. Once the column is created, you can set up a Data Analysis Expressions (DAX) formula.

***Removing and hiding columns***

In Chapter 3, I advised you to not import a column that you don't need in the model. However, if this ever happens, you can fix it in two ways. First, you can open the table definition by clicking the Table Properties button in the Design ribbon tab. Then set up a column filter to exclude the unwanted column, and re-import the table data. Or, you can right-click the column header in Data View and then click Delete Columns. If you open the table definition after deleting a column, you'll see that the column still appears, but it's not checked. You can add the column by selecting its checkbox in the table definition. Note that the tasks of removing and adding columns are not reversible and the Undo/Redo buttons are not available. If the column participates in a relationship, removing the column removes the associated relationship(s).

**TIP** There is a caveat with deleting columns in Data View and the containing table uses a custom query to import data. If you open the table definition and make a change to the SQL query, all the columns you've deleted from Data View will reappear. As a best practice, always remove columns in the table definition. This will refresh the table data. Deleting columns in Data View could be useful when you want to save time with large tables because PowerPivot won't reimport the data.

Suppose you need the column in the model but you don't want to show it to end users. For example, you might need a primary key column or foreign key column to set up a relationship. Since such columns usually contain system values you might want to exclude them from showing up in client tools by simply hiding them. The difference between removing and hiding a column is that hiding a column allows you to use the column in the model, such as in hierarchies or custom sorting, and in DAX formulas.

**NOTE** A drillthrough action shows all table columns including hidden columns. Therefore, don't hide columns for security reasons because another user can drill through and see the column. If the column isn't needed or contains sensitive information, exclude that column when you import data.

To hide a column, right-click the column header and click "Hide From Client Tools". A hidden column appears grayed out in Data View. If you change your mind later on, you can unhide the column by right-clicking the column and clicking "Unhide from Client Tools" (see **Figure 4.6**).

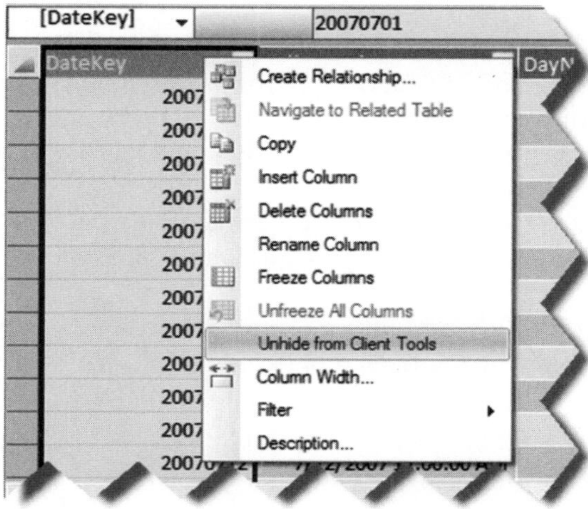


**Figure 4.6** A hidden column appears grayed out in Data View.

Finally, the Copy operation allows you to copy the content of the selected columns and paste it in another application, such as Microsoft Excel. You can't paste the column content inside PowerPivot. Again, that's because PowerPivot window is read-only.

### 4.1.5 Working with Tables and Columns ▶

Now that you're familiar with tables and columns, let's turn our attention to the Adventure Works model and spend some time exploring and refining it. The following steps will help familiarize you with the common tasks you'll use when working with tables and columns.

***Sorting data***

You can gain insights into your imported data by sorting and filtering it. Suppose that you want to find which employees have been with the company the longest.

1. In Excel, open your copy of the "Adventure Works.xlsx" workbook that includes your changes from Chapter 3.

**NOTE** If you haven't completed the Chapter 3 exercises, you can use the Adventure Works Excel workbook from the \Source\Ch03 folder. However, remember that my samples import data from several data sources, including the Adventure Works cube and the Product Catalog 2008 report, and you need to update all the data sources to reflect your specific setup. To do so, open the Adventure Works workbook in Excel, and then click the PowerPivot Window button. In the PowerPivot window (Design tab), click the Existing Connections button. Click each connection, and then click Edit. In the Edit Connection dialog box, change the connection settings as needed.

2. Click the PowerPivot tab in the ribbon, and then click the PowerPivot Window button.
3. In the PowerPivot window, click the Employees tab at the bottom of the window.
4. Click any cell in the HireDate column.
5. In the Home tab of the ribbon, click the "Sort Oldest to Newest" button in the Sort and Filter group. Note that Guy Gilbert is the first person on the list, and he was hired on 7/31/1996.
6. Expand the drop-down arrow in the HireDate column header. Note that the context menu includes the same sort options.
7. Click the "Clear Sort from HireDate" menu to remove the sort and to revert to the original order in which data was imported from the data source.

***Filtering data***

PowerPivot also provides flexible options to filter data. However, filtering in the PowerPivot window is very different from setting up row filters during an import. Filtering in the PowerPivot window helps you analyze data while the row filtering excludes data from being imported in the model.

1. Suppose that you want to see only married employees. Click the drop-down arrow inside the MaritalStatus column header. Notice that the drop-down list shows the distinct values of MaritalStatus (M and S) across all the rows in the table.
2. Uncheck the (Select All) value to clear the filter and check the checkbox next to the M value. PowerPivot then filters the Employee table to show only the married employees.
3. Besides selecting individual values for filtering, you can use PowerPivot to specify more complex filtering criteria for numeric data types. Suppose you want to further filter the employee list to married employees with an hourly rate of $50 or more. Click the drop-down arrow in the BaseRate column header, and then click Number Filters ⇨ Greater Than or Equal To. In the Custom

Filter dialog box that follows, enter 50 in the first field, and then click OK. PowerPivot filters the table to show that only three employees meet the filtered criteria.

4. In the ribbon's Home tab (Sort and Filter group), click the "Clear All Filters" button to remove all filters.

***Renaming tables***

As it stands, the Adventure Works data model includes seven tables. The name of the table is included in the metadata that you'll see when you create reports. Therefore, it's important to have a naming convention for tables. In this case, we will use a plural naming convention for the table that keeps the history of the measures (ResellerSales), and a singular naming convention for the rest of the tables.

1. Double-click the FactResellerSales table tab at the bottom of the window, change its name to *ResellerSales*, and then press Enter.
2. Rename the DimDate table to *Date*, SalesTerritories to *SalesTerritory*, Resellers to *Reseller*, Employees to *Employee*, Currencies to *Currency*, and Products to *Product*.
3. (Optional) Right-click each table tab, click Description, and then provide descriptive text to describe the table, such as "Stores wholesale sales data" for the ResellerSales table.

***Working with columns***

Next, let's revisit each table and make changes as necessary.

1. Click the Date tab at the bottom of the window. Double-click the column header of the FullDateAlternateKey column, and then rename it to *Date*. Decrease the Date column width by dragging the column's right border so it's wide enough to accommodate the content in the column. Rename the EnglishDayNameOfWeek column to *DayNameOfWeek* and EnglishMonthName to *MonthName*. Hide the DateKey column.
2. Click the ResellerSales tab. The foreign key columns (with the "Key" suffix) are useful for data relationships but not for data analysis. Click the column header of the ProductKey column to select the column. Hold the Shift key, and then click the column header of the SalesTerritoryKey column. This selects all key columns. Right-click the selection, and then click Hide From Client Tools.
3. Change the format of all the currency columns to two decimal places. To save time, click the column header of the first column (UnitPrice) to select the column, hold the Shift key, and then click the header of the last column (Freight). This selects all the adjacent columns. Or you can click the first column and while still holding the mouse button drag the selection to the adjacent columns. Then, click the Increase Decimal button twice in the Formatting group on the ribbon's Home tab (see **Figure 4.7**).
4. Click the SalesTerritory table tab. If you've imported the SalesTerritory table from the Adventure Works cube, the Table Import Wizard has assigned very long names to the columns in this table. Rename the "Sales TerritorySales Territory GroupSales Territory Group" column to *TerritoryGroup*, "Sales TerritorySales Territory CountrySales Territory Country" to *TerritoryCountry*, "Sales TerritorySales Territory RegionSales Territory Region" to *TerritoryRegion*, and "MeasuresSales Amount" to *Revenue*.

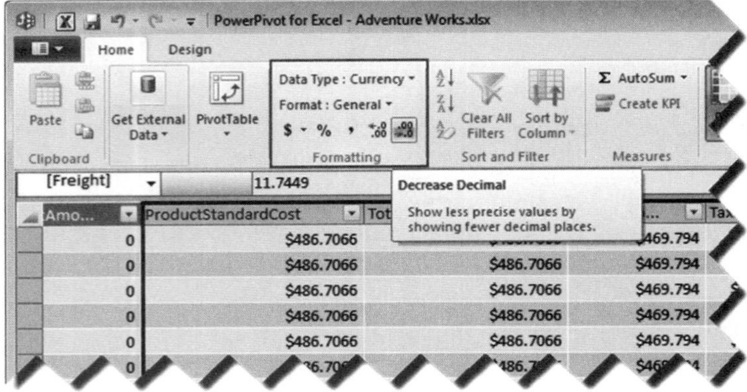


Figure 4.7 Use the Formatting group to change the column data type and format.

5. If you've imported the SalesTerritory table from the cube, click any cell in the Revenue column. In the ribbon's Home tab, notice that the Data Type drop-down menu is set to Decimal Number. That's how PowerPivot interpreted the column data type when importing its data from Analysis Services. In the ribbon's Home tab, expand the Data Type drop-down menu, and then click Currency. Accept the prompt that warns you about the data lost as a result of a narrowing data type conversion. Click the Decrease Decimal button to format the number with no decimals.
6. Click the Employee table tab. Hide the EmployeeKey, ParentEmployeeKey, and SalesTerritoryKey columns.
7. Click the Reseller table tab. Change the data type of the AnnualSales and AnnualRevenue columns to the Decimal Number data type. Format the columns with a thousands separator and no decimals.
8. Assuming you want the ResellerKey to remain in place while you scroll the table to the right, right-click the column header, and then click Freeze Columns. Hide the column from client tools.
9. Click the Product table tab. Right-click the ShowDescription column, and then click Delete to remove the column since it's not useful for analysis.
10. If you've imported the Product table from the Product Catalog 2008 report, rename the ProdCat2 column to *ProductCategory*. Increase the column width to accommodate the content. Rename ProdSubCat column to *ProductSubcategory*, ProdModel to *ProductModel*, and ProdName to *ProductName*.
11. Suppose that for data exploration purposes you want the ProductName column to be the first column in the table. Click the ProductName column header to select the column, and then drag the column all the way to the left. You can also freeze this column (right-click it, and then click Freeze Column) to make it visible while you scroll. If you freeze a column, PowerPivot automatically moves the column at the beginning of the table.
12. Change the data type of the StandardCost and ListPrice columns to Currency, and then reformat them with two decimal places.
13. Click the Currency table tab, and then hide the AW ID column. Rename the Currency Code and Currency Name columns to *CurrencyCode* and *CurrencyName*, respectively.
14. (Optional) Provide column descriptions as needed. To enter a column description, right-click a column, and then click Description. In the Column Description dialog box, enter the description text.

## 4.2 Managing Schema and Data Changes

To review, once PowerPivot for Excel imports data, it saves the data in the Excel workbook. The model schema and data is *not* automatically synchronized with changes in the data sources. Typically, after the initial load, you'll need to refresh the model data on a regular basis, such as when you receive a new source file. PowerPivot for Excel provides features to keep your model up to date.

### 4.2.1 Managing Connections and Tables

It's not uncommon for a PowerPivot model to have many tables connected to different data sources so that you can integrate data from multiple places. As a modeler, you need to understand how to manage connections and tables. This will help you reuse connections and minimize the maintenance effort required to import data.

***Managing connections***

Suppose you need to import additional tables from a data source that you've already set up a connection to. One option is to repeat the same steps and continue creating new connections for each new table. However, increasing the number of connections will increase the effort required to manage them. For example, if the database name or security credentials change, you'll need to update multiple connection definitions. Or, if you want to schedule a data refresh after you publish the workbook to SharePoint, you need to define the refresh settings for all the connections to that data source. Instead, consider reusing the existing connection to import new tables, as follows:

1. In the PowerPivot window, click the Design tab on the ribbon, as shown in **Figure 4.8**.

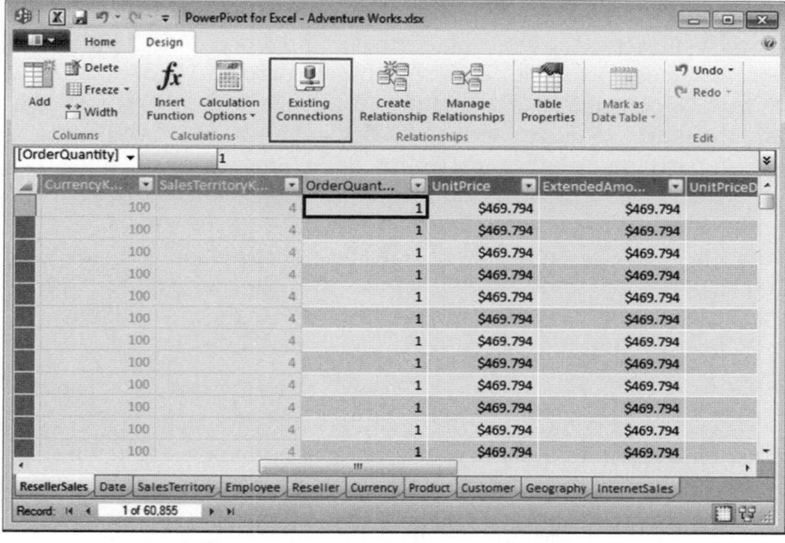


**Figure 4.8** Click the Existing Connections button to manage all the data source connections defined in a PowerPivot model.

2. Click the Existing Connections button to open the Existing Connections dialog box, as shown in **Figure 4.9**).

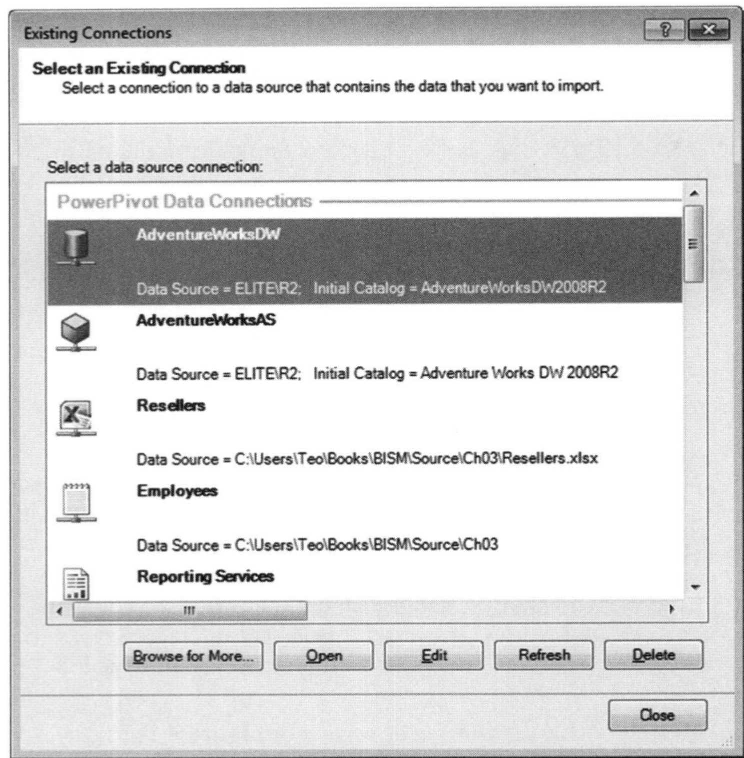


**Figure 4.9** The Existing Connection dialog box shows all connections defined in the model.

The PowerPivot Data Connections section lists the connections that you defined in the model. If you scroll down the list, the Local Connections section (not shown in **Figure 4.9**) shows all Office connection files (*.odc files) in your Documents\My Data Sources folder. And, the Workbook Connections section (not shown in **Figure 4.9**) lists connections defined in the Excel workbook.

Use the "Browse for More" button to import other connection definitions stored in Office Data Connection (*.odc) files. The Open button opens the familiar Table Import Wizard, so you could import other tables from that connection. Use the Edit button to change the connection definition, such as the connection string. The Refresh button refreshes the data in all the tables that are associated with that connection. The Delete button removes the connection if there are no associated tables. If you have tables that use the connection, you must delete the tables before deleting the connection.

### *Managing tables*

You don't need to delete and re-create a PowerPivot table if the underlying schema changes or if you need to make other modifications, such as adding or removing columns or changing the column and row filters. The Table Properties button on the Design ribbon's tab brings you to a dialog box where you can make the necessary changes. For example, if the PowerPivot table is bound to a relational table or a SQL view, you'll see the "Edit Table Properties" dialog box, as shown in **Figure 4.10**. This dialog box allows you to set up new row and column filters. Or, if you want to use a custom query to have more control over the data import process, expand the Switch To drop-down, and then click Query Editor. The Switch To option is only available when you're sourcing data from relational data sources.

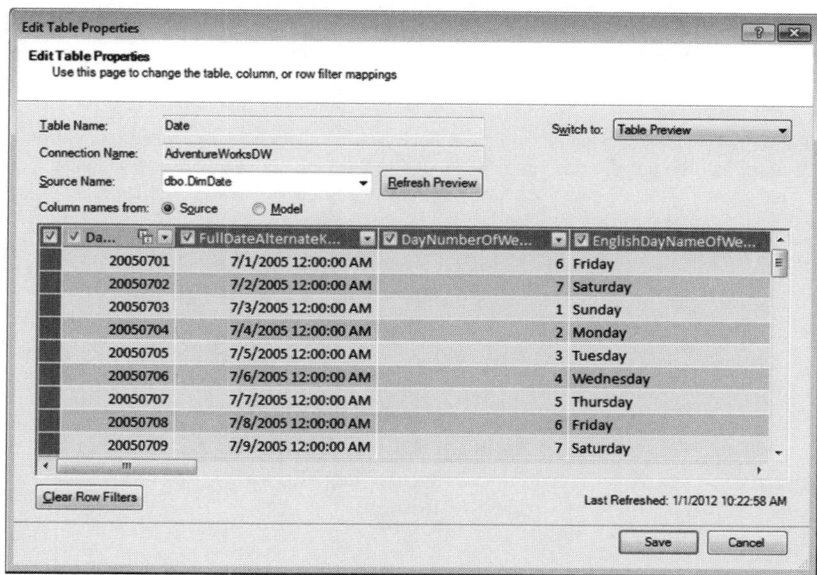


**Figure 4.10** Use the "Edit Table Properties" dialog box to change the table definition.

## 4.2.2 Managing Data Refresh

We previously covered that, by default, Tabular and PowerPivot cache data to give you the best performance when you query the model and aggregate the data. The only option to synchronize data changes with PowerPivot for Excel is to refresh the data manually.

***Refreshing data***

PowerPivot supports several refresh options. You can refresh all the data in the model or a subset of data, depending on which refresh option you use. To refresh all the tables, expand the Refresh drop-down menu in the ribbon's Home tab of the PowerPivot window, and then click Refresh All to open the "Data Refresh Progress" dialog box, as shown in see **Figure 4.11**.

**Figure 4.11** PowerPivot for Excel refreshes tables sequentially and cancels the entire operation if a table fails to refresh.

PowerPivot refreshes tables sequentially, one table at the time. The Data Refresh Progress dialog box shows the number of rows imported. When you refresh a table, PowerPivot for Excel discards the entire table data and then reloads the data from the data source. There is no incremental data refresh option.

**NOTE** Based on usability feedback, Microsoft decided on the sequential PowerPivot for Excel data refresh for easier failure analysis. If a table fails to refresh, the entire refresh operation stops so that the user can more easily identify which table failed. This isn't a technical limitation. PowerPivot for SharePoint and Analysis Services Tabular refresh tables in parallel.

Instead of refreshing all the data, you might want to refresh specific tables to save some time. For example, you might know that only one table have data changes. You can then click the Refresh button in the ribbon's Home tab to refresh the active table in Data View. As I mentioned, the Refresh button in the Existing Connections dialog box (in the Design ribbon tab, click Existing Connections) refreshes all the tables associated with the selected connection.

VertiPaq uses the same state-of-the-art processing architecture as Multidimensional for refreshing data. Because of this, it's capable of importing more than 100,000 rows per second. The actual data refresh speed depends on many factors, including how fast the data source returns rows, the network speed, your machine hardware configuration, and so on.

**REAL LIFE** I was called a few times to troubleshoot slow processing issues with both Multidimensional and PowerPivot. In all the cases, I've found that the external factors impacted the processing speed. For example, a large fact table might be missing an index, or the data warehouse server could be overwhelmed. In one case, it turned out that the IT department has decided to throttle the network speed on all non-production network segments in case a computer virus takes over.

You can cancel the refresh operation by clicking the Stop Refresh button. Tables that were imported successfully up to that point will be added to the model; the rest will be ignored.

***Troubleshooting data refresh***

If a table fails to refresh, such as when there is no connectivity to the data source, the Data Refresh dialog box shows an error indicator and displays an Error message in the Status column, as shown in **Figure 4.12**.

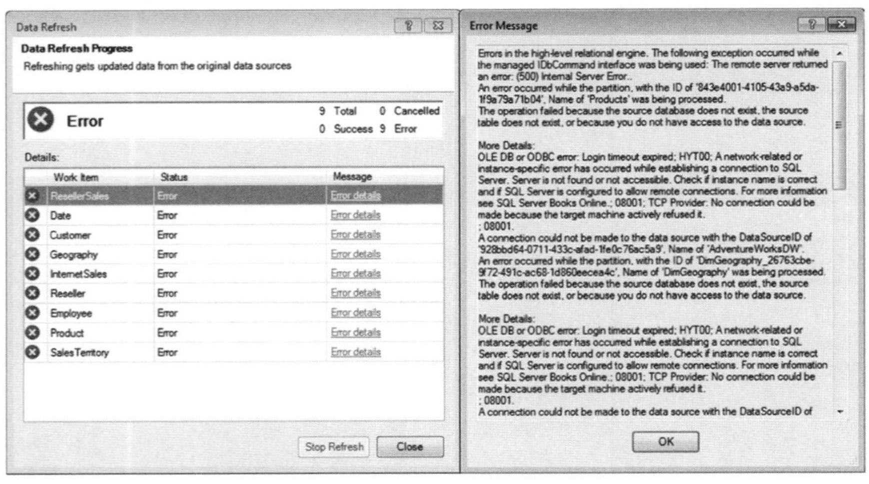


**Figure 4.12** If the refresh operation fails, click the Error details link to find out what went wrong.

Unfortunately, the Data Refresh Progress dialog box reports the error across all the tables, making it difficult to understand which specific table failed to refresh. Because of this, you need to do some investigation work on your part. Click the Error details link in the Message column and then inspect the error message. Its usefulness depends on the type of data provider that failed and the specific error. In this case, there was an issue establishing a connection to the Adventure-WorksDW2008R2 database.

## 4.2.3 Performing Management Tasks ▶

The following practice will help you become familiar with the management tasks required to update the model schema and data. Specifically, you'll practice importing new tables and then you'll practice synchronizing the model data.

***Importing additional tables***

Besides wholesale data, the Adventure Works data warehouse stores retail data for direct sales to individual customers. Suppose that you need to extend the Adventure Works model to analyze retail sales. Follow these steps to import three additional tables reusing the existing connection to the AdventureWorksDW2008R2 database:

1. In the PowerPivot Window, click the Design ribbon tab. Click the Existing Connections button.
2. In the Existing Connections dialog box, make sure that the AdventureWorksDW connection is selected, and the click the Open button to start the Table Import Wizard.
3. In the "Choose How to Import the Data" step, leave the default choice to select from a list of tables.
4. In the Select Tables and Views steps, check the DimCustomer, DimGeorgraphy, and FactInternetSales tables. In the AdventureWorksDW2008R2 database, the DimGeography table isn't related directly to the FactInternetSales table. Instead, DimGeography joins DimCustomer, which joins FactInternetSales. This is an example of a snowflake schema that I discussed in Section 3.1.1 in Chapter 3.
5. Select FactInternetSales and click the "Preview & Filter" button. Uncheck the RevisionNumber, CarrierTrackingNumber, and CustomerPONumber columns to exclude them from the import process.
6. In the Friendly Name column, enter *Customer* as a friendly name for DimCustomer, *Geography* for DimGeography, and *InternetSales* for FactInternetSales.
7. Click Finish to add the three tables to the Adventure Works model and to import the data.
8. Notice that the PowerPivot Importing dialog box shows Details link next to the last row. Click the Details link. A Details dialog box opens to inform you that PowerPivot has detected two table joins (referential integrity relationships) in the AdventureWorksDW2008R2 database and has carried them to the model. Click Close to go back to the PowerPivot window.

***Refreshing data***

Suppose that you've been notified about changes in the ResellerSales table, and now you need to refresh its data.

1. Click the ResellerSales table tab at the bottom of the PowerPivot window to activate the ResellerSales table. Next, click the Refresh button in the ribbon's Home tab. Notice that PowerPivot only refreshes the ResellerSales table. Click the Close button.
2. Suppose you want to refresh all the data in the model to synchronize it with changes in all the data sources. In the ribbon's Home tab, expand the Refresh button, and then click Refresh All.

3. Click the Design ribbon tab, and then click Existing Connections. With the AdventureWorksDW connection selected, click the Refresh button. Note that PowerPivot for Excel refreshes only the ResellerSales, Date, Customer, Geography, and InternetSales tables because only these tables are associated with this connection.

## 4.3 Relationships Revisited

One of the PowerPivot strengths is that it can analyze data across multiple tables. Back in Chapter 3, I explained that as a prerequisite for aggregating data in one table by columns in another table, you must set up a relationship between the two tables. When you import tables from a relational database that supports referential integrity and has table relationships defined, PowerPivot detects these relationships and applies them to the model. However, when you import tables as separate steps, when no table joins are defined in the data source, or when you import data from different data sources, PowerPivot is unable to detect relationships upon import. Because of this, you must revisit the model and create appropriate relationships before you analyze the data.

### 4.3.1 Relationship Rules and Limitations

A relationship is a join between two tables. When you define a table relationship, you're telling PowerPivot that there is a logical one-to-many relationship between a row in the lookup (dimension) table and corresponding rows in the fact table. For example, the relationship between the Reseller and ResellerSales tables in **Figure 4.13** means that each reseller in the Reseller table can have many corresponding rows in the ResellerSales table. Indeed, Progressive Sports (ResellerKey=1) recorded a sale on August 1st 2006 for $100 and another sale on July 4th 2007 for $120. In this case, the ResellerKey column in the Reseller table is the primary key in the lookup (dimension) table. The ResellerKey column in the ResellerSales table fulfills the role of a foreign key in the fact table.

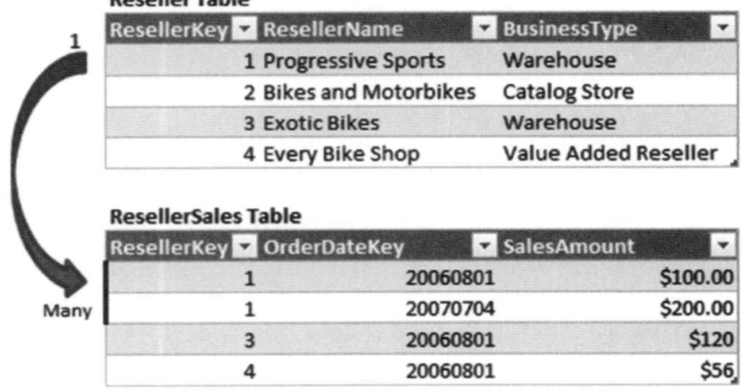


**Reseller Table**

| ResellerKey | ResellerName | BusinessType |
|---|---|---|
| 1 | Progressive Sports | Warehouse |
| 2 | Bikes and Motorbikes | Catalog Store |
| 3 | Exotic Bikes | Warehouse |
| 4 | Every Bike Shop | Value Added Reseller |

**ResellerSales Table**

| ResellerKey | OrderDateKey | SalesAmount |
|---|---|---|
| 1 | 20060801 | $100.00 |
| 1 | 20070704 | $200.00 |
| 3 | 20060801 | $120 |
| 4 | 20060801 | $56 |

**Figure 4.13** There is a logical one-to-many relationship between the Reseller table and the ResellerSales table because each reseller can have multiple sales recorded.

***Understanding relationship rules***

A relationship can be created under the following circumstances:

- The two tables have matching columns, such as a ResellerKey column in the Reseller lookup table and a ResellerKey column in the ResellerSales table. The column names don't have to be the same but the columns must have matching values. For example, you can't relate the two tables if the ResellerKey column in the ResellerSales table has reseller codes, such as PRO for Progressive Sports.

- The key column in the lookup (dimension) table must have unique values, similar to a primary key in a relational database. In the case of the Reseller table, the ResellerKey column fulfills this requirement because its values are unique across all rows in the tale. If you attempt to establish a join to a column in the lookup table that doesn't contain unique values, you'll get the following error:

The relationship cannot be created because each column contains duplicate values. Select at least one column that contains only unique values.

**TIP** If the lookup table doesn't have a column with unique values, you can add another table that contains only the unique values of the lookup table used for the join, such as by copying the column values in Excel, using the Excel Remove Duplicates feature, and then by linking the table to the model. You can then define appropriate relationships, such as Account ⇨ AccountCustomer, Customer ⇨ AccountCustomer, and Account ⇨ Balances. And, you can then use DAX calculations to handle the many-to-many relationships, as I'll demonstrate in Chapter 6.

Interestingly, PowerPivot doesn't require the two columns to have matching data types. For example, the ResellerKey column in the Reseller table can be of a Text data type while its counterpart in the ResellerSales table could be defined as the Whole Number data type. Behind the scenes, PowerPivot resolves the join by converting the values in the latter column to the Text data type. However, to improve performance and to reduce storage space, use numeric data types whenever possible.

***Understanding relationship limitations***
Relationships have the following limitations:

- Only one column can be used on each side of the relationship. If you need a combination of two or more columns so the key column can have unique values, you can add a calculated column that uses a DAX expression to concatenate the values, such as =[ResellerKey] & [SourceID]. Then, you can use this column for the relationship.
- You can't create redundant relationships. For example, given the relationships Table1 ⇨ Table2 and Table2 ⇨Table3, you can't set an active relationship Table1 ⇨ Table3. Such a relationship isn't needed anyway because you'll be able to analyze the data in Table3 by Table 1 with only the first two relationships in place. Attempting to create a Table1 ⇨ Table3 will succeed but it will create an inactive relationship. Inactive relationships are explained in Section 4.3.3.

## 4.3.2 Auto-detecting Relationships

PowerPivot is capable of auto-detecting and creating missing relationships when you author a pivot report that uses multiple tables. This behavior is enabled by default but you can disable it by turning off the Relationship Detection button in the Excel PowerPivot ribbon tab, as shown in **Figure 4.14**.

***Understanding missing relationships***
What happens when you don't have a PowerPivot relationship between two tables and attempt to analyze the data in a pivot report? You'll get repeating values in the report and a "Relationship may be needed" warning in the PowerPivot Field List. In this case, I attempted to aggregate the SalesAmount column from the ResellerSales table across the ResellerName column in the Reseller table, but there is no relationship defined between these two tables. You must define a relationship to resolve this issue.

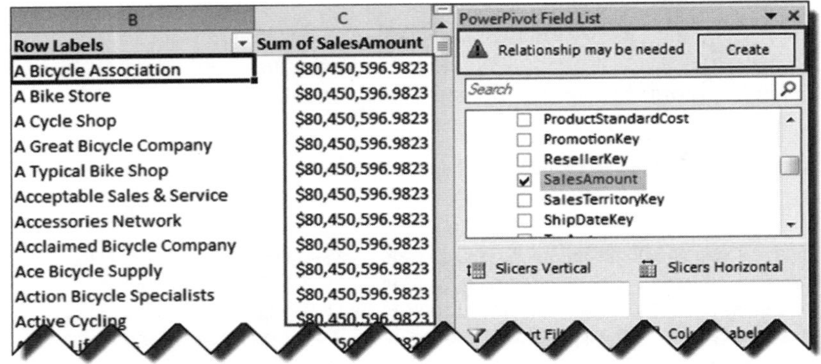


**Figure 4.14** PowerPivot detects missing relationships and warns you about them.

**NOTE** If you're a BI pro and you are experienced in multidimensional cubes, you might know that the same behavior occurs in Multidimensional when there is no relationship between a dimension and a measure group and when the IgnoreUnrelatedDimensions measure group setting is set to True (default setting). Therefore, the Multidimensional equivalent of PowerPivot relationships is the relationships in the Dimension Usage tab in the Cube Designer and not the relationships in the data source view.

### *Letting PowerPivot create relationships*

The lazy approach to handle missing relationships is to let PowerPivot create them by clicking the Create button in the PowerPivot Field List. PowerPivot follows certain rules to detect relationships, such as analyzing the column names and data types. If PowerPivot detects a suitable relationship candidate, it creates the relationship and displays the Relationship dialog box, as shown in **Figure 4.15**.

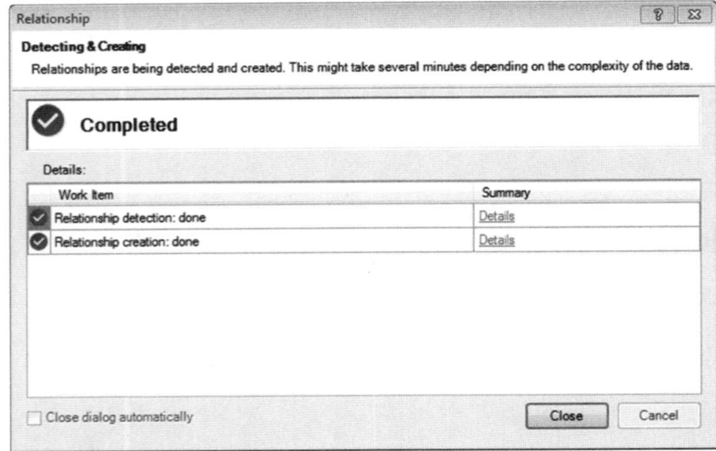


**Figure 4.15** The Relationship dialog box shows that PowerPivot has created a relationship successfully.

In case of an unsuccessful detection process, the Relationship dialog box shows a "No relationships detected" warning message. If this happens, review the relationship rules and limitations in Section 4.3.1.

**NOTE** If you a BI pro, note that the automatic relationship detection isn't available in Analysis Services Tabular projects in SQL Server Data Tools (SSDT). This feature is specific to PowerPivot only.

## 4.3.3 Creating Relationships Manually

Since table relationships are very important in PowerPivot, I'd recommend that you configure them manually. You can do this by using the Create Relationship dialog box or by using Diagram View.

***Steps to create a relationship***

Follows these steps to set up a relationship in Data View:

1. Identify a foreign key column in the table on the Many side of the relationship.
2. Identify a primary key column that uniquely identifies each row in the lookup table.
3. In Data View, right-click the foreign key column and click Create Relationship. Or you can click the Create Relationship button found in the Relationships group (Design ribbon tab).
4. Select the related lookup table and related lookup column.

***Understanding the Create Relationship dialog box***

**Figure 4.16** shows the Create Relationship dialog box when setting up a relationship between the ResellerSales and Reseller tables. If you right-click the ResellerKey column in the ResellerSales table and click Create Relationship, you'll have the Table and Column fields pre-populated but the Related Lookup Table and Related Lookup Columns fields will be empty. You need to expand the drop-down lists and specify the correct matching lookup table and lookup column.

If you attempt to set up a relationship in the wrong direction, the Create Relationship dialog box displays a warning sign in front of the Related Lookup Column drop-down list. If you hover your mouse over it, a tooltip pops up, informing you that the relationship can't be created in the requested direction. When you click Create, PowerPivot reverses the direction so the relationship is valid.

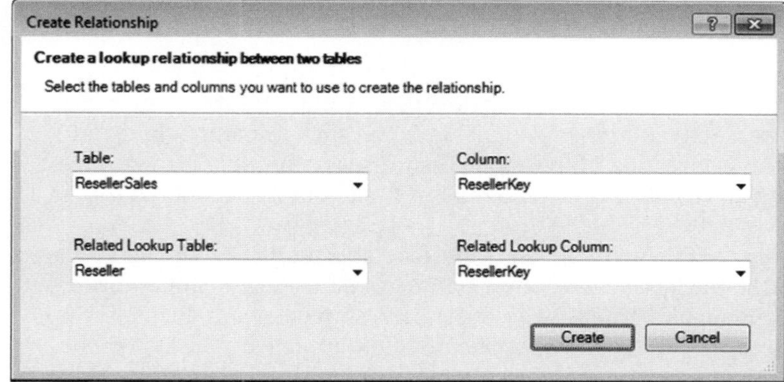


**Figure 4.16** Use the Create Relationship dialog box to specify the columns used for the relationship.

***Managing relationships***

You can manage all the relationships defined in your model by using the Manage Relationships dialog box, which you can open by clicking the Manage Relationships button in the Relationships group (in Design ribbon tab). In **Figure 4.17**, the Manage Relationships dialog box shows that there are five relationships defined in the Adventure Works model.

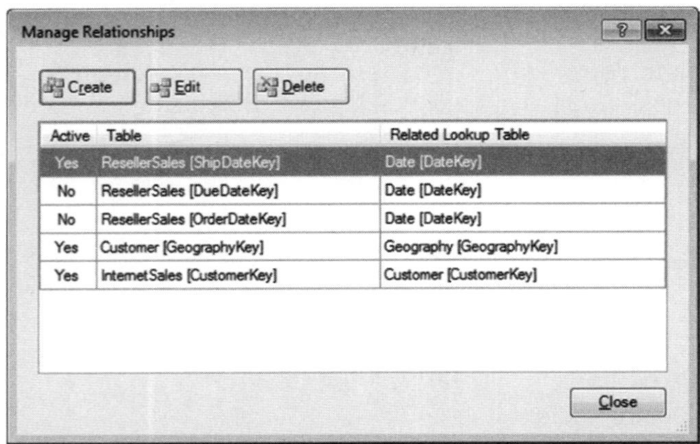


**Figure 4.17** Use the Manage Relationships dialog box to view all the relationships defined in the model and to change them.

In the Manage Relationships dialog box, the Create Relationship button brings you to an empty Create Relationship dialog box. The Edit button opens the Edit Relationship dialog box, which is the same as the Create Relationship dialog box, but with all fields pre-populated. Finally, the Delete button removes the selected relationship.

**NOTE** I'll use the TableName [ColumnName] notation as a shortcut when I refer to a table column. For example, Customer [CustomerKey] means the CustomerKey column in the Customer table. This notation will help you later on with DAX formulas because DAX follows the same syntax. When referencing relationships, I'll use a right arrow (⇨) to denote a relationship from a fact table to a lookup table. For example, ResellerSales [OrderDateKey] ⇨ DimDate [DateKey] means a relationship between the OrderDateKey in the ResellerSales table to the DateKey in the DimDate table.

***Understanding active and inactive relationships***

Besides regular relationships, where a lookup table joins directly a fact table, Tabular supports more advanced relationship types. Some of these relationship types, such as parent-child and many-to-many, require DAX knowledge, and I'll postpone their discussion until Chapter 6. One common relationship type that you've already encountered but I've left unexplained is a role-playing relationship.

A role-playing lookup table is a table that joins the same fact table multiple times and thus plays multiple roles. For example, the ResellerSales table has the OrderDateKey, ShipDateKey, and DueDateKey columns because a sales order has an order date, ship date, and due date. Suppose you want to analyze the reseller sales by these three dates. One approach is to import the Date table three times with different names and to create relationships to each date table. This approach gives you more control because you now have three separate Date tables and their data doesn't have to match. For example, you might want the ShipDate table to include only valid ship dates instead of a continuous range of dates. On the downside, you increase the number of tables and duplicate data and metadata definitions.

Another approach is to join the three ResellerSales date columns to the Date table. Use this approach to reuse the same Date table three times. However, Tabular supports only one active role-playing relationship. An active relationship is a relationship that PowerPivot follows to automatically aggregate the data between two tables. The Active flag in the Manage Relationship dialog box indicates if the relationship is active. In our case, the ResellerSales [ShipDateKey] ⇨ DimDate

[DateKey] relationship is active because this happens to be the first of the three relationships between the DimDate and FactResellerSales tables that PowerPivot imported. Consequently, when you create a report that slices reseller dates by Date, PowerPivot automatically aggregates by the ship date.

**NOTE** Supporting only one active role-playing relationship is a limitation with Tabular. Multidimensional doesn't have this restriction and it supports multiple active role-playing dimensions.

If you want the default aggregation to happen by the order date, you must set ResellerSales [OrderDateKey] ⇨ DimDate [DateKey] as an active relationship. To do so, first select the ResellerSales [ShipDateKey] ⇨ DimDate [DateKey] relationship, and then click Edit. In the Edit Relationship dialog box, uncheck the Active checkbox, and then click OK. Finally, edit the ResellerSales [OrderDateKey] ⇨ DimDate [DateKey] relationship, and then check the Active checkbox.

What if you want to be able to aggregate data by other dates without importing the Date table multiple times? The workaround is to create DAX calculated measures, such as ShippedSalesAmount and DueSalesAmount, that use the DAX USERELATIONSHIP function to navigate inactive relationships, as I'll show you in Chapter 6.

***Understanding unknown members***

Consider the model shown in **Figure 4.18**, which consists of a Reseller lookup table and Sales fact table. The Reseller table has only two resellers. However, the Sales table has data for two additional resellers with keys of 3 and 4. This is a common data integrity issue when the source data originates from heterogeneous data sources and when there isn't an ETL process to validate and clean the data.

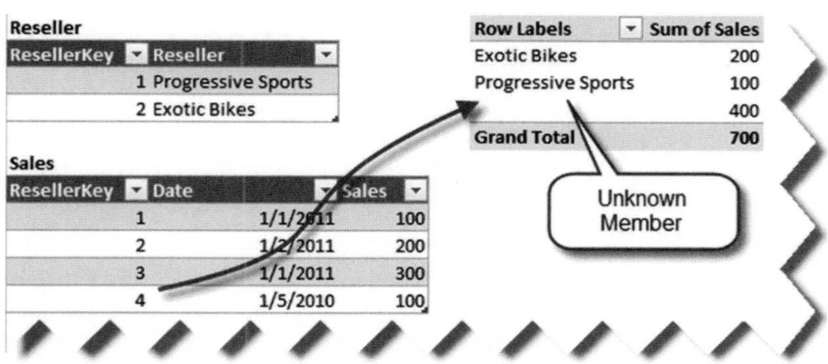


**Figure 4.18** PowerPivot enables an unknown member to the lookup table when it encounters missing rows.

Tabular has a simple solution for this predicament. When creating a relationship, PowerPivot checks for missing rows in the lookup table. If it finds any, it automatically configures the lookup table to include a special unknown member. That's why all unrelated rows appear grouped under a blank row in a pivot report. This row represents the unknown member in the Reseller table.

**NOTE** If you have experience with Multidimensional, the unknown member concept might be familiar to you. Tabular supports dimension properties to control the unknown member appearance and name. As it stands, Tabular doesn't have equivalent settings and you're stuck with the blank row. As a best practice, consider handling unknown members and other data integrity issues at the data source or with custom queries upon import if possible.

## 4.3.4 Understanding Diagram View

One of the top requested features for PowerPivot in the past was a graphical representation of the model schema and relationships, similar to the Data Source View in Multidimensional or the Relationships view in Microsoft Access. The Analysis Services team addressed this need by introducing Diagram View in PowerPivot and SQL Server Data Tools. You can use Diagram View to:

- Visualize the model schema
- Create and manage relationships
- Make other limited schema changes, such as renaming, hiding, deleting objects, and changing column data types
- Create and manage hierarchies (discussed in Chapter 5)
- Visualize perspectives (discussed in Chapter 5)

***Visualizing the model schema***
One of the strengths of Diagram View is that you can quickly visualize and understand the model schema and relationships. **Figure 4.19** shows a subset of the Adventure Works model schema in Diagram View.

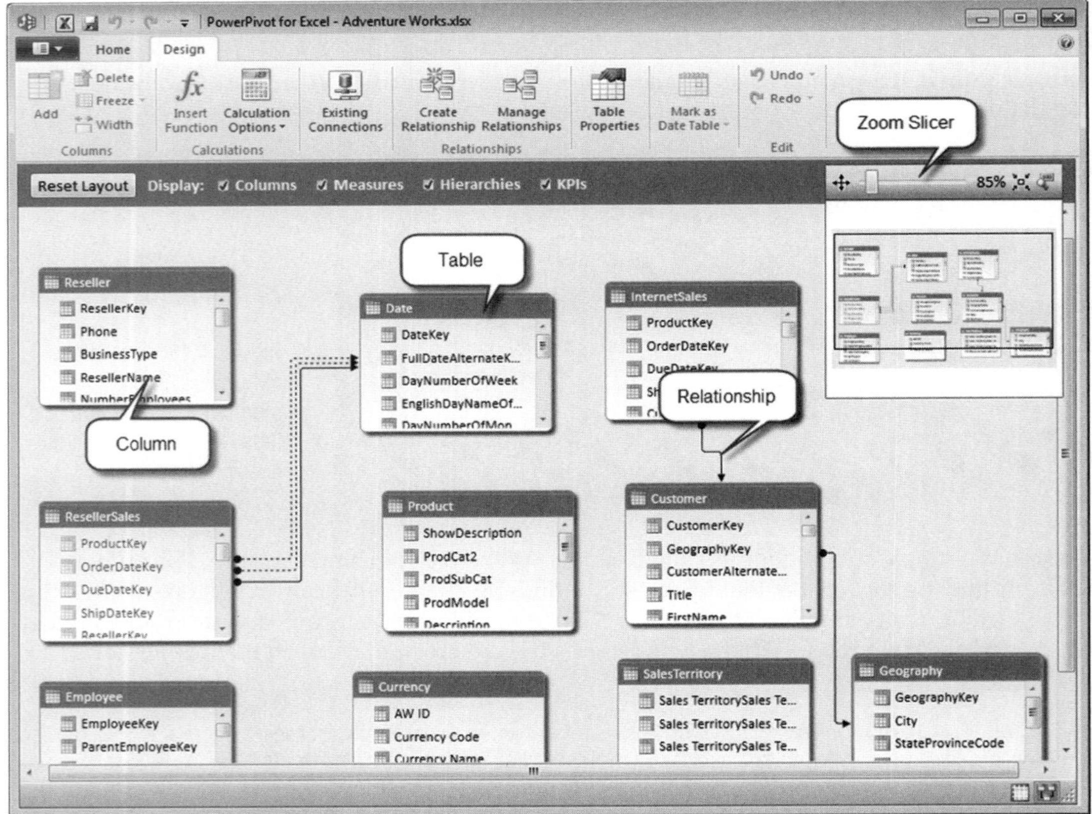


**Figure 4.19** Diagram View helps you understand the model schema.

Glancing at the model, you can immediately see what relationships exist in the model. To help you navigate the data schema, Diagram View supports several zooming modes. First, there is a zoom slicer in the top-right corner that allows you to zoom the schema in and out. You can use the interactive zoom feature (the directional cross to the left of the zoom slicer) to interactively select and zoom a particular area of interest.

The Fit to Screen button to the right of the zoom slicer will zoom out the model to fit to the screen size. The Original Size button next to the Fit to Screen button will restore the diagram to its original size. The Reset Layout button above the diagram rearranges the tables, such as to move related tables closer to each other. Finally, you can manually move a table around by dragging its header to a new location. That's a lot of freedom to navigate and control your Diagram View!

Models with many tables and end-user features could make Diagram View crowded. You can use the checkboxes at the top to toggle the visibility of certain object types. For example, you can uncheck the Columns checkbox to show only the table names in the diagram.

***Making schema changes***

You can make limited schema changes in Diagram View. When you right-click an object, a context menu opens up to show the supported operations, as shown in **Table 4.2**.

**Table 4.2 This table shows the schema operations by object type.**

| Object Type | Supported Operations | Object Type | Supported Operations |
|---|---|---|---|
| Table | Delete, Create Relationship, Create Hierarchy, Hide, Rename | Measure | Delete, Rename |
| Column | Delete, Create Relationship, Create Hierarchy, Hide, Rename | Hiearchy | Delete, Rename |
| Relationship | Delete, Activate, Edit | KPI | Delete, Rename |

***Managing relationships***

Since we are on the subject of relationships, let's take a closer look at how Diagram View represents relationships. A relationship is visualized as a connector between two tables. The arrow points to the lookup table and the dot on the other end points to the fact table. For example, after examining **Figure 4.20**, you can see that there is a relationship between the Reseller table and ResellerSales table and that the Reseller table is a lookup table.

When you click a relationship to select it, Diagram View highlights it in a blue color. When you hover your mouse over a relationship, Diagram View highlights the corresponding columns in the joined tables to indicate visually which columns are used in the relationship. For example, pointing the mouse to the highlighted relationship between the ResellerSales and Date tables reveals that the relationship is created between the ResellerSales[ShipDateKey] column and Date[DateKey] column.

As I mentioned, PowerPivot has a limited support of role-playing relationships where a lookup table joins multiple times to a fact table. The caveat is that only one role-playing relationship can be active. Diagram Views shows the inactive relationships with dotted lines. To make another role-playing relationship active, first you need to deactivate the currently active relationship. To do so, select the active relationship, right-click it, and then click "Mark as Inactive". Or, you can double-click the active relationship and use the Edit Relationship dialog box to uncheck the Active flag. Finally, you can select the other role-playing relationship, right-click it, and then click "Mark as Active".

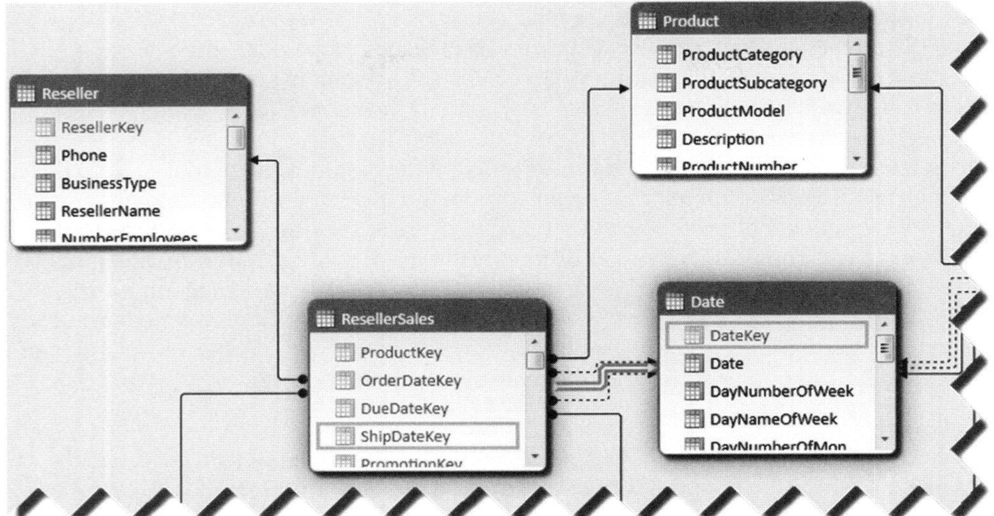


**Figure 4.20** Diagram View helps you understand the relationship type and related columns.

A great feature of Diagram View is creating relationships by dragging a column from the fact table and dropping it onto the matching column in the lookup table. For example, if there wasn't a relationship between the ResellerSales and Reseller table, you can set up a relationship by dragging the ResellerKey column in the ResellerSales table and dropping it onto the ResellerKey column in the Reseller table. Or you can right-click a column or a table, and then click Create Relationship. This brings you to the familiar Create Relationship dialog box. To delete a relationship, simply click the relationship to select it, and then press the Delete key. Or, right-click the relationship line, and then click Delete.

## 4.3.5 Working with Relationships ▶

As it stands, the Adventure Works PowerPivot model has ten tables and many of the tables are not related. Next, you'll set up appropriate relationships in Data View and Diagram View. In the process, you'll learn how you can use a custom query to construct missing columns required for a relationship.

***Creating relationships in Data View***

The Adventure Works model has two fact tables (ResellerSales and InternetSales) and eight lookup tables. Start by setting up relationships from the ResellerSales tables to the Reseller, Employee, and Currency tables.

1. In the PowerPivot window (Data View), click the ResellerSales table tab. When creating a relationship, start with the table that's on the many side. In our case, a row in the Reseller table is associated with many rows in the ResellerSales table. Therefore, ResellerSales is on the many side of the relationship.
2. Right-click the ResellerKey column header in the ResellerSales table, and click Create Relationship.
3. In the Create Relationship dialog box that follows, expand the Related Lookup Table drop-down list, and the click the Reseller table.

4. Expand the Related Lookup Column drop-down list, and then select the ResellerKey column. Click the Create button to create the relationship and to return to Data View. Notice that the OrderDateKey column header has a special icon to inform you that it's related to another table and that's on the many side of the relationship.
5. Hover your mouse cursor over the column header of the ResellerKey column. Notice that a tooltip pops up with the text "Related to column [ResellerKey] in table [Reseller]".
6. Right-click the ResellerKey column header, and then click Navigate to Related Table to browse the Reseller table. Click the ResellerSales table tab to activate the ResellerSales table again.
7. Create a relationship between ResellerSales [EmployeeKey] and Employee [EmployeeKey].
8. Create a relationship between ResellerSales [CurrencyKey] and Currency [AW ID].

***Handling missing lookup columns***

Sometimes, a table might not have a suitable column to set up a relationship. You can use the following approaches to resolve the issue:

- Import the required column from the data source, such as a key column that uniquely identifies rows in a lookup table. I'll demonstrate this approach with the SalesTerritory table.
- Create a new column that uses a DAX formula to construct the required key values. Suppose that a Product table has a ProductNumber column that contains both the product category and part number, such as A-H123, B-M005. Let's say that the ResellerSales table has a ProductNumber column that has only the part number. You can add a calculated column to the Product table that uses a DAX formula to extract the part number so you can join the two tables.

**NOTE** If you've imported the SalesTerritory table from the AdventureWorksDW2008R2 database, jump to step 11 in this section because the DimSalesTerritory table already includes the SalesTerritoryKey column.

If you've imported the SalesTerritory table from the Adventure Works multidimensional cube, let's use the first approach to create a missing relationship between ResellerSales and SalesTerritory tables. Assuming that the Sales Territory dimension in the Adventure Works cube has the database column you need, you can add a calculated member to the MDX query that returns that column.

**NOTE** This exercise uses calculated members for customizing MDX queries. If you source your data from a relational database, you could use a custom query that does whatever is necessary to derive a matching column, such as joining tables. Custom queries are not supported with other data sources, such as text files. In this case, consider a PowerPivot calculated column that uses a DAX formula.

1. Click the ResellerSales table tab and note that the SalesTerritoryKey column contains integer values.
2. Click the SalesTerritory table tab. Notice that the SalesTerritory table doesn't include an integer column that identifies each region uniquely.
3. With the SalesTerritory table tab active, switch to the Design ribbon tab, and then click Table Properties.
4. In the Edit Table Properties dialog box, click the Design button to open the MDX query designer.
5. In the Table Import Wizard, click the Add Calculated Member toolbar button.
6. In the Calculated Member Builder dialog box, enter *SalesTerritoryKey* as the name for the calculated member. In the Expression field, enter the following MDX expression:

```
iif ( KPIValue("Revenue") = 0, null,
[Sales Territory].[Sales Territory Region].CurrentMember.Properties("MEMBER_KEY"))
```

This expression uses the MDX IIF operator to check if the value of the Revenue key performance indicator (KPI) is zero. If this is the case, the expression returns null. Since by default the MDX query designer asks for non-empty cells, the net result is that the query will exclude sales territories that have no data. If the KPI value isn't zero, the expression requests a special MEMBER_KEY property for each sales territory. MEMBER_KEY returns the value of the column used to set up the dimension key attribute in the Sales Territory dimension. In the case of the Adventure Works cube, this is the SalesTerritoryKey column in the DimSalesTerritory table, which is exactly what you need.

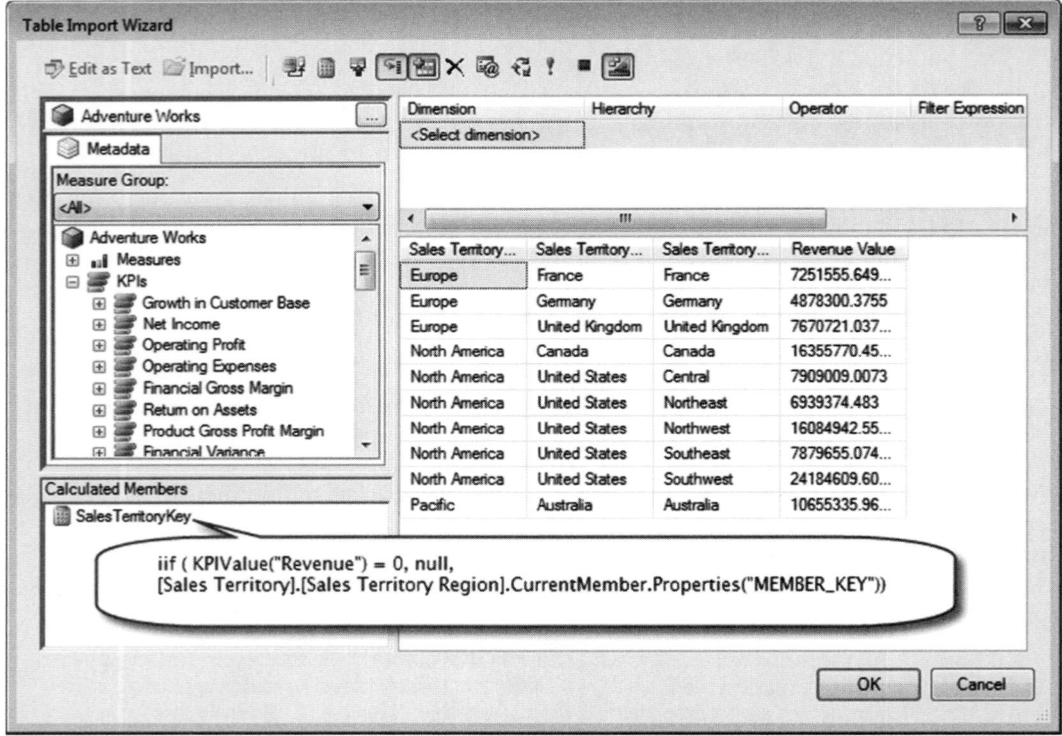


**Figure 4.21** The SalesTerritoryKey calculated member returns the key value of each territory.

7. Click OK to close the "Calculated Member Builder" dialog box. Right-click the SalesTerritoryKey member in the Calculated Members pane, and then click "Add to Query". Compare your results with **Figure 4.21**. Click OK to close the Table Import Wizard.
8. In the "Edit Table Properties" dialog box, you should see the following MDX query:

```
WITH MEMBER [Measures].[SalesTerritoryKey] AS
iif ( KPIValue("Revenue") = 0, null,
[Sales Territory].[Sales Territory Region].CurrentMember.Properties("MEMBER_KEY"))
SELECT NON EMPTY { KPIValue("Revenue"), [Measures].[SalesTerritoryKey] } ON COLUMNS, NON EMPTY { ([Sales Territory].[Sales
Territory Group].[Sales Territory Group].ALLMEMBERS * [Sales Territory].[Sales Territory Country].[Sales Territory Country].ALLMEMBERS *
[Sales Territory].[Sales Territory Region].[Sales Territory Region].ALLMEMBERS)} DIMENSION PROPERTIES MEMBER_CAPTION,
MEMBER_UNIQUE_NAME ON ROWS FROM [Adventure Works] CELL PROPERTIES VALUE, BACK_COLOR, FORE_COLOR,
FORMATTED_VALUE, FORMAT_STRING, FONT_NAME, FONT_SIZE, FONT_FLAGS
```

9. Click the Save button. PowerPivot adds a SalesTerritoryKey column to the SalesTerritory table and refreshes the table data. Back in the PowerPivot window, rename the MeasuresSalesTerritoryKey column to *SalesTerritoryKey*. Change the column date type to Whole Number. Hide the SalesTerritoryKey column.
10. Click the ResellerSales table tab, and then create a relationship between ResellerSales [SalesTerritoryKey] and SalesTerritory [SalesTerritoryKey].

***Working with custom queries***

Previously, you imported the Product table from a Reporting Services report. Similar to the SalesTerritory table, the Product table doesn't include a suitable key column that you can relate to the ProductKey column in the ResellerSales table. One way to solve this predicament is to create a custom SQL query to join the ResellerSales table to the Product table in the AdventureWorksDW2008R2 database so that you can import the product model in the ResellerSales table, on which a join can be made.

**NOTE** If you've imported the Product table from the AdventureWorksDW2008R2 database, you can skip the steps in this section and join the ResellerSales and InternetSales tables to the Product table on the ProductKey column. However, I recommend you follow the steps so you could practice custom queries and your model matches the book source code.

1. Click the ResellerSales table. In the Design ribbon tab, click the Table Properties button.
2. In the "Edit Table Preview" dialog box, expand the Switch To drop-down list, and then click Query Editor.
3. The "Edit Table Properties" dialog box shows the source SQL query.
4. You can change the query manually, but you'll need knowledge of SQL. Since the database server is SQL Server, you can use the graphical query designer to make changes. Click the Design button.
5. PowerPivot opens the Table Import Wizard by default in text mode. Click the "Edit as Text" button (if it's depressed) to switch to the graphical query designer. When PowerPivot prompts you to confirm switching to the visual designer, accept the prompt. This prompt exists because the graphical query designer can't reverse-engineer the source query to its visual representation.
6. In the Database View pane, click the checkbox next to the FactResellerSales table to select all of its columns, as shown in **Figure 4.22**.
7. Scroll up the table list, and then click the checkbox next to the ProductAlternateKey column of the DimProduct table. Since there is a join between the two tables in the AdventureWorksDW2008R2 database, the query designer knows how to join the two tables. In absence of joins in the database, you can use the Relationships section of the graphical query designer to set up a join manually (click the Auto Detect button before you do that in order to disable automatic relationship discovery).

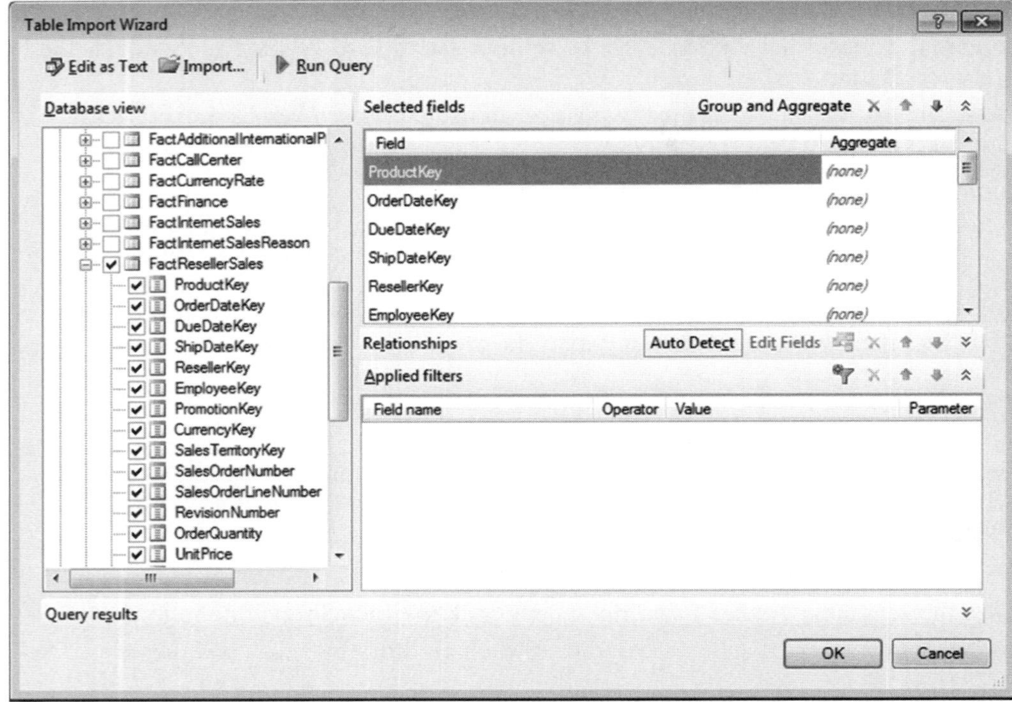


**Figure 4.22** The visual query designer auto-generates the SQL query.

8. Click OK to return to the Edit Table Properties dialog box, which should show this query:

```
SELECT
 FactResellerSales.ProductKey
 ,FactResellerSales.OrderDateKey
 ,FactResellerSales.DueDateKey
 ,FactResellerSales.ShipDateKey
 ,FactResellerSales.ResellerKey
 ,FactResellerSales.EmployeeKey
 ,FactResellerSales.PromotionKey
 ,FactResellerSales.CurrencyKey
 ,FactResellerSales.SalesTerritoryKey
 ,FactResellerSales.SalesOrderNumber
 ,FactResellerSales.SalesOrderLineNumber
 ,FactResellerSales.RevisionNumber
 ,FactResellerSales.OrderQuantity
 ,FactResellerSales.UnitPrice
 ,FactResellerSales.ExtendedAmount
 ,FactResellerSales.UnitPriceDiscountPct
 ,FactResellerSales.DiscountAmount
 ,FactResellerSales.ProductStandardCost
 ,FactResellerSales.TotalProductCost
 ,FactResellerSales.SalesAmount
 ,FactResellerSales.TaxAmt
 ,FactResellerSales.Freight
 ,FactResellerSales.CarrierTrackingNumber
 ,FactResellerSales.CustomerPONumber
 ,DimProduct.ProductAlternateKey
FROM DimProduct INNER JOIN FactResellerSales ON DimProduct.ProductKey = FactResellerSales.ProductKey
```

9. Click the Save button to re-import the reseller sales data and the new ProductAlternateKey column.
10. In the ResellerSales table tab, hide the ProductAlternateKey column.
11. Repeat the same steps to add the ProductAlternateKey column to the InternetSales table.
12. Back in the ResellerSales table in the PowerPivot window, establish a relationship between ResellerSales [ProductAlternateKey] and Product [ProductNumber]. Don't create a relationship between InternetSales [ProductAlternateKey] and Product [ProductNumber] because you'll use Diagram View to do so next.

***Creating relationships in Diagram View***

Next, you'll use the Diagram View to set up the remaining relationships.

1. In the PowerPivot window (in the Home ribbon tab), click the Diagram View button. Take some time to explore the model schema and to experiment with the Diagram View features, such as zooming.
2. Zoom to the InternetSales table.
3. Drag the ProductAlternateKey column from the InternetSales table, and then drop it on the ProductNumber column in the Product table, as shown in **Figure 4.23**. If the Product table isn't near the InternetSales table, right-click the ProductAlternateKey column in the InternetSales table, and click Create Relationship. Then select Product as a lookup table and ProductNumber as the lookup column.

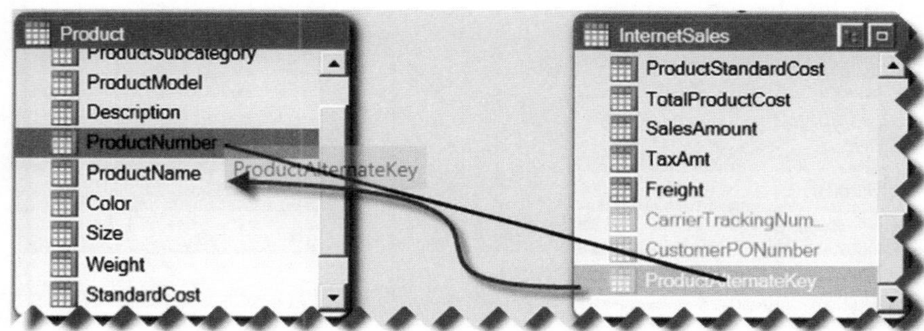


**Figure 4.23** Use Diagram View to create a relationship by dragging and dropping a column.

4. Hover your mouse over the relationship line. Notice that Diagram View highlights the related columns.
5. Use the same drag-and-drop technique or the Create Relationship dialog box to create the following relationships:
   InternetSales [OrderDateKey] ⇨ Date [DateKey]
   InternetSales [DueDateKey] ⇨ Date [DateKey]
   InternetSales [ShipDateKey] ⇨ Date [DateKey]
   InternetSales [CurrencyKey] ⇨ Currency [AW ID]
   InternetSales [SalesTerritoryKey] ⇨ SalesTerritory [SalesTerritoryKey].

***Working with active and inactive relationships***

Notice that there are three relationships between the Date table and the ResellerSales table.

1. Hover your mouse over the solid line that connects these two tables. Notice the relationship uses the ShipDateKey column in the ResellerSales table. Therefore, this role-playing relationship is active while the other two are inactive and are shown as dotted lines.

2. Suppose that you prefer to use the order date when slicing the ResellerSales table by date. Click the ResellerSales [ShipDateKey] ⇨ Date [DateKey] relationship to select it, right-click it, and then click "Mark as Inactive". If you have trouble with the context menu now showing, double-click the relationship, and then uncheck the Active checkbox. Next, click the ResellerSales [OrderDateKey] ⇨ Date [DateKey] relationship, right-click it, and then click "Mark as Active".
3. Use similar steps to make the relationship active between the InternetSales [OrderDateKey] and Date [DateKey] columns.
4. Hold the CTRL key, and then click the CustomerKey, GeographyKey, CustomerAlternateKey, SpanishEducation, FrenchEducation, SpanishOccupation, and FrenchOccupation columns in the Customer table. Right-click the selection, and then click Hide from Client Tools. Double-click the EnglishEducation column, and then rename it in place to *Education*. Use the same steps to rename the EnglishOccupation column to *Occupation*.
5. In the Geography table, hide the GeographyKey, SpanishCountryRegionName, FrenchCountryRegionName, and SalesTerritoryKey columns. Rename the EnglishCountryRegionName column to *CountryRegionName*.
6. In the InternetSales table, hide all the columns whose names end with "Key" (the first eight columns), as well as the RevisionNumber, CarrierTrackingNumber, and CustomerPONumber columns.
7. In the Design ribbon tab, click the Manage Relationship button, and then review the existing relationships. Compare your results with **Figure 4.24**. As it stands, the Adventure Works model has 15 relationships. Click the Close button, and then save the Adventure Works workbook.

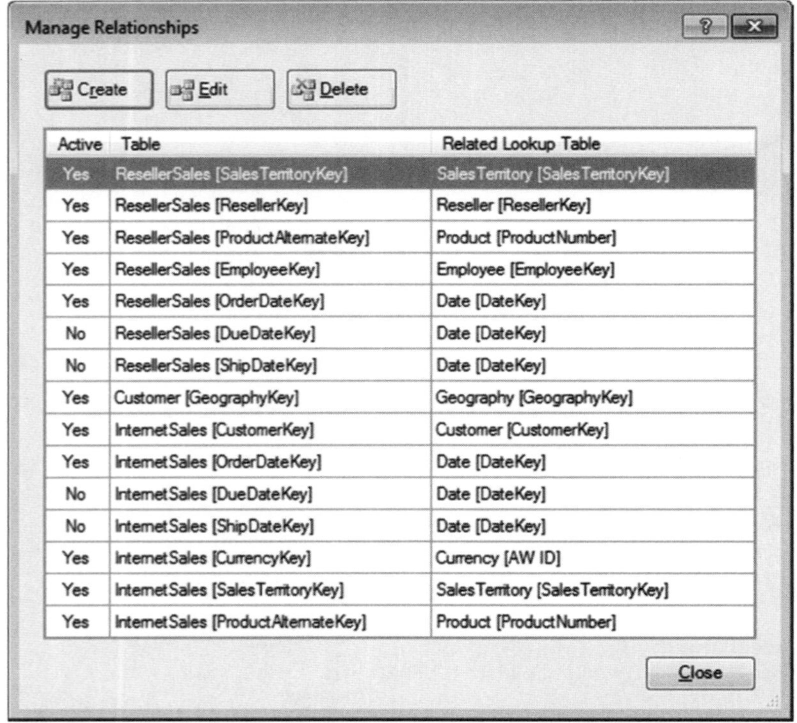


| Active | Table | Related Lookup Table |
|---|---|---|
| Yes | ResellerSales [SalesTerritoryKey] | SalesTerritory [SalesTerritoryKey] |
| Yes | ResellerSales [ResellerKey] | Reseller [ResellerKey] |
| Yes | ResellerSales [ProductAlternateKey] | Product [ProductNumber] |
| Yes | ResellerSales [EmployeeKey] | Employee [EmployeeKey] |
| Yes | ResellerSales [OrderDateKey] | Date [DateKey] |
| No | ResellerSales [DueDateKey] | Date [DateKey] |
| No | ResellerSales [ShipDateKey] | Date [DateKey] |
| Yes | Customer [GeographyKey] | Geography [GeographyKey] |
| Yes | InternetSales [CustomerKey] | Customer [CustomerKey] |
| Yes | InternetSales [OrderDateKey] | Date [DateKey] |
| No | InternetSales [DueDateKey] | Date [DateKey] |
| No | InternetSales [ShipDateKey] | Date [DateKey] |
| Yes | InternetSales [CurrencyKey] | Currency [AW ID] |
| Yes | InternetSales [SalesTerritoryKey] | SalesTerritory [SalesTerritoryKey] |
| Yes | InternetSales [ProductAlternateKey] | Product [ProductNumber] |

**Figure 4.24** The Manage Relationships dialog box shows 15 relationships defined in the Adventure Works model.

## 4.4 Summary

Once you import the initial set of tables, you should spend some time exploring the model data and refining the model schema. Data View supports various column operations to help you explore the model data and to make necessary changes. Revisit each column and configure its data type and formatting properties.

Avoid creating more connections if you need to import additional tables from the same data source. Use the table definition to change the row and column filters, or to define a custom query if you need more control over the data import process.

You must set up table relationships in order to integrate data across multiple tables. In some cases, PowerPivot might be capable of auto-detecting any missing relationships when you create reports. However, as a best practice, you should set up relationships manually by using Data View's Create Relationship feature or by using the drag-and-drop technique in Diagram View.

You've come a long way in designing the Adventure Works model. In Chapter 5, let's see how we can gain data insights by analyzing the model in Excel.

# Chapter 5

# Analyzing Data



Up until now, you have seen how to implement and refine a PowerPivot model. This was the necessary ground work required before you can analyze data. After all, the whole purpose of creating a PowerPivot model is to derive knowledge from the data. With PowerPivot for Excel, you can build meaningful and attractive tabular, crosstab, and chart reports with a just few mouse clicks.

This chapter teaches you how to create Excel pivot reports to analyze PowerPivot models. You'll learn how to implement end-user features that further enrich the model and make it more intuitive to end users. I'll show you different new ways to filter data and to build interactive reports. You'll also implement an Excel-based dashboard for historical and trend data analysis.

## 5.1 Understanding Excel Data Analysis

Microsoft positions Excel as its premium business intelligence (BI) tool, and PowerPivot is one of the manifestations of this strategy. Instead of having to purchase and learn a new reporting tool, with PowerPivot you can analyze data right inside Excel. PowerPivot even adds new features to make the process easier and more user-friendly.

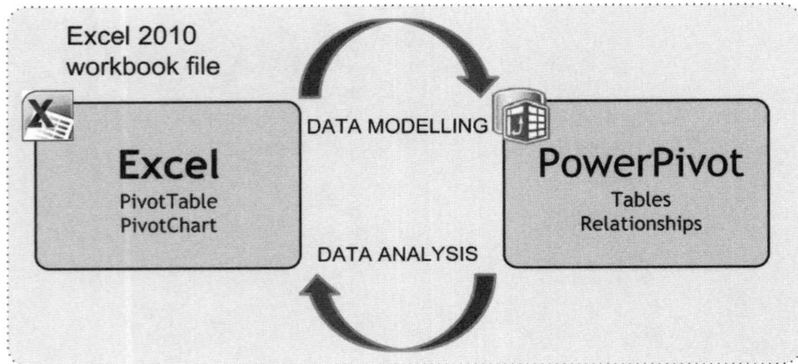


**Figure 5.1** PowerPivot uses Excel pivot reports for data analysis and reporting.

**Figure 5.1** shows the Excel modeling and analysis lifecycle. PowerPivot for Excel is implemented as an Excel add-in. As you've seen, model development takes place in the PowerPivot window that represents the PowerPivot modeling environment. PowerPivot falls back on Excel for data analysis and reporting. The PowerPivot model, data, and reports are saved in a single Excel workbook file.

## 5.1.1 Understanding Pivot Reports

Before we continue any further, let me clarify something important. A common misconception is that PowerPivot supersedes Excel reporting or adds some cool reporting capabilities not found in Excel. The PowerPivot name contributes to this confusion because it implies more than pivot reporting! To the contrary, PowerPivot uses the Excel PivotTable and PivotChart reports and adds only incremental features to facilitate integration with PowerPivot models. Don't be disappointed though, since you can do a lot with pivot reports. You can use PivotTable to create tabular and crosstab reports and PivotChart to visualize data in charts.

**NOTE** Covering Excel's PivotTable and PivotChart in detail is outside the scope of this book. For a closer look, you might find the following reading list useful (http://amzn.to/pivotbooks). This chapter focuses on the Excel pivot features that are specific to PowerPivot.

***Understanding PivotTable types***

PivotTable reporting is the main tool for data analysis in Excel. You would typically use a PivotTable to build interactive reports that aggregate large amounts of data. The PivotTable debuted in Excel 5.0, which was released almost two decades ago! Depending on your background, you probably have experience with two types of PivotTable reports:

- Native (PivotCache) – Uses an Excel worksheet as a data source or uses external data imported with Microsoft Query.
- Online analytical processing (OLAP) – Connects to an Analysis Services cube.

PowerPivot for Excel adds a third PivotTable type, which I'll refer to as a *PowerPivot* report. You can think of this type as a hybrid of the above two types. Although it's technically an OLAP PivotTable, the PowerPivot Field List will trick you into believing that it's a native PivotTable.

***Comparing PivotTable types***

**Table 5.1** provides a high-level comparison of the three pivot report types.

**Table 5.1 Comparing PivotTable report types.**

| Feature | Native | OLAP | PowerPivot |
|---|---|---|---|
| Data Storage | Cached locally | External | Cached locally |
| Compression | Good compression | Better compression | Best compression |
| Model | One table | Dimensions and measures | One or more tables |
| Calculations | Excel formulas | MDX calculations defined in the cube | DAX calculated columns and measures |
| Processing | Local | Server | Local |
| Field List | PivotTable Field List (one table) | PivotTable Field List (cube metadata) | PowerPivot Field List (tables and columns) |

In terms of data storage, native pivot reports can source data from an Excel worksheet or import data from an external data source and then cache the data in the Excel file. OLAP pivot reports connect to an external cube. Similar to native reports, PowerPivot imports and saves the data in the Excel file. Native pivot reports have a good compression with smaller datasets. PowerPivot compresses data the best but differences show up with larger datasets (above 100,000 rows). Native pivot reports are limited to one Excel list as a data source, while a PowerPivot model can have multiple related tables.

Native pivot reports use Excel formulas for calculated fields. An OLAP cube can include server-side Multidimensional Expressions (MDX) calculations but an OLAP pivot report won't let you define custom calculations except named sets in Excel 2010 (the object model supports this feature, but there is no user interface for it). With PowerPivot, you can create Data Analysis Expressions (DAX) calculated columns and measures. A native report aggregates data locally on your machine, and it has its own internal mechanism for querying data. An OLAP report sends an MDX query to the server, which does the data crunching. A PowerPivot report sends an MDX query to the PowerPivot model inside the Excel workbook, so the data processing and aggregation happens locally on your computer.

**NOTE** One area with PowerPivot reports to watch for is detail-level (transactional) reporting. Due to the way Excel formulates MDX queries, Excel transitional reports, such as a report that shows customers and sales orders, might not give you good performance. I provided more details in my blog post, "Transactional Reporting with BISM Tabular" at http://bit.ly/pivotdetailed.

Each pivot type comes with its own Field List. The Field List of a native pivot report shows only one table. When connected to a cube, the Field List of an OLAP report shows the cube metadata. The PowerPivot Field List shows the tables and columns defined in the model.

## 5.1.2 Understanding Report Layouts

PowerPivot includes predefined report layouts to help you get started with pivot reports. You can access these layouts by expanding the PivotTable drop-down button found in two places: the Home ribbon tab in the PowerPivot window and the PowerPivot tab in the Excel ribbon. **Figure 5.2** shows the two menus stacked with the available layout options to the right.

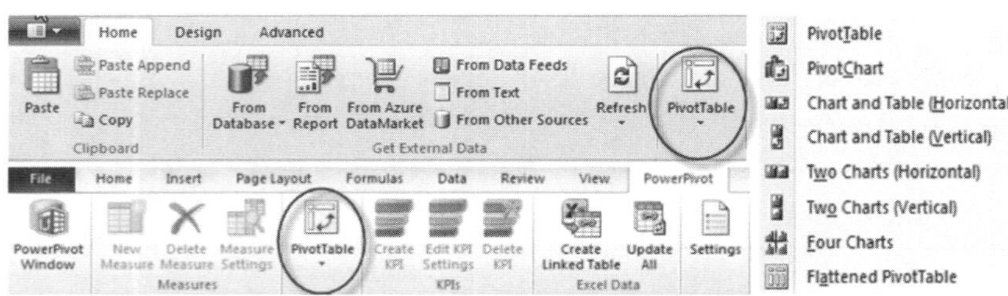


**Figure 5.2** PowerPivot provides several predefined pivot report layouts.

Next, I'll review only PivotTable, PivotChart, and Flattened PivotTable layouts since the rest are just different combinations of those. For example, Chart and Table (Horizontal) combines PivotTable and PivotChart layouts arranged horizontally.

***PivotTable report layout***

The PivotTable option creates an empty PivotTable report. **Figure 5.3** shows a PivotTable report that I created, based on the PivotTable layout. Notice that the PowerPivot Field List on the right includes several zones, as follows:

- Slicers Vertical and Slicers Horizontal – You can use these zones to add interactive visual filters called *slicers* (not used in the report shown in **Figure 5.3**).
- Report Filter – The fields added to this area can be used to filter the report data. They appear in an area above the report. The PivotTable report shown in **Figure 5.3** doesn't have a report filter.

- Column Labels – The report pivots on columns by the fields added to this area so you can implement crosstab reports. In my case, the report pivots on CalendarYear.
- Row Labels – The report groups data on rows by fields that are added to Row Labels area. The report in **Figure 5.3** groups data by the ProductCategory and ProductSubcategory fields.
- Values – The pivot report aggregates fields that are added to this area. My report aggregates the SalesAmount field.

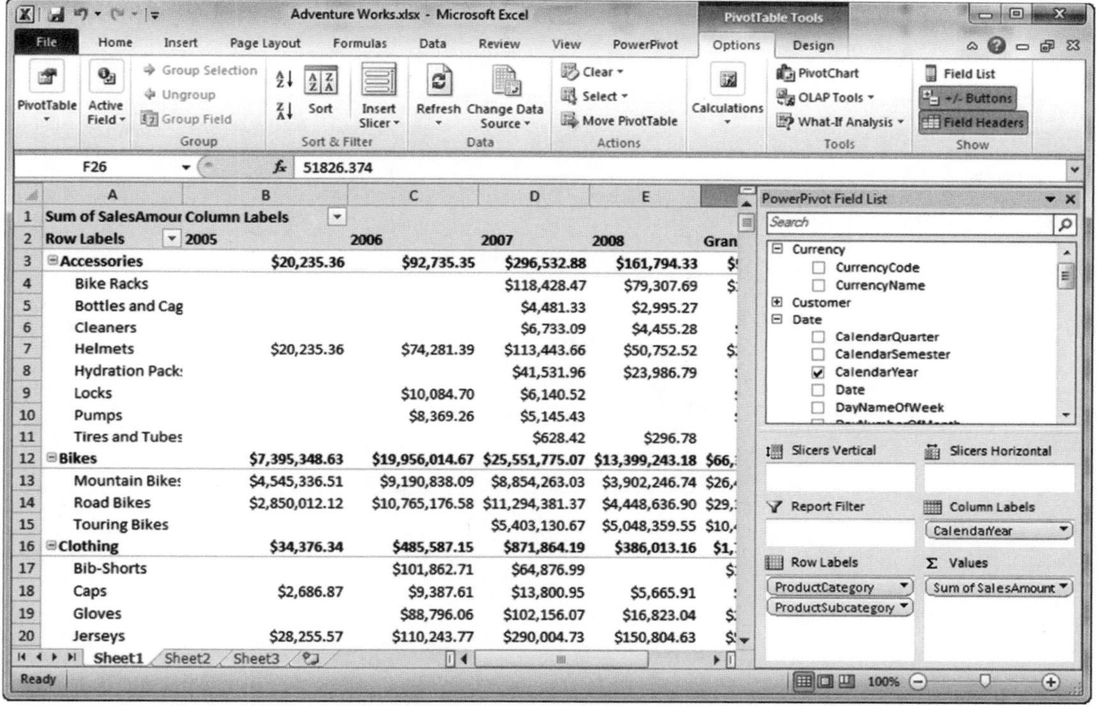


**Figure 5.3** The PivotTable layout creates a PivotTable report with stacked columns.

The PivotTable layout option is preconfigured for a compact layout that stacks fields in the same area on top of each other. For example, both the ProductCategory and ProductSubcategory fields occupy the same (first) column. The compact layout is the default PivotTable layout starting with Excel 2007. It is suitable for grouping data by multiple fields because it minimizes the report size and the level of detail shown on the report. The user can drill-down to see more details by expanding the plus sign next to the field value. For example, to drill down the Accessories product category, simply expand the plus sign to the left of it.

The Excel Options ribbon tab includes buttons to perform common PivotTable-related tasks. Click a cell inside the pivot report to see the Options menu appear in the Excel main menu. For example, you can use the Move PivotTable button to move the report to another location. To delete the entire report, expand the Select drop-down button, click Select Entire PivotTable, and then press the Delete key.

The Design ribbon tab gives you control over the report layout and colors. For example, if you want to remove all grand totals, expand the Grand Totals drop-down button, and then click Off for Columns and Rows. Or, if you don't like the default colors, choose any of the predefined styles in the PivotTable Style group or create your own style.

***PivotChart report layout***

The second main layout option is a PivotChart layout. This adds an empty chart that's preconfigured as a column chart. You can use this chart type to create reports similar to the one shown in **Figure 5.4**.

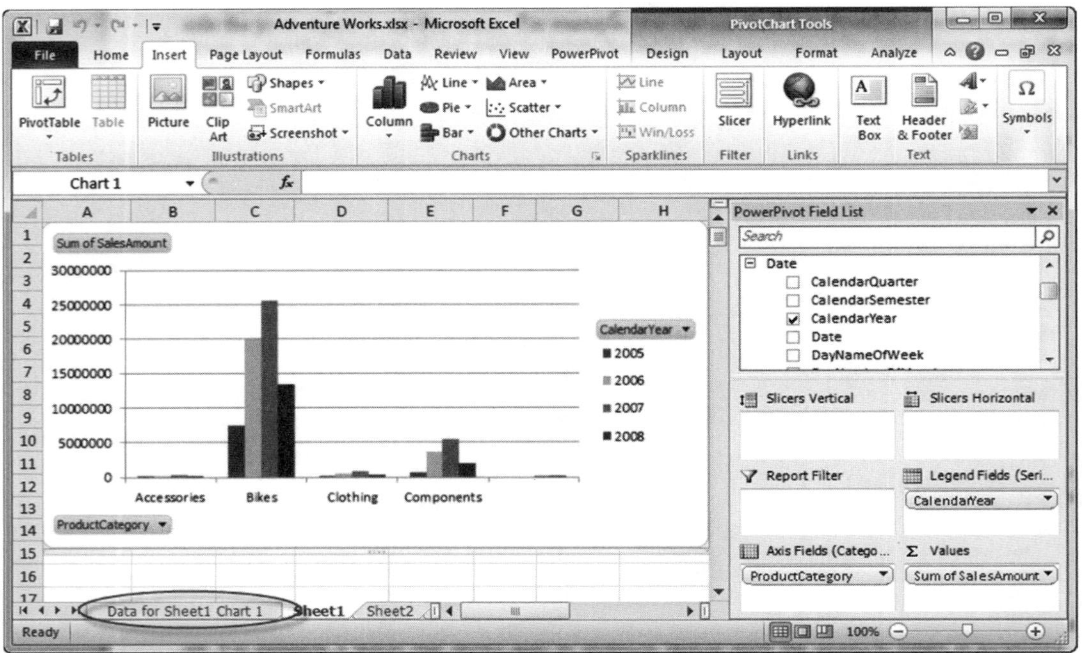


**Figure 5.4** The PivotChart layout option to visualize data as a chart.

Due to the way Excel charting works, a chart report uses a PivotTable as a data source. This is why PowerPivot generates a new worksheet for each PivotChart report and names it "Data for Sheet <SheetN> Chart <ChartN>", where <SheetN> is the name of the sheet where the chart is located and <ChartN> is the name of the chart. Consider hiding these supporting worksheets to reduce clutter especially if you plan to share the workbook with other users.

**TIP** You don't have to use the PivotChart layout if you simply want to visualize a PivotTable as a chart. Instead, click any cell in the PivotTable, and from the Excel Insert ribbon tab, click the chart type you want. This will add a chart to the same sheet where the PivotTable report is located and will synchronize the chart with the PivotTable.

Notice also that the PowerPivot Field List for PivotCharts is somewhat different than it is for PivotTables. Fields added to the Legend Fields area define the chart series. In this case, the chart uses the CalendarYear field for its data series (corresponding to Column Labels in a PivotTable). Use the Axis Fields area to set up chart categories (similar to row groups in a PivotTable). This report groups data by the ProductCategory field. You can right-click any chart element to open a context menu to configure its properties. For example, to change the chart type, right-click the chart area, and then click "Change Chart Type".

***Flattened PivotTable***

Instead of stacked columns, some types of reports, such as financial reports, might require separate columns (one column per field). This is where the Flattened PivotTable layout could be useful. **Figure 5.5** shows the same report that's in **Figure 5.3**, but this time it has a flattened layout.

| Sum of SalesAmount | | CalendarYear | | | |
|---|---|---|---|---|---|
| **ProductCategory** | **ProductSubcategory** | **2005** | **2006** | **2007** | **2008** |
| **Accessories** | Bike Racks | | | $118,428.47 | $79,307.69 |
| | Bottles and Cages | | | $4,481.33 | $2,995.27 |
| | Cleaners | | | $6,733.09 | $4,455.28 |
| | Helmets | $20,235.36 | $74,281.39 | $113,443.66 | $50,752.52 |
| | Hydration Packs | | | $41,531.96 | $23,986.79 |
| | Locks | | $10,084.70 | $6,140.52 | |
| | Pumps | | $8,369.26 | $5,145.43 | |
| | Tires and Tubes | | | $628.42 | $296.78 |
| **Accessories Total** | | **$20,235.36** | **$92,735.35** | **$296,532.88** | **$161,794.33** |
| **Bikes** | Mountain Bikes | $4,545,336.51 | $9,190,838.09 | $8,854,263.03 | $3,902,246.74 |
| | Road Bikes | $2,850,012.12 | $10,765,176.58 | $11,294,381.37 | $4,448,636.90 |
| | Touring Bikes | | | $5,403,130.67 | $5,048,359.55 |
| **Bikes Total** | | **$7,395,348.63** | **$19,956,014.67** | **$25,551,775.07** | **$13,399,243.18** |
| **Clothing** | Bib-Shorts | | $101,862.71 | $64,876.99 | |

**Figure 5.5** The Flattened PivotTable layout option doesn't stack columns.

The main difference is that the ProductCategory and ProductSubcategory fields now occupy separate columns. To improve the report appearance, I suppressed the ProductCategory labels from repeating. To do so, I right-clicked a cell in the ProductCategory column, and then I clicked Field Settings from the context menu. In the Field Settings dialog box, I clicked the Layout & Print tab, and then I unchecked the "Repeat Item Labels" option. To highlight the subtotals, I went to the Design ribbon tab, and then I selected the third style (Pivot Style Light 1) in the PivotTable Styles ribbon group.

**TIP** You don't have to start from scratch if you want to change the PivotTable layout. Instead, click any cell inside the pivot report, and then click the Excel Design ribbon tab. Expand the Report Layout drop-down button, and then select the desired layout, such as Show in Tabular Form if you prefer a flattened layout. Use the other options in the Design ribbon tab to refine the report appearance. For example, the PivotTable Styles group includes about 70 predefined styles and allows you to create custom styles to jazz up your PivotTables.

## 5.1.3 Understanding PowerPivot Field List

As I mentioned, PowerPivot reports are technically OLAP reports because Excel sees a PowerPivot model as an Analysis Services cube and sends MDX queries to it as you interact with the report. PowerPivot comes with its own field list called PowerPivot Field List. The PowerPivot Field List replaces the Excel PivotTable Field List when you create reports from PowerPivot models.

***Comparing PowerPivot and PivotTable field lists***

When you create a PowerPivot report, the PowerPivot Field List shows up docked on the right. If it doesn't show, go to the Excel PowerPivot ribbon tab, and click the Field List button. To see the OLAP version of the PivotTable Field List so you can compare the two field lists, right-click anywhere on report, and then click Show Field List. **Figure 5.6** shows both field lists side by side.

Here are the main differences between the two field lists:

- The PowerPivot Field List shows the model metadata as tables and columns (fields). The PivotTable Field List uses OLAP artifacts, such as measures, measures groups, and dimensions.

The PivotTable Field List shows the system-defined "__No measures defined" measure in a Values measure group to get around a limitation with OLAP reports where must be at least one measure defined in the cube.

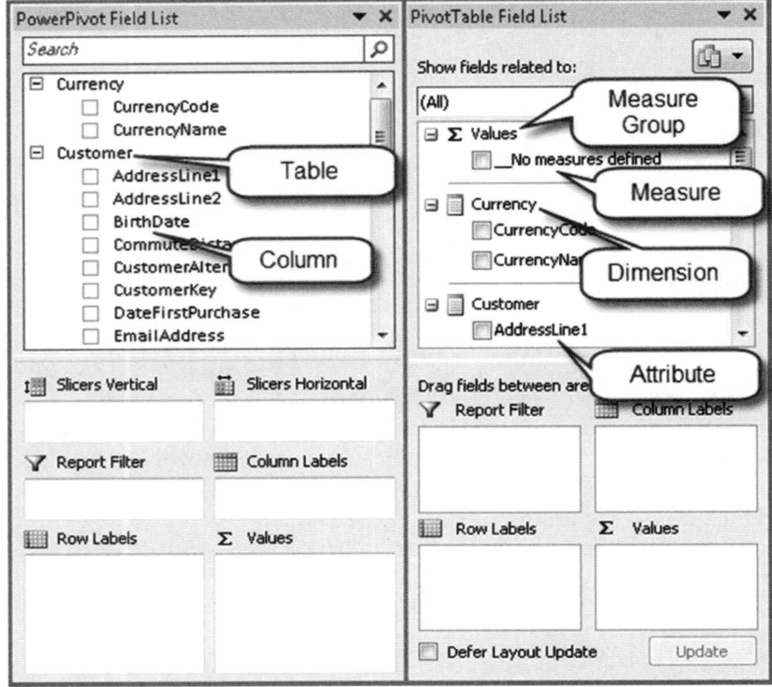


**Figure 5.6** Comparing the PowerPivot Field List and PivotTable Field List side by side.

- The PowerPivot Field List allows you to aggregate any field added to the Values zone. By contrast, the PivotTable Field List allows you to aggregate only measures. If a table has implicit measures (columns added to the Values zone in the PowerPivot Field List) or explicit measures (measures with custom DAX formulas), it will appear twice in the PivotTable Field List: as a measure group and as a dimension.
- The PowerPivot Field List doesn't support in-place filtering, such as to filter customers whose names begin with "Teo" before you add the customer's Name field on the report. Because of this, you might experience performance degradation when you add high-cardinality columns, such as Customer and Account, to the report. As a workaround, consider setting up a report filter or a slicer to filter data before adding such columns.
- The PowerPivot Field List includes two additional zones, Slicer Vertical and Slicers Horizontal, to help you configure slicers.
- The PowerPivot Field List doesn't have a "Defer Layout Update" checkbox. As a result, any change in the report layout results in a query to the model.

**NOTE** When enabled, the Defer Layout Update option in the PivotTable Field List doesn't query the cube after each report change, such as after adding a new field to the report. You need to press the Update button to refresh the report. It would have been useful to have this option especially with PowerPivot detail-level reports, which could be quite resource intensive.

- The PowerPivot Field List supports metadata searching, such as typing *Customer* in the Search field on the top of the pane to find objects whose names contain "Customer". This feature searches only metadata and not the data in the model.

Microsoft did a great job of improving the PowerPivot metadata appearance for OLAP clients and the PivotTable Field List is now much more intuitive. However, since PowerPivot is a very different model than OLAP, you should use the PowerPivot Field List for the best possible experience when creating PowerPivot reports.

***Understanding implicit aggregation***

A PivotTable is an excellent tool for analyzing large datasets because it automatically aggregates data depending on what fields you've used on the report. There are three options to add a field to the report:

- Right-click a field in the PowerPivot Field List, and then select which zone you want to add the field to, such as Add to Values to add the field to the Values zone.
- Drag the field, and then drop it into the desired zone.
- Check the checkbox to the left of the field in the PowerPivot Field List.

When you use the last option, PowerPivot follows some basic rules to decide where to place the field. If the field is numeric, PowerPivot assumes you want to aggregate it and puts it in the Values zone. If the field is text-based, it puts it in the Row Labels zone. If a field ends up in the wrong zone, you can always drag it away from that zone and drop it into the correct zone. A new feature in this release of PowerPivot is the ability to add values to rows and columns in order to create more flexible report layouts. For more information about this feature, read the "Adding Values to Rows and Columns" blog post by Julie Strauss (a Microsoft PowerPivot Program Manager) at http://bit.ly/values2rc.

When you add a field to the Values zone, PowerPivot automatically creates an implicit measure to aggregate the field's values. PowerPivot supports several common aggregation functions, including Sum, Count, Min, Max, Average, and DistinctCount. How does PowerPivot choose an aggregation function? PowerPivot inspects the field type and uses the Sum function for numeric fields and the Count function for text fields. For example, when you add the SalesAmount field to the Values zone, PowerPivot creates a "Sum of SalesAmount" implicit measure that uses the Sum function, as shown in **Figure 5.7**.

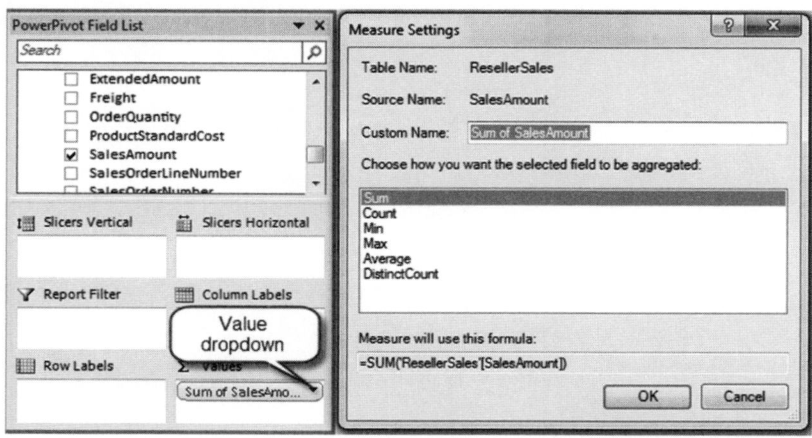


**Figure 5.7** The Measure Settings dialog box allows you to change the name of the implicit measure and its aggregation function.

To overwrite the aggregation behavior, expand the drop-down list next to the field in the Values zone, and then click the Summarize By option in the context menu. Or, you can right-click the field in the Values zone, and then click Edit Measure. Use the Measure Settings dialog box to change the field name on the report and the aggregation function. The only aggregation functions available for text fields are the Count and DistinctCount functions.

> **TIP** Excel supports various Show As options to display aggregated values, such as to show them as % of Grand Total. To use this feature, simply right-click on an aggregated cell in the pivot report, and then click Show Values As. For more information about this feature, please read the "A Few More PivotTable Improvements in Excel 2010" blog post by the Excel team at http://bit.ly/showas.

## 5.1.4 Understanding Integration with Excel

The PowerPivot model gets saved in the Excel workbook file in an Analysis Services backup (*.abf) file format. When the report queries the model, the PowerPivot add-in hops into action, extracts the file into the VertiPaq in-memory engine, and presents it as a multidimensional cube (called "Model") to Excel. When you interact with the report, Excel auto-generates MDX queries and sends them to the PowerPivot model. Before we get started with report authoring, let's take a moment to understand how this integration works.

***Understanding connectivity***

Excel reports communicate with the PowerPivot model via a special workbook connection. To see this connection, click any cell on a PowerPivot report, go to the Data tab in the Excel ribbon, and then click Connections. In the Workbook Connections dialog box, you'll see a connection called PowerPivot Data. **Figure 5.8** shows the properties of the PowerPivot Data connection.

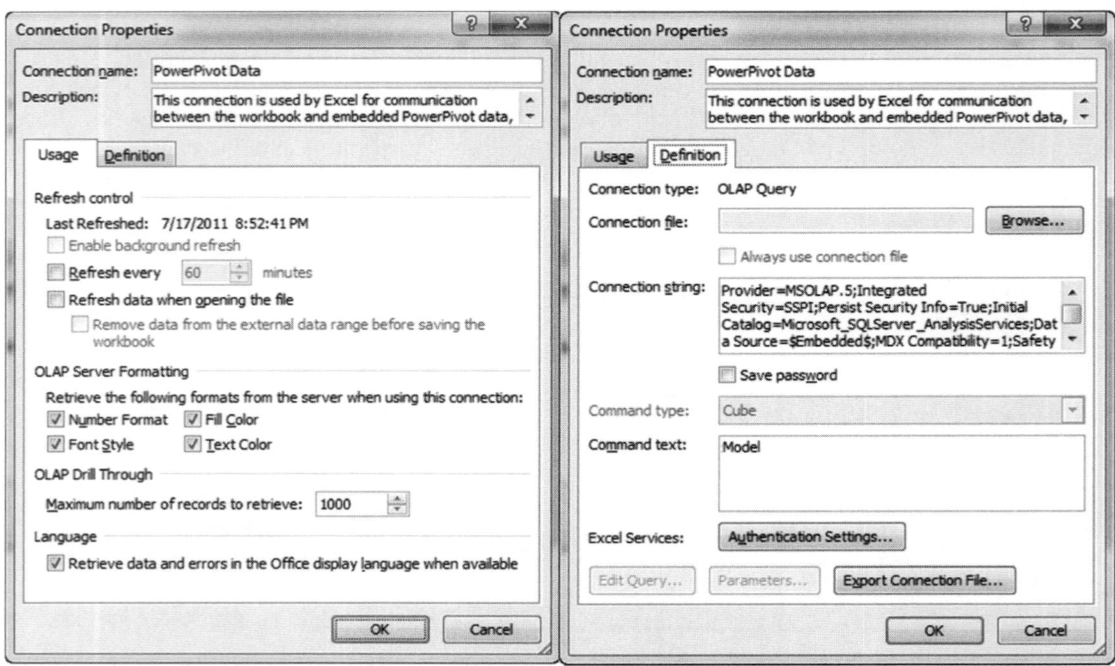


**Figure 5.8** Excel communicates with PowerPivot via the PowerPivot Data connection.

The Layout tab has various settings, many of which don't apply to PowerPivot. Pivot reports maintain their own data cache inside the workbook file. This is why you can see the report immediately when you open the Excel file. The options in the "Refresh control" section specify how often pivot reports query the data source to show the latest data. However, since the PowerPivot model caches data inside the Excel workbook, refreshing PowerPivot reports on a schedule or upon opening the file isn't very useful because Excel doesn't tell PowerPivot to open the connections defined in the model in order to refresh the data imported in the model.

**NOTE** Currently, there isn't a way to configure Excel to refresh the PowerPivot model data on open. What's needed in a future version is a PowerPivot object model and VBA API to automate the process, as I suggested in the "Object Model for PowerPivot for Excel" Connect suggestion at http://bit.ly/powerpivotvba (Ashvini Sharma, Microsoft PowerPivot Program Manager Lead, responded that the request is in consideration for a future release).

The only option from the OLAP Server Formatting section that applies to PowerPivot is the Number Format option. If you uncheck this option, the format settings in the model won't carry to Excel reports. The OLAP Drill Through option specifies that when you drill through a cell, Excel will display the first 1,000 rows. You can increase the threshold if necessary. Finally, the Definition tab shows the connection string that you shouldn't modify except in rare cases, such as when you need to change how PowerPivot reacts to errors. Vidas Matelis, SQL Server MVP, demonstrates this approach in his blog post, "Changing how PowerPivot handles DAX errors", (http://bit.ly/powerpivoterrors).

**TIP** Now that you know about the PowerPivot Data connection, there is another way to add a PivotTable or PivotChart report (besides using the PivotTable drop-down menu). Go to the Insert tab in the Excel ribbon, expand the PivotTable button (the first button on the left), and then select PivotTable or PivotChart. In the Create PivotTable dialog box, select the Use an External Data Source option, and then click the Choose Connection button. In the Existing Connections dialog box, select the PowerPivot Data connection, which should be the first connection listed, and then click Open. Back in the Create PivotTable dialog, specify the location of the report, and then click OK.

### *Detecting metadata changes*

During the model development phase, you might find that you constantly switch between the model (to make changes) and the Excel pivot report (to test these changes). The PowerPivot Field List uses the PowerPivot Data connection to probe for metadata changes. If it detects any, it displays the "PowerPivot data was modified" message shown in **Figure 5.9**.

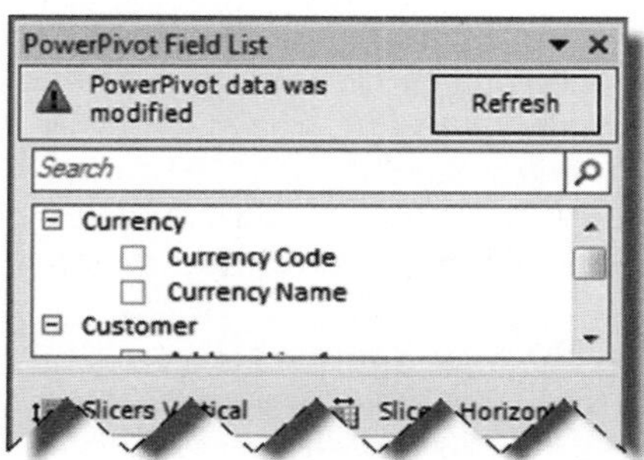


**Figure 5.9** The PowerPivot window prompts you to refresh the metadata.

For example, you'll get this message, if you change the format settings of a column and then switch to the pivot report. Click the Refresh button to synchronize the PowerPivot Field List and reports with the model changes.

**NOTE** Don't confuse the PowerPivot Field List refresh action with refreshing the model data, which I discussed in Chapter 4. The former refreshes the PowerPivot Field List and reports with the metadata changes that you've made in the model, while the latter reloads the data in the model.

## 5.1.5 Understanding Slicers

Slicers are visual controls that allow you to quickly and easily filter data in a more interactive way than the traditional pivot report filtering options. Slicers are very useful for implementing global filters that restrict data in multiple pivot reports with just one click.

***Understanding Excel slicers***

Slicers were introduced in Excel 2010. They are not a PowerPivot-specific feature and they can be used with native, OLAP, and PowerPivot pivot reports. You can add a slicer to a native pivot report, as follows:

1. Click any cell in the report. In the Insert tab in the Excel ribbon, click the Slicer button.
2. In the Insert Slicers dialog box that follows, select the fields you want to filter, and then click OK.

You can attach multiple slicers to a report. **Figure 5.10** shows a pivot report with two slicers to filter the report data by product category and subcategory. Notice that although the Product-Category field is added to the report, it's also used as a slicer. That's because slicers are independent of the pivot reports they're attached to.

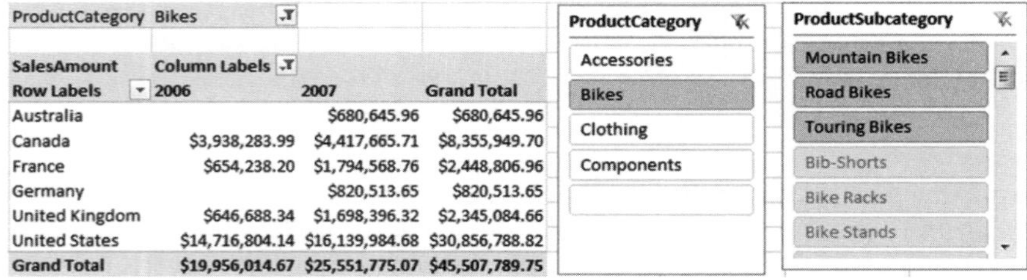


**Figure 5.10** You can add slicers to interactively filter the report data.

To filter data by a given item, simply click that item in the slicer. This will filter data in all the pivot reports attached to the slicer. You can hold the Ctrl key to select multiple values or the Shift key to select adjacent values. An interesting feature is the cross-slicer filter where selecting a value in one slicer highlights the values in another slicer that exist with the first value. For example, in **Figure 5.10**, the ProductSubcategory slicer highlights Mountain Bikes, Road Bikes, and Touring Bikes because these subcategories belong to the Bikes product category that I selected in the ProductCategory slicer. To clear the slicer filter and see all the report data, simply click the Clear Filter button in the top-right corner of the slicer.

Slicers support various settings that control their layout and behavior. You can access these settings from the context menu when you right-click the slicer. The PivotTable Connections menu allows you to specify which pivot reports are connected to the slicer. This is useful because Pivot-Table filters can't filter multiple pivot reports but slicers can. You can use the Size and Properties menu to change the slicer appearance, including the size and number of columns. Another way to access these settings is to select the slicer, and then click the Excel ribbon's Options table, which also includes predefined slicer styles to choose from. For more information about customizing slicers, read the "Dressing up your Slicers" blog post by the Excel team at http://bit.ly/customexcelslicers.

**TIP** Slicers are most useful to filter fields with a few values. Since slicers don't support hierarchies and searching, they are not very practical with long lists because you need to scroll down the list to find a particular value. In this case, consider pivot report filters because they support searching and filtering by different criteria.

***Understanding PowerPivot slicers***

PowerPivot for Excel adds features to make slicers easier to use. The PowerPivot Field List adds Slicers Vertical and Slicers Horizontal zones to help you work with slicers. **Figure 5.11** shows the effect of adding slicers to the Slicers Vertical zone.

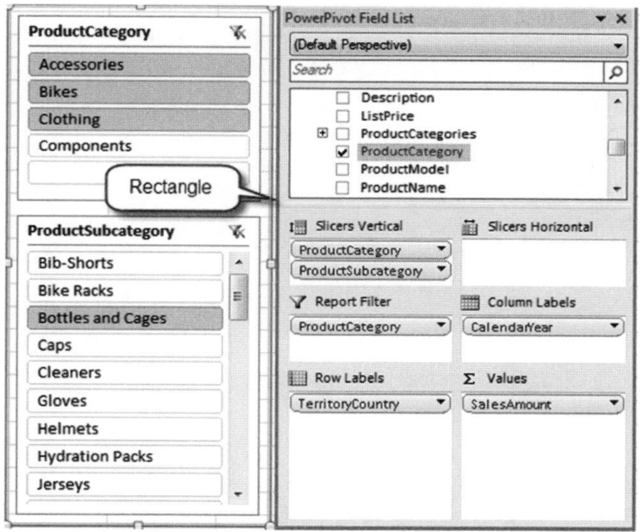


**Figure 5.11** The PowerPivot Field List includes slicer zones to facilitate configuring slicers with PowerPivot pivot reports.

When you add fields to a slicer zone, PowerPivot encloses the slicers in a bounding rectangle. Using PowerPivot Field List slicer zones has the following advantages:

- You can automatically arrange multiple slicers in a vertical and horizontal layout.
- You can rearrange the slicers within a zone by dragging them around.
- You can easily resize or move the slicers to a new location in the Excel worksheet by dragging the bounding rectangle.

Excel draws the bounding rectangle around the slicer zone only when you interact with the pivot report. To avoid clutter and to improve the report presentation, the rectangle disappears when you click outside the report. You won't be able to precisely configure the slicer size and position because the bounding rectangle auto-sizes the embedded slicers. If you find this too restricting, consider dragging the slicer outside the rectangle.

## 5.1.6 Understanding OLAP Pivot Features

Since PowerPivot reports are disguised online analytical processing (OLAP) pivot reports, you can use pivot features specific to OLAP. These features include named sets and cube formulas.

***Understanding named sets***

As its name suggests, a named set is an aliased set of column values. Suppose that you frequently analyze European sales. Instead of filtering every pivot report by territory, you need a predefined set that includes the countries assigned to you. This is where a named set could be useful. To create a named set:

1. Click any cell in the PowerPivot report to activate it. In the Options tab in the Excel ribbon, expand the "Fields, Items, & Sets" drop-down button (Calculations group) and click Manage Sets.
2. In the Set Manager dialog box, expand the New button, and then click "Create Set Based on Row Items" if you want to create a set based on a field that you added to the pivot Row Labels zone. Or, click "Create Set Based on Column Items" if you want to create a set based on a field that you added to the Column Labels zone.
3. In the New Set dialog box (see **Figure 5.12**), enter *My Territories* as a set name.
4. Remove the items that you don't need by selecting each item and clicking the Delete Row button.

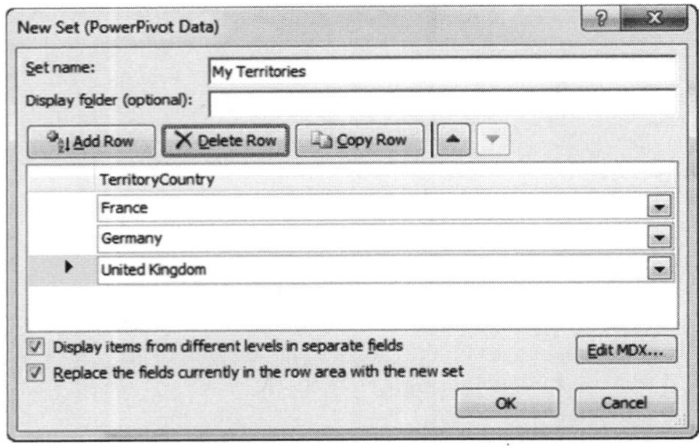


**Figure 5.12** You can create a named set for a subset of field values that you frequently analyze.

5. (Optional) Rearrange the items by clicking the up or down arrows. Click OK. Excel adds a new folder (Sets) in the PowerPivot Field List, and then adds the named set to it.

The named set is saved in the Excel workbook and can be used with any PowerPivot report in the workbook. Once the set is defined, you can add it to the Row Labels or Column Labels zones just like a regular field. With some knowledge of MDX, you can create more advanced named sets. To do so, use the Create Set using MDX option or click the Edit MDX button in the New Set dialog box. For example, the following MDX expression returns the top ten products whose standard cost exceeds $100.

```
TopCount(Exists([Product].[ProductName].[ProductName].Members,
Filter ([Product].[StandardCost].[StandardCost].Members,
[Product].[StandardCost].CurrentMember.MemberValue>100)), 10,
[Measures].[Sum of SalesAmount 2])
```

**NOTE** Since Tabular doesn't support member properties, the Filter function uses the MDX MemberValue property to filter the StandardCost column.

***Understanding cube formulas***

Although pivot reports are a great tool for quick interactive analysis, you might find their layout restrictive. For example, a pivot report won't let you insert a column or have a freeform layout. This is where cube formulas can help. With cube formulas, you can convert each cell of an OLAP pivot report to a formula. Once the pivot report is converted to formulas, it's no longer a pivot report and you can manipulate each cell individually. To convert a pivot report to formulas:

1. Click a cell on a pivot report.
2. In the Options tab in the Excel ribbon, expand the OLAP Tools drop-down button (Tools group), and then click "Convert to Formulas". If Excel asks you to confirm, accept the prompt.

**Figure 5.13** shows a pivot report converted to formulas. The original report layout is shown in **Figure 5.10**. Each report cell uses a special Excel function to look up a value from the model using MDX. For example, the CUBEVALUE function returns a single value given the current cell coordinates, such as the aggregated SalesAmount value for the United States in 2009. For more information about Excel cube formulas, read the "Cube Functions" blog post by the Excel team at http://bit.ly/cubformulas.

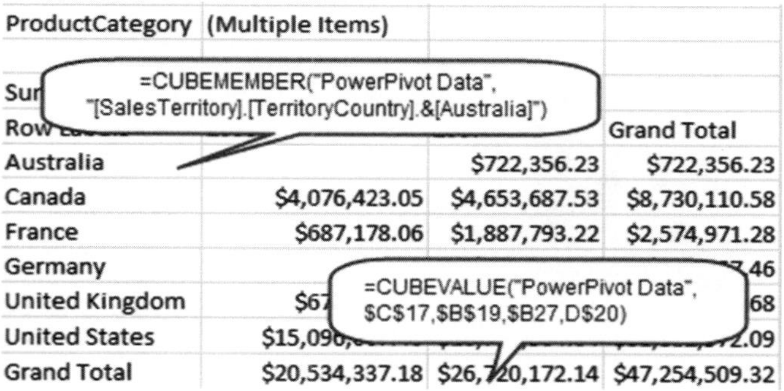

| ProductCategory | (Multiple Items) | | |
|---|---|---|---|
| Su[illegible] | | | |
| Row [illegible] | [illegible] | [illegible] | Grand Total |
| Australia | | $722,356.23 | $722,356.23 |
| Canada | $4,076,423.05 | $4,653,687.53 | $8,730,110.58 |
| France | $687,178.06 | $1,887,793.22 | $2,574,971.28 |
| Germany | [illegible] | [illegible] | [illegible].46 |
| United Kingdom | $67[illegible] | [illegible] | [illegible]68 |
| United States | $15,09[illegible] | [illegible] | [illegible].09 |
| Grand Total | $20,534,337.18 | $26,720,172.14 | $47,254,509.32 |

=CUBEMEMBER("PowerPivot Data", "[SalesTerritory].[TerritoryCountry].&[Australia]")

=CUBEVALUE("PowerPivot Data", $C$17,$B$19,$B27,D$20)

**Figure 5.13** Once a report is converted to formulas, each cell sends a query to the PowerPivot model.

Cube formulas can be useful to implement freeform reports, such as the summary report shown in **Figure 5.14**.

| Total Customers | Bike Buyers | Bike Buyers First Year |
|---|---|---|
| 18,484 | 9,132 | 1,013 |

**Figure 5.14** This freeform report uses cube formulas.

To plug in a cube formula in a cell, type in the function name in the Excel formula bar. Excel AutoComplete will show you the function arguments. In this case, I used the following formulas:

```
Total Customers
=CUBESETCOUNT(CUBESET("PowerPivot Data", "[Customer].[CustomerKey].[CustomerKey].Members"))

Bike Buyers
=CUBESETCOUNT(CUBESET("PowerPivot Data", "Exists([Customer].[CustomerKey].[CustomerKey].Members,
[Product].[ProductCategory].[Bikes],'InternetSales')"))

Bike Buyers First Year
=CUBESETCOUNT(CUBESET("PowerPivot Data", "Exists([Customer].[CustomerKey].[CustomerKey].Members,
[Product].[ProductCategory].[Bikes] * Head([Date].[CalendarYear].[CalendarYear].Members, 1), 'InternetSales')"))
```

The Total Customers formula uses the CUBESET function to return a set of all the customers. The CUBESETCOUNT function wraps the CUBESET function to calculate the set count. The Bike Buyers formula uses the MDX EXISTS function to return the subset of customers who have purchased bikes. To do so, the EXISTS function cross-joins all the customers with the Bikes product category via the InternetSales table, which stores the direct sales to customers. Finally, the Bike Buyers First Year formula works in the same way, but it further filters the results to the first year from the Date table.

## 5.2 Implementing Basic Pivot Reports

Next, you'll practice what you've learned about pivot reports, and you'll implement the Sales by Country report (see **Figure 5.15**) to analyze the Adventure Works reseller sales. This report is a combination of a PivotTable and PivotChart that are arranged vertically.

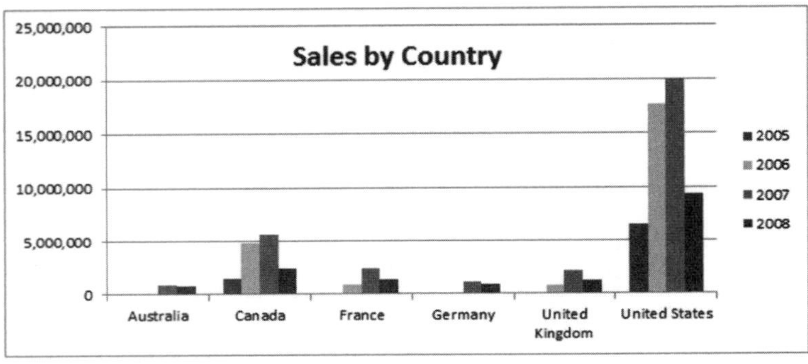


| ProductCategory | All |
|---|---|

| Sum of SalesAmount | Column Labels | | | | |
|---|---|---|---|---|---|
| Row Labels | 2005 | 2006 | 2007 | 2008 | Grand Total |
| Australia | | | $847,430.96 | $746,904.41 | $1,594,335.38 |
| Canada | $1,513,359.46 | $4,822,999.20 | $5,651,305.43 | $2,390,261.51 | $14,377,925.60 |
| France | | $857,123.18 | $2,373,804.04 | $1,376,610.72 | $4,607,537.94 |
| Germany | | | $1,098,866.68 | $885,121.35 | $1,983,988.04 |
| United Kingdom | | $841,757.76 | $2,160,145.83 | $1,277,105.23 | $4,279,008.83 |
| United States | $6,552,075.85 | $17,622,549.51 | $20,071,116.48 | $9,362,059.37 | $53,607,801.21 |
| Grand Total | $8,065,435.31 | $24,144,429.65 | $32,202,669.43 | $16,038,062.60 | $80,450,596.98 |

**Figure 5.15** The Sales by Country report consists of a chart section, which is implemented as a PivotChart, and a crosstab section, which is implemented with a PivotTable.

### 5.2.1 Implementing a PivotTable Report ▶

Start by creating the crosstab report that shows sales data grouped by country on rows and years on columns with the ability to filter the data by product category. This is a job for the Excel PivotTable component, and authoring such reports takes a few mouse clicks.

***Creating a report layout***

In this exercise, you'll use the Chart and Table (Vertical) report layout.

1. Open the Adventure Works workbook with your changes from Chapter 4.
2. Click the Excel ribbon's PowerPivot tab, and then click the PowerPivot Window button. The PowerPivot window opens.

3. On the Home ribbon tab, expand the PivotTable drop-down button, and then click the Chart and Table (Vertical) layout.
4. In the "Create PivotChart and PivotTable (Vertical)" dialog box that follows, select the Existing Worksheet option.
5. Click the Selector button, as shown in **Figure 5.16**. To place the report on the existing Sheet1, click Sheet1 to make it active, and then select the B2 cell. This is where the top-left corner of the report will be placed. Click OK to close the Range Selection dialog box, and then click OK to create the report.

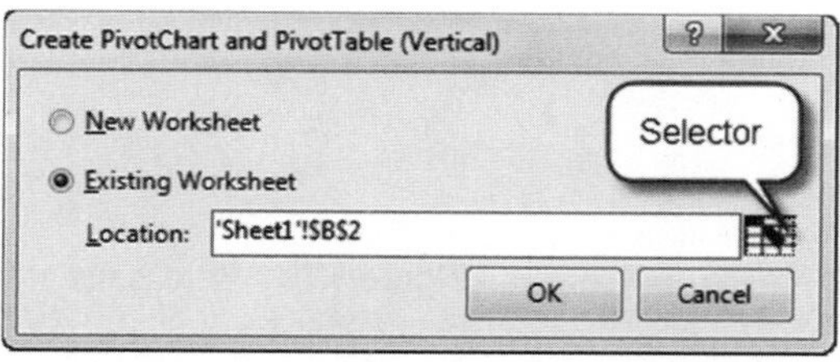


**Figure 5.16** Use the "Create PivotChart and PivotTable (Vertical)" dialog box to select a location for the report, which could be either a new worksheet or an existing worksheet.

PowerPivot creates a new report with empty PivotChart and PivotTable sections arranged vertically. It also adds a worksheet called "Data for Sheet1 Chart 1" that serves as a data source for the chart. The PivotTable report is active and the PowerPivot Field List shows the model metadata.

***Authoring the crosstab report***

Next, follow these steps to add data to PivotTable and create the crosstab report.

1. In the PowerPivot Field List, expand the ResellerSales table. Check the checkbox next to the SalesAmount field.
2. PivotTable shows a number that correspond to the grand total sales amount aggregated across all other tables, as shown in **Figure 5.17**.

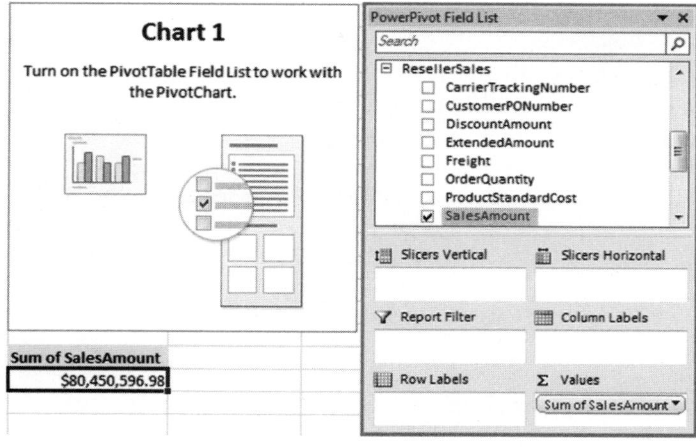


**Figure 5.17** The PivotTable report shows the grand total Sales Amount.

3. To show sales grouped by country on rows, in the PowerPivot Field List expand the SalesTerritory table, and then check the TerritoryCountry field. Or, you can right-click the TerritoryCountry field, and then click "Add to Row Labels". Or, you can simply drag the field to the Row Labels zone. If you make a mistake and the TerritoryCountry field ends up in a wrong zone, you can drag the field away to remove it from the zone and then drop it into the right zone.

4. To show the report data grouped by years on columns, expand the Date table in the PowerPivot Field List, and then drag the CalendarYear field to the Column Labels zone. Be sure to drag the field instead of checking its checkbox. If you check it, PowerPivot will add the CalendarYear field to the Values zone because it's numeric and because PowerPivot assumes that the field needs to be aggregated. Compare your results with **Figure 5.18**.
5. In the PowerPivot Field List, right-click the Sum of SalesAmount field in the Values zone, and then click Edit Measure. In the Measure Settings dialog box, enter *SalesAmount* as a custom name to rename the field. Or, you can double-click the Sum of SalesAmount cell in the report and rename it in place.

| Sum of SalesAmount | Column Labels | | | | |
|---|---|---|---|---|---|
| Row Labels | 2005 | 2006 | 2007 | 2008 | Grand Total |
| Australia | | | $847,430.96 | $746,904.41 | $1,594,335.38 |
| Canada | $1,513,359.46 | $4,822,999.20 | $5,651,305.43 | $2,390,261.51 | $14,377,925.60 |
| France | | $857,123.18 | $2,373,804.04 | $1,376,610.72 | $4,607,537.94 |
| Germany | | | $1,098,866.68 | $885,121.35 | $1,983,988.04 |
| United Kingdom | | $841,757.76 | $2,160,145.83 | $1,277,105.23 | $4,279,008.83 |
| United States | $6,552,075.85 | $17,622,549.51 | $20,071,116.48 | $9,362,059.37 | $53,607,801.21 |
| Grand Total | $8,065,435.31 | $24,144,429.65 | $32,202,669.43 | $16,038,062.60 | $80,450,596.98 |

**Figure 5.18** Here is the report after adding the SalesAmount, TerritoryCountry, and Year fields.

6. To filter data by product category, in the PowerPivot Field List, expand the Product table, and then drag the ProductCategory field to the Report Filter zone. At this point, your PivotTable report should look like the one shown in **Figure 5.15**.
7. Expand the ProductCategory drop-down list on the report, and then select "Bikes" to filter the report to show only data for the Bikes product category.
8. Suppose you want to see the level of details behind a cell, such as to understand which rows contribute to the Australia sales for the year 2007. Right-click that cell, and then click Show Details.

   Notice that PowerPivot adds a new worksheet that shows the first 1,000 rows contributing to that cell. As I mentioned in Section 5.1.4, you can use the connection properties to display more rows if needed. Notice also that the drillthrough sheet shows all columns from the ResellerSales table including hidden columns. Unlike Multidimensional, PowerPivot doesn't support custom drillthrough actions for you to request columns from other tables. As a workaround, you can add calculated columns to the ResellerSales table to bring related columns from other tables that you want the user to see when drilling through. Another limitation of drillthrough actions is that you can't customize the column headers on the drillthrough sheet, such as "Order Date" instead of "[ResellerSales].[$Date.Date]".
9. (Optional) Expand the "Row Labels and Column Labels" drop-down lists to select specific countries and years.

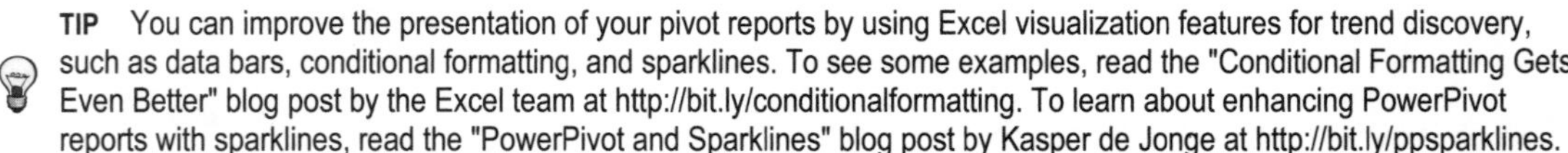

**TIP** You can improve the presentation of your pivot reports by using Excel visualization features for trend discovery, such as data bars, conditional formatting, and sparklines. To see some examples, read the "Conditional Formatting Gets Even Better" blog post by the Excel team at http://bit.ly/conditionalformatting. To learn about enhancing PowerPivot reports with sparklines, read the "PowerPivot and Sparklines" blog post by Kasper de Jonge at http://bit.ly/ppsparklines.

### 5.2.2 Implementing a PivotChart Report ▶

Next, you'll author the chart section to help you visualize the data in the crosstab report. Although a PivotChart can be completely independent from the PivotTable report and show different data, your chart will show the same information as the PivotTable report.

***Adding data to the chart***
Follow similar steps to author the chart report.

1. Click anywhere in the PivotChart section to select it. Notice that the PowerPivot Field List refreshes and no fields are selected because the chart is empty. In addition, the PowerPivot Field List zones have different names that correspond to the chart areas. For example, the Column Labels zone has been renamed to the Legend Fields (Series) zone.
2. Check the SalesAmount field in the ResellerSales table.
3. Expand the SalesTerritory table. Drag the TerritoryCountry field, and then drop it in the Axis Fields (Categories) zone.
4. To show the chart data grouped by years, expand the Date table in the PowerPivot Field List, and then drag the CalendarYear field to the Legend Fields (Series) zone.
5. To filter data by product category, in the PowerPivot Field List expand the Product table, and then drag the ProductCategory field to the Report Filter zone.

***Refining the chart appearance***
Let's spend some time improving the chart appearance.

1. Right-click the Y-axis (the vertical chart axis), and then click Format Axis.
2. In the Format Axis dialog box, click the Number tab. Select the Number category, and then check the "Use 1000 Separator (,)" checkbox if it's not checked. Enter *0* in the Decimal Places field. Click Close.
3. Double-click the chart title, and then enter *Sales by Country*. If the chart doesn't have a title, select the chart, click the Excel Layout menu, expand the Chart Title drop-down button, and then click Centered Overlay Title. Move the title as necessary.
4. Right-click any of the gray field buttons, and then click Hide All Field Buttons on Chart.
5. Resize the chart area to align it with the PivotTable component.
6. Rename the Sheet1 worksheet to *Sales by Country*.
7. Rename the "Data for Sheet1 Chart 1" worksheet to *Sales by Country Chart Data*. Right-click the *Sales by Country Chart Data* worksheet, and then click Hide to hide it from end users.

## 5.3 Implementing Dashboards

Similar to an automobile's dashboard, a business intelligence (BI) digital dashboard enables users to get a "bird's eye view" of the company's health and performance. A dashboard page typically hosts several sections that display data visually in charts, graphs, or gauges, so that data is easier to understand and analyze. You can use PowerPivot to create dashboard pages consisting of PivotTable and PivotChart reports. And, as with any Excel report, once you deploy the workbook to SharePoint, the dashboard becomes immediately available to all users who have SharePoint rights to view it.

**NOTE** Excel isn't the only Microsoft-provided tool that can be used to create a dashboard connected to a PowerPivot model. For example, a BI pro might favor PerformancePoint Services, which is bundled with SharePoint Server 2010 Enterprise edition, to implement balanced scorecards. Or, a BI pro can use Reporting Services to author dashboard-looking reports.

## 5.3.1 Creating a Dashboard Report ▶

In this practice, you'll implement the dashboard page shown in **Figure 5.19**. This dashboard page includes four chart sections and two slicers arranged vertically to filter data by year and month.

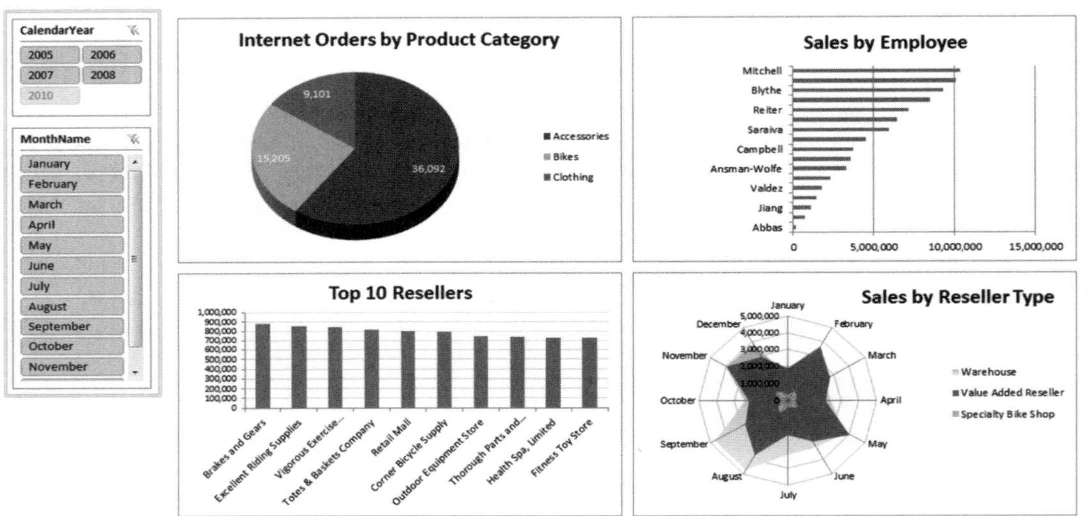


**Figure 5.19** This dashboard page includes four charts and slicers.

***Implementing the Internet Orders by Product Category chart***

Start by implementing the Internet Orders by Product Category chart. This pie chart displays the number of orders grouped by product category.

1. In the PowerPivot window (Home ribbon tab), expand the PivotTable drop-down menu, and then click Four Charts.
2. In the "Create Four PivotCharts" dialog box that follows, select the Existing Worksheet option. Click the Selector button, click the Sheet2 tab, and then click the B2 cell. Click OK. PowerPivot adds four empty PivotChart charts to the Sheet2 worksheet. In addition, PowerPivot creates four new worksheets to supply data for the charts. Click the Sheet2 tab if it's not active.
3. Right-click Chart 1, and then click Change Chart Type. In the Change Chart Type dialog box, select the Pie chart type. In the Pie section in the right pane, click the second pie variation (Pie in 3-D), and then click OK. Don't worry that the chart appearance doesn't change. That's because the chart zones are not configured yet.
4. With the chart selected, in the PowerPivot Field List, expand the InternetSales table. Check the OrderQuantity field to add this field to the Values zone.
5. In the PowerPivot Field List, expand the Product table, and then check the ProductCategory field to add it to the Axis Fields (Categories) zone.

6. Assuming you want to remove empty product categories, expand the ProductCategory drop-down field in the chart area, and then uncheck the last checkbox.
7. Right-click the chart, and then click 3-D Rotation. In the Format Chart Area dialog box, set the Y angle to 50 and the perspective to 0.1. Click Close.
8. Right-click the chart and click Add Data Labels.
9. Right-click any of the data labels, and then click Font. In the Font dialog box, change the font color to white and the font style to bold. Click Close.
10. Right-click any of the data labels in the pie chart, and then click Format Data Labels. In the Format Data Labels dialog box, click the Number tab. In the right pane, click the Number category, and then enter 0 in the Decimal Places field. Click Close.
11. Click the white area around the pie chart, but make you click close to the pie chart to select the chart. Resize the chart as needed.
12. Right-click the chart title, and then click Edit Text in the context menu. Enter *Internet Orders by Product Category*.
13. Compare your results with **Figure 5.20**.

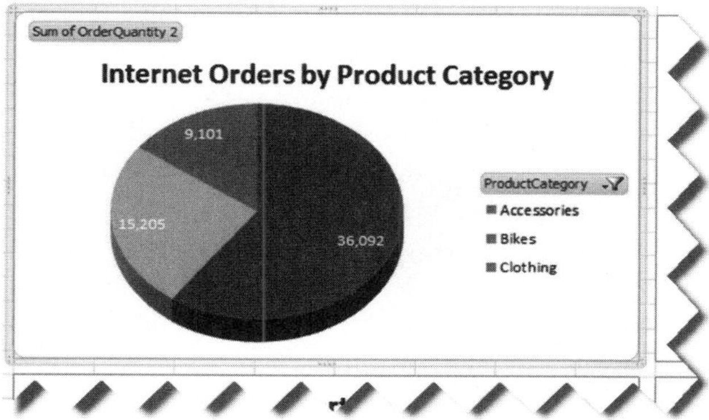


**Figure 5.20** Here is the finished Internet Orders by Product Category chart.

***Implementing the Top 10 Resellers chart***

Next, you'll implement the Top 10 Resellers Chart in the Chart 2 section.

1. Click Chart 2 to select it.
2. In the PowerPivot Field List, expand the ResellerSales table. Check the SalesAmount field to add it to the Values zone.
3. In the PowerPivot Field List, expand the Reseller table, and then check the ResellerName field to add it to the Axis Fields (Categories) zone.
4. In the chart area, expand the ResellerName drop-down field. Click the Value Filter option, and then click Top 10. In the Top 10 Filter dialog box that follows, click OK to accept the default settings.
5. To sort resellers in descending order of sales, expand the ResellerName drop-down list again, and then click More Sort Options. In the Sort (ResellerName) dialog box, select the Descending option (Z to A). Expand the drop-down list below it, and then select Sum of Sales Amount. Click OK.
6. Click the chart legend to select it, and then press the Delete key to remove the legend.
7. Right-click the chart title, and then click Edit Text. Enter *Top 10 Resellers*.

8. Right-click the Y-axis, and then click Format Axis. In the Format Axis dialog box, click the Number tab. In the right pane, click the Number category, and then enter 0 in the Decimal Places field. Click Close. Compare your results with **Figure 5.21**.

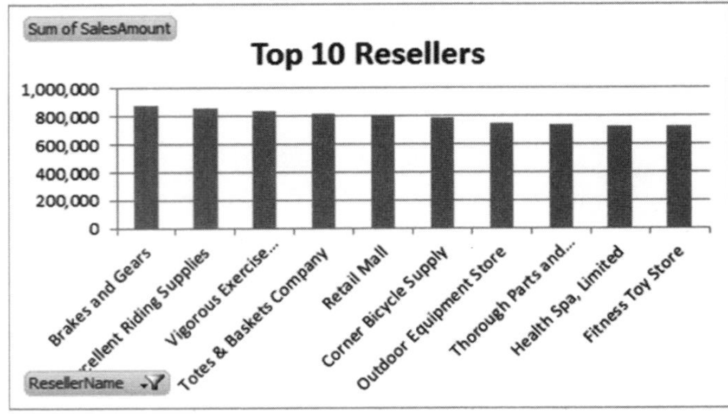


**Figure 5.21** Here is the finished Top 10 Resellers chart.

***Implementing the Sales by Employee chart***

The Sales by Employee chart shows the sales by the Adventure Works sales persons.

1. Click Chart 3 to select it, and then change the chart type to Bar (Clustered Bar).
2. In the PowerPivot Field List, expand the ResellerSales table. Check the SalesAmount field to add it to the Values zone.
3. In the PowerPivot Field List, expand the Employee table, and then check the LastName field to add it to the Axis Fields (Categories) zone.
4. To sort employees in descending order of sales, expand the LastName drop-down list, and then click More Sort Options. In the Sort (ResellerName) dialog box, select the Ascending option (A to Z). Expand the drop-down list below it, and then select Sum of Sales Amount. Click OK.
5. Click the chart legend inside the chart area to select it, and then press the Delete key to remove the legend.
6. Right-click the chart title, and then click Edit Text. Enter *Sales by Employee*.
7. Right-click the X-axis, and then click Format Axis. In the Format Axis dialog box, click the Number tab. In the right pane, click the Number category, and then type *0* in the Decimal Places field. Click Close. Compare your results with **Figure 5.22**.

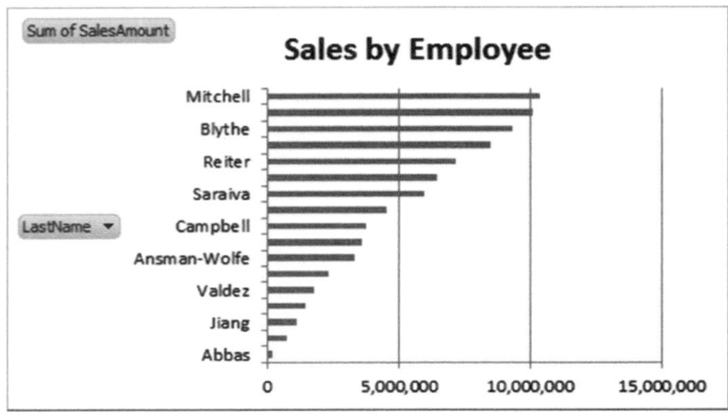


**Figure 5.22** Here is the finished Sales by Employee chart.

***Implementing the Sales by Reseller Type chart***

A radar chart helps you analyze data by several subject areas. The Sales by Reseller Type chart is implemented as a radar chart that shows the reseller sales by reseller type grouped by months.

1. Change the Chart 4 chart to Radar (Filled Radar).
2. Click Chart 4 to select it.
3. In the PowerPivot Field List, locate the ResellerSales table. Check the SalesAmount field to add it to the Values zone.
4. In the PowerPivot Field List, expand the Date table, and then check the MonthName field to add it to the Axis Fields (Categories) zone.
5. In the PowerPivot Field List, expand the Reseller table. Drag the BusinessType field, and then drop it onto the Legend Fields (Series) zone.
6. To bring resellers with least sales on top, right-click the chart series (the colored area), click Sort and Filter, and then click More Sort Options. In the Sort dialog box, select the Descending option (Z to A). Expand the drop-down list below it, and then select Sum of SalesAmount. Click OK.
7. Right-click the chart series again, and then click Format Data Series. In the Format Data Series dialog box, click the Marker Fill tab. In the right pane, select the Gradient Fill option, and then click Close.
8. Format the chart axis to show the sales numbers as Number with no decimal places.
9. Right-click the Y-axis labels, and then click the Font menu. Decrease the Y-axis label font to 8 pt.
10. Increase the chart plot area to occupy as much space on the chart as possible.
11. Select the Excel Layout menu. Expand the Chart Title drop-down list, and then select Centered Overlay Title. Once the title is added to the chart, move the title to an empty spot so it doesn't overlay the chart. Change the title text to *Sales by Reseller Type*. Compare your results with **Figure 5.23**. Don't worry that months sort alphabetically instead of by their natural order, such as January, February, March, and so on. We will fix it in Section 5.4.

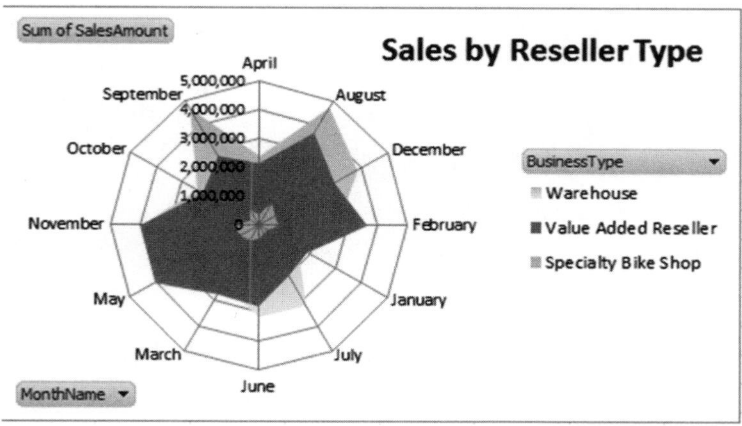


**Figure 5.23** Here is the finished Sales by Reseller Type chart.

## 5.3.2 Working with Slicers ▶

Excel slicers are attached at the database connection level. As a result, a slicer can filter all PivotTable and PivotChart reports in the workbook. PowerPivot further extends Excel slicers by adding slicer zones in the PowerPivot Field List.

***Adding slicers***

PowerPivot supports vertical and horizontal slicer layouts. Follow these steps to add two slicers to filter data by year and month.

1. In the PowerPivot Field List, expand the Date table.
2. Drag the CalendarYear field, and then drop it on the Slicers Vertical zone. PowerPivot creates a new slicer zone with a vertical layout to the left of the report area and adds the CalendarYear field to it. Notice that the 2010 value appears grayed out because it there is no data in the InternetSales table for year 2010.
3. The slicer shows all the years and the user can click a year or multiple years to filter the data. By default, all the years are selected. To try slicer filtering, click 2007 to filter data for that year only. Click the Clear Filter button to remove the filter and to show the data for all years.
4. You can add multiple slicers. In the PowerPivot Field List, drag the MonthName field to the Slicers Vertical zone, and then drop it after the CalendarYear field. PowerPivot adds a second slicer below the CalendarYear field in the vertical zone.

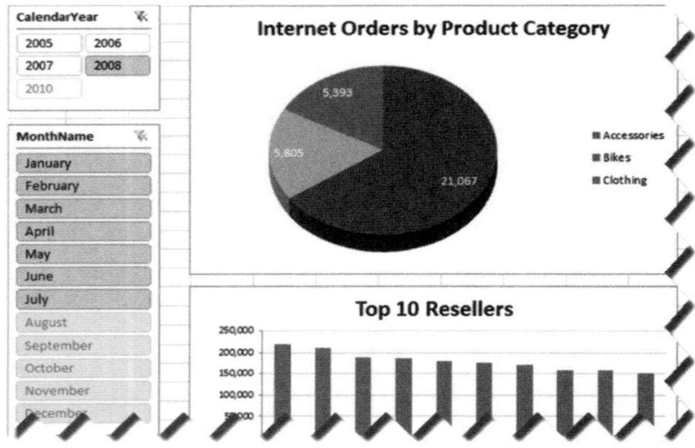


**Figure 5.24** Selecting a year in the CalendarYear slicer cross-filters the MonthName slicer.

5. Slicers can be cross-filtered. Click 2008 in the CalendarYear slicer. Notice that the MonthName slicer highlights a few months, as shown in **Figure 5.24**. That's because the PowerPivot application has data for these months only in the year 2008.
6. Click the Clear Filter buttons in the CalendarYear and MonthName slicers to clear all the filters.

***Cleaning up***

Let's spend some time cleaning up the Excel reports and improving their visual appearance.

1. Rename the Sheet2 worksheet to *Dashboard*.
2. Hide the following four supporting worksheets: "Data for Sheet 2 Chart 1", "Data for Sheet 2 Chart 2", "Data for Sheet 2 Chart 3", and "Data for Sheet 2 Chart 4" supporting worksheets.

3. Click the Internet Orders by Product Category chart (the first chart you created) to select it. In the Analyze tab in the Excel ribbon, expand the Field Buttons drop-down list, and then check the Hide All option to hide all the fields in the chart area.
4. Repeat the last step to hide all of the fields for the other three charts. Unfortunately, you can't select the remaining charts to apply formatting changes to all the selected charts at once. Instead, you must apply the changes one chart at the time.

## 5.4 Implementing End-User Features

This release of PowerPivot packs additional capabilities for you to implement end-user features that further enrich the model. This section discusses features that don't require the Data Analysis Expressions DAX experience, including configuring a Date table, custom sorting, perspectives and hierarchies. Chapter 6 covers key performance indicators (KPIs) and advanced relationships.

### 5.4.1 Working with Dates ▶

Most models require analyzing data by time, such as to show sales by quarters. Follow these best practices (as with Multidimensional) to work with dates in Tabular:

- Date table – While online transactional processing (OLTP) systems almost never have a designated Date table, analytical models can benefit greatly from having one. A separate Date table includes additional columns for flexible time exploration, such as Quarter, Year, Fiscal Quarter, Fiscal Year, Holiday Flag, and so on.
- Day granularity – Your Date table should have a day granularity. If you need to analyze data by time, add a separate table with the time fractions you need, such as Hour, Minute, Second, and so on.
- Continuous dates – Your Date table should contain a continuous range of dates to support time calculations, such as parallel period or previous period.
- Date type column – The Date table must include a column of the date type so that you can mark the table as a Date table. This column must come from the data source, and it can't be a calculated column.

**NOTE** Unlike Multidimensional, Tabular doesn't include a feature to auto-generate a server Date table or to auto-generate and populate a dimension table with dates. As a best practice, you should include a separate Date table in a Tabular model. If you can't obtain this table from a data warehouse database, you can create an Excel table as I demonstrated in Chapter 2. Or, you can import the Date table from the DateStream feed in the Azure Marketplace as SQL Server MVP, Boyan Penev, explains in his "Introducing Project DateStream" blog post at http://bit.ly/datestream.

You can configure multiple tables as Date tables if needed. This could be useful when you need to analyze your model by multiple dates, such as by OrderDate, ShipDate, and DueDate, and you decide to import a table with dates multiple times instead of configuring role-playing relationships.

***Why configure a Data table?***

Marking a table as a Date table achieves two things. First, DAX calculations for implementing time intelligence won't require you to explicitly reference the Date table as an argument. Second, Excel pivot reports enable date filters for all the columns in the Date Table, such as a filter to use relative dates (see **Figure 5.25**).

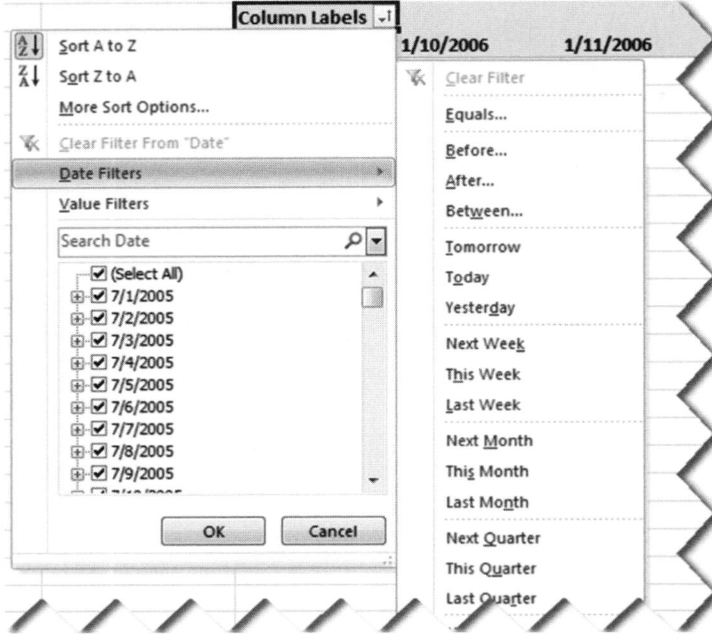


**Figure 5.25** Excel enables date filters for all the columns in a table marked as a Date table.

Let's now discuss additional settings that are specific to Date tables.

***Configuring a Date table***

Follow these steps to configure a Date table in the Adventure Works model:

1. In the PowerPivot Window (Data View), click the Date table tab.
2. In the Design ribbon tab, expand the Mark as Date Table button, and then click Mark as Date Table. The "Mark as Date Table" dialog box opens, as shown in **Figure 5.26**.
3. Expand the Date drop-down list, and then select the column that's of the date type. In our case this is the Date column. Click OK.

If you want to change the Date table settings later on, expand the Mark as Date Table button, and then click Date Table Settings to open the "Mark as Date Table" dialog box. Or, if you want to reconfigure the Date table as a regular table, expand the Mark as Date Table button, and then click the "Mark as Date Table" checkbox to uncheck it.

***Understanding custom sorting***

By default, PowerPivot sorts column values in ascending order. In most cases, this is the expected behavior. For example, a report that shows sales by products should probably show the products sorted in ascending order by name. In some cases, however, the default sorting behavior isn't desirable. For example, the Sales by Reseller Type chart report (see **Figure 5.23** again) sorts the months in alphabetical order. However, chances are that you would need the months sorted in their natural order.

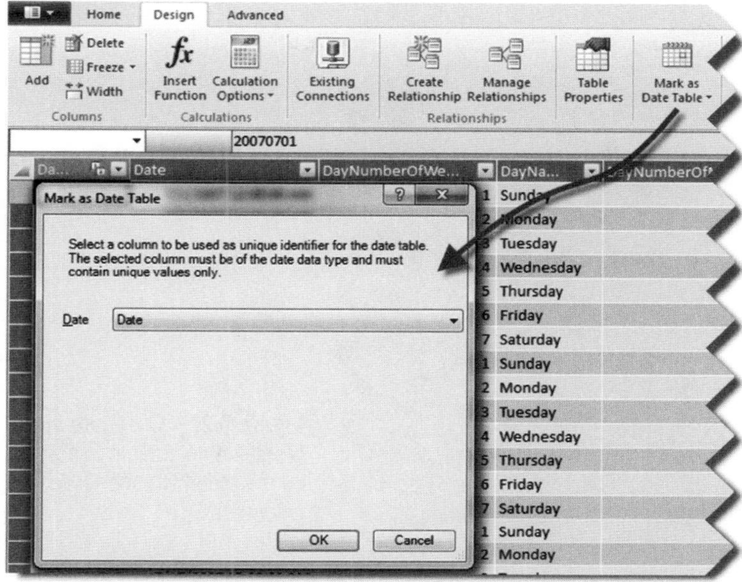


**Figure 5.26** To mark a Date table, specify a column of the date type.

Fortunately, PowerPivot allows you sort the values of a column by another column. To get the right sort order, the column you're sorting by must have the same granularity as the sorted column. For example, if the sorted column is MonthName with the values of January, February, and so on, and you want to sort months in their natural order, then you would need an integer column that returns the month ordinal number, such as 1 for January, 2 for February, or so on. If the MonthName column combines the month and year, such as Jan 2008, Feb 2008, and so on, then the column to sort by should have integer values that combines the year and the month, such as 200801, 200802, and so on. Note that Chapter 2 demonstrated the latter scenario in Section 2.1.3.

**NOTE** The Multidimensional equivalent of PowerPivot custom sorting is setting the OrderBy and OrderByAttribute properties to configure attribute sorting by another attribute. However, unlike Multidimensional, which uses attribute relationships to detect the sort order, Tabular requires that the two columns have the same granularity.

Follow these steps to sort columns in the Date table in their natural order:

1. In the PowerPivot window (Data View), click the Date tab to activate the Date table.
2. Click the column header of the MonthName column to select it.
3. In the Home ribbon tab, click the Sort by Column button.
4. In the Sort by Column dialog box, expand the right drop-down list, and then select the MonthNumberOfYear column to sort the MonthName column in the same order, as shown in **Figure 5.27**. You can't select the DateKey column or the Date column as a sorting column because it has lower granularity. Click OK.
5. (Optional) Repeat the same steps to set up the sort order for other columns in the Date table and other tables if needed.

If later on you want to remove the custom sort order, select the column, expand the Sort by Column drop-down list, and then click Clear Sort by Column.

**Figure 5.27** Configure the MonthName column to sort by the MonthNumberOfYear column.

## 5.4.2 Working with Perspectives ▶

As the number of tables increase, your model might become difficult to understand and navigate, especially if you plan to deploy it to SharePoint and allow other users to create reports from it. How will the user know which tables are related when building a report? This is where perspectives can help.

***Understanding perspectives***

A perspective represents a subset of the model metadata. Its main purpose is to reduce the perceived complexity of a busy model and to expose a subset of the model metadata. For example, if you frequently analyze the Adventure Works reseller sales, you can define a perspective that includes only the ResellerSales fact table and its associated lookup tables. The model always includes a default perspective that exposes the entire schema.

**NOTE** Tabular perspectives fulfill the same role as perspectives in Multidimensional. In both models, perspectives are not a security mechanism and you can't use them to enforce restricted access to parts of the model. From an end-user standpoint, perspectives are entirely optional.

A perspective can include the following objects: entire tables, columns, hierarchies, measures, and KPIs. By default, new objects are created in the default perspective and they're not added to the user-defined perspectives. For example, when you create a new calculated column, the column is assigned to the default perspective, but it's not added to any user-defined perspectives although you might have prior selected the entire table to be included in the perspective. You must explicitly assign new objects to a perspective if you want them to be included in that perspective.

***Implementing perspectives***

PowerPivot considers perspectives an advanced feature that doesn't show in the default ribbon configuration. Follow these steps to create Internet Sales and Reseller Sales perspectives:

1. In the PowerPivot window, expand the drop-down menu in the Quick Access toolbar, and then click Switch to Advanced Mode (see **Figure 5.28**).

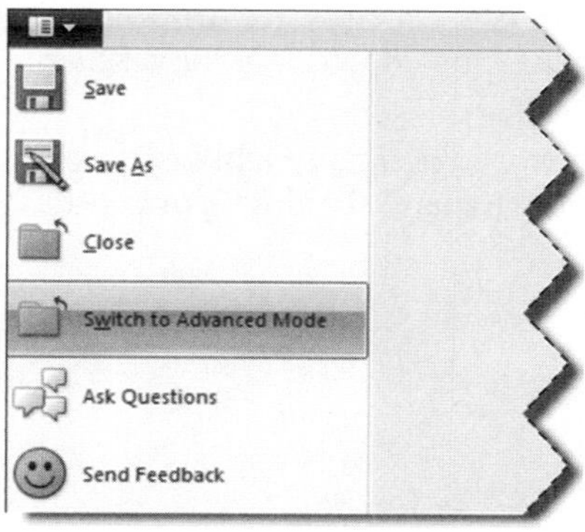


**Figure 5.28** PowerPivot supports advanced properties, including perspectives and reporting properties.

2. PowerPivot adds a new Advanced tab to the ribbon. Click the Advanced ribbon tab, and then click the Perspectives button.
3. Click the New Perspective button. Type in *Reseller Sales* as a name for the new perspective, and then press Enter.
4. Check the Currency, Date, Employee, Product, Reseller, ResellerSales, and SalesTerritory tables.
5. Follow similar steps to create an Internet Sales perspective that includes the Currency, Customer, Date, Geography, Internet Sales, Product, and Sales Territory tables. Compare your results with **Figure 5.29**.

   If you point the mouse cursor to the column header of a perspective, PowerPivot displays three buttons so that you can delete, rename, or copy that perspective. Click OK to close the Perspectives dialog box.

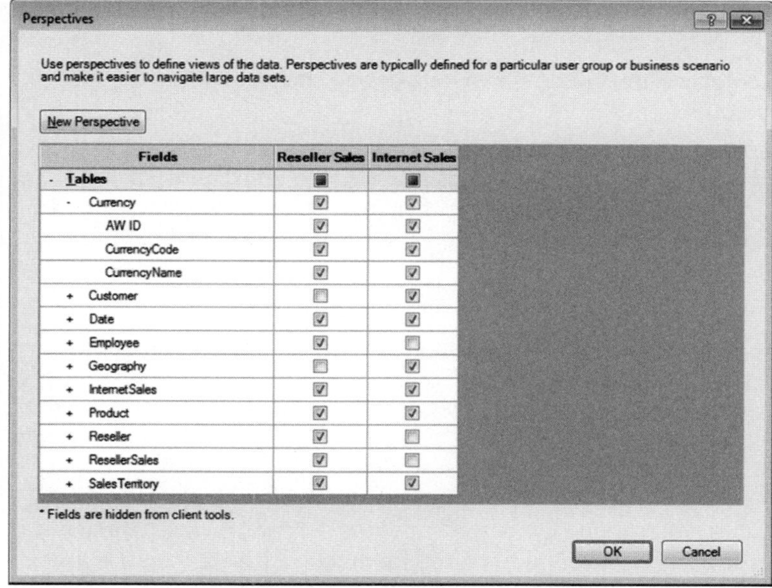


**Figure 5.29** The Reseller Sales and Internet Sales perspectives include specific tables.

***Testing perspectives***
You can test perspectives with Diagram View and with Excel pivot reports.

1. To test the new perspectives, switch to Diagram View. Expand the Select Perspective drop-down list, and then select the Reseller Sales perspective. Note that that diagram shows only the reseller-related objects.
2. To test perspectives with Excel, create a pivot report. Notice that the PowerPivot Field List recognizes perspectives and adds a drop-down list at the top of the pane. Expand the drop-down list, and then select the Reseller Sales perspective, as shown in **Figure 5.30**.

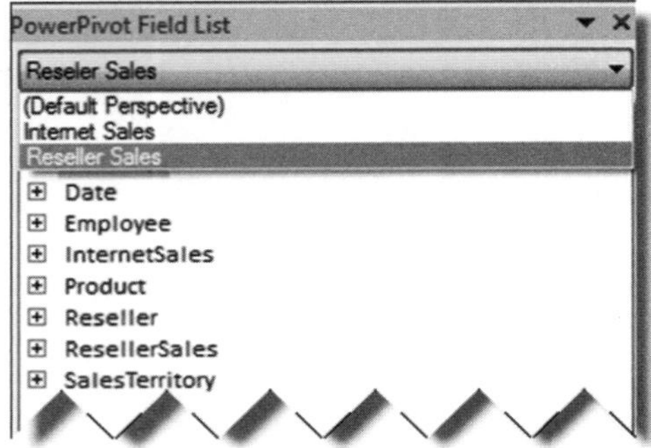


**Figure 5.30** Use the PowerPivot Field List to select a perspective.

Notice that the PowerPivot Field List filters the metadata to show only the objects included in the Reseller Sales perspective.

## 5.4.3 Working with Hierarchies ▶

A hierarchy is a combination of columns that defines a navigational drilldown path in the model. Tabular is a flexible model that allows you to use any column for slicing and dicing data in related tables. However, some columns form logical navigational paths for data exploration and drill-down. You can define hierarchies to group such columns. A hierarchy offers two important benefits:

- Usability – You can add all columns for drilling down data in one click by adding the hierarchy instead of individual columns.
- Performance – Suppose you drag a high-cardinality column, such as CustomerName, to a pivot report. You might end up with a huge report. This might cause unnecessary performance degradation. Instead, you can hide the Customer field and you can define a hierarchy with levels, such as State, City, and Customer levels, to enforce this navigational path for browsing data by customers.

***Understanding hierarchies***
The easiest way to understand a hierarchy is to see it in action, such in the pivot report shown in **Figure 5.31**. Suppose that the Product table in the PowerPivot Field List includes a ProductCategories hierarchy with Category, Subcategory, and Product levels. Once you add the hierarchy to the report, you can drill-down data by expanding its levels. A hierarchy can include columns from a single table only. If you have a snowflake schema with cascading relationships, such as InternetSales ⇨ Customer ⇨ Geography, and you want to form a hierarchy with columns from the Customer and Geography tables, you can use calculated columns to "denormalize" these relationships, and then bring the Geography columns in the Customer table. Chapter 6 demonstrates this technique.

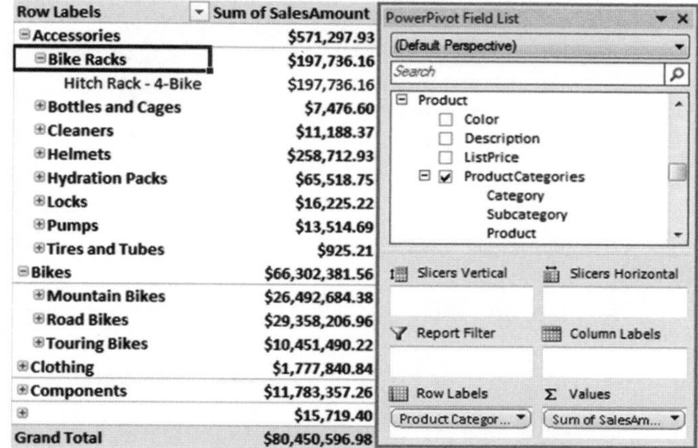

| Row Labels | Sum of SalesAmount |
|---|---|
| ⊟Accessories | $571,297.93 |
| ⊟Bike Racks | $197,736.16 |
| Hitch Rack - 4-Bike | $197,736.16 |
| ⊞Bottles and Cages | $7,476.60 |
| ⊞Cleaners | $11,188.37 |
| ⊞Helmets | $258,712.93 |
| ⊞Hydration Packs | $65,518.75 |
| ⊞Locks | $16,225.22 |
| ⊞Pumps | $13,514.69 |
| ⊞Tires and Tubes | $925.21 |
| ⊟Bikes | $66,302,381.56 |
| ⊞Mountain Bikes | $26,492,684.38 |
| ⊞Road Bikes | $29,358,206.96 |
| ⊞Touring Bikes | $10,451,490.22 |
| ⊞Clothing | $1,777,840.84 |
| ⊞Components | $11,783,357.26 |
| ⊞ | $15,719.40 |
| Grand Total | $80,450,596.98 |



**Figure 5.31** Hierarchies encourage users to follow common navigational paths in the model and to facilitate drilldown.

Typically, a hierarchy combines columns with logical one-to-many relationships, such as one year can have multiple quarters, and one quarter can have multiple months. This doesn't have to be the case though. For example, you can create a reporting hierarchy with ProductModel, Size, and Product columns, if you wish to analyze products that way.

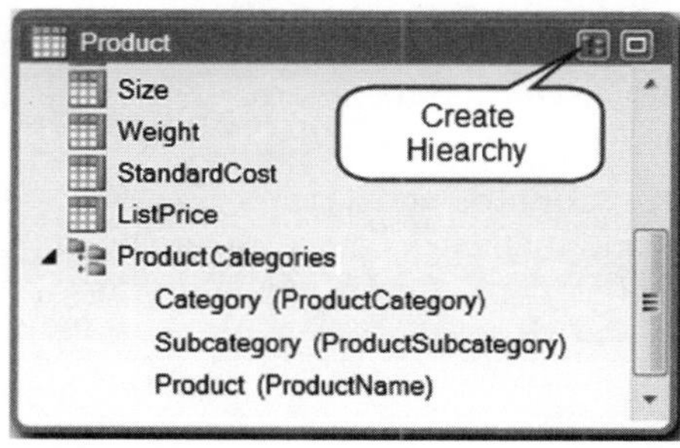



**Figure 5.32** You can use the Create Hierarchy button to create an empty hierarchy.

You can use Diagram View to create hierarchies. One way to set up a hierarchy is to click the Create Hierarchy button found in the top-right corner of the table, as shown in **Figure 5.32**. This creates an empty hierarchy called Hiearchy1. Then, you can select one or more columns, right-click the selection, and then click Add to Hierarchy ⇨ Hiearchy1. A faster approach is to select the columns first, right-click the selection, and then click Create Hierarchy.

When you use the multi-select technique, PowerPivot detects the cardinality of the columns and attempts to order the levels in a correct way. You should review the hierarchy levels and reorder them if necessary. To change the level order, right-click the level and click Move Up or Move Down. Or, you can simply drag the level to the desired position in the hierarchy. The level name doesn't need to match the column name. To rename a level, right-click it, and then click Rename.

Once you have a hierarchy in place, you might want to hide high-cardinality columns in order to prevent the user from adding them directly to the report and to avoid performance issues. For example, you might not want to expose the Date column in the Date table, in order to avoid allowing users to add it to a report outside the hierarchies it participates in. To do so, right-click the Date level in the hierarchy, and then click "Hide Source Column Name". Or, right-click the Date column in the table (the one outside any hierarchies) and click "Hide from Client Tools".

**NOTE** Readers familiar with Multidimensional might remember that an important optimization technique when setting up a dimension is to define attribute relationships among attributes with logical one-to-many relationships. In that process, the modeler has to set up unique and sometimes composite attribute keys, such as (City, State, and Country) to configure each city to be unique with respect to its state and country. This complexity disappears with Tabular and you don't need to set up intra-column relationships within a table. However, you lose some flexibility, such as the ability to use multiple key columns to properly differentiate two people named "John Smith".

### *Implementing hierarchies*

You must use Diagram View to work with hierarchies. Follow these steps to implement the ProductCategories and SalesTerritories hierarchies:

1. In the PowerPivot window, click the Home ribbon tab, and then click the Diagram View button to switch to Diagram View.
2. Make sure that the Select Perspective drop-down list shows the Default perspective. That's because new hierarchies are assigned to the active perspective. For example, if you create a hierarchy with the Reseller Sales perspective selected, the hierarchy won't show up in the Internet Sales perspective.
3. Zoom to the Product table and click the Create Hierarchy button.
4. Double-click the new Hierarchy1 hierarchy and rename it to *ProductCategories*.
5. Right-click the ProductCategory column and click Add to Hierarchy ⇨ ProductCategories. Add also the ProductSubcategory and ProductName columns to the hierarchy.
6. Right-click the ProductCategory level in the ProductCategories hierarchy, click Rename, and then type in *Category*. Rename the ProductSubcategory level to *Subcategory* and the ProductName level to *Product*. Compare your results with **Figure 5.32**.
7. Hold the Ctrl key, and then select the TerritoryGroup, TerritoryCountry, and TerritoryRegion columns in the SalesTerritory table. Right-click the selection, and then click Create Hierarchy in the context menu. Rename the new hierarchy in place to *SalesTerritories*. Compare you results with **Figure 5.33**.

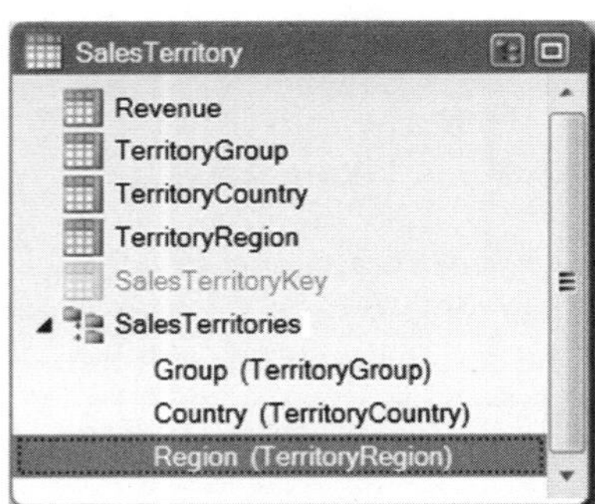


**Figure 5.33** The SalesTerritories hierarchy includes Year, Semester, Quarter, Month, and Date attributes.

8. Because you created the two hierarchies in the default perspective, they're not automatically assigned to the Reseller Sales and Internet Sales perspectives. Click the Advanced ribbon tab, and then click the Perspectives button. Check the checkboxes of the Product and Sales Territories tables for both perspectives to re-assign the entire tables, including the new hierarchies, to the user-defined perspectives.
9. (Optional) Create a PivotTable report to test the new hierarchies. For example, create a pivot report that has the Sales Territories hierarchy in the Row Labels zone, as shown in **Figure 5.34**.

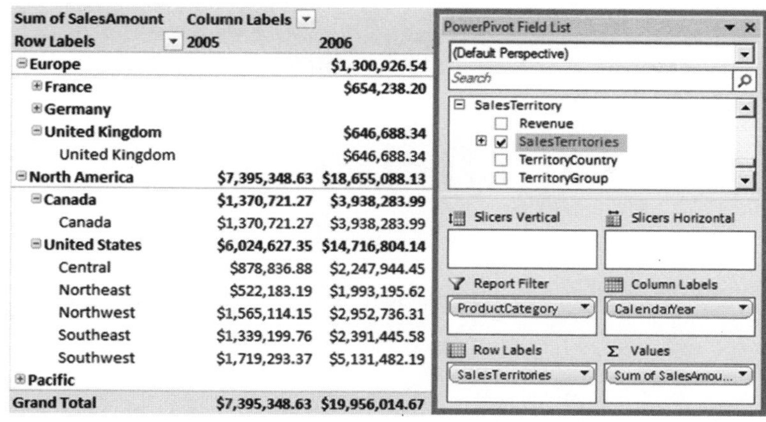

| Sum of SalesAmount | Column Labels | |
|---|---|---|
| Row Labels | 2005 | 2006 |
| ⊟Europe | | $1,300,926.54 |
| ⊞France | | $654,238.20 |
| ⊞Germany | | |
| ⊟United Kingdom | | $646,688.34 |
| United Kingdom | | $646,688.34 |
| ⊟North America | $7,395,348.63 | $18,655,088.13 |
| ⊟Canada | $1,370,721.27 | $3,938,283.99 |
| Canada | $1,370,721.27 | $3,938,283.99 |
| ⊟United States | $6,024,627.35 | $14,716,804.14 |
| Central | $878,836.88 | $2,247,944.45 |
| Northeast | $522,183.19 | $1,993,195.62 |
| Northwest | $1,565,114.15 | $2,952,736.31 |
| Southeast | $1,339,199.76 | $2,391,445.58 |
| Southwest | $1,719,293.37 | $5,131,482.19 |
| ⊞Pacific | | |
| Grand Total | $7,395,348.63 | $19,956,014.67 |



**Figure 5.34** The SalesTerritories hierarchy is an unbalanced hierarchy because only United States has states.

Under normal circumstances, each branch in a hierarchy has the same number of levels. Such hierarchies are called *balanced*. An example of a balance hierarchy is the ProductCategories hierarchy because each product has a subcategory and each subcategory has a category. An *unbalanced* hierarchy has branches with inconsistent depths. For example, an organization chart hierarchy is likely to be unbalanced. Finally, a *ragged* hierarchy is a hierarchy in which each level has a consistent meaning, but the branches have inconsistent depths because at least one level is unpopulated. The SalesTerritories hierarchy shown in **Figure 5.34** is an example of an unbalanced hierarchy because only United States has regions. The other countries repeat the country name when you drill down to the Region level.

**NOTE** In Multidimensional, you can avoid repeating or empty members in different levels by setting the HideMemberIf level property. While Analysis Services supports HideMemberIf for tabular models internally, neither PowerPivot nor SQL Server Data Tools include user interface to set this property.

## 5.5 Summary

Excel pivot reports are the main tool for analyzing PowerPivot models and for presenting information in a variety of ways that range from basic tabular reports to dashboards. Use the PivotTable report to author crosstab reports. The PivotChart report layout enables you to visualize data as a chart. Besides the pivot report filtering options, you can use slicers to set up visual interactive filters. You can further customize the report by using OLAP features, such as named sets and cube formulas.

PowerPivot supports end-user features to make the model more intuitive. By default, PowerPivot sorts column values in ascending order. You can sort a column by another column when you need a specific sort order. Perspectives hide the perceived complexity of the model and expose a subset of the model metadata. And, hierarchies define navigational paths for data exploration.

In the next chapter, you'll learn how to enhance the model with business calculations.

## Chapter 6

# Implementing Calculations



PowerPivot promotes rapid personal business intelligence (BI) for essential data exploration and analysis. Chances are, however, that in real life you might need to go beyond basic models. Business needs might require extending the model with calculations. Data Analysis Expressions (DAX) gives you the needed programmatic power to travel the "last mile" and unlock the full potential of Tabular.

This chapter teaches you how to use DAX to extend your models with business logic. It starts by introducing you to DAX and its arsenal of functions. Next, you'll learn how to implement custom calculated columns, measures, and key performance indicators (KPIs). Finally, I'll show you how to handle advanced table relationships with DAX. The Adventure Works.xlsx workbook in the Ch06 folder extends the Adventure Works model with DAX calculations.

## 6.1 Understanding Data Analysis Expressions

Data Analysis Expressions (DAX) is a formula-based language in Tabular that allows you to define custom calculations. DAX isn't related to Multidimensional Expressions (MDX), which is the query and expression language for Multidimensional. Instead, DAX is designed to extend the Excel formula language. DAX was introduced in the first version of PowerPivot (released in May 2010) with the following design goals:

- Simplicity – To get you started quickly with implementing business logic, DAX uses the Excel standard formula syntax and inherits many Excel functions. As a business analyst, Alice already knows many Excel functions, such as SUM and AVERAGE. When she uses PowerPivot, she appreciates the fact that DAX has the same functions.
- Tabular – DAX is designed with Tabular in mind and supports its artifacts, including tables, columns, and relationships. For example, if Alice wants to sum the SalesAmount column in the ResellerSales table, she can use the following formula: =SUM(ResellerSales[SalesAmount])
- Integration with Excel reports – DAX integrates well with Excel pivot reports. For example, when Alice creates a report, she can add DAX calculations to the report, such as to show the year-to-date sales.

PowerPivot version 2 (with SQL Server 2012) adds new functions, including new statistical functions, information functions, functions for parent-child hierarchies, and filter functions. In addition, Microsoft extended DAX with query constructs to allow external clients to query tabular models. This chapter focuses on DAX as an expression language to extend PowerPivot models. Chapter 10 covers DAX queries.

### 6.1.1 Understanding DAX Calculations

You can use DAX as an expression language to implement custom calculations that range from simple expressions, such as to concatenate two columns together, to complex measures that aggregate data in a specific way, such as to implement weighted averages. Based on the intended use, DAX supports two types of calculations: calculated columns and measures.

***Introducing calculated columns***

A calculated column is a table column that uses a DAX formula to derive its values. For example, you can add a FullName calculated column to the Customer table that uses the following formula to concatenate the customer's first name and last name:

```
=[FirstName] & " " & [LastName]
```

**NOTE** The closest Multidimensional equivalent of a calculated column is a named calculation defined in the data source view. Similar to a named calculation, a calculated column is stored to disk. However, unlike a named calculation, changing a calculated column doesn't require reprocessing the table or the entire model.

When a column contains a formula, PowerPivot computes the value for each row. PowerPivot calculates the column as soon as you create the formula. As I mentioned in Section 2.2.2 (Chapter 2), when the Calculation Options drop-down button in the Design ribbon tab is set to "Automatic Calculation Mode", PowerPivot automatically recalculated the values as necessary, such as when the underlying data is refreshed. By contrast, when the Calculation Options button is set to "Automatic Calculation Mode", you have to click the Calculate Now option (in the same button) to calculate columns manually. This could be useful if your model has complex formulas or very large datasets and you want to control when to update the column formulas.

In terms of reporting, you can use calculated columns to group and filter data. For example, you can add a calculated column to the Row Labels, Column Labels, Report Filter, Slicers Vertical, and Slicers Horizontal zones of a PivotTable report. One interesting implementation detail is that calculated columns store their values to disk just like regular columns do. To use a techie term, their values get "materialized" or "persisted". Therefore, from a performance standpoint, calculated columns and regular columns perform equally well. The difference is that regular columns import their values from a data source, while calculated columns are evaluated and saved after the regular columns are loaded. Because of this, the formula of a calculated column can reference regular columns and other calculated columns.

**NOTE** Calculated columns are designed to be static in nature. However, if a BI pro secures data (row-level security) in an Analysis Services Tabular model, the calculated columns are evaluated and their values stored before row filters are applied. Because of this, calculated columns can't reference the USERNAME and CUSTOMDATA functions, which are typically used to implement dynamic data security. Ideally, a future version should include dynamic calculated columns that are not persisted, as I requested in the "(BISM Tabular) Dynamic Calculated Columns" Connect suggestion at http://bit.ly/bismcalculatedcolumn. (Ashvini Sharma, Microsoft PowerPivot Program Manager Lead, responded that the request is considered for a future release.)

Every DAX formula is evaluated in a specific context. The formulas of calculated columns are evaluated for each row (row context). Because its formula is evaluated for each row in the Customer table (see **Figure 6.1**), the FullName column returns the full name for each customer.

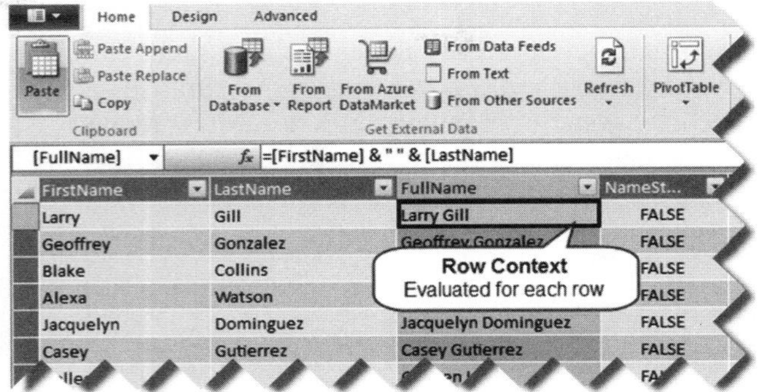


**Figure 6.1** Calculated columns operate in row context and their formulas are evaluated for each table row.

***Introducing measures***

Besides calculated columns, you can use DAX formulas to define measures. Measures are typically used to aggregate numeric columns, such as to summarize a SalesAmount column or to calculate a distinct count of customers who have placed orders. Measures are typically added to the Values zone of the PowerPivot Field List. PowerPivot supports two types of measures:

- Implicit measures – To get you started as quick as possible with data analysis, Microsoft felt that PowerPivot shouldn't require you to specify which columns should be aggregated and what their aggregation behavior is. Any column added to the Values zone of the Excel PowerPivot Field List is treated as an implicit measure and automatically aggregated based on the column data type.
- Explicit measures – Sometimes, you might need an aggregation behavior that goes beyond the standard aggregation functions. For example, you might need a year-to-date (YTD) calculation that uses a custom formula. Explicit measures are measures that have a custom DAX formula you specify.

**NOTE** The closest Multidimensional equivalent of an implicit measure is a regular measure that binds to a fact column and that has an associated aggregation function. Following the same logic, a calculated member added to the Measures dimension of a cube is similar to a DAX explicit measure.

**Table 6.1** summarizes the differences between implicit and explicit measures.

**Table 6.1 Comparing implicit and explicit measures.**

| Criterion | Implicit Measures | Explicit Measures |
|---|---|---|
| Design | Automatically generated | Manually created |
| Accessibility | Excel PowerPivot reports only | All report clients |
| Customization | Use the PowerPivot Field List to change the name or choose another function | Use the PowerPivot Field List, Excel UI, or PowerPivot window to change the name or formula |
| DAX support | Standard aggregation formulas only | Can use DAX functions |
| Organizational models | Not supported and converted to explicit measures | Preserved |

Implicit measures are automatically generated by Excel when you add a field to the Values zone of the PowerPivot Field List. Implicit measures are an Excel-specific feature, and they're not accessible by other report clients, such as Power View. By contrast, explicit measures are available to all report clients. Once the implicit measure is created, you can use the PowerPivot Field List to rename the measure or to change its aggregation function. You can't edit implicit measures in the PowerPivot window. By contrast, you can edit explicit measures and change their formulas in the PowerPivot window, Excel window, and PowerPivot Field List.

Implicit measures can use only the PowerPivot standard aggregation functions: Sum, Count, Min, Max, Average, and DistinctCount. By contrast, explicit measures can use any DAX function, such as to define a custom aggregation behavior. Finally, if a BI pro decides to upgrade a PowerPivot model to an organizational model, as I'll demonstrate in Chapter 10, Analysis Services Tabular doesn't support implicit measures, and it automatically converts them to explicit measures.

As you can see, implicit measures are somewhat less flexible than explicit measures. To make things worse, PowerPivot doesn't support converting an implicit measure to an explicit measure. Suppose that you want to customize the aggregation behavior of the "Sum of SalesAmount" implicit measure on the Sales by Country pivot report that you authored in Chapter 5. Since an implicit measure can't have a custom DAX formula, you need to remove the implicit measure, add a new explicit measure, and then update all reports to use the new measure. Because of these limitations, I suggest you define most of your measures as explicit measures, even if they all use standard aggregation functions, such as SUM. As I'll show you in Section 6.3.2, this is actually quite easy to do.

***Comparing calculated columns and measures***

The most important difference between calculated columns and measures is that measures are evaluated at run time for each *cell* as opposed to each row. The result of the measure formula is never saved. Moreover, measures are evaluated in the filter context of each cell, as shown in **Figure 6.2**.

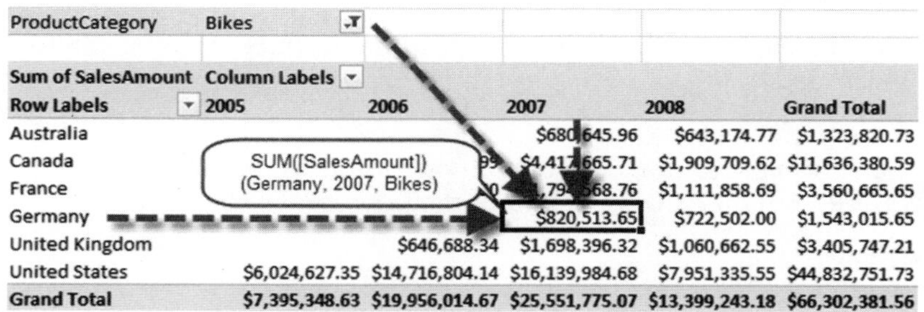

| ProductCategory | Bikes | | | | |
|---|---|---|---|---|---|
| **Sum of SalesAmount** | **Column Labels** | | | | |
| **Row Labels** | **2005** | **2006** | **2007** | **2008** | **Grand Total** |
| Australia | | | $680,645.96 | $643,174.77 | $1,323,820.73 |
| Canada | | [illegible] | [illegible] | $1,909,709.62 | $11,636,380.59 |
| France | | [illegible] | [illegible] | $1,111,858.69 | $3,560,665.65 |
| Germany | | | $820,513.65 | $722,502.00 | $1,543,015.65 |
| United Kingdom | | $646,688.34 | $1,698,396.32 | $1,060,662.55 | $3,405,747.21 |
| United States | $6,024,627.35 | $14,716,804.14 | $16,139,984.68 | $7,951,335.55 | $44,832,751.73 |
| **Grand Total** | **$7,395,348.63** | **$19,956,014.67** | **$25,551,775.07** | **$13,399,243.18** | **$66,302,381.56** |



**Figure 6.2** Measures are evaluated for each cell, and they operate in the cell filter context.

This figure shows the Sales by Country crosstab report that you've authored in the previous chapter. The report summarizes the SalesAmount measure by countries on rows and by years on columns. The report is further filtered to show only sales for the Bikes product category.

In Chapter 5, I explained that when you place a numeric column in the Values zone of the PowerPivot Field List, PowerPivot automatically creates an implicit measure. What you might not know is that behind the scenes the measure formula uses the DAX SUM function. The filter context of the highlighted cell is the Germany value of the SalesTerritory[TerritoryCountry] column, the 2007 value of the Date[CalendarYear] column, and the Bikes value of the Product [ProductCategory] column.

If you're familiar with the SQL language, you can think of the filter context as a WHERE clause that's determined dynamically and then applied to each cell. When Tabular calculates the expression for that cell, it scopes the formula accordingly, such as to sum the sales amount from rows in the ResellerSales table where the TerritoryCountry value is Germany, the CalendarYear value is 2007, and the ProductCategory value is Bikes.

## 6.1.2 Understanding DAX Syntax

As I mentioned, one of the DAX design goals is to extend the Excel formula language. Because of this, the DAX syntax resembles the Excel formula syntax. The DAX formula syntax is case-insensitive. For example, the following two expressions are both valid:

```
=YEAR([Date])
=year([date])
```

That said, I suggest you have a naming convention and stick to it. I personally prefer the first example where the function names are in an uppercase case and the column references match the column names in the model. This convention helps me quickly identify functions and columns in DAX formulas.

***Understanding expression syntax***

A DAX formula consists of an equal sign (=) followed by an expression that evaluates to a scalar (single) value. Expressions can contain operators, constants, or column references to return literal or Boolean values. The following formula returns the customer's full name and it's an example of a simple expression that concatenates two values:

```
=[FirstName] & " " & [LastName]
```

Expressions can also include functions to perform more complicated operations, such as aggregating data. Back in **Figure 6.2**, the DAX formula references the SUM function to aggregate the SalesAmount column. Functions can be nested. For example, the following formula nests the COUNTROWS and DISTINCT functions to calculate the count of distinct resellers:

```
=COUNTROWS(DISTINCT(ResellerSales[ResellerKey]))
```

DAX supports up to 64 levels of function nesting but going beyond two or three levels makes the formulas more difficult to understand.

***Understanding operators***

DAX supports a set of common operators to support more complex formulas, as shown in **Table 6.2**. DAX also supports TRUE and FALSE as logical constants.

**Table 6.2 DAX supports the following operators.**

| Category | Operators | Description | Example |
|---|---|---|---|
| Arithmetic | +, -, *, /, ^ | Addition, subtraction, multiplication, division, and exponentiation | =[SalesAmount] * [OrderQty] |
| Comparison | >, >=, <, <=, <> | For comparing values | =FILTER(RELATEDTABLE(Products),Products[UnitPrice]>30)) |
| Logical | \|\|, && | Logical OR and AND | =FILTER(RELATEDTABLE(Products),Products[UnitPrice]>30 && Products[Discontinued]=TRUE()) |
| Concatenation | & | Concatenating text | =[FirstName] & " " & [LastName] |
| Unary | +, -, NOT | Change the operand sign | = -[SalesAmount] |

***Referencing columns***

One of the DAX strengths over regular Excel formulas is that it can traverse table relationships and reference columns. This is much simpler and more efficient than referencing Excel cells and ranges with the VLOOKUP function. In Tabular, the column name is unique within a table. You can reference a column using its fully qualified name in the format <TableName>[<Column-Name>], such as in this example:

```
ResellerSales[SalesAmount]
```

If the table name includes a space or is a reserved word, such as Date, enclose it with single quotes:

```
'Reseller Sales'[SalesAmount]
'Date'[CalendarYear]
```

When a calculated column references a column from the same table, you can omit the table name. The PowerPivot AutoComplete feature helps you avoid syntax errors when referencing columns. As **Figure 6.3** shows, the moment you start typing the fully qualified column reference in the formula bar of the PowerPivot window, it displays a drop-down list of matching columns.

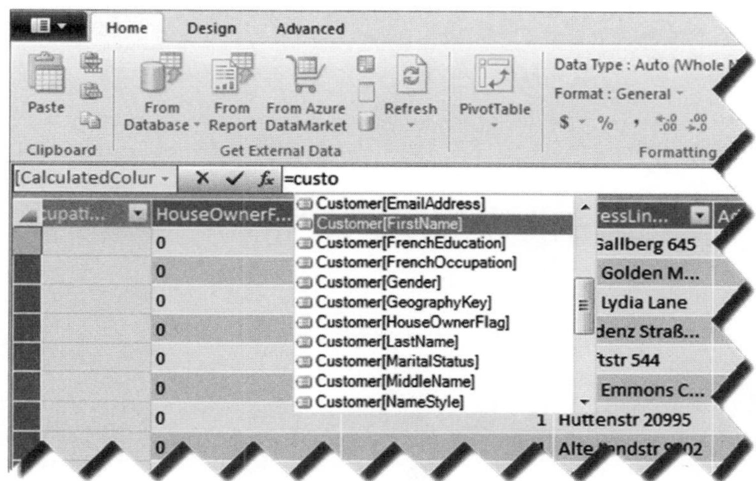


**Figure 6.3** PowerPivot AutoComplete helps you with column references in the PowerPivot window.

## 6.1.3 Understanding DAX Functions

DAX supports over a hundred functions that encapsulate a prepackaged programming logic to perform a wide variety of operations. If you type in the function name in the formula bar of the PowerPivot window, AutoComplete shows the function syntax and its arguments. For the sake of brevity, this book doesn't cover the DAX functions and their syntax in details. For more information, please refer to the DAX language reference by Ed Price at http://bit.ly/daxfunctions, which provides a detailed description and example for each function. Another useful resource is "DAX in the BI Tabular Model Whitepaper and Samples" (http://bit.ly/daxwhitepaper).

**NOTE** Tabular doesn't include functions for navigating hierarchies, such as DESCENDANTS, ANCESTOR, PREVMEMBER, and others that readers with Multidimensional experience might be familiar with. In many cases, it's possible to use DAX functions to return the desired results, although the resulting formulas can get rather complex.

***Functions from Excel***

DAX supports approximately 80 Excel functions. The big difference is that DAX formulas can't reference Excel cells or ranges. References such as A1 or A1:A10, which are valid in Excel formulas, can't be used in DAX functions. Instead, when data operations are required, the DAX functions must reference columns or tables. **Table 6.3** shows the subset of Excel functions supported by DAX, grouped by category with examples.

**Table 6.3 DAX supports a subset of Excel functions.**

| Category | Functions | Example |
|---|---|---|
| Date and Time | DATE, DATEVALUE, DAY, EDATE, EOMONTH, HOUR, MINUTE, MONTH, NOW, SECOND, TIME, TIMEVALUE, TODAY, WEEKDAY, WEEKNUM, YEAR, YEARFRAC | =YEAR([Date]) |
| Information | ISBLANK, ISERROR, ISLOGICAL, ISNONTEXT, ISNUMBER, ISTEXT | =IF(ISBLANK([MonthName]), "N/A", [MonthName]) |
| Logical | AND, IF, NOT, OR, FALSE, TRUE | =IF(ISBLANK(Customers[MiddleName]),FALSE(),TRUE()) |
| Math and Trigonometry | ABS,CEILING, ISO.CEILING, EXP, FACT, FLOOR, INT, LN, LOG, LOG10, MOD, MROUND, PI, POWER, QUOTIENT, RAND, RANDBETWEEN, ROUND, ROUNDDOWN, ROUNDUP, SIGN, SQRT, SUM, SUMSQ, TRUNC | =SUM(ResellerSales[SalesAmount]) |
| Statistical | AVERAGE, AVERAGEA, COUNT, COUNTA, COUNTBLANK, MAX, MAXA, MIN, MINA | =AVERAGE(ResellerSales[SalesAmount]) |
| Text | CONCATENATE, EXACT, FIND, FIXED, LEFT, LEN, LOWER, MID, REPLACE, REPT, RIGHT, SEARCH, SUBSTITUTE, TRIM, UPPER, VALUE | =SUBSTITUTE(Customer[Phone],"-", "") |

Besides Excel functions, DAX adds new functions that I'll introduce next.

***Date and number formatting***

Instead of the Excel TEXT function, DAX introduces a FORMAT function that works in the same way as the Visual Basic FORMAT function. The following example uses the FORMAT function to format the Cost column in the Product table as a currency with two decimal places:

```
=FORMAT(Product[StandardCost],"$#,###.00")
```

The FORMAT function returns a text value that can't be aggregated. If all you need is to format a numeric column, consider the PowerPivot built-in formatting capabilities.

***Aggregation functions***

As you've seen, PowerPivot "borrows" the Excel aggregation functions, such as SUM, MIN, MAX, COUNT, and so on. However, the PowerPivot equivalent functions accept a table column as an input argument instead of a cell range. Since referencing columns only can be somewhat limiting, PowerPivot adds X-version of these functions: SUMX, AVERAGEX, COUNTAX, MINX, MAXX. All functions take two arguments. The first one is a table and the second is an expression. These functions work by evaluating the expression for each row in the table that's passed as the first argument.

Suppose you want to calculate the total order amount for each row in the ResellerSales table using the formula [SalesAmount] * [OrderQuantity]. You can accomplish this in two ways. First, you can add an OrderAmount calculated column that uses the above expression and then use the SUM function to summarize the calculated column. Or, you can perform the calculation in one step by using the SUMX function, as follows:

```
=SUMX(ResellerSales, [SalesAmount] * [OrderQuantity])
```

Although the result in both cases is the same, the calculation process is very different. In the case of the SUM function, PowerPivot simply aggregates the column. When you use the SUMX function, PowerPivot will compute the expression for each row in the table and then aggregate the result. What makes the X-version functions flexible is that the table argument can also be a function that returns a table of values. For example, the following formula calculates the simple average (arithmetic mean) of the SalesAmount column for rows in the InternetSales table whose unit price is above $100:

```
=AVERAGEX(FILTER(InternetSales, [UnitPrice]>100), [SalesAmount])
```

This formula uses the FILTER function, which returns a table of rows matching the criteria that you pass in the second argument.

***Statistical functions***

DAX adds new statistical functions. The COUNTROWS(Table) function is similar to the Excel COUNT functions (COUNT, COUNTA, COUNTX, COUNTAX, COUNTBLANK) but it takes a table as an argument and returns the count of rows in that table. For example, the following formula returns the number of rows in the ResellerSales table:

```
=COUNTROWS(ResellerSales)
```

Similarly, the DISTINCTCOUNT(Column) function, which debuts in SQL Server 2012, counts the distinct values in a column. PowerPivot 2.0 also adds new statistical functions: STDEV.S, STDEV.P, STDEVX.S, STDEVX.P, VAR.S, VAR.P, VARX.S, and VARX.P for calculating standard deviation and variance. Similar to Count, Sum, Min, Max, and Average, the Analysis Services team wrote their own implementation of these functions for better performance instead of just using the Excel standard library.

***Filter functions***

This category includes functions for navigating relationships and filtering data, including the ALL, ALLEXCEPT, ALLNOBLANKROW, CALCULATE, CALCULATETABLE, DISTINCT, EARLIER, EARLIEST, FILTER, LOOKUPVALUE, RELATED, RELATEDTABLE, and VALUES functions. Next, I'll provide examples for the most popular filter functions.

You can use the RELATED(Column), RELATEDTABLE(Table), and USERELATIONSHIP (Column1, Column2) functions for navigating relationships in the model. The RELATED function follows a many-to-one relationship, such as from a fact table to a lookup table. Consider a calculated column in the ResellerSales table that uses the following formula:

```
=RELATED(Product[StandardCost])
```

For each row in the ResellerSales table, this formula will look up the standard cost of the product in the Product table. The RELATEDTABLE function can travel a relationship in either direction. For example, a calculated column in the Product table can use the following formula to obtain the total reseller sales amount for each product:

```
=SUMX(RELATEDTABLE(ResellerSales), ResellerSales[SalesAmount])
```

For each row in the Product table, this formula finds the corresponding rows in the ResellerSales table that match the product and then it sums the SalesAmount column across these rows. The USERELATIONSHIP function can use inactive role-playing relationships, as I'll demonstrate in Section 6.4.1.

The FILTER (Table, Condition) function is useful to filter a subset of column values, as I've just demonstrated with the AVERAGEX example. The DISTINCT(Column) function returns a table of unique values in a column.

For example, this formula returns the count of unique customers with Internet sales:

```
=COUNTROWS(DISTINCT(InternetSales[CustomerKey]))
```

PowerPivot 2.0 adds a LOOKUPVALUE (ResultColumn, SearchColumn1, SearchValue1 [, SearchColumn2, SearchValue2]...) function to look up a single value from another table, even if the two tables are not related. The following formula looks up the sales amount of the first line item bought by customer 14870 on August 1st, 2007:

```
=LOOKUPVALUE(InternetSales[SalesAmount],[OrderDateKey],"20070801",[CustomerKey],"14870",
[SalesOrderLineNumber],"1")
```

If multiple values are found, the LOOKUPVALUE function will return the error "A table of multiple values was supplied where a single value was expected". If you expect multiple values, use the FILTER function instead.

The CALCULATE(Expression, [Filter1],[Filter2]..) function is a very popular and useful function, especially for implementing measures. It evaluates an expression in its filter context that could be modified by optional filters. Suppose you need to add a TxnCount calculated column to the Customer table that computes the count of transactions (order line items) posted by each customer. On a first attempt, you might try the following expression to count the order line items:

```
=COUNTROWS(InternetSales)
```

However, this expression won't work as expected (see the left screenshot in **Figure 6.4**). Specifically, it returns the count of all the rows in the InternetSales table instead counting the line items for each customer.

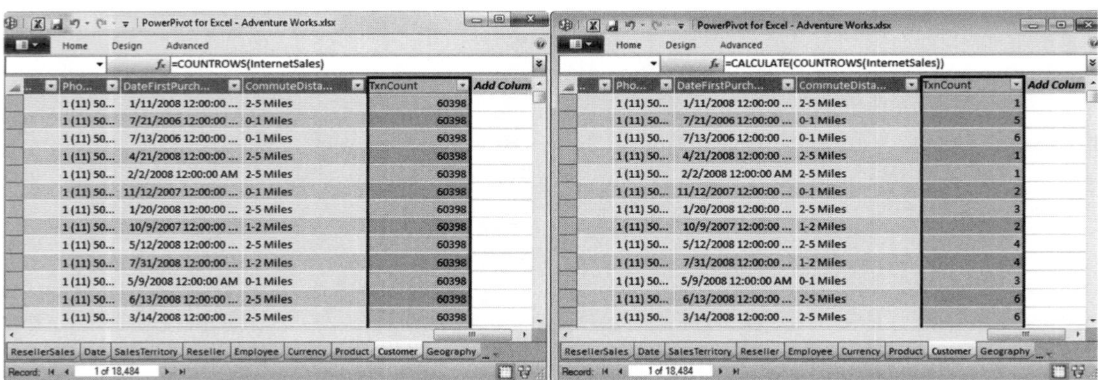

**Figure 6.4** Using the CALCULATE function to pass the row context.

To fix this, we need to force the COUNTROWS function to execute in the current row context. To do this, we will use the CALCULATE function as follows:

```
=CALCULATE(COUNTROWS(InternetSales))
```

The CALCUATE function determines the current row context and applies the filter context to the formula. For example, if the CustomerKey for the first row is 11602, the filter context for the first execution is COUNTROWS(InternetSales, CustomerKey=11602).

The CALCULATE function can take one or more filters as optional arguments. The filter argument can be a Boolean expression or a table. The following expression returns the transaction count for each customer for year 2007 and Bikes product category:

```
=CALCULATE(COUNTROWS(InternetSales), 'Date'[CalendarYear]=2007, Product[ProductCategory]="Bikes")
```

This expression counts rows in the InternetSales table for each customer where the product category is "Bikes" or missing:

```
=CALCULATE(COUNTROWS(InternetSales), FILTER(Product, Product[ProductCategory]="Bikes" || ISBLANK(Product[ProductCategory])))
```

The Filter function returns a table that contains only the rows from the Product table where ProductCategory="Bikes". When you pass the returned table to the CALCULATE function, it will filter away any combination of column values that don't exists in the table.

**TIP** When the expression to be evaluated is a measure, you can use the following shortcut for the CALCULATE function: =MeasureName(optional SetFilters). For example: =[SalesAmount1]('Date'[CalendarYear]=2006)

***Context functions***

DAX has functions to help you discover the filter context, including the ISFILTERED, ISCROSSFILTERED, HASONEVALUE, FILTERS, and HASONEFILTER functions. Consider the pivot report shown in **Figure 6.5**.

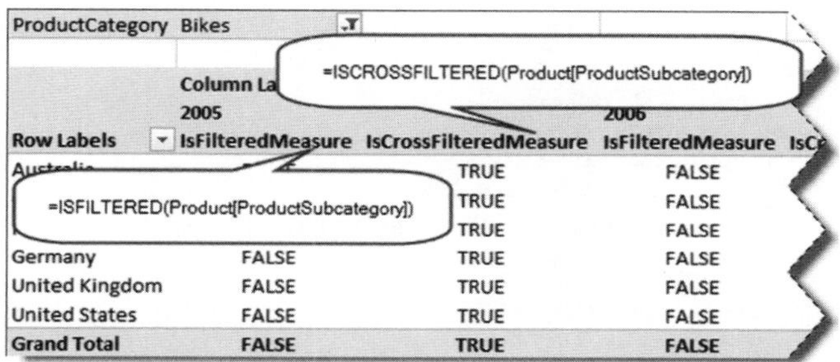


**Figure 6.5** You can use context functions to discover if a column is directly filtered.

This report has a direct filter on Product[ProductCategory] because this column was added to the Report Filter zone. In addition, each cell is directly filtered by SalesTerritory[Country] and Date[CalendarYear] columns because these columns were added to the Row Labels and Column Labels zones respectively. However, although not immediately obvious, the report data is also cross-filtered. For example, each cell is indirectly filtered on product subcategories (Product[ProductSubcategory] column) that exist with the Bikes category. The context functions can help you discover the effect of direct filtering and cross filtering. For example, suppose you want to aggregate a measure one way when the Bikes category is selected and another way for other categories.

```
=IF(HASONEVALUE(Product[ProductCategory]) && VALUES(Product[ProductCategory]) = "Bikes",
 SUM([SalesAmount]), AVERAGE([SalesAmount]))
```

This formula uses the IF statement to check if the report is filtered by only one product category and this product category is Bikes. If this is the case, the formula sums the SalesAmount column. Otherwise, it averages the column.

**TIP** Suppose you want to add a status field to the report that shows what filters are applied. Unfortunately, DAX currently doesn't have functions for metadata discovery. As a workaround, consider manually enumerating and testing all potential filter columns, and then concatenate the first value of all the columns that have slicers/page filters into a big string, as follows:
If(IsFiltered(T[C1]), "T[C1]: " & TopN(1, Filters(T[C1]), [C1]) & "; ") & If(IsFiltered(T[C2]), "T[C2]: " & TopN(1, Filters(T[C2]), [C2]) & "; ") & ...

While we are on the subject of filtering, DAX has the ALL, ALLEXCEPT, and ALLSELECTED functions to fully or partially ignore the filter context. Suppose you want to calculate the percentage contribution of each sales territory to all sales territories. The following measure formula gets the job done:

```
=SUM([SalesAmount])/CALCULATE(SUM([SalesAmount]), ALL(SalesTerritory))
```

The formula divides the aggregated sales for each territory by the sales across all the territories. The denominator uses the CALCULATE function because of its filtering capabilities. The second argument uses the ALL(Table or Column) function to remove the SalesTerritory table from the filter context. The ALLEXCEPT function works in the reverse way. It ignores the filter context from all the tables except the tables you specify.

With the ALLSELECTED(Table or Column) function, you can get to the report visual totals. This function retains all the explicit filters, such as report filters, slicers, report parameters, label filters, and value filters, but the function ignores the context filter for the current row or column. Consider the report shown in **Figure 6.6**.

| ProductCategory | Bikes | | | | |
|---|---|---|---|---|---|
| | | | | | |
| Sum of SalesAmount | Column Labels | | | | |
| Row Labels | 2005 | 2006 | 2007 | 2008 | Grand Total |
| Australia | | | $680,645.96 | $643,174.77 | $1,323,820.73 |
| Canada | $1,370,721.27 | $3,938,283.99 | $4,417,665.71 | $1,909,709.62 | $11,636,380.59 |
| France | | $654,238.20 | $1,794,568.76 | $1,111,858.69 | $3,560,665.65 |
| Germany | | | [illegible] | [illegible] | [illegible] |
| United Kingdom | | $646,688.34 | [illegible] | [illegible] | [illegible] |
| United States | $6,024,627.35 | $14,716,804.14 | [illegible] | [illegible] | [illegible] |
| **Grand Total** | **$7,395,348.63** | **$19,956,014.67** | **$25,551,775.07** | **$13,399,243.18** | **$66,302,381.56** |

=CALCULATE (SUMX(ResellerSales, [SalesAmount]), ALLSELECTED ())

**Figure 6.6** The ALLSELECTED function ignores the row and column context.

Here are some formula examples that use the ALLSELECTED function.

```
Removes the row and column filter, and returns the report grand total
=CALCULATE (SUMX(ResellerSales, [SalesAmount]), ALLSELECTED())

Removes the row filter and returns the horizontal (SalesTerritory) grand totals
=CALCULATE (SUMX(ResellerSales, [SalesAmount]), ALLSELECTED(SalesTerritory))

Removes the column filter and returns the vertical (Date) grand totals
=CALCULATE (SUMX(ResellerSales, [SalesAmount]), ALLSELECTED('Date'))
```

**NOTE** The subject of cross-filtering can get rather complex. For more information about how filter context and cross-filtering work, read the blog post, "The Logic behind the Magic of DAX Cross Table Filtering" by Jeffrey Wang at http://bit.ly/daxcalculate.

***Time intelligence functions***

One of the most common analysis needs is implementing time calculations, such as year-to-date, parallel period, previous period, and so on. The time intelligence functions require a Date table. The Date table should contain one row for every date that might exist in your data. DAX uses the Data table to construct a set of dates for each calculation depending on the DAX formula you specify. For more information about how DAX uses the Date table, read the blog post, "Time Intelligence Functions in DAX" by Howie Dickerman (http://bit.ly/daxtifunctions).

DAX has about 35 functions for implementing time calculations. The first set of functions returns a single date, such as the FIRSTDATE, LASTDATE, STARTOFMONTH, STARTOFQUARTER, STARTOFYEAR, ENDOFMONTH, ENDOFQUARTER, ENDOFYEAR, FIRSTNONBLANK, and LASTNONBLANK functions. For example, the FIRSTDATE(Column) function returns the first date from the Date table within the current context. The report shown in **Figure 6.7** pivots by FiscalYear on columns and uses a measure with the following formula:

```
=FIRSTDATE('Date'[Date])
```

| Measure 5 | Column Labels | | | |
|---|---|---|---|---|
| Row Labels | 2006 | 2007 | 2008 | 2009 |
| Australia | 7/1/2005 0:00 | 7/1/2006 0:00 | 7/1/2007 0:00 | 7/1/2008 0:00 |
| Canada | 7/1/2005 0:00 | 7/1/2006 0:00 | 7/1/2007 0:00 | 7/1/2008 0:00 |
| France | 7/1/2005 0:00 | 7/1/2006 0:00 | 7/1/2007 0:00 | 7/1/2008 0:00 |
| Germany | 7/1/2005 0:00 | 7/1/2006 0:00 | 7/1/2007 0:00 | 7/1/2008 0:00 |
| United Kingdom | 7/1/2005 0:00 | 7/1/2006 0:00 | 7/1/2007 0:00 | 7/1/2008 0:00 |
| United States | 7/1/2005 0:00 | 7/1/2006 0:00 | 7/1/2007 0:00 | 7/1/2008 0:00 |
| **Grand Total** | **7/1/2005 0:00** | **7/1/2006 0:00** | **7/1/2007 0:00** | **7/1/2008 0:00** |

**Figure 6.7** The FIRSTDATE function returns the first date within the current context.

FIRSTDATE returns July 1st, 7/1/2005 because that's the first date in the Adventure Works 2006 fiscal year. If I group the report further by FiscalQuarter, FIRSTDATE returns 7/1/2005 for Q1/2005, 10/1/2005 for Q2/2005, and so on. The FIRSTNONBLANK and LASTNONBLANK functions can be used to find the first (or last) date (or any other column value as well) where an expression that's passed as a second argument has a non-blank value. I'll provide an example in Section 6.4.3.

The second set of time intelligence functions return a table of dates, including the PREVIOUSDAY, PREVIOUSMONTH, PREVIOUSQUARTER, PREVIOUSYEAR, NEXTDAY, NEXTMONTH, NEXTQUARTER, and NEXTYEAR functions. Given the current context, these functions calculate the previous (or next) period and then return that period as a single column table. For example, the following formula calculates the sales amount for the previous year:

```
=CALCULATE(SUM(ResellerSales[SalesAmount]),PREVIOUSYEAR('Date'[Date]))
```

There are also to-date functions that return a table with multiple periods, including the DATESMTD, DATESQTD, DATESYTD, and SAMEPERIODLASTYEAR. For example, the following measure formula returns the YTD reseller sales:

```
=CALCULATE(SUM(ResellerSales[SalesAmount]),DATESYTD('Date'[Date]))
```

Finally, the DATEADD, DATESBETWEEN, DATESINPERIOD, and PARALLELPERIOD functions can take an arbitrary range of dates. The following formula returns the reseller sales between July 1st 2005 and July 4th 2005.

```
=CALCULATE(SUM(ResellerSales[SalesAmount]), DATESBETWEEN('Date'[Date],DATE(2005,7,1),DATE(2005,7,4)))
```

***Ranking functions***

SQL Server 2012 introduces the RANK.EQ, RANKX, and TOPN ranking functions. The RANK.EQ(Value, Column, [Order]) function allows you to implement a calculated column that returns the rank of a number in a list of numbers. Consider the Rank calculated column in the SalesTerritory table (see **Figure 6.8**).

The formula uses the RANK.EQ function to return the rank of each territory, based on the value of the Revenue column. If multiple territories have the same revenue, they will share the same rank. However, the presence of duplicate numbers affects the ranks of subsequent numbers. For example, had Southwest and Canada had the same revenue, their rank would be 1, but the Northwest rank would be 3. The function can take an Order argument, such as 0 (default) for descending order or 1 for ascending order.

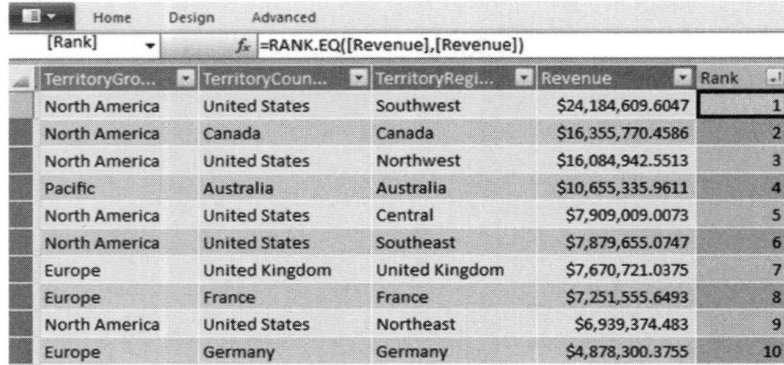

Home Design Advanced

[Rank] =RANK.EQ([Revenue],[Revenue])

| TerritoryGro... | TerritoryCoun... | TerritoryRegi... | Revenue | Rank |
|---|---|---|---|---|
| North America | United States | Southwest | $24,184,609.6047 | 1 |
| North America | Canada | Canada | $16,355,770.4586 | 2 |
| North America | United States | Northwest | $16,084,942.5513 | 3 |
| Pacific | Australia | Australia | $10,655,335.9611 | 4 |
| North America | United States | Central | $7,909,009.0073 | 5 |
| North America | United States | Southeast | $7,879,655.0747 | 6 |
| Europe | United Kingdom | United Kingdom | $7,670,721.0375 | 7 |
| Europe | France | France | $7,251,555.6493 | 8 |
| North America | United States | Northeast | $6,939,374.483 | 9 |
| Europe | Germany | Germany | $4,878,300.3755 | 10 |

**Figure 6.8** The RANK.EQ function ranks each row based on the value in the REVENUE column.

The RANKX(Table, Expression, [Value],[Order],[Ties]) function is similar to RANK.EQ but it's more flexible. It takes a table as an argument so you can implement a rank measure. In addition, it takes an optional Ties argument that specifies if numbers for tied ranks are skipped. The TOPN(Value, Table, [OrderByExpression],[Order1], [OrderBy2Expression],[Order2]...) function returns the top N rows of the specified table and sorts them in a given way. For example, the following formula sums the SalesAmount column for the top ten transactions in the ResellerSales table, ordered by SalesAmount in descending order:

```
=SUMX(TOPN(10, ResellerSales, [SalesAmount]), [SalesAmount])
```

**NOTE** The DAX TOPN function doesn't behave exactly as its T-SQL counterpart. For example, the T-SQL TOP(5) function returns no more than five rows. By contrast, TOP(5) in DAX might return more rows if the they have the same OrderByExpression values.

### *Information functions*

A newcomer in this category is the CONTAINS (Table, Column1, Value1, [Column2], [Value2]...) function that allows you to search a table for matching values. The function returns TRUE if there is at least one row matching the criteria. For example, the following formula searches the Product table and returns TRUE if there is a row with the "Accessories" product category and the "Cable Lock" product model.

```
=CONTAINS (Product,[ProductCategory],"Accessories",[ProductModel],"Cable Lock")
```

### *Table functions*

To support Power View, new functions were introduced that generate tables, including the SUMMARIZE, ADDCOLUMNS, ROW, CROSSJOIN, and GENERATE functions. As its name suggests, the SUMMARIZE(Table, GroupBy1 [,GroupBy2]...[,ColumnName1, ScalarExpression1][, ColumnName2, ScalarExpression2]...) function create a summary table of data. Suppose you want to group the SalesTerritory table by the TerritoryGroup column and sum the Revenue column, as shown in **Figure 6.9**.

| TerritoryGroup | TerritoryCountry | TerritoryRegion | Revenue |
|---|---|---|---|
| Europe | United Kingdom | United Kingdom | $7,670,721.04 |
| Europe | France | France | $7,251,555.65 |
| Europe | Germany | Germany | $4,878,300.38 |
| North America | United States | Southwest | $24,184,609.60 |
| North America | Canada | Canada | $16,355,770.46 |
| North America | United States | Northwest | $16,084,942.55 |
| North America | United States | Central | $7,909,009.01 |
| North America | United States | Southeast | $7,879,655.07 |
| North America | United States | Northeast | $6,939,374.48 |
| Pacific | Australia | Australia | $10,655,335.96 |

| TerritoryGroup | Revenue |
|---|---|
| Europe | $19,800,577.06 |
| North America | $79,353,361.18 |
| Pacific | $10,655,335.96 |

SUMMARIZE(SalesTerritory, [TerritoryCountry], "SalesAmount", SUM([Revenue]))

**Figure 6.9** The SUMMARIZE function returns a summary table of data.

The following formula gets the job done:

```
=SUMMARIZE(SalesTerritory, [TerritoryCountry], "SalesAmount", SUM([Revenue]))
```

**NOTE** Although the example shows an Excel table to help you visualize the results of the SUMMARIZE function, you can use the table functions only in formulas or DAX queries (I'll introduce you to the DAX query syntax in Chapter 10). You can't use the table functions to add new physical tables to the PowerPivot model.

Since the SUMMARIZE function returns a table, you can pass the result to any function that accepts a table, such as a ranking function or X-versions of the aggregate functions. The ADDCOLUMNS (Table, Name1, Expression1 [,Name2, Expression2]...) function adds new columns to a table that's passed as a first argument, such as when you need columns to hold intermediate results before aggregating these columns. Note that ADDCOLUMNS is a query-time function and it doesn't add physical columns to a PowerPivot table. Instead, it returns a table variable with the new columns added. For example, the following formula returns an in-memory copy of the SalesTerritory table with two new columns that calculate the overall sum and average across all rows in the SalesTerritory table:

```
= ADDCOLUMNS(InternetSales,"C1",SUM(InternetSales[SalesAmount]),"C2",AVERAGE(InternetSales[SalesAmount]))
```

The ROW function is very similar to ADDCOLUMNS except that it doesn't add columns to an existing table. Instead, it creates a new table that has only one row. This function was introduced to support Power View summary reports that request only grand totals.

```
=ROW("TotalQty", SUM(ResellerSales[OrderQuantity]),"TotalAmount",SUM(ResellerSales[SalesAmount]))
```

The CROSSJOIN (Table1, [Table2] ...) function returns a cross-joined set of two tables where every row of one table relates to every row of the other table. And, the GENERATE(Table1, Table2) function enumerates each row in the table passed as the first argument, and in the context of the row, it evaluates the expression passed as a second argument. The following DAX query uses the GENERATE function to return the top three products for each year, as shown in **Figure 6.10**.

```
EVALUATE GENERATE(VALUES('Date'[CalendarYear]), TOPN(3, VALUES(Product[ProductName]),
CALCULATE(SUM(ResellerSales[SalesAmount]))))
```

| Date[CalendarYear] | Product[ProductName] |
|---|---|
| 2005 | Mountain-100 Black, 42 |
| 2005 | Mountain-100 Black, 44 |
| 2005 | Mountain-100 Black, 38 |
| 2006 | Mountain-200 Silver, 42 |
| 2006 | Mountain-200 Black, 42 |
| 2006 | Mountain-200 Black, 38 |
| 2007 | Mountain-200 Silver, 38 |
| 2007 | Mountain-200 Black, 38 |

**Figure 6.10** The GENERATE function generates a table by enumerating each row in the CalendarYear column and then by evaluating the expression passed in the second argument.

Now that I've introduced you to the DAX syntax and functions, let's practice creating DAX calculations. The first practice teaches you how to use DAX to create calculated columns.

## 6.2 Implementing Calculated Columns

As I previously mentioned, calculated columns are columns that use DAX formulas for their values. Unlike the regular columns you get when you import data into your PowerPivot model, you add calculated columns after the data is imported by entering DAX formulas. When you create a report, you can place a calculated column in any zone of the PowerPivot Field List, although you would typically use calculated columns to group and filter data on the report. Because of this, you would place a calculated column in the Row Labels, Column Labels, Report Filter, or the slicer zones of the PowerPivot Field List.

### 6.2.1 Creating Basic Calculated Columns ▶

DAX includes various operators to create basic expressions, such as expressions for concatenating strings and for performing arithmetic operations. You can use these operators to create simple expression-based columns.

***Concatenating text***

Follow these steps to create a calculated column that shows the employee's full name:

1. Open the Adventure Works workbook with your changes from Chapter 5.
2. Click the PowerPivot ribbon tab (in the Excel window), and then click the PowerPivot Window button to open the PowerPivot window.
3. Click the Employee table tab at the bottom of the window to make the Employee table active.
4. To add the new column before the MiddleName column, right-click the MiddleName column header, and then click Insert Column. PowerPivot inserts a new empty column named CalculatedColumn1. Or, you can click the Insert Function button in the Design ribbon tab. This will bring you to the Insert Function dialog box where you can select a DAX function. Finally, to add a column at the end of the table, you can click the Add button, which is also found in the Design ribbon tab.

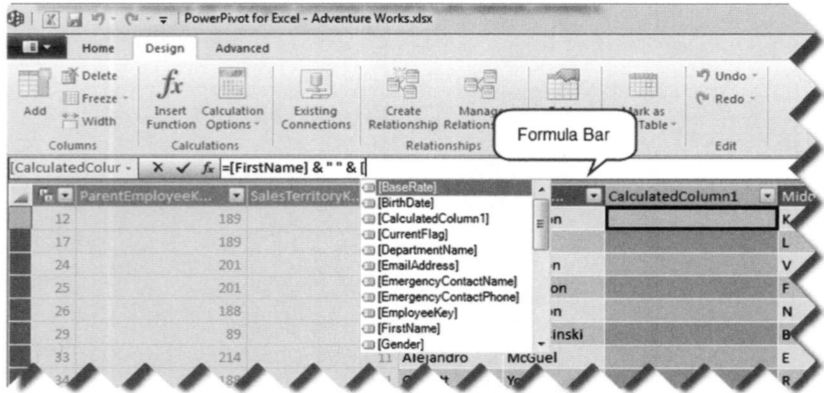


**Figure 6.11** Auto-Complete helps you with the DAX syntax.

5. With the new column selected, type an equal sign in the formula bar. To reference the FirstName column, simple click the FirstName column. The formula bar shows the following expression:

```
=[FirstName]
```

**TIP** You can use this technique to reference a column in other tables as well. When you need to reference a column in another table and you don't want to type the column name, simply click the table tab, and then click a cell in the column you need. Also, you can click the button to the right of the formula bar to expand it so you can write the formula text in multiple lines.

6. You can use the concatenation (&) operator to concatenate text. Type in *& " " &* after the formula text, so the formula now reads =[FirstName] & " " &.
7. AutoComplete helps you with the formula syntax although you must know some basic rules, such as that a column reference must be enclosed in square brackets. In the formula bar, enter a left square bracket, as shown in **Figure 6.11**. PowerPivot understands that you want to reference a column in the active table and it opens a drop-down list that shows the columns in the Employee table.
8. Scroll down the list and select the [LastName] column, or press the L key to jump to columns starting with the letter "L". At this point, the formula should be the following:

   ```
   =[FirstName] & " " & [LastName]
   ```

   This expression uses the concatenation operator to concatenate the FirstName and LastName columns and to add an empty space in between them.
9. Press Enter or click the checkmark button to the left of the formula bar. PowerPivot evaluates the expression and refreshes the CalculatedColumn1 column to show the employee's full name.
10. Rename the column to *FullName*.
11. Follow similar steps to implement a FullName calculated column in the Customer table that concatenates the FirstName and LastName columns.

***Working with date columns***

Some columns in the Date table don't have user-friendly values. For example, you might want to show Q1 2007 as opposed to 1 when the user slices data by quarters.

1. In the Date table, add the calculated columns shown in **Table 6.4** to assign user-friendly names to months, quarters, and semesters.

**Table 6.4 Add the following calculated columns in the Date table.**

| Column Name | Expression | Example |
|---|---|---|
| MonthNameDesc | =[MonthName] & " " & [CalendarYear] | July 2007 |
| CalendarQuarterDesc | ="Q" & [CalendarQuarter] & " " & [CalendarYear] | Q1 2008 |
| FiscalQuarterDesc | ="Q" & [FiscalQuarter] & " " & [FiscalYear] | Q3 2008 |
| CalendarSemesterDesc | ="H" & [CalendarSemester] & " " & [CalendarYear] | H2 2007 |
| FiscalSemesterDesc | ="H" & [FiscalSemester] & " " & [FiscalYear] | H2 2007 |

2. Sort the MonthNameDesc column by the MonthNumberOfYear column.
3. Switch to the Diagram View, and then add a Calendar hierarchy to the Date table that has the CalendarYear, CalendarSemesterDesc, CalendarQuarterDesc, MonthNameDesc, and Date columns (refer to Section 5.4.3 or watch the video tutorial for this section if you need step-by-step instructions of how to set up a hierarchy).

4. Rename the hierarchy levels, and then remove the "Desc" suffix. For example, rename CalendarSemesterDesc to *CalendarSemester*, CalendarQuarterDesc to *CalendarQuarter*, and MonthNameDesc to *Month*. Compare your results with **Figure 6.12**.

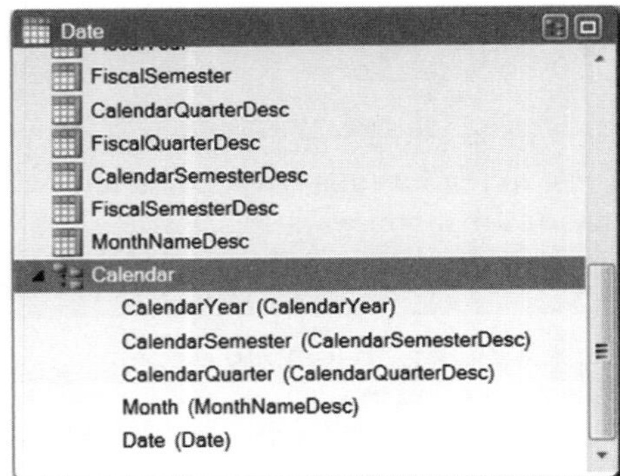


**Figure 6.12** The Calendar hierarchy in the Date table includes the CalendarYear, CalendarSemester, CalendarQuarter, Month, and Date levels.

5. To reduce clutter, hide the CalendarQuarter and CalendarSemester columns in the Date table. These columns show the quarter and semester ordinal numbers, and they're not that useful for analysis. Make sure to hide the columns and not the levels in the Calendar hierarchy.
6. (Optional) Follow similar steps to implement a Fiscal hierarchy consisting of FiscalYear, FiscalSemester, FiscalQuarter, Month, and Date levels.
7. Click the Save button to save your changes.

***Performing arithmetic operations***

Another common requirement is to create a calculated column that performs some arithmetic operations, such as multiplication and addition. Follow these steps to create a LineTotal column that calculates the total amount in the ResellerSales table by multiplying the order quantity, discount, and unit price.

1. In the PowerPivot window, click the ResellerSales tab to activate the ResellerSales table.
2. In the Design tab of the PowerPivot ribbon, click the Add button.
3. In the formula bar, type in an equal sign, and then click the *fx* button to the left of the formula bar to open the Insert Function dialog box. Expand the Select a Category drop-down list, and then select the Logical category to see a list of the DAX logical functions. Click a function, such as the IF function, as shown in **Figure 6.13**. Notice that the dialog box shows the function syntax. Click Cancel because the DAX formula you'll write won't use any functions.
4. Back in the formula bar, enter the following formula. I've intentionally misspelled the OrderQty column reference to show you how you can troubleshoot errors in formulas.

```
=([UnitPrice] * (1-[UnitPriceDiscountPct])) * [OrderQty]
```

This expression multiplies UnitPrice times UnitPriceDiscountPrc times OrderQty. Notice that when you type in a recognized function in the formula bar and enter a parenthesis "(", AutoComplete shows the function syntax.

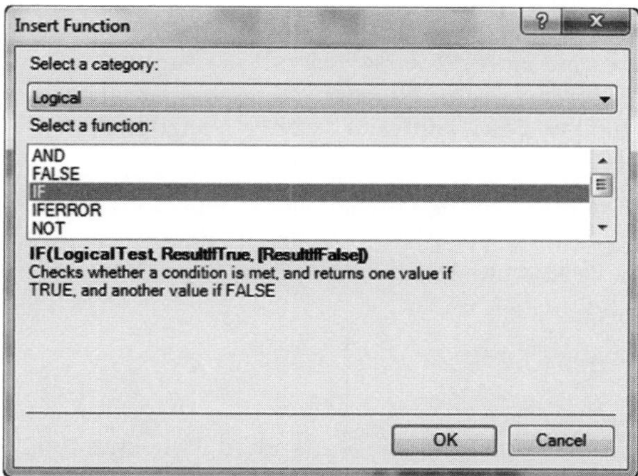


**Figure 6.13** The Insert Function dialog box shows the supported DAX functions and their syntax.

5. Press Enter to commit the formula. Notice that PowerPivot displays a #ERROR message, as shown in **Figure 6.14**. In addition, both the calculated column and the Reseller tab show a warning icon to indicate that there is an issue with that column and table.

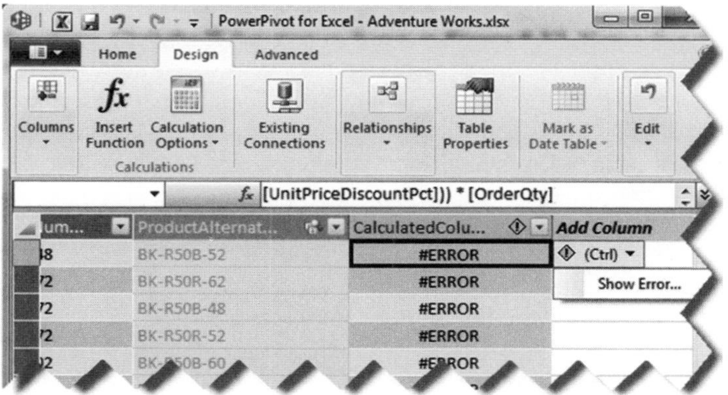


**Figure 6.14** PowerPivot displays #Error when the DAX formula contains an invalid column reference.

6. Click any cell in the calculated column. Expand the (Ctrl) drop-down list, and then click Show Error. Or, press Ctrl+Enter. PowerPivot displays the following informational message:

```
Cannot find column 'OrderQty'
```

7. Click OK to close the message dialog box. Click the calculated column to activate it. In the formula bar, replace the OrderQty reference with OrderQuantity as follows:

```
=([UnitPrice] * (1-[UnitPriceDiscountPct])) * [OrderQuantity])
```

8. Press Enter. Now, the column should work as expected. Rename the column to *LineTotal*.

## 6.2.2 Creating Advanced Calculated Columns

PowerPivot supports formulas that allow you to create more advanced calculated columns. For example, you can use the RELATED function to look up a value from a related table. Another popular function is the SUMX function, with which you can sum values from a related table.

***Implementing a lookup column***

Suppose you want to calculate the net profit for each row in the ResellerSales table. You would calculate the line item net profit by subtracting the product cost from the line item total. As a first step, you need to look up the product cost in the Product table.

1. In the PowerPivot window, click the ResellerSales table tab.
2. Add a new calculated column that uses the following expression:

```
=RELATED(Product[StandardCost])
```

This expression uses the RELATED function to look up the value of the StandardCost column in the Product table. Since a calculated column inherits the current row context, this expression is evaluated for each row. Specifically, for each row PowerPivot obtains the current product, joins to the Product table, and retrieves the standard cost for that product.

3. To calculate the net profit, change the expression as follows:

```
=[LineTotal] - RELATED(Product[StandardCost])
```

Note that when the line item's product cost exceeds the line total, the result is a negative value.

4. Rename the column to *NetProfit*.

**NOTE** Changing the formula of a calculated column invalidates other calculated columns that depend on it. For example, the NetProfit calculated column references the LineTotal calculated column. If you change the LineTotal formula, you must refresh the ResellerSales table.

***Aggregating values***

You can use the SUMX function to aggregate related rows from another table. Suppose you need a calculated column in the Product table that returns the reseller sales for each product.

1. Switch to the Product table.
2. Add a new calculated column with the following expression:

```
=SUMX(RELATEDTABLE(ResellerSales), ResellerSales[SalesAmount])
```

The RELATEDTABLE function follows a relationship in either direction (many-to-one or one-to-many) and returns a table containing all the rows that are related to the current row from the specified table. In this case, this function returns a table with all the rows from the ResellerSales table that are related to the current row in the Product table. Then, the SUMX function sums the SalesAmount column.

3. Rename the new calculated column to *ResellerSales*. Notice that the formula returns a blank value for some products because these products don't have any reseller sales, as shown in **Figure 6.15**.

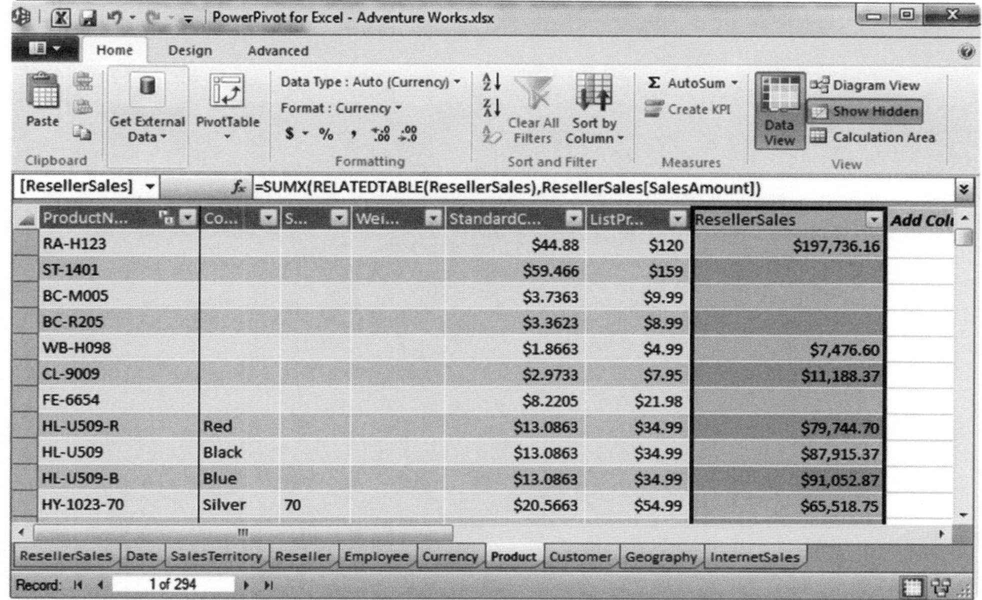


**Figure 6.15** The ResellerSales calculated column uses the RELATEDTABLE function.

***Counting rows***

PowerPivot provides a COUNTROWS function that you can use to count rows in a table. Let's add a LineItemCount column to the Employee table that returns the number of line items from the ResellerSales table with a sales amount greater than $1,000 for each employee. From a business standpoint, the result might represent the count of high volume line items associated with each sales person.

1. Switch to the Employee table.
2. Add a new calculated column with the following expression:

```
=COUNTROWS(FILTER(RELATEDTABLE(ResellerSales), ResellerSales[SalesAmount] >1000))
```

COUNTROWS is similar to the other COUNT functions (COUNT, COUNTA, COUNTX, COUNTAX, and COUNTBLANK) but it takes a table as its argument and returns the count of rows in that table. The FILTER function filters only the rows in the ResellerSales table whose SalesAmount exceeds 1,000. Notice that the formula returns a blank value for most employees because they don't have sales. But if you scroll all the way down the Employee table, you should see some employees who are sales people and have sales, as shown in **Figure 6.16**.

3. Change the column name to *LineItemCount*.

***Ranking values***

Suppose you want to rank each customer based on the customer's overall sales. The RANKX function can help you implement this requirement.

1. Switch to the Customer table.
2. Add a new calculated column, SalesRank, to the Customer table that uses the following formula:

```
=RANKX(Customer, SUMX(RELATEDTABLE(InternetSales), [SalesAmount]),,,Dense)
```

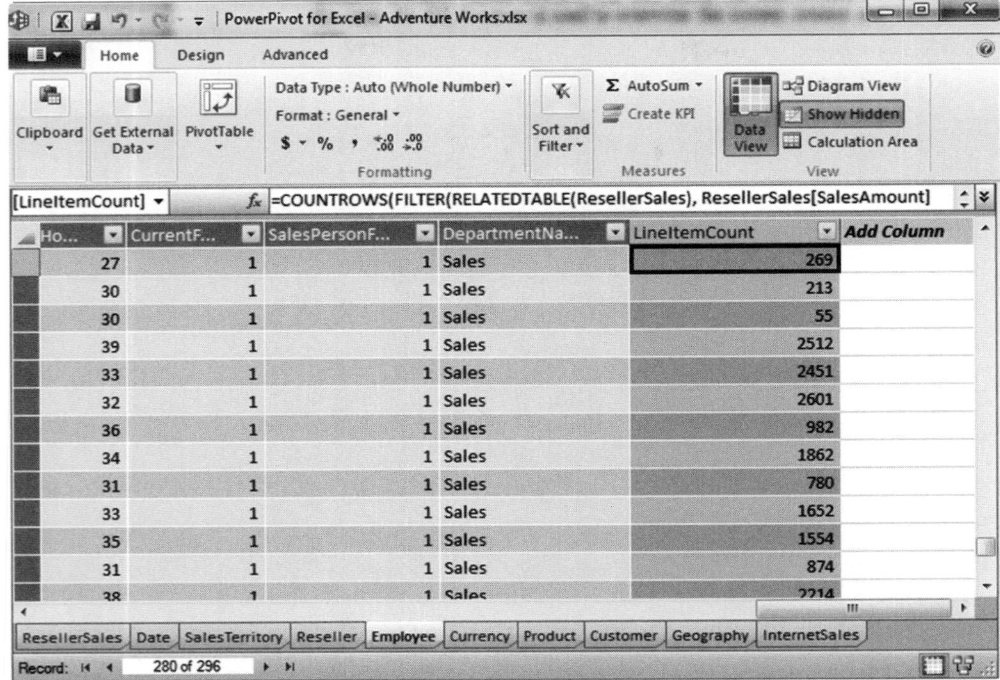

Figure 6.16 The COUNTROWS function counts the number of sales transactions exceeding $1,000.

This function uses the RANKX function to calculate the rank of each customer, based on the customer's overall sales recorded in the InternetSales table. Similar to the previous example, the SUMX function is used to aggregate the [SalesAmount] column in the InternetSales table. The Dense argument is used to avoid skipping numbers for tied ranks (ranks with the same value).

## 6.3 Implementing Measures

Measures are typically used to aggregate values. Unlike calculated columns whose expressions are evaluated at design time for each row in the table, measures are evaluated at run time for each cell on the report. PowerPivot applies the row, column, filter, and slice selections when it calculates the formula. PowerPivot supports implicit and explicit measures. An implicit measure is a regular column that's added to the Values zone of the PowerPivot Field List. An explicit measure has a custom DAX formula. For more information about the differences between implicit and explicit measures, see **Table 6.1** again.

### 6.3.1 Implementing Implicit Measures ▶

In this exercise, you'll work with implicit measures. This will help you understand how implicit measures aggregate and you how you can control their default aggregation behavior.

***Changing the default aggregation behavior***

In Chapter 5, I explained that by default PowerPivot aggregates implicit measures using the SUM function for numeric columns and the COUNT function for text-based columns. When you add a column to the Values zone of a pivot report, PowerPivot automatically creates an implicit measure, whose name follows the convention "<Aggregation Function> of <Column Name>". For example, when you added the SalesAmount column to the Sales by Country report, behind the scenes PowerPivot created a "Sum of SalesAmount" implicit measure. If needed, you can change the default aggregation function for numeric columns from the PowerPivot advanced properties.

1. In the PowerPivot window, click the Data View button in the Home ribbon tab.
2. If the Advanced tab doesn't appear in the ribbon, in the top-left corner of the menu bar, expand the PowerPivot File drop-down menu, and then click Switch to Advanced Mode. This adds the Advanced tab to the PowerPivot ribbon.
3. Click the Advanced ribbon tab. Note that it has a Summarize By drop-down button, as shown in **Figure 6.17**.

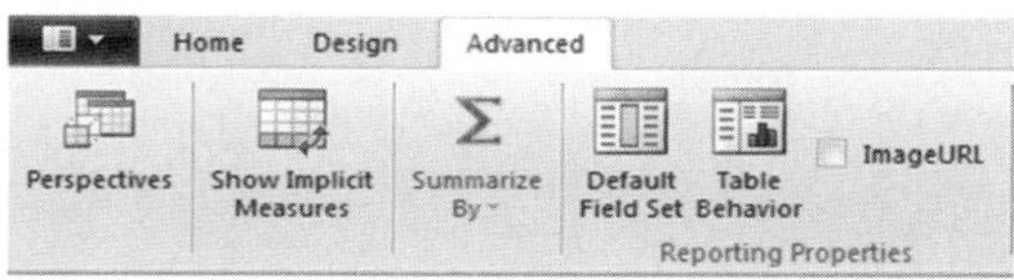


**Figure 6.17** The Summarize By button gives you the ability to change the default aggregation behavior of implicit measures.

The ResellerSales table includes a ProductStandardCost column. Suppose that when you add this column to the Values zone in the PowerPivot Field List, you want to average its values by default as opposed to summing them up.

4. In the ResellerSales table, click the ProductStandardCost column header to select the column.
5. In the Advanced ribbon tab, expand the Summarize By drop-down list, and then click Average.
6. Switch to the Excel window. Click the Sales by Country worksheet tab to see the pivot report that you implemented in the previous chapter. Click any cell in the crosstab report to activate it.
7. In the PowerPivot Field List, click the Refresh button. Expand the ResellerSales table, and then add the ProductStandardCost column to the Values zone. Notice that the name of the implicit measure is "Average of ProductStandardCost".
8. In the Values zone, right-click the "Average of the ProductStandardCost" measure, and then click Edit Measure to open the Measure Settings dialog box, as shown in **Figure 6.18**. Notice that the measure aggregation function is Average and you can overwrite it as needed.

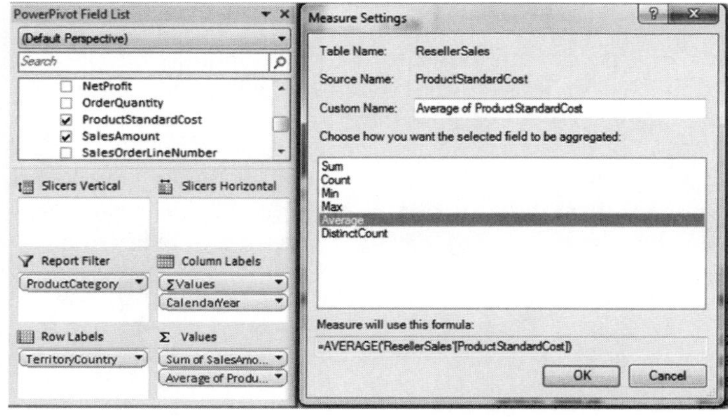


**Figure 6.18** This measure defaults to the Average aggregate function.

9. (Optional) Crosstab reports typically group data by columns and then by measures. To change the report layout, the Column Labels zone drag the Values item and drop it below CalendarYear so that CalendarYear appears before Values.

Some numeric columns can't be aggregated in a meaningful way. For example, the ResellerSales and InternetSales tables include a SalesOrderLineItem numeric column that doesn't make sense to aggregate. You can use the Summarize By feature and set these columns to Do Not Summarize to inform report clients, such as Power View, not to aggregate these columns when they're added on the report. The Do Not Summarize option doesn't work with Excel pivot reports.

***Showing implicit measures***

By default, implicit measures are not shown in the PowerPivot window. However, you can click the Show Implicit Measures button in the Advanced tab of the PowerPivot ribbon to see the implicit measures in both Diagram View and the Calculation Area of Data View (I'll introduce the Calculation Area in Section 6.3.2). **Figure 6.19** shows the implicit measures in the ResellerSales table shown in Diagram View.

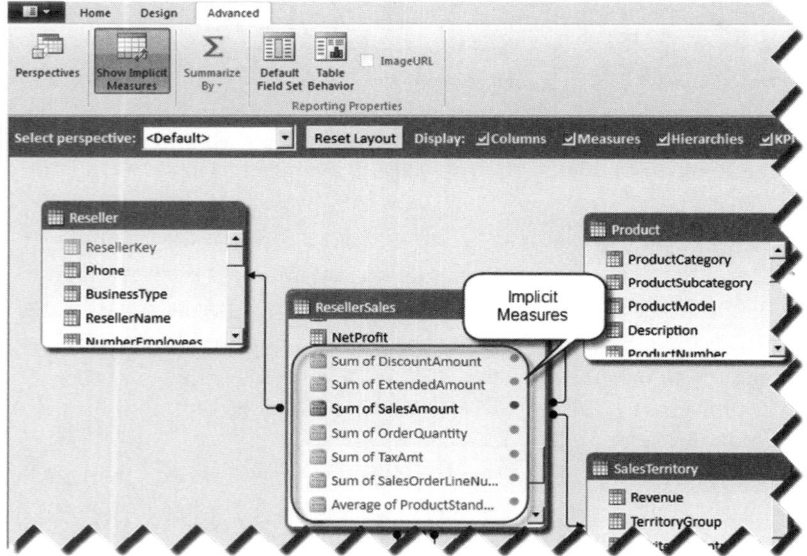


**Figure 6.19** If the Show Implicit Measures button is pressed in the Advanced menu, the Diagram View shows the implicit measures with an orange dot icon.

Each implicit measure has an orange dot icon. If the measure isn't used in a pivot report, it appears grayed out. For example, the Sum of Sales Amount measure isn't grayed out because it's used in the pivot reports you authored in Chapter 5. However, the rest of the implicit measures (created with the Summarize By feature) are grayed out because they're not used on any report in the workbook.

Inactive implicit measures are not accessible by external clients. To reduce clutter, you should revisit inactive implicit measures and remove them if they're no longer needed. To delete an implicit measure in Diagram View, simply click the measure to select it, press the Delete key, and then accept the confirmation prompt that follows.

## 6.3.2 Implementing Explicit Measures ▶

Explicit measures are more flexible than implicit measures because you can use custom DAX formulas. Similar to implicit measures, explicit measures are typically used to aggregate data and are placed in the Values zone in the PowerPivot Field List. PowerPivot supports several ways to implement an explicit measure (the last two are only available in PowerPivot and are not supported in SQL Server Data Tools):

- Use the AutoSum button found in the Home tab in the PowerPivot window (Data View). This creates an explicit measure that uses a standard aggregation function.
- Use the Calculation Area to type in the formula directly.
- Click the New Measure button in the Excel's PowerPivot ribbon tab.
- Right-click a table in the PowerPivot Field List, and then click New Measure.

These tasks are not exclusive. For example, you can create a basic explicit measure using the AutoSum button, but then edit the formula in the Calculation Area.

***Implementing a basic explicit measure***

Let's start by implementing a basic explicit measure that returns the same result as an implicit measure. This will help you understand how the filter context is applied to measures. You'll use the PowerPivot AutoSum feature to implement the measure.

1. In the PowerPivot window (Data View), click the ResellerSales tab. Select the SalesAmount column by clicking its column header.
2. In the Home ribbon tab, expand the AutoSum button. Notice that it lists six standard aggregation functions (Sum, Average, Count, Distinct Count, Max, and Min), as shown in **Figure 6.20**.

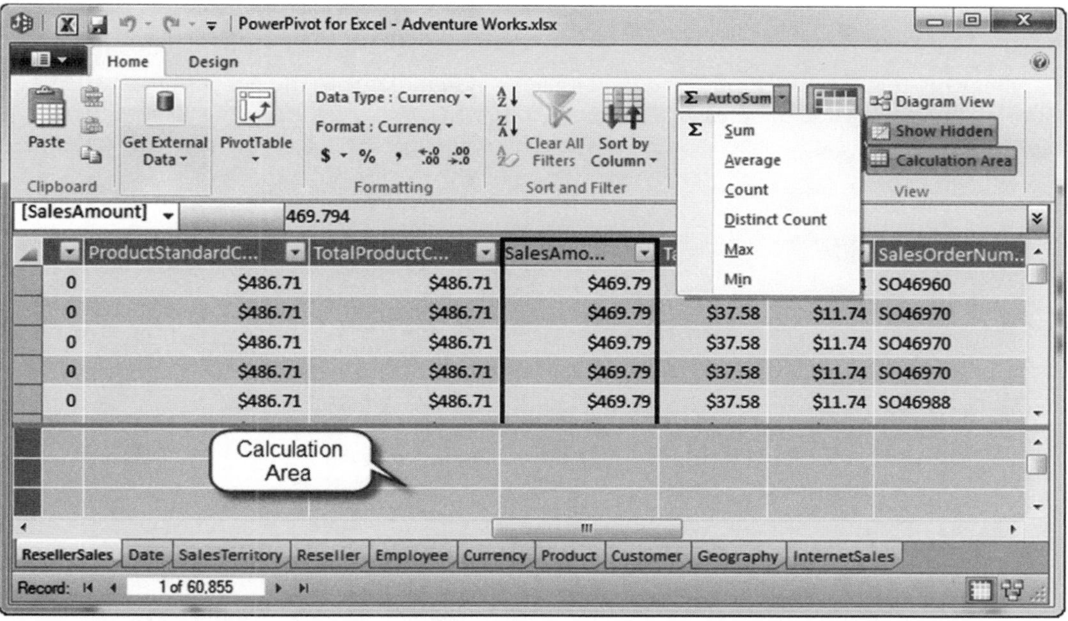


**Figure 6.20** Use AutoSum to create an explicit measure that uses a standard aggregation function.

3. Click the Sum aggregation function from the drop-down list. PowerPivot creates a new measure called "Sum of SalesAmount 3" that uses the following formula:

```
=SUM([SalesAmount])
```

4. PowerPivot shows the new measure in the Calculation Area below the SalesAmount column.

**NOTE** Suppose you want to create a measure TotalSalesAmount using the following formula: =SUM(InternetSales[SalesAmount] + SUM(ResellerSales[SalesAmount])

Given that this formula spans two tables, the TotalSalesAmount measure doesn't logically belong to either table. However, because Tabular doesn't support display folders, it's currently not possible to place the measure in a virtual table, such as a Summary table. Instead, you must always assign the measure to an existing table. Or, you can create a "dummy" table (with no rows and one hidden column) that just holds your calculated measures.

### *Understanding the Calculation Area*

One of the most common roadblocks for implementing explicit measures in the previous release of PowerPivot was that the users couldn't understand the difference between a calculated column and a measure. They would create a calculated column, such as to add two regular columns together, and then try to create a measure using the same formula, only to find out that the formula doesn't work as expected.

The Calculation Area was introduced in this release to help you differentiate between calculated columns and measures. You can use it to create measures, change the measure formulas, and test measures. If you don't see the Calculation Area, toggle the Calculation Area button in View group of the Home ribbon tab. The Calculation Area works similarly to aggregating cells in Excel. You can click any cell and type in a DAX formula in the formula bar. When you press Enter, PowerPivot evaluates the formula and displays the result. The Calculation Area supports this syntax:

```
MeasureName:=Formula
```

If you enter only the formula, PowerPivot will assign a system name to the new measure, such as Measure1. You can rename the measure by typing a new name in the formula bar before the := operator. You can also right-click the measure in the Calculation Area to open a context menu, as shown in **Figure 6.21**.

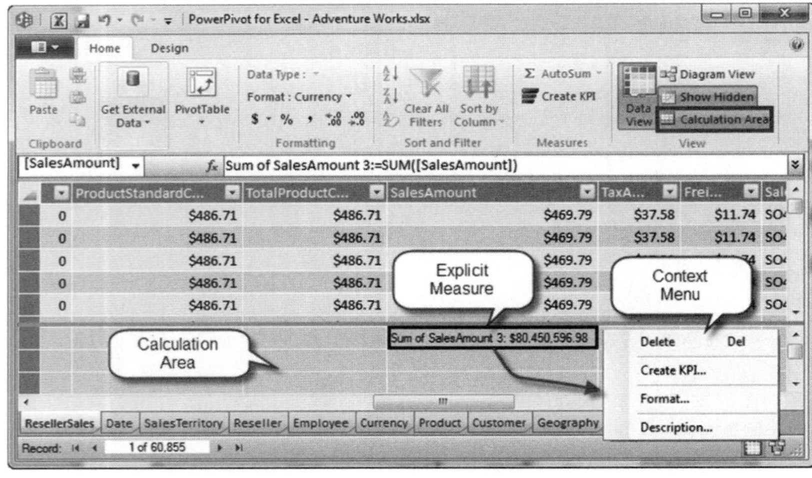


**Figure 6.21** Explicit measures are shown in the Calculation Area.

To delete a measure, simple select its cell in the Calculation Area, and then press the Delete key or use the Delete command from the context menu. Use the Format menu to change the measure's format settings and the Description menu to enter some text that describes the measure. The Create KPI menu deserves more attention, as I'll explain in Section 6.3.3.

1. In the formula bar, replace the "Sum of SalesAmount 3" text with *SalesAmount1* to rename the measure.
2. Switch to the Excel window, and then click the Sales By Country pivot report. Click the Refresh button in the PowerPivot Field List to refresh the metadata.
3. In the PowerPivot Field List, expand the ResellerSales table. Notice that the SalesAmount1 measure shows up (see **Figure 6.22**). It has a special icon next to it so that you can easily tell explicit measures apart from other fields.

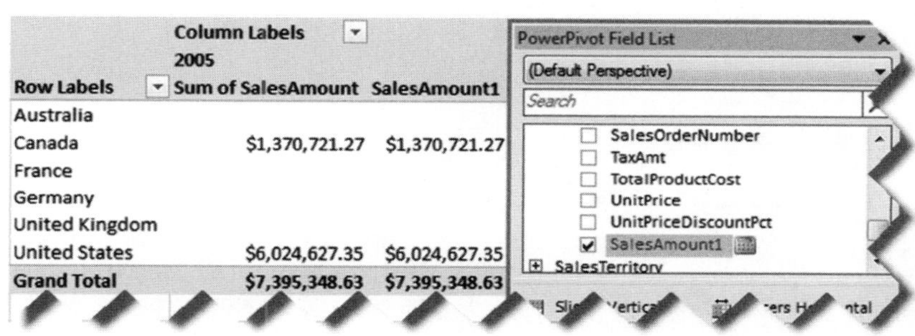


**Figure 6.22** The special icon appears to the right of explicit measures in the PowerPivot Field List.

4. Right-click the SalesAmount1 measure in the PowerPivot Field List. Notice that its context menu allows you to perform additional actions, such as to rename and delete the measure, or to change its formula.
5. Check the checkbox of the SalesAmount1 measure to add it to the crosstab report. If the report pivots by values first, move the Values item below the CalendarYear item in the Column Labels zone.
6. Compare your results with **Figure 6.22**. Notice that the SalesAmount1 measure returns the same results as the SalesAmount implicit measure. Just like implicit measures, PowerPivot calculates explicit measures for each cell on the report within the current context consisting of the current row value, column value, filter and slicer selections.
7. Once you're done testing, right-click the SalesAmount1 measure in the PowerPivot Field List, and then click Delete to remove the measure from the model.

***Implementing a distinct count measure***

A common data analytics requirement is to implement a distinct count measure that counts unique occurrences. Suppose that you need to count unique customers who have placed orders within a given time period. If a customer has multiple orders, the customer must be counted only once. Implementing a distinct count formula in a native Excel pivot report isn't a trivial task, but with PowerPivot it takes only a few clicks.

**NOTE** Since PowerPivot 2.0 adds DistinctCount to the list of standard aggregation functions for implicit measures, you could simply drag the field you want to count distinct values on to the Values zone, and then change its aggregation function to DistinctCount. This will create an implicit measure. However, as I mentioned before, I favor explicit measures because they're more flexible and available to all report clients.

1. In the PowerPivot window, select the InternetSales table.

2. In the Calculation Area, click a cell. Since you'll use the CustomerKey column for the distinct count, you might want to click the cell that's immediately below the CustomerKey column, but you can also use any other cell.
3. In the formula bar, enter the following formula and press Enter:

```
DistinctCustomerCount:=COUNTROWS(DISTINCT([CustomerKey]))
```

4. Unfortunately, this formula doesn't work and the cell shows a warning icon (see **Figure 6.23**).

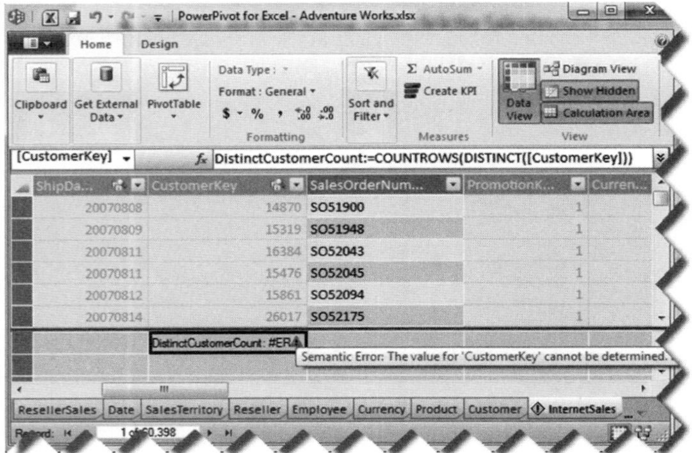


**Figure 6.23** The Calculation Area shows #Error (at the end of the cell) and a warning icon if the measure formula is invalid.

5. Point your mouse cursor to the warning icon. You'll see the following error text:

Semantic Error: The value for 'CustomerKey' cannot be determined. Either 'CustomerKey' doesn't exist, or there is no current row for a column named 'CustomerKey'.

8. The issue here is that we didn't use a fully qualified column reference. To fix this, change the formula to:

DistinctCustomerCount:=COUNTROWS(DISTINCT(**InternetSales**[CustomerKey]))

The expression uses the DISTINCT function which returns a table containing the unique values within the specified column (CustomerKey). Then, the COUNTROWS function counts the values.

9. Right-click the DistinctCustomerCount cell in the Calculation Area, and then click Format. Format the measure with no decimal places and with a thousand separator. Or, you can use the Formatting group in the Home ribbon tab to change the format, just like you can do with regular and calculated columns.
6. You can use the Sales by County report to test the new measure. If the report has only the DistinctCountMeasure in the Values zone, it will look like the report in **Figure 6.24**.

| ProductCategory | Bikes | | | | |
|---|---|---|---|---|---|
| | | | | | |
| **DistinctCustomerCount** | **Column Labels** | | | | |
| **Row Labels** | **2005** | **2006** | **2007** | **2008** | **Grand Total** |
| Australia | 394 | 859 | 1,442 | 1,396 | 2,155 |
| Canada | 47 | 226 | 275 | 332 | 656 |
| France | 59 | 233 | 423 | 510 | 816 |
| Germany | 76 | 233 | 520 | 603 | 904 |
| United Kingdom | 96 | 265 | 592 | 643 | 1,032 |
| United States | 341 | 861 | 1,623 | 1,967 | 3,569 |
| **Grand Total** | **1,013** | **2,677** | **4,875** | **5,451** | **9,132** |

**Figure 6.24** The DistinctCustomerCount measure calculates the count of unique customers within the current context.

TIP Filtering a column in Data View applies to the Calculation Area. For example, if you filter the OrderDateKey in the InternetSales table to a given day, the DistinctCustomerCount measure will show the number of distinct customers for that day only. This feature allows you test explicit measures by just filtering data.

***Implementing a percent of total measure***

Suppose you need a measure for calculating a ratio of current sales compared to overall sales. For example, if the TerritoryCountry field is used on the report, the measure calculates the ratio between the sales for the current territory and the sales across all the territories. Instead of using the Calculation Area, this time you'll create the measure in the Excel pivot report to practice this approach for creating measures.

1. Click any cell in the Sales by Country crosstab report.
2. In the Excel window's PowerPivot ribbon tab, click the New Measure button to open the Measure Settings dialog box, as shown in **Figure 6.25**.

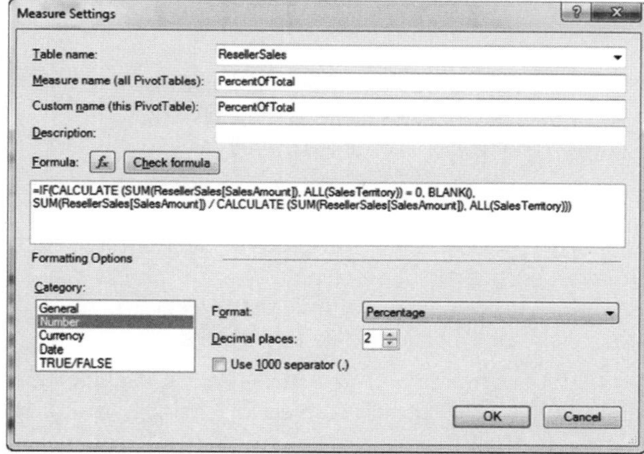

**Figure 6.25** Using the Measure Settings dialog box to implement a percent of total measure.

3. Expand the Table Name drop-down list, and then click ResellerSales to assign the measure to the ResellerSales table.
4. In the Measure Name field, enter *PercentOfTotal*. If you want to change the measure caption inside the active pivot report, you can provide another measure name in the Column Name field.
5. In the Formula field, enter the following formula:

```
=IF(CALCULATE (SUM(ResellerSales[SalesAmount]), ALL(SalesTerritory)) = 0, BLANK(),
SUM(ResellerSales[SalesAmount]) / CALCULATE (SUM(ResellerSales[SalesAmount]), ALL(SalesTerritory)))
```

To avoid division by zero, the expression uses the IF operator to check if the denominator is zero or a blank value (blank values are treated as zeros). If this is the case, the BLANK function returns a blank (NULL) value. Otherwise, the expression performs the actual calculation. The SUM function sums the SalesAmount column. The denominator uses the CALCULATE and ALL functions to ignore the current context so that the expression calculates the overall sales across *all* the sales territories.

**TIP** When blank values are acceptable, write your expressions to return a blank value instead of zero. Similar to Multidimensional, Tabular evaluates sparse datasets more efficiently. This is especially important for measures and less important for calculated columns, unless those calculated columns are then later used by explicit measures or other calculated columns.

6. Click the Check Formula button to verify the formula syntax. You should see the message "No errors in formula".
7. In the Formatting Options section, change the format settings as shown in **Figure 6.25**.
8. Click OK. PowerPivot creates the measure and adds it to the report so you can test it immediately.
9. Compare your results with **Figure 6.26**.

| ProductCategory | Bikes | | | | |
|---|---|---|---|---|---|
| **PercentOfTotal** | **Column Labels** | | | | |
| **Row Labels** | **2005** | **2006** | **2007** | **2008** | **Grand Total** |
| Australia | | | 2.66 % | 4.80 % | 2.00 % |
| Canada | 18.53 % | 19.73 % | 17.29 % | 14.25 % | 17.55 % |
| France | | 3.28 % | 7.02 % | 8.30 % | 5.37 % |
| Germany | | | 3.21 % | 5.39 % | 2.33 % |
| United Kingdom | | 3.24 % | 6.65 % | 7.92 % | 5.14 % |
| United States | 81.47 % | 73.75 % | 63.17 % | 59.34 % | 67.62 % |
| **Grand Total** | **100.00 %** | **100.00 %** | **100.00 %** | **100.00 %** | **100.00 %** |

**Figure 6.26** The PercentOfTotal measure calculates the ratio of the current territory's sales to the overall sales.

***Implementing YTD calculation***

DAX supports many time intelligence functions for implementing common date calculations, such as YTD, QTD, and so on. These functions require a column of the Date data type in the Date table. The Date table in the Adventure Works model includes a Date column that meets this requirement. Let's implement an explicit measure that returns year-to-date (YTD) sales.

1. Switch to the Excel window. To try yet another way to define an explicit measure, right-click the ResellerSales table in the PowerPivot Field List and click Add New Measure. This brings you to the familiar Measure Settings dialog box. The Table Name field is automatically set to ResellerSales.
2. Define a new SalesAmountYTD measure with the following formula:

```
=TOTALYTD(Sum([SalesAmount]), 'Date'[Date])
```

This expression uses the TOTALYTD function to calculate the SalesAmount aggregated value from the beginning of the year to date. Notice that the second argument must reference the column of the Date data type. To test the SalesAmountYTD measure, create a report that has the Calendar hierarchy in the Row Labels zone (or Column Labels zone) and both the SalesAmount and SalesAmountYTD measures in the Values zone, such as the one shown in **Figure 6.27**. Notice that the quarter values in the SalesAmountYTD column are running totals. For example, the SalesAmountYTD value for Q4 2005 ($8,065,435) is calculated by summing the sales of all previous dates from the beginning of year 2005.

7. Save the Excel workbook.

**NOTE** Readers familiar with Multidimensional might have implemented date calculations using a Date utility dimension and scope assignments. Since Tabular doesn't support scope assignments, you must define explicit measures for each column that needs date calculations, such as SalesAmountYTD, SalesAmountQTD, OrderQtyYTD, OrderQtyMTD, and so on.

| Row Labels | Sum of SalesAmount | SalesAmountYTD |
|---|---|---|
| ⊟2005 | $8,065,435.31 | $8,065,435.31 |
| ⊟H2 2005 | $8,065,435.31 | $8,065,435.31 |
| ⊞Q3 2005 | $3,193,633.97 | $3,193,633.97 |
| ⊞Q4 2005 | $4,871,801.34 | $8,065,435.31 |
| ⊟2006 | $24,144,429.65 | $24,144,429.65 |
| ⊟H1 2006 | $8,223,006.46 | $8,223,006.46 |
| ⊟Q1 2006 | $4,069,186.04 | $4,069,186.04 |
| ⊞January 2006 | $713,116.69 | $713,116.69 |
| ⊞February 2006 | $1,900,788.93 | $2,613,905.62 |
| ⊞March 2006 | $1,455,280.41 | $4,069,186.04 |
| Q2 2[illegible] | 153[illegible]2 | 223[illegible]6 |

**Figure 6.27** The SalesAmountYTD measure calculates year to date sales.

## 6.3.3 Implementing Key Performance Indicators ▶

Many organizations use key performance indicators (KPIs) to gauge their business performance. KPIs are quantifiable measures that represent critical success factors, and analysts use them to measure company performance, over time, against a predefined goal. For example, Sales Profit, Revenue Growth, Growth in Customer Base, and so on, are good KPI candidates.

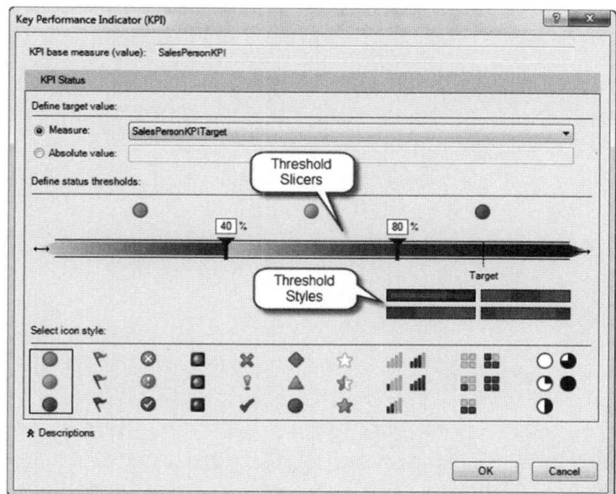


**Figure 6.28** Use the Key Performance Indicator (KPI) dialog box to configure the KPI target and status thresholds.

***Understanding PowerPivot KPIs***

In PowerPivot, a KPI is an extended explicit measure that has three properties:

- Value – The KPI Value property represents the current value of the KPI. You must use an explicit measure for the KPI Value.
- Target – This property defines what the KPI value should be in the perfect world. It could be set to an absolute number, such as 0.40 for 40 percent. Or set it to an explicit measure.
- Status – The Status property indicates how the KPI value compares to its target, based on predefined thresholds that you specify.

**NOTE** In Multidimensional, a KPI could have a Trend property to indicate how the KPI is performing over time. KPIs in Tabular don't support a Trend property.

You can use the Key Performance Indicator (KPI) dialog box to configure the KPI settings, as shown in **Figure 6.28**. In the Define Target Value section, you can choose between an absolute value and an explicit measure to define the KPI target. You can choose one of the four predefined threshold styles: Increasing is Better, Decreasing is Better, Closer to Target is Better, and Away from Target is Better. To set up the status thresholds, simply drag the slicers. For example, by default the threshold that defines good performance for the Increasing is Better style is set to 80% of the target value but you can drag the slicer to the right to change it to 90%. Or, you can type in the value directly in the slicer's label.

You can choose one of the predefined icon styles to visualize the KPI status although it's up to the report client to interpret and visualize the icon style. Finally, you can expand the Descriptions section and provide descriptive information for the KPI properties and for the KPI itself.

**NOTE** Report clients vary in their support of Analysis Services KPIs. For example, Excel fully supports KPIs, but Power View doesn't currently support visualizing the KPI Status property as an image.

***Importing the FactSalesQuota table***

Suppose you want to track the performance of the Adventure Works sales representatives. The FactSalesQuota table in the Adventure Works data warehouse database stores the sales person quota on a per-calendar-quarter basis. Follow these steps to import the FactSalesQuota table so you can define a KPI that uses the sales person's quota:

1. In the PowerPivot window (Data View), click the Design ribbon tab, and then click the Existing Connections button.
2. In the Existing Connections dialog box, make sure that the AdventureWorksDW connection is selected, and then click the Open button to start the Table Import Wizard.
3. In the Choose How to Import the Data step, leave the Select from a List of Tables option selected, and click Next.
4. In the Select Tables and Views step, check the FactSalesQuota table. In the Friendly Name column, enter *SalesQuotas*, and then click Finish.
5. Use Data View or Diagram View to set up the two relationships:
SalesQuotas[EmployeeKey] ⇨ Employee[EmployeeKey]
SalesQuotas[DateKey] ⇨ Date[DateKey].

***Implementing the KPI***

Next, you'll create a KPI that compares the sales person's actual performance against her quota.

1. In the ResellerSales table, click an empty cell in the Calculations Area, and then type the following formula to add a SalesPersonKPI explicit measure that sums the SalesAmount column:

```
SalesPersonKPI:=SUM([SalesAmount])
```

2. For the KPI target, add a SalesPersonKPITarget explicit measure with the following formula:

```
SalesPersonKPITarget:=CALCULATE(SUM(SalesQuotas[SalesAmountQuota]))
```

3. Format the SalesPersonKPI and SalesPersonKPITarget measures as Currency.

There are several ways to open the Key Performance Indicator (KPI) dialog box:

- Right-click the measure in the Calculation Area, and then click Create KPI.
- Select the measure in the Calculation Area, and then click the Create KPI button in the PowerPivot's Home ribbon tab (Measures group).

- In the PowerPivot Field List, click an explicit measure, and then click the Create KPI button in Excel's PowerPivot ribbon tab.
- In the PowerPivot Field List, right-click an explicit measure, and then click Create KPI.

4. In the Calculation Area, right-click the SalesPersonKPI measure, and then click Create KPI.
5. In the Key Performance Indicator (KPI) dialog box, expand the Measure drop-down list, and then select the SalesPersonKPITarget measure (see **Figure 6.28** again).
6. Assuming you want to define the start of the good zone at 85% of the sales person's quota, drag the right slicer to 85%. Click OK.
7. To test the KPI, create a pivot report with the FullName field (Employee table) in the Row Labels zone, Calendar hierarchy (Date table) in the Column Labels zone, and the Value, Target, and Status properties of the SalesPersonKPI (ResellerSales table) in the Values zone (see **Figure 6.29**). You can find this report in the Reports tab of the Adventure Works.xlsx workbook in the \Source\Ch06 folder.

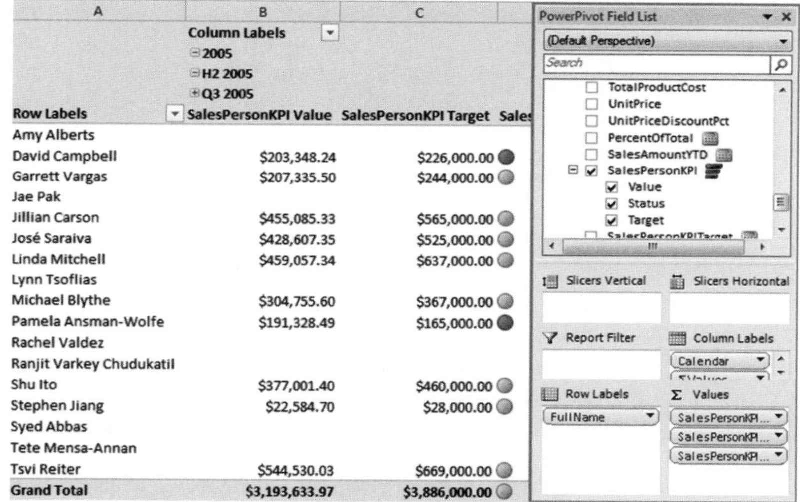

**Figure 6.29** A KPI is an extended measure with Value, Status, and Target properties.

Glancing at the report in **Figure 6.29**, you can see that the KPI statuses for David and Pamela are green, which means that they're within the 85% of the KPI target. You can use more complicated DAX expressions for the KPI value and target to meet more advanced requirements. For example, if you can use the following formula to define the KPI target as 10% more of the last year sales:

```
=CALCULATE(SUM(ResellerSales[SalesAmount]), PREVIOUSYEAR('Date'[Date])) * 1.10
```

## 6.4 Implementing Advanced Relationships

Besides regular table relationships where a lookup table joins the fact table directly, you might need to model more advanced relationships, including role-playing, parent-child, and many-to-many relationships. Unlike Multidimensional, Tabular doesn't support a declarative way to set up these relationship types and for the server to automatically aggregate data based on the relationship type you define. The only way to handle advanced relationships with Tabular is to use DAX formulas.

## 6.4.1 Implementing Role-Playing Relationships

In Chapter 4, I explained that a lookup table can be joined multiple times to a fact table. The dimensional modeling terminology refers to such a lookup table as a role-playing dimension. For example, in the Adventure Works model the Date table is joined three times to the OrderDateKey, DueDateKey, and ShipDateKey columns in the ResellerSales and InternetSales tables.

***Revisiting role-playing relationships***

As it stands, Tabular doesn't fully support role-playing relationships. Although a lookup table can relate multiple times to a fact table, only one relationship can be active at a time. You've marked the ResellerSales[OrderDateKey] ⇨ Date[DateKey] relationship as active for the ResellerSales table and InternetSales[OrderDateKey] ⇨ Date[DateKey] relationship as active for the InternetSales table. As a result, when you slice data in these fact tables by the Date table, PowerPivot uses the OrderDateKey column to find matching rows.

Chances are that you might want to compare the ordered sales amount and shipped sales amount side by side, such as to calculate a variance. To address this requirement, you can implement measures that use DAX formulas to navigate inactive relationships.

***Using DAX role-playing functions***

Follow these steps to implement a ShipSalesAmount measure in the InternetSales table.

1. In the PowerPivot window (Data View), click the InternetSales table to activate it.
2. In the Calculation Area, click an empty cell, such as a cell below the ShipDateKey, and then define a ShipSalesAmount explicit measure with the following formula:

```
ShipSalesAmount:=CALCULATE(SUM([SalesAmount]), USERELATIONSHIP('Date'[DateKey], InternetSales[ShipDateKey]))
```

The formula uses the USERELATIONSHIP function to travel the inactive relationship between the ShipDateKey column in the InternetSales table and the DateKey column in the Date table.

3. In the Home tab of the PowerPivot ribbon, click the PivotTable button.
4. In the PowerPivot Field List, expand the InternetSales table, and then check the SalesAmount and ShipSalesAmount fields. Expand the Product table, and then check the ProductCategories hierarchy to add it to Row Labels zone. Expand the Date table, and then drag the Calendar hierarchy to the Column Labels zone.
5. On the report, double-click the SalesAmount column, and then enter *OrderSalesAmount* in the Custom Name field on the Value Field Settings dialog box. Compare your report to the one shown in **Figure 6.30**. Notice that the ShipSalesAmount measure is different than the OrderSalesAmount measure.

| | Column Labels | | | |
|---|---|---|---|---|
| | ⊞2007 | | ⊞2008 | |
| Row Labels | OrderSalesAmount | ShipSalesAmount | OrderSalesAmount | ShipSalesAmount |
| ⊞Accessories | $293,709.71 | $278,639.84 | $407,050.25 | $422,120.12 |
| ⊞Bikes | $9,359,102.62 | $9,107,439.98 | $9,162,324.85 | $9,528,138.36 |
| ⊞Clothing | $138,247.97 | $131,468.71 | $201,524.64 | $208,303.90 |
| Grand Total | $9,791,060.30 | $9,517,548.53 | $9,770,899.74 | $10,158,562.38 |

**Figure 6.30** The ShipSalesAmount measure uses the USERELATIONSHIP function.

## 6.4.2 Implementing Parent-Child Relationships

A parent-child relationship is a hierarchical relationship formed between two entities. Common examples of parent-child relationships include an employee hierarchy, where a manager has subordinates who in turn have subordinates, and an organizational hierarchy, where a company has offices and each office has branches. DAX includes functions that are specifically designed to handle parent-child relationships.

***Understanding parent-child relationships***

In your Adventure Works model, the EmployeeKey and ParentEmployeeKey columns in the Employee table have a parent-child relationship, as shown in **Figure 6.31**. Specifically, the ParentEmployeeKey column points to EmployeeKey column for the employee's manager. For example, Kevin Brown (EmployeeKey = 2) has David Bradley (EmployeeKey=7) as a manager who in turn reports to Ken Sánchez (not shown in the screenshot). Ken Sánchez's ParentEmployeeKey is blank, which means that he's the top manager. Parent-child hierarchies typically have an arbitrary number of levels. Such hierarchies are called *unbalanced* hierarchies.

| EmployeeKey | ParentEmployeeKey | FirstName | LastName |
|---|---|---|---|
| 1 | 18 | Guy | Gilbert |
| 2 | 7 | Kevin | Brown |
| 3 | 14 | Roberto | Tamburello |
| 4 | 3 | Rob | Walters |
| 5 | 3 | Rob | Walters |
| 6 | 267 | Thierry | D'Hers |
| 7 | 112 | David | Bradley |
| 8 | 112 | David | Bradley |
| 9 | 23 | JoLynn | Dobney |
| 10 | 189 | Ruth | Ellerbrock |
| 11 | 3 | Gail | Erickson |
| 12 | 189 | Barry | Johnson |
| 13 | 3 | Jossef | Goldberg |

**Figure 6.31** The ParentEmployeeKey column contains the identifier of the employee's manager.

***Implementing a parent-child relationship***

Next, you'll use DAX functions to flatten the parent-child relationship before you can create a hierarchy to drill down the organizational chart.

1. Start by adding a Path calculated column to the Employee table that constructs the parent-child path for each employee. The Path calculated column has the following formula:

```
=PATH([EmployeeKey],[ParentEmployeeKey])
```

**Figure 6.32** shows the results of this DAX formula. Notice that the formula uses the PATH DAX function, which returns a delimited list of IDs, (using a vertical pipe as the delimiter) starting with the top/root of a hierarchy and ending with the current employee identifier. For example, the path for Kevin Brown is 112|7|2, meaning that the intermediate manager Kevin (EmployeeKey=2) is the employee with the EmployeeKey value of 7, whose manager has an EmployeeKey value of 112.

The next step is to flatten the parent-child hierarchy by adding a column for each level. This means that you need to know beforehand the maximum number of levels that the employee hierarchy might have. To be on the safe side, add one or two more levels to accommodate future growth.

[Path] =PATH([EmployeeKey],[ParentEmployeeKey])

| EmployeeKey | ParentEmployeeKey | FirstName | LastName | Path |
|---|---|---|---|---|
| 1 | 18 | Guy | Gilbert | 112\|23\|18\|1 |
| 2 | 7 | Kevin | Brown | 112\|7\|2 |
| 3 | 14 | Roberto | Tamburello | 112\|14\|3 |
| 4 | 3 | Rob | Walters | 112\|14\|3\|4 |
| 5 | 3 | Rob | Walters | 112\|14\|3\|5 |
| 6 | 267 | Thierry | D'Hers | 112\|14\|3\|267\|6 |
| 7 | 112 | David | Bradley | 112\|7 |
| 8 | 112 | David | Bradley | 112\|8 |
| 9 | 23 | JoLynn | Dobney | 112\|23\|9 |
| 10 | 189 | Ruth | Ellerbrock | 112\|23\|189\|10 |
| 11 | 3 | Gail | Ericks[illegible] | 112\|[illegible]\|3\|11 |

**Figure 6.32** The PATH DAX function returns the complete parent-child path for each employee.

2. Add a Level1 calculated column that has the following formula:

```
=LOOKUPVALUE(Employee[FullName],Employee[EmployeeKey],PATHITEM([Path],1))
```

This formula uses the PATHITEM function to parse the Path calculated column and to return the first identifier, such as 112 in the case of Kevin Brown. Then, it uses the LOOKUPVALUE function to return the full name of the corresponding employee which in this case is Ken Sánchez.

3. Add five more calculated columns for Levels 2-6 that use similar formulas to flatten the hierarchy. Compare your results with **Figure 6.33**. Notice that most of the cells in the Level 5 and Level 6 columns are empty, and that's okay because only a few employees have more than four indirect managers.

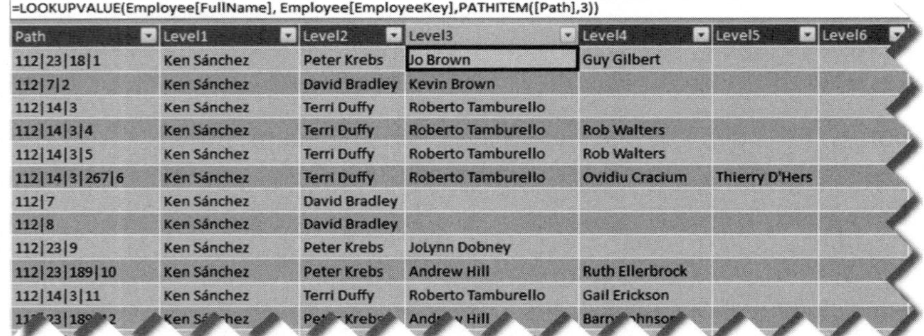

=LOOKUPVALUE(Employee[FullName], Employee[EmployeeKey],PATHITEM([Path],3))

| Path | Level1 | Level2 | Level3 | Level4 | Level5 | Level6 |
|---|---|---|---|---|---|---|
| 112\|23\|18\|1 | Ken Sánchez | Peter Krebs | Jo Brown | Guy Gilbert | | |
| 112\|7\|2 | Ken Sánchez | David Bradley | Kevin Brown | | | |
| 112\|14\|3 | Ken Sánchez | Terri Duffy | Roberto Tamburello | | | |
| 112\|14\|3\|4 | Ken Sánchez | Terri Duffy | Roberto Tamburello | Rob Walters | | |
| 112\|14\|3\|5 | Ken Sánchez | Terri Duffy | Roberto Tamburello | Rob Walters | | |
| 112\|14\|3\|267\|6 | Ken Sánchez | Terri Duffy | Roberto Tamburello | Ovidiu Cracium | Thierry D'Hers | |
| 112\|7 | Ken Sánchez | David Bradley | | | | |
| 112\|8 | Ken Sánchez | David Bradley | | | | |
| 112\|23\|9 | Ken Sánchez | Peter Krebs | JoLynn Dobney | | | |
| 112\|23\|189\|10 | Ken Sánchez | Peter Krebs | Andrew Hill | Ruth Ellerbrock | | |
| 112\|14\|3\|11 | Ken Sánchez | Terri Duffy | Roberto Tamburello | Gail Erickson | | |
| 11[illegible]23\|18[illegible]2 | Ken S[illegible]hez | Pe[illegible] Kreb[illegible] | Andr[illegible] Hill | Barr[illegible]hnso[illegible] | | |

**Figure 6.33** Use the PATHITEM function to flatten the parent-child hierarchy.

4. To be able to drill down the organizational chart, switch to Diagram View, and then define an Employees hierarchy in the Employee table, as shown in **Figure 6.34**.

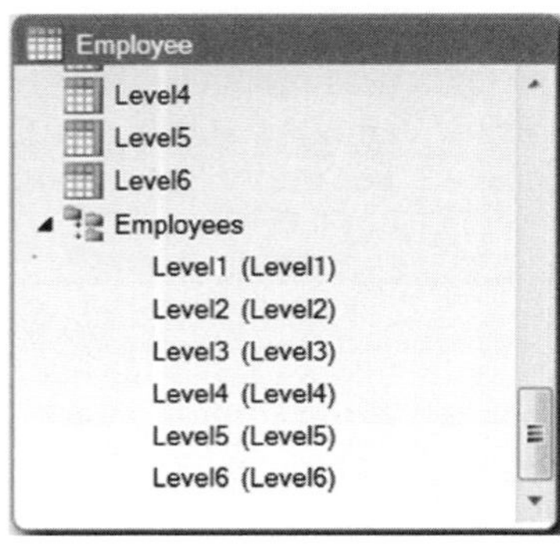


**Figure 6.34** The Employees hierarchy allows you to drill down the organizational chart.

5. Create a pivot report to test the Employees hierarchy, such as the one shown in **Figure 6.35**.

| Sum of SalesAmount | Column Labels | | | | |
|---|---|---|---|---|---|
| Row Labels | 2005 | 2006 | 2007 | 2008 | Grand Total |
| Ken Sánchez | $8,065,435.31 | $24,144,429.65 | $32,202,669.43 | $16,038,062.60 | $80,450,596.98 |
| Brian Welcker | $8,065,435.31 | $24,144,429.65 | $32,202,669.43 | $16,038,062.60 | $80,450,596.98 |
| Amy Alberts | | $3,457,549.94 | $7,967,661.67 | $4,110,734.65 | $15,535,946.26 |
| | | $86,380.60 | $547,374.88 | $98,322.96 | $732,078.44 |
| Jae Pak | | $2,522,835.94 | $4,172,459.45 | $1,808,043.26 | $8,503,338.65 |
| Rachel Valdez | | | $961,127.59 | $829,512.64 | $1,790,640.23 |
| Ranjit Varkey Chudukatil | | $848,333.40 | $2,286,699.75 | $1,374,855.78 | $4,509,888.93 |
| Stephen Jiang | $8,065,435.31 | $20,686,879.71 | $23,387,576.80 | $11,180,423.53 | $63,320,315.35 |
| Syed Abbas | | | $847,430.96 | $746,904.41 | $1,594,335.38 |
| Grand Total | $8,065,435.31 | $24,144,429.65 | $32,202,669.43 | $16,038,062.60 | $80,450,596.98 |

**Figure 6.35** Use this report to test the Employees hierarchy.

You can find the finished report in the Reports tab of the Adventure Works workbook (\Source\Ch06 folder). To create this report, I've added the Employees hierarchy (Employee table) to the Row Labels zone, the Calendar hierarchy (Date table) to the Column Labels zone, and the SalesAmount column (ResellerSales table) to the Values zone. Notice that you can expand Ken Sánchez and drill down the Employees hierarchy recursively.

### 6.4.3 Implementing Many-to-Many Relationships

Typically, a row in a lookup table relates to one or more rows in a fact table. For example, a given customer has one or more orders. This is an example of a one-to-many relationship that all of our tables used so far. Sometimes, you might run into a scenario where two tables have a logical many-to-many relationship. Since Tabular doesn't provide a native support for many-to-many relationships, you need to use DAX formulas to aggregate values in the correct way.

***Understanding many-to-many relationships***

The PowerPivot model in the M2M.xlsx workbook (\Source\Ch06 folder) demonstrates a popular many-to-many scenario that you might encounter if you model joint bank accounts. It consists of five tables, as shown in **Figure 6.36**.

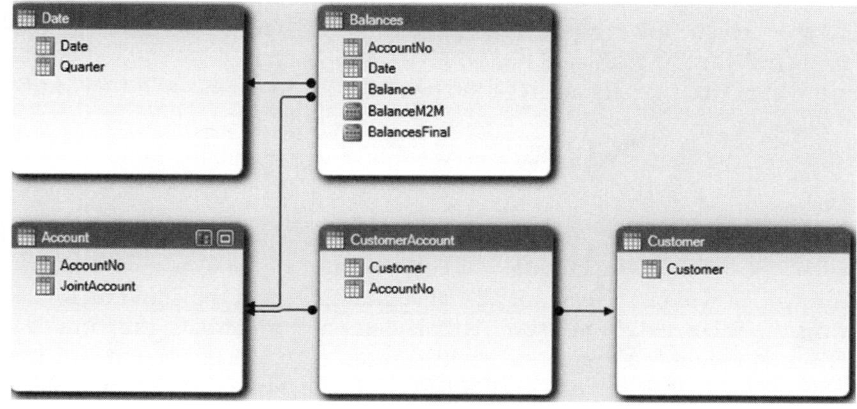


**Figure 6.36** This PowerPivot diagram models joint bank accounts.

The Customer table has a row for each customer. The Account table stores the bank accounts. A customer might have multiple bank accounts and a single account might be owned by two or more customers, such as a personal or business savings account. The CustomerAccount table is a bridge table that indicates which account is owned by which customer. The Balances table records the account balances over time. Finally, as a best practice, the model has a designated Date table, although the calculations will work even if there isn't one.

***Implementing a many-to-many aggregation***

If you create a report that aggregates the Balance measure, you'll find that the report produces wrong results. Specifically, the grand totals at the customer or account levels are correct, but the rest are incorrect. Instead of using the Balance column, you'll add a new measure that aggregates balances correctly.

1. Add a BalanceM2M explicit measure to the Balances table that uses the following formula:

```
=CALCULATE(SUM(Balances[Balance]), SUMMARIZE(CustomerAccount, Account[AccountNo]))
```

This formula uses the SUM function to sum the Balance column in the Balances table. The trick to get the result right is to aggregate the balance over a distinct set of accounts. The SUMMARIZE function is used to group the CustomerAccount table only for the subset of accounts in the current row context.

**TIP** Another way to rewrite the above formula and to make it more succinct is to create a new calculated measure SumBalance, with the expression =SUM(Balances[Balance]). Then, the BalanceM2M formula could use the abbreviated syntax: =[SumBalance] (SUMMARIZE(CustomerAccount, Account[AccountNo]))

If the Balance measure was fully-additive (can be summed across all lookup tables that are related to the Balances table), then you're done. However, semi-additive measures, such as account balances and inventory quantities, are trickier because they can be summed across all the tables except for the Date table. To understand this, take a look at the report shown in **Figure 6.37**.

| BalanceM2M | Column Labels | | | | | |
|---|---|---|---|---|---|---|
| Row Labels | 1/1/2011 | 2/1/2011 | 3/1/2011 | 4/1/2011 | 5/1/2011 | Grand Total |
| Alice | $100 | $200 | $300 | | | $600 |
| Bob | $600 | $700 | $300 | | | $1,600 |
| John | $100 | $200 | | | | $300 |
| Sam | | $100 | $100 | $200 | $50 | $450 |
| Grand Total | $700 | $1,000 | $400 | $200 | $50 | $2,350 |

**Figure 6.37** This report shows wrong date grand totals for account balances.

The customer grand totals are correct. However, the date grand totals are wrong. For example, the Alice's closing account balance should be $300 and not $600. Clearly, we have some more work to do. You'll add another measure that fixes the aggregation behavior of the BalanceM2M measure across dates.

2. Add a BalanceFinal measure to the Balances table that uses the following formula:

```
=IF(ISFILTERED([Date]), [BalanceM2M],
[BalanceM2M] (LASTNONBLANK(DATESBETWEEN ('Balances'[Date], BLANK(), LASTDATE('Balances'[Date])), SUM([Balance]))))
```

First, the IF operator uses the ISFILTERED function to check the context of the Date column. If ISFILTERED returns TRUE, which will be the case for all Date columns except the grand total column, the formula returns the BalanceM2M measure. To calculate the grand totals, the formula uses the LASTNONBLANK function to find the last date with a recorded balance. Then, it returns the BalanceM2M measure value for that date. The DATESBETWEEN function returns a range of dates in the Date table. The BLANK function is used in the first argument because we are not interested in any particular start date.

The report in **Figure 6.38** uses the BalanceFinal measure and then produces the correct results.

| BalancesFinal | Column Labels | | | | | | | |
|---|---|---|---|---|---|---|---|---|
| | Q1 2011 | | | Q1 2011 Total | Q2 2011 | | Q2 2011 Total | Grand Total |
| Row Labels | 1/1/2011 | 2/1/2011 | 3/1/2011 | | 4/1/2011 | 5/1/2011 | | |
| Alice | $100 | $200 | $300 | $300 | | | | |
| Bob | $600 | $700 | $300 | $300 | | | | |
| John | $100 | $200 | | | | | | |
| Sam | | $100 | $100 | $100 | $200 | $50 | $50 | $50 |
| Grand Total | $700 | $1,000 | $400 | $400 | $200 | $50 | $50 | $50 |

**Figure 6.38** This report shows correct grand totals for account balances.

**NOTE** For readers familiar with Multidimensional, the BalanceFinal measure behaves the same way as the LastNonEmpty aggregate function. If you're puzzled as to why the vertical Grand Total column shows empty balances for Alice, Bob, and John, read my blog post, "Last Non Empty Affairs" (http://bit.ly/teolastnonempty). The short answer is that these customers have no recorded balances for the second quarter and the calculation assumes that their balances are zero.

## 6.5 Summary

One of the most compelling reasons to favor PowerPivot is that its Data Analysis Expressions (DAX) language makes it easy to define custom business logic that's difficult or impossible to implement with standard Excel formulas. This chapter introduced you to the DAX calculations, syntax, and formulas. You can use the DAX formula language to implement calculated columns and measures.

Calculated columns are custom columns that use DAX formulas to derive their values. The column formulas are evaluated for each row in the table, and the resulting values are saved in the model. The practices walked you through the steps for creating basic and advanced columns.

Measures are evaluated for each cell in the report. PowerPivot automatically creates an implicit measure for every column that you add to the Values zone of the PowerPivot Field List. You can create explicit measures that use custom DAX formulas you specify. You can also use DAX to implement a key performance indicator (KPI), which is an extended measure that has Value, Target, and Status properties.

As it stands, Tabular doesn't support declarative role-playing, parent-child, and many-to-many relationships. However, you can use DAX formulas to navigate inactive relationships, to flatten parent-child hierarchies, and to change the measure aggregation behavior.

# PART 2

# *Team Business Intelligence*

Team BI empowers business users to share their BI artifacts with other users in a trustworthy and scalable environment. Microsoft SharePoint is a platform for document sharing and collaboration. SharePoint Server 2010 adds appealing BI features, including PowerPivot model hosting and reporting. The technology that powers Microsoft team BI is PowerPivot for SharePoint

This part of the book is for both business users and IT professionals. If you're a business user who has started on the personal BI road with PowerPivot, you might find that e-mailing large Excel files to your coworkers is impractical. Instead, consider deploying PowerPivot models to SharePoint. Once the model is deployed, it becomes immediately available for reporting to users who are given SharePoint rights to view it. Your teammates can gain data insights by creating a variety of reports from the published model, ranging from viewing the pivot reports embedded in the workbook to authoring new operational or ad-hoc reports that use the model as a data source.

SQL Server 2012 brings a new end-user data exploration tool called Power View. With a click of a button, an end user can launch Power View and create quickly an interactive report using a PowerPivot model as a data source. Transcending traditional "canned" reports without requiring prior report authoring experience, Power View allows you to gain knowledge by having fun with data.

Team BI is great but "managed" team BI is even better. This part of the book gives IT administrators the necessary background to install and configure the server environment. PowerPivot for SharePoint provides a management dashboard to for IT pros to gain insights about the server and model utilization and to be proactive. Finally, the book teaches IT professionals how to manage deployed models, including setting up automatic data refresh, managing PowerPivot workbook files, configuring version history, setting up shared data sources and approval workflow

## Chapter 7

# Team BI Basics



We all need to share information. If your organization has formalized its information sharing needs by adopting tools and business processes to support that effort, chances are your company is already using SharePoint to manage documents and collaborate online. As a power user who is also implementing personal business intelligence (BI) models, wouldn't it be nice if you could upload these models to a SharePoint site to quickly disseminate insightful information with your teammates? Or, how about publishing a digital dashboard to help a management team understand company business and make decisions?

To meet these needs, PowerPivot supports SharePoint integration features that allow you to deploy your PowerPivot models to SharePoint, to view the pivot reports included in the models, and to create new reports that connect to the PowerPivot models. This chapter starts with an overview of SharePoint Products and Technologies. Then, I'll explain how PowerPivot integrates with SharePoint. Next, IT pros will learn how to install PowerPivot for SharePoint on a test server. Finally, I'll show you how you can publish PowerPivot models and troubleshoot setup issues.

## 7.1 Understanding Team Business Intelligence

Team BI empowers business users to share their PowerPivot models. The technology that drives Microsoft team BI on top of Tabular is the second flavor of PowerPivot – PowerPivot for SharePoint. PowerPivot for SharePoint enables the following scenarios:

- Allows users to upload PowerPivot workbooks with embedded reports to SharePoint. Once Alice is done with her PowerPivot model, she can publish the model to SharePoint to make it accessible to her teammates.
- Allows users to view these reports in the browser without having Excel installed on the desktop. For example, Alice's teammates can navigate to the SharePoint library where Alice published the Adventure Works model and view the Sales by Country and Dashboard reports online.
- Empowers users to create new reports that connect to the PowerPivot models. Not only can Alice's teammates view the pivot reports in the Alice's model online, but they can also create their own reports. For example, they can use Power View to create interactive reports that are connected to the Adventure Works model.
- Facilitates "managed" personal BI by enabling IT pros to establish BI governance policies, to monitor the server utilization, and to automate refreshing data in the PowerPivot workbooks. For example, Bob from the Adventure Works IT department can set up an approval process for publishing PowerPivot models so he can review the Alice's model before it becomes available for everyone else. Once the model is approved, Bob can track how people are using the

Alice's model. If the model gains popularity, Bob can consider upgrading the model to an organizational model running on a dedicated Analysis Services Tabular server. Bob can also schedule an automatic data refresh to synchronize the model with changes in the source data.

Before delving into the team BI specifics, I'll introduce you to SharePoint Products and Technologies and explain at a high level how PowerPivot integrates with it.

**REAL WORLD** The personal-team-organizational BI continuum is just one of the paths to implement Tabular solutions. In one of my projects, a solution provider was looking for ways to provide Excel-based financial reports to its clients. The solution provider was envisioning a custom application that would support both online and offline viewing. After realizing the breadth of SharePoint features, they went for a SharePoint-centered solution that significantly reduced the implementation effort. It this case, there weren't any business users implementing personal BI models. Instead, we developed the PowerPivot models and then deployed them to SharePoint as a prepackaged product offering.

## 7.1.1 Introducing Microsoft SharePoint

Nowadays, many organizations leverage Microsoft SharePoint Products and Technologies for web-based document management and collaboration. Microsoft SharePoint 2010 is the collective name for two applications: SharePoint Foundation and SharePoint Server, as shown in **Figure 7.1**.

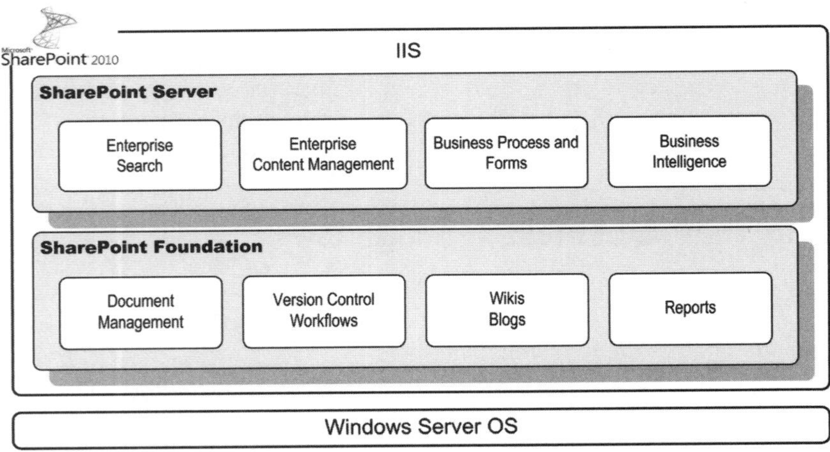


**Figure 7.1** Microsoft SharePoint is a collective name for SharePoint Foundation and SharePoint Server products.

Let's briefly take a look at each of these components to understand its role in the PowerPivot for SharePoint ecosystem.

***SharePoint Foundation***

SharePoint Foundation 2010, previously known as Windows SharePoint Services (WSS), is a free download (http://bit.ly/getsharepointfoundation) that runs on Windows Server operating systems. SharePoint Foundation is a core technology upon which other Microsoft web-centric applications are based, including Microsoft SharePoint Server and Microsoft Project Server.

With its fourth major version released in 2010, SharePoint Foundation provides essential services for document management and collaboration, including document editing, document organization and version control capabilities. It also includes other popular content features, such as wikis, blogs, to-do lists, alerts, discussion boards, and workflows.

SharePoint Foundation also provides essential features for you to quickly build web pages for showing content. For example, information workers could implement personalized web pages that consist of multiple web parts. A SharePoint web part is an ASP.NET control that exposes content, such as a report. A SharePoint site includes a collection of SharePoint pages. A SharePoint web application hosts a collection of sites and runs under IIS. SharePoint uses SQL Server databases to store documents, metadata, and configuration information, such as security policies. SharePoint requires a Windows Server operating system with IIS and ASP.NET enabled. SharePoint Foundation integrates well with Microsoft Office so you can open and publish documents to and from SharePoint sites and libraries.

As far as BI goes, SQL Server Reporting Services can integrate with SharePoint Foundation to allow viewing and managing operational and ad hoc reports inside the SharePoint environment. The rest of the Microsoft BI products and services, including PowerPivot, PerformancePoint, and Excel Services, require SharePoint Server Enterprise edition and are not available with SharePoint Foundation.

***SharePoint Server***

SharePoint Server 2010, previously known as Microsoft Office SharePoint Server (MOSS) is built on top of SharePoint Foundation and adds more features, web parts, and infrastructure. Specifically, it offers enterprise search capabilities across multiple SharePoint sites and external resources. It extends the SharePoint content management features by consolidating content from multiple sources into a centrally managed and scalable repository. Microsoft InfoPath Form Services, which is a component of SharePoint Server, can streamline business processes by allowing information workers to fill in Web Forms.

Microsoft positions the Enterprise edition of SharePoint Server as a central repository for BI assets that adds several important BI features. Its Excel Services component allows you to execute PowerPivot models and Excel spreadsheets on the server. For example, you can author an Excel PivotTable report connected to an Analysis Services cube and then publish the workbook to SharePoint Server. Or, you can deploy a workbook with an embedded PowerPivot model and pivot reports. When the user navigates to the Excel workbook in his web browser, Excel Services refreshes the workbook on the server and renders it in HTML format. Because of this, end users don't need to have Microsoft Excel installed locally on the desktop to view these reports.

With PerformancePoint Services, you can monitor and analyze your business by implementing dashboards and scorecards with key performance indicators (KPIs). Another interesting BI-related feature is Business Connectivity Services. Organizations can leverage Business Connectivity Services to present business data from back-end server applications, such as SAP or Siebel, without writing any code. SharePoint Server also provides additional web parts that are not available in the SharePoint Foundation technology download, including chart and filter web parts.

***Microsoft Office 365***

SharePoint 2010 is also available online as a part of the Microsoft Office 365 cloud initiative (http://www.microsoft.com/en-us/office365). Microsoft Office 365 is a collection of cloud services that provide online access to email, web conferencing, documents, and calendars. As of this writing, the Office 365 version of SharePoint doesn't include BI features.

For more information about Microsoft SharePoint 2010 products, editions, and licensing, visit the SharePoint official web page at http://sharepoint.microsoft.com.

## 7.1.2 Understanding PowerPivot for SharePoint

PowerPivot for SharePoint is a collection of components and services that allow you to view and manage PowerPivot models in SharePoint 2010. PowerPivot for SharePoint extends SharePoint Server 2010 and its Excel Services component to add server-side processing, collaboration, and document management support for the PowerPivot workbooks that you publish to SharePoint.

***Understanding components and service interaction***

SharePoint supports different deployment configurations, as follows:

- Single-tier deployment – SharePoint and the database server are installed on a single machine.
- Two-tier deployment – SharePoint and the database server are installed on two machines.
- Three-tier deployment – SharePoint front-end components are installed on a front-end server, SharePoint application components are installed on an application server, and the SharePoint configuration and content databases are hosted on a third server.

To ensure that PowerPivot reports are available within the SharePoint collaborative environment, PowerPivot for SharePoint includes a set of features that allow you to deploy and manage PowerPivot models. **Figure 7.2** shows the logical components and services that enable the PowerPivot functionality in a SharePoint environment.

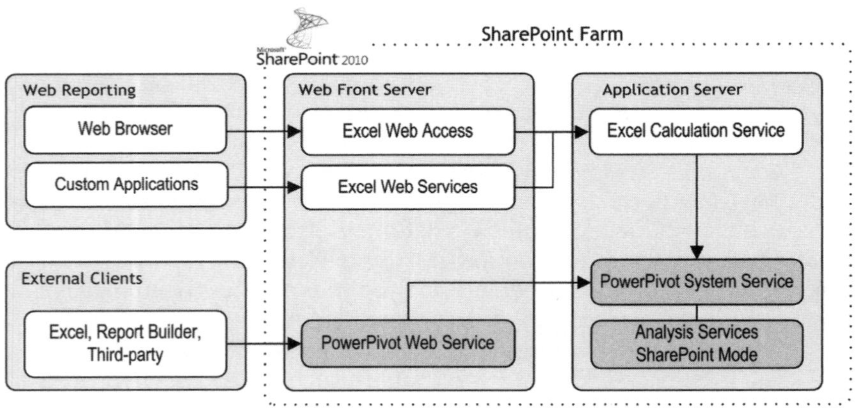


**Figure 7.2** PowerPivot for SharePoint uses the built-in SharePoint services and adds new services.

PowerPivot for SharePoint leverages some of the SharePoint services and adds new services (the boxes with the shaded background), including PowerPivot Web Service, PowerPivot System Service, and an Analysis Services instance running in SharePoint (VertiPaq) integration mode.

***Excel Web Access***

The Excel Web Access service was introduced in SharePoint 3.0. It renders Excel workbooks in HTML without requiring Excel on the desktop. The service doesn't impose restrictions on the Excel content and can render any workbook, including regular Excel sheets with data and formulas, or sheets with native, OLAP, and PowerPivot reports. When the user points the web browser to the workbook, a special Excel Web Access web part embedded on the web page calls Excel Calculation Services to recalculate and render the workbook.

***Excel Web Services***

This service provides programmatic access to workbooks. Custom applications can call its web methods to calculate, set, and extract values from workbooks, and to refresh external data connections.

**NOTE** Since PowerPivot doesn't integrate with the Excel object model, currently it's not possible to programmatically refresh PowerPivot data connections. However, you can use PowerPivot for SharePoint to schedule a data refresh for PowerPivot models.

***Excel Calculation Service***

This service loads and calculates PowerPivot workbooks in much the same way as other Excel workbooks. When the user performs an interactive report action, such as drill down or changing a slicer, this service interacts with the PowerPivot System Service to query the Analysis Services instance.

***PowerPivot Web Service***

This service exposes PowerPivot workbooks that are deployed to SharePoint as data sources to external applications, such as Excel or Report Builder. External applications communicate with PowerPivot Web Service through the XML for Analysis (XML/A) protocol, which is the same protocol that Multidimensional uses. As a result, client applications can send Multidimensional Expressions (MDX) queries to query PowerPivot data in workbook applications that are hosted in a SharePoint farm.

***PowerPivot System Service***

This service is the workhorse of PowerPivot for SharePoint. It communicates with the Analysis Services instance for any action that requires querying or managing the PowerPivot models. Such actions include managing the application database, monitoring server health, coordinating client requests for load balancing, collecting usage data, and performing automatic data refresh for PowerPivot workbooks.

***Analysis Services in SharePoint mode***

Do you remember that tabular models are powered by an in-memory VertiPaq engine? To provide enterprise-level scalability, PowerPivot models are actually hosted in an Analysis Services instance running in a special SharePoint (VertiPaq) mode. This instance must be installed on the SharePoint application server. The Analysis Services instance is dedicated to SharePoint only and can't be used to deploy Multidimensional or Tabular organizational models. That said, you can install additional instances of Analysis Services on the same server if needed.

Let's gain a better understanding of how PowerPivot for SharePoint interacts with Analysis Services.

## 7.1.3 Understanding Runtime Interaction

PowerPivot for SharePoint engages different services, depending on the specific action initiated by the end user. Next, I'll provide a few examples so you can understand at a high level the most significant activities.

***Uploading models and viewing reports***

Uploading an Excel workbook with a PowerPivot model isn't much different than uploading a regular Office document. SharePoint saves the file in its content database and then shows a link to the workbook in the document library where the document is uploaded.

**NOTE** There are additional activities that take place when you deploy the workbook to the PowerPivot Gallery document library, which is specifically designed to host PowerPivot models. For example, a special event handler executes the program GetSnapshot.exe in the background to load the PowerPivot workbook and to obtain an image snapshot of its content.

Unless you initiate an interactive report action, viewing a pivot report that's embedded in the workbook involves only the Excel Web Access service and Excel Calculation Services. No requests are made to PowerPivot System Service or to Analysis Services.

***Performing report interactive actions***

When you perform an interactive action that requires querying the PowerPivot model, such as drilling down or filtering a PowerPivot report, more services hop into action. The PowerPivot System Service extracts the PowerPivot model data, which is saved in an Analysis Services backup format, and it restores the database on the Analysis Services instance. From that point on, all the queries are directed to that database. The entire process is completely transparent to the end user. You can see these Analysis Services databases when you connect to the Analysis Services instance on the SharePoint application server, as shown in **Figure 7.3**. You should never create reports or custom applications that query these databases directly because they're exclusively owned and managed by PowerPivot for SharePoint.

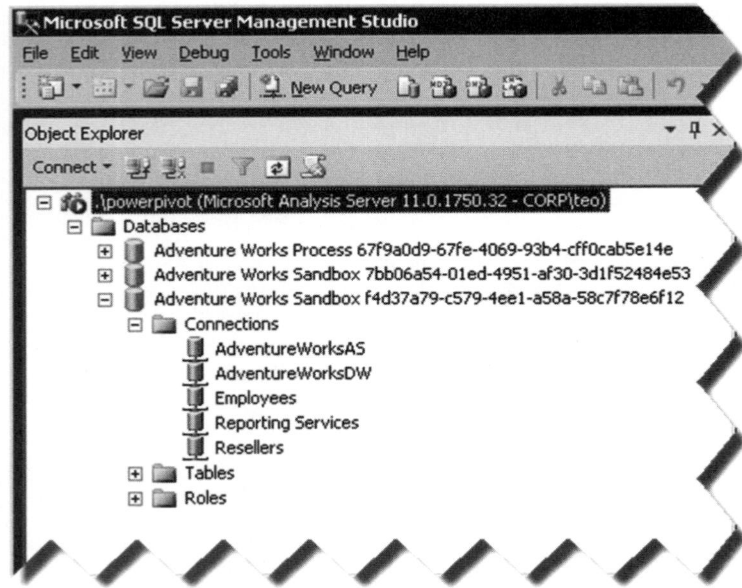


**Figure 7.3** PowerPivot for SharePoint creates a temporary Analysis Services database for each workbook.

***Unloading databases***

The PowerPivot System Service periodically scans and unloads the Analysis Services databases if needed. In general, this happens when the database has been inactive for some time or when the Excel workbook has been refreshed. Dave Wickert, from the Microsoft Analysis Services team, provides more details on this subject in his blog post, "A Peek Inside: Unloading PowerPivot Data" at http://bit.ly/unloadpp.

## 7.2 Installing PowerPivot for SharePoint

Due to the complexity of SharePoint itself, installing PowerPivot for SharePoint is much more complicated than installing PowerPivot for Excel. In this section, I'll walk you through the steps required to install PowerPivot for SharePoint on a single server for testing purposes. I would recommend this setup if you're new to SharePoint because it will help you work out any issues before attempting a production setup.

Setting up PowerPivot for SharePoint on an existing farm requires more planning. For more information, see the "Install PowerPivot for SharePoint" topic (http://bit.ly/ppsonexistingfarm) and the "Deployment Checklist: Multi-Server Installation of PowerPivot for SharePoint" topic in Books Online (http://bit.ly/ppsonmultiserver).

### 7.2.1 Understanding Prerequisites

Before you start, review the Hardware and Software Requirements (PowerPivot for SharePoint) document at http://bit.ly/ppsrequirements.

***Planning hardware***
Your test server must have a 64-bit processor because SharePoint 2010 is available only in 64-bit. It should have also at least 8 GB of RAM. If you plan to set up a virtual machine, you need 64-bit virtualization software, such as Hyper-V in Windows Server 2008 and later, or VMware by VMware Inc., or VirtualBox by Oracle Corporation. As of the time of this writing, Microsoft Virtual PC doesn't support 64-bit guest operating systems, and you can't use it to install SharePoint 2010 on your computer.

***Planning software***
Review the following prerequisites specific to the steps required to set up a test server:

- I recommend the Windows Server 2008 R2 operating system. The computer must belong to an Active Directory domain. If the machine has been added to a domain already, you must obtain a domain service account. If the machine doesn't belong to a domain and if adding it to an existing domain isn't an option, you need to install Active Directory Domain Services (see the installation steps in the next section), and then set up a standalone domain.
- You need to have local administrator rights to the server.
- You need to obtain SharePoint 2010 Server Enterprise edition. You can download the evaluation version at http://technet.microsoft.com/en-us/evalcenter/ee388573.
- You need SQL Server 2012 Evaluation, Developer, Business Intelligence, or Enterprise Edition. You can obtain an evaluation copy from the SQL Server 2012 website at http://www.microsoft.com/sqlserver.

### 7.2.2 Installing Active Directory Domain Services

PowerPivot for SharePoint requires that Active Directory domain accounts be used as service accounts. Therefore, you can't install PowerPivot for SharePoint on a machine that's running in a workgroup mode. You can skip this section if the server has been already added to a corporate domain. If the server doesn't belong to a domain and it's not possible to add it to an existing domain, follow these steps to install Active Directory Services on a test server, and then promote it to a domain controller.

*Installing the Active Directory Domain Services role*

Start by installing the Active Directory Domain Services (AD DS) role on the server.

1. Open the Server Manager, and then click Server Roles.
2. Check the Active Directory Domain Services role, and then click Next, as shown in **Figure 7.4**.
3. Accept the defaults in the next steps.

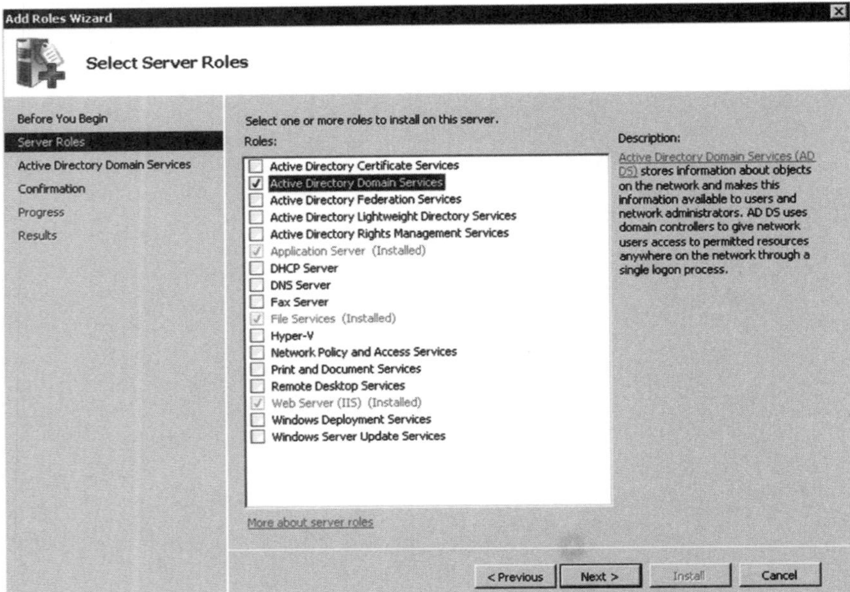


**Figure 7.4** Select the Active Directory Domain Services role.

4. Installing only the AD DS role doesn't promote the server to a domain controller. You need to do this by running the dcpromo.exe tool. To do so, click the "Close the wizard and launch the Active Directory Domain Services Installation Wizard (dcpromo.exe)" link in the Installation Results step (see **Figure 7.5**).

*Running the Active Directory Installation Wizard*

After you click the link, the setup starts the Active Directory Installation Wizard.

1. In the Choose a Deployment Configuration step, select the Create a New Domain in a New Forest option since you'll set up a standalone domain.
2. In the Name the Forest Root Domain step, enter the name of the root domain, such as *adventureworks.com*. In my case, I entered *prologika.com*, as shown in **Figure 7.6**.
3. In the Set Forest Functional Level, choose Windows Server 2008 R2. Since you're setting a standalone domain, you don't need to worry about compatibility with other domains.
4. In the Additional Domain Controller Options step, uncheck the DNS Server checkbox. That's because you're doing a single-server installation, and you don't need a Domain Name System (DNS). Click Next, and then accept the DNS Registration Failure prompt that follows.
5. Accept the default settings for Location for Database, Log Files, and SYSVOL, assuming you want to install the domain files on the C drive.
6. In the Directory Services Restore Mode Administrator Password step, enter a password that you'll use if you ever need to restore the domain settings.

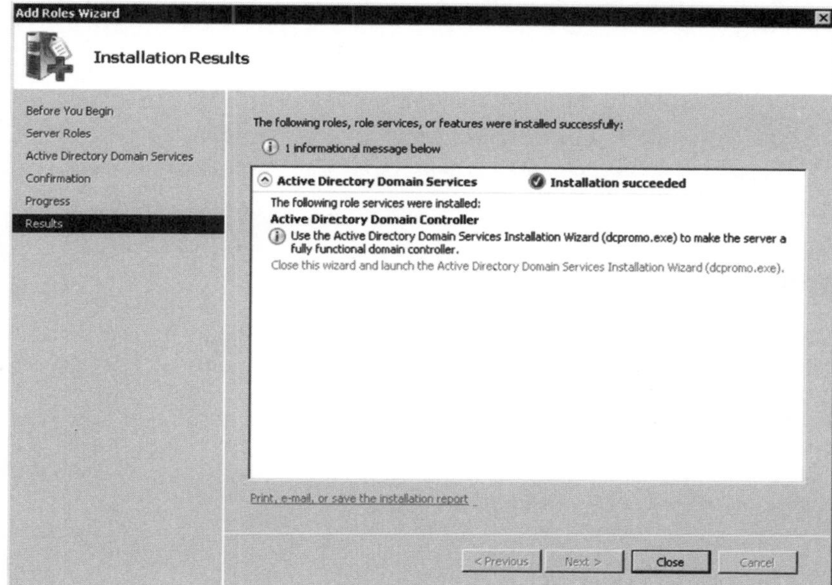


**Figure 7.5** Click the link to promote the server to a domain controller.

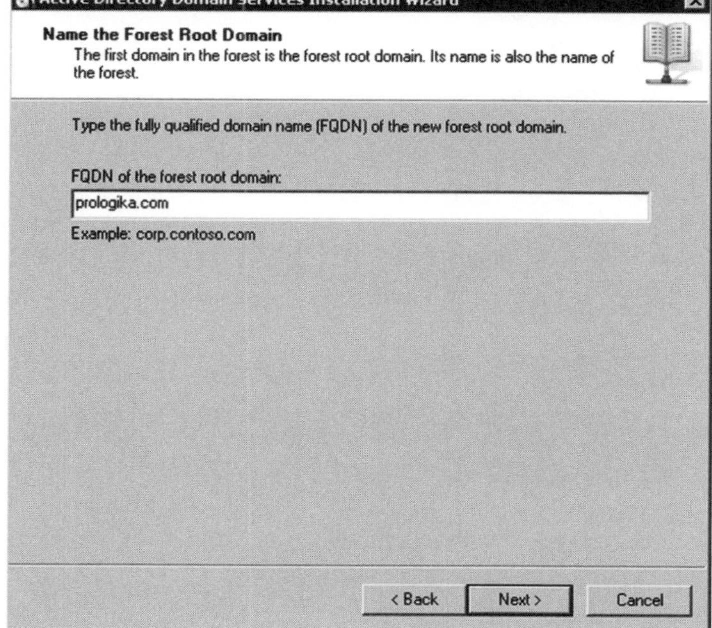


**Figure 7.6** Enter the name of the forest domain.

7. Review the settings in the Summary page, and then click Next to start the domain promotion process.
8. Once the wizard is done, reboot the server, and then log in using your domain login credentials. You won't be able to log in with your local Windows account anymore. For example, if your user name is "administrator" and you chose "prologika.com" as a root domain, log in as

"prologika\administrator". This works because the promotion process has automatically mapped your local login to a domain login.

9. Click All Programs ⇨ Administrative Tools. Observe that you have several Active Director applets, including Active Directory Users and Computers.
10. Click Active Directory Users and Computers, and then select the Users folder. Create a new user account, such as *powerpivotsvc*. You'll use this account as a service account later on to run the PowerPivot for SharePoint services under it.

## 7.2.3 Installing SharePoint Server

Once Active Directory is configured, the next step is to install SharePoint Server 2010 Enterprise edition. This involves installing the SharePoint prerequisites and a new SharePoint farm.

***Installing the SharePoint prerequisites***
Before you set up SharePoint, you need to install several software components and services.

1. If the setup doesn't start automatically when you insert or mount the SharePoint Server DVD, double-click the default.hta file.
2. Click the Install Software Prerequisites link (see **Figure 7.7**) to start the Microsoft SharePoint 2010 Products Preparation Tool wizard.

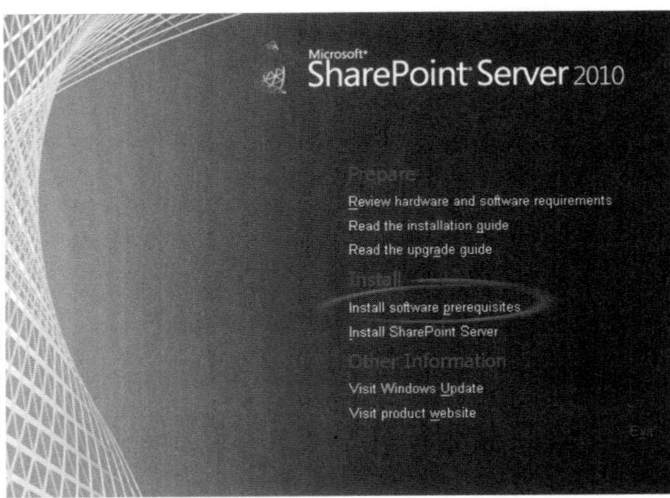


**Figure 7.7** Click the "Install software prerequisites" link to install the SharePoint prerequisites.

3. The next step shows you what prerequisites will be installed. Click Next.
4. Accept the licensing agreement, and then click Next to start the installation process.

After installing the prerequisites, I suggest you reboot the server.

***Installing SharePoint***
The next step is to set up SharePoint, as follows:

1. Double-click the default.hta file to open the splash screen again.
2. Click the Install SharePoint Server link.
3. In the next steps, accept the licensing agreement and enter the product key.

**NOTE** If you install SharePoint on a machine that isn't a domain controller, the wizard shows the "Choose the Installation Type You Want" step, and then you need to select Server Farm, which is the only SharePoint setup option supported by PowerPivot for SharePoint. Next, in the Server Type step, accept the default option of Complete. However, in our case the wizard detects that you're installing SharePoint on a domain controller, and it defaults to these options because that's the only supported configuration. Therefore, you won't see these steps.

4. (Important) In the last step Run Configuration Wizard, uncheck the "Run the SharePoint Products Configuration Wizard Now" checkbox. That's because you'll use the PowerPivot Configuration Tool later on to configure the SharePoint farm. This is the easiest way to configure the SharePoint farm for testing purposes.
5. Download and install SharePoint Server 2010 Service Pack 1 from http://www.microsoft.com/download/en/details.aspx?id=26623. SharePoint Server 2010 Service Pack 1 is a required prerequisite for this release of PowerPivot for SharePoint.

***Installing SQL Server***

Next, you need to run the SQL Server 2012 setup to install PowerPivot for SharePoint. The SQL Server setup program has a specific workflow just for this purpose. Note that you can't install other SQL Server services, such as Reporting Services or Analysis Services in Tabular mode, at the same time you're installing PowerPivot for SharePoint. You must run the setup again after PowerPivot for SharePoint is installed to add the additional services you need.

1. Run the SQL Server 2012 setup program.
2. In the SQL Server Installation Center screen, click the Installation link, and then click the "New SQL Server Stand-alone Installation or Add Features to an Existing Installation" link.
3. Click OK in the Setup Support Rules step. Enter the product key in the Product Key step, and then accept the license terms in the License Terms step. The SQL Server setup program installs the setup files and then starts a setup wizard that walks you through the setup process.
4. The Setup Support Rules step checks for known problems that might fail the setup process. Assuming all rules pass, click Next.
5. In the Setup Role step, select the "SQL Server PowerPivot for SharePoint" option, and then check the "Add SQL Server Database Relational Engine Services" checkbox, as shown in **Figure 7.8**. This configuration will set up PowerPivot for SharePoint and install the SQL Server Relational Database Engine to host the SharePoint databases.

**NOTE** If you want to host the SharePoint database on another SQL Server instance, leave the Add SQL Server Database Relational Engine Services to this Installation checkbox unchecked. You can use the PowerPivot Configuration Tool later on to specify that SQL Server instance. Another reason to leave this checkbox unchecked is when the SharePoint farm is already configured and you just want to add PowerPivot for SharePoint to it.

6. Assuming you want to install the files in the default C:\Program Files\Microsoft SQL Server folder, click Next on the Feature Selection page.
7. The Installation Rules runs a set of rules to ensure that the setup won't be blocked. If the setup discovers any critical issues, you click on the link next to the issue to get more information. You must address critical issues and restart the setup. An example of a critical issue that I ran into was that I had to upgrade an existing Visual Studio 2010 installation to Service Pack 1. If there are no critical issues detected, click Next in the Installation Rules step.
8. In the Instance Configuration step, notice that by default the setup will install SQL Server and Analysis Services on a named instance called POWERPIVOT. If you prefer, you can change the instance name. Click Next.

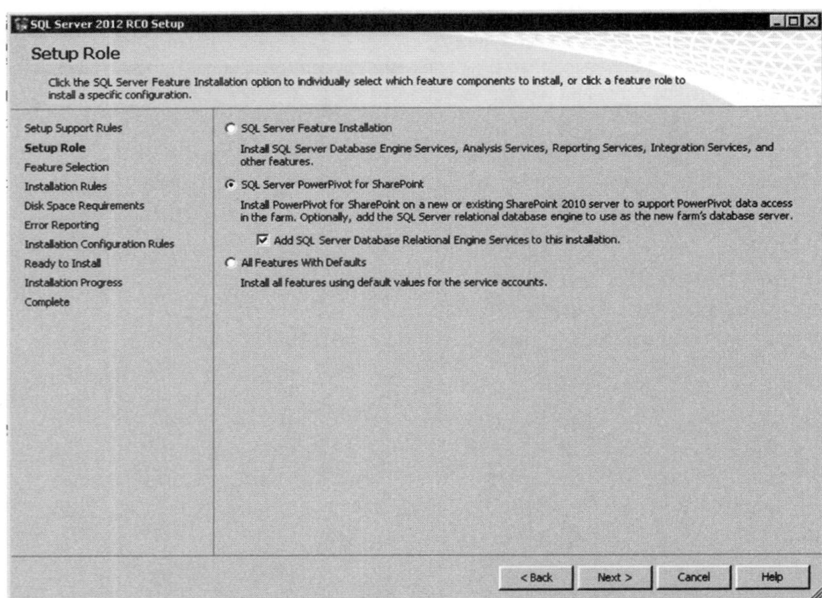


**Figure 7.8** Select the SQL Server PowerPivot for SharePoint option to set up PowerPivot for SharePoint.

9. In the Server Configuration step, enter a domain service account for Analysis Services, as shown in **Figure 7.9**. PowerPivot for SharePoint requires a domain account for the Analysis Services service so that you can manage this account in the SharePoint Central Administration application.

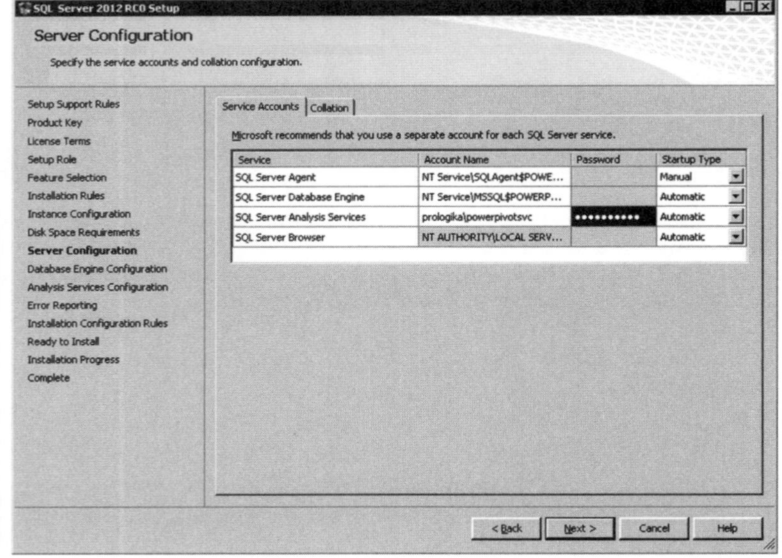


**Figure 7.9** The SQL Server Analysis Services service must use a domain account.

10. In the Database Engine Configuration step, I recommend you enable Mixed Mode for SQL Server authentication. Enter a password for the SQL Server system administrator (SA) user. Click the Add Current User button to add yourself as a SQL Server administrator. Consider adding the local

Administrators group as well in order to grant all Windows local administrators the SQL Server administrator rights.

11. In the Analysis Services Configuration step, click the Add Current User button to add yourself as an Analysis Services administrator. There is no need to add the local Administrators group because by default this group gains system administrator rights to Analysis Services anyway (the default value of the Analysis Services BuiltinAdminsAreServerAdmins setting is set to True).
12. The Installation Configuration Rules step validates another set of rules to determine if the installation process will be blocked. Assuming there aren't any blocking rules, click Next.
13. Review the setup summary in the Ready to Install step, and then click the Install button to start the installation process.

The SQL Server setup installs the requested features. If all is well, once the setup finishes, the Complete step should show a successful status for all the features.

## 7.2.4 Configuring PowerPivot for SharePoint

In the previous release, the SQL Server setup program would install and configure the SharePoint farm and PowerPivot for SharePoint. However, due to the complexity of SharePoint itself, it was difficult to troubleshoot setup issues when something went wrong. Microsoft attempts to address this situation by refactoring the setup in this release. The SQL Server setup program would only install the PowerPivot for SharePoint bits and start services. Installation won't be complete until the server is configured as a post-installation task, using one of the following approaches:

- PowerPivot Configuration Tool
- Central Administration
- PowerShell

***Running the PowerPivot Configuration Tool***

This release of SQL Server brings a new PowerPivot Configuration Tool for configuring and repairing PowerPivot for SharePoint. Next, I'll walk you through the steps to run the PowerPivot Configuration Tool and complete the PowerPivot for SharePoint setup.

1. Open the PowerPivot Configuration Tool from the Microsoft SQL Server 2012 ⇨ Configuration Tools program group.
2. Once the tool examines the system, it shows a menu with three options:
   - Configure or Repair PowerPivot for SharePoint (default) – Use this option to perform a new installation or to repair a failed PowerPivot for SharePoint installation.
   - Remove Features, Services, Applications, and Solutions – Use this option to uninstall PowerPivot for SharePoint from your SharePoint farm.
   - Upgrade Features, Services, Applications, and Solutions – Use this option when you want to upgrade from SQL Server 2008 R2 or SQL Server 2012 Release Candidate 0 (RC 0). Note that this task upgrades only the program files and application pages; it doesn't upgrade PowerPivot workbooks.
3. Leave the Configure or Repair PowerPivot for SharePoint option selected, and then click OK.

The tool validates the requested action and then displays the main screen, as shown in **Figure 7.10**. On the left side, the tool shows a list of the tasks that need to be performed to bring PowerPivot for SharePoint to an operational state. The task list will vary depending on your setup. For example, if the SharePoint farm is already configured, you'll see fewer actions. In the right pane, the Parameters tab shows a few fields that need to be filled, in order to configure PowerPivot for SharePoint. The Script tab shows the PowerShell script for each task. If you're new to PowerShell for SharePoint, watch the "Windows PowerShell for SharePoint Server 2010 Administrators" video by Todd Klindt to get you started at http://bit.ly/sharepointpowershell. Finally, to help you troubleshoot failed tasks, the Output tab shows the execution log for each task.

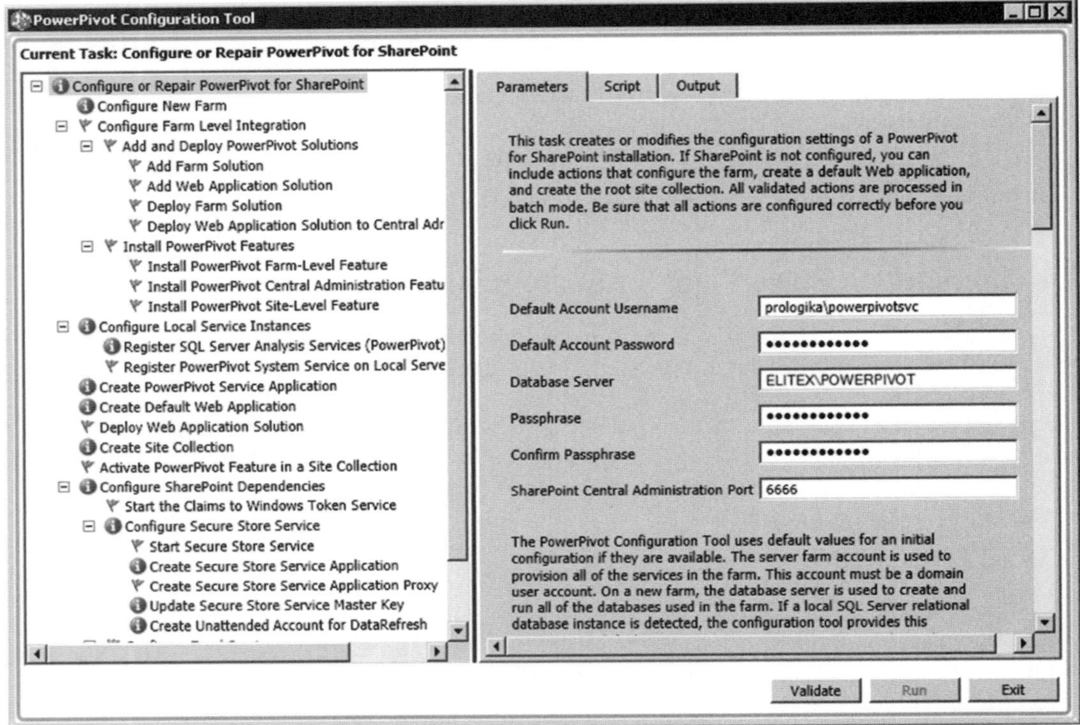


**Figure 7.10** The PowerPivot Configuration Tool shows each step that needs to be performed.

4. In the Parameters tab in the right pane, enter a domain service account that will be used as a default account. This account is used to provision shared services in the farm, and it's used as a service account for PowerPivot for SharePoint. It defaults to your domain account, but you should change it to a designated service account instead.
5. In the Database Server field, enter the SQL Server instance that will host the SharePoint databases.
6. In the Passphrase and Confirm Passphrase fields, enter a passphrase that SharePoint will use as the basis for encryption between members of a SharePoint farm. If SharePoint is already configured, enter the passphrase you specified when you installed the SharePoint farm.
7. If the SharePoint farm isn't configured, in the SharePoint Central Administration Port field, enter the port for the SharePoint Central Administration web application. I suggest you enter a port that you can easily remember. For example, if you enter 9999, the SharePoint Central Administration URL will be http:/<server>:9999.
8. Click Validate for the PowerPivot Configuration Tool to validate the entries. You should get a message that the validation was successful.

9. Click the Run button to execute the tasks. Click Yes in the confirmation prompt that asks you if the configuration settings will be applied to the SharePoint farm.
10. The PowerPivot Configuration Tool displays an Activity Progress dialog box so that you know which task is being executed. The PowerPivot Configuration Tool executes tasks sequentially.

    PowerPivot for SharePoint should be in an operational state when all tasks execute successfully. Once the PowerPivot Configuration Tool is done, reboot the server. Or, start the Windows Command Prompt as an administrator, type in *iisreset*, and then press Enter to restart Internet Information Services (IIS).

    ***When things go wrong***
    If a task fails, you need to analyze the issue and fix it. Then, you can restart the PowerPivot Configuration Tool to continue with the remaining tasks. In some cases, the tool suggests corrective actions. For example, **Figure 7.11** shows that it failed to install the PowerPivot Farm-Level feature, and it suggests the use of the Force attribute to overwrite the feature.

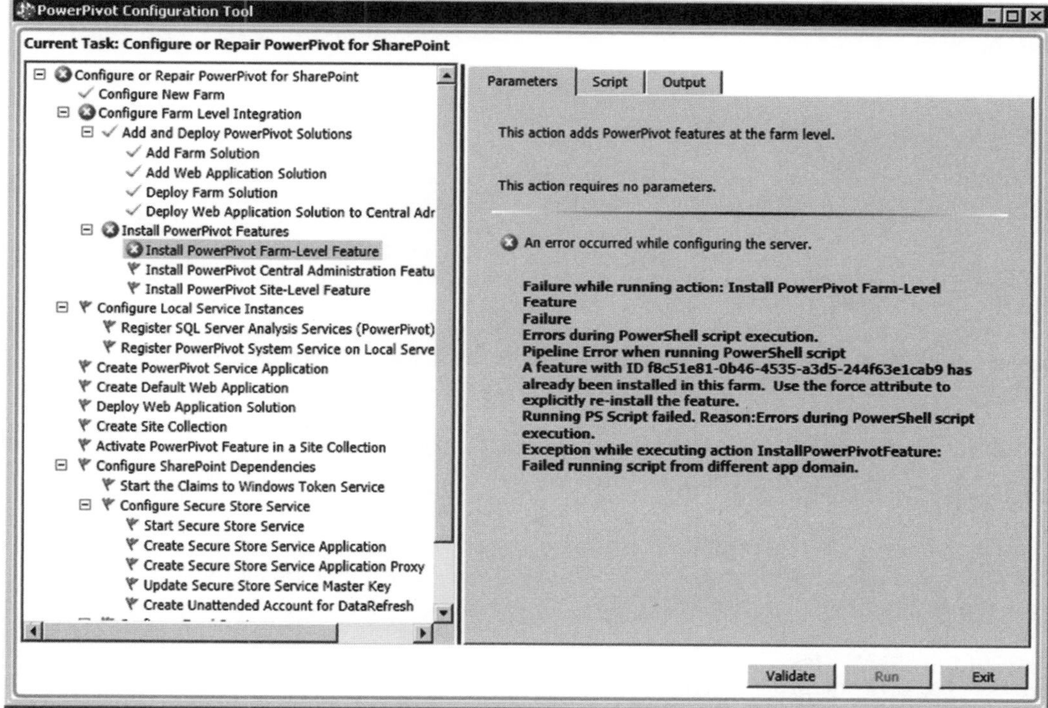


**Figure 7.11** The PowerPivot Configuration Tool reports configuration errors.

In this particular case, I followed these steps to correct this issue:

1. I switched to the Script tab, and then copied the PowerShell script for this action. Notice that in this case the task informs you that it requires loading a ConfigurePowerPivot.ps1 custom library from the \Microsoft SQL Server\110\Tools\PowerPivotTools\ConfigurationTool\Resources folder, as follows:

```
# Open PowerShell library from: C:\Program Files\Microsoft SQL Serv-
er\110\Tools\PowerPivotTools\ConfigurationTool\Resources\ConfigurePowerPivot.ps1
Install-SPFeature -path PowerPivot
```

2. I started the SharePoint 2010 Management Shell as an administrator from the Microsoft SharePoint 2010 Products program group.
3. To load the custom library, I executed this command in the Windows Command Prompt:

```
cd "C:\Program Files\Microsoft SQL Server\110\Tools\PowerPivotTools\ConfigurationTool\Resources"
```

4. I loaded the PowerPivot for SharePoint custom library. **Figure 7.12** shows how to load the ConfigurePowerPivot.ps1 library in SharePoint 2010 Management Shell before you can call its functions.

```
Administrator: SharePoint 2010 Management Shell
PS C:\Program Files\Microsoft SQL Server\110\Tools\PowerPivotTools\Configuration
Tool\Resources> .\ConfigurePowerPivot.ps1
PS C:\Program Files\Microsoft SQL Server\110\Tools\PowerPivotTools\Configuration
Tool\Resources> _
```

**Figure 7.12** Loading the ConfigurePowerPivot.ps1 library in PowerShell.

5. I pasted the PowerShell script that I obtained from the Script tab, and then executed it with the force attribute as the PowerPivot Configuration Tool suggested.

```
Install-SPFeature -path PowerPivot –force
```

6. Back in the PowerPivot Configuration Tool, I clicked the Validate button, and then clicked the Run button to continue with the configuration process.

   If you encounter another error, perform similar steps to correct the issue, and then re-run the PowerPivot Configuration Tool until all the steps are successfully installed.

**REAL WORLD** As someone who has done a fair share of manual SharePoint configuration troubleshooting, I really like the PowerPivot Configuration Tool. In one installation, the tool failed to create the default SharePoint web application (SharePoint – 80). I created the web application manually and reran the tool, which continued with its remaining tasks to configure a fully functional PowerPivot for SharePoint installation. The tool can save you many hours of troubleshooting and searching the Internet for a solution!

## 7.2.5 Upgrade Considerations

If you installed the SQL Server 2008 R2 version of PowerPivot for SharePoint, you can upgrade that instance to use the new features. Next, I'll provide a few considerations for you to keep in mind when planning the upgrade process.

***Understanding upgrade steps***

In a nutshell, the upgrade process requires the following steps:

1. Run the SQL Server 2012 setup program to upgrade the program files on each application server in the SharePoint Farm.
2. Run the PowerPivot Configuration Tool, and then select the "Upgrade Features, Services, Applications, and Solutions" option to perform the SharePoint upgrade actions.
3. (Optional) Upgrade PowerPivot workbooks (see the section below).

***Using PowerPivot version 1 (SQL Server 2008 R2) workbooks***

PowerPivot for SharePoint supports version 1 and version 2 workbooks side by side. Keeping the legacy PowerPivot models without upgrading could be useful if you have a lot of published workbooks and if you don't plan to use the PowerPivot for Excel version 2 features. Or, you might want to allow users who haven't upgraded to PowerPivot version 2 to deploy their models to PowerPivot for SharePoint 2012. Version 1 workbooks are not automatically upgraded, but they continue to work via backward compatibility interfaces.

I previously covered that Excel connects to the embedded PowerPivot model using the Analysis Services OLE DB Provider. PowerPivot 1.0 (and PerformancePoint Services) uses the version 4 of this provider (MSOLAP.4), which might not be installed on a new server. One quick way to find out if the MSOLAP.4 provider is installed is to check for the existence of the \Program Files\Microsoft Analysis Services\AS OLEDB\10 folder. If the provider isn't installed and you want to deploy PowerPivot version 1 workbooks or use PerformancePoint Services to connect to them, download and install the provider from the SQL Server 2008 R2 Feature Pack page at http://bit.ly/msolap4provider. Scroll down the page until you find the "Microsoft Analysis Services OLE DB Provider for Microsoft SQL Server 2008 R2" section, and then download the x64 version of the SQLServer2008_ASOLEDB10.msi installation program.

***Upgrading PowerPivot R2 workbooks***

PowerPivot for SharePoint is capable of auto-upgrading PowerPivot version 1 workbooks, but this behavior isn't enabled by default. For more information about how to enable auto-upgrading, read the "Upgrade PowerPivot for Excel and PowerPivot Data" topic in Books Online at http://bit.ly/upgradepps. Once the feature is activated, all the legacy workbooks that are scheduled for an automatic data refresh will get upgraded on the next refresh. If you publish a PowerPivot workbook created with PowerPivot version 1, and then enable data refresh, it will get upgraded on the first refresh.

Besides auto-upgrading on data refresh, there is no other way to batch upgrade PowerPivot workbooks. You need to open each workbook in Excel, click the PowerPivot Window button to initiate a manual update, and then republish the workbook to the server.

The "Upgrading PowerPivot for SharePoint" topic in the MSDN Library (http://bit.ly/ppssharepointupgrade) provides more details of how to upgrade PowerPivot for SharePoint on an existing SharePoint farm.

## 7.3 Verifying the SharePoint Setup

By now, you have gone through the steps required to configure SharePoint, SQL Server, and PowerPivot for SharePoint. Next, you need to verify that the server is functional before you let new users access it. To do this, you need to deploy a PowerPivot model to the SharePoint server, and then test a PowerPivot report, as I'll show you next.

### 7.3.1 Publishing PowerPivot Models

You can deploy a PowerPivot model directly from Microsoft Excel or by uploading it using the SharePoint document management capabilities. The natural place for published PowerPivot models is the PowerPivot Gallery document library.

***Introducing the PowerPivot Gallery***

As a part of the installation process, PowerPivot for SharePoint creates a special library in the default SharePoint site. This library is called PowerPivot Gallery, and it's specifically designed to host PowerPivot models. The setup program adds a PowerPivot Gallery link to the left navigation menu, as shown in **Figure 7.13**.

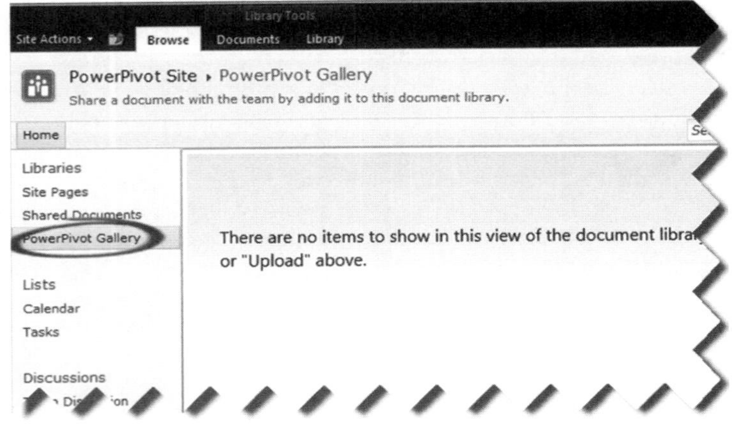


**Figure 7.13** PowerPivot Gallery is a special document library for storing PowerPivot models.

PowerPivot Gallery requires Microsoft Silverlight version 5 to be installed on the client computer. If Silverlight isn't present, PowerPivot Gallery will prompt you to download and install it.

**TIP** What if you want to add a PowerPivot Gallery document library to an existing site? You can do so by expanding the Site Actions drop-down menu, and then click More Options. In the Create page, click the Library section, and then click the PowerPivot Gallery template. If you can't find the PowerPivot Gallery template, make sure the Power View Integration Feature is activated at the Site Collection level. To verify this, go to Site Actions ⇨ Site Settings, and then click the Site Collection Features link in the "Site Collection Administration" section. Make sure that the Power View Integration Feature has a status of Active.

***Publishing PowerPivot models with Excel***

Follow these steps to publish the Adventure Works model from Excel:

1. In Excel, open the Adventure Works.xlsx workbook with your changes from Chapter 6.
2. In the Excel File menu, click Save & Send. In the Save & Send page, select the Save to SharePoint option, as shown in **Figure 7.14**.

**Figure 7.14** Use the Excel Save & Send menu to publish a PowerPivot model to SharePoint.

**NOTE** If you're running Excel on Windows Server 2008 or Windows Server 2008 R2 operating system, you might find that you won't be able to browse the content of the SharePoint site in the Save As dialog box. The most likely reason is that the Desktop Experience feature isn't installed. As a result the WebDAV protocol, which SharePoint uses to make a SharePoint site look like a file share, isn't enabled. To resolve this issue, open the Windows Server Manager, click the Features folder, and then click Add Features. In the Add Features Wizard, select the Desktop Experience feature, and then proceed to install it. Be aware that the Desktop Experience feature includes a number of other desktop components, such as Windows Media Player, and installing them increases the attack surface (the code that can be accessed by hackers) of your SharePoint application server.

3. If you're publishing to SharePoint for the first time, double-click the "Browse for a Location" option on the right (see **Figure 7.14**). Once you've published a workbook, Excel will remember the link and show it in the Recent Locations section for your convenience.

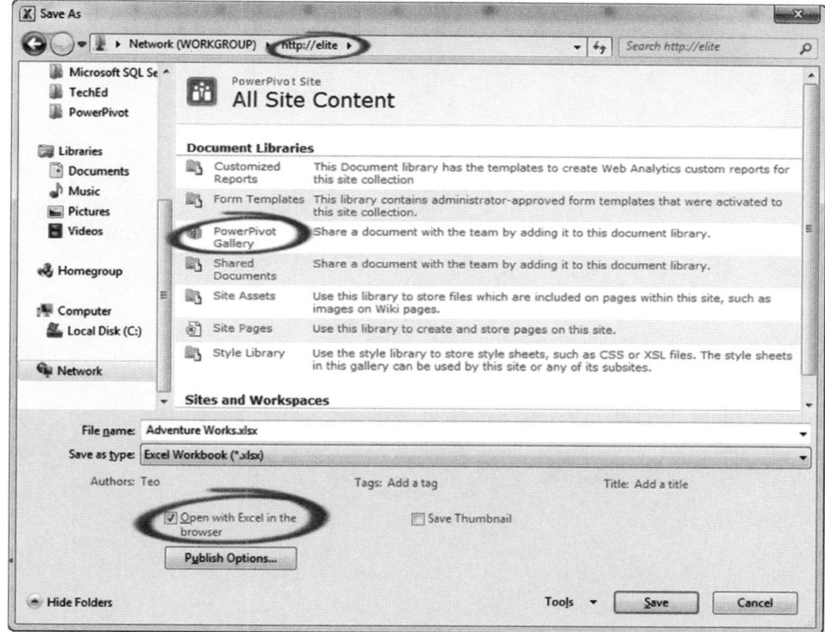


**Figure 7.15** Publish PowerPivot models to the SharePoint PowerPivot Gallery document library.

4. In the Save As dialog box, enter the URL of the SharePoint site that you want to publish to in the navigation field at the top of the dialog box, and then press Enter. In **Figure 7.15**, you can see that I intend to publish the Adventure Works.xlsx workbook to a SharePoint site at *http://elite*.

5. Excel connects to the site and then retrieves its content. You should see the site content in the middle-right pane of the Save As dialog box. Double-click the PowerPivot Gallery link to navigate to it.

**NOTE** There is a difference between the Excel Save As option and the Save & Send option in the File tab of the ribbon. Although both options display the Save As dialog box for you to save to SharePoint, the Save & Send option adds a Publish Options button. You can use Publish Options to select which items in the Excel workbook will be published, and then you can configure optional parameters. I'll discuss these options in more detail in Chapter 8.

6. Notice that the "Open with Excel in the browser" checkbox is checked by default. Click the Save button to publish the workbook and navigate to it in your Web browser.

*Uploading PowerPivot models*

Another option to publish your PowerPivot model is to upload it using the SharePoint document management features.

1. In SharePoint, navigate to the PowerPivot Gallery document library, and then click the Documents tab in the SharePoint ribbon.
2. Expand the Upload Document button, and then click Upload Document to upload one workbook, or click Upload Multiple Documents to upload several Excel files (see **Figure 7.16**).

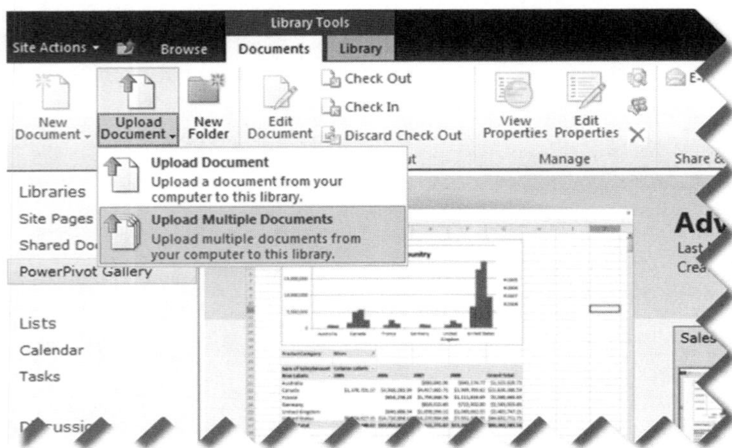


**Figure 7.16** Use the Upload Document feature to upload PowerPivot models to the PowerPivot Gallery document library.

**NOTE** Uploading documents by using the SharePoint UI is a synchronous (sequential) operation that blocks the user interface until the files are uploaded. By contrast, Excel uses the Office Upload Center to upload the file asynchronously (simultaneously) to SharePoint. For more information about how this feature works, read the blog post by Denny Lee (from Microsoft's SQL Customer Advisory Team), "Uploading #PowerPivot for Excel workbook using "Save As" vs. SharePoint UI" (http://bit.ly/ppexcelsaveas).

*Testing interactivity*

Once you have uploaded a PowerPivot model, you can perform a quick test to verify that PowerPivot for SharePoint is functional. Do the following steps:

1. If you used Excel to publish the model and the "Open with Excel in the browser" checkbox was checked (again see **Figure 7.15**), Excel renders the workbook in the web browser. If you uploaded the workbook manually, click the Dashboard report in the Adventure Works PowerPivot model (see **Figure 7.17**).

   You might remember that the initial report rendering doesn't involve the PowerPivot System Service and Analysis Services. Therefore, you must initiate an interactive action to involve all the services to be sure that PowerPivot for SharePoint is fictional.

2. Click a slicer item, or change a PivotTable filter. For example, in the case of the Adventure Works model, click the year 2008 in the CalendarYear slicer, as shown in **Figure 7.18**.

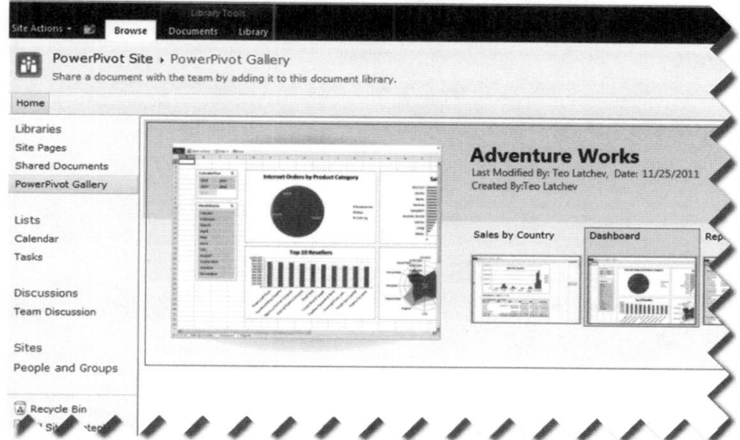


**Figure 7.17** PowerPivot Gallery shows preview images of PowerPivot reports.

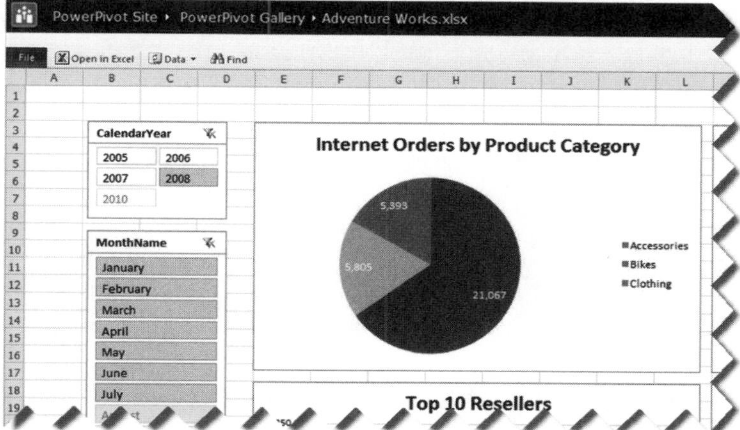


**Figure 7.18** Initiate an interactive feature to test that PowerPivot for SharePoint is functional.

The filtering action should complete successfully. This confirms that PowerPivot for SharePoint is functional. If the operation fails and you see an error, you have a setup issue that you need to resolve. Read the next section for troubleshooting steps.

## 7.3.2 Troubleshooting Techniques

SharePoint is a very valuable and feature-rich product, but it's also complex. Due to the number of layers involved, troubleshooting SharePoint can be a daunting experience. Here are some tips that can help you identify and fix PowerPivot for SharePoint issues.

***SharePoint Unified Logging Service logs***

SharePoint logs error information in text logs that are produced by the SharePoint Unified Logging Services (ULS). The default log location is \Program Files\Common Files\Microsoft Shared\Web Server Extensions\14\LOGS.

1. Navigate to that folder and double-click the latest file with a *.log extension to open it in Notepad, as shown **Figure 7.19**.

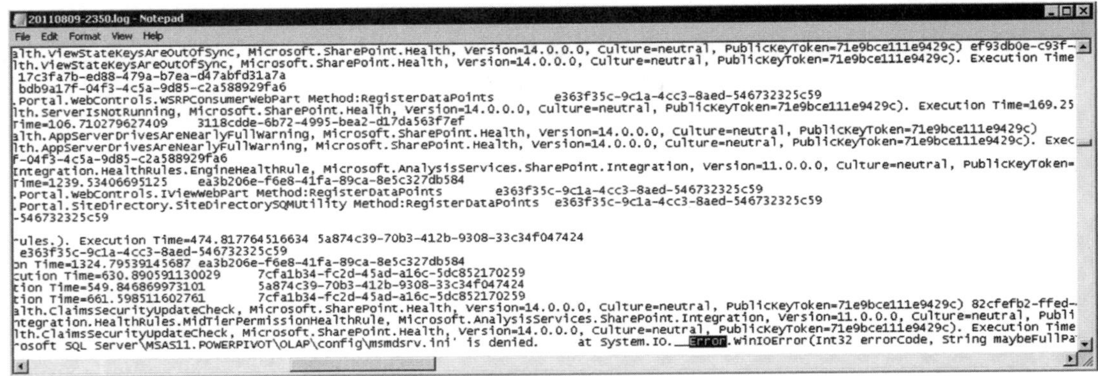

**Figure 7.19** SharePoint logs error messages in ULS log files.

2. Search for "error" or "exception". If SharePoint has reported the correlation identifier of the error message, search for that identifier.

   Sieving through large text files in an attempt to find some important information that could help you troubleshoot the error could be somewhat tedious. Instead, consider using the SharePoint LogViewer (http://sharepointlogviewer.codeplex.com) by Overroot Inc. or the Stefan Gordon's ULS Log Viewer (http://ulsviewer.codeplex.com/).

   ***Using the SharePoint LogViewer***
   I personally prefer the SharePoint LogViewer for its live-monitoring feature that allows you to watch errors as they occur in real time. Follow these steps to use the SharePoint LogViewer to monitor the activity:

1. Start the SharePoint LogViewer. Click the Open File(s) button, or press Ctrl+O to open the current SharePoint log file (the one with the latest timestamp).
2. Enter "*error*" in the filter field to monitor for any messages that contain "error".
3. Click the Start Live Monitoring button.
4. If the error is easily reproducible, initiate the action that triggers the error, such as clicking an item in an Excel slicer.
5. At this point, you should see the error(s) logged in the SharePoint LogViewer. Click the corresponding row, and then examine the error message in the Message area, as shown in **Figure 7.20**.

   If the cause of the error and the resolution steps are not immediately obvious, look up the error message on the Internet to see if you can find more information in the product documentation, blogs, or other resources.

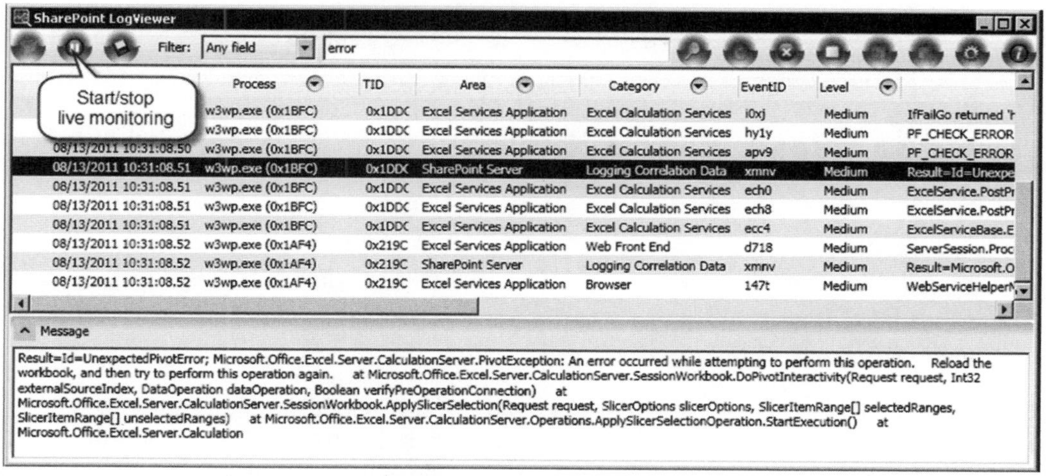

**Figure 7.20** Use the SharePoint LogViewer to monitor errors in real-time.

## 7.4 Summary

PowerPivot for SharePoint allows teams to collaborate and share personal BI solutions through SharePoint Server 2010. This chapter introduced you to PowerPivot for SharePoint and its capabilities. PowerPivot for SharePoint extends the SharePoint BI features and adds new components and services. It requires an Analysis Services instance that's configured in SharePoint integration mode in order to process the PowerPivot models on the server.

I showed you how to perform a standalone installation of PowerPivot for SharePoint for testing purposes. First, you need to install Active Directory services and promote the server to a domain controller. Next, you need to install the Enterprise edition of SharePoint Server 2010. Once SharePoint is installed, run the SQL Server 2012 setup, and then install PowerPoint for SharePoint. Finally, you need to run the PowerPivot Configuration Tool to configure the SharePoint farm and to install the required components and services.

Finally, this chapter provided steps to verify that PowerPivot for SharePoint is functional and to troubleshoot setup issues by examining the SharePoint ULS log files. Now that PowerPivot for SharePoint is up and running, Chapter 8 shows you how you can gain insights from the published PowerPivot models.

# Chapter 8

# SharePoint Insights



Publishing a PowerPivot model to SharePoint gives you several options to gain insights from the data in the model. Your co-workers can browse the Excel pivot reports included in the workbook. They can build interactive Excel pivot reports and Power View reports that use the model as a data source. And, power users can author operational reports with the Reporting Services Report Builder.

This chapter walks you through various ways to build reports from PowerPivot models. It starts by comparing report options so that you can choose the right tool for the task at hand. Next, it shows you how you can interact with and customize Excel reports. You'll learn how to build interactive reports with Power View. Finally, I'll show you how you can author operational reports using Report Builder. You'll find the finished reports in the Ch08 folder. If you haven't done it already, follow the steps in Chapter 7 to deploy the Adventure Works model to the SharePoint PowerPivot Gallery library.

## 8.1 Understanding SharePoint Insights

The fact that tabular models can be queried via Multidimensional Expressions (MDX) allows every online analytical processing (OLAP) client to automatically become a Tabular client. Microsoft provides several report tools that fulfill various report needs, ranging from web-based reporting to standard "canned" reports. This section helps you understand how these tools integrate with PowerPivot for SharePoint and how they compare with each other.

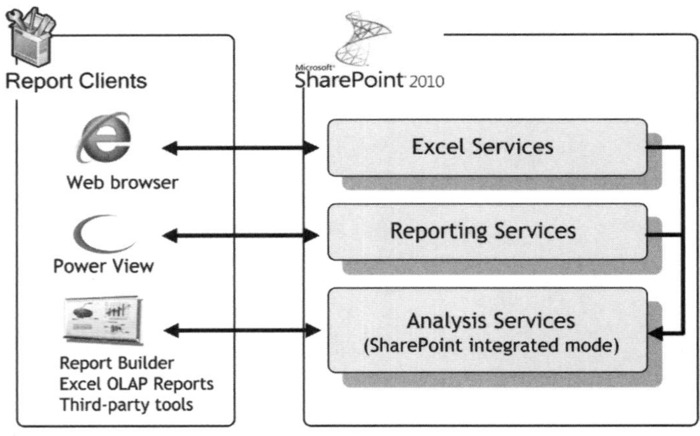


**Figure 8.1** This diagram shows how the Microsoft-provided report tools integrate with PowerPivot for SharePoint.

### 8.1.1 Understanding Integration Options

For the sake of brevity, I'll limit the report clients covered in this chapter to the most popular tools that target business users: Excel, Power View, and Report Builder. **Figure 8.1** shows how these clients integrate with PowerPivot for SharePoint. Other OLAP-capable tools, such as PerformancePoint, Report Designer, and third-party tools, can connect to published models as though they're Multidimensional cubes, which is exactly how Excel OLAP reports and Report Builder integrate with PowerPivot for SharePoint. For more information about the Microsoft-provided business intelligence (BI) tools, read the whitepaper "How to Choose the Right Business Intelligence Technology to Suit Your Style" by John Lauer et al (http://bit.ly/chooseBI).

***Excel web reports***

In Chapter 5, you saw that you can author Excel pivot reports that connect to the PowerPivot model and then include these reports in the same workbook where the PowerPivot model resides. As you've already seen, once you publish the workbook to PowerPivot for SharePoint, these reports immediately become available online to other users, subject to SharePoint security policies. Microsoft Internet Explorer 7.0 (or higher) and Mozilla Firefox 3.5 (or higher) fully support the HTML format produced by Excel Services. And, the December Cumulative Update 2011-12 for SharePoint 2010 (http://bit.ly/sspdeccu) added support for Apple iPad devices.

The natural place for PowerPivot-enhanced Excel workbooks is the PowerPivot Gallery. When you view and interact with the report, a set of services, which **Figure 8.1** refers to as Excel Services, communicate with an Analysis Services instance to query the PowerPivot model and then to render it in HTML format. The Analysis Services instance is configured for SharePoint integrated mode.

***Power View***

Another option for web-based reporting is Power View. Power View is a new interactive data exploration and visualization tool developed by the Microsoft Reporting Services team. It's designed to use Tabular models as data sources. Power View empowers business users to author ad hoc, web-based reports without requiring report authoring experience. Power View is available only in a SharePoint environment, and it requires Microsoft Silverlight version 5 to be installed on the client. Review the "Get Microsoft Silverlight" article at http://bit.ly/slbrowsers for more information about Silverlight browser support.

Power View requires Reporting Services to be installed and configured in SharePoint integrated mode. Power View reports communicate with Reporting Services server components, which in turn communicate with an Analysis Services instance configured for SharePoint integrated mode.

***Other clients***

Excel OLAP pivot reports, Report Builder, and third-party OLAP clients can query PowerPivot models published for SharePoint by sending MDX queries. Report Builder is an ad hoc reporting tool that provides full support for the Reporting Services report authoring features. The tool targets power users willing to author reports from variety of data sources, including PowerPivot models. SQL Server 2008 R2 introduced the third version of Report Builder, which remains unchanged in SQL Server 2012.

Report Builder can connect to a PowerPivot model as it connects to a multidimensional cube. Report Builder includes the MDX query designer that's capable of auto-generating MDX queries for basic reports. Another option for ad hoc reporting is Excel OLAP pivot reports that are connected to a PowerPivot model. This works in the same way as connecting Excel to a multidimensional cube.

## 8.1.2 Comparing Report Tools

Before we jump into report authoring, let's start with a high-level comparison of the tool capabilities and usage scenarios. **Table 8.1** provides a high-level feature comparison between Excel reports, Power View, and Report Builder. It's meant to help you choose the right tool for the reporting task at hand.

**Table 8.1 Feature comparison of report clients that support PowerPivot for SharePoint.**

| Feature | Excel Web Reports | Excel OLAP Reports | Power View | Report Builder |
|---|---|---|---|---|
| Intended audience | Business users | Business users | Business users | Power users |
| Client type | Online | Desktop | Online | Desktop |
| Requires SharePoint | Yes | No | Yes | No |
| Query language | MDX | MDX | DAX | MDX |
| Report type | Ad hoc/operational | Ad hoc | Ad hoc | Ad hoc/operational |
| Report layout | Fixed (limited interactivity) | Interactive | Interactive | Fixed |
| Customization | High | High | Basic | Highest |
| Offline reporting | Yes | No | No | No |
| Query performance | Medium | Medium | Excellent | Medium |

***Excel web reports***

Consider Excel web reports when you need to allow users to view pivot reports online. Once deployed to SharePoint, Excel reports are available for all users across the enterprise without requiring Excel on the desktop. Since the reports have already been authored, there is a low learning curve required for end users to use the reports. And, because the reports are packaged in the same file where the model is, you can view these Excel reports online (inside SharePoint) and offline by downloading the workbook. Online Excel reports are rendered in HTML and don't require installing any software on the client.

On the downside, Excel web reporting is available in SharePoint only. Excel reports have a fixed layout, and the end user can't make layout changes, such as adding or removing a field. However, users can perform interactive actions, such as drilling down a hierarchy and changing report filters. Because Excel reports are not optimized for Tabular, you might encounter performance issues with detail-level reports, such as a report that shows customers and invoices.

***Excel OLAP reports***

As I mentioned, you can author Excel OLAP pivot and chart reports that are connected to a published PowerPivot model. Consider this scenario when you don't have PowerPivot for Excel installed, such as when you have Excel 2007, but you want to author ad hoc reports from published PowerPivot models. Unlike embedded PowerPivot reports, OLAP reports don't support PowerPivot natively, and they present the model metadata as dimensions and measures. In other words, you'll get the PivotTable Field List as opposed to the PowerPivot Field List. As a result, you'll need to understand and adjust to the OLAP-based metadata format. In addition, the modeler will need to define DAX calculations in the PowerPivot workbook itself, since without the PowerPivot Field List, you can't add or change DAX calculations.

Similar to Excel web reports, Excel OLAP reports send MDX queries to the model. This might present performance challenges with detail-level reports.

***Power View reports***
Consider Power View when you need to author basic reports that allow you to explore data interactively. The target audience for Power View reports is business users and no authoring experience is assumed. Power View provides a highly-interactive and visual experience that end users are likely to appreciate. Because Power View was designed specifically to support Tabular, it performs equally well with summarized and detail-level reports.

Similar to Excel reports, Power View is a SharePoint-based tool. Embracing the "more is less" paradigm as a guiding design principle, Power View supports basic reports. For example, Power View doesn't support expressions and it's not extensible.

***Report Builder***
Users familiar with Reporting Services might remember that Report Builder enables power users to create ad hoc reports from a variety of data sources. Implemented as a desktop application, Report Builder is a good option when you need paper-oriented operational reports, such as reports with a page header, footer, groups, and so on. Similar to the Report Designer included in SQL Server Data Tools (SSDT), Report Builder gives you access to all the report authoring features of Reporting Services. You can create flexible layouts and deliver Report Builder reports on demand or through subscriptions.

On the downside, there is a steeper learning curve to become productive with Report Builder. Once the report is designed and published, its layout is fixed and can't be changed without opening the report in Report Builder. Similar to Excel OLAP reports, Report Builder sees a PowerPivot model as a cube and sends MDX queries to it. Unlike Excel reports, report authors can access and fine-tune the MDX query, although this requires MDX skills that business users are unlikely to have.

Now that you know what report options are available in SharePoint environment and how they compare, let's see how you can exercise these reporting options.

## 8.2 Working with Excel Reports

I previously mentioned that the preferred way to share PowerPivot models across the enterprise is to publish them to a SharePoint server that's integrated with PowerPivot. Once the PowerPivot model has been published, end users can view the PowerPivot reports published with the workbook. In addition, end users can author Excel OLAP reports that use the published PowerPivot model as a data source.

### 8.2.1 Working with Excel Web Reports ▶

In Chapter 7, you've deployed the Adventure Works model to the server, ran a PowerPivot report, and tested an interactive action to validate the server setup. Let's now gain further understanding about the capabilities of Excel web reports.

***Viewing reports***
Follow these steps to view the reports published with the Adventure Works model:

1. Open your web browser and navigate to PowerPivot Gallery, such as http://<server>/PowerPivot Gallery.

2. You should see the Adventure Works model, as shown in **Figure 8.2**. The default document library view is Gallery (requires Microsoft Silverlight 5.0 to be installed on the client). This view shows a snapshot image of each spreadsheet. You might see an hourglass icon if the server is currently processing the snapshot image.

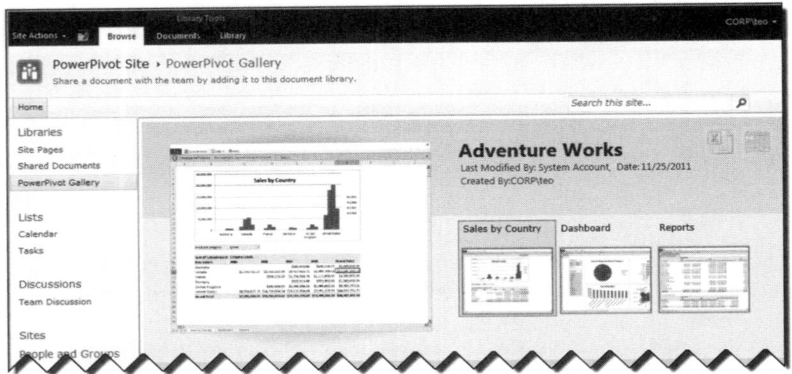


**Figure 8.2** Use the default Gallery view of the PowerPivot Gallery to preview reports.

3. Point your mouse cursor to the Sales by Country thumbnail image. Notice that PowerPivot for SharePoint shows a preview of this report. Point the mouse cursor to the Dashboard image to preview this report as well.

> **TIP** If you like animated effects and get tired of the Gallery view, there are two additional views (Theater and Carousel) that you can try. To change the default PowerPivot Gallery view, go to the Library tab, and then expand the Current View drop-down list. If you're not a fan of Silverlight animation, change the view to All Documents. Changing the document library view is an example of SharePoint personalization. SharePoint isolates such changes to the interactive user so that they don't affect other users.

4. To view the Sales by Country report, click the Sales by Country snapshot image. SharePoint renders the report in a "thin client" mode by exporting the spreadsheet in HTML (see **Figure 8.3**).

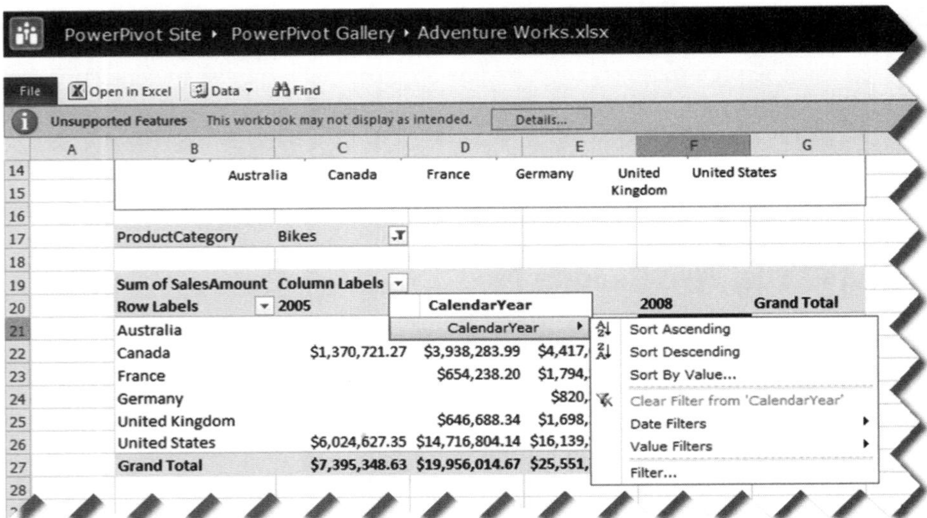


**Figure 8.3** SharePoint renders the report in HTML so you don't Excel to be installed on the desktop.

Notice that the PowerPivot Field List is missing. That's because Excel web reports are rendered in read-only mode and you can't make layout changes. However, interactive features, such as slicers, filtering, and sorting, are supported.

**NOTE** Don't worry about the Unsupported Features prompt caused by the fact that PowerPivot slicers are enclosed in a rectangle. Since the Excel Web Service can't render shapes, it removes the rectangle and displays the warning message. For more information about Excel features that are not supported in Excel Services, read the "Differences between using a workbook in Excel and Excel Services" article at http://bit.ly/excelservicesunsupported.

5. Expand the Column Labels drop-down list. Notice that you can sort and filter the CalendarYear column just like you can in Excel.
6. (Optional) Click the Dashboard tab to view the Dashboard report. Click a slicer item to filter the report by a given year or month.

Not all Excel interactive options are supported. For example, you can't drill through a cell or use the Show Value As feature. Another disappointing limitation is that native printing isn't supported. As a result, you must rely on the browser printing capabilities to print reports, or you can open the workbook in Excel and then use the Excel print feature.

***Working with Excel workbooks***

Excel web reports allows you to make changes to the original workbook and embedded reports.

1. Click the Open in Excel menu (again see **Figure 8.3**). A dialog box pops up to ask you if you want to open the workbook in Read Only (default) more or Edit mode.
2. Select the Edit mode, and then click OK.
3. If you have Excel 2010 installed on your desktop, Excel opens the Adventure Works 2010 workbook. This lets you make changes to the report or to the PowerPivot model if PowerPivot for Excel is installed.
4. For example, to improve the report appearance, click the Excel View ribbon tab, and uncheck the Gridlines checkbox to remove the Excel gridlines, as shown in **Figure 8.4**.

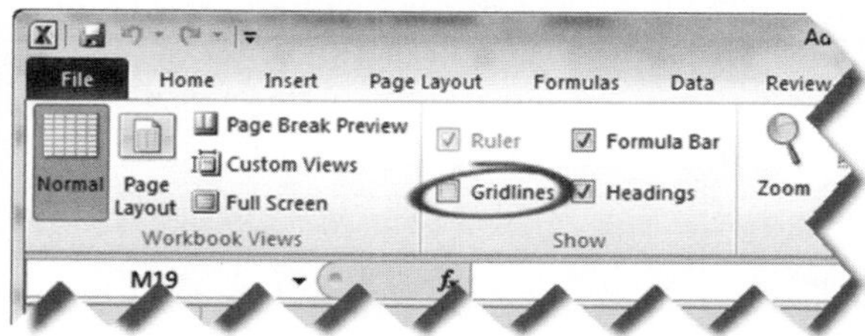


**Figure 8.4** Turn off gridlines to improve the report appearance.

5. Click the Save button in the Quick Access toolbar (above the File tab) to save the workbook back to SharePoint.

The File ribbon tab in the Excel web report (again see **Figure 8.3**) provides additional download options, such as downloading the workbook as a file or a snapshot. A snapshot contains only the reports and not the data. A snapshot can be useful when you want to print the report using the Excel printing capabilities, but you don't want to download the entire workbook with the PowerPivot data. The Reload Workbook option in the File tab reloads the workbook in SharePoint from its original location.

The options in the Data tab are not that useful for PowerPivot for SharePoint. For regular pivot reports, the Refresh Selected Connection option and the Refresh All Connections option connect to the data source and refresh the report data. In the case of PowerPivot reports, however, these options read the cached data in the PowerPivot model. If you have a large report, use the Find tab to search for text on the report.

## 8.2.2 Working with Advanced Publishing Options

Suppose you want to parameterize an Excel web report so that you can pass a filter or slicer value on the report URL. Unfortunately, the Excel Viewer web page (xlviewer.aspx) doesn't accept parameters. However, you can create a custom page that uses SharePoint web parts to address this requirement. This is the approach I'll discuss next. It builds upon a code sample provided by Rob Collie of PowerPivotPro (http://powerpivotpro.com).

***Defining report parameters***

Start by defining workbook parameters. In my case, I want the end user to filter the Dashboard report by passing a calendar year as a parameter. Since the Dashboard report has a CalendarYear slicer, I'll promote this slicer to a report parameter.

1. Open the Adventure Works workbook in Excel either from SharePoint or from disk.
2. In the File tab, click Save & Send, and then click Save to SharePoint. In the right pane, click the Publish Options button to open the Publish Options dialog box.

   The Show tab allows you to select which workbook items, such as worksheets or ranges, you want to publish. Notice that by default, Excel publishes the entire workbook. However, you can decide to publish certain items only. For example, to publish specific worksheets, expand the drop-down list, select the Sheets option, and then check the worksheets you want to publish to SharePoint.
3. Click the Parameters tab, and then click the Add button. Notice that the Add Parameters dialog box that follows allows you to promote any report filter or slicer to a report parameter. Check the Slicer_CalendarYear parameter, and then click OK.
4. Back in the Publish Options dialog box, compare your results with **Figure 8.5**. Click OK, and then click the Save button to publish the workbook to the PowerPivot Gallery library, as you did in Chapter 7.

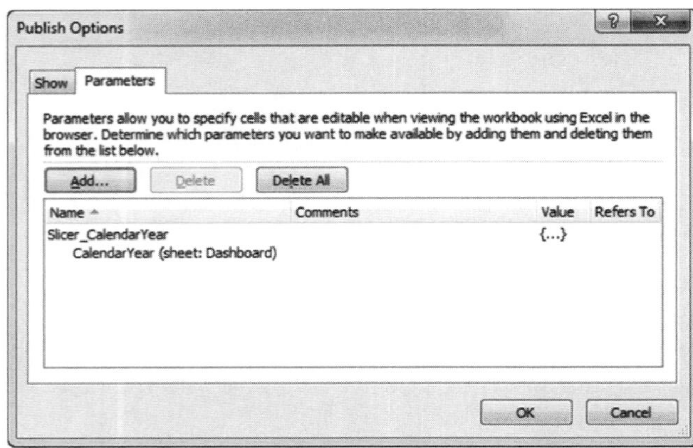


**Figure 8.5** The CalendarYear slicer is promoted as a report parameter.

***Implementing a web part page***

Next, I'll show you how to implement a SharePoint page that uses the Excel Web Access and Query String (URL) Filter web parts to pass the parameter value to the slicer in the Dashboard report. As a prerequisite for using the Excel Web Access web part, you need to enable the "SharePoint Server Enterprise Site Features" feature.

1. In SharePoint, expand the Site Actions menu, and then click Site Settings. In the Site Settings page, click the Manage Site Features link found under the Site Actions group. If the "SharePoint Server Enterprise Site Features" isn't active, click the Activate button.
2. Expand the Site Actions drop-down menu, and then click More Options.
3. In the Create page that follows, click the Page option found under the Filter category. Select the Web Part Page template and click the Create button.
4. In the "New Web Part Page" screen, enter *ParameterDemo* as a page name. Accept the default layout template of "Header, Footer, 3 Columns". Expand the Document Library drop-down list, and then select Site Pages to save the new page to the Site Pages document library. Click the Create button.

***Adding web parts***

SharePoint opens the page in Edit mode. You can add a web part to the page by clicking the Add a Web Part link in whatever zone you want the web part to appear.

1. Click the "Add a Web Part" link in the Header zone.
2. In the Categories pane, click the Filters category, select the "Query String (URL) Filter" web part, and then click the Add button. Query String (URL) Filter isn't visible to the end user, but it's very useful because it can extract the query parameters from the URL and send them to other web parts on the page.
3. Click the "Open the Tool Pane" link to configure the web part. In the tool pane, enter *Parameter* in the Filter Name field, *CalendarYear* in the Query String Parameter Name field, and *[Date].[CalendarYear].&[2006]* in the Default Value field, as shown in **Figure 8.6**.

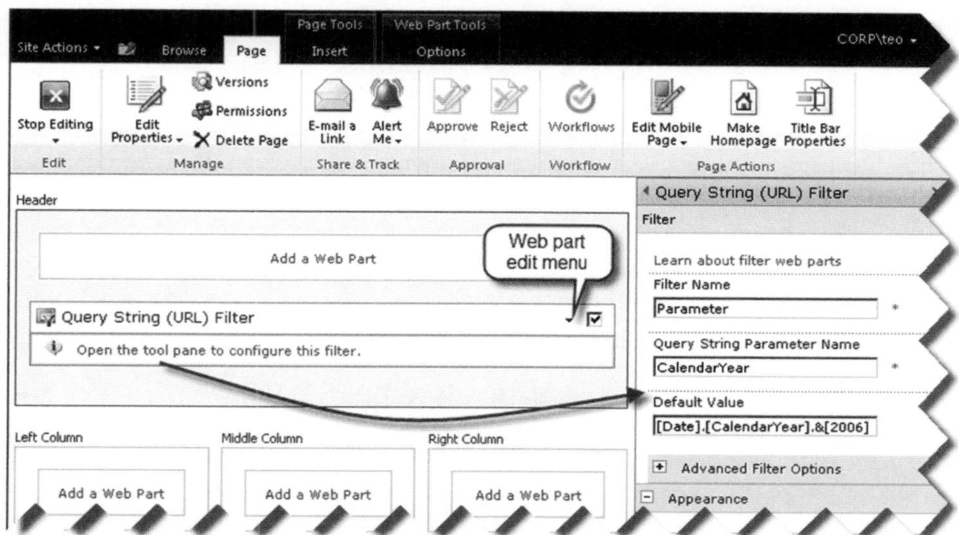


**Figure 8.6** Click the Open the Tool Pane link to configure the Query String (URL) Filter web part.

As a result, the filter web part will look for a URL query parameter called CalendarYear. Since Excel sees a PowerPivot model as a cube, you need to use the MDX UniqueName syntax for the selected slicer item. If you plan to pass multiple years, expand the Advanced Filter Options section, and then select Send All Values.

4. Scroll down the tool pane, and then click Apply to apply the settings.
5. Click the "Add a Web Part" link in the Left Column zone. In the Categories pane, click the Business Data category. Select the Excel Web Access web part, and then click the Add button.
6. With the Excel Web Access web part added to the page, click the "Click Here to Open the Tool Pane" link to edit the web part.
7. In the tool pane, enter the URL to the Adventure Works workbook, such as *http://<site>/PowerPivot Gallery/Adventure Works.xlsx*, where <site> is your server name. Expand the Appearance section, and then change the web part height to 800 pixels. Click the Apply button.

***Connecting web parts***
Next, you'll connect the "Query String (URL) Filter" web part to the Excel Web Access web part using the SharePoint connectable web part infrastructure.

1. Expand the "Web part edit menu" drop-down button of the Query String (URL) Filter web part (see **Figure 8.6** again). Click Connections ⇨ Send Filter Values To ⇨ Excel Web Access – Adventure Works.
2. In the Choose Connection – Webpage Dialog, expand the Connection Type drop-down list, and then select Get Filter Values From, as shown in **Figure 8.7**.

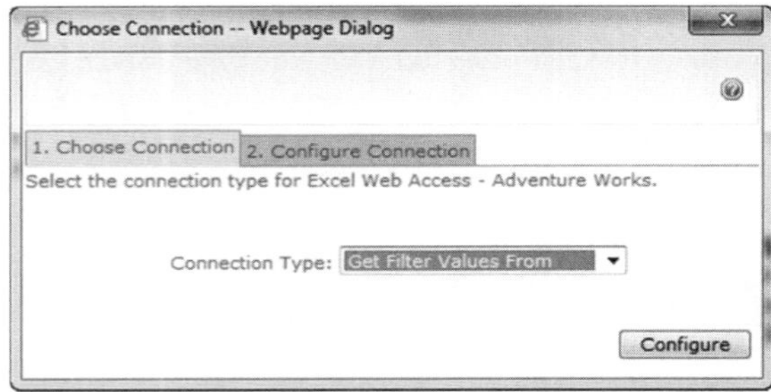


**Figure 8.7** Use the "Choose Connection – Webpage Dialog" dialog box to configure a web part connection.

3. Click the Configure Connection tab. Expand the Filtered Parameter drop-down list, and then select Slicer_CalendarYear. Click the Finish button.
4. Back on the ParameterDemo page, click the Stop Editing toolbar button to save the changes and to exit the Edit mode.
5. To test the changes, open your web browser, and then enter the following URL:

http://<site>/SitePages/ParameterDemo.aspx?CalendarYear=[Date].[CalendarYear].%26[2007]

If you select the Dashboard tab you should see its CalendarYear slicer value set to 2007. Note that I escaped the ampersand in the parameter value with %26, so SharePoint doesn't interpret it as another query parameter. If you want to pass multiple years, append them as query parameters to the page URL. For example, use the following URL to pass the years 2006 and 2007:

http://<site>/SitePages/ParameterDemo.aspx?
CalendarYear=[Date].[CalendarYear].%26[2006]&CalendarYear=[Date].[CalendarYear].%26[2007]

## 8.2.3 Authoring Excel OLAP Reports ▶

Based on my experience, the unfortunate truth is that not many organizations have moved to Excel 2010 yet. Suppose that some of your teammates have Excel 2007, and they want to author pivot reports from a published PowerPivot model. In this scenario, the PowerPivot model serves as a data source while Excel 2007 is a front-end reporting tool that connects to the model.

***Connecting Excel to the model***

While you can set up the Excel connection manually, the PowerPivot Gallery makes it easy to get started with Excel online analytical processing (OLAP) reports.

1. In SharePoint, navigate to the PowerPivot Gallery document library.
2. Notice that two icons appear in the top-right corner next to the Adventure Works model: the "Open New Excel Workbook" icon and "Manage Data Refresh" icon, as shown in **Figure 8.8**. Click the "Open New Excel Workbook" icon. Accept the security prompt to download and open the Office Data Connection (*odc) file.

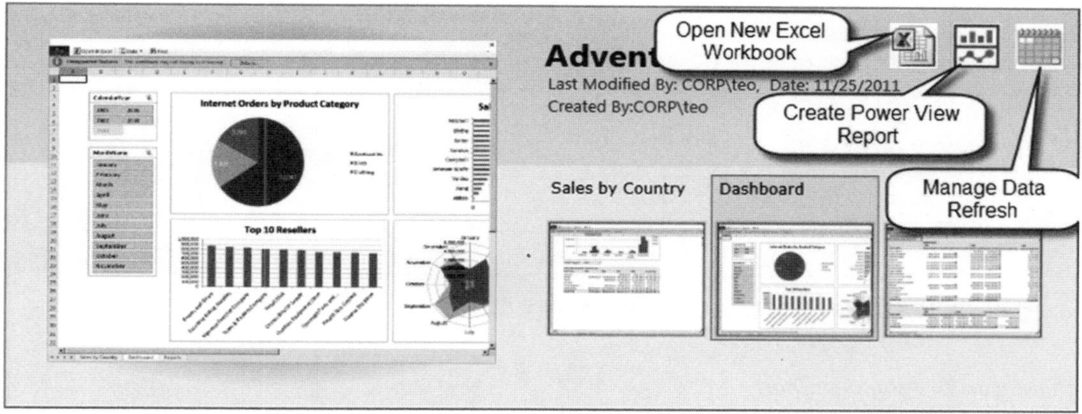


**Figure 8.8** Click "Open New Excel Workbook" to connect Excel to a published PowerPivot model.

**NOTE** Once you install Power View, a third "Create Power View Report" icon appears between the "Open New Excel Workbook" icon and the "Manage Data Refresh" icon. Click it to author a Power View report connected to the PowerPivot model.

3. In the Select Table dialog box, select the "Model" cube, which represents the entire model, and then click OK. Notice that you can select a perspective, such as Internet Sales, if you prefer to work with a subset of the model metadata.

   Excel opens a new workbook and adds an empty PivotTable report. The PivotTable Field List shows the model metadata. Next, you'll create the PivotTable report shown in **Figure 8.9**.

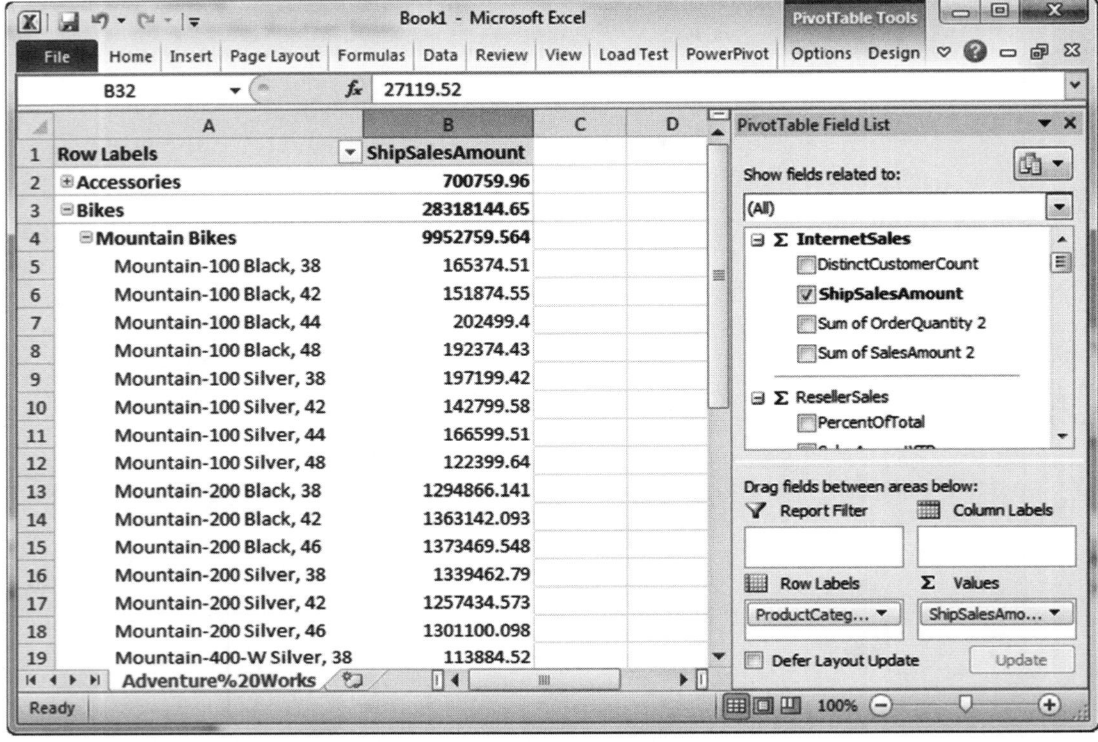


**Figure 8.9** The PivotTable Field List shows the model metadata.

***Authoring an OLAP pivot report***

Now that you have experience with pivot reports from Chapter 5, authoring an OLAP PivotTable report should be easy. You might remember that the PivotTable Field List shows the model metadata as Multidimensional artifacts, such as measure groups and dimensions. The measure groups include numeric measures that can be added to the Values zone. The dimensions include fields that you can add to Report Filter, Row Labels, and Column Labels zones.

1. In the PivotTable Field List, expand the InternetSales measure group. Notice that it includes both explicit measures (such as DistinctCustomer Count and ShipSalesAmount) and implicit measures (such as "Sum of Order Quantity 2" and "Sum of SalesAmount 2"). There is no visual indicator for the measure type (implicit or explicit).
2. Check the ShipSalesAmount measure to add it to the Values zone.
3. Expand the Product dimension, and then check the ProductCategories hierarchy to add it to the Row Labels zone (see **Figure 8.9** again).

You can save the workbook locally, or you can click File ⇨ Save & Send to save it back to SharePoint. Once the workbook is published to SharePoint, users can view the Excel OLAP reports in HTML just like they can do so with PowerPivot reports.

## 8.3 Working with Power View Reports

SQL Server 2012 introduces a new SharePoint-based reporting tool that allows business users to author interactive reports from Tabular models, including personal models published to SharePoint and organizational models deployed to Analysis Services Tabular. Next, I'll introduce you to Power View and its architecture, and I'll walk you through the steps to author two reports.

### 8.3.1 Understanding Power View

Power View is an interactive data exploration tool that further expands the reach of BI to business users. Transcending traditional "canned" reports, Power View is about gaining knowledge by having fun with data.

***Understanding design principles***

Although it's developed by the Reporting Services team, Power View doesn't have a lot in common with Report Designer or Report Builder that you might have used in the past. In fact, you might better off forgetting everything you know about Reporting Services so that you don't have any preconceived ideas about Power View. To understand Power View better, you need to understand its design tenets. Don't worry if some are not immediately clear.

1. One way to do things
2. Two clicks to a Return on Investment (ROI)
3. All tasks are done in context
4. Everything happens on the canvas, with the data
5. Less is more
6. Choose the right default, by default
7. Easy for the end user, hard on Microsoft
8. Highly efficient

At the same time it's important to understand what Power View is not. Power View isn't meant to replace Report Designer and Report Builder, which target professional developers and power users willing to author paper-oriented, operational reports. Power View isn't a high-end analysis tool for implementing complex calculations, forecasting, or what-if analysis. It's not meant to replace PerformancePoint Services, which is still the Microsoft premium tool for scorecards and management dashboards. As it stands, Power View isn't extensible and you can't plug in custom controls or widgets to enhance its capabilities.

***Understanding Power View architecture***

**Figure 8.10** shows how the Power View components fit into the SharePoint architecture. Unlike Report Builder, Power View is a web-based reporting tool that uses Microsoft Silverlight technology so you can author interactive reports in your web browser.

While report viewing happens on the client, the actual report processing takes place on the server. One welcome improvement in SQL Server 2012 is that it's easier to set up Reporting Services in SharePoint integrated mode. You don't need to install a separate report server anymore. Instead, Reporting Services plugs in the SharePoint shared service infrastructure. Besides a simplified setup, this architectural change brings other benefits, including centralized configuration via SharePoint Central Administration, leveraging the SharePoint scale-out model, supporting claim-based authentication, SharePoint cross-farm report viewing, utilizing the SharePoint backup, and ULS logging.

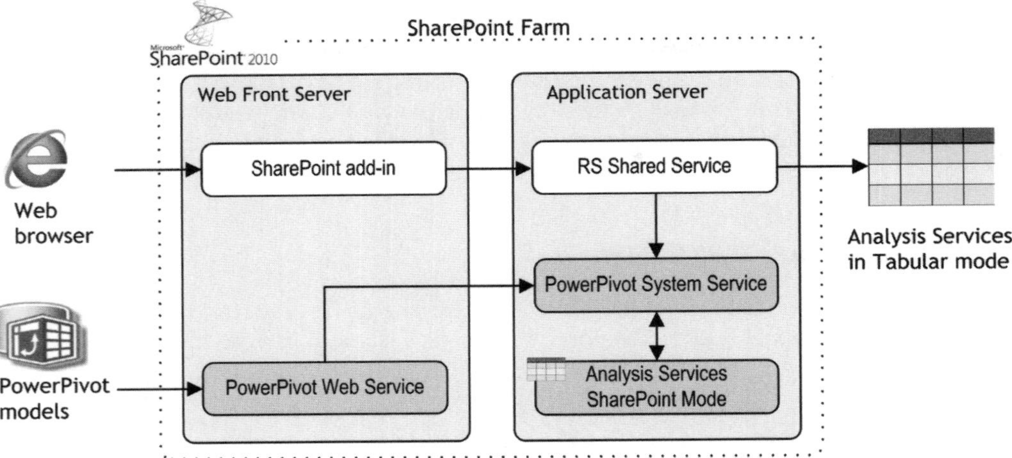


**Figure 8.10** Power View integrates with SharePoint and supports Tabular models as data sources.

As a part of setting up Reporting Services in SharePoint integrated mode, you need to install a Reporting Services for SharePoint add-in on the SharePoint web front-end server and the Reporting Shared Service (shown as Reporting Services in the SQL Server setup) on the SharePoint application server. The server components allow you to manage and run operational reports and Power View reports in the SharePoint environment. PowerPivot for SharePoint is required if you plan to author Power View reports from PowerPivot models. PowerPivot for SharePoint isn't required if all you need is to create Power View reports that are connected to organizational tabular models deployed to Analysis Services Tabular.

**NOTE** In this release of SQL Server, Power View can connect only to Tabular models. This includes published PowerPivot models and organizational models deployed to Analysis Services running in Tabular mode. Microsoft plans to extend Power View to support multidimensional cubes as a data source in a later release.

## 8.3.2 Installing Reporting Services

Assuming you want to create Power View reports from PowerPivot models and PowerPivot for SharePoint is already configured, then installing Power View requires only a few simple steps.

***Installing Reporting Services in SharePoint mode***

Start by running the SQL Server 2012 setup to install Reporting Services on the SharePoint application server. The following steps don't describe the setup process in detail. These steps only highlight the important points that you need to pay attention to when installing Reporting Services. In this case, I assume that you're installing Reporting Services on a single SharePoint server (a single-tier SharePoint deployment).

1. In the SQL Server Installation Center screen, click the Installation link, and then click "New SQL Server Stand-alone Installation or Add Features to an Existing Installation".
2. In the Installation Type step, select "Perform a New Installation of SQL Server 2012".
3. In the Setup Role step, leave the "SQL Server Feature Installation" option preselected.

4. In the Feature Selection step, check the "Reporting Services – SharePoint" and "Reporting Services Add-in for SharePoint Products" checkboxes, as shown in **Figure 8.11**. Accept the defaults in the next steps.

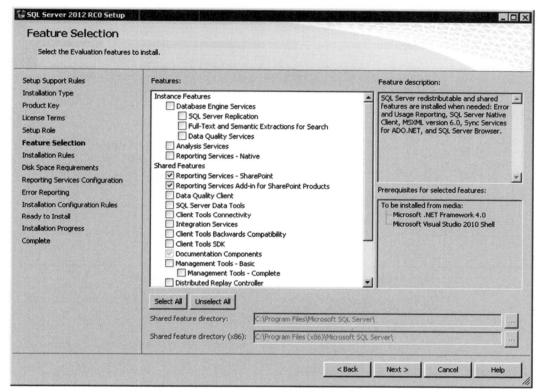

**Figure 8.11** Install Reporting Services – SharePoint and Reporting Services Add-in for SharePoint Products.

**NOTE** With multi-tier SharePoint deployments, you need to install "Reporting Services – SharePoint" on the SharePoint application server and "Reporting Services Add-in for SharePoint Products" on each web front-end (WFE) server.

***Creating a Reporting Services service application***

Next, you need to set up a Reporting Services service application using the SharePoint Central Administration application. You need to have SharePoint farm administrator rights to do this.

1. Open SharePoint Central Administration, and then click Manage Service Applications in the Application Management section.
2. Expand the New drop-down button, and the click SQL Server Reporting Services Service Application, as shown in **Figure 8.12**.
3. In the "Create SQL Server Reporting Services Service Application" page, specify the appropriate settings that match your setup, and then click OK.
4. **Table 8.2** describes these settings and provides examples.

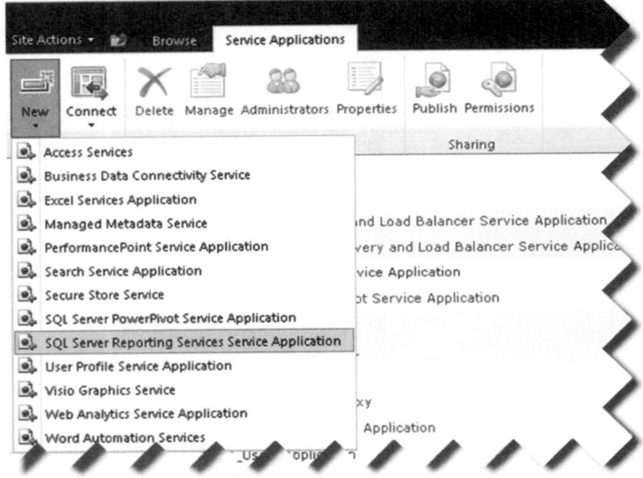


**Figure 8.12** Create a new SQL Server Reporting Services service application.

**Table 8.2 Reporting Services Service Application system settings**

| Setting | Description | Example |
|---|---|---|
| Name | Name of the service application | Default SSRS Service Application |
| Application Pool | Existing or new IIS application pool | SSRSApplicationDomain (new application pool) |
| Database Server | SQL Server instance for SSRS databases | <your SQL Server instance name> |
| Database Name | Name of the SSRS database | ReportingService_412d96a923a44ddfa534cd2bcb03a7ae |
| Database Authentication | Windows or standard authentication | Windows |
| Web Application Association | Web applications associated with SSRS | SharePoint - 80 |

To learn more about setting up a new Reporting Services application, read the "Install Reporting Services SharePoint Mode as a Single Server Farm" topic in the MSDN Library at http://bit.ly/SSRSSharePoint.

**NOTE** Reporting Services (both Native mode and SharePoint mode) supports installing the SSRS database on SQL Server 2008 or higher. You can choose to install the SSRS databases on the SQL Server instance that hosts the SharePoint configuration databases or to install them on a different instance. However, make sure that you have the appropriate database edition requirements fulfilled. For example, Reporting Services Enterprise can't connect to a SQL Server Developer edition. For more details, read the "Create a Report Server Database" topic in the MSDN Library at http://bit.ly/SSRSdatabase.

### *Enabling content types*

The PowerPivot Gallery document library is pre-configured for Power View reporting. If you plan to author and manage operational reports with Report Builder, you also need to enable the BI-related content types by following these steps:

1. Navigate to your SharePoint site, such as the default SharePoint site on http://<site>/. In the left navigation menu, click the document library, such as Shared Documents or PowerPivot Gallery, where you plan to deploy your reports.
2. Click the Library ribbon tab, and then click the Library Settings button.
3. In the Document Library Settings page, click the Advanced Settings link found in the General Settings section. In the Document Library Settings page, select Yes for the "Allow Management of Content Types?" setting, and then click OK.
4. In the Document Library Settings page, click the "Add From Existing Site Content Types" link.
5. In the Add Content Types page, select the BI Semantic Model Connection (installed by PowerPivot for SharePoint), Report Builder Model, Report Builder Report, and Report Data Source content types in the Available Site Content Types list, and then click the Add button to add them to the "Content Types to Add" list (see **Figure 8.13**). Click OK. **Table 8.3** explains the content types.

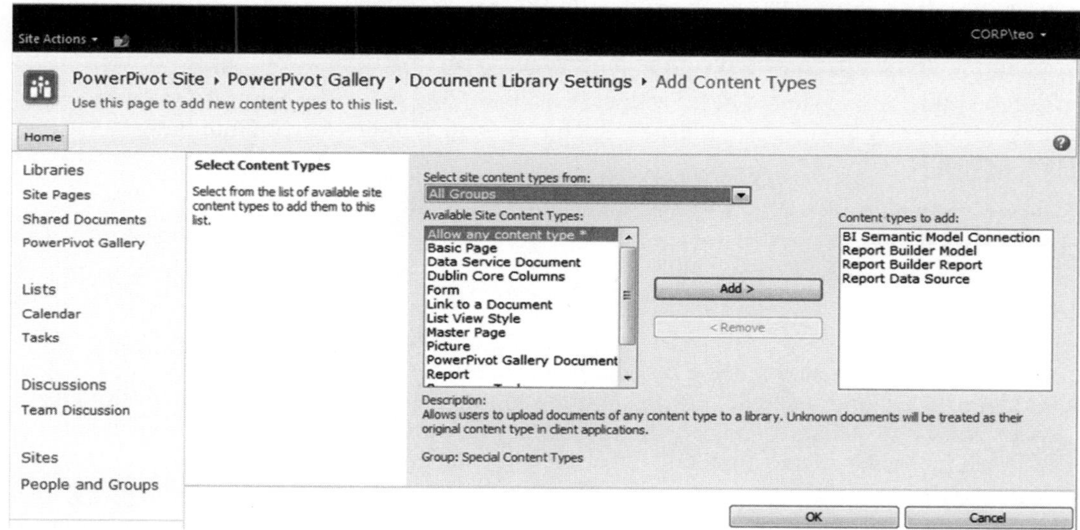


**Figure 8.13** Add the BI content types to a document library.

**Table 8.3 BI content types**

| Content Type | Purpose |
|---|---|
| BI Semantic Model Connection | A connection to a PowerPivot model or a tabular model hosted in Analysis Services Tabular |
| Report Builder Model | A Report Builder (*.smdl) model (deprecated in SQL Server 2012) |
| Report Builder Report | An ad hoc report that's authored with Report Builder |
| Report Data Source | A Reporting Services shared data source |

At this point, your Reporting Services installation should be operational, and you can author Power View reports from published PowerPivot models.

### 8.3.3 Understanding Reporting Properties

Back in Chapter 6, I mentioned that PowerPivot supports a set of advanced properties, known as reporting properties, which provide additional metadata to report clients. Power View reads these properties and applies them to improve the report presentation and make the model more intuitive to end users. These properties are described in the "Power View Reporting Properties (SSAS)" topic in Books Online at http://bit.ly/bismreportproperties.

***Importing image columns***

To demonstrate how these report properties apply to Power View, I've made a few changes to the Adventure Works model in the Ch08 folder.

1. I deleted the Product table that was initially imported from the Product Catalog 2008 report. This was to demonstrate how to import data from reports as data feeds.
2. I imported the DimProduct table in the AdventureWorksDW2008R2 database. This table includes a LargePhoto column that stores the photo image for each product. PowerPivot 2.0 supports image columns and sets their data type to the Binary data type.
3. I applied the same settings to the new Product table, including renaming columns, recreated relationships, configuring the ProductCategories hierarchy, and adding calculation in the ResellerSales table.

***Configuring report properties***

Next, let's set reporting properties for the Product table in the Adventure Works model:

1. In the PowerPivot window, expand the File drop-down menu, and then click Switch to Advanced Properties.
2. Click the Product table tab to select it. In the Advanced ribbon tab, click the Default Field Set button. In the Default Field Set dialog box that follows, select the ProductName and ProductModel fields, and then click the Add button to move them to the Default Fields list. Click OK. As a result of this change, Power View adds these columns to the report when you click the Product table in the metadata pane.
3. Click the Table Behavior button to open the Table Behavior dialog box, as shown in **Figure 8.14**.
4. Expand the Row Identifier drop-down list, and then select the ProductKey column. This tells Power View that this column uniquely identifies each row in the table. A row identifier column is required to set the other reporting properties in this dialog box.
5. By default, Power View groups identical values when a column is added to the report and aggregates data across these values. For example, the ProductName column includes duplicated product names to keep history when the product standard cost changes. When you add the ProductName column to the report, the report will show one row for each product even if two rows in the table have the same product name. In most cases, this is the expected behavior. However, if you want Power View to show separate rows, in the Keep Unique Row list, check the ProductName column.
6. Expand the Default Label drop-down list, and then select the ProductName column. Power View uses this column to show a display name, such as to pop up a tooltip that shows the product name when you hover your mouse over the product image.
7. Expand the Default Image drop-down list, and then select the LargePhoto column so that you can visualize product images on the report. Click OK.

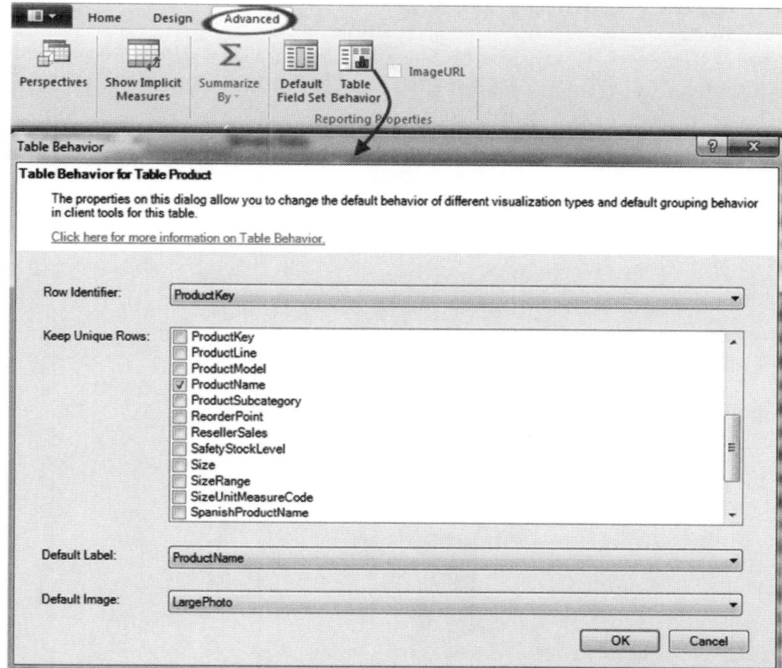


**Figure 8.14** Use the Table Behavior dialog box to configure Power View-specific table properties.

**NOTE** Power View supports three options to visualize images: external, text, and binary. If the images are external, such as images that are located on a web server, select the column that contains the image URL in Data View, and then check the ImageURL checkbox in the Advanced ribbon tab. Power View also supports text (base64-encoded string) images and binary images that are stored in a database.

**8.** (Optional) Apply similar changes to set up report properties for other tables. Remember to apply the appropriate format settings to columns in order to carry these format settings over to Power View reports. If you don't want Power View to summarize a numeric column by default, consider specifying a different aggregation function by using the Summarize By button in the Advanced ribbon tab.

**NOTE** Power View examines table relationships and disallows invalid combinations based on which fields are used on the report. For example, Power View won't allow you to aggregate reseller sales by customers because no relationship exists between the Customer and ResellerSales tables. You'll be able to select only explicit measures that are defined in the ResellerSales table although they will probably show no data or repeating data.

Now that I've introduce you to Power View, I'll show you how you can author Power View reports from the Adventure Works model. Due to its highly interactive and visual nature, attempting to cover the Power View capabilities in one section does it little justice. Remember to watch the video that accompanies this section for the best learning experience. Also, note that Chapter 10 includes another exercise for authoring Power View reports. For a more in-depth look of Power View, I recommend you review the "Abundantly "Crescent": Demos Galore" presentation by Carolyn Chau and Sean Boon at http://channel9.msdn.com/Events/TechEd/NorthAmerica/-2011/DBI208 and that you follow Sean Boon's blog at http://blogs.msdn.com/b/seanboon.

## 8.3.4 Implementing the Sales by Country View ▶

In this section, I'll walk you through the steps to author the Sales by Country report, shown in **Figure 8.15**. This report demonstrates the following features:

- Implementing clustered column and scatter charts
- Copying and pasting sections
- Automatic highlighting
- Implementing global and visualization-level filters
- Working with multiple views
- Exporting and printing

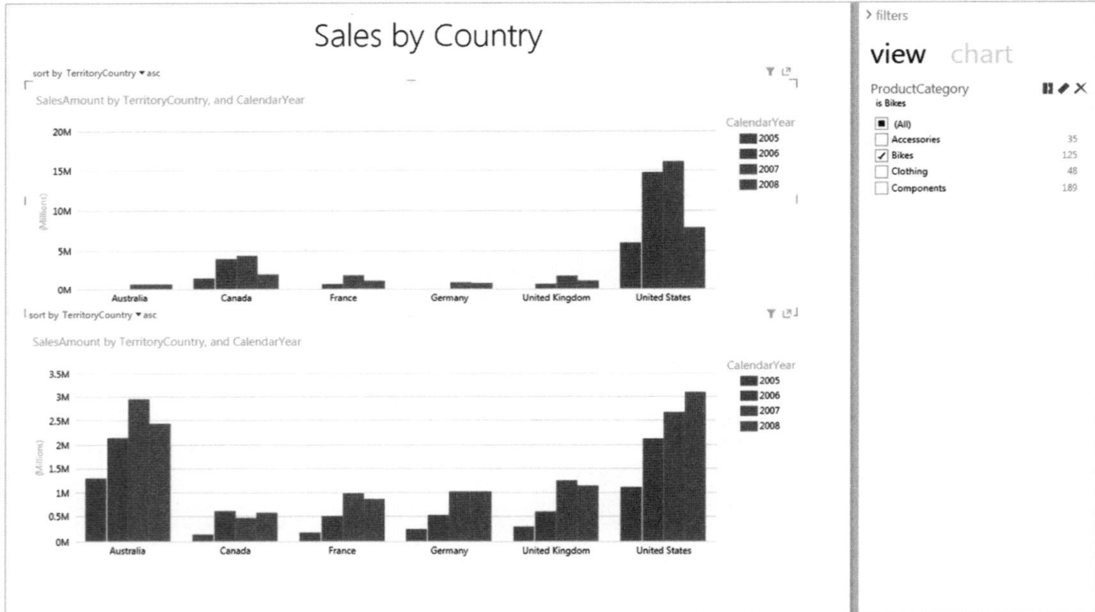


**Figure 8.15** This report includes two charts that show reseller sales and Internet Sales side by side.

***Getting started with Power View***

PowerPivot Gallery makes it easy to create a Power View report.

1. Deploy the Adventure Works.xlsx workbook to the SharePoint PowerPivot Gallery library, as I demonstrated in Section 7.3.1.
2. In PowerPivot Gallery, click the "Create Power View Report" icon (see **Figure 8.8** again).

   Power View creates an empty report connected to the Adventure Works model, as shown in **Figure 8.16**. Similar to the PowerPivot Field List in Excel, the Fields pane shows the model metadata, which consists of tables and fields (columns). You can use the Layout pane to define the report layout by dragging fields from the Fields pane.
3. Expand the Product table. Notice that some fields have icons.

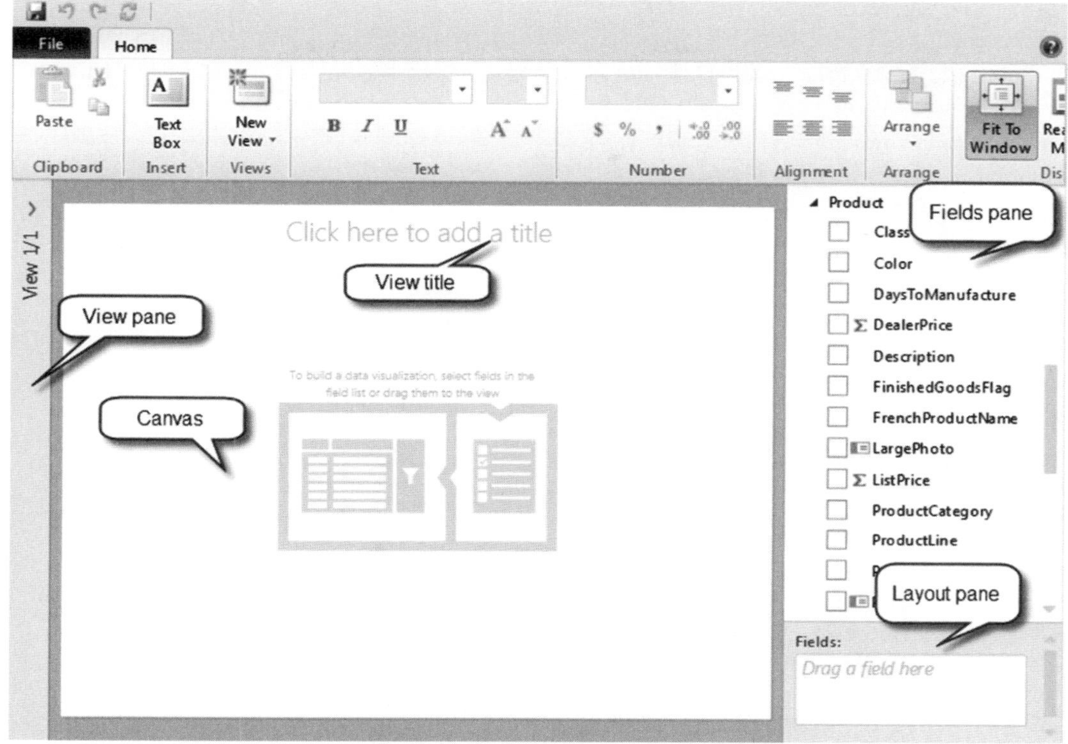


**Figure 8.16** The Field List pane shows the model metadata, which consists of table and columns.

A table icon indicates that that field has additional properties applied to it. For example, there is table icon preceding the ProductName field because you configured this column to keep unique rows. A Sigma icon precedes numeric fields, such as the DealerPrice and ListPrice fields, to indicate that the field can be aggregated. The report canvas represents the report layout. To keep things simple, Power View has no margins, page breaks and other pagination settings. Instead, a report can have one or more views in a landscape orientation, just like a PowerPoint presentation has one or more slides. In fact, when you export the report to PowerPoint, a view is exported as a slide. You can add multiple report sections (called *visualizations*) to a view. If you need more visualizations that exceed the size of the first (default) view, you can add more views by clicking the New View button in the ribbon. Again, similar to PowerPoint, the View pane shows preview images of the report views and allows you to navigate to a particular view by clicking its image (not shown in **Figure 8.16** because the View pane isn't expanded).

There are three ways to add a field to the report canvas. First, you can check its checkbox in the Fields pane. Second, you can drag a field and drop it in the Layout pane (the zones in the Layout pane change based on the visualization). Third, you can simply drag it on the report. Similar to Excel, Power View is capable of creating implicit measure when you add fields to the report. Unless you have set the Summarize By property in the model to another aggregation function, Power View defaults to the Sum aggregation function for numeric fields and to the Count aggregation function for the other data types. Unlike Excel, Power View doesn't save implicit measures in the PowerPivot model (they're only saved in the report definition).

4. To change the view title, double-click "Click Here to Add a Title" and type *Sales by Country*.

***Creating a chart report***

Follow these steps to create a chart report that shows the reseller sales:

1. In the Field List, expand the ResellerSales table, and then check the SalesAmount field. Notice that Power View adds the SalesAmount field to the Layout pane, as shown in **Figure 8.17**.

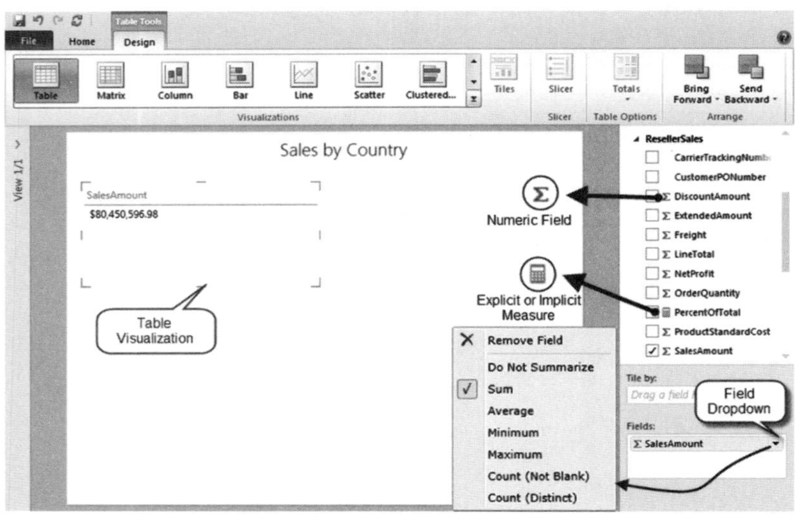


**Figure 8.17** Power View defaults to a Table visualization.

Similarly to Excel, you can expand the Field drop-down list and overwrite the aggregation function for regular fields if needed (a regular field is a field that isn't defined as a measure in the model). You can't overwrite the aggregation function of implicit and explicit measures that are defined in the PowerPivot model. To make this distinction clearer, the Fields pane prefixes implicit and explicit measures with a calculator icon, and the regular numeric fields with the sigma (Σ) icon. To remove a field from the report, select it in the Layout pane, and then press Delete. Or, click Remove Field in the field's drop-down list.

Unlike other reporting tools that you might be familiar with, such as Report Builder, Power View is always presentation-ready and doesn't require switching between a design and preview mode. Each time you add a new report section, Power View uses a Table visualization to display the data in a tabular layout. For optimal performance, Power View doesn't fetch all the data at once when showing tables. As you scroll through the table, Power View brings more data in the background. Power View supports other visualizations for authoring tabular, crosstab, and chart reports (see **Table 8.4**).

**Table 8.4 Power View supports different visualizations to present data on the report.**

| Visualization Category | Visualizations | Purpose |
|---|---|---|
| Chart | Column, 100% Column, Clustered Column, Bar, 100% Bar, Clustered, Line, Scatter | Create chart reports. |
| Table | Table, Matrix | Create tabular and crosstab reports. |
| Other | Card | Display data in a card format, like an index card. |

You can change the visualization, such as from a table to a chart, at any time by using the Visualizations group in the Design ribbon tab. A report view can include multiple visualizations side by side, and visualizations can overlap each other.

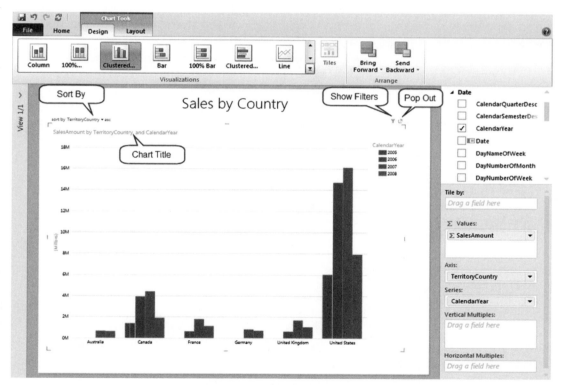

**NOTE** Make sure that the visualization you're working with is active by clicking it before you make changes to it. An active section has resize handles around it. If you click outside a visualization, it becomes inactive. As a result, if you check a field in the Fields pane, Power View assumes that you want a new visualization and adds a new report section.

2. In the Visualizations group of the Design ribbon tab, scroll down the list, and then select the Clustered Column chart visualization. Power View changes the visualization to a chart. Notice that Power View examines the value range and it automatically scales the Y-axis to millions. This is just one example of how Power View applies the right default settings by default.
3. Drag the resize handles of the chart to enlarge it.
4. Expand the SalesTerritory table, and then check TerritoryCountry to add it to the Axis zone.
5. In the Fields pane, expand the Date table, and then check the CalendarYear field to add it to the chart Series zone in the Layout section, as shown in **Figure 8.18**.

**Figure 8.18** Power View applies the right defaults as you configure the chart.

If a field ends up in a wrong zone in the Layout pane, you can drag it to the correct zone just like you can with the Excel PowerPivot Field List. If you've made a mistake, you can click the Undo button in the Quick Access toolbar (above the ribbon) to undo the last step (or press Ctrl+Z). You can click the Redo button (or press Ctrl+Y) to redo the last step.

6. Hover your mouse cursor over the chart. Notice that a new area (known in some circles as "floatie") appears above the chart. The Sort By area lets you sort the chart series or categories. On the right side, you can use the Show Filters button to set up a visualization-specific filter. The Pop Out button opens the chart in full-screen mode. This helps you zoom out the chart in a busy report to see its data in more details. Click the button again to zoom in the chart.
7. (Optional) Make sure that the chart is selected. In the Fields pane, expand the Product table, and then drag the ProductCategory field to the Vertical Multiples zone in the Layout pane. The chart breaks into four charts, and each chart shows the reseller sales for a given product category, such as bikes. As you can see, multiples make it easy to generate several views for a side-by-side comparison and for trend discovery. Press Ctrl+Z to undo the chart changes and clear the Vertical Multiples zone.

***Copying and pasting objects***

Next, you'll add a new chart to show the Internet sales. This chart will use the same fields as the existing chart, with the exception that instead of showing the SalesAmount field from the ResellerSales table, it will use the SalesAmount field from the InternetSales table. Instead of starting from scratch with the new chart, you can copy and paste the existing chart.

1. Click the chart to select it and then press Ctrl+C. A prompt pops up asking you to confirm that Power View can access the Windows Clipboard. To avoid this prompt in the future, check Remember my Answer checkbox, and then click Yes. Press Ctrl+V to paste the chart in the same view.
2. Click the new chart to select it. In the Layout pane, expand the drop-down list of the SalesAmont field in the Values zone, and then click Remove Field. Or, you can remove a field by dragging it away from the Layout zone and dropping it onto the Fields pane.
3. With the new chart selected, in the Fields pane, expand the InternetSales table. Drag the Sales Amount field, and then drop it on the Values zone. You should see a blue right arrow when the field enters the Value zone, indicating that the operation is permitted. Or, you can drag the field from the Fields pane and drop it onto the chart area.

**NOTE** So, where have all context menus gone? As you might notice, right-clicking an object in the report canvas doesn't open a context menu like you'd expect. This is by design. Microsoft felt that context menus would complicate the user experience and contradict the "one way to do things" design tenet.

***Automatic highlighting***

At this point your version of the Sales by Country view should resemble the report shown in **Figure 8.15**. Examining the report, you can deduce that the sales in the United Sales far exceed the sales in other countries. However, because of the series grouping, it might be difficult to understand how the sales for a specific year compare. Automatic highlighting facilitates this type of analysis.

1. Click the 2005 value in the legend of the Reseller Sales chart, as shown in **Figure 8.19**. Notice that Power View highlights the 2005 series in all the countries in both charts. Even if other visualizations don't have the CalendarYear field, selecting 2005 in the chart would act as a filter to all visualizations and it would highlight the 2005 contributions. You can hold Ctrl to select multiple values in the legend.
2. Click the chart area of the Reseller Sales chart to remove the automatic highlights.

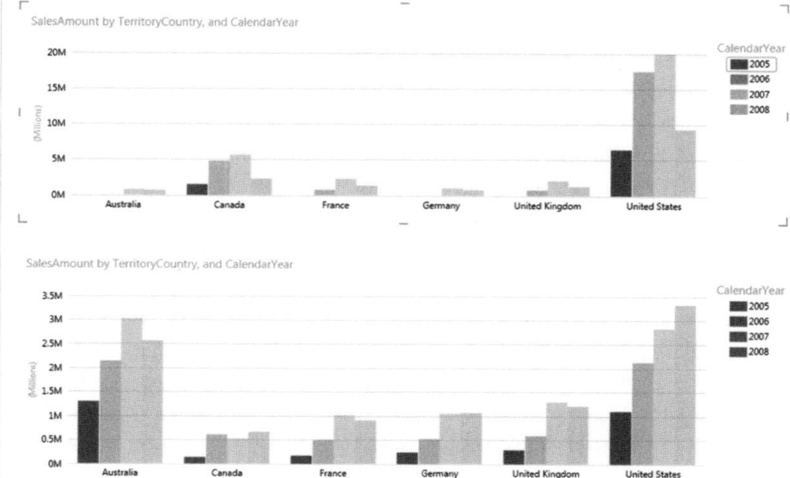


**Figure 8.19** You can click a value in the chart legend to highlight the contribution of this value to the chart series.

***Filtering report data***

Power View supports comprehensive filtering options. You can set global filters that apply to all the visualizations in a view or you can create visualization-specific filters. Follow these steps to set up a global filter that filters the two charts by product category.

1. Click to the Home ribbon tab, and then click the Filters Area button to show the filter area on the right side of the canvas.
2. To filter the report on product category, expand the Product table in the Fields pane. Drag the ProductCategory field to the filter area.

By default, Power View sets the filter in a basic filtering mode, where it shows a list of column values so that you can check the values you want to see on the report (see **Figure 8.20**). Basic filtering could be useful when filtering low-cardinality columns with a few values, such as ProductCategory. Power View shows the count of rows in the Product table for each product category. You can click the ProductCategory label to collapse the filter and to hide the values. This could be useful to preserve space when you have multiple filters in the filter area.

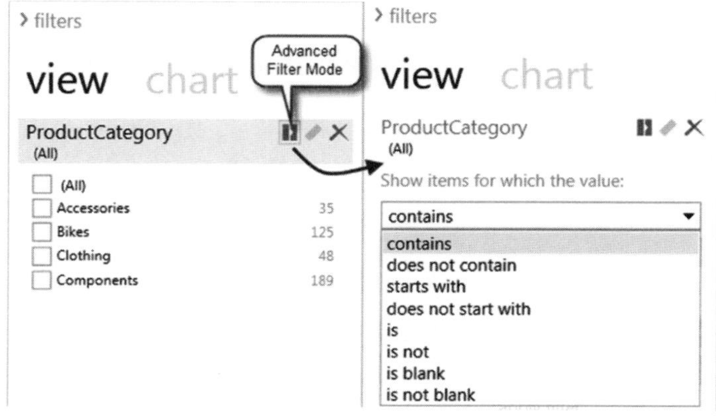


**Figure 8.20** The Filter Area supports basic and advanced filter modes.

Longer lists could benefit from the advanced filtering mode (click the Advanced Filter Mode button to toggle between modes), which supports different filter criteria, based on the data type of the column. You can also use the AND or OR conditions, such as the filter "ProductName Contains 'Bike'" AND "ProductName Does Not Start With 'Mountain'". Finally, filters on integer columns, such as CalendarYear or CalendarQuarter, are visualized as slicers in the filter area. To clear the filter selection and to see all the data, click the Clear Filter button which is located to the right of the Advanced Filter Mode button. To remove a filter from the report, click the Delete Filter button. You can filter on multiple columns. Each new filter acts as an AND clause, such as "ProductCategory='Bikes'" AND "CalendarYear=2006".

3. In the ProductCategory filter, check Clothing. Both charts change to show clothing sales only.
4. Sometimes, you might want to filter a given visualization without affecting other visualizations. You can do so by setting up a visualization-specific filter. Click the Show Filters button in the "floatie" of the Reseller Sales chart (see **Figure 8.18** again). Or, with the chart selected, click the Chart option in the filter area (see **Figure 8.20**). By default, the Filters area shows only the fields used in the chart but you can drag other fields from the Fields pane, if needed.

***Slicers and tiles***

Another way to filter all the visualizations in a view is to set up a slicer. Power View slicers resemble Excel slicers. To create a slicer, you need to first create a single-column table from any field, and then convert the table into a slicer. Suppose that you want to filter reseller sales for a given product by clicking on the product image.

1. In the Fields list, expand the Product table. Expand the drop-down list next to the LargePhoto column, and then click Add to Table to create a table showing the product images.
2. In the Design ribbon tab, click the Slicer button to convert the table to a slicer. Reposition the slicer so it doesn't obscure the report data.
3. Click a product image in the slicer. Notice that the two charts show data for that product only.
4. Select the LargePhoto slicer, and then press Delete to remove the slicer from the report.
5. (Optional) Click the Reseller Chart to select it. Drag the LargePhoto field from the Fields pane, and then drop into the Tile By zone in the Layout pane. This action adds a tile area to the reseller sales chart, which allows you to filter the chart data by clicking on a product image. You might need to resize the chart to see both the tile area and the chart.

***Saving the report***

You can save a Power View report back to SharePoint. You can save the report to any document library. However, saving it to PowerPivot Gallery allows you to see preview images of the report views, just like you can see thumbnail images of pivot reports embedded in PowerPivot workbooks. To save a Power View report, follow these steps:

1. Click the File ribbon tab, and then click the Save (or Save As) button to open the Save As dialog box.
2. In the Save As dialog box, verify that the PowerPivot Gallery library is preselected.
3. In the File Name field, enter *Adventure Works Sales*, and then click OK.
4. In SharePoint, navigate to PowerPivot Gallery. Notice that it shows a preview image of the report.
5. Click the Adventure Works Sales image. The report opens in reading mode for faster viewing. You can click the Edit Report menu to switch to Design mode if you want to make changes to the report.

**NOTE** Power View saves report files with the *.rdlx file extension. Although RDLX extends the RDL format, you can't open Power View reports in another Reporting Services designer, such as Report Builder. In fact, the RDLX files are saved as zip files to further discourage you from experimenting with them. Power View RDLX files are just for Power View. You can't set them up for subscriptions, caching, or any other management options available with traditional RDL reports.

## 8.3.5 Implementing the Sales Person Performance View ▶

Power View visualizations are not limited to static tabular and chart reports. You can create animated views to visualize data trends, such as to watch how sales change across time. Next, you'll add a Sales Person Performance view to the Adventure Works Sales report, as shown in **Figure 8.21**. This view has a scatter chart that plots the performance of each Adventure Works sales person. In this case, the performance is plotted as a bubble. The coordinates are the actual sales on the X axis, and the sales quota is on the Y axis. The NetProfit measure controls the size of the bubble.

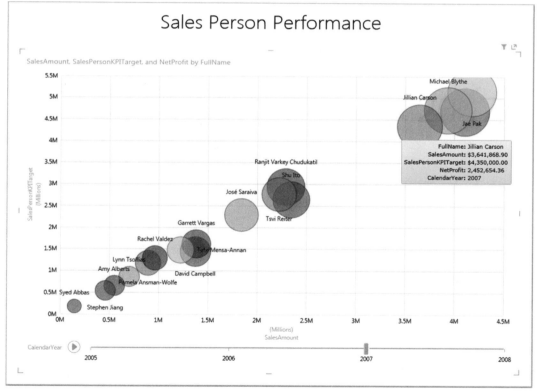

**Figure 8.21** This scatter chart displays the sales person performance.

What's more interesting is that the scatter chart has a play axis that's bound to the CalendarYear column in the Date table. You can click the Play button to start the animation. In play mode, the chart queries the sales person metrics for each year, and then plots them on the chart.

***Authoring a scatter chart***

Follow these steps to add a new view and to create the chart:

1. With the Adventure Works Sales report open in Edit mode, click the Home menu and click the New View button. Change the title of the new view to *Sales Person Performance*.
2. In the Fields pane, expand the ResellerSales table, and then check the SalesAmount measure to create a new Table visualization.
3. Click the Scatter visualization in the Design ribbon tab to change the visualization to a scatter chart.
4. In the Fields pane, check the SalesPersonKPITarget field to add it to the Y Value zone. You implemented the SalesPersonKPITarget measure in Chapter 6 when you configured a key performance indicator (KPI).
5. Check the NetProfit field to add it to the Size zone. This field will control the size of the bubble.
6. Expand the Employee table in the Fields list, and then check the FullName field to add it to the Details zone. This displays the sales person's full name next to each bubble.
7. Expand the Date table, and then check CalendarYear to add it to the Play Axis zone.
8. Click the Play button to the left of the play axis to start the animation.

   Watch the animation to see how the sales persons' performance changes over time.

***Enabling tracking***

It might be difficult to track the performance of a specific employee in a busy chart. Fortunately, Power View supports highlighting and tracking.

1. Click the bubble with Jillian Carson's name. Notice that Power View grays out the other bubbles.
2. Play the chart. Notice that now it's much easier to track Jillian's performance. Her sales increase up to 2007 and then plummet in 2008, probably due to the economy downturn.

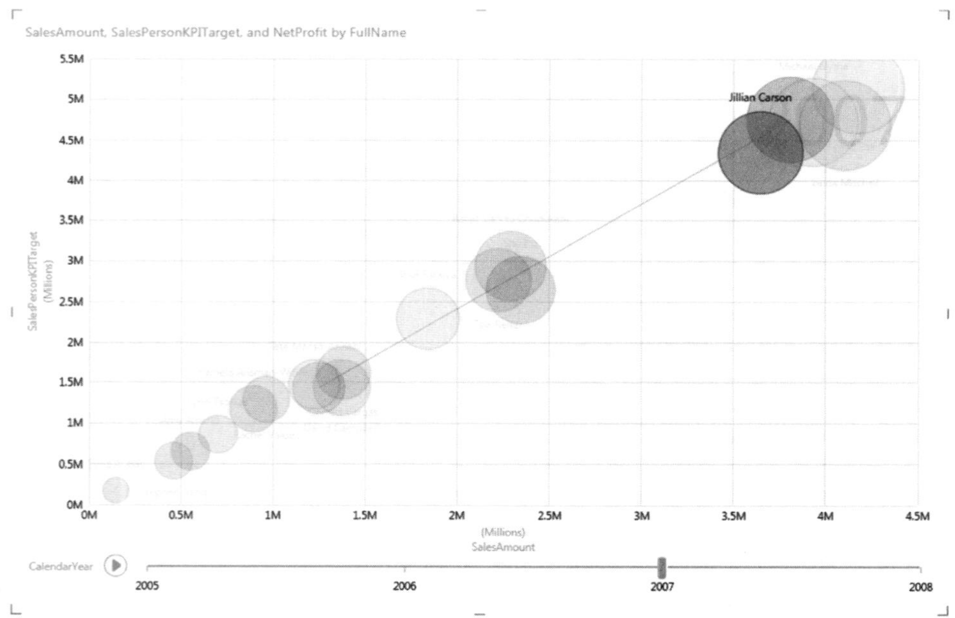


**Figure 8.22** Tracking helps you visualize the historical performance of a sales person.

3. Another option to monitor the performance of a specific employee is to enable tracking. Play the chart, and then click the Jillian's bubble. Notice that Power View highlights the track as the bubble moves in time, as shown in **Figure 8.22**. Now it's easier to see how Jillian has been performing. You can see more detailed information by hovering the mouse cursor over the bubble.
4. Save the report back to SharePoint. Notice that PowerPivot Gallery shows thumbnail images for both views in the Adventure Works Sales report. You can click a view to open the report in a preview mode.

***Refreshing data and metadata***

There is a difference between refreshing the model data and refreshing the metadata in Power View. If all you need is to view the latest data, click the Refresh button in the upper-left screen above the ribbon. This action executes the report queries and shows the latest data. If you've made changes to the model, such as adding a new column, and redeployed the PowerPivot workbook, then you need to refresh the browser (press F5 in Internet Explorer). This action reconnects Power View to the model and refreshes the Fields pane.

***Exporting and printing Power View reports***

Power View can export reports to PowerPoint. Each view becomes a separate PowerPoint slide.

1. In Power View with the Adventure Works Sales report open, click the File ribbon tab, and then click Export to PowerPoint.
2. In the Save As dialog box, choose a folder on your hard drive, and then enter *Adventure Works Sales* as a name of the PowerPoint file. Click Save.
3. Open PowerPoint, and then open the Adventure Works Sales.pptx file. Or, double-click the file in Windows Explorer.

   Notice that the presentation has two slides that correspond to the two views in the Power View report. The slides contain static images of the report views. However, if you have connectivity to SharePoint, you can interact with the slides.
4. In PowerPoint, click the Enable Editing button in the status bar.
5. In the lower-right corner, click the Reading View button or the Slide Show button. Notice that when you hover your mouse over an image, PowerPoint shows the "Click to Interact" button.
6. Click the "Click to Interact" button to switch to interactive mode. Notice that all report interactive features work. For example, you can click the Play button in the Sales Person Performance report.

**NOTE** Behind the scenes, the interactive mode uses a Silverlight alternative hosting control (right-click the object on the slide and click View Code) that connects to the deployed report on the SharePoint server. I provided more details about this control in my blog post, "What's New in Power View RC0" (http://bit.ly/pvhostingcontrol).

7. In Power View, click the File menu, and then click Print to open the Print dialog box. Select a printer, and then click Print. Unlike Reporting Services operational reports, Power View doesn't use an ActiveX control for printing, so you don't have to download and install any controls. Instead, it implements its own printing mechanism built on top of Silverlight printing that sends the print output in PostScript to printers that support it.

   Power View prints the current view. The view always prints in landscape orientation, regardless of settings in the Print dialog box. The printed page shows exactly what you see on the screen. Unlike Reporting Services operational reports, Power View Power View doesn't use an ActiveX control for printing, so you don't have to download and install any controls. Instead, it implements its own printing mechanism that's built on top of Silverlight printing.

# 8.4 Authoring Operational Reports

As you've seen in the preceding practices, non-technical users can implement ad hoc Excel pivot and Power View reports from published PowerPivot models. While very useful for interactive analysis, these tools are not designed for paper-oriented operational reports. Fortunately, Reporting Services includes Report Designer and Report Builder tools to fill this need for developers and for power users. In this section, I'll show you how a power user can author the "Territory Sales by Product Category" report, which is shown in **Figure 8.23**.

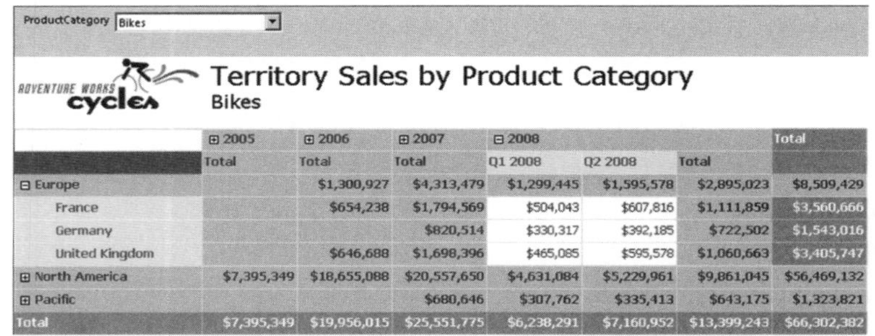


| | 2005 | 2006 | 2007 | 2008 | | | Total |
|---|---|---|---|---|---|---|---|
| | Total | Total | Total | Q1 2008 | Q2 2008 | Total | |
| Europe | | $1,300,927 | $4,313,479 | $1,299,445 | $1,595,578 | $2,895,023 | $8,509,429 |
| France | | $654,238 | $1,794,569 | $504,043 | $607,816 | $1,111,859 | $3,560,666 |
| Germany | | | $820,514 | $330,317 | $392,185 | $722,502 | $1,543,016 |
| United Kingdom | | $646,688 | $1,698,396 | $465,085 | $595,578 | $1,060,663 | $3,405,747 |
| North America | $7,395,349 | $18,655,088 | $20,557,650 | $4,631,084 | $5,229,961 | $9,861,045 | $56,469,132 |
| Pacific | | | $680,646 | $307,762 | $335,413 | $643,175 | $1,323,821 |
| Total | $7,395,349 | $19,956,015 | $25,551,775 | $6,238,291 | $7,160,952 | $13,399,243 | $66,302,382 |

**Figure 8.23** This is an example of an operational report that sources data from the Adventure Works PowerPivot model.

This is a crosstab report that shows the Adventure Works reseller sales grouped by territories on rows and by years on columns. You can expand the Territory Group and Year levels to drill down to the Country and Quarter levels respectively.

## 8.4.1 Getting Started with Report Builder

Report Builder is implemented as a desktop application that allows power users to author reports from a variety of data sources, including Multidimensional and Tabular models. It supports the full report authoring capabilities of Microsoft Reporting Services. You can download the Report Builder stand-alone installer from the Microsoft download center (http://bit.ly/getrb) and install it on your machine. Another installation option is to launch Report Builder from SharePoint via Microsoft .NET ClickOnce technology, as I will demonstrate next.

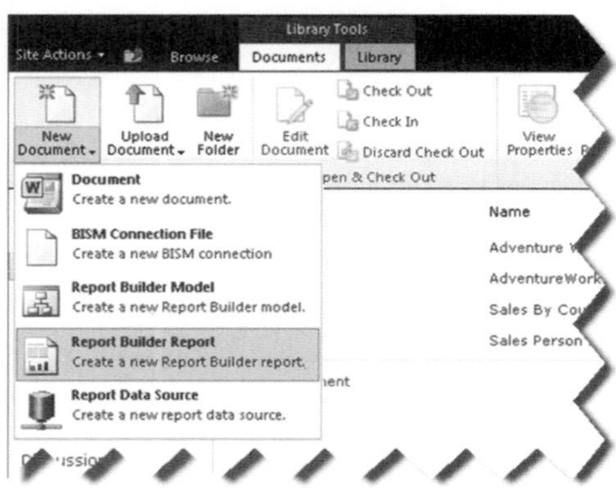


**Figure 8.24** Use the Report Builder Report option to create a new Report Builder report.

***Launching Report Builder***

Follow these steps to launch Report Builder from SharePoint.

1. In the SharePoint, go to the Shared Documents library, and then click the Documents menu.
2. Expand the New Document drop-down button, as shown in **Figure 8.24**. If you don't see the report content types listed in the list, follow the steps in Section 8.3.2 to add the content types to the document library.
3. Click the Report Builder Report option.
4. Accept the prompt that follows to download the Report Builder file.

The first time you launch Report Builder, the ClickOnce technology will download it and install it on your machine. The next time you click the Report Builder Report option, ClickOnce will check your version against the server and then re-install Report Builder only if upgrade is required.

***Setting up a connection***

Once Report Builder is successfully installed, ClickOnce launches it and displays a Getting Started window. While it's possible to create a report from scratch, you can also use one of the Report Builder wizards to create a report in a few steps. Next, you'll use the "New Table or Matrix" wizard to create the "Territory Sales by Product Category" report.

1. In the Getting Started window, click the "New Table or Matrix" wizard.
2. In the Choose a Dataset step, leave "Create a Dataset" selected, and then click Next.
3. In the "Choose a Connection to a Data Source" step, click New to set up a new connection.

**NOTE** Report Builder supports embedded and shared connections. To simplify management, you can set up a shared data source definition, and then deploy it to SharePoint. In this case, the user can simply click the Browse button and then select the shared connection. The user doesn't need to specify the connection specifics, such as the server name and database name. Report Builder processes the report differently based on the connection type. In the case of an embedded data source, the user specifies the connection details, and then the report executes entirely on the client. By contrast, when the user chooses a shared data source, the report is processed on the server.

4. In the Data Source Connection dialog box, expand the Select Connection Type drop-down list, and then select the "Microsoft SQL Server Analysis Services provider", as shown in **Figure 8.25**.

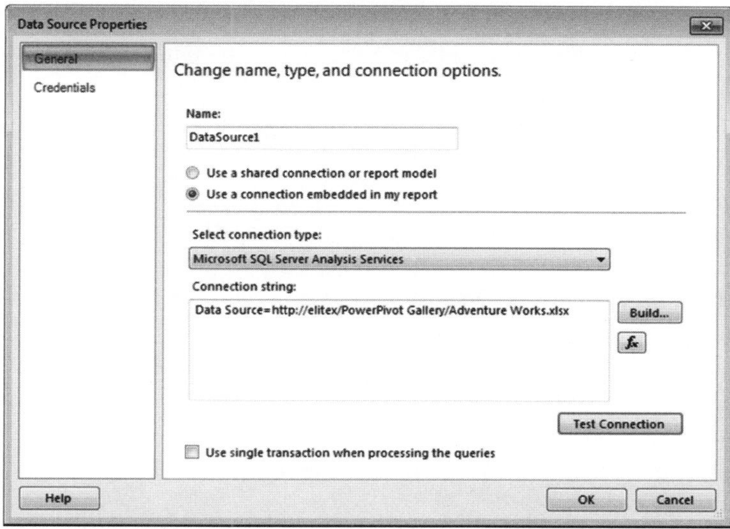


**Figure 8.25** To connect to a published PowerPivot model, use the Microsoft SQL Server Analysis Services provider, and then enter the SharePoint URL.

5. In the Connection String field, enter the URL of the PowerPivot model in the following syntax:

```
Data Source=http://<site>/PowerPivot Gallery/<workbook file name>
```

6. Click the Credentials tab, and then select the first option "Use Current User". As a result, you'll connect to the PowerPivot model under your Windows credentials.
7. Back in the General tab, click the Test Connection button to test connectivity. If all is well, click OK to close the Data Source Properties dialog box.
8. Back in the Table or Matrix wizard, click Next to advance to the "Design a query" step.

***Designing the report query***

Because you're connecting to the PowerPivot model using the Multidimensional interfaces, Report Builder shows the MDX query designer. This is the same query designer you used when you imported a dataset from the Adventure Works cube in Chapter 3. Remember that this query designer is capable of auto-generating MDX queries as you drag entities from the Metadata pane and drop them in the Query Results pane. As a result, you can author basic reports without having to know MDX.

1. Expand the Perspectives drop-down list, and then select "Model" to see all the metadata.
2. In the Metadata pane, expand the Measures folder, and then expand the Reseller Sales folder under it. Similar to Excel OLAP reports, the Metadata pane shows explicit and implicit measures. Drag the Sum of Sales Amount measure to the Query Results pane. Or, right-click it, and then click Add to Query.

   The MDX query designer auto-generates an MDX query that requests the overall reseller sales. You can toggle the Design Mode toolbar button to see the actual MDX query statement.
3. To slice the measures by territory, in the Metadata pane, expand the Sales Territory table. Drag the SalesTerritories hierarchy to the Query Results pane.

   As you might remember, the SalesTerritories hierarchy allows users to browse data by the Group ⇨ Country ⇨ Region navigational path. However, our report needs to show data grouped only by territory groups and countries. In the next step, you'll remove Region from the navigational path.
4. In the Query Results pane, click a cell inside the Region column, and then click the Delete toolbar button to remove the Region column. Or, you can remove a column by dragging the column header away from the Query Results pane.
5. In the Metadata pane, expand the Date table. Drag the Calendar hierarchy to the Query Results pane, and then drop it in, after the Country column.
6. Since the report needs to show data at the quarter level, remove the Month and Date columns from the Query Results pane. Also remove the CalendarSemester column.

   Let's define a report parameter to filter the report data by product category. Because the MDX query designer is capable of auto-generating the report parameters, we can do this with just a few mouse clicks.
7. In the Metadata pane, expand the Product dimension. Drag the ProductCategory field to the Filter pane.
8. To set the Bikes category as the default value for the parameter, expand the drop-down list in the Filter Expression column, and then check the Bikes category.
9. Check the Parameters checkbox in the last column.
10. Compare your dataset configuration with the one shown in **Figure 8.26**. Click Next to create the dataset.

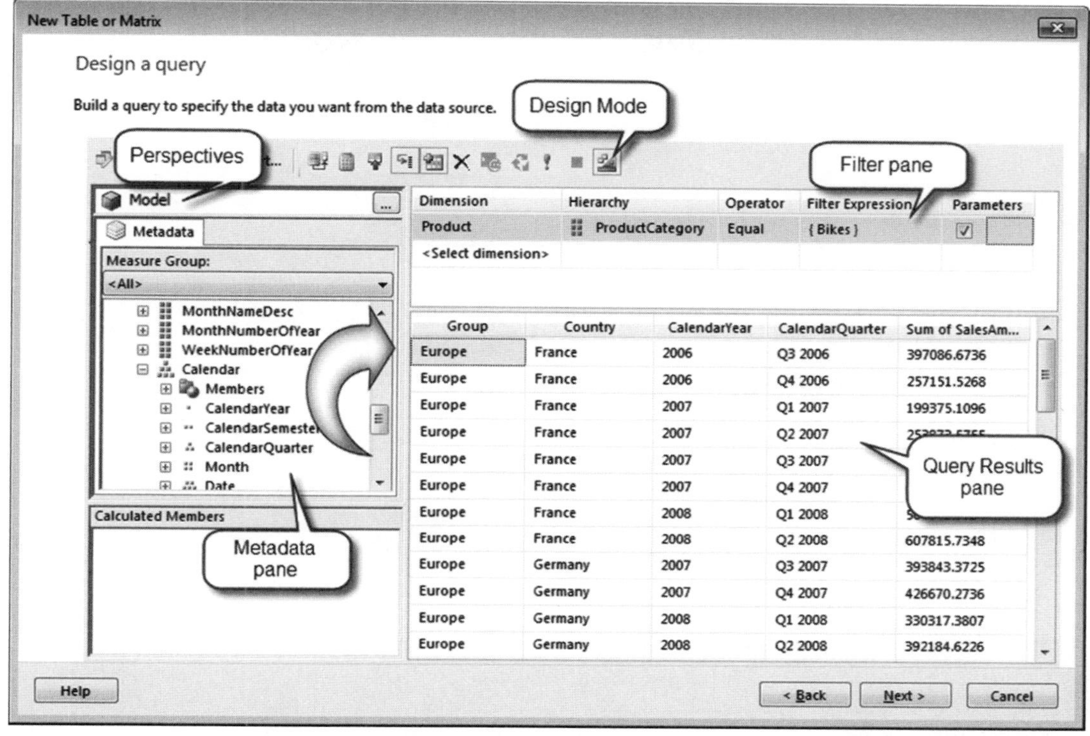


**Figure 8.26** Use the MDX query designer's drag-and-drop feature to set up the report query.

***Defining the report layout and appearance***

Use the next steps to define the report layout, including row and column groups, as well as the report appearance.

1. In the Arrange Field step, drag the Group and Country fields to the Row Groups pane, drag CalendarYear and CalendarQuarter to the Column Groups pane, and then drag Sum_of_Sales_Amount to the Values pane. Later on, the wizard will generate a crosstab layout that groups sales amount by Group and Country on rows, and CalendarYear and CalendarQuarter on columns.
2. In the Choose the Layout step, select the "Stepped, Subtotals Above" layout. Notice that the Expand/Collapse Groups checkbox is enabled by default so that you can toggle the visibility of row and column groups when you run the report. Click Next.
3. In the Choose a Style step, accept the default Ocean style, and then click Finish. The wizard generates the new report and opens it in Design mode.

## 8.4.2 Working with Report Builder

**Figure 8.27** shows the new report open in Design mode in Report Builder. Next, you'll get familiar with the Report Builder designer environment and perform various tasks to refine the report appearance.

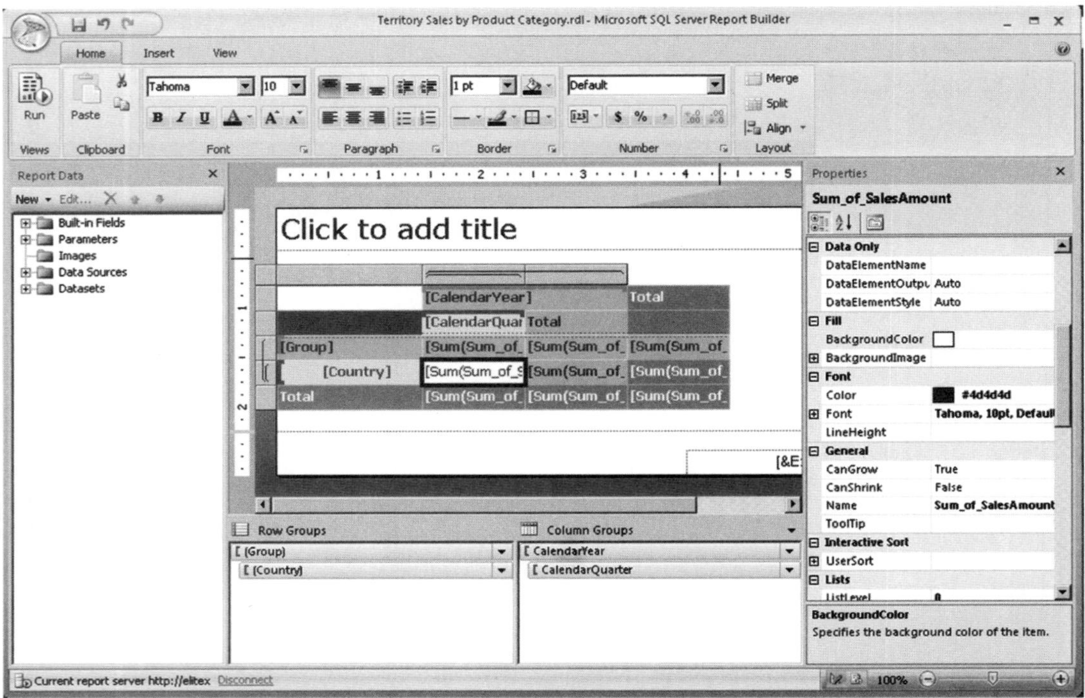


**Figure 8.27** The Territory Sales by Product Category report in Design mode.

***Understanding the design environment***

Report Builder is a collection of graphical query and design tools hosted in a desktop application that has the Microsoft Office look and feel. The white area in the center represents the report itself. If the report has groups, the Grouping pane at the bottom of the window shows the row and column groups defined on the report. The Report Data contains data objects, such as dataset fields, that can be dragged on the report. If the Report Data pane isn't visible, go to the View ribbon tab, and then check Report Data. In the Properties window (on the right), you can view and change the properties of the currently selected item on the report.

In the Home ribbon tab, you can carry out common formatting tasks, such as changing the font options, text alignment, and format settings. The Insert ribbon tab contains report items that you drag onto the design area to lay out the report. The View ribbon tab controls the visibility of the Report Data, Grouping, Ruler, and Properties panes. Finally, the Report Builder button (with the logo) saves and opens reports.

A report has a body section and optional page header and page footer sections. The body of the report contains the report data. You can place any report item in the body, including tables, matrices, lists, and charts. In our case, the report has a single Matrix region. You can use the page header section to include information on the top of each page of the report, such as the report title and company logo. The "Territory Sales by Product Category report" doesn't have a page header section. Similarly, the page footer repeats information on the bottom of each page, such as the page number. In our case, the wizard has added a text box in the page footer that uses an expression to show the report execution time.

Report Builder has design and preview modes. You can click the Run Report button on the Home menu (or press F5) to preview the report. If the report is in Preview mode, you can click the Design button to go back to Design mode. During the report design phase, you'll frequently switch between layout and preview modes to make and test report changes.

***Configuring the report page***

As I mentioned, operational reports are typically designed to look good when printed. Report Builder supports options to control the page size and margins. Since our report is a crosstab report that can expand horizontally as the user drills down years, let's change the report layout to Landscape.

1. Right-click an empty blue area outside the report body, and then click Report Properties.
2. In the Report Properties dialog box (Page Setup tab), select the Landscape orientation. Click OK to close the Report Properties dialog box.

***Changing the report header***

Let's change the report header to show a report title and subtitle, as well as the Adventure Works company logo.

1. Double-click the report title, and then replace its text with *Territory Sales by Product Category*.
2. Resize the report title to free some text on the left for the report title.
3. Suppose you want to add a report subtitle that shows the product category that you select as a report parameter when you run the report. Double-click the report title box again to enter edit mode. Put the mouse cursor at the end of the report title text, and then press Enter to create a new paragraph.
4. In the Report Data pane, expand the Parameters folder, and then drag the ProductProduct-Category parameter to the new line in the title box.
5. Press F5 to run the report. Notice that the subtitle shows #Error. That's because the report parameter is configured for multi-valued selection so that you can select multiple product categories. To fix this, you need to use an expression to concatenate the selected parameter values. Report Builder allows you to define expressions using Visual Basic as an expression language.
6. Right-click the [@ProductProductCategory] placeholder, and then click Expression. In the Expression dialog box, enter the following expression:

   ```
   =Trim(Join(Parameters!ProductProductCategory.Label, ","))
   ```

   This expression (see **Figure 8.28**) uses the Visual Basic Join function to concatenate the selected parameter values into a comma-delimited string. Then, it uses the Trim function to remove the trailing empty spaces.
7. To add a company logo, click the Insert ribbon tab, and then click the Image button.
8. In the Image Properties dialog box (General tab), click the Import button. In the Open dialog box, navigate to the Ch08 folder. Select the AWC.jpg image, and then click Open. Then, click OK to close the Image Properties dialog box. Report Builder embeds the image inside the report and shows it next to the report title.

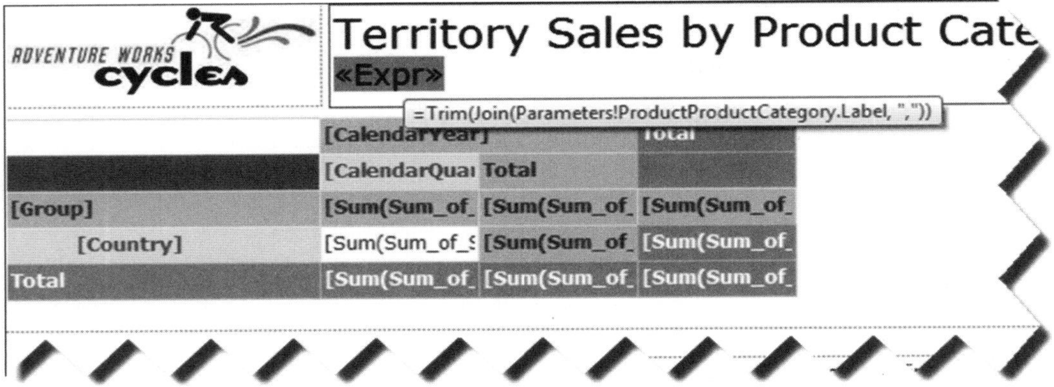


Figure 8.28 You can add images to reports, such as to show a company logo.

***Changing formatting***

Next, you'll refine the report appearance by resizing columns and by changing the formatting.

1. Press F5 to preview the report. Expand Europe. Notice that United Kingdom wraps to the next line because the first column isn't wide enough. Also, notice that the numeric cells wrap because they're formatted with four decimal places by default.
2. Click the Design button to switch to Design mode.
3. Drag the right border of the first column to the right to increase its width.
4. Right-click any of the numeric cells (the ones whose content starts with =Sum), and then click Text Box Properties.
5. In the Text Box Properties dialog box, click the Number tab, and then format the text box as Currency with a thousand separator with no decimal places. Click OK.
6. In the Properties pane, locate the Format property. Select its value (it should be '$'#,0;('$'#,0)), and then press Ctrl+C to copy it to the Windows Clipboard.
7. Select all the numeric cells on the report (you can hold the Shift key for an extended selection). In the Properties window, paste the format string in the Format property to apply the same formatting to all the cells.

***Saving the report to SharePoint***

You can save a Report Builder report locally to your hard drive or to the server.

1. Click the Report Builder button, or press Ctrl+S to open the Save As Report dialog box.
2. Because you launched Report Builder from SharePoint, Report Builder shows the structure of the SharePoint site. Navigate to the Shared Documents folder.
3. In the Name field, enter *Territory Sales by Product Category.rdl* as a report name. Click Save to publish the report to SharePoint.

**NOTE** Report Designer and Report Builder are very flexible and feature-rich tools. As usual, however, flexibility comes with complexity. To get productive with them, you need to study Reporting Services. My book, Applied Microsoft SQL Server 2008 Reporting Services (http://bit.ly/ssrsbook), is designed to help you master this technology.

## 8.5 Summary

Once you publish a PowerPivot model to SharePoint, there are various options to gain insights from it. Use Excel Services for thin-client rendering of pivot reports and charts without requiring Excel on the desktop. Users with Excel 2007 or later can author OLAP pivot reports by connecting to a published PowerPivot model.

Power View is a new web-based reporting tool that's specifically designed to support Tabular. Business users can use Power View to author interactive reports with tabular, crosstab, and chart sections. Power View includes capabilities not found in other reporting tools, such as automatic highlighting and animation.

Finally, power users can use Report Builder to implement operational "canned" reports. Report Builder includes wizards and the MDX query designer to help you get started. Once the report is ready, it can be saved to disk or to a SharePoint library.

SharePoint provides additional features that help IT professionals manage and monitor PowerPivot for SharePoint. That's what I'll discuss in the next chapter.

Chapter 9

# Managing PowerPivot for SharePoint



Allowing business users to deploy models to a wide-open shared environment without supervision is asking for trouble. Uncontrolled deployment to PowerPivot for SharePoint will sooner or later lead to "spreadmarts". Undefined and unverified data will be floating from spreadsheet to spreadsheet, and can be used to draw false conclusions that lead to wrong decisions. While team business intelligence (BI) gives business users the tools to share their BI models and to collaborate online, managed team BI gives the IT department the means to establish the necessary limits for these processes to happen in a controlled and trustworthy manner.

This chapter is for IT professionals, and I assume that you have some basic knowledge and experience with SharePoint. It teaches you how to manage PowerPivot for SharePoint. You'll learn how to perform common management tasks, including managing PowerPivot workbooks, configuring version history, and setting up shared data sources and approval workflows. You'll also understand how to secure PowerPivot for SharePoint and how to refresh PowerPivot models on a schedule. Finally, I'll show you how to monitor the server utilization and workbook activity.

## 9.1 Managing PowerPivot Workbooks

When you upload a PowerPivot model to SharePoint, the Excel workbook file is saved in the SharePoint content database. As far as SharePoint is concerned, a PowerPivot model is no different than any other document type, such as a regular Excel workbook. As a result, you can use the built-in SharePoint features to manage the PowerPivot workbooks.

### 9.1.1 Managing Application Settings and Files

Since its original release, SharePoint has offered comprehensive document management features. Common file management tasks include creating folders, uploading and downloading files, making changes, and removing, sending, and versioning files.

***Managing application settings***
Before allowing users to publish models to SharePoint, review and change if necessary the PowerPivot for SharePoint application settings, such as the maximum upload file size and session timeout.

1. Open the "SharePoint Central Administration" application, and then click the "Manage Service Applications" link found in the Application Management section.
2. In the Service Applications tab, click the ExcelServiceApp1 link.
3. In the "Manage Excel Services Application" page, click the "Trusted File Locations" link.
4. In the "Trusted File Locations page", click the http:// link.

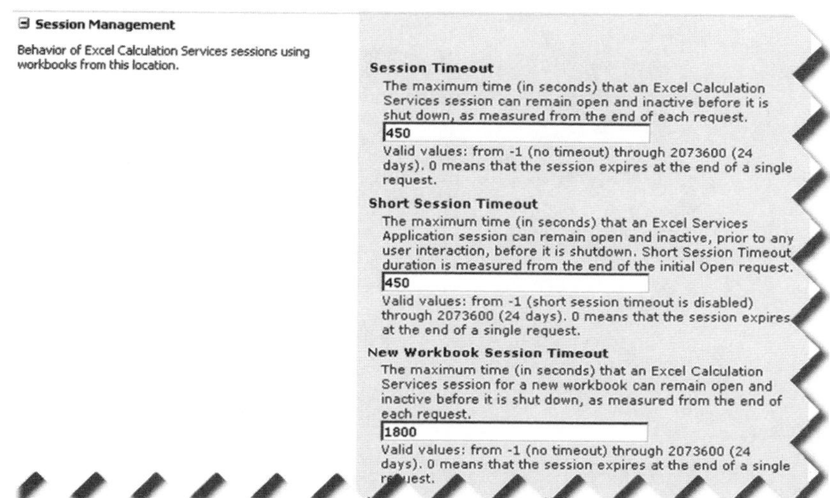


**Figure 9.1** The "Excel Service Application" settings control the session timeout of a web report.

5. In the "Edit Trusted File Location" page, scroll down the Session Management settings (see **Figure 9.1**). Notice that the Short Session Timeout setting is set to 450 seconds. As a result, if the user browses an Excel web report and doesn't interact with the report for 7.5 minutes, the session times out. If the user attempts an interactive action and the session has timed out, then the user sees the following message:

   Your session has timed out because of inactivity. To reload the workbook, click OK.

   If the end users find the default session timeout too short, consider increasing the "Short Session Timeout" setting.

   **NOTE** There are actually several session timeout settings, as explained in the "Short Session Timeout and Session Timeout in Excel Services" blog post by Shahar Prish, Principal Software Engineer at Microsoft, at http://bit.ly/PPSSessiontimeout.

6. Scroll further down until you see the Workbook Settings section. Notice that the maximum workbook size is set to 200 MB. This setting throttles the maximum file size across all the SharePoint sites, and it should be sufficient for most installations.
7. Go back to the SharePoint Central Administration home page, and then click the "Manage Web Applications" link. Select the "SharePoint – 80" web application and click the General Settings menu. Scroll down the "Web Application General Settings" page. Observe that the Maximum Upload Size setting is 2,047 MB. This setting overwrites the maximum workbook size limit on the "Trusted File Location" page. If you need to upload larger workbooks, make sure to check and adjust both settings.

*Managing files*

All the file management tasks can be performed using the SharePoint Documents ribbon tab.

1. In the web browser, navigate to PowerPivot Gallery, such as http://<site>/PowerPivot Gallery.
2. Click the Documents ribbon tab, as shown in **Figure 9.2**.

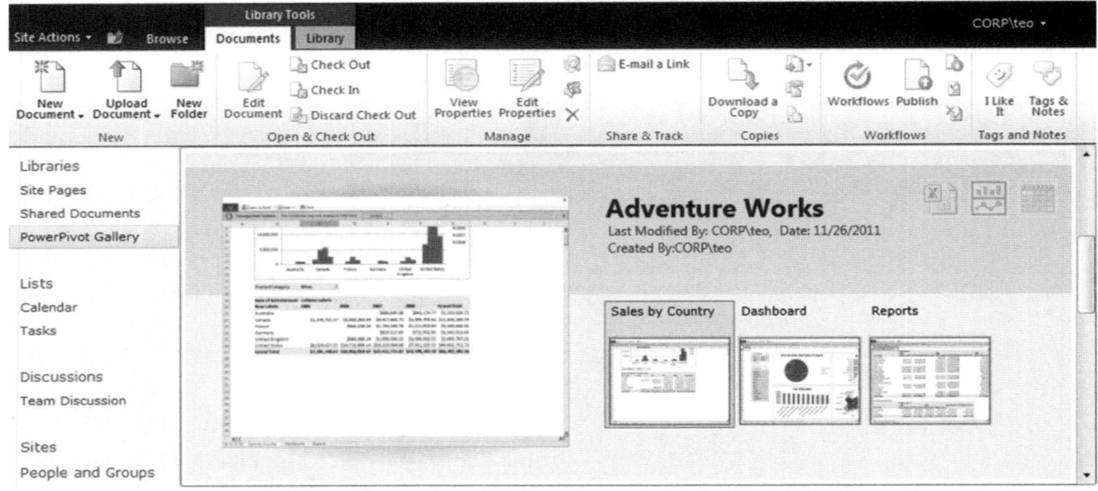


**Figure 9.2** Use the SharePoint Documents ribbon tab to initiate content management tasks.

**Table 9.1** describes the menu options in the Documents ribbon tab that relate to managing documents in PowerPivot Gallery.

**Table 9.1 This table describes the menu options in the Documents ribbon tab and how they relate to PowerPivot models.**

| Menu Button | Submenu Drop-Down List | Task |
|---|---|---|
| New Document | PowerPivot Gallery Document | Opens Microsoft Excel |
| Upload Document | Upload Document | Uploads a single Excel workbook |
| | Upload Multiple Documents | Uploads multiple files |
| New Folder | | Creates a new folder to organize content |
| Check Out, Check In | | Maintains document history |
| View Properties | | Shows who created the document and when it was last updated |
| Edit Properties | | Change document properties, such as the document name |
| Delete Document | | Removes the document and places it in the Recycle bin |
| E-mail a Link | | Sends an e-mail with a link to the document |
| Download a Copy | | Downloads the workbook to your machine |
| Send To | Other Location | Copies the document to another location, such as another folder |

## 9.1.2 Managing Data Sources

In Chapter 8, you saw that PowerPivot Gallery makes it easy to start with Power View reporting. The user can click the "Create Power View Report" button in the PowerPivot Gallery to launch a new report that uses the selected PowerPivot model as a data source. The caveat with this approach is that the connection information gets embedded in the Power View report. If the PowerPivot workbook file is renamed or moved to a new location, all the reports that reference it will be invalided, and then you must update the data source properties for each report. When this happens, you need to complete the following steps to change the data source properties:

1. If the Power View report is saved in PowerPivot Gallery, use the Library ribbon tab to change the library view to All Documents.
2. Hover your mouse over the report, expand the report drop-down menu, and click Manage Data Sources.
3. Change the data source definition.

To avoid these steps for each report that uses the same connection, consider setting up a shared data source to centralize connection management for operational reports and for Power View reports.

***Setting up a connection***

Follow these steps to create a shared data source for Power View reports and to configure it to connect to the Adventure Works model:

1. In the web browser, navigate to the document library where you want to create the connection, such as http://<site>/PowerPivot Gallery.
2. Click the Documents tab in the SharePoint ribbon. Expand the New Document drop-down menu (see **Figure 9.3**), and then click "BI Semantic Model Connection". If you don't see the "BI Semantic Model Connection" option, then you must import the BI content types, as I explained in Chapter 8.

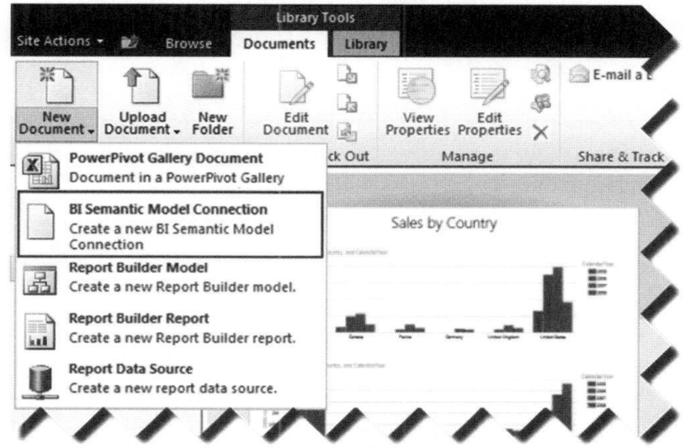


**Figure 9.3** Click the "BI Semantic Model Connection" option to set up a new shared connection for Power View reports.

3. In the "New BI Semantic Model Connection" page, enter the data source name and description, as shown in **Figure 9.4**. In the "Workbook URL or Server Name" field, enter the workbook URL. Don't fill in the Database field because it's reserved for organizational models that are deployed to an Analysis Services instance in Tabular mode. Click OK to create the connection.

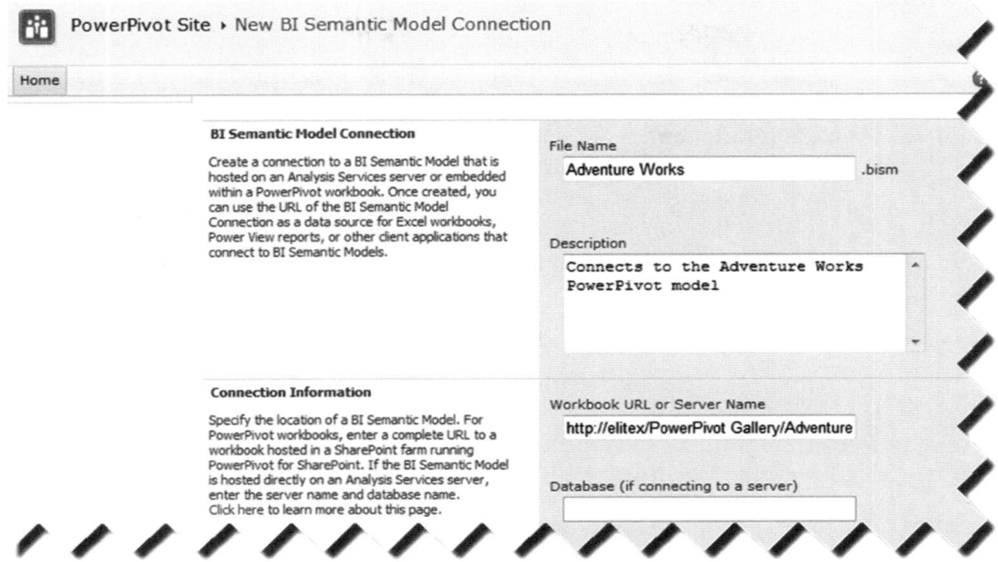


**Figure 9.4** Set up a new BI Semantic Model Connection by specifying the workbook URL.

BI semantic model connections have a *.bism file extension. Once the connection is created, the user can use it for Power View reports. If you decide to save the connection in PowerPivot Gallery, you'll see a thumbnail image that helps you differentiate it from the reports. The user can simply click the "Create Power View Report" icon next to the thumbnail image of the connection file to create a new Power View report that uses this connection.

If you save the connection file to another library, the end user can hover the mouse cursor over it, expand the drop-down menu, and then click "Create Power View Report" to launch Power View. If you decide to rename or to move the workbook, you only need to update the connection file, and then all the existing reports will pick up the changes. Unfortunately, PowerPivot Gallery doesn't give you a shortcut to view or edit the connection definition. You can edit the connection by following these steps:

4. Click the Library ribbon tab. Expand the Current View drop-down menu, and then click All Documents.
5. Once SharePoint switches to the new view, hover your mouse over the Adventure Works connection. Expand the drop-down list, and then click "Edit BI Semantic Model Connection".

***Creating a report data source***

One limitation of BI semantic model connections is that they use Windows integrated security to pass the identity of the interactive user to Analysis Services. This could be an issue when the client and server don't belong to the same Active Directory domain. However, you can create a report data source instead of a BI Semantic Model Connection in order to get additional security options, such as using stored credentials.

1. In the New Document drop-down menu, click Report Data Source (see **Figure 9.3** again).
2. In the Data Source Properties page, expand the Data Source Type drop-down list, and then select "Microsoft BI Semantic Model for Power View". In the Connection String field, enter the workbook URL, as shown in **Figure 9.5**.

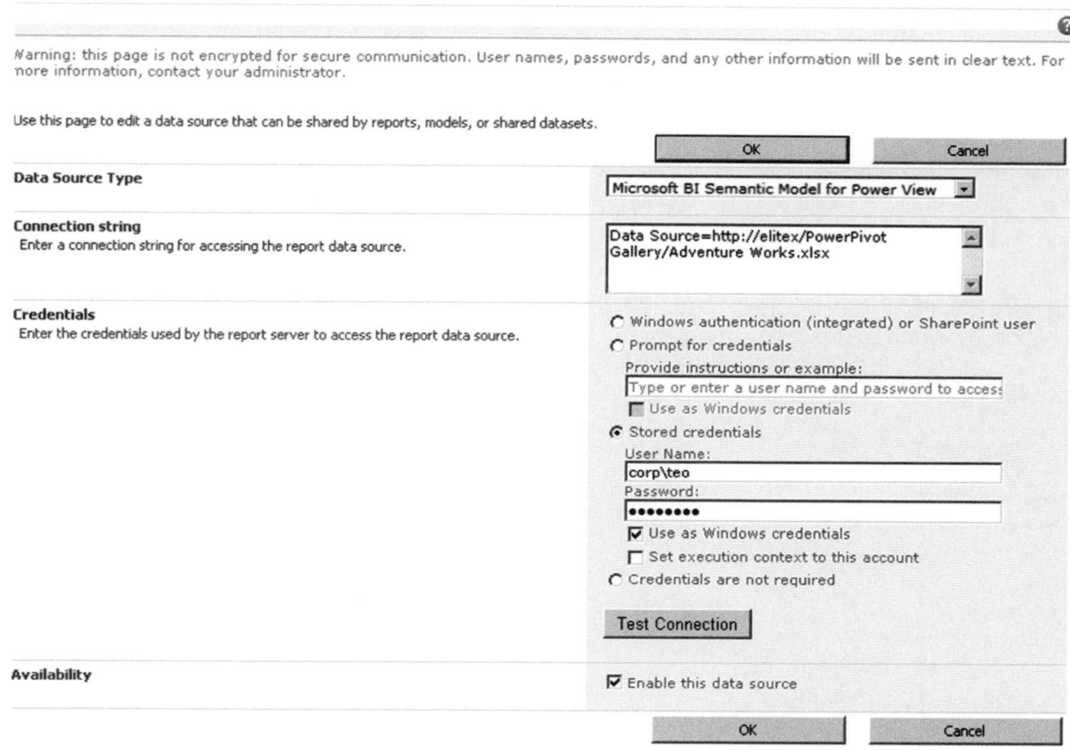


**Figure 9.5** Report data sources support additional security options.

3. The only supported credential options for tabular models are Windows Authentication and Stored Credentials. For example, if you want all the requests to go under a single Windows login account, select the Stored Credentials option, specify the Windows credentials, and then check "Use as Windows credentials". Click OK to create the report data source. It gets saved as a file with an *.rsds extension.

Once the connection is created, you can hover the mouse over it, expand the drop-down menu, and then click "Create Power View Report" to launch Power View. If you've created the connection in the PowerPivot Gallery library, use the Library tab in the SharePoint ribbon to change the Current View drop-down list to All Documents. The reason is because the other views (Gallery, Theater, and Carousel) don't provide context menus for report data sources.

**TIP** As noted in Chapter 8, operational reports can also benefit from shared report data sources. When the user creates a new report in Report Builder, they can browse and select a shared data source that includes the connection details. Specifically, in the "Choose a Connection to a Data Source" step of the Report Builder wizard, they'd click Browse and then navigate to a SharePoint library or folder where the data source definition is located.

## 9.1.3 Configuring Version History

Suppose regulatory or audit requirements dictate that you must maintain report versions each time the report definition or data is updated. Fortunately, document versioning is one of the SharePoint standard document management features. Once a document library is configured for versioning, users can check out and check in documents, including PowerPivot workbooks. And, each time the document is checked in, a new version is created.

***Enabling versioning support***

Before you can create versions, you need to configure PowerPivot Gallery for versioning.

1. In SharePoint, navigate to PowerPivot Gallery, click the Library tab, and then click the Library Settings button in the ribbon.
2. In the "Document Library Settings" page, click the Versioning Settings link to open the Versioning Settings page, which is shown in **Figure 9.6**.

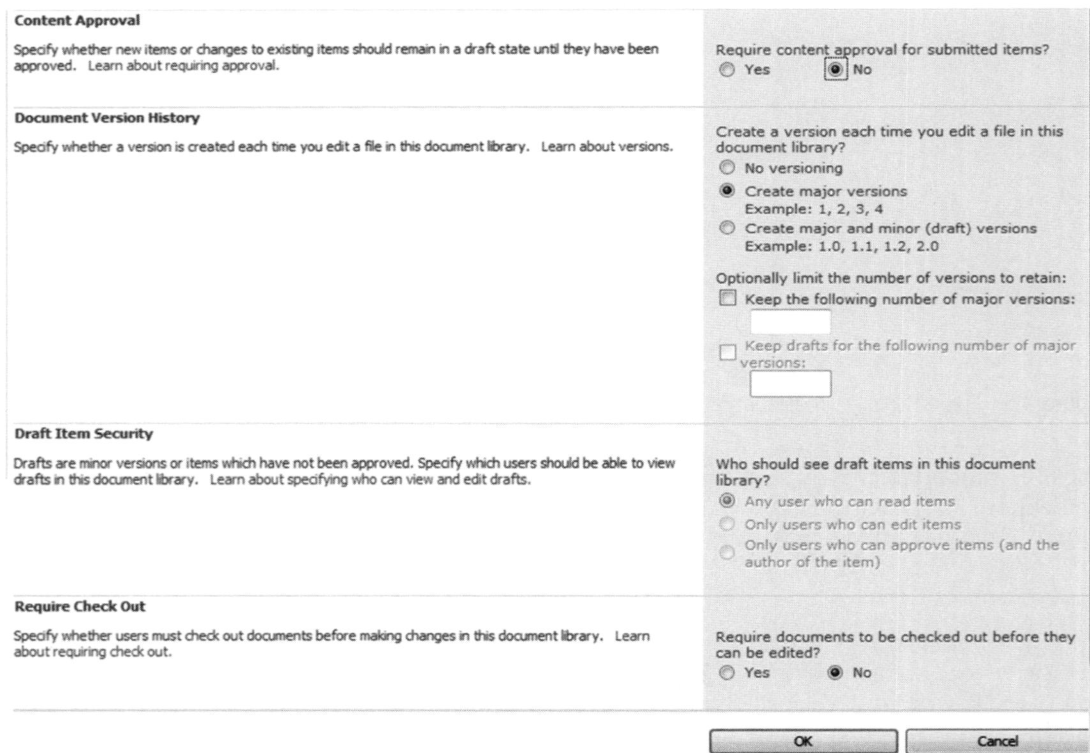


**Figure 9.6** Before users can check out and check in workbooks, you must enable versioning.

3. Assuming you want to maintain report changes in the history, in the "Document Version History" section, select the preferred numbering option, such as Create Major Versions. Click OK.

**NOTE** Since SharePoint saves the entire workbook when a new version is created, the size of the content database can swell considerably when versioning large PowerPivot workbooks. Consider retaining a limited number of versions by configuring the "Keep the following number of major versions" setting in the Versioning Settings page. Also, beware that if you configure the workbook for automate data refresh, PowerPivot for SharePoint will create a new version for each data refresh. For example, an hourly automated refresh on a 1 GB PowerPivot workbook requires 24 versions and 24 GB of version history storage per day.

*Managing versions*

Once versioning is enabled, any change to the workbook (including automatic data refresh) automatically creates a new version. Subject to security rights, the end user can explicitly check out the model, make changes, and then check it back to SharePoint by using the Check Out and Check In buttons in the Documents ribbon tab. When a user checks in a file, the user can include comments to describe the changes.

1. To see the version history, select the PowerPivot model in PowerPivot Gallery, click the Documents ribbon tab, and then click Version History to open the dialog box shown in **Figure 9.7**.
2. To view a prior version, simply click the version's link. The Version History dialog box allows you to restore and delete versions.

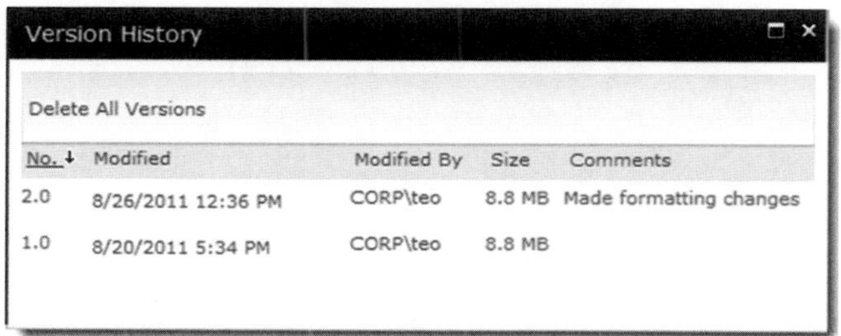


**Figure 9.7** The Version History dialog box lets you review the document history, restore versions, and delete versions.

## 9.1.4 Approving Published Models

Suppose your users can upload workbooks, but you want someone to review and approve the published models before they become publicly available. SharePoint includes comprehensive document approval and routing capabilities that can help you enforce BI governance policies and avoid "spreadmarts".

*Configuring content approval*

The easiest way to implement formal approval is to configure the versioning settings, as follows:

1. In the Versioning Settings page (see **Figure 9.6** again), select Yes for the "Require content approval for submitted items?" Once this setting is enabled, the workbooks are published in a draft status.
2. In the "Draft Item Security" section, specify who can view the draft workbook. For example, if you select the "Only users who can approve items" option, users who don't have approval rights won't see the workbook.

   Once the draft is published, users with Approve rights, such as a user who is a member of the SharePoint Members security group, can review and approve the workbook.
3. In PowerPivot Gallery, click the workbook to select, and then click the Approve/Reject button in the Documents ribbon tab.

4. In the Approve/Reject dialog box, select one of the following statuses: Approved, Rejected, or Pending. You can enter a comment to explain the status change. Click OK to update the document status.

***Implementing an approval workflow***

SharePoint Server includes a set of specialized workflows that give you more control and customization over document processes. One of these workflows is the Document Approval workflow. This workflow is disabled by default. Follow these steps to enable and configure the Document Approval workflow.

1. Expand the Site Actions drop-down menu, and then click Site Settings. In the Site Settings page, click the "Site Collection Features" link found in the "Site Collection Administration" section. In the Features page, scroll down the page all the way to the end, and then click the Activate button next to the Workflows feature.
2. After you enable the Document Approval workflow at the site level, you can add it to PowerPivot Gallery and configure it. In PowerPivot Gallery, click the Library ribbon tab. Expand the Workflow Settings drop-down menu, and then click Add a Workflow. This starts a wizard to help you configure the workflow.

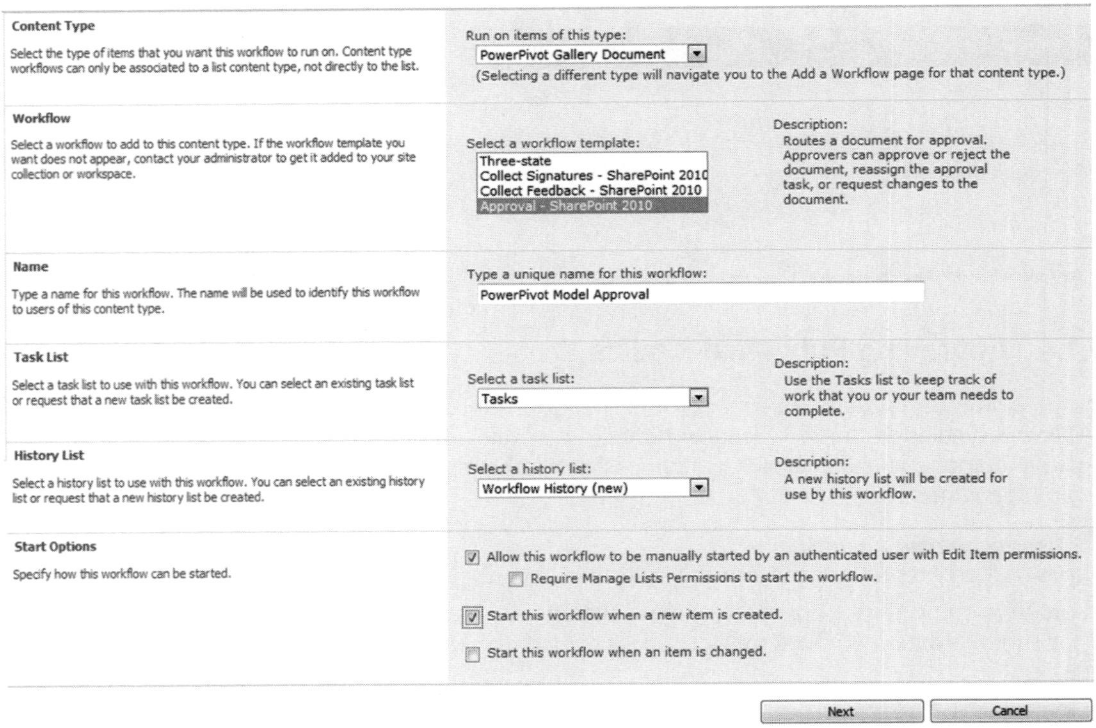

**Figure 9.8** Use the Approval workflow to approve PowerPivot models.

3. On the first step, expand the Content Type drop-down list, and then select "PowerPivot Gallery Document" (assuming you want to apply the workbook to PowerPivot workbooks only). In the Workflow section, select the "Approval – SharePoint 2010" workflow. In the Name section, enter *PowerPivot Model Approval* as a workflow name. Check the "Start this workflow when a new Item

is created" checkbox to start the workflow automatically when a user publishes a model. Compare your settings with **Figure 9.8**, and then click Next.

**NOTE** At this point, you might get an error "The form cannot be rendered. This might be due to a misconfiguration of the Microsoft SharePoint Server State Service. For more information, contact your server administrator." The reason for this error is that the SharePoint State Services isn't configured. Follow the steps in the "Form not rendered due to misconfiguration of State Service" blog post by Alexander Meijer at http://bit.ly/stateserviceconfig. In my case, I used the Farm Configuration Wizard approach to resolve the issue.

4. On the second step, assign approvers and the task specifics, such as the duration of the approval task. Click the Save button to finalize the workflow configuration.
5. To test the workflow, upload a workbook in PowerPivot Gallery. This will start the workflow. Each approver will receive a task assigned to them and an e-mail notification if e-mail delivery is configured.

   Assuming you've assigned yourself as an approver, click the Tasks link in the SharePoint navigation menu to review the tasks assigned to you, as shown in **Figure 9.9**. In this case, the workflow was triggered by uploading the "Top 10 Products by Internet Sales" PowerPivot workbook.

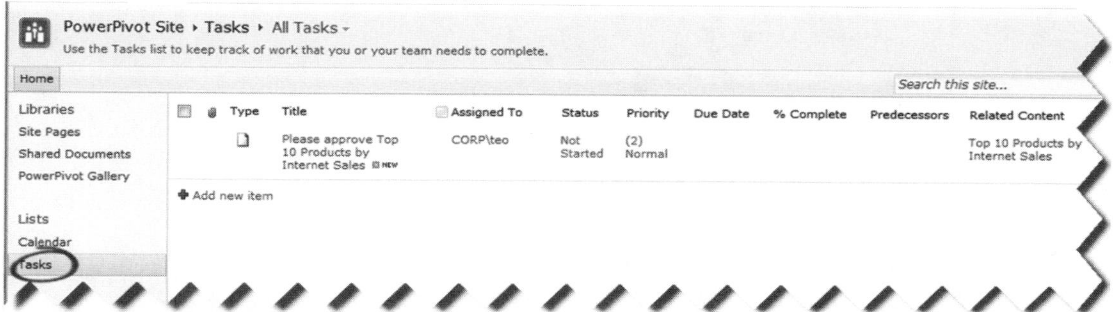


**Figure 9.9** The approvers receive a task to review and approve the model.

6. Click the link in the Related Content column to download and open the workbook, so that you can review the PowerPivot model and embedded reports. Click the link in the Title column to open a dialog box where you can change the task status, such as to approve a task, reject it, request a change, or reassign a task.

**NOTE** This section of the chapter only gave you a sneak preview of the SharePoint workflow capabilities. When the predefined workflows are not enough, you can customize them in SharePoint Designer. Or, developers can implement more sophisticated workflows in Visual Studio. For more information about SharePoint approval workflows, review the "Understand Approval Workflows In SharePoint 2010" topic in the product documentation at http://bit.ly/approvalworkflow.

# 9.2 Managing Data Refresh

Once the data is imported into PowerPivot, data is cached in the Excel workbook file. In time, the data in the original data sources might change, and the PowerPivot cached data won't reflect these changes. As you might remember, when you work with PowerPivot for Excel, you can manually refresh data. However, once the application is deployed to the server, refreshing data requires opening the application in Excel, reimporting data, and redeploying the application. This process can become cumbersome. Fortunately, PowerPivot for SharePoint allows you to configure automatic data refresh for published PowerPivot workbooks.

## 9.2.1 Understanding Data Refresh

Data refresh for PowerPivot in SharePoint is an automated process that involves several components. **Figure 9.10** shows how the process works at a high level. Microsoft has written a whitepaper, "Everything You Always Wanted to Know About PowerPivot Data Refresh but Were Afraid to Ask" (http://bit.ly/datarefresh) that provides additional insights. Another great resource is the "PowerPivot Data Refresh in SharePoint" video by Lee Graber at http://bit.ly/datarefreshvideo.

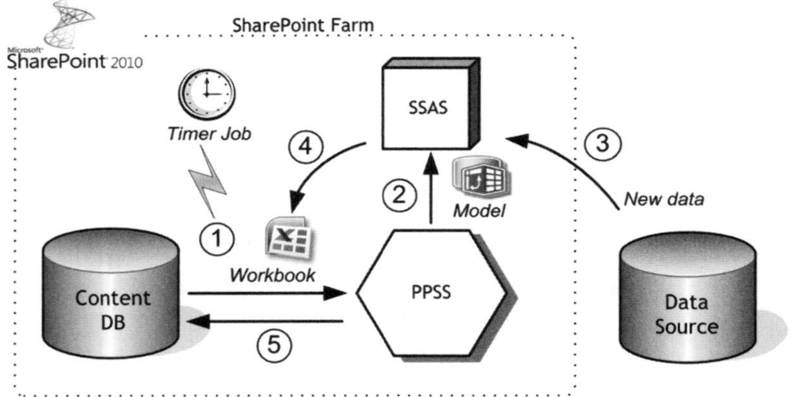


**Figure 9.10** This diagram shows the runtime interaction between components that are involved in a PowerPivot data refresh.

***Understanding components***

The following components are involved in the data refresh operation:

- Timer Service – Data refresh is a scheduled operation. As a part of configuring data refresh you need to specify a schedule, such as to refresh the PowerPivot model data on a daily basis. The SharePoint Timer Service is responsible to monitor which schedules are due and to create timer jobs.

**TIP** Normally, the SharePoint Timer Service checks schedules about once per minute. However, it won't run jobs if the system is under pressure, such as when CPU or memory utilization is high. If you find that a scheduled data refresh doesn't happen as expected, examine the current activity on the SharePoint server, and then free up some resources.

- PowerPivot System Service (PPSS) – This component is responsible for the actual data refresh operation, including retrieving data from the data source and updating the PowerPivot model.
- Analysis Services in SharePoint Integrated Mode (SSAS) – As you might know by now, PowerPivot for SharePoint hosts PowerPivot models on a dedicated Analysis Services instance.

- Windows account for data refresh (not shown on the diagram) – As a part of configuring the data refresh, you specify a Windows account that PowerPivot System Service will use to connect to the SharePoint content database and to external data sources when Windows integrated security is used.

Currently, it's not possible to trigger a data refresh programmatically, such as by a custom application that monitors data changes. Your only option is to initiate the refresh job on a set schedule.

***Understanding runtime interaction***
The data refresh process starts when the timer job discovers that a schedule is due according to the schedule specification. The timer job then notifies the PowerPivot System Service (PPSS). PPSS uses the Windows account for data refresh to connect and extract (1) the Excel workbook from the SharePoint content database. PPSS instructs (2) Analysis Services to load the embedded database with PowerPivot data from the workbook and to attach it as a read/write database that's designated for a data refresh only.

Next, PPSS uses again the Windows account for data refresh to send processing commands to the Analysis Services database. Analysis Services connects (3) to the external data source under this account and then it retrieves the latest data. Once the data is loaded, PPSS saves the Analysis Services database (4) back to the Excel workbook.

PPSS uses the Windows account for data refresh for a third time to connect to the SharePoint content database and to update the Excel workbook. If PowerPivot Gallery is the document library where the workbook is located, an event is triggered to start the snapshot generation process (GetSnapshot.exe) to update the workbook thumbnail image. PPSS updates the schedule status and the data refresh history. Finally, the Analysis Services database is detached and then attached as a read-only database to service report queries.

## 9.2.2 Configuring Data Refresh

Now that you have a better understanding of how SharePoint data refresh works, let's see how you can configure it. As it stands, the Adventure Works model imports data from several data sources, including the Adventure Works data warehouse. Suppose that the data warehouse is updated every day. Your objective is to schedule an automatic data refresh that will synchronize the Adventure Works PowerPivot model with the changes in the data warehouse.

***Preparing for a data refresh***
Before configuring a data refresh, review the connections in the Adventure Works model and make adjustments as needed.

1. In Excel, open the Adventure Works.xlsx workbook with your changes from Chapter 8. Click the PowerPivot ribbon tab in Excel, and then click the PowerPivot Window button.
2. In the PowerPivot window, click the Design ribbon tab, and then click Existing Connections.
3. In the Existing Connections dialog box (see **Figure 9.11**), review the connection strings.

When you work with PowerPivot for Excel you can import data from virtually everywhere, including local servers and files. However, chances are that the SharePoint server might not be able to reach these data sources. For example, the Resellers and Employees data sources point to local files on the C drive. When the SharePoint server executes the refresh job, it will try to find the files on *its* C drive, and it will fail if the files are not there. The same consideration applies to connection strings using *(local) or localhost*. Also, SharePoint 2010 is 64-bit only and requires 64-bit drivers to be installed on the SharePoint application server. Whereas your Excel 2010 installation might be 32-bit and might require 32-bit drivers.

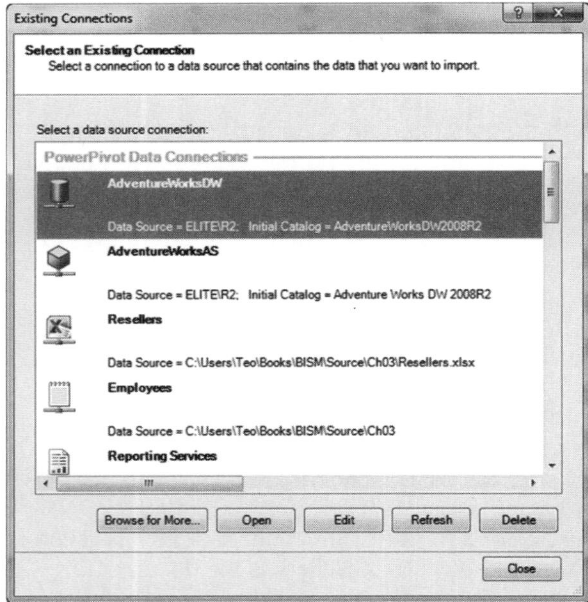


**Figure 9.11** Make sure that the PowerPivot connections specify data sources that are accessible by the SharePoint server.

In general, you have two options to fix the connection strings when they reference local resources:

- (Recommended) For files, click the Edit button, and then change the connection string to point to a network share that the SharePoint server can access. For databases, use the server NETBIOS name instead of using (local) or localhost.
- Make sure that the appropriate 64-bit drivers are installed on the SharePoint application server. Also, make sure that the SharePoint server can connect to the data sources that need to be refreshed.

### *Planning security*

The next decision point to make is what authentication option you'll use to connect to the data sources. For most data sources, such as flat files or Reporting Services reports, the only option is Windows security. Because of this, you need to make sure that the Windows account that you specify for data refresh has the necessary rights to access these data sources.

For database servers that support Windows integrated security, such as SQL Server, Windows security is preferred because you don't need to specify a password and because the Windows accounts can be centrally managed in Active Directory. However, while you're working out the kinks of the data refresh, you might consider standard security to eliminate issues with Active Directory.

**NOTE** You can also overwrite the credentials during the process of configuring the data refresh. Unfortunately, besides changing the security credentials, SharePoint doesn't allow you to change other settings in the connection string, such as the server name and database name. Normally, SharePoint data refresh doesn't require Kerberos authentication when connecting to external data sources (except the scenario where you configure SQL Server to use a linked server with Windows authentication). This is explained in more detail in the "Microsoft PowerPivot for SharePoint: Security Context of Connections in a Farm" video by Lee Graber at http://bit.ly/pprefreshsecurity.

Once you've made the required changes, deploy the workbook to PowerPivot Gallery.

***Setting up a refresh job***

Next, you'll schedule a data refresh job. This requires SharePoint Contributor rights.

1. In PowerPivot Gallery, click the "Manage Data Refresh" button (the Calendar icon) next to the Adventure Works model, as shown in **Figure 9.12**.

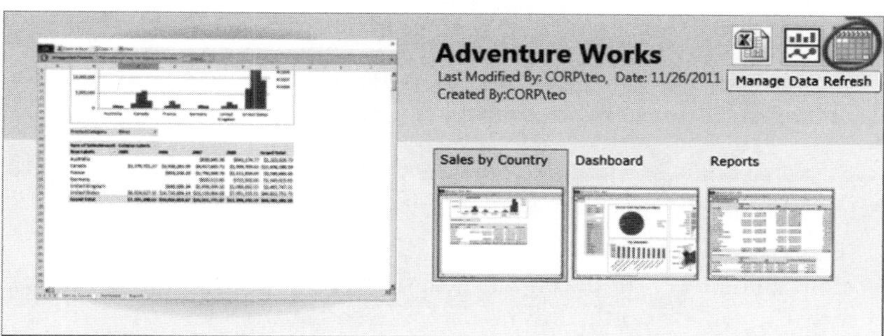


**Figure 9.12** Click the "Manage Data Refresh" button to schedule a data refresh for the selected model.

2. If you've deployed the model to another library, however, hover the mouse cursor over the model, expand the context drop-down menu, and then click "Manage PowerPivot Data Refresh" to open the configuration page, as shown in **Figure 9.13**.

OK Cancel

**Data Refresh**

Specify if you would like to turn Data Refresh on or off.

☑ Enable

**Schedule Details**

Define the frequency (daily, weekly, monthly or once) and the timing details for the refresh schedule.

◉ Daily ◉ Every 1 day(s)
○ Weekly ○ Every weekday
○ Monthly ○ On the following days:
○ Once
☐ Sunday ☐ Monday ☐ Tuesday ☐ Wednesday
☐ Thursday ☐ Friday ☐ Saturday

☑ Also refresh as soon as possible

Check this checkbox if you want to start data refresh as soon as possible

**Earliest Start Time**

Specify the earliest start time that the data refresh will begin

◉ After business hours
○ Specific earliest start time:
12 : 00 ◉ am ○ pm

**E-mail Notifications**

Specify e-mail address of the users to be notified in the event of data refresh failures.

**Credentials**

Provide the credentials that will be used to refresh data on your behalf.

◉ Use the data refresh account configured by the administrator
○ Connect using the following Windows user credentials
○ Connect using the credentials saved in Secure Store Service (SSS) to log on to the data source. Enter the ID used to look up the credentials in the SSS ID box

**Figure 9.13** You can schedule a data refresh on a schedule.

3. In the Data Refresh section, click the Enable checkbox to enable a data refresh for the Adventure Works model.
4. In the Schedule Details section, select the schedule frequency, such as daily, weekly, or monthly.

**TIP** Unlike what you might think, the Once option doesn't mean that you'll run the refresh job immediately. Instead, it means to run it once, at the time that you specify in the "Earliest Start Time section". To schedule a data refresh as soon as possible, don't use the Once option. Instead, select another option as you would normally do, such as Daily, but check the "Also refresh as soon as possible" checkbox in addition to selecting the frequency, and then schedule the start time (in the "Earliest Start Time" section) ahead of the current time, or select the "After business hours" option.

5. In the "Earliest Start Time" section, specify specific time or select the After Business Hours option. You can review and change the definition of "business hours" in the PowerPivot Management Dashboard.
6. If SharePoint is configured for e-mail delivery, in the E-mail Notification section, you can specify the e-mail addresses of the users who will be notified if the data refresh fails.

***Configuring credentials***

The Credentials section deserves more explanation. As I mentioned previously, the PowerPivot System Service uses a Windows account to log in to the SharePoint content database and data sources whose data needs to be refreshed, when Windows integrated security is specified in the PowerPivot data source connection. You have three choices for this Windows account (see the Credentials section in **Figure 9.13**):

- Use the data refresh account configured by the administrator – This is the default option, and it uses the PowerPivot unattended data refresh account. By default, the unattended account is the SharePoint service account that you specify when you run the PowerPivot Configuration Tool. For more information about the unattended account, read the "How to: Configure the PowerPivot Unattended Data Refresh Account" topic in the MSDN Books Online (http://bit.ly/ppunattended).
- Connect using the following Windows user credentials – Specify the credentials (user name and password) of a domain account that has rights to read from the external data sources.
- Connect using the credentials saved in Secure Stored Service (SSS) – Specify the identifier of a Secure Store Service application that you've previously set up. For more information about how to do this, read the "Configure the Secure Store Service" topic (http://bit.ly/configuresss).

As a best practice, I suggest you use either the first or third option, especially if you schedule multiple workbooks for refresh. That way you don't have to update the account in multiple places if it its credentials gets changed.

**NOTE** If you get the error "Logon failure: the user has not been granted the requested logon type at this computer" during the data refresh, the issue could be that the Windows account doesn't have the rights to log on locally to the SharePoint server. You can either add the Windows account to the pre-defined "Server Operators Windows" group or use the "Local Security Policy" applet to grant the account this right.

***Configuring data sources***

Once you decide on which Windows account to use, select the data sources you want to refresh:

1. Scroll down the "Manage Data Refresh" page to the Data Sources section, as shown in **Figure 9.14**. Notice that only connections to external data sources are shown. For example, linked tables and tables that you imported by copy and paste from the Windows Clipboard can't be refreshed.

2. Checking the "All Data Sources" option will schedule all your connections to refresh. In our case, we want to refresh only the data from the Adventure Works data warehouse. Only check the AdventureWorksDW data source.

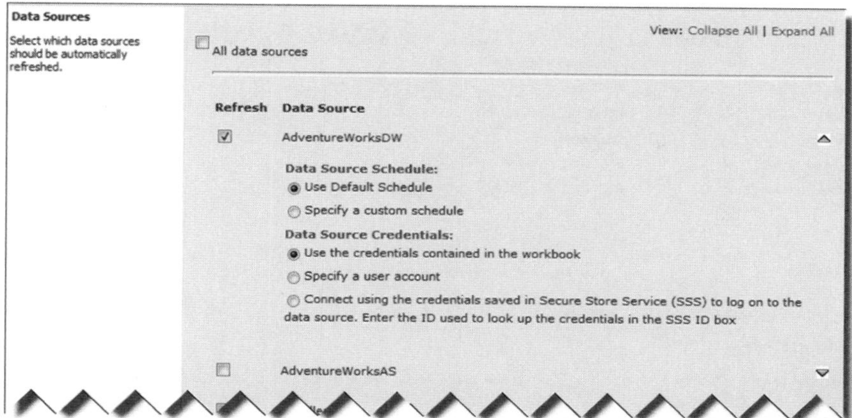


**Figure 9.14** Select which data sources to automatically refresh.

3. Expand the AdventureWorksDW section. Notice that you can specify a data-source-specific schedule and credentials that overwrite the previous settings. For example, you might want to schedule several data sources to refresh daily, except a flat file data source, which you want to refresh monthly. You can use the global schedule for most refresh jobs, and you can configure a data source schedule that executes monthly to refresh the flat file connection.

   By default, the "Data Source Credentials" option is set to "Use the credentials contained in the workbook". This means that SharePoint connects to the data sources using the credentials that you specified for that connection in the PowerPivot "Existing Connections" dialog box. For example, if you've decided to use the standard security, SharePoint will use the specified logon and password to connect to a database server. If Windows security is used, the SharePoint Windows account will be used according to your settings in the Credentials section. You can specify data-source-specific credentials, which could be either a specific Windows account or a Secure Store Service ID.

4. Leave the default settings for the AdventureWorksDW data source, and then click OK.

***Monitoring the data refresh***

Besides receiving e-mail notifications in case of a data refresh failure, you can proactively monitor the data refresh status, as follows:

1. In the PowerPivot Gallery library, click the "Manage Data Refresh" button again next to the Adventure Works workbook. PowerPivot detects that you've already configured a data refresh for this workbook. Instead of opening the "Manage Data Refresh" page, PowerPivot navigates you to the "Data Refresh History" page, as shown in **Figure 9.15**.

   The header section shows statistics about the data refresh operations, such as the date and time when the data refresh task was last executed and when the next refresh will occur. Below the Schedule Information section, it shows a detailed history record of all the refresh tasks, including their status and error messages, in the cases where failures occur. You can click the Configure Schedule link if you want to change the data refresh settings.

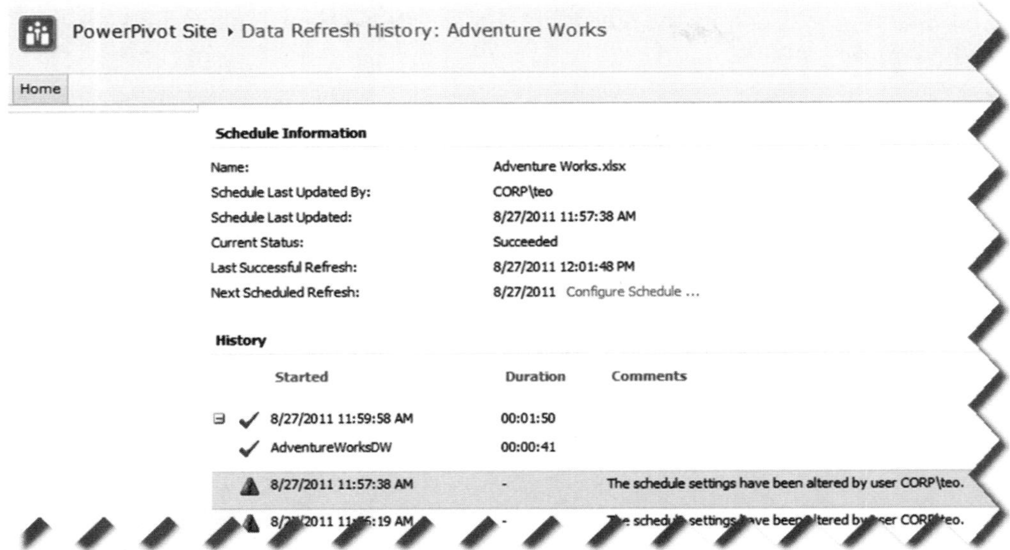


**Figure 9.15** Use the "Data Refresh History" page to see data refresh tasks and their execution status.

## 9.3 Monitoring Server Utilization

Team (business intelligence) BI shouldn't lead to chaos and "spreadmarts". A better BI is a managed BI, where the administrator understands how business users are utilizing PowerPivot for SharePoint to answer questions, such as whether the server can handle the report payload, which workbooks are the most utilized, which refresh operations fail, and so on. This is where the PowerPivot Management Dashboard can help.

### 9.3.1 Understanding PowerPivot Management Dashboard

PowerPivot for SharePoint periodically gathers statistics about the server utilization and then exposes the collected data in the PowerPivot Management Dashboard for reporting purposes. As an administrator, you can control what's collected and how often the usage statistics are updated.

***Understanding usage collection***

The following steps describe how the usage collection processes work at the high-level activity:

1. PowerPivot for SharePoint components occasionally call SharePoint APIs to log events, such as query usage, load, unload, and connection events. The event details are saved as usage files with the extension *.usage in the SharePoint log directory (\Program Files\Common Files\Microsoft Shared\Web Server Extensions\14\LOGS).
2. Two SharePoint timer jobs move usage data from usage files to the PowerPivot database. You can see these jobs and manually run them in SharePoint Central Administration (Monitoring ⇨ Review Job Definitions ⇨ Expand the View drop-down list, and then click All). These two jobs are:
   - Microsoft SharePoint Foundation Usage Data Import -- This job imports the usage files from the log directory to the SharePoint logging database, and it runs every 30 minutes.

- Microsoft SharePoint Foundation Usage Processing -- This timer job extracts usage data from the SharePoint logging database and then loads it into the PowerPivot database. It runs once every day, between 1 AM and 3 AM. The PowerPivot database is hosted in the database server that you specified when you ran the PowerPivot Configuration Tool. The name of the database is DefaultPowerPivotServiceApplicationDB-<guid>.

3. Another timer job, PowerPivot Management Dashboard Processing Timer Job, runs daily, between 3 AM and 5 AM, to update each Excel workbook that's used by the reports in the PowerPivot Management Dashboard. To view this job in SharePoint Central Administration, go to PowerPivot Management Dashboard ⇨ Review Timer Job Definitions.

To learn more about the inner workings and about troubleshooting the PowerPivot Management Dashboard, review the document, "Diagnostic Guide for Usage and the PowerPivot Management Dashboard" by Ankur Goyal, Microsoft Tester, at http://bit.ly/ppdashboardfix.

***Understanding dashboard web parts***

Open the PowerPivot Management Dashboard as follows:

1. Open SharePoint 2010 Central Administration.
2. Click the PowerPivot Management Dashboard, which is found under the "General Application Settings" section. This displays the dashboard page, as shown in **Figure 9.16**.

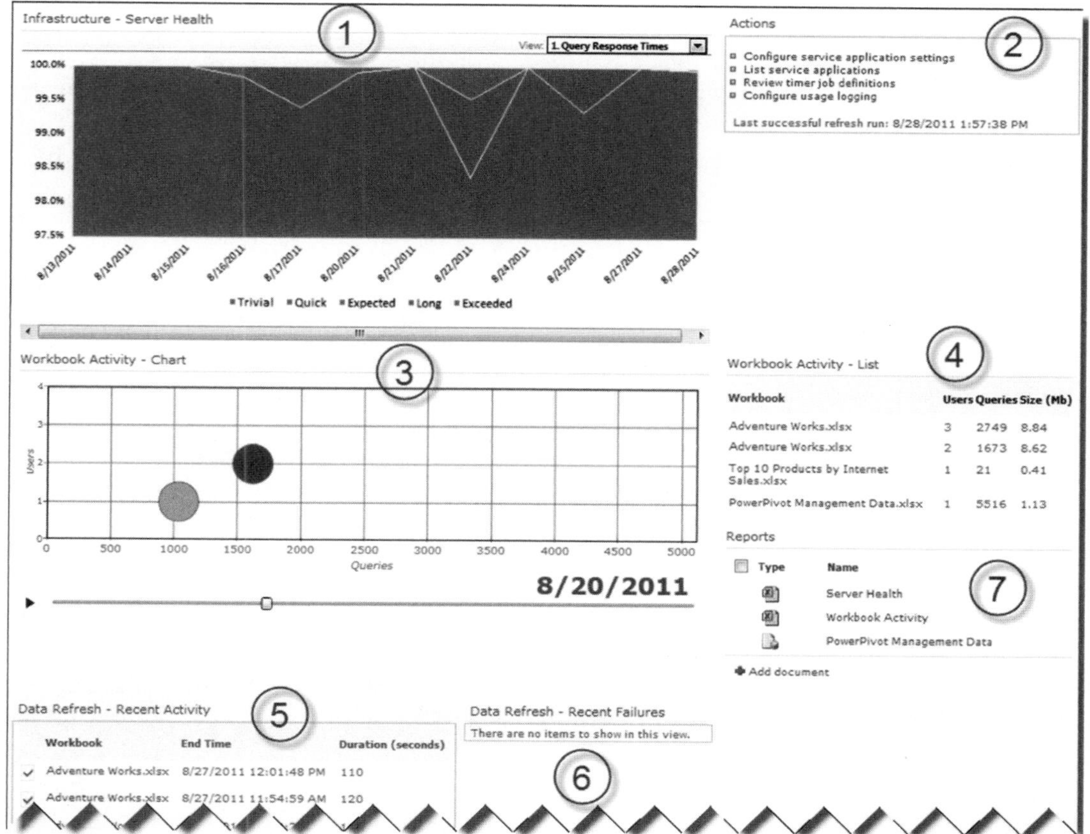


**Figure 9.16** Use the PowerPivot Management Dashboard to understand server utilization and activity.

The PowerPivot Management Dashboard is implemented as a SharePoint web page consisting of the following web parts (the numbers next to the web part name correspond to the numbers in the diagram):

- Infrastructure – Server Health (1) – Provides several reports that show the server utilization, such as CPU, memory usage, and query times.
- Actions (2) – Gives you the ability to configure the dashboard configuration settings.
- Workbook Activity – Chart (3) – Shows the PowerPivot workbook activity as an animated chart with number of queries on the X-axis and number of users on the Y-axis.
- Workbook Activity – List (4) – Shows the PowerPivot workbook as a list that displays the number of users who have used the workbook, the number of queries sent to the PowerPivot model, and the size of the workbook file.
- Data Refresh – Recent Activity (5) – Displays the data refresh history including failures. Each row shows the status of a data refresh job, the workbook that's refreshed, the end time of the operation, and the duration.
- Data Refresh – Recent Failures (6) – Lists the workbooks whose data refresh jobs failed.
- Reports (7) – Includes links to other supporting reports.

***Understanding dashboard settings***

Next, let's spend some time getting familiar with the dashboard settings.

1. In the Actions web part, click the "Configure Service Application Settings" link. Scroll down to the Data Refresh section. Notice that the default business hours are 4 AM – 8 PM. As a result, when you schedule a data refresh to run after business hours, PowerPivot for SharePoint will run the job after this time range. You can adjust the business hours as needed.
2. Scroll further down to the Usage Data Collection section, as shown in **Figure 9.17**. Examine the following settings:
   - Query Reporting Interval – By default, the dashboard data is refreshed every 300 seconds.
   - Usage Data History – By default, usage data is retained for 365 days.
   - Query Upper Limits – These last four settings define the thresholds for the trivial, quick response, expected response, and long response metrics for the Query Response Times chart in the Server Health section. For example, by default the chart considers query times up to 500 milliseconds as trivial.
3. Click Cancel to return to the dashboard. Click the "Review timer job definitions" link in the Actions web part (again see **Figure 9.16**). Notice that "PowerPivot Management Dashboard Processing Timer Job" is one of the timer jobs listed.
4. Back in the dashboard, click the "Configure usage logging" link (also in the Actions web part). Notice that by default, PowerPivot logs connections, loads and unloads, and query usage events.

**TIP** You can customize to some extent the PowerPivot Management Dashboard, such as to add your own management reports. If this sounds interesting, read the "Customizing the PowerPivot Management Dashboard" whitepaper by Ankur Goyal, Software Development Engineer, at http://bit.ly/ppdashboardcustomize.

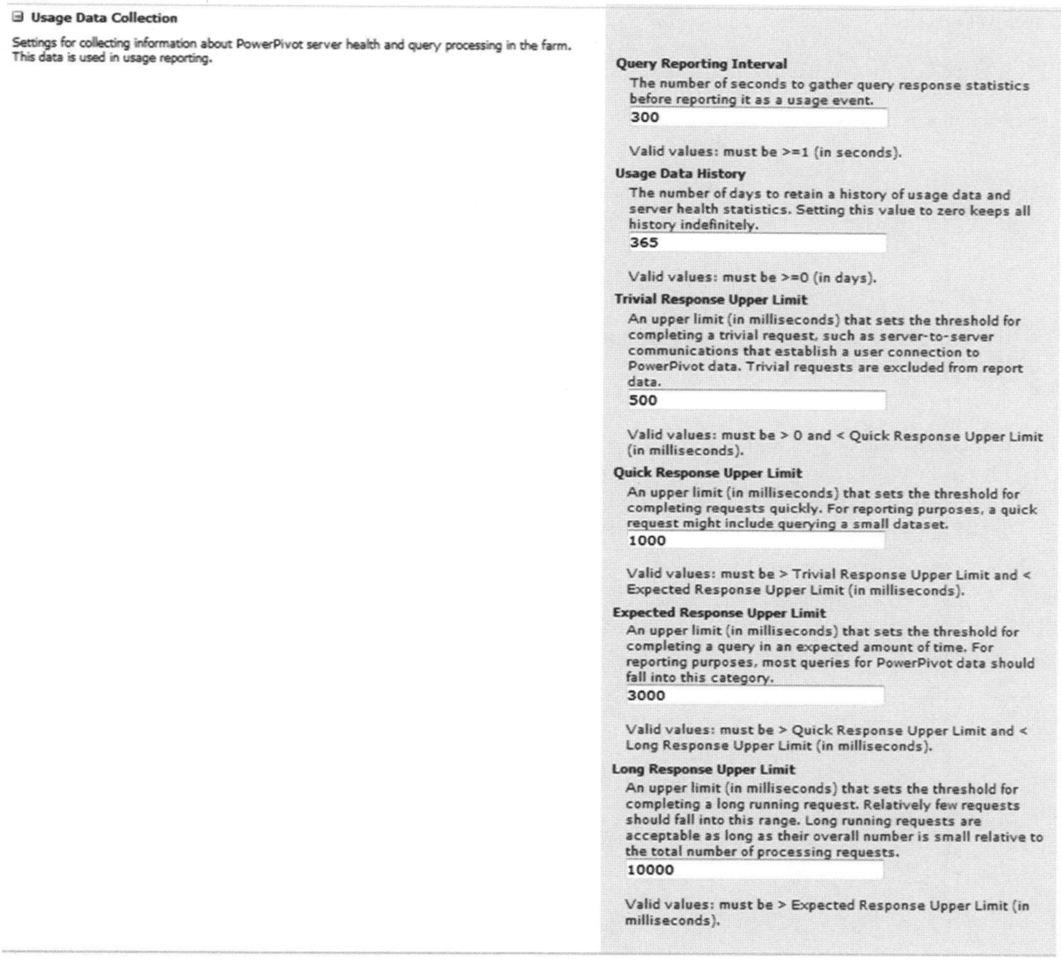

**Usage Data Collection**

Settings for collecting information about PowerPivot server health and query processing in the farm. This data is used in usage reporting.

**Query Reporting Interval**

The number of seconds to gather query response statistics before reporting it as a usage event.

300

Valid values: must be >=1 (in seconds).

**Usage Data History**

The number of days to retain a history of usage data and server health statistics. Setting this value to zero keeps all history indefinitely.

365

Valid values: must be >=0 (in days).

**Trivial Response Upper Limit**

An upper limit (in milliseconds) that sets the threshold for completing a trivial request, such as server-to-server communications that establish a user connection to PowerPivot data. Trivial requests are excluded from report data.

500

Valid values: must be > 0 and < Quick Response Upper Limit (in milliseconds).

**Quick Response Upper Limit**

An upper limit (in milliseconds) that sets the threshold for completing requests quickly. For reporting purposes, a quick request might include querying a small dataset.

1000

Valid values: must be > Trivial Response Upper Limit and < Expected Response Upper Limit (in milliseconds).

**Expected Response Upper Limit**

An upper limit (in milliseconds) that sets the threshold for completing a query in an expected amount of time. For reporting purposes, most queries for PowerPivot data should fall into this category.

3000

Valid values: must be > Quick Response Upper Limit and < Long Response Upper Limit (in milliseconds).

**Long Response Upper Limit**

An upper limit (in milliseconds) that sets the threshold for completing a long running request. Relatively few requests should fall into this range. Long running requests are acceptable as long as their overall number is small relative to the total number of processing requests.

10000

Valid values: must be > Expected Response Upper Limit (in milliseconds).

**Figure 9.17** Use the "Configure Service Application Settings" page to change the usage collection settings.

## 9.3.2 Analyzing Utilization and Activity

Now that you're familiar with the dashboard, let's see how you can use it to analyze the server utilization and activity. Naturally, your results will be different than mine and they will match your PowerPivot for SharePoint setup and activity.

***Analyzing server health***

The administrator can use the Server Health section to track the server utilization over time. The default view shows the query response times. Glancing back at **Figure 9.16**, you can see that most of the queries fall in the trivial category (blue area), which means that they were very fast, and few queries were categorized as quick (red) and expected (green). Again, you can use the "Configure Service Application Settings" page to customize the query thresholds if needed.

1. Expand the drop-down list in the "Infrastructure – Server Health" web part, and then select "Average Instance CPU". You'll see a line chart, as shown in **Figure 9.18**.

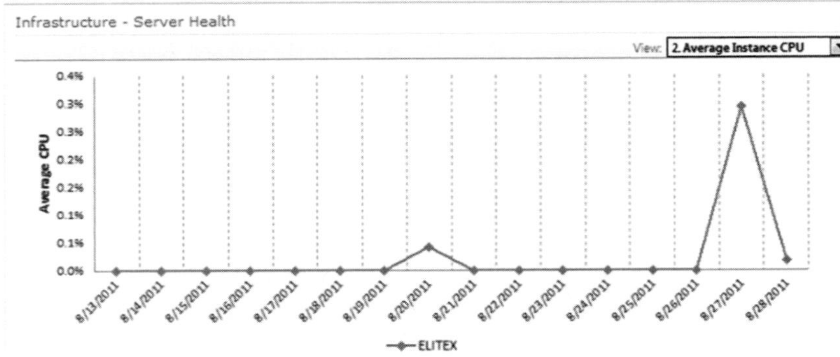


**Figure 9.18** This chart shows the average CPU utilization over time.

The line chart shows the average CPU utilization across the SharePoint application servers in the farm that have PowerPivot for SharePoint installed (there's only one in **Figure 9.18**). In this case, CPU utilization isn't a concern because PowerPivot for SharePoint has utilized less than one percent on average the CPU resources of the server.

2. Expand the drop-down list, and then select "Average Instance Memory" to see the line chart shown in **Figure 9.19**. Memory utilization can be an issue with many published workbooks and large PowerPivot models because of the in-memory VertiPaq storage. In this case, the highest memory utilization (of 300 MB) was recorded on the last date.

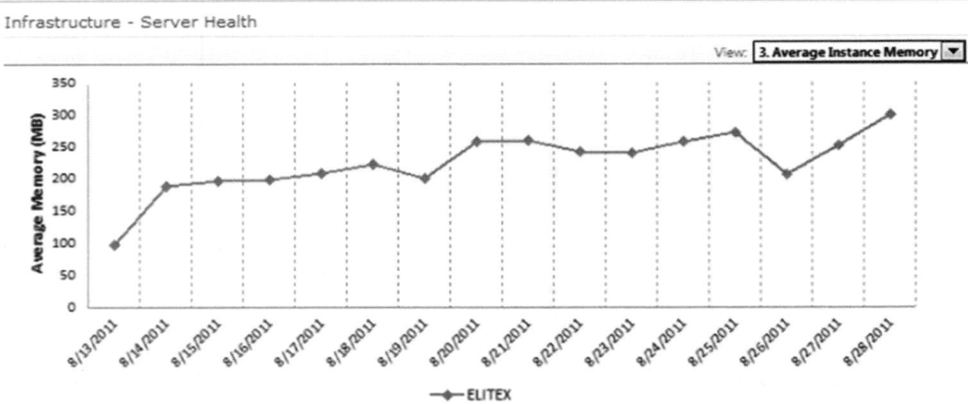


**Figure 9.19** This chart shows the average memory utilization for each application server.

3. You can see the server activity and performance in the Infrastructure section by changing the drop-down list, but you'll get a better view by opening the supporting Excel workbook directly. In the Reports web part, click the Server Health workbook. Once the workbook is shown, expand View drop-down list in the top-right corner, and then select Activity. The Activity report provides detailed information about how many connections, queries, application loads, unloads, and users occurred per day, together with line charts to help you analyze this information visually (see **Figure 9.20**).

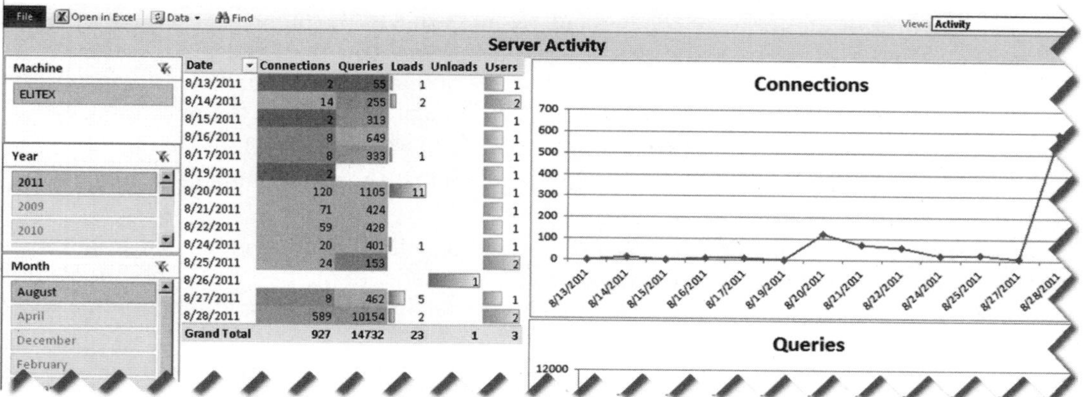

**Figure 9.20** Use the Server Health workbook to see summarized views of the PowerPivot model activity.

4. Another useful report is Workbook Activity. Back in the dashboard, click the Workbook Activity link in the Reports section to open the "Workbook Activity by Document" report, as shown in **Figure 9.21**. This report displays the number of users, queries, and load sizes for each PowerPivot model that's queried on the server.

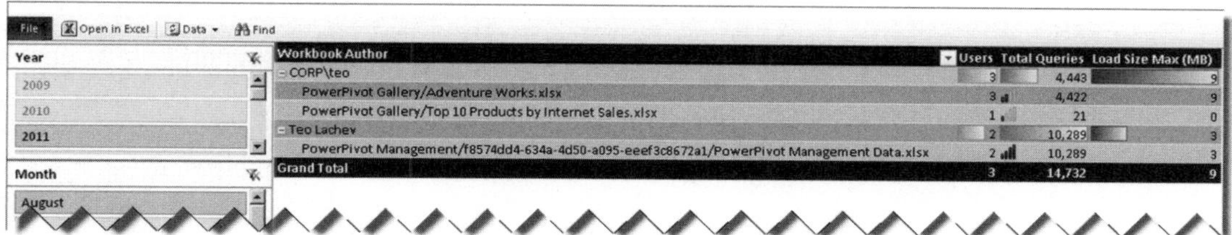

**Figure 9.21** The Workbook Activity report shows utilization for each PowerPivot model.

***Analyzing workbook activity***

Another way to analyze the PowerPivot model utilization is to examine the Workbook Activity web parts, which are labeled with numbers 3 and 4 back in **Figure 9.16**. The "Workbook Activity – Chart" web part (see **Figure 9.22**) is implemented as a Silverlight control that allows you to analyze the utilization over time expressed as the number of queries plotted on the x-axis and the number of users plotted on the y-axis. Each bubble represents a published workbook. The size of the bubble is proportional to the data size of the workbook.

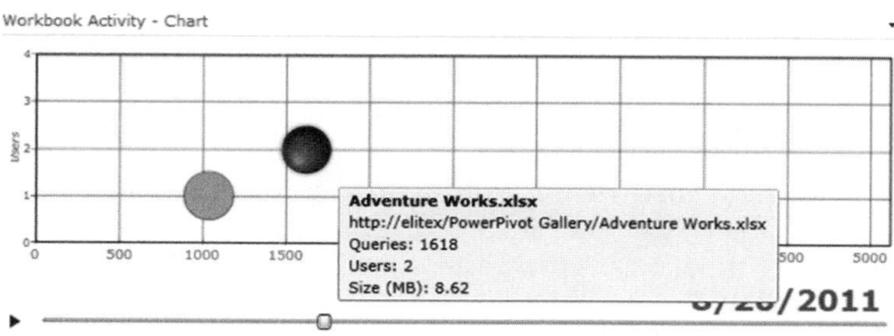


**Figure 9.22** This chart provides an animated view that shows the workbook utilization over time.

1. Click the play button to activate the chart animation. The bubbles will move as the time slicer progresses. As an administrator, you'll be particularly interested in the highly-utilized PowerPivot models that are used by most users and handle the most queries (the ones that move to the top-right corner) over time. These models are probably good candidates to be converted to organizational models that run on a dedicated Analysis Services Tabular instance. At the same time, you should review and delete models that are not utilized and consider removing them.
2. Hover your mouse cursor over a bubble. A tooltip pops up that shows the number of queries, the number of users, and the workbook size.
3. The Workbook Activity – A list web part that shows the same information in text format, but it also enables you to sort the data by the number of users, number of queries, and application size. For example, click the Queries column header to sort the applications by the number of queries so you can see which models are queried the most.

## 9.4 Managing Security

One important task that every administrator needs to master is managing security. You won't get very far with a SharePoint deployment if you don't have a good grasp of its security model. Out of the box, only SharePoint administrators have access to PowerPivot for SharePoint. You're responsible for defining security policies that grant end users selective rights to view or edit PowerPivot models.

Because the SharePoint security model is layered on top of Windows, understanding security isn't easy, and explaining this topic in detail is beyond the scope of this book. Therefore, I'll assume that you have a basic knowledge of how Windows authentication and authorization work. The Microsoft MSDN Security Center (http://msdn.microsoft.com/security) is a great place to start if you want to get up to speed with Windows security.

### 9.4.1 Understanding SharePoint Security

To understand PowerPivot for SharePoint security, you need to understand the SharePoint security framework. You can use SharePoint security to provide restrictive access to the entire workbook. PowerPivot for SharePoint doesn't allow you to secure data in the model (row-level security), such as for managers to see their own data but not the data for other managers. If row-level security is a requirement, you must upgrade your PowerPivot models to organizational models, and then use SQL Server Data Tools (SSDS) to implement row filters.

***Understanding security terminology***

You'll probably find the SharePoint security model similar to other Microsoft or home-grown security frameworks that you've come across. In a nutshell, the user is authenticated based on the user's Windows identity (assuming SharePoint is configured for Windows authentication), and the user is authorized according to the security policies that the administrator has set up. A security policy applies permissions to a SharePoint securable object for specific users and groups, as shown in **Figure 9.23**. Let's explain these terms in more details.

- Permission – Permissions are the most granular security rights. They represent specific tasks that can be authorized, such as View Items or Delete Items. SharePoint has a fixed list of permissions that you can't change. To see the standard permissions, in SharePoint Central Administration, click Manage Web Applications, then select an application, such as "SharePoint – 80", and then click the User Permissions button in the ribbon.

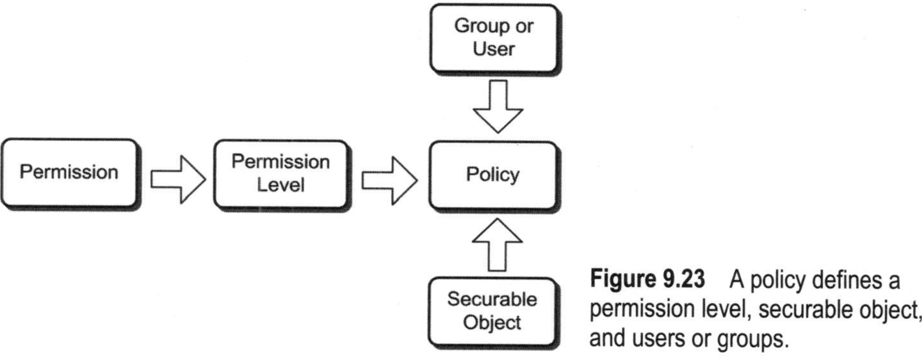


**Figure 9.23** A policy defines a permission level, securable object, and users or groups.

- Permission level – A permission level is a predefined set of permissions that the administrator can grant users to access content. The default permission levels vary depending on the site template. **Figure 9.24** shows the six permission levels for a site that's based on the Team Site template. When the predefined permission levels are not enough, you can create your own.

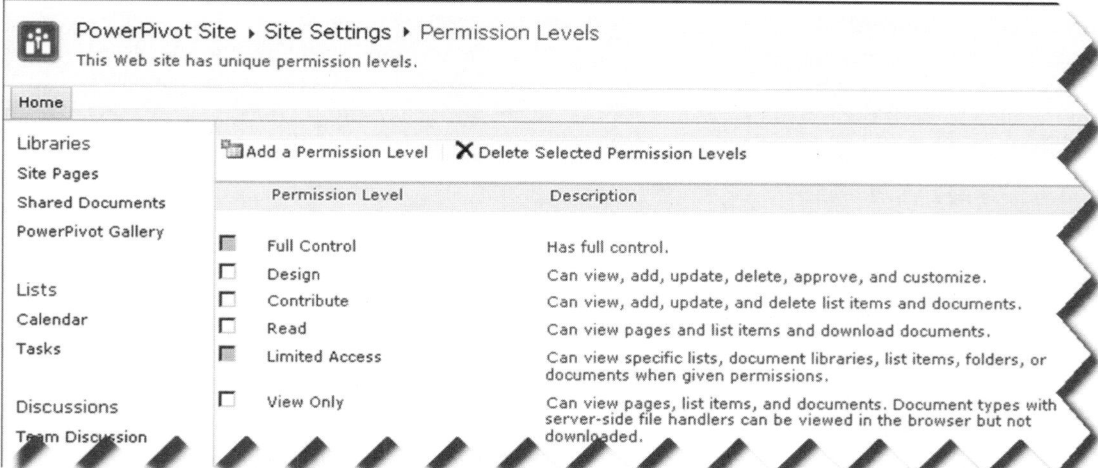


**Figure 9.24** The Team Site template defines six permission levels.

- User – Represents the end user or group that you want to authorize. To simplify security maintenance, consider grouping users into Active Directory groups, such as an ACCOUNTING group whose members are users from the Accounting department. Active Directory groups can be nested. For example, the ACCOUNTING group can nest ACCOUNTING_RECEIVABLES and ACCOUNTING_PAYABLE Active Directory groups.
- Securable object – A securable object is a SharePoint item that can be secured, such as a library, a folder, or an Excel workbook.
- Security group – A SharePoint group includes users who have identical rights. SharePoint creates security groups according to the site template chosen when the site is created. **Table 9.2** lists the SharePoint standard groups.

Table 9.2 **SharePoint includes pre-defined security groups.**

| Security Group | Template | Purpose |
|---|---|---|
| Site Collection Administrators | All templates | Full rights to all sites within a SharePoint site collection |
| <Site Collection Name> Owners | All templates | Full Control permission level |
| <Site Collection Name> Members | All templates | Contribute permission level |
| <Site Collection Name> Visitors | All templates | Read permission level |
| Viewers | Collaboration and Meeting | View Only permission level |
| Approvers | Enterprise and Publishing | Approval permission level |
| Designers | Enterprise and Publishing | Design permission level |
| Hierarchy managers | Enterprise and Publishing | Manage Hierarchy permission level |
| Restricted readers | Enterprise and Publishing | Restricted Read permission level |

The administrator controls access to content by defining security policies. A security policy is a combination of a securable item, user (or group), and one or more permission levels. Security policies are additive, meaning that if a user is granted multiple permission levels, such as by adding the user to both the Owners and Members security groups, the user will get the union of all permissions.

***Understanding security inheritance***

Similar to Windows ACL permissions, permissions are inherited by default from the parent folder. In the example shown in **Figure 9.25**, the user is given the View Only permission level to a SharePoint site. Thanks to security inheritance, you don't need to define explicit policies for the PowerPivot Gallery and Shared Documents libraries and their content. That's because SharePoint automatically propagates the View Only permission level down the hierarchy. However, you can break the security inheritance at any level or a securable item. Suppose that the same user needs Contributor rights for PowerPivot Gallery so that he can upload PowerPivot models and create reports. You can break the security inheritance at that library and then define a policy that grants the user the Contributor permission level. The Contributor permissions will flow down to the descendants until the inheritance chain is severed again. The administrator can always restore security inheritance at any level to inherit from its parent.

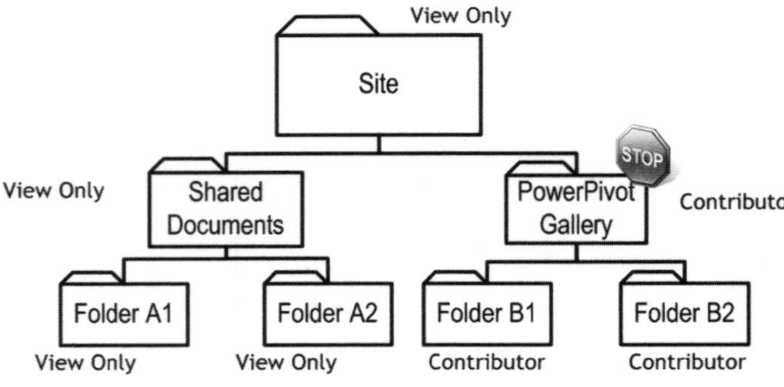


**Figure 9.25** Permissions are inherited from a parent, but permission inheritance can be broken.

To simplify security management, I suggest you stick with security inheritance as much as possible. I recommend enforcing the minimum set of permissions at the site level, such as granting users View Only rights. Then, expand the user rights down the content on an as-needed basis. It's important to understand that if the user doesn't have rights to view a given securable item, the user won't be able to see that item. Therefore, make sure you grant the user at least the View Only permission level to content hierarchy above the user's working folder so the user can navigate the folder hierarchy and get to the folder.

**TIP** As a best practice, keep the folder hierarchy flat as much as possible, such as not to exceed two or three levels deep. Add users to Active Directory groups, and then assign these groups to SharePoint security groups. Use security inheritance to inherit permissions from parent items, and only break the security inheritance when needed.

***Understanding PowerPivot for SharePoint security***

Now that you're familiar with SharePoint security, you need to know how it applies to PowerPivot for SharePoint. **Table 9.3** shows the allowed tasks for different permission levels. I limit the permission levels to Full Control, Contribute, Read, and View Only.

**Table 9.3 How SharePoint security applies to PowerPivot models and reports.**

| Permission Level | PowerPivot Model and Excel Reports | Operational and Power View Reports |
|---|---|---|
| Full Control | Includes Contribute permission level rights. Activate PowerPivot feature integration at the site collection level. Activate online help. Create a PowerPivot Gallery library. | Includes Contribute permission level rights. Create, manage, and secure report server items and operations. |
| Contribute | Includes Read permission level rights. Add, edit, delete, and download PowerPivot workbooks. Configure data refresh. Create new workbooks and Excel web reports that are based on PowerPivot workbooks on a SharePoint site. | Includes Read permission level rights. Create and publish reports and models from design tools to a SharePoint library. Save Power View reports. |
| Read | Includes View Only permission level rights. Allow external clients to connect to deployed models. | Includes View Only permission level rights. Download the source file for a report definition or a report model. View and edit Power View reports. |
| View Only | View PowerPivot workbooks. View data refresh history. | View operational and interactive reports. Create, change, and delete subscriptions that are owned by the user. |

## 9.4.2 Securing PowerPivot Models and Reports

By default, end users don't have access to SharePoint so they won't be able to browse SharePoint content, upload PowerPivot models, or create reports. As an administrator, you need to set up security policies that grant the users the minimum permissions required without compromising security.

In this practice, you'll implement partially the security scenario shown in **Figure 9.25**. Specifically, you'll grant a user View Only rights to the top-level site so that the user can browse the site content. Then, you'll break the security inheritance for the PowerPivot Gallery library by granting the user Contribute rights so that the user can upload PowerPivot models and create reports.

***Setting up users and verifying access***

If you don't have a test Windows user account, start by creating a new account. The following steps assume that you've installed SharePoint on a standalone domain controller and that you have administrator rights to Windows and SharePoint:

1. On the SharePoint server, open the "Active Directory Users and Computers" applet from the Administrative Tools program group. If SharePoint is installed on a machine that's already added to an Active Directory domain, then you can use the Computer Management applet in the Administrative Tools program group to create a local user.
2. In the "Active Directory Users and Computers" applet, right-click the Users folder, and then click New ⇨ User.
3. In the "New Object – User" dialog box, enter *Bob* in the First Name field and *Bob* in the "User Logon Name" field. Click Next.
4. In the second step, enter and confirm a password. Uncheck the "User Must Change Password at Next Login" checkbox. Check the "Password Never Expires" checkbox. Click Next.
5. In the confirmation step, click Finish to create the account.
6. (Optional) Assign the user to an Active Directory group if you want to grant permissions to the group and not the user.
7. In the web browser, navigate to the SharePoint top-level site, such as http://<site>.
8. You should be able to browse the site home page successfully since you have SharePoint administrator rights.
9. SharePoint makes it easy to impersonate another Windows user if you know the user's password. Expand the drop-down list in the top-right corner of the home page (see **Figure 9.26**), and then click Sign in as Different User. In the security dialog box that follows, select the "Use Another Account" option, and then enter Bob's credentials. Click OK.

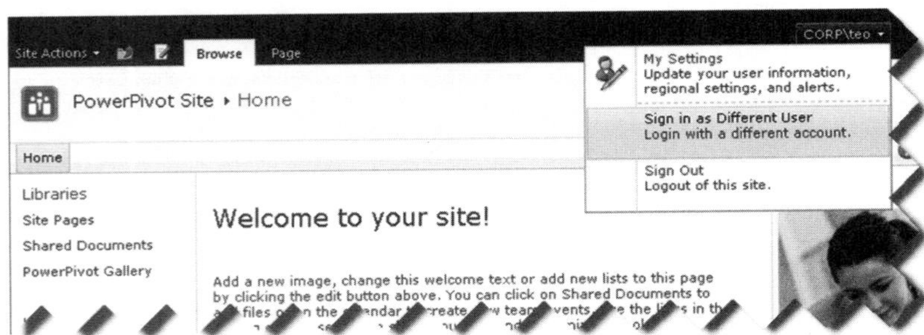


**Figure 9.26** Impersonate another user by clicking the "Sign in as Different User" option.

10. Notice that SharePoint displays an Access Denied error message, as shown in **Figure 9.27**. As I mentioned, by default, users don't have rights to SharePoint.

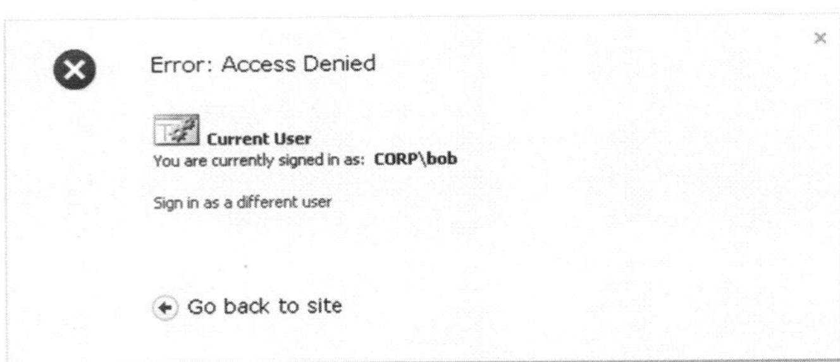


**Figure 9.27** Users don't have access to SharePoint unless they're given explicit rights.

11. Click the "Sign in as a Different User" link, and then sign in with your credentials.

***Setting up security policies***
Next, you'll grant View Only permissions to the top-level SharePoint site by adding the user to the Viewers security group.

1. In the browser, navigate to the SharePoint top-level site.
2. Expand the Site Actions drop-down menu, and then click Site Permissions.
3. In the Permissions page, click the Viewers group.
4. In the "Peoples and Groups" page, expand the New drop-down menu, and then click Add Users, as shown in **Figure 9.28**.

**Figure 9.28** Add a user to the Viewers security group so that the user can browse SharePoint content.

5. In the Grant Permissions dialog box, enter *Bob,* and then click OK to add Bob to the Viewers group.
6. Impersonate Bob again. Notice that now he can browse the site content, including the Shared Documents and PowerPivot Gallery libraries.
7. Navigate to the PowerPivot Gallery library, and then click the Adventure Works model. Notice that Bob can view the reports in the workbook. However, Bob can't download the workbook either by using the SharePoint document management features, or by using the Excel web report (the "Open in Excel" button is missing). Bob can run operational reports, but he can't view Power View reports. Bob also can't upload workbooks to SharePoint.

***Breaking security inheritance***
Suppose that you want to grant Bob rights to upload workbooks to the PowerPivot Gallery library, but you also want to restrict him to View Only permissions elsewhere on the site. You can achieve this by breaking the security inheritance at the PowerPivot Gallery library, and then grant Bob a Contributor permission level.

1. While browsing the SharePoint site under your identity, navigate to PowerPivot Gallery.
2. Click the Library tab in the ribbon and then click the Library Permissions button.
3. The Permissions Tools page (see **Figure 9.29**), allows you to carry several security-related tasks. You can click the Manage Parent button to view or change the security settings of the parent object. The Stop Inheriting Permissions button breaks the security inheritance chain. Use the Check Permissions button to see what permissions are granted to a given user. Click the Stop Inheriting Permissions button to break the security inheritance.

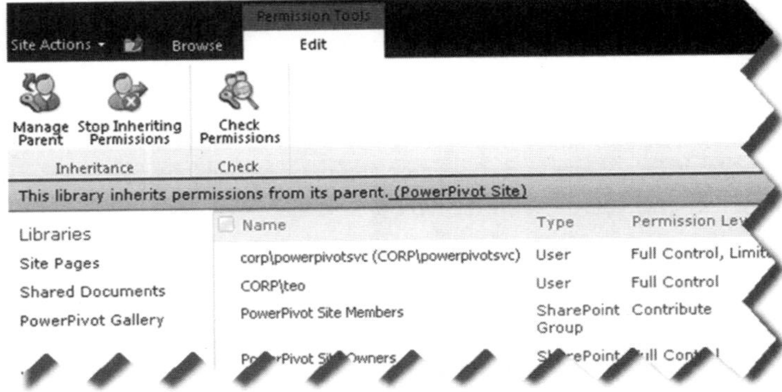


**Figure 9.29** Click the Stop Inheriting Permissions button to break the security inheritance.

4. Accept the following prompt that warns you about the effects of breaking security inheritance:

You are about to create unique permissions for this document library. Changes made to the parent site permissions will no longer affect this document library.

**NOTE** Once you accept the prompt, the Permissions Tools page removes the Manage Parent button and the Stop Inheriting Permissions button and it adds an Inherit Permissions button. Clicking the Inherit Permissions button restores security inheritance and remove all custom permissions.

5. Click the Grant Permissions button.
6. In the Grant Permissions page (see **Figure 9.30**), you can grant Bob rights by assigning him to SharePoint security groups (recommended) or by giving him direct permissions.

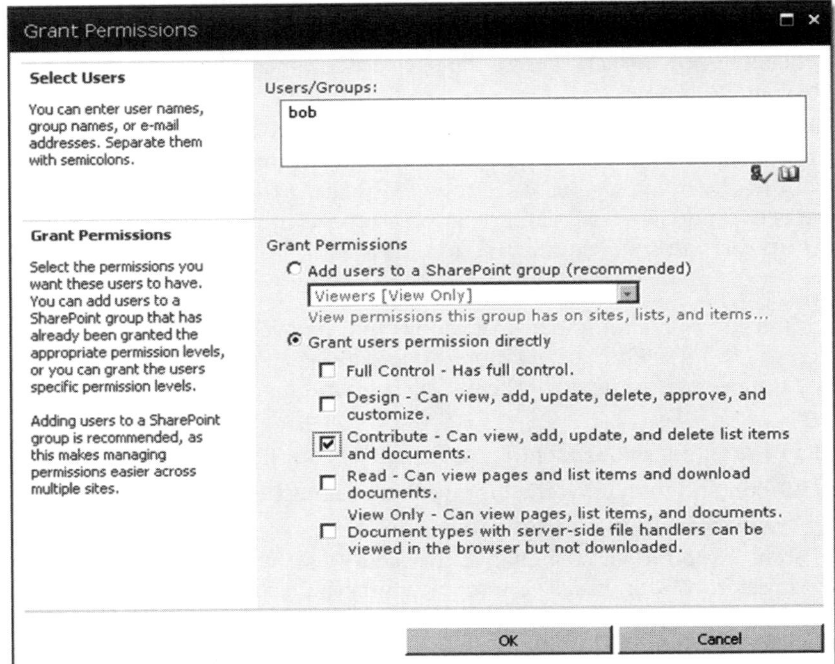


**Figure 9.30** Once you stop security inheritance, you can grant the user direct permissions to the securable object.

After a first look, you might decide to add Bob to the Members group, which has Contribute rights. However, because this group has rights to the top site as well, Bob will gain Contributor rights to the entire site. This contradicts our objective to restrict the Contributor rights to the PowerPivot Gallery library only. One option to achieve this is to create a new custom security group, such as PowerPivot Gallery Contributors, to grant this group Contributor rights to PowerPivot Gallery, and then assign Bob to this group. Another option is to grant Bob (or an Active Directory group he belongs to) direct permissions to the library, which is the approach we will take.

7. Select the "Grant users permissions directly" option, and then check the Contribute checkbox. Click OK.
8. Back in SharePoint, impersonate Bob again.
9. Navigate to PowerPivot Gallery, and then click the Documents tab in the SharePoint ribbon. Observe that the Upload Document button is now enabled, which means that Bob can upload workbooks.
10. Click the Shared Documents library link in the SharePoint navigation menu on the left, and then click the Documents tab. Notice that the Upload Document button is disabled, meaning that Bob doesn't have Contributor rights.

## 9.5 Summary

In this chapter, you've learned how to manage PowerPivot for SharePoint. You can use the SharePoint document management features to perform routine content management tasks, including uploading, deleting, renaming, and moving workbooks. You can benefit from other useful features to address a variety of more advanced needs that would otherwise require custom code, such as versioning and document approval.

PowerPivot for SharePoint supports a scheduled data refresh to periodically synchronize PowerPivot models with changes in the data sources. The PowerPivot Management Dashboard is your first stop to track the server utilization and to troubleshoot data refresh failures.

Out of the box, SharePoint is configured for Windows security, and end users are not authorized to access PowerPivot models and reports. As an administrator, you can set up security policies to grant users selective rights to perform the required tasks. Simplify security management by adding users to groups and by configuring SharePoint items to inherit security polices from the parent level.

The next chapter continues the personal-team-organizational continuum and introduces you to organizational BI powered by Analysis Services in Tabular mode.

PART 

# Organizational Business Intelligence

Organizational BI with Tabular is as the last stop of the personal-team-organizational continuum. It lets you travel the last mile of BI journey to extend the reach of your tabular models and BI across the enterprise. While personal and team business intelligence with PowerPivot have been possible since its first release in May 2010, using the VertiPaq technology to implement corporate analytical models is new with SQL Server 2012. Organizational BI is powered by Analysis Services configured in a Tabular mode (new in SQL Server 2012) that's capable of hosting scalable and secure tabular models.

This part of the book is for BI pros. Because personal and organizational models share the same modeling framework and features, this part of the book doesn't cover modeling concepts. If you're new to Tabular and wonder how we got here, go back and read the first part of the book about personal BI with PowerPivot for Excel. Once you know PowerPivot, you'll find that for the most part, the only difference from a modeling standpoint is the hosting environment. Unlike the Excel-centric environment for implementing personal PowerPivot models, organizational BI projects are designed using a professional toolset that's included in the SQL Server Data Tools.

Analysis Services Tabular adds new features for organizational use which don't exist in PowerPivot, including options for configuring security and data management. Increased data volumes demand more flexible storage options. You will learn how to partition large tables to refresh and manage data selectively. When real-time data access is needed, you can configure the model in a special pass-through mode to query directly SQL Server databases. And, you can apply data security to restrict end users to a subset of data they're authorized to view.

As with any other software development lifecycle, it's unlikely that your Tabular journey will end when the model design is complete. You must know how to manage organizational models to ensure they're operational and perform as expected. The good news is that if you have ever managed multidimensional cubes, you can seamlessly transfer your knowledge to managing Tabular models.

Chapter 10

# Organizational BI Basics



So far, the focus of this book has been the PowerPivot technology that empowers business users to create solutions for personal business intelligence (BI) and for team BI. Back in Chapter 1, I mentioned that the second flavor of Tabular is Analysis Services running in a Tabular mode. Analysis Services Tabular allows BI professionals to implement organizational BI models when scalability and security requirements outgrow the PowerPivot capabilities.

This chapter introduces you to organizational BI. You'll learn about its building blocks and how it compares with personal BI. Next, the chapter walks you through the process of installing the required components. You'll learn different options to implement tabular models for organizational use, including how to import from PowerPivot and how to use SQL Server Data Tools. Finally, you'll create a Power View dashboard report that's powered by a tabular model, and you'll understand how Power View queries the model. The code samples for the practices in this chapter are located in the \Source\Ch10 folder.

## 10.1 Understanding Organizational Tabular Models

Organizational BI is a set of technologies and processes for implementing an end-to-end BI solution. Unlike personal and team BI applications, which are typically developed by business users, organizational BI solutions are provisioned and sanctioned by IT pros. Business Intelligence Semantic Model (BISM) in SQL Server 2012 allows BI pros to build scalable and secure tabular models.

Chapter 1 explained that BISM provides two paths for building organizational BI solutions: Multidimensional and Tabular. Tabular is the natural choice for transitioning personal and team BI models to organizational models on a single platform (when you've outgrown the PowerPivot capabilities). BI pros starting new projects might find Tabular appealing because of its low learning curve for the rapid implementation of simple analytical models.

### 10.1.1 Understanding Professional Features

If you know PowerPivot, you'll discover that you can seamlessly transition your knowledge to organizational projects. Indeed, an organizational tabular model is a superset of all the features in PowerPivot, plus some optional enterprise-oriented and advanced features, such as options for configuring security, scalability, and low latency.

***Introducing professional features***
Organizational Tabular adds the following features not found in PowerPivot:

- Data security – Unlike PowerPivot models, where security is an all-or-nothing proposition, organizational BI models can have row-level data security, such as to allow a sales representative to see only the data for resellers that he's responsible for.
- Enterprise scalability – You might remember that PowerPivot workbooks are confined within the 2GB maximum file size. This limits the imported data to a few million rows. However, organizations models must be capable of handling larger data volumes. Just by deploying the model to an Analysis Services instance, you gain better scalability that's boosted by the hardware resources of a dedicated server. Also, to reduce the data load window and to process data incrementally, you can divide large tables in partitions. Unlike PowerPivot data refresh, organizational models support processing tables in parallel, in order to better utilize the resources of a dedicated server.
- Low latency – Similar to PowerPivot, organizational BI models cache data by default to give you the best performance for aggregating large data volumes. However, some scenarios require real-time data access to see data changes immediately in reports. You can implement a low latency solution by configuring your tabular model in a special pass-through mode (called DirectQuery) where the server directly queries a SQL Server database.

***Comparing personal and organizational features***
**Table 10.1** provides a side-by-side comparison between personal and organizational features.

**Table 10.1 This table compares Tabular's personal BI and organizational BI characteristics.**

| Feature | Personal BI | Organizational BI |
|---|---|---|
| Target users | Business users | Professionals |
| Environment | Excel and PowerPivot | Visual Studio (SSDT) |
| VertiPaq Engine | In-process | Out of process (dedicated Analysis Services instance) |
| Size | One file (2 GB max) | Large data volumes, partitions |
| Refreshing data | Sequential table refresh | Parallel table refresh, incremental processing, partitions |
| Development | Ad-hoc development | Project (business case, plan, dates, hardware, source control) |
| Lifespan | Weeks or months | Years |

Next, let me introduce you to the toolset for implementing organizational BI with Tabular.

## 10.1.2 Understanding the Professional Toolset

Enterprise development requires professional tools for developing and managing tabular models. **Figure 10.1** shows the toolset that Microsoft provides for designing, deploying, and managing organizational tabular models.

***SQL Server Data Tools***
Unlike the Excel-centric environment for implementing self-service PowerPivot models, organizational BI projects are designed in SQL Server Data Tools (SSDT). SSDT succeeds Business Intelligence Development Studio (BIDS), which you might be familiar with from previous SQL Server

releases. It gives you the power of the Visual Studio 2010 Integrated Development Environment at no additional cost. You can install SSDT from the SQL Server 2012 setup program. SSDT installs only SQL Server development projects, including database projects (requires running a web installer), Analysis Services projects, Reporting Services projects, and Integration Services projects.

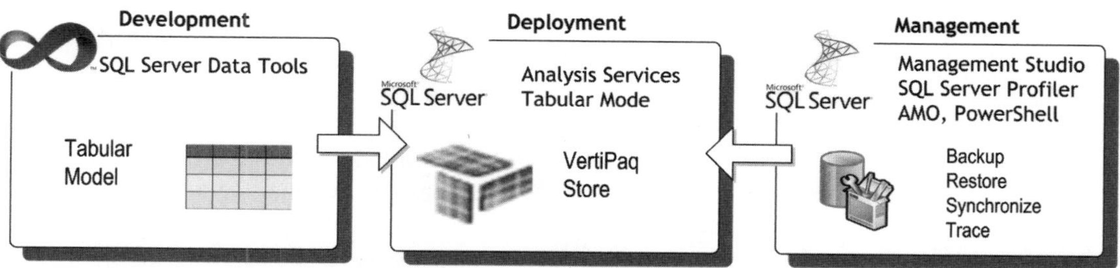


**Figure 10.1** Microsoft provides tools for designing, hosting, and managing organizational models.

If you install the full-blown version of Visual Studio 2010, the SQL Server setup program integrates the SQL Server project templates in your Visual Studio installation. As a result, developers can use Visual Studio to work with solutions that include code projects and SQL Server projects. SQL Server Data Tools is supported on Windows Vista SP2 or above and on Windows Server 2008 and above.

***Analysis Services in Tabular mode***

Similar to PowerPivot for SharePoint and to Multidimensional, deployed tabular models are powered by a dedicated instance of Analysis Services. The difference is that the Analysis Services instance is running in a Tabular mode. The model data is saved in a compressed format to disk on the server for durable storage. At run time, data is loaded in the in-memory VertiPaq store.

From a hardware perspective, you should plan for enough memory capacity on the server to ideally load the entire VertiPaq cache in RAM. As a rule of thumb, the RAM capacity should be at least twice the size of the disk footprint of all the models that are hosted on the server. Why? Because additional memory is required to process the models. If there isn't enough memory, the server will start paging out data to disk, and then the performance will degrade. I provide more information about configuring data paging and memory in Chapter 12.

***Management tools***

Thanks to the fact that Tabular is a component of Analysis Services, administrators can use familiar tools to manage tabular models. SQL Server Management Studio (SSMS) is the Microsoft premium tool to carry out common management tasks, such as backing up, restoring, and synchronizing Tabular databases.

**NOTE** Although Tabular and Multidimensional are both part of Analysis Services, Microsoft currently doesn't support mixed deployment where a single instance can host both Multidimensional and Tabular databases. An Analysis Services instance configured in a Tabular mode can host only tabular models. Similarly, you can't deploy PowerPivot for SharePoint models to Analysis Services in Tabular mode. And, you can't deploy SSDT projects to Analysis Services configured in SharePoint integrated mode.

You can use the tracing capabilities of SQL Server Profiler to capture Analysis Services events, such as to obtain the duration of a query execution. Finally, developers can write code that integrates with the Analysis Management Objects (AMO) library, SQL Server Integration Services, and PowerShell to automate management tasks.

## 10.1.3 Understanding the Development Lifecycle

If you've ever built an Analysis Services multidimensional cube, you'll find the process for implementing organizational tabular models to be very similar. However, there are also differences that are due to the nature of the tabular models.

***Steps for implementing tabular projects***

In a nutshell, implementing a Tabular model involves the following steps:

1. Create an Analysis Services Tabular project in SSDT. A project is a blueprint of a tabular model.
2. Import you data, and then design the raw model as a set of tables, columns, relationships, and calculations, just like you would do in PowerPivot for Excel. Unlike PowerPivot, however, as a BI pro you'd probably need to plan for additional effort to design the data model and the extraction, transformation, and loading (ETL) processes in order to clean the data.
3. Make and test design changes iteratively until the model is complete.
4. Deploy the model to a remote Analysis Services server for shared access, such as for quality assurance (QA) testing or for production use.

***Understanding workspace databases***

In review, the two design tenets of Tabular are simplicity and performance. To promote rapid development and to avoid explicit deployment steps during the design phase, SSDT applies each model change immediately. For example, if you add a new calculated column to a table, SSDT applies the change automatically to a deployed model, and the column is immediately available and populated with data. Similar to PowerPivot, almost every design action corresponds to a query or a commit operation to the model.

Again similar to PowerPivot, the SSDT design environment is always data-ready, meaning that when you make model changes, you work with the actual data as opposed to just the metadata. This is a paradigm shift for readers with a Multidimensional background who might remember that design changes are first applied offline to the cube metadata in the project, and you must explicitly deploy the cube in order to see the effect of the changes. By contrast, in Tabular each design change is followed by an implicit deployment step so you don't have to deploy the project explicitly.

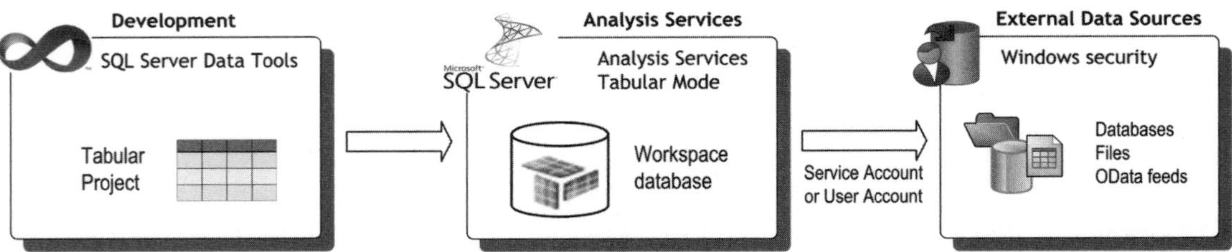


**Figure 10.2** During development, design changes are applied to a workspace database.

The constant "preview" mode requires a live Analysis Services instance that's configured in Tabular mode. The moment that you open the model in the tabular designer, SSDT automatically creates a shadow workspace database on the Analysis Service instance, as shown in **Figure 10.2**. Think of a workspace database as your private database that's always synchronized with the changes you make to the model. To guarantee that the database name is unique across projects and users, SSDT assigns it a name in this format <ProjectName>_<UserWindowsLogon>_<guid>. For example, Adventure Works_teo_34a282bb-62c1-4e58-b4d8-6fb781d837d7.

**NOTE** At this point, you might question the complexity of workspace deployment, and you might wonder why Microsoft didn't host an in-process VeritPaq engine in SSDT, as they did with PowerPivot for Excel. Unfortunately, Visual Studio is 32-bit only, and 32-bit applications are restricted to 2 GB of memory. Unlike PowerPivot, chances are that even during development, you might need to work with larger datasets that can exceed the 2 GB memory space.

Once the model is ready, you can periodically publish it to a test server or production server. A deployed database is completely independent from your workspace database and has an indefinite lifetime. Due to the transient nature of the workspace database, you should never create production reports that use it as a data source. Remember that a workspace database is for modeling and testing only. However, you're encouraged to use the workspace database during highly iterative model and report development, provided that you'll change the data source once the model is finished and deployed.

***Understanding workspace retention policies***

The workspace database has retention policy settings that control its lifetime. When you create a project in SSDT, you specify one of the following retention settings:

- Keep in memory – This is the recommended setting if your workspace is installed locally. The workspace server keeps the database in memory when you close SSDT. When you open the project again, you'll save time because you don't have to wait for Analysis Services to create a new workspace database. Analysis Services automatically mounts the workspace database after you restart the computer or the Analysis Services Tabular service. However, you're responsible to clean up the workspace databases off the server if these databases are not needed anymore.
- Keep on disk but unload from memory – If you use a remote workspace server, consider this setting to unload the workspace database from memory but keep it on disk when you close the project. This option conserves memory in a shared environment where multiple developers use the same server, and it avoids the spread of unused workspace databases.
- Delete workspace database – This option deletes the workspace database when it's not in use. As a result, you lose all imported data, and each time you open the project, you'll experience a delay until a new workspace database is created on the server and the data is imported.

***Understanding data backup settings***

SSDT supports creating backup files of the workspace database in the project folder. By default, a backup file (an Analysis Services *.abf file) isn't created, in order to avoid longer save times with larger data volumes. A backup file could be useful when you want to share workspace databases or undo changes, as explained in the blog post, "Working with backups in the tabular designer" by Cathy Dumas at http://bit.ly/TabularBackups. If these scenarios are important for you, consider enabling data backup. If you decide to do so, this is a simplified workflow describing how the workspace and backup interact:

- If the metadata in the project matches the metadata in the workspace database, connect to the workspace database, and then start modeling ELSE…
- If the metadata in the project matches the metadata in the backup, restore the backup to the workspace database, and then start modeling ELSE…
- Remove the workspace database, apply the metadata in the project to the workspace, and then start modeling. This effectively removes all the imported data.

For more details about the workspace synchronization, read the blog post, "Where does data come from when you open a BIM file" by Cathy Dumas at http://bit.ly/tabularsync.

You need to make two upfront decisions when setting up your development environment:

1. Where will you install the Analysis Services instance (workspace server) that will host the workspace database?
2. What Windows account will be used as a service account?

***Where to install the workspace server***

The Analysis Services Tabular instance that you'll use as a workspace server can be installed either locally on your development machine or on a remote server. A local instance might be preferable because it allows you to host the entire development environment on your machine. In addition, you don't need to worry about resource contention in a shared environment, such as the server running out of memory. A remote instance might be a better choice when you need to import large data volumes and your development machine is underpowered. Or, when you don't have Analysis Services Tabular installed locally. Three are functionality differences between local and remote workspace servers, as shown in **Table 10.2**.

**Table 10.2 Considerations for installing the workspace server locally or remotely**

| Feature | Local Workspace Server | Remote Workspace Server |
|---|---|---|
| SSDT backups | Supported | Not supported |
| Importing from PowerPivot | Import data and metadata | Import metadata only<br>See the blog post, "Recovering from cryptic errors thrown when importing from PowerPivot" by Cathy Dumas at http://bit.ly/ppimport |
| Analysis Services Tabular | On your machine | On the remote server |

Don't worry too much if you've made a wrong choice though because you can always switch between local and remote deployment, just by changing the project settings.

***Planning service accounts***

When you install Analysis Services Tabular, you need to decide what Windows account you want the service to run under. By default, when connecting to data sources that support Windows integrated security, the Analysis Services instance will use this account to connect and read data. Therefore, the service account must have read access to the external databases or folders where the files are located. In addition, the service account needs access to the project folder if you've configured the project to take backups of the workspace database.

Besides a service account, another option (to connect to data sources that require Windows security) is to use specific Windows credentials, such as your credentials. However, SSDT doesn't save the password, and you'll be prompted to enter it each time that you close and reopen the project for each data source. This can become rather annoying. Therefore, I recommend you use the service account to connect to external data sources whenever possible. Here are some considerations to help you choose a service account:

- Local development server – Choose the built-in Local System account, which has administrator access to local SQL Server databases. Or, for stricter security, choose the Local Service system account. When refreshing data from external data sources in SSDT, use standard security by entering a login name and password (ask your database administrator (DBA) to give you a login that has read access to the database). For data sources that support Windows security only, such as Analysis Services or files on a network share, enter specific Windows credentials, such as your Windows account credentials.

- Remote workspace, test, or production server – Choose a domain account. Grant the service account write access to the project folder on your machine if you configure the project to take backups. Grant the service account read access to data sources that require Windows security.

Don't worry if this sounds too complicated. You can always change the service account later on in the SQL Server Configuration Manager, which you can find in the Microsoft SQL Server 2012 ⇨ Configuration Tools program group.

***Development best practices***

To summarize, here are some best practices to streamline your development experience:

1. Although Tabular is somewhat more flexible than Multidimensional (because it treats all tables the same), in most cases your projects will benefit from a dimensional (star) schema. A star schema is preferable because it reduces the number of tables and because it makes the model more intuitive to end users and more efficient for data retrieval. Therefore, when you start a new tabular project, consider implementing a dimensional (star) schema and ETL processes to load clean and trusted data. For more information about dimensional modeling, I recommend the book, "The Data Warehouse Lifecycle Toolkit" by Ralph Kimball.
2. Prepare a small dataset to import into your model in order to speed up development. A small dataset cuts down processing time and facilitates testing business rules and expected results.
3. Once you've created the project in SSDT, put it under source control, such as by using Microsoft Team Foundation Server or Visual SourceSafe. This way you can review code changes and restore older versions if necessary.
4. Install a local instance of Analysis Services Tabular to host your workspace database. Use the built-in Local System account as a service account. If you decide to use another system or domain service account, grant this account rights to the project folder and to all the external data sources.
5. Use a domain service account for remote servers. Grant this account read rights to the external data sources and write rights to the local project folder.

## 10.1.4 Installing Analysis Services in Tabular Mode

Now that you know about the Tabular architecture and development lifecycle, let me walk you through the steps to install the required software. This includes installing Analysis Services in Tabular mode and SQL Server Data Tools from the SQL Server setup program. The following steps assume that you're setting up a development environment on your computer. Setting up a dedicated testing or production server involves similar steps although you don't have to install SSDT if you don't plan to work with projects.

***Selecting the required components***

Start by installing Analysis Services and SSDT to set up your development environment as follows:

1. Run the SQL Server setup program. In the SQL Server Installation Center page, click the Installation link in the left pane, and then click "New SQL Server Stand-alone Installation or add features to an existing installation". Accept the default options in the next steps to obtain the product updates and to install the setup files.
2. In the Installation Type step, leave the default option of "Perform a New Installation" selected.
3. In the Setup Role step, leave the default option of "SQL Server Feature Installation" selected.
4. In the Feature Selection step, select Analysis Services and select SQL Server Data Tools, as shown in **Figure 10.3**. This is the minimum set of features that you need in order to develop organizational models locally on your development machine. However, based on your needs, you might

need additional components. For example, if you'll perform management tasks, you should also select the "Management Tools – Basic" option to install SQL Server Management Studio (SSMS).

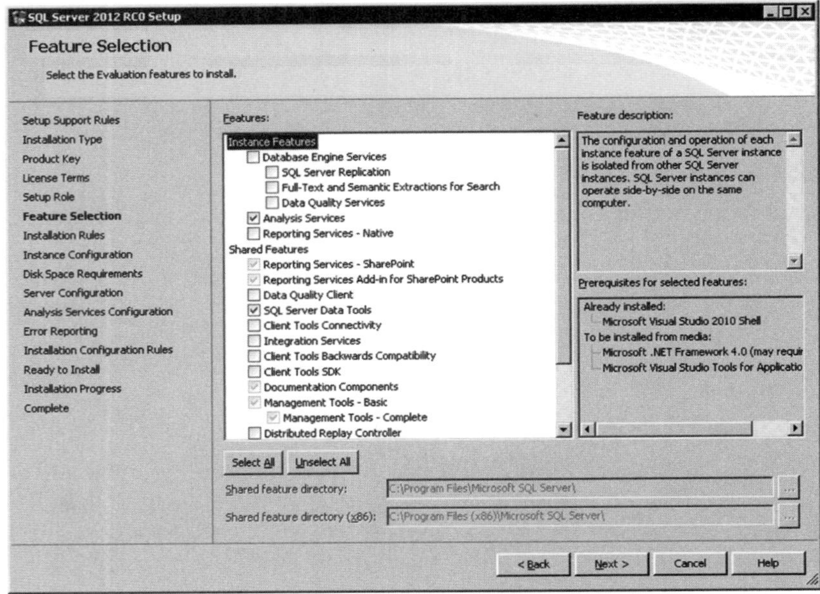


**Figure 10.3** At minimum, install Analysis Services and SQL Server Data Tools to develop organizational tabular models.

5. In the Instance Configuration step, specify which SQL Server instance you want to install Analysis Services on. The available options will depend on your setup. For example, if you don't have any SQL Server services installed, you can install Analysis Services on the default instance, which is called MSSQLSERVER. Otherwise, the only option available is to install it on a named instance and you must provide an instance name, such as *TABULAR*.

***Configuring a service account***

As I mentioned, you need to be careful when choosing the Analysis Services service account in order to avoid an account that's overly restricted. For development purposes, consider using Local System if you're installing a local instance of Analysis Services.

1. In the Server Configuration step, expand the Account Name drop-down list next to SQL Server Analysis Services, and then click <<Browse…>>. To use the Local System account, in the dialog box that follows, enter *<MachineName>\SYSTEM*, where <MachineName> is your computer name (see **Figure 10.4**). Or, specify the credentials of a domain service account, if you're configuring a remote server, such as a production server. Click the Check Names button to verify the account, and then click OK. You don't need to specify a password for a system account.
2. In the Analysis Services Configuration step, select the Tabular Mode option. Click the Add Current User button to add yourself as a server administrator, as shown in **Figure 10.5**. If you need to grant other users or Active Directory (AD) groups rights to manage the server, click the Add button. You don't need to add the local Administrators group (<MachineName>\Administrators) because the setup grants it system rights by default (the BuiltinAdminsAreServerAdmins server property is set to True).

**NOTE** Any developer, who wants to use a remote Analysis Services Tabular instance as a workspace server, must have administrator rights to that instance. It's convenient to add the developers in the Analysis Services Configuration step.

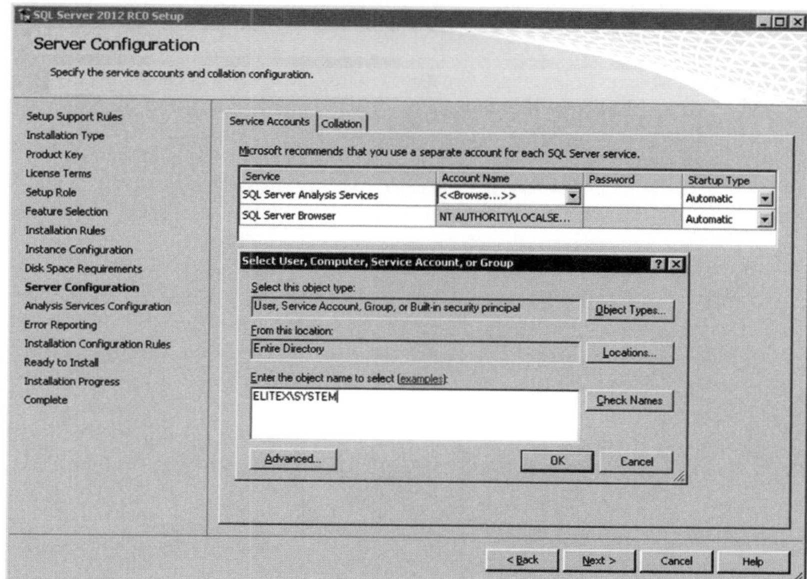


**Figure 10.4** For development, consider using the Local System account as an Analysis Services service account.

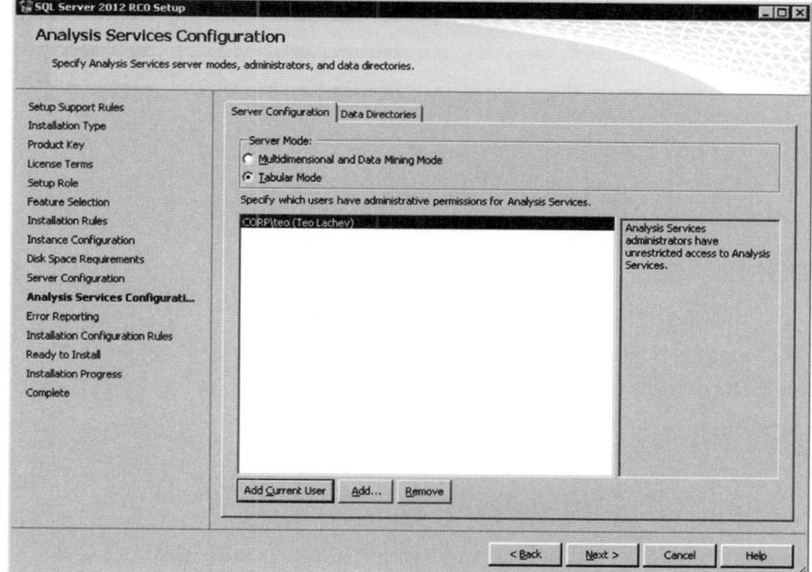


**Figure 10.5** Install Analysis Services in Tabular mode to develop organizational BI models.

3. Accept the default options in the next steps, and then proceed to install the software.

***Installing Microsoft Excel***

Now that Microsoft retired Office Web Components, SSDT doesn't include a built-in browser for testing Tabular models. As a result, you need Microsoft Excel to browse the model and to test changes your during the development phase. If Excel isn't present, when you click the "Analyze in Excel" button in SSDT, you'll get an error that the Office Data Connection (ODC) file can't be open. Any Excel version that supports ODC files can be used. Although for a better experience, you should target Excel 2007 or later.

**NOTE** If you plan to import data from text files, consider carefully whether to install Excel 32-bit or 64-bit. As I explained in Chapter 2, you can't install Office 32-bit and 64-bit side by side. If you have a 64-bit Windows OS, you should install the 64-bit version of Excel. If you have the 32-bit of Excel and you install the 64-bit version of SQL Server, the workspace server won't be able to load the Microsoft ACE provider, and then importing from text files will fail with the error, "The provider Microsoft.ACE.OLEDB.12.0 is not registered." Cathy Dumas describes these considerations in more detail in the blog post, "Working with the ACE provider in the tabular designer" at http://bit.ly/aceprovider.

If you can't install Excel on your local machine, you can install it on a remote machine. Then, you can connect to your workspace database, so that you can have your project on one machine, Excel on another, and still see the data live as you're modeling. However, installing Excel on a test server or on a production server is rarely a possibility. Another option to browse deployed models is to use the MDX query designer included in SSMS. This is the same query designer that PowerPivot for Excel uses for importing data from multidimensional databases but the SSMS implementation is enhanced to support security options, such as specifying roles or impersonating users.

***Installing data providers***

During development, the workspace server connects to the data sources to import data. Once you deploy the model to the production server, the production instance of Analysis Services Tabular establishes the connections. Therefore, you must install all the required data providers on the machine where Analysis Services Tabular is installed. Again, you must obtain the correct version (32-bit or 64-bit) of the providers, so that they match the bitness of SQL Server.

For example, suppose that the model imports data from flat files and that the server doesn't have Microsoft Office installed (which includes the ACE provider). Suppose that the server is running the 64-bit version of Windows Server 2008 R2 and the 64-bit version of SQL Server 2012. You need to install the 64-bit version of the Microsoft Access Database Engine 2010 Redistributable from the Microsoft Download Center (http://bit.ly/downloadace).

## 10.2 Designing Models

Now that you've installed the required components, you're ready to start designing organizational models. As I mentioned, professional modeling takes place in the SQL Server Data Tools (SSDT). In this section, I'll introduce you to project development and walk you through different options to implement organizational models.

### 10.2.1 Getting Started with Project Development

Next, let's practice a few common tasks that will help you get familiar with SSDT and Analysis Services Tabular projects. If you have both SSDT and Visual Studio 2010 installed, you can use either one to complete the practices that follow.

***About projects and solutions***

Implementing an organizational tabular model requires an Analysis Services Tabular project. The Analysis Services Tabular project represents an Analysis Services database that hosts the tabular model when the project is deployed to the server. **Figure 10.6** shows the relationship between projects and databases.

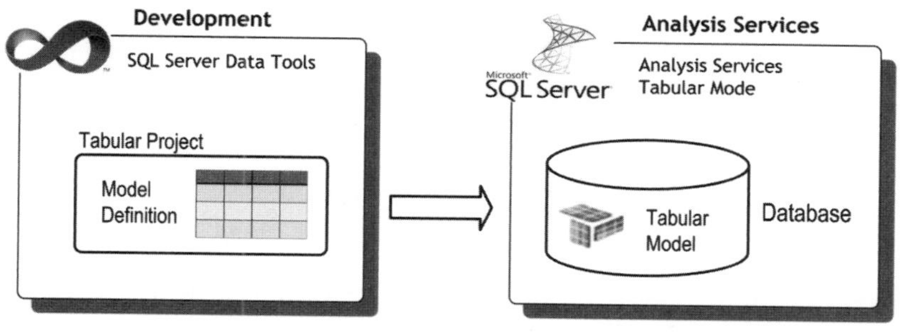


**Figure 10.6** A Tabular project represents an Analysis Services database.

When you create an Analysis Services Tabular project, SSDT automatically adds a Model.bim file that contains the entire XML-based definition of the tabular model, which consists of a set of tables, columns, relationships, and other tabular elements. This is different than a Multidimensional project that has one file per item, such as a file for each dimension. A Tabular project always contains only one tabular model (one Model.bim file). When the project is synchronized with the workspace server or when you explicitly deploy to a server, Analysis Services creates a database that hosts the model. Since a database (and its corresponding Analysis Services Tabular project) can contain only one model, I'll use the terms "database" and "model" interchangeably.

It's completely up to you to define the project scope. In most cases, you would probably end up with a single project that has all the tables required for analysis. However, security or operational requirements might necessitate multiple models and therefore multiple projects (and multiple Analysis Services databases). For example, if you upgrade PowerPivot workbooks to organizational models, you might decide to have a separate project per workbook. As it stands, SSDT doesn't allow you to automatically consolidate projects by merging the model metadata. However, if you start from scratch, you might decide to make your project less granular and to include more tables.

**TIP** The BISM Normalizer (http://bit.ly/normalizer) is a free tool that allows you to compare the metadata of two Tabular models and optionally copy parts of one model to the other. It can be useful when you want to consolidate the metadata of multiple PowerPivot workbooks into a single organization model.

An Analysis Services Tabular project includes the same design environment as PowerPivot. As a result, you can seamlessly transfer your PowerPivot modeling knowledge to organizational models. If you know PowerPivot, you already know 90% of the organizational BI feature set. The difference is the hosting environment. There are two notable differences between SSDT and PowerPivot design environments:

- SSDT doesn't support implicit measures (all measures are explicit).
- When you connect to a Tabular model in Excel, the field list is different. PowerPivot for Excel uses the PowerPivot Field List, whereas Tabular models use the PivotTable Field List.

Visual Studio supports solutions. A solution consists of one or more projects. For example, you can add an Analysis Services project and a Reporting Services project to the same solution, and then you can work with them in a single instance of SSDT. Or, if you have the full-blown version of Visual Studio, a solution can include BI and code projects so that you can work with all the project artifacts in a single SSDT instance.

**NOTE** Unlike Multidimensional, Tabular doesn't support online mode where you can connect to a deployed database and then apply changes directly to it. In other words, the File ⇨ Open ⇨ Analysis Service Database menu in SSDT applies only to Multidimensional. You must work in project mode to design Tabular models, and the project must be constantly connected to the workspace server during development.

***Setting up data modeling options***

To avoid failed attempts to create a new project caused by SSDT not being able to connect to the workspace server, configure the default workspace settings before you create the project, as follows:

1. Start SQL Server Data Tools from the Microsoft SQL Server 2012 program group.
2. Click the Tools menu, and then click Options.
3. In the Options dialog box, click the Data Modeling node under the Analysis Services section, as shown in **Figure 10.7** (selecting the Analysis Services node shows the Data Modeling options too). This page allows you to specify default settings for the workspace server that can be overwritten by model-specific settings on a per-project basis.

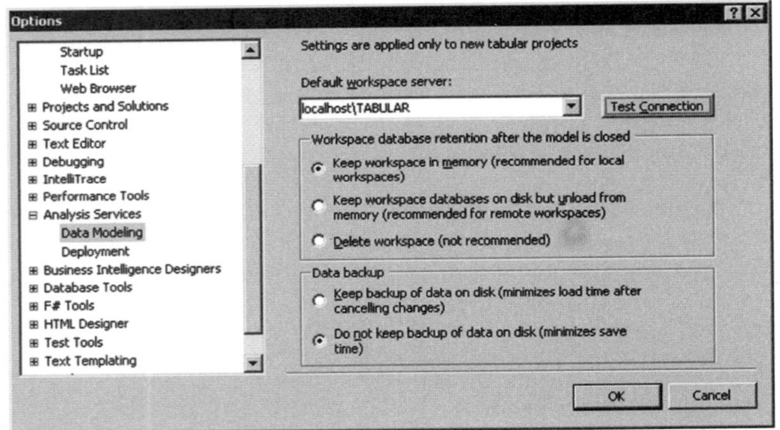


**Figure 10.7** Use the Analysis Services options in SSDT to configure the workspace retention policies and data backup.

If you don't see the Analysis Services section in Visual Studio, SQL Server Data Tools isn't installed. Earlier I explained that you must install SSDT from the SQL Server setup program to get the BI project templates.

4. The Default Workspace Server drop-down list includes all the local instances of Analysis Services. Expand the drop-down list, and then select your Analysis Services Tabular instance that will host the workspace database, such as localhost\TABULAR if you've installed Analysis Services in tabular mode on a named instanced called TABULAR on your machine. Or, to use a remote workspace server, enter that instance name. Remember that you must have administrator rights to that instance.
5. Click the Test Connection button to test connectivity. You should see a confirmation message that the connection has succeeded. In Section 10.1.3, I explained the workspace retention and data backup policies. Leave the default settings.
6. (Optional) In the left pane, click the Deployment node in the Analysis Services section. In the "Default Deployment Server" drop-down list, enter the name of the server that you're planning to deploy your project by default to, such as a test server or a production server. If you don't have a

remote server, enter your local Analysis Services Tabular instance, such as localhost\TABULAR, or select it from the drop-down list. Click OK.

***Understanding Tabular project templates***

SSDT provides a set of Business Intelligence project templates, including templates to get you started with Analysis Services Tabular projects. Follow these steps to view these templates:

1. In SSDT, click File ⇨ New ⇨ Project or click the New Project toolbar button to open the New Project dialog box.
2. In the Installed Templates pane, click Analysis Services found under the Business Intelligence node, as shown in **Figure 10.8**.

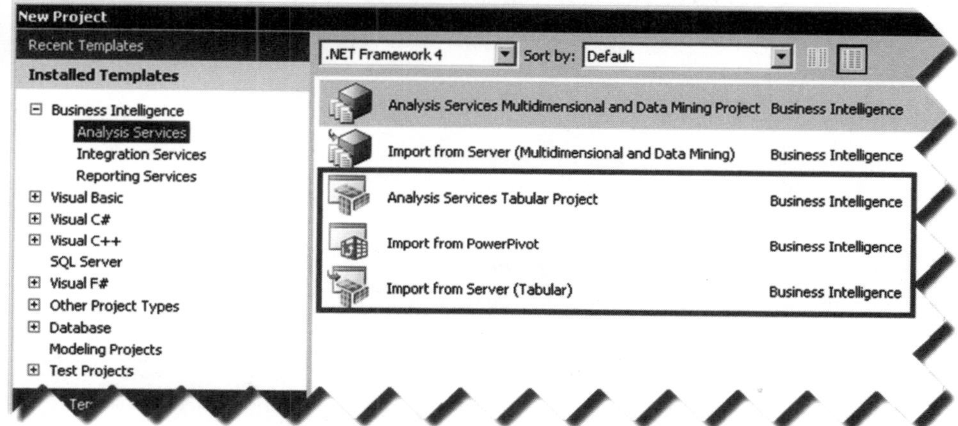


**Figure 10.8** SSDT includes three templates for Analysis Services Tabular projects.

You can use the last three templates to implement Tabular projects, as follows:

- Analysis Services Tabular Project – Creates an empty tabular project.
- Import from PowerPivot – Creates a project by importing from a PowerPivot workbook.
- Import from Server (Tabular) – Imports the model definition from a deployed database.

Let's practice these three options, starting with importing from PowerPivot.

## 10.2.2 Importing from PowerPivot

It's time to go back to Alice and the Adventure Works model that she implemented for personal BI analysis and exploration. Since Alice has deployed the model to SharePoint, it has gathered momentum and other business users and managers have been using it to gain insights. However, data volumes have increased too, and Alice realizes that more hardware resources are required to handle and process data. Moreover, management is requesting data security, such as to authorize sales persons to see only their sales data.

These requirements go beyond Alice's skill set, and so she turns the model over to you. Your job as a BI pro is to migrate what has started as a humble personal BI model to a scalable and secure solution. In this chapter, you'll learn how to create and deploy the tabular project. In the next chapter, you'll extend the model with data management and security features.

*Importing the Adventure Works workbook*

Follow these steps to create an Analysis Services Tabular project by importing the Adventure Works PowerPivot model:

1. In the New Project dialog box, select the "Import from PowerPivot" option.
2. In the Name field, enter *Adventure Works* as your project name.
3. In the Location field, enter the path to the folder where you want the project files to be saved. Click OK.

**NOTE** If the service account of the workspace server doesn't have the rights to access the folder where the PowerPivot workbook is located, you'll get a warning message that SSDT will be able to import the metadata but not the data. If you want to get the data, move the PowerPivot workbook to another location that the service account can access. Or, grant the account explicit read rights to that folder.

4. In the Open dialog box that follows, navigate to the Ch08 folder, select the Adventure Works.xlsx file, and then click Open.

SSDT starts the import process. The status bar shows progress messages, such as "Preparing workspace database from extracted content..." Once the import task is complete, SSDT loads the project and opens the model in a Data View mode.

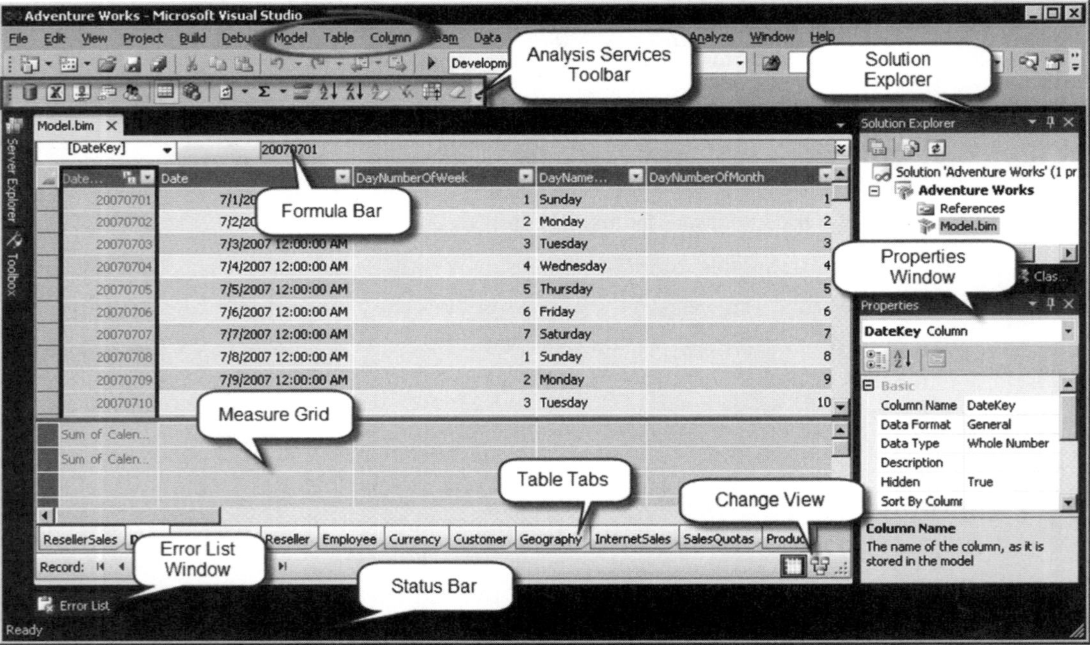


**Figure 10.9** The Adventure Works project is open in the SSDT tabular designer.

To learn more about the behind-the-scenes mechanics of the import process and how to adjust data source references of embedded PowerPivot reports, read the blog post, "What does Import from PowerPivot actually do?" by Cathy Dumas at http://bit.ly/importfrompp.

*Understanding the SSDT environment*

**Figure 10.9** shows the Adventure Works project open in SSDT. The Solution Explorer pane on the right shows that SSDT has created an Adventure Works solution (Adventure Works.sln file), which includes the Adventure Works project (Adventure works.smproj file). Ignore the References folder, which was inherited from Visual Studio code projects. It has no relevance to BI projects. You can also ignore the Class View tab for the same reason. The Model.bim file represents the tabular model, and its name is irrelevant. You can rename the file without affecting anything.

**TIP** You can add other files to your projects, such as Microsoft Word documents or HTML files with supporting help documentation. When you do so, SSDT automatically sets the Build Action property to None to avoid a deployment error. If the solution is under source control and if you want to share the layout settings with other developers, then I suggest you add the Model.bim.layout file to the project, and then add it to source control. Cathy Dumas explains the .layout file in more detail in her blog post, "New for RC0 – the .layout file" at http://bit.ly/bismlayout.

1. Double-click the Model.bim file to open it in the tabular designer.
2. In the Solution Explorer, click the Model.bim file to select it.

The Properties window shows the properties of the currently selected object. When you select the model file (Model.bim), the Properties window shows the model properties. Notice that you can overwrite the workspace server instance and retention settings if you want them to be different than the default settings that you specified in the SSDT Tools ⇨ Options menu.

The pane to the left of Solution Explorer represents the modeling environment, which is also known as a tabular designer. Since PowerPivot and SSDT share the same design framework, discussing its features in details will be redundant. Instead, I'll focus on the differences only. The SSDT menus and toolbars replace the Excel ribbon interface. Specifically, the Model, Table, and Column menus (see **Figure 10.10**) allow you to configure the model, table, and column definitions respectively or to carry out specific actions, such as deleting a table.

**Figure 10.10** The Model, Table and Column menus replace the Excel PowerPivot ribbon.

You can configure item properties in the Properties window. For example, when you select a column, you can use the Properties window to change the column description, data type, format settings, and advanced properties. If you want to import data from the Windows Clipboard, the copy and paste features are available in the Edit menu, including the Copy Data, Paste Append, and Paste Replace features. The Analysis Services toolbar (again see **Figure 10.9**) provides another way to carry out modeling tasks. For example, you can click the Existing Connections button (the third from the left) to open the Existing Connections dialog box. If you accidentally close the Analysis Services toolbar, you can turn it back on from the SSDT View ⇨ Toolbars menu.

3. Expand the Model menu, and then click Existing Connections. This opens the familiar Existing Connections dialog box. If the PowerPivot model wasn't designed by you, check and change the connections as needed so that the workspace server can connect to the data sources.
4. Select the AdventureWorksDW data source, and then click Edit. Unlike PowerPivot, notice that the Edit Connection dialog box has an Impersonation button. Click this button to open the Impersonation Information dialog box, as shown in **Figure 10.11**.

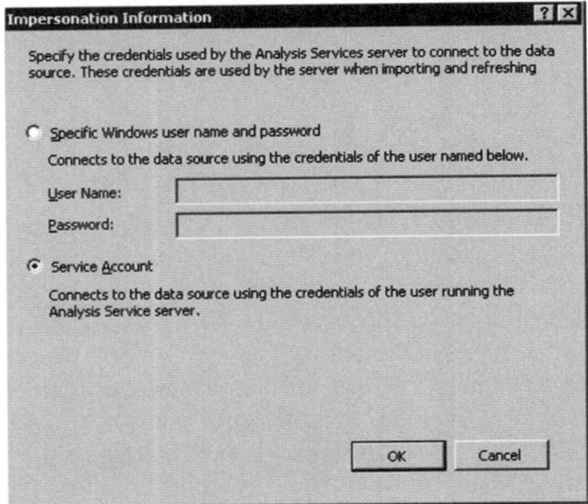


**Figure 10.11** You can configure the workspace server to open a data source connection under a specific user account or under the service account.

Notice that you have two authentication options for data sources that support Windows security. By default, the workspace server will use its service account to connect. Or, select the "Specific Windows user name and password" option to use a specific Windows account to connect, such as your account. As I explained in Section 10.1.3, the caveat with the latter option is that SSDT doesn't save the password between restarts, and so you need to reenter it. This is why I recommend that you use the service account option. Because it runs outside of SSDT, the workspace server doesn't support an option to impersonate the current user.

**NOTE** If you double-click a connection in a Tabular database in SQL Server Management Studio (SSMS), and then go to the Impersonation Info settings, you'll see four impersonation options (Specific User Name, Service Account, Inherit, and User the Credentials of the Current User). Since, SSMS shares the same UI with Multidimensional, the last two options were inherited from Multidimensional but don't apply to Tabular models.

***Understanding changes***

I explained in Chapter 6 that PowerPivot supports implicit and explicit measures. Implicit measures are numeric columns that are added to the Values zone of the Fields pane in Excel PowerPivot reports. Analysis Services Tabular and SSDT don't support implicit measures. When SSDT encounters implicit measures upon import from PowerPivot, it converts them to explicit hidden measures. The measure grid (called Calculation Area in PowerPivot for Excel), displays both internal and explicit measures, as shown in **Figure 10.12**.

You can define new explicit measures using the following two options:

- To create a measure that uses a standard aggregation function (Sum, Average, Count, DistinctCount, Min, Max), click on a column, and then expand the Sum button (Σ) on the

Analysis Services toolbar. Or, with the column selected, click the Column ⇨ AutoSum button.

- To create a measure that has a custom Data Analysis Expressions (DAX) formula, click an empty cell in the measure grid, and then type a DAX formula in the formula bar. When you press Enter, the measure appears in the selected cell in the measure grid. SSDT doesn't include the Excel UI dialog boxes for implementing explicit measures, such as the "PowerPivot Measure Settings" dialog box.

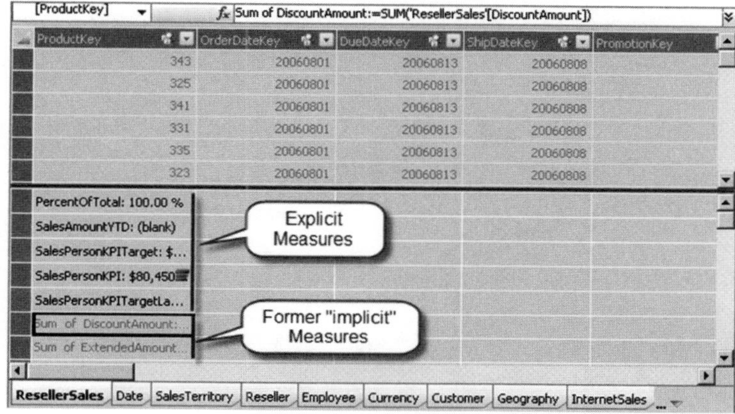


**Figure 10.12** PowerPivot implicit measures are converted to hidden explicit measures on import.

**NOTE** Microsoft has provided an unsupported DAX Editor (http://daxeditor.codeplex.com/) that's implemented as an extension of SQL Server Data Tools (SSDT). Among other things, the DAX Editor supports DAX syntax highlighting and IntelliSense support for keywords, functions, columns, and measures. You can use the DAX editor for measure authoring instead of, or in addition to, using the measure grid.

**TIP** If you don't prefix the formula with an equal sign (=) when you enter a new explicit measure in the measure grid, you'll get a comment and not a measure. You can differentiate comments from measures by looking at the font (comments are in italics). If you know the name you want, the best way to create a measure is to type in the measure using the syntax Measure Name:=DAX Formula.

***Working with measures***

Because organizational models typically have a much broader audience and scope, you should spend some time refining the model metadata. When doing so, consider what reporting tools will be used to produce reports and what the limitations are of these tools. For example, the ResellerSales and InternetSales tables have columns with identical names. If an end user creates a Power View report that shows both reseller sales and Internet sales side by side, then the user won't be able to tell them apart by just looking at the field names on the report. Follow these steps to refine the model metadata:

1. Delete all inactive measures (measures that appear grayed out in the measure grid) from the ResellerSales and InternetSales tables since you don't need them for reporting purposes. These measures were former implicit measures in the PowerPivot model. For example, click the "Sum of DiscountAmount" measure in the measure grid, and then press the Delete key. To delete multiple measures, hold the Ctrl key, click on each measure, and then press Delete. Also, delete the "Sum of SalesAmount" measure from the ResellerSales table.
2. Click the PercentOfTotal measure in the measure grid to select it. In the Properties grid, change the Measure Name property to *ResellerSalesPercentOfTotal*. Or, you can rename a measure in the

formula bar (replace the text before the := operator). Rename the SalesAmountYTD measure to *ResellerSalesAmountYTD*.

3. Click a cell in the OrderQuantity column. Click the Sum drop-down button (the one with the Sigma sign) in the Analysis Services toolbar to create an explicit measure that sums this column. This creates a "Sum of OrderQuantity" explicit measure, which appears immediately under the column in the measure grid, as shown in **Figure 10.13**.

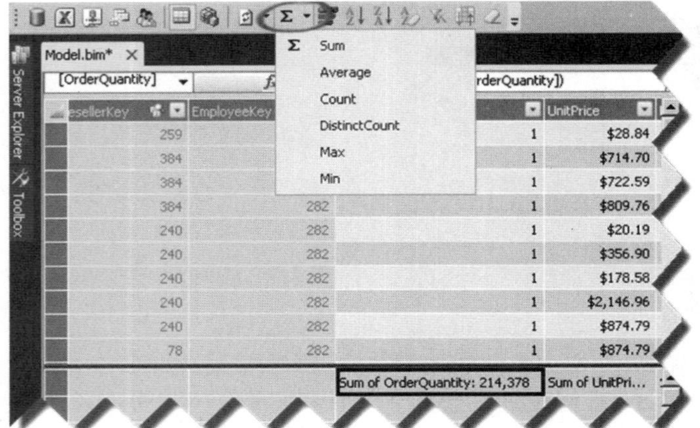


**Figure 10.13** Use the Sum toolbar button to create explicit measures.

4. Rename the new "Sum of OrderQuantity" measure to *ResellerOrderQuantity*. Right-click the column header of the OrderQuantity column (not OrderQuantity in the measure grid), and then click "Hide from Client Tools". This hides the column, but it leaves the explicit measure visible to report clients.

5. Create explicit measures for the rest of the numeric columns in the ResellerSales table. Rename the new measures by replacing the "Sum of " with "Reseller", such as rename "Sum of UnitPrice" to *ResellerUnitPrice*. Hide the source columns.

**TIP** You can quickly create explicit measures for multiple columns by selecting the columns (drag the mouse cursor horizontally across the columns you want to select), and then click the Sum toolbar button.

6. Perform similar steps to create explicit measures for all the numeric columns in the InternetSales table. Rename the new measures by replacing the "Sum of " with *"Internet"*, and then hide the source columns.

7. Click the Date table tab. Click the Column menu in the SSDT menu bar, and then click Add Column. In the formula bar, type in the following DAX formula, and then press Enter:

```
=[CalendarYear] * 100 + [CalendarQuarter]
```

8. Double-click the header of the new column to enter edit mode. Rename it to *QuarterSort*.

9. Click a cell in the CalendarQuarterDesc column, and then click the "Sort by Column" button in the Analysis Services toolbar (or click the Column menu ⇨ Sort ⇨ Sort by Column). In the "Sort By Column" dialog box, expand the By drop-down list, and then select the QuarterSort column. As a result, when you add the CalendarQuarterDesc column to a report, calendar quarters will sort in their natural order. This will be useful for the exercise in Section 10.3.1, when you'll create a Power View chart that groups data by quarters.

10. (Optional) Repeat the last step to sort the FiscalQuarterDesc column by the QuarterSort column. Right-click the column header of the QuarterSort column, and then click "Hide from Client Tools" to hide it.

***Handling errors***

There are three types of errors when working with DAX formulas: syntax, semantic, and calculation errors. If the formula has a syntax error, such as missing brackets, you can't commit a formula (you're stuck in the formula bar). A semantic error, such as an unknown column name, or a calculation error, such as overflow, will allow you to commit the formula, but an error icon appears in the table tab and in the column header of the table designer (same as in PowerPivot). In addition, semantic and calculation errors appear in the SSDT Error List window (click View ⇨ Error List to open it if it's hidden), as shown in **Figure 10.14**.

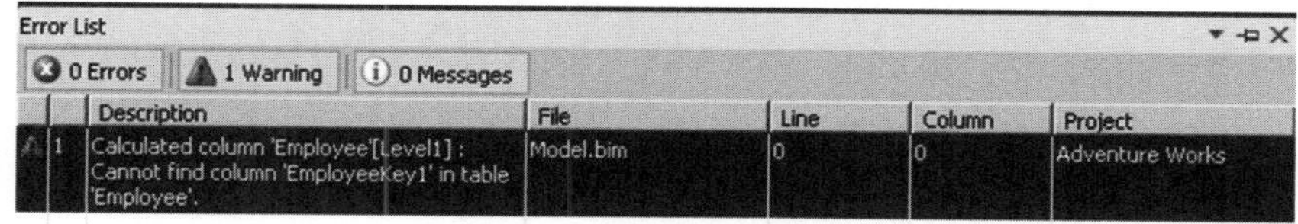


**Figure 10.14** The Error List window shows an error in a calculated column.

When you double-click the error, SSDT navigates you to the corresponding table and then highlights the failed column or measure.

***Browsing the model***

Naturally, you would need to test model changes during the design phase. As I mentioned, SSDT doesn't include a built-in browser. Instead, you need to have Microsoft Excel installed locally or on a remote machine. You can use Excel to create (online analytical processing (OLAP) reports that use the model as a data source.

1. Click the "Analyze in Excel" toolbar button (the one with the Excel icon) in the Analysis Services toolbar. Or, start Excel by clicking Model ⇨ "Analyze in Excel" menu in the SSDT menu bar.

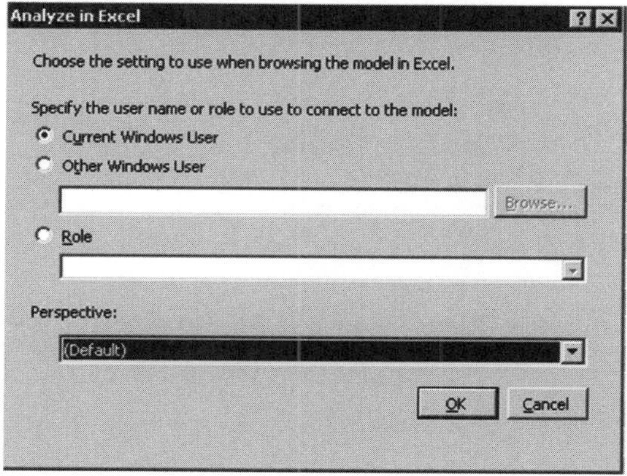


**Figure 10.15** Use the "Analyze in Excel" dialog box to specify impersonation options and select a perspective.

2. SSDT opens the "Analyze in Excel" dialog box, as shown in **Figure 10.15**. By default, Excel will open under your identity, but there are other options that are useful when testing security. If your

model includes perspectives, you can use the Perspective drop-down list to select a specific perspective. Or, you can accept the (Default) selection to see the entire model metadata. Click OK.

3. Once Excel opens, you'll see model metadata in the PivotTable Field List, and you'll see an empty pivot report. Click the Data ribbon tab, and then click Connections. In the Workbook Connections dialog box, click the Properties button, and then click the Definition tab. Notice that Excel connects to the workspace database. As a result, you can leave Excel open while you're making model changes, and then click the Refresh button in Excel to see the effect of these changes.

***Deploying the project***

You'd probably want to publish the model periodically for testing or reporting purposes. By explicitly deploying the model to a dedicated Analysis Services Tabular server you make the model scalable and accessible by other users who have rights to connect to it.

1. In Solution Explorer, right-click the Adventure Works project (the Adventure Works .smproj file), and then click Properties to open the Property Pages dialog box (see **Figure 10.16**).

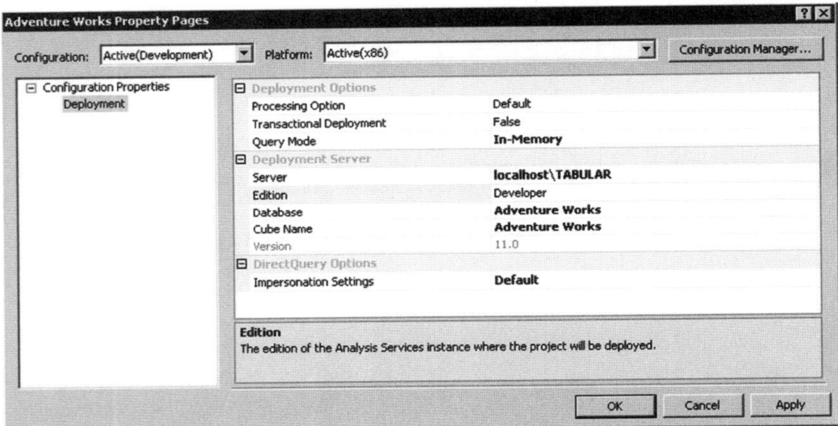


**Figure 10.16** Use the project properties to specify settings for deployment to a remote server.

2. If needed, change the Server property to match the Analysis Services Tabular instance where you want to deploy the model. If you don't have a remote server, you can deploy to your workspace server to complete the exercises in this chapter.

3. Change the Cube Name setting to a more user-friendly cube name for OLAP clients, such as *Adventure Works*.

Going quickly through the rest of the properties, the Processing Option property supports three settings: Default, Do Not Process, and Full. The default setting is Default, meaning that SSDT applies the minimum processing tasks, depending on the metadata changes needed to bring the model to a fully functional state. These tasks might include loading data for unprocessed partitions, recalculating relationships, hierarchies, and calculated columns. However, not all the metadata operations mark objects as unprocessed. For example, if you change the partition definition query, this doesn't mark the partition as unprocessed, and by default the partition won't be re-processed if you do Process Default. Moreover, Process Default doesn't detect when rows in your data sources have changed, so you might be unknowingly looking at stale data.

The "Do Not Process" setting deploys only the metadata changes without importing the data. This could be useful if you plan to synchronize the server with the latest changes, but you want to import data at a later time, such as by using SSMS to process the model or by running an ETL job. Finally, the Full setting applies the metadata changes and refreshes all the data. SSDT treats synchronizing metadata and importing data as two separate steps. Set Transactional Deployment to *True* if you want both steps to occur within an atomic transaction. If there is an error during the data import, the metadata changes will be undone and the model will be left in its previous state.

Let's postpone discussing the Query Mode and Impersonation Settings for the next chapter. The Edition setting allows you to target a specific SQL Server edition. You'll get design-time errors if you use features that the target edition doesn't support. This setting doesn't really apply to Analysis Services Tabular because tabular models are supported with Enterprise, Business Intelligence, and Developer editions with no difference in their features.

**NOTE** Readers with prior BI development experience might have used SSDT project configurations to maintain deployment settings and connection strings for different environments, such as production or testing. Analysis Services Tabular projects don't support project configurations.

4. Click OK to close the Property Pages dialog box. In Solution Explorer, right-click the Adventure Works project, and then click Deploy. Or, expand the Build menu, and then click "Deploy Adventure Works".

   SSDT opens the Deploy dialog box, which is very similar to the Data Refresh dialog box in PowerPivot for Excel. The Deploy dialog box displays the deployment progress.

***Troubleshooting deployment***

Chances are that your first deployment won't be successful. If deployment fails, the likely reason is the connection strings are wrong (go to Model ⇨ Existing Connections menu and check). Another possible culprit could be that the service account of the target Analysis Services Tabular instance doesn't have read rights to the data sources. Follow these steps to troubleshoot and fix deployment issues:

1. In the Deploy dialog box, click one of the error details links. In the Error Message dialog box, examine the error message to understand which connection has failed.
2. If the failed connection is AdventureWorksDW, in SQL Server Management Studio (SSMS), connect to the SQL Server instance hosting the AdventureWorksDW2008R2 database. Make sure that a SQL Server login exists for the SSAS service account, and then grant that login read rights to AdventureWorksDW2008R2. Normally, this step isn't needed if the SSAS service account is Local System (NT AUTHORITY\SYSTEM) and if the database server is on the same machine.
3. If the failed connection is AdventureWorksAS, then in SSMS, connect to the Analysis Services instance hosting the Adventure Works DW 2008 database. Expand the Roles folder, and then create an Analysis Services role. Assign the Analysis Services Tabular service account to that role, and then grant the role rights to read from the Adventure Works cube. Normally, this step isn't needed if the Analysis Services Tabular service account is Local System and if the source Analysis Services server is on the same machine.
4. As I explained in Section 10.1.4, you won't be able to connect with the Service Account option if Analysis Services Tabular and the data source are on two different machines and if the Analysis Services Tabular service account is a local account, such as Local System. If using a domain service account isn't an option, configure the data source to impersonate with the "Specific Windows user name and password" option, and then enter the credentials of a Windows account that has read rights to the data source.

*Testing deployment*

Once the model is deployed, you can use SSMS to test the model by following these steps:

1. Open SQL Server Management Studio from the "Microsoft SQL Server 2012" program group.
2. In the Object Explorer pane, click the Connect button, and then connect to the Analysis Services Tabular instance that you deployed the model to.
3. Expand the Databases folder, and then verify that the Adventure Works database exists, as shown in **Figure 10.17**. This figure also shows the workspace database because I used the same Analysis Services instance as a workspace and test server.

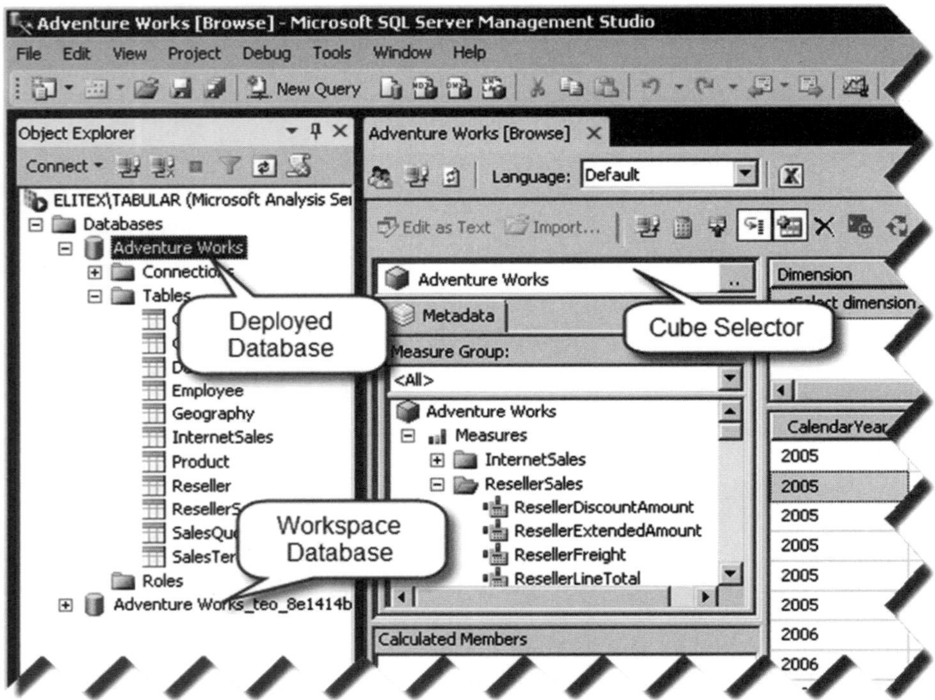


**Figure 10.17** Use SSMS to query and manage tabular databases.

4. To browse the model, right-click the Adventure Works database, and then click Browse. This opens the familiar MDX query designer, which you used in Chapter 3 to import data from multi-dimensional databases. By default, the Metadata pane shows the entire model metadata. However, you can use the Cube Selector drop-down list to select a perspective in order to see a subset of the metadata (if perspectives exist in the model).
5. (Optional) Drag measures from the Measures folder and dimension attributes to the Results pane to query the model and to test the data.

**NOTE** Tabular projects don't support Excel linked tables, which is an Excel-specific feature. If the PowerPivot workbook contains linked or pasted tables, SSDT converts them to internal data source upon import. For example, if you expand the Connections folder in SSMS, you'll see a "PushedDataSource <guid>" connection whose connection string is "Provider=None". This is an internal data source for the Currency table because this table was created by copying and pasting data.

## 10.2.3 Implementing New Models

You don't have to necessarily follow the personal-organizational continuum and implement organizational models by importing them from existing PowerPivot workbooks. Next, I'll show you how to implement a new tabular model in SSDT to analyze call-center operations. This model will use the FactCallCenter table in the Adventure Works data warehouse. This table captures the activity of the Adventure Works call center, including calls received and issues raised per day. This exercise will help you practice various SSDT modeling tasks. In the next chapter, you'll extend the CallCenter model to query data in real time.

***Creating a project***

Start by creating a new Analysis Services Tabular project in SSDT.

1. In SSDT, click File ⇨ New ⇨ Project.
2. In the New Project dialog box, select the Analysis Services Tabular Project template.
3. In the Name field, enter *CallCenter* for the project name.
4. Choose a location for the project, and then click OK to create it.
5. (Optional) In Solution Explorer, right-click the CallCenter project, and then click Properties. In the Property Pages dialog box, change the Cube Name property to *CallCenter*.

***Importing data***

Next, you'll import two tables from the Adventure Works data warehouse. As a prerequisite, grant the service account of your workspace server read access to the AdventureWorksDW2008R2 database.

1. With the model open in the tabular designer, click the "Import From Data Source" button in the Analysis Services toolbar. Or, expand the Model menu, and then click "Import From Data Source". This opens the familiar Table Import Wizard.
2. In the "Connect to a Data Source" step, leave Microsoft SQL Server selected, and then click Next.
3. In the "Connect to a Microsoft SQL Server Database" step, change the Friendly Connection Name to *AdventureWorksDW*. In the Server Name field, enter the SQL Server instance name. Expand the Database Name drop-down list, and then select the AdventureWorksDW2008R2 database. Click Next.

**NOTE** If you decide to open and test the CallCenter project from the Ch10 folder, then you need to change the connection string from the Existing Connections dialog box to match your environment. If you don't, you'll get an error message when you try to process the model.

4. In the Impersonation Information step, select the Service Account option. This assumes that the service account of the workspace server has access to the AdventureWorksDW2008R2 database.
5. In the "Choose How to Import the Data" step, leave the default option to select tables, and then click Next.
6. In the "Select Tables and Views" step, check the FactCallCenter and DimDate tables, and then click Finish.
7. The Importing step of the Table Import Wizard shows the progress of the data import task. The task should complete successfully. Click Close.

***Making metadata changes***

Let's make a few changes to refine the model. The following steps should be familiar to you from the PowerPivot practices, so I won't go into details. The goal of this practice is to understand how the SSDT modeling environment differs from PowerPivot and not to implement a production-ready model. As an optional exercise, follow similar steps to what you did in Chapter 4 in order to refine the model metadata.

1. Rename the DimDate table to *Date* and the FactCallCenter table to *CallCenter*.
2. In the Date table, right-click the DateKey column, and then click "Hide from Client Tools". Rename the FullDateAlternateKey column to *Date*. To sort months in their natural order, select the EnglishMonthName column, and then click the "Sort by Column" button in the Analysis Services toolbar. In the "Sort by Column" dialog box, expand the second drop-down list, select the MonthNumberOfYear column, and then click OK.
3. Switch to the CallCenter table. Hide the FactCallCenterID and DateKey columns.
4. Most of the numeric measures in the CallCenter table are fully additive because they can be summed across all lookup tables, including the Date table. Select the LevelOneOperators column. Holding the Shift key, and then click the IssuesRaised column to select multiple columns. Expand the Sum drop-down button in the Analysis Services toolbar (the one with the Sigma sign), and then click Sum to create explicit measures that sum these columns. This action adds seven explicit measures to the measure grid that use the Sum aggregation function.
5. With these seven columns still selected, expand the Data Format drop-down list in the Properties window, and then select Whole Number. Changing the data format to a whole number shows additional properties in the Properties window. Expand the "Show Thousands Separator" property, and then select True to format these measures with a thousands separator.
6. Click the AverageTimePerIssue column, and then change its Data Format property in the Properties window to Decimal Number. Select the ServiceGrade column, and then change its Data Format property to Decimal Number and its Decimal Places property to 4.
7. The AverageTimePerIssue and ServiceGrade columns can't be meaningfully summed. Instead, you'll define explicit measures that average these columns. Select the AverageTimePerIssue and ServiceGrade columns, expand the AutoSum drop-down menu, and then click Average.
8. (Optional) Hide the source columns for the explicit measures that you've created. For example, to hide the LevelOneOperators column, right-click its column header, and then click "Hide from Client Tools".
9. Click the "Analyze in Excel" button in the Analyses Services toolbar. Create the pivot report shown in **Figure 10.18** to analyze the number of calls by the Date field (Date table) on rows and the Shift field (CallCenter table) on columns.

> **TIP** A line chart might be a preferred visualization for this dataset. To add a line chart, click any cell in the pivot report, click the Excel Insert tab, and then click Line chart. This creates a PivotChart report that's synchronized with the PivotTable report.

10. Back in SSDT, save the project. In Solution Explorer, right-click the CallCenter node, and then click Deploy to deploy the model to the server and to make it available for reporting.

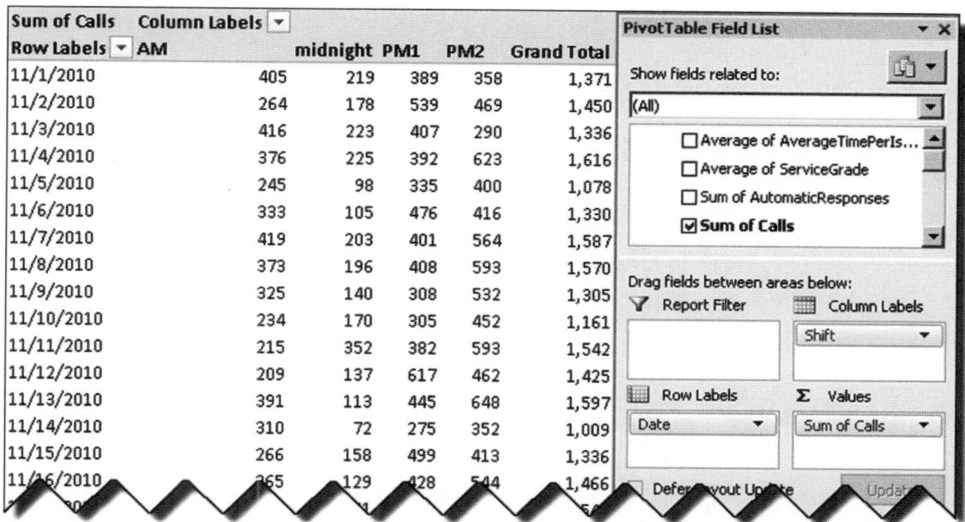

| Sum of Calls | Column Labels | | | | |
|---|---|---|---|---|---|
| Row Labels | AM | midnight | PM1 | PM2 | Grand Total |
| 11/1/2010 | 405 | 219 | 389 | 358 | 1,371 |
| 11/2/2010 | 264 | 178 | 539 | 469 | 1,450 |
| 11/3/2010 | 416 | 223 | 407 | 290 | 1,336 |
| 11/4/2010 | 376 | 225 | 392 | 623 | 1,616 |
| 11/5/2010 | 245 | 98 | 335 | 400 | 1,078 |
| 11/6/2010 | 333 | 105 | 476 | 416 | 1,330 |
| 11/7/2010 | 419 | 203 | 401 | 564 | 1,587 |
| 11/8/2010 | 373 | 196 | 408 | 593 | 1,570 |
| 11/9/2010 | 325 | 140 | 308 | 532 | 1,305 |
| 11/10/2010 | 234 | 170 | 305 | 452 | 1,161 |
| 11/11/2010 | 215 | 352 | 382 | 593 | 1,542 |
| 11/12/2010 | 209 | 137 | 617 | 462 | 1,425 |
| 11/13/2010 | 391 | 113 | 445 | 648 | 1,597 |
| 11/14/2010 | 310 | 72 | 275 | 352 | 1,009 |
| 11/15/2010 | 266 | 158 | 499 | 413 | 1,336 |
| 11/16/2010 | 365 | 129 | 428 | 544 | 1,466 |



**Figure 10.18** Create an Excel pivot report to test the model.

## 10.2.4 Importing from Server

The third and final option to create an Analysis Services Tabular project is to reverse-engineer it from a deployed database. Consider the following scenario. Going back to Alice's quest for a more scalable model, suppose that the PowerPivot model doesn't need new enhancements. Instead of creating a new project and importing the PowerPivot model, you decide to restore the PowerPivot model on a dedicated production server in order to make it immediately available for reporting.

**TIP** Here is another scenario that can benefit from importing the source from a server database. Imagine you're a consultant who's going to a client site, and they ask you to modify an existing Tabular database. However, they have lost the original source. You can use this option to regenerate the project from the existing database.

***Restoring PowerPivot workbooks***

Let's first restore Alice's workbook to the server. You can use SQL Server Management Studio (SSMS) to restore PowerPivot workbooks, as follows:

1. In SSMS, connect to the target Analysis Services Tabular instance.
2. Right-click the Databases folder, and then click "Restore from PowerPivot".
3. In the "Restore from PowerPivot" dialog box, specify the location of the workbook, the name of the new Analysis Services database, and then click OK. SSMS extracts the PowerPivot model from the workbook and then creates a new database.

***Importing projects***

Now suppose that end users have requested model changes. Since you prefer to work in a professional environment, you decide to create an Analysis Services Tabular project from the deployed database.

1. In SSDT, click File ⇨ New ⇨ Project. In the New Project dialog box, select the "Import from Server (Tabular)" template. Specify a project name and location, and then click OK.

2. In the "Import from Analysis Services" dialog box that follows, specify the server instance and the database that you'll use for the import operation (see **Figure 10.19**). Once the import process completes, you can continue modeling in SSDT.

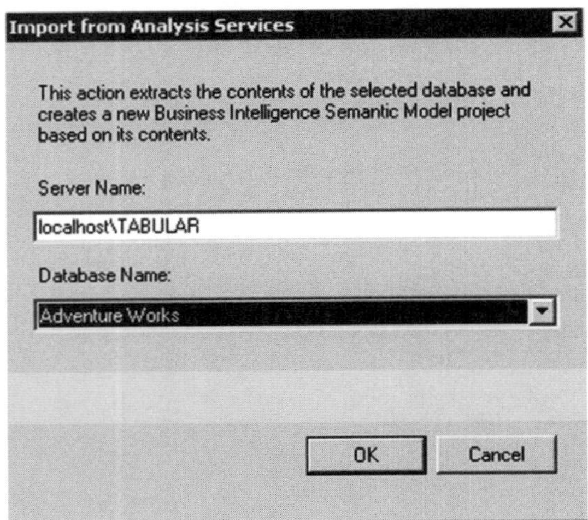


**Figure 10.19** Specify the Analysis Services Tabular instance and database to import the project from.

## 10.3 Authoring Reports

Next, I'll show you how to author Power View reports from deployed models. While there aren't any reporting features specific to organizational models deployed to an Analysis Services Tabular instance, this exercise will give you another chance to hone your report authoring skills with Power View (please review Section 8.3 if you're new to Power View). Moreover, it will help you understand how Power View connects and queries Analysis Services Tabular. As a prerequisite, you must have a functional SharePoint Server 2010 with SQL Server 2012 Reporting Services. Chapter 7 provides step-by-step instructions to install SharePoint and Reporting Services.

### 10.3.1 Implementing a Dashboard

**Figure 10.20** shows the Adventure Works Dashboard report that you'll implement in this practice. You can find the finished report definition (Adventure Works Dashboard.rdlx) in the \Source\Ch10 folder (you need to upload it to SharePoint in order to run it). Designed as a typical management dashboard, the report includes four visualizations that consolidate, aggregate, and arrange sales measures in a visual representation. This is a single-page report on purpose so that information can be analyzed at a glance.

Adventure Works Dashboard

Internet vs. Reseller Sales

Employee Sales vs. Target

Reseller Sales by Product Subcategory

| ProductSubcategory | 2005 | 2006 | 2007 | Total |
|---|---|---|---|---|
| Road Bikes | 50,012.12 | $10,765,176.58 | $11,294,381.37 | **$24,909,570.** |
| Mountain Bikes | 45,336.51 | $9,190,838.09 | $8,854,263.03 | **$22,590,437.** |
| Touring Bikes | | | $5,403,130.67 | **$5,403,130.** |
| Mountain Frames | 71,587.79 | $1,400,331.68 | $2,067,908.64 | **$3,839,828.** |
| Road Frames | 43,887.19 | $1,618,391.51 | $1,631,377.27 | **$3,493,655.** |
| Touring Frames | | | $1,032,154.04 | **$1,032,154.** |
| Wheels | | $452,122.12 | $226,947.94 | **$679,070.** |
| Jerseys | 28,255.57 | $110,243.77 | $290,004.73 | **$428,504.** |
| Shorts | | $49,261.57 | $179,301.33 | **$228,562.** |
| Helmets | 20,235.36 | $74,281.39 | $113,443.66 | **$207,960.** |
| Tights | | $122,895.93 | $78,937.08 | **$201,833.** |

Internet Sales

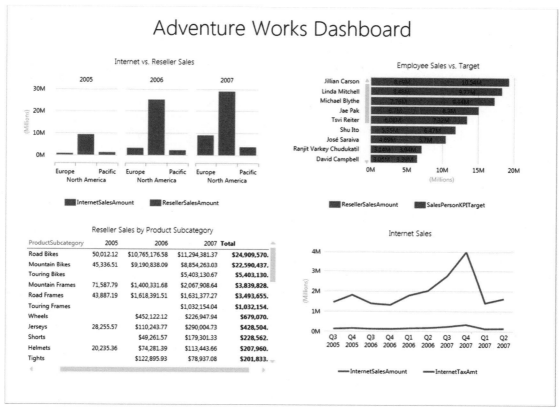

**Figure 10.20** The Adventure Works Dashboard report presents an interactive summary of sales data.

***Setting up a connection***

While setting up a connection to a PowerPivot workbook is optional, a BI Semantic Model connection (or a report data source) that points to an organizational model is a required prerequisite for creating reports. Follow similar steps as the ones in Section 9.1.2 to set up a new BI Semantic Model connection to the Adventure Works model. You must have at least SharePoint Contribute permissions to create a connection file.

**NOTE** The BI Semantic Model Connection content type is installed by PowerPivot for SharePoint. If you plan to author reports that connect to Analysis Services Tabular and you don't need PowerPivot for SharePoint, set up a report data source, as I demonstrated in Section 9.1.2.

1. In SharePoint, navigate to the document library where you want to save the connection, such as to PowerPivot Gallery.
2. Click the Documents tab in the ribbon. Expand the New Document drop-down menu, and then click "BI Semantic Model Connection".
3. In the "New BI Semantic Model Connection" page, enter *Adventure Works Tabular* as a data source name. In the "Workbook URL or Server Name" field, type in the Analysis Services Tabular instance that hosts the Adventure Works database that you deployed in Section 10.2.1. For example, type ELITEX\TABULAR if the server name is ELITEX and the instance name is TABULAR.

4. In the Database field, enter *Adventure Works*.
5. Click OK. SharePoint validates and saves the connection. If the validation fails, SharePoint displays an error message and gives you an option to save the connection without validation.

> **NOTE** SharePoint validates the connection using the PowerPivot service account. The connection uses the EffectiveUserName setting to check if the end user has permissions. If the validation fails, make sure that the PowerPivot service account has Analysis Services administrator rights. To grant the PowerPivot service administrator rights, in SSMS, connect to the Analysis Services Tabular instance, right-click on the server, and then click Properties. In the Analysis Services Properties dialog box, click Security, and then click Add to add the PowerPivot service account. Or, you could simply ignore the SharePoint validation and save the connection after verifying that the instance name and database name are correct.

6. Back in PowerPivot Gallery, click the "Create Power View Report" icon next to the Adventure Works Tabular connection. This opens Power View with an empty report.

***Implementing the Internet vs. Reseller Sales section***

This section shows Internet and reseller sales grouped by year and territory. It's implemented as a column chart with vertical multiples.

1. In the Fields pane, check the InternetSalesAmount field (InternetSales table) and the ResellerSalesAmount field (ResellerSales table).
2. Click the Design tab in the ribbon, and then change the visualization to Column (column chart).
3. In the Fields pane, check the TerritoryGroup field (SalesTerritory table) to add it to the Axis zone in the Layout pane.
4. In the Fields pane, check the CalendarYear field (Date table) to add it to the Vertical Multiples zone in the Layout pane.
5. Click the Layout button in the ribbon. Expand the Chart Title drop-down menu, and then click None to hide the chart title.
6. Expand the Legend button, and then click "Show Legend at Bottom" to move the chart legend below the chart.
7. Click the Home tab in the ribbon. Click the Text Box button to add a new textbox. With the textbox in edit mode, enter *Internet vs. Reseller Sales*. Move the textbox above the chart.

***Implementing the "Employee Sales vs. Target" section***

Implemented as a bar chart, this section shows the Adventure Works sales persons' sales and quotas. Follow these steps to implement it:

1. Click on a blank area outside and to the right of the "Internet vs. Reseller Sales" chart.
2. In the Fields pane, check the ResellerSalesAmount and SalesPersonKPITarget fields in the ResellerSales table.
3. Click the Design tab in the ribbon, and then change the visualization to Bar (bar chart).
4. In the Fields pane, check the FullName field (Employee table) to add it to the Axis zone in the Layout pane.
5. Click the Layout button in the ribbon. Expand the Chart Title drop-down menu, and then click None to hide the chart title.
6. Expand the Legend button, and then click "Show Legend at Bottom" to move the chart legend below the chart.
7. Expand the Data Labels button, and then click Show to display the chart labels.

8. Hover your mouse over the chart. In the "floatie", click the "Sort by FullName" drop-down menu, and then change it to ResellerSalesAmount to sort the chart data by this field. Click the Asc button to toggle it to Desc (descending order) in order to see the employees with most sales on the top of the chart.
9. Click the Home tab in the ribbon. Click the Text Box button to add a new textbox. With the textbox in edit mode, enter *Employee Sales vs. Target*. Move the textbox above the chart.
10. Move and resize the chart as needed.

***Implementing the "Reseller Sales by Product Subcategory" section***
This section shows the Adventure Works reseller sales grouped by product subcategory on rows and calendar year on columns. It's implemented as a crosstab report that uses the Matrix visualization.

1. Click on a blank area outside and below the "Internet vs. Reseller Sales" chart.
2. In the Fields pane, check the ResellerSalesAmount field (ResellerSales table).
3. Click the Design tab in the ribbon, and then change the visualization to Matrix.
4. In the Fields pane, check the ProductSubcategory field (Product table) to add it to the Row zone in the Layout pane.
5. In the Fields pane, drag the CalendarYear field (Date table) to the Column Groups zone in the Layout pane.
6. In the visualization, click the Total column to sort the report in descending order by the Total column.
7. Click the Home tab in the ribbon. Click the Text Box button to add a new textbox. With the textbox in edit mode, enter *Reseller Sales by Product Subcategory*. Move the textbox above the matrix.
8. Move and resize the matrix visualization as needed.

***Implementing the Internet Sales section***
This section shows the Adventure Works Internet sales and tax amounts. It's implemented as a line chart.

1. Click on a blank area outside and to the right of the "Reseller Sales by Product Subcategory" visualization.
2. In the Fields tab, check the InternetSalesAmount and InternetTaxAmount fields (InternetSales table).
3. Click the Design ribbon tab, and then change the visualization to Line (line chart).
4. In the Fields pane, check the CalendarQuarterDesc field (Date table) to add it to the Axis zone in the Layout pane. Because you've set up a custom sort on this column, quarters should sort in their natural order.
5. Click the Layout button in the ribbon. Expand the Chart Title drop-down menu, and then click None to hide the chart title.
6. Expand the Legend button, and then click "Show Legend at Bottom" to move the chart legend below the chart.
7. Click the Home ribbon tab. Click the Text Box button to add a new textbox. With the textbox in edit mode, enter *Internet Sales*. Move the textbox above the chart.
8. Move and resize the chart as needed.

***Setting up a report filter***

Suppose you want to filter the report by calendar year.

1. Click the Home ribbon tab, and then click the Filters Area.
2. In the Fields pane, drag CalendarYear (Date table), and then drop it onto the Filters Area.

   Because the data type of the CalendarYear field is a whole number, Power View shows a slider. You can drag the slider to filter a subset of years. For example, slide the right handle to the left to set up a "is less than or equal to" criterion, such as to filter years from 2005 and 2007.

3. Use the File ⇨ Save menu to save the report to PowerPivot Gallery as *Adventure Works Dashboard*.

## 10.3.2 Introducing DAX Queries

Chapter 1 covered how Business Intelligence Semantic Model (BISM) provides two external interfaces for querying Tabular models: Multidimensional Expressions (MDX) and Data Analysis Expressions (DAX). OLAP clients, such as Microsoft Excel, can query the model with MDX while Tabular-aware clients can send DAX queries. Since DAX is the native expression language of Tabular, the DAX interface is more efficient when querying tabular models. However, only Power View is capable of generating DAX queries. Microsoft hasn't extended other reporting tools, such as Excel and Report Builder, to support DAX.

**TIP** Irrespective of the fact that Reporting Services doesn't include a DAX query designer, you could use Report Builder or the Report Designer in SSDT to create operational reports that send DAX queries to a tabular model. Besides a solid knowledge of DAX, you need to set up a data source that uses the Microsoft OLE DB Provider for Analysis Services. If the report is parameter-driven, you can concatenate the parameter values to the query text. Or, consider using an Analysis Services data source (instead of the OLE DB Provider), and then click the DMX button in the query designer, which allows you to run DAX queries with parameters using the DMX tab.

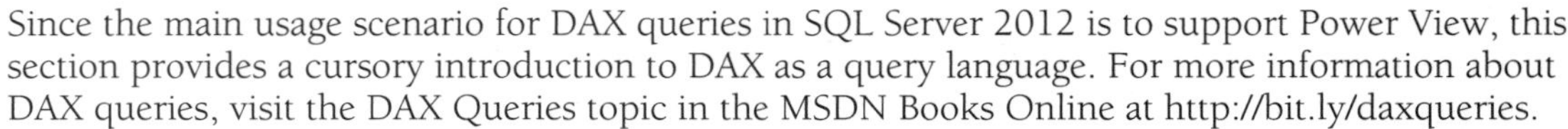

Since the main usage scenario for DAX queries in SQL Server 2012 is to support Power View, this section provides a cursory introduction to DAX as a query language. For more information about DAX queries, visit the DAX Queries topic in the MSDN Books Online at http://bit.ly/daxqueries.

***Understanding the DAX query syntax***

Tabular provides a DAX query variant centered on the EVALUATE clause. The basic DAX query syntax is as follows:

```
[DEFINE {MEASURE <TableName>[<MeasureName>] = <expression>}
EVALUATE <table>
[ORDER BY {<expression> [{ASC | DESC}]}[, ...]
[START AT {<value>|<@parameter>} [, ...]]]
```

Let's explain this syntax one step at a time. The DEFINE clause is an optional clause that allows you to define query-scoped measures using DAX formulas (similar to query-level MDX calculated members in Multidimensional). Similar to explicit measures, you can specify a query-scoped measure by using the TableName[MeasureName] syntax and by entering an expression that returns a single scalar value. A query-scoped measure can reference other query-scoped measures defined before or after that measure.

The EVALUATE clause contains a table expression that returns the query results in a tabular (two-dimensional) format. The expression must return a table. It can reference query-scoped measures that were previously introduced with the DEFINE clause. An optional ORDER BY clause can be added to sort the results.

The optional START AT clause provides a mechanism to request the results at a particular spot in the ordered set. The ORDER BY and START AT clauses are closely related, and you can't use START AT without using ORDER BY. Each item following the START AT clause maps to one of the ORDER BY expressions. The query might specify either a starting value or the name of a parameter that will contain the starting value, such as @Month.

**NOTE** Given the relational nature of Tabular, you might wonder why Microsoft didn't opt for T-SQL as a query language for tabular models instead of the new and proprietary EVALUATE syntax. Although this scenario was strongly considered, SQL is a standard of the American National Standards Institute (ANSI). Therefore, introducing new extensions, which were required to support the Power View interactive features, turned out to be a difficult proposition.

DAX isn't case-sensitive, and you can use upper or lower case, such as *EVALUATE* or *evaluate*. DAX queries don't support multiple axes and pivoting. The report tool is responsible for pivoting the results, such as to present data in a crosstab report, which groups by year on columns.

***Working with basic queries***

You can use SQL Server Management Studio (SSMS) to write and execute DAX queries by following the same steps that you would use to write MDX queries. The Queries.mdx file included in the \Source\Ch10\DAX folder includes the sample DAX queries for this exercise.

1. In SSMS, connect to the Analysis Services Tabular instance.
2. Right-click the Adventure Works database, and then click New Query ⇨ MDX.
3. Enter the following query in the MDX Editor:

```
EVALUATE (ResellerSales)
```

   SSMS hasn't been extended to support DAX queries, and IntelliSense isn't available. Although a red squiggly line underlines the EVALUATE clause, the query syntax is correct.

4. Click the Execute button to run the query. As shown in **Figure 10.21**, this query returns all the rows and columns from the ResellerSales table.

The EVALUATE clause can use any function that returns a table, such as the FILTER function. The following query returns the rows with SalesAmount exceeding 20,000:

```
EVALUATE FILTER(ResellerSales, [SalesAmount]>20000)
```

The following query adds the ORDER BY clause to sort the results by OrderDateKey in an ascending order, followed by SalesAmount in a descending order:

```
EVALUATE FILTER(ResellerSales, [SalesAmount]>20000)
ORDER BY [OrderDateKey], [SalesAmount] DESC
```

The following query uses the START AT clause to limit the results to start at January 1st, 2006 just like a SQL query can use a WHERE clause:

```
EVALUATE FILTER(ResellerSales, [SalesAmount]>20000)
ORDER BY [OrderDateKey], [SalesAmount] DESC
START AT 20060101
```

The following query returns the same results without using the START AT clause.

```
EVALUATE FILTER(ResellerSales, [SalesAmount]>20000 && [OrderDateKey]>=20060101)
ORDER BY [OrderDateKey], [SalesAmount] DESC
```

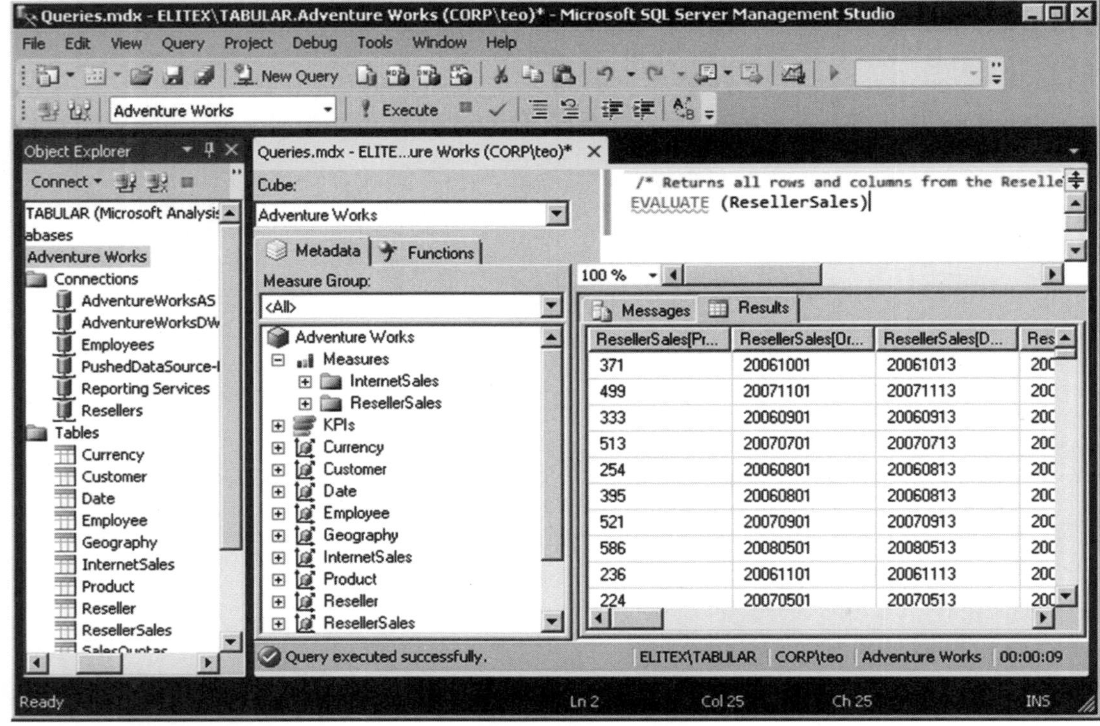


**Figure 10.21** You can use SSMS to write and execute DAX queries.

### *Grouping data*

As with other query languages, DAX queries are capable of aggregating data. The following query uses the SUMMARIZE function, which I introduced in Chapter 6, to group reseller sales by OrderDateKey and ProductKey. It also adds the SumOfSalesAmount and AvgOfSalesAmount columns that calculate the sum and average of the SalesAmount column, as shown in **Figure 10.22**.

```
EVALUATE SUMMARIZE(ResellerSales, [OrderDateKey], [ProductKey],
"SumOfSalesAmount", SUM(ResellerSales[SalesAmount]),
"AvgOfSalesAmount", AVERAGE(ResellerSales[SalesAmount]))
ORDER BY [OrderDateKey], [SumOfSalesAmount] DESC
```

| ResellerSales[OrderDateKey] | ResellerSales[ProductKey] | [SumOfSalesAmount] | [AvgOfSalesAmount] |
|---|---|---|---|
| 20050701 | 350 | 46574.862 | 6653.5517 |
| 20050701 | 348 | 44549.868 | 6364.2669 |
| 20050701 | 351 | 40499.88 | 4499.9867 |
| 20050701 | 319 | 40240.524 | 2515.0328 |
| 20050701 | 349 | 32399.904 | 4049.988 |
| 20050701 | 314 | 30057.468 | 3005.7468 |
| 20050701 | 34 | 28559 | 3173 |

**Figure 10.22** Use the SUMMARIZE function to aggregate data.

The SUMMARIZE function can aggregate by columns in another table. The following query aggregates by the CalendarYear column in the Date table, as shown in **Figure 10.23**:

```
EVALUATE SUMMARIZE('Date', 'Date'[CalendarYear],
"SumOfSalesAmount", SUM(ResellerSales[SalesAmount]),
"AvgOfSalesAmount", AVERAGE(ResellerSales[SalesAmount]))
ORDER BY [CalendarYear], [SumOfSalesAmount] DESC
```

| Date[CalendarYear] | [SumOfSalesAmount] | [AvgOfSalesAmount] |
|---|---|---|
| 2005 | 8065435.3053 | 1949.1144 |
| 2006 | 24144429.654 | 1447.855 |
| 2007 | 32202669.4252 | 1203.4782 |
| 2008 | 16038062.5978 | 1207.4127 |
| 2010 | | |

**Figure 10.23** Use the SUMMARIZE function to aggregate by a related table.

The following query uses the FILTER and ISBLANK functions to remove the row for year 2010, since no sales exist for that year:

```
EVALUATE FILTER (SUMMARIZE('Date', 'Date'[CalendarYear],
"SumOfSalesAmount", SUM(ResellerSales[SalesAmount]),
"AvgOfSalesAmount", AVERAGE(ResellerSales[SalesAmount]))
, NOT(ISBLANK('ResellerSales'[ResellerSalesAmount])))
ORDER BY [CalendarYear], [SumOfSalesAmount] DESC
```

Another way to produce the same results as the previous query is to aggregate on the ResellerSales table. Because the query aggregates this table first, the 2010 year is excluded automatically because it has no data.

```
EVALUATE SUMMARIZE(ResellerSales, 'Date'[CalendarYear],
"SumOfSalesAmount", SUM(ResellerSales[SalesAmount]),
"AvgOfSalesAmount", AVERAGE(ResellerSales[SalesAmount]))
ORDER BY [CalendarYear], [SumOfSalesAmount] DESC
```

Finally, a query can insert a ROLLUP function to get additional rows with aggregations that might be needed for subtotals and grand totals. The following query uses the ROLLUP function to return additional rows with subtotals at a CalendarQuarter level, as shown in **Figure 10.24**. The ISSUBTOTAL function is used to identify these rows.

```
EVALUATE SUMMARIZE(ResellerSales, 'Date'[CalendarYear],
ROLLUP('Date'[CalendarQuarter]),
"SumOfSalesAmount", SUM(ResellerSales[SalesAmount]),
"AvgOfSalesAmount", AVERAGE(ResellerSales[SalesAmount]),
"IsSubtotal", if(ISSUBTOTAL('Date'[CalendarQuarter]), "Yes", "No"))
ORDER BY [CalendarYear], [SumOfSalesAmount] DESC
```

| Date[CalendarYear] | Date[CalendarQuarter] | [SumOfSalesAmount] | [IsSubtotal] |
|---|---|---|---|
| 2005 | | 8065435.3053 | Yes |
| 2005 | 4 | 4871801.3366 | No |
| 2005 | 3 | 3193633.9687 | No |
| 2006 | | 24144429.654 | Yes |
| 2006 | 3 | 8880239.4384 | No |
| 2006 | 4 | 7041183.7534 | No |

**Figure 10.24** The ROLLUP function returns subtotal rows.

***Working with measures***

Suppose you need a query that returns the reseller sales grouped by year. First, you need to group the Date table by year. To do so, use the DISTINCT function to get the distinct years.

```
DISTINCT('Date'[CalendarYear])
```

Or, you could use the SUMMARIZE function. Unlike Transact-SQL (T-SQL), where GROUP BY outperforms DISTINCT, the DAX SUMMARIZE and DISTINCT functions should perform equally well.

```
SUMMARIZE('Date', 'Date'[CalendarYear])
```

Next, you can use the ADDCOLUMNS function to add columns. ADDCOLUMNS is very similar to SUMMARIZE, except that it keeps all the columns in the table expression passed as the first argument. It simply adds calculated columns to that table.

```
EVALUATE ADDCOLUMNS(SUMMARIZE('Date', 'Date'[CalendarYear]),
"Sales", CALCULATE(SUM(ResellerSales[SalesAmount])))
```

| Date[CalendarY... | [Sales] |
|---|---|
| 2005 | 8065435.3053 |
| 2006 | 24144429.654 |
| 2007 | 32202669.4252 |
| 2008 | 16038062.5978 |
| 2010 | |

**Figure 10.25** ADDCOLUMNS adds columns to an existing table.

Now, suppose that you want the query to return the last year's sales as well. This is where you can benefit from refactoring the query and defining the measures. This makes the query easier to read since you avoid using the CALCULATE function in each measure. Moreover, the query is easier to maintain because you can define new measures on top of existing measures, as the following query demonstrates.

```
DEFINE MEASURE ResellerSales[TotalSales] = Sum([SalesAmount])
MEASURE ResellerSales[LastYearSales] = [TotalSales](SAMEPERIODLASTYEAR('Date'[Date]))
EVALUATE ADDCOLUMNS (SUMMARIZE('Date', 'Date'[CalendarYear]),
"TotalSales", [TotalSales], "LastYear", [LastYearSales])
```

First, the query defines a TotalSales query-scoped measure that sums the SalesAmount column. Next, the query defines a LastYearSales measure using the abbreviated syntax <MeasureName> (<optional SetFilters>). For example, the following two expressions are equivalent:

```
CALCULATE ([TotalSales], SamePeriodLastYear('Date'[Date]))
[TotalSales](SamePeriodLastYear('Date'[Date]))
```

The query produces the results shown in **Figure 10.26**.

| Date[CalendarY... | [TotalSales] | [LastYear] |
|---|---|---|
| 2005 | 8065435.3053 | |
| 2006 | 24144429.654 | 8065435.3053 |
| 2007 | 32202669.4252 | 24144429.654 |
| 2008 | 16038062.5978 | 18878869.3757 |
| 2010 | | |

**Figure 10.26** The LastYear column is defined as a query-scoped measure.

### *Tracing queries*

Now that I've introduced you to DAX queries, let me show you how you can use SQL Server Profiler to trace the queries that Power View sends to the server. Once you capture the auto-generated queries, you can study them to enhance your DAX knowledge. In addition, tracing allows you to monitor the query execution times.

**NOTE** Tracing Analysis Services events requires server administrator rights to capture all the events generated by the server, or it requires database administrator rights to see only the events that are associated with that database.

1. Open SQL Server Profiler from the Microsoft SQL Server 2012 ⇨ Performance Tools program group. Or, you can start it from within SSMS by clicking Tools ⇨ SQL Server Profiler.
2. Click File ⇨ New Trace (or press Ctrl+N) to start a new trace.
3. In the "Connect to Server" dialog box, expand the Server Type drop-down list, and then select Analysis Services. In the Server Name field, enter the Analysis Services Tabular instance in the format ServerName\InstanceName, such as ELITEX\TABULAR. Click the Connect button.
4. In the Trace Properties dialog box, accept the default settings, and then click Run to start the trace.
5. In SharePoint, navigate to PowerPivot Gallery, and then click the Adventure Works Dashboard report. As SharePoint processes the report, you should see various events in SQL Server Profiler, including Query Begin and Query End events, as shown in **Figure 10.27**.

| EventClass | EventSubclass | TextData | NTUserName | Duration | ConnectionID |
|---|---|---|---|---|---|
| Query Begin | 3 - DAXQuery | EVALUATE CALCULATETABLE( SUMM... | teo | | 100 |
| Query End | 3 - DAXQuery | EVALUATE CALCULATETABLE( SUMM... | teo | 341 | 100 |
| Query Begin | 3 - DAXQuery | EVALUATE CALCULATETABLE( ADDC... | teo | | 100 |
| Query End | 3 - DAXQuery | EVALUATE CALCULATETABLE( ADDC... | teo | 65 | 100 |
| Query Begin | 3 - DAXQuery | EVALUATE CALCULATETABLE( ADDC... | teo | | 100 |
| Query End | 3 - DAXQuery | EVALUATE CALCULATETABLE( ADDC... | teo | 20 | 100 |

```
EVALUATE
  CALCULATETABLE(
    ADDCOLUMNS(
      KEEPFILTERS(
        TOPN(
          1002,
          FILTER(
            KEEPFILTERS(
              SUMMARIZE(
                KEEPFILTERS(VALUES('Employee')),
                'Employee'[FullName],
                "ResellerSalesAmount_FullName", 'ResellerSales'[ResellerSalesAmount]
              )
            ),
            OR(
              NOT(ISBLANK('ResellerSales'[ResellerSalesAmount])),
              NOT(ISBLANK('ResellerSales'[SalesPersonKPITarget]))
            )
          ),
          [ResellerSalesAmount_FullName],
          0,
          'Employee'[FullName],
          1
        )
      ),
      "ResellerSalesAmount", 'ResellerSales'[ResellerSalesAmount],
      "SalesPersonKPITarget", 'ResellerSales'[SalesPersonKPITarget]
    ),
```

**Figure 10.27** Use SQL Server Profiler to trace DAX queries.

6. The server generates a Query Begin event when it receives the query and a Query End event when the query is processed. The Duration column shows you the query execution time in milliseconds. The NTUserName column displays the Windows logon of the interactive user. And, the

TextData column includes the actual query text. I have selected the query that Power View generates to populate the Employee Sales vs. Target chart. There are a few DAX functions that deserve more explanation so that you can better understand how Power View generates queries.
The CALCULATETABLE function (CALCULATETABLE(<expression>, <filter1>, <filter2>, ...) is similar to the CALCULATE function, except that the expression and the result are both tables. CALCULATETABLE changes the context in which the data is filtered, and it evaluates the expression in the new context that's specified by the filter arguments. For each column used in a filter argument, any existing filters on that column are removed, and the filter arguments are applied instead. In other words, CALCULATETABLE changes the filter context and then constructs a table in that new context.

The KEEPFILTERS function preserves any previous filters so that both the new and previous filters are applied. Suppose you want to filter the table T on the column C. The following expression returns rows from T where [C] = 1 or [C] = 2. Only the latest (innermost) filter takes effect.

```
CALCULATETABLE(CALCULATETABLE (T, T[C]=1 || T[C]=2), T[C]=2 || T[C]=3)
```

Whereas, the next formula returns rows from T where [C] = 2. In other words, KEEPFILTERS returns the intersection of both filters.

```
CALCULATETABLE(CALCULATETABLE(T, KEEPFILTERS(T[C]=1 || T[C]=2)), T[C]=2 || T[C]=3)
```

Power View uses the TOPN function to return data in chunks of 1,002 rows at a time. As you scroll down row-based visualizations, such as tables or matrices, Power View fetches more rows as needed.

## 10.4 Summary

This chapter introduced you to organizational BI with Analysis Services Tabular. Consider "upgrading" to organizational BI when you've outgrown the PowerPivot capabilities and your operational requirements demand scalability and security. The good news is that you can seamlessly transition your PowerPivot design knowledge from personal BI to organizational models.

As a BI pro, you would use SQL Server Data Tools (SSDT) to design tabular models. SSDT supports three ways to create Analysis Services Tabular projects: import from existing PowerPivot workbooks, create a new project, or reverse-engineer the project source from an existing Analysis Services database. Project development requires a live Analysis Services Tabular instance to host the workspace database. Once the model is ready, you can deploy it to a dedicated Analysis Services Tabular instance to make it available for reporting. Once the model is deployed, you can author the same type of reports as you do with published PowerPivot workbooks. This chapter walked you through the steps to implement a Power View dashboard report, and it introduced you to DAX queries.

So far, you haven't seen any new features that are specific to Analysis Services Tabular. This will change in the next chapter, where you'll learn why Analysis Services Tabular is the preferred choice for implementing organizational models.

Chapter 11

# Designing Storage and Security



Organizational business intelligence (BI) might pose interesting challenges related to larger data volumes and stricter security restrictions. Analysis Services Tabular supports features that help you tackle advanced requirements. Partitions allow you to process data selectively. When real-time data access is needed, you can configure the model in a special pass-through mode to send queries directly to the data source. And, you can apply row-level security to allow end users to see only the data that they're authorized to view.

This chapter discusses different ways to configure the storage of tabular models. It shows you how to partition large tables and discusses different options to refresh data. Next, it explains how you can configure DirectQuery settings to implement low-latency tabular models. Finally, you'll learn how to implement security roles that restrict data the user can view. You'll find the sample projects in the Ch11 folder. If you haven't done already, follow the steps in Chapter 10 to implement the Adventure Works and Call Center models.

## 11.1 Designing VertiPaq Storage

Tabular supports two main storage modes:

- Cached (VertiPaq) – This is the default storage mode for organizational models and the only storage option for PowerPivot. Remember that by default Tabular imports and caches data. Data is first saved to disk on the server (or the user's computer with PowerPivot) and then loaded into the VertiPaq in-memory engine. To reduce the storage footprint, data is highly compressed. The cached storage mode is the default mode because it gives you the best query performance. However, you have to process (refresh) the model periodically in order to synchronize it with changes in the data sources.
- DirectQuery – This mode is supported by organization models only. When the model is configured for DirectQuery, the server generates and sends queries to the data source. The DirectQuery mode doesn't require the data to be imported in the model. Section 11.2 discusses the inner workings and limitations of the DirectQuery mode.

As you've probably guessed, choosing a storage mode is a tradeoff between query performance, data latency, and functionality. Next, I'll discuss options to get the most out of the VertiPaq storage mode, including partitioning large tables and optimizing processing.

**NOTE** Readers familiar with Multidimensional might remember that it supports three storage modes (MOLAP, HOLAP, and ROLAP). Think of the VertiPaq storage mode as the equivalent of MOLAP and of DirectQuery as the equivalent of ROLAP. As it stands, Tabular doesn't support aggregations (pre-calculated summaries of data).

### 11.1.1 Understanding Partitions

Analysis Services stores data in physical units called *partitions*. A partition defines the slice of the source data that's loaded into a table. By default, a table has only one partition that contains all data from the source table in the data source. While a Tabular table with one partition is the easiest to design and understand, it might not be necessarily optimized, particularly as the table grows larger. Creating additional partitions can benefit larger tables in two ways:

- Reduced processing times – With larger data volumes, partitions provide the means to import data selectively and reduce data processing-time windows in order to meet service level agreements. For example, if a fact table in the data warehouse undergoes changes for the latest month only, you can process the most recent partition instead of the entire table to synchronize the data changes in your model.
- Improved manageability – Partitions can be managed independently. For example, you can delete a partition, change the partition slice, and merge partitions without having to reprocess the model. Another example when partitions can be beneficial from a manageability standpoint is to reduce the time to synchronize two models, such as to synchronize only the changed data between two servers that are physically located in separate regions.

Partitioning is available in all of the three SQL Server editions that include Tabular: Enterprise, Business Intelligence, and Developer.

***Choosing a partition slice***

You would typically partition time-dependent tables that include a date column or are related to a Date table. Therefore, a natural strategy would be to partition by date, such as by year, quarter, or month. Determining the partition slice definition – that is, the number of rows stored in the partition—is not an exact science. It all depends on how granular you want data processing to be and depends on your manageability goals. How often do you need to fetch new data and at what granularity, such as hour, day, week, month, and so on? How often do you clear your old data? What is your processing-time window?

In general, it's preferable to have fewer partitions in a table. Because Tabular can't process partitions in parallel, having many partitions doesn't help you reduce the time to process a table. Here are some general guidelines for partitioning tables:

- For smaller tables (less than 100 million rows), don't partition at all assuming that fully processing the entire table completes within the desired processing-time window.
- For larger tables, aim for no more than 100 partitions. A large number of partitions might overwhelm the server's data management and retrieval jobs.

**Figure 11.1** shows three partition definitions. In the first case, the table is partitioned by year and the partition slices are uniform. Uniform slice definitions are the most common because they are easier to set up and manage. This doesn't have to be the case though. For example, the second table has more granular partitions for newer data. This strategy allows you to implement volatile "hot" partitions that stores the most recent data and can be processed faster and more frequently than older partitions.

Partitions need not use a single table as a source. The third example shows a table that has three partitions mapped to different source tables. In this case, the containing table essentially combines actual, budget, and scenario data into a single table. As long as the source tables have the same schema, you can bind partitions to separate tables. Another application of this design is having a partition bound to a separate SQL view or to a table that returns new data only.

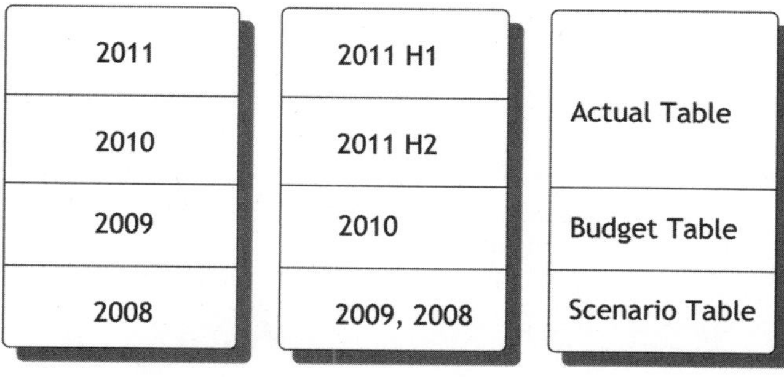


**Figure 11.1** This diagram shows three different partitioning strategies.

**NOTE** Readers with a Multidimensional background likely know that Multidimensional supports partitioning measure groups (fact tables) only. Since all tables are equal citizens in Tabular, this restriction is removed and you can partition any table in a tabular model, such as a large Customer lookup (dimension) table.

You can partition tables that obtain data from any data source that supports row filters, including text files. You can't partition tables whose data was imported from linked Excel tables, data feeds, or pasted from the Windows Clipboard.

Partition Manager

Use partitions to divide a table into logical parts that can be processed independently.

Table: CallCenter

Search Partition Names

| Partition Name | # Rows | Size (KB) | Last Processed |
|---|---|---|---|
| FactCallCenter | 120 | 2 | 12/3/2011 10:36:56 AM |

New | Copy | Delete

Details - FactCallCenter

Partition Name: FactCallCenter

Connection: AdventureWorksDW

Source Name: dbo.FactCallCenter | Refresh Preview

Query Editor

Table Preview

| FactCallCenterID | DateKey | WageType | Shift | LevelOneOperators | LevelT | TotalO |
|---|---|---|---|---|---|---|
| 1 | 20101101 | weekday | AM | 2 | | |
| 2 | 20101101 | weekday | PM1 | 2 | 10 | |
| 3 | 20101101 | weekday | PM2 | 3 | 11 | |
| 4 | 20101101 | weekday | midnight | 1 | 4 | |
| 5 | 20101102 | weekday | AM | 2 | 8 | |
| 6 | 20101102 | weekday | PM1 | 3 | 10 | |
| 7 | 20101102 | weekday | PM2 | 3 | 12 | |

Clear Row Filters

Last Processed: 12/3/2011 10:36:56 AM

OK | Cancel

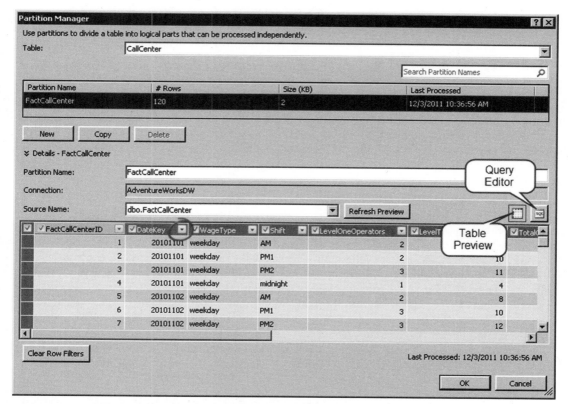

**Figure 11.2** Use Partition Manager to change the table partition design.

***Understanding Partition Manager***

After you decide on the partition slice range, you're ready to partition the table. You can create partitions during the design cycle by using SQL Server Data Tools (SSDT) or after the model is deployed by using SQL Server Management Studio (SSMS). Although these two options have somewhat different user interfaces, they both produce the same results. In general, you would use SSDT if you wanted your partition design to be included in the project, but to change the partition design after the model is deployed, the administrator might prefer to use SSMS. **Figure 11.2** shows Partition Manager which is included in SSDT. To open Partition Manager, select a table, and then click the Partitions button in the Analysis Services toolbar. Or, click Table ⇨ Partitions.

As I mentioned, by default, a table has a single (default) partition that loads all the rows from the source table. This is why the Partitions section shows only one partition that has the same name as the source table. In addition, the Partition section shows the number of rows loaded in the partition, the partition size in kilobytes, and the last time its data was processed (refreshed). If new partitions use the same source table, before adding a new partition, you must first narrow the slice of the default partition to leave space for new partitions.

***Setting a partition slice***

If you're loading data from a relational database and you don't use a custom query, you have two options to configure the partition slice, which you can toggle by clicking the Table Preview and Query Editor buttons. With the Table Preview mode, you can specify the partition slice interactively by setting up row filters. This is very similar to filtering data upon import. For example, to partition by date, expand the drop-down list in the DateKey column header, click Number Filters ⇨ Between, and then specify the range criteria in the Custom Filter dialog box that follows.

**TIP** Besides using Partition Manager, another way to change the default partition slice is to set up a row filter in the table definition and then reload the data. You can set up an import filter in the Table Properties dialog box (Table menu ⇨ Table Properties). This approach works if there is only one (default) partition in the table.

Another option to set up a partition slice is to switch to the Query Editor mode (click the Query Editor button), and then manually specify the partition slice query. This requires entering a SQL SELECT statement with a WHERE clause. For example, the following SELECT statement selects rows for January 2010 only assuming that the DateKey column is of an integer data type and uses the YYYYMMDD convention:

```
SELECT * FROM [dbo].[FactCallCenter] WHERE [DateKey] BETWEEN 20100101 AND 20100199
```

The Query Editor mode is the only option if the table uses a custom query to load data. If you decide to switch to query mode after you've set up a Table Preview filter, Partition Manager will auto-generate the WHERE clause. While in the Query Editor mode, you can click the Validate button (not shown in **Figure 11.2**) to validate that the SELECT statement is syntactically correct. If you struggle with the query syntax, click the Design button (not shown in **Figure 11.2**) to open the familiar query designer (see Section 3.2.2 in Chapter 3). Remember that the query designer allows you to write the query statement and to execute the query to see the results. If you target SQL Server, the query designer supports a graphical mode. Remember that once you've switched to Query Mode to set up the partition slice, you can't go back to the Table Preview mode without losing the changes that you've made to the query.

***Creating new partitions***

Once you've changed the default partition, adding the rest of the partitions is a matter of few simple steps, as follows (here, I just mention the steps; the actual exercise is in Section 11.1.3):

1. Click the Copy button to copy the definition of an existing partition.

2. Set the partition slice using Table Preview or Query Editor.
3. Rename the new partition to have a more descriptive name, such as *FactCallCenter 201002* for a partition that loads February 2010 data.
4. Repeat the above steps to add partitions that cover all the date periods in the table.
5. Consider creating extra partitions that cover future time periods, such as a few extra years. For the last partition, I suggest you use a partition query with an open-ended WHERE clause, such as DateKey >= 20150101, to include all the future periods, in case the modeler ever "forgets" to add a new partition in time.

Be extra careful when you define the partition slice query. The partition slice query determines what table rows will be loaded into the partition. When adding a new partition, specify a correct WHERE clause so that no rows are lost or duplicated. For example, suppose that you copy a partition for January 2010 but forgot to change the partition query. When you process the two partitions, you'll find that the data for January 2010 is loaded twice and you won't get a warning about this issue.

**REAL LIFE** I was called once to help with an existing cube after the resident BI developer had left the company. The cube was supposed to go live but testers kept discovering strange defects. As it turned out, two cube partitions had identical slice queries, and the data was duplicated. After fixing this issue, many QA defects magically disappeared. Triple verify the partition slice queries!

As I mentioned, you can bind partitions to different tables or SQL views to present these tables as a single logical table to the end user, such as an AccountBalances SQL view that consolidates Actual, Budget, and Scenario tables. Assuming the tables have the same schema, to change the partition table binding, simply expand the Source Name drop-down list (see **Figure 11.2** again), and then select the appropriate source table.

***Changing the table definition***

Once you've partitioned a table, changing the table definition using the Edit Table Properties dialog box (Table menu ⇨ Table Properties) becomes somewhat trickier than a table with only one partition or than PowerPivot. That's because table changes are not automatically synchronized with the partition design. Specifically, the following changes require manual intervention:

- Row filtering – Setting a row filter in the Edit Table Properties dialog box has no effect on a partitioned table. Even though you can see the filter in the Edit Table Properties dialog box, it's ignored at processing time. Instead, the partition definition queries are used to filter the data.
- Adding a column – As with PowerPivot and a single-partition table, you must use the Edit Table Properties dialog box to add a column to a table. However, you must also update the definition of each partition to include the new column. If you don't, you'll get the following error upon process: "The operation failed because the source doesn't contain the requested column. You can fix this problem by updating the column mappings."
- Removing a column – Removing a column in the Edit Table Properties dialog box removes that column from the table definition. However, for a partitioned table, you should exclude the column from the partition definition query to avoid unnecessary data that's coming down the wire during processing.

To warn you about these conditions, the Edit Table Properties dialog box displays the following message with partitioned tables:

This table has partitions. If you make changes to the set of columns in the table using this dialog, you must use Partition Manager to update the partition definitions to match. Do not set row filters in this dialog. Use Partition Manager to update the set of rows in the table instead.

**TIP** As a best practice, avoid using custom queries to import data so that you don't have to synchronize partition queries with table definition changes. Instead, if you source data from a relational database, use a SQL view to wrap the source table and to only return the columns you need to import. Then, the partition slice query could use the "SELECT * FROM" syntax to return all the columns.

## 11.1.2 Understanding Processing

Processing (or refreshing) a model is the act of loading the model with data. Remember that the default storage mode for a tabular model is VertiPaq. VertiPaq caches the source data in the computer main memory. Since VertiPaq doesn't automatically synchronize the model with changes in the data sources, you must process the model objects explicitly to apply any changes.

***Understanding processing options***

A database contains one or more tables. A table contains one or more partitions. Data is loaded in partitions. To meet different requirements for processing-time windows, Tabular supports several processing options, as follows:

- Process Default – Detects the state of the object, and then it performs the minimum processing that's necessary to bring the object to a fully processed state. For example, processing a new partition with Process Default will load the partition data and then recalculate any related objects, such as relationships, hierarchies, and calculated columns. This option doesn't detect whether data has changed in the data source. It simply detects and processes any unprocessed objects.
- Process Full – Discards existing storage, and it processes the object and all the objects that it contains. This type of processing is required when a structural change has been made to an object, such as after you add a new column. Fully processing a database processes all of its tables and partitions. Process Full Process full is also useful to eliminate fragmentation (see the Process Defrag option below).
- Process Data – Loads data without rebuilding related objects (hierarchies, relationships, and calculated columns). Use Process Data when you need to process specific partitions, followed by Process Recalc on the database to rebuild related objects.
- Process Clear – Discards the storage content of an object. This option can be useful when you want to empty specific partitions without deleting them, such as when you need to experiment with different data loads and when you need to test the model performance.
- Process Add – Adds rows to a table or a partition. Use this option to process a partition incrementally by loading only new rows. Process Add doesn't handle deletes or updates. It only adds rows from another table or by using a filter condition that returns the new rows. Be careful with Process Add because it doesn't check for existing rows, so you might end up duplicating rows each time you process the partition. In other words, make sure that the partition slice query returns new rows only.
- Process Recalc – This is a new option that's specific for tabular models, and it doesn't have a Multidimensional equivalent. Process Recalc rebuilds certain database-level objects, such as hierarchies, relationships, and calculated columns, which are invalidated after Process Add, Process Clear, and Process Data. Any time after you use any of these processing options, you must use the Process Recalc option.
- Process Defrag – This is another processing option that's specific to Tabular. Incrementally adding and deleting many partitions to a table will result in table dictionary (.dictionary) files

that are growing continuously. Similar to defragmenting a SQL Server index, this option defragments dictionaries to remove entries that no longer exist in the data, and then it rebuilds the partition data based on the new dictionaries. Imagine the situation where you have 12 partitions and based on your rolling processing-time window, you drop the first partition (January 2011) and then add another one for January 2012. Now many of the column values that were referenced by the January 2011 partition might no longer be referenced by any rows in the table even though there might not be any rows in the table that reference these values. Process Defrag explicitly cleans up those useless entries in order to save space and to improve performance. However, note that the algorithm used for defragmentation uses a lot of memory (more than for actually processing data), so be careful with this option. It isn't necessary to defragment a table if you fully process the table every once in a while.

**NOTE** Readers familiar with Multidimensional are probably curious about the absence of the Process Update option that's used to update a dimension with new, changed, and deleted members without invalidating cubes. Process Update is an expensive option because it has to reimport all the data and compare it with all the original data in the dimension so that it can keep the old data identifiers (DataIDs). In addition, Process Update on a dimension would require Process Indexes on partitions to restore indexes and aggregations in order to avoid fully reprocessing all the partition data. Due to architectural changes in Tabular, you can now fully re-process a table without having to process other tables. Therefore, Process Update isn't needed.

**Table 11.1** shows how these processing options apply to tabular objects.

**Table 11.1 Processing options supported by Tabular and how they apply to objects.**

| Object | Process Default | Process Full | Process Data | Process Clear | Process Add | Process Recalc | Process Defrag |
|---|---|---|---|---|---|---|---|
| Database | ✓ | ✓ | | ✓ | | ✓ | (via script) |
| Table | ✓ | ✓ | ✓ | ✓ | | | ✓ |
| Partition | ✓ | ✓ | ✓ | ✓ | ✓ | | |

### *Understanding processing scenarios*

Let's go through a few scenarios to understand how to apply these processing options. Suppose that you have a relatively small database, and refreshing all the tables takes a few minutes. You need a simple way to process all the data in the model. As with Multidimensional, fully processing (Process Full) the entire database is the easiest and cleanest way to process the entire database.

Suppose that your model has grown in size, and now you need a more lightweight option to reduce the processing-time window. Let's say only some recent data in the FactInternetSales table has undergone changes. You need to process only the recent partitions of FactInternetSales and all related lookup (dimension) tables whose data might have changed too. Process the latest FactInternetSales partitions and related lookup tables with Process Data, followed by processing the database with Process Recalc.

Finally, suppose that only new data is added to the FactCallCenter table. Again, you're after the fastest processing option that lets you import only new rows in FactCallCenter and to synchronize changes to any related lookup tables. There are different ways to meet this requirement. The easiest way is to set up a SQL view that returns only the new rows and then to create a new partition that's bound to the view and that you process with Process Add. This new partition can then be merged with an existing partition if you'd like. You need to process the related lookup tables with Process Data, followed by Process Recalc on the database. If you do this frequently, you'll want to use Process Defrag too.

**NOTE** Only SSMS gives you the ability to merge partitions. To merge partitions, right-click the table, and then click Partitions. In the Partitions dialog box, select the partitions that you want to merge, and then click the Merge button. In the Merge Partitions dialog box, review the changes, and then click OK.

***Considerations for processing partitions***

Now that you know about processing objects, let's go back to partitions and see how you can process partitions during the design cycle. Remember that changing the partition design is a metadata (not data) operation. SSDT doesn't immediately start the process of reloading the model data into the new partitions to reflect changes to the partition design. **Figure 11.3** shows that the InternetSales table has two partitions prefixed with asterisks (*) as a visual clue to indicate that the partition design isn't saved yet.

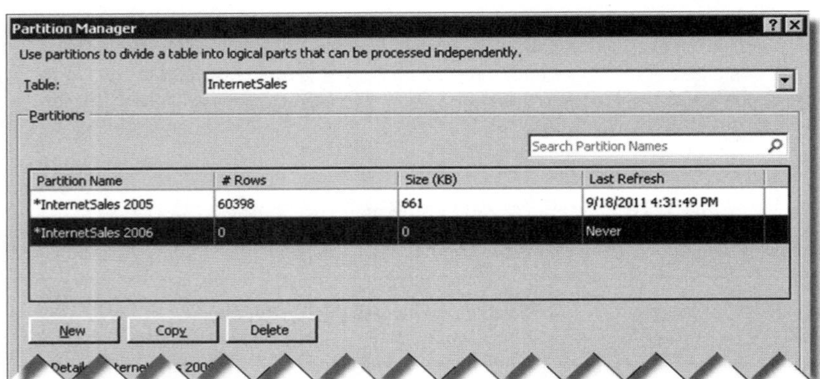


**Figure 11.3** Changing the partition design is a metadata operation that doesn't affect the data.

The default partition still has 60,398 rows, while the second partition doesn't have any rows because it hasn't been refreshed (processed). You must explicitly process partitions to reflect changes to the partition design. You can initiate the processing task from the Process Partitions drop-down button on the Analysis Services toolbar, as shown in **Figure 11.4**.

You're probably already familiar with two of the processing options from PowerPivot. Process Table fully processes the active table and reloads all the partitions with source data. Process All fully processes all tables. The Process Partitions option is specific to organizational models because only organizational models can have partitions. This option opens the Process Partitions dialog box, which allows you to specify a processing option and to select which partitions you want to process. When in doubt about which processing option to choose, accept the default option, Process Default. Or, don't use Process Partitions at all, and use the Process Table option instead to reload the entire table.

**NOTE** Unlike Multidimensional, Tabular can't process partitions within a table in parallel. It can only process partitions across tables in parallel. So, while partitions across TableA and TableB will be processed simultaneously, the partitions within TableA (and TableB) will be read sequentially, one at a time. Therefore, the processing time for a Tabular model is likely to take much longer than Multidimensional. On the positive side, you'll save some time because you no longer have to process indexes (ProcessIndex) on partitions after updating (ProcessUpdate) tables, as you have to do with Multidimensional.

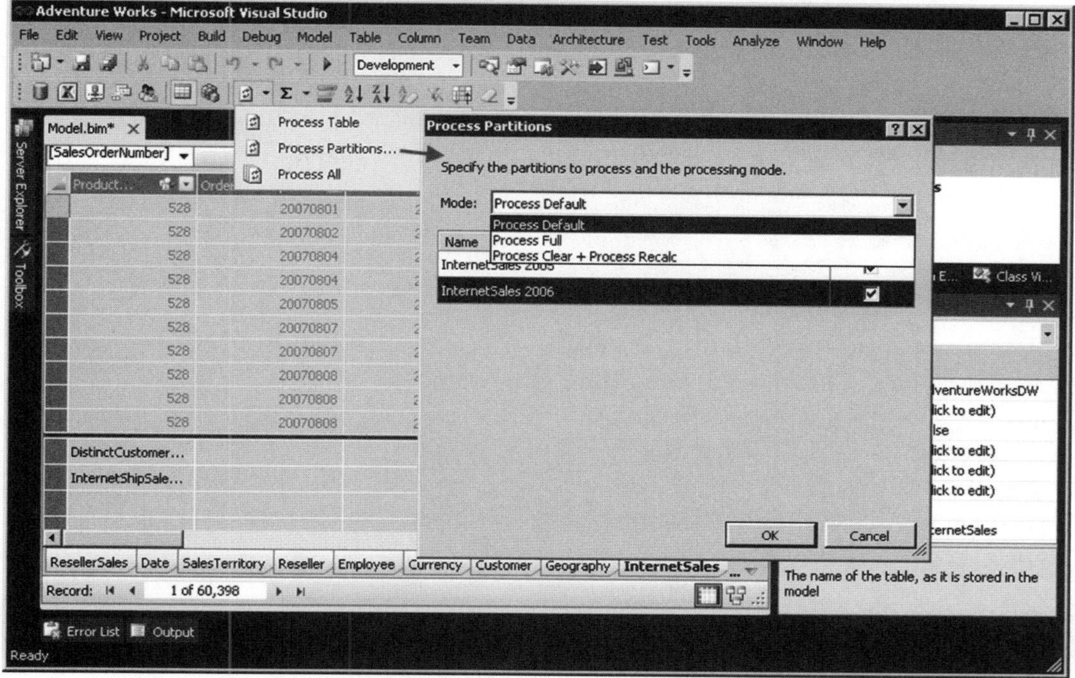


**Figure 11.4** Use the Process Partitions dialog box to process partitions.

**TIP** Suppose that you work with a large table during the development lifecycle. You can process only the first (default) partition, and then leave the rest of the partitions unprocessed (use Process Clear to delete their data if you have previously imported any data). To use the rest of the partitions, simply deploy the project to a dedicated server. Now you have a small dataset for development and a large dataset for testing. This works because design changes are applied to the workspace database. When you deploy the project to a dedicated server, Process Default in project properties will load all the partitions. For this strategy to be effective, remember to filter the data in the Table Import Wizard; otherwise you'll just waste time importing all the data only to drop it later.

## 11.1.3 Working with Partitions

Now that you know about the benefits of partitioning, you'll partition the ResellerSales and InternetSales tables in the Adventure Works model that you implemented in Chapter 10. These tables load data for four years (2005 to 2008). Suppose that the corresponding fact tables in the data warehouse store about 200 million rows each with an estimated growth of 50 million rows per year. Given the size of these data loads, suppose that you decide to partition the tables by year.

***Partitioning tables***

Start by partitioning the ResellerSales table. Follow these steps:

1. Open the Adventure Works project from the Ch10 folder in SSDT.
2. Click the ResellerSales table to make it active, and then click the Partitions button in the Analysis Services toolbar to open Partition Manager. Or, expand the Table menu, and then click Partitions.

3. Notice that the default partition is named "_Count ResellerSales" and it has the same SELECT statement as the custom query that's used to load the ResellerSales table. In the Partition Name field, overwrite the default name to *ResellerSales 2005*.
4. Since the ResellerSales table uses a custom query to load data, the only option to configure the partition slice is to use Query Editor. In the SQL Statement field, scroll until the end of the query, and then add the following WHERE clause to load the data for the year 2005 only:

```
. . .
FROM
 DimProduct INNER JOIN FactResellerSales
  ON DimProduct.ProductKey = FactResellerSales.ProductKey
WHERE OrderDateKey BETWEEN 20050101 AND 20051299
```

5. Click the Validate button to check the query syntax.
6. Click the Copy button three times to create three new partitions.
7. Rename the second partition to *ResellerSales 2006*, the third partition to *ResellerSales 2007*, and the fourth partition to *ResellerSales 2008*.
8. Change the WHERE clause in the partition queries of the new partitions to return data for years 2006, 2007, and 2008, as shown in **Figure 11.5**. Click OK to close Partition Manager.

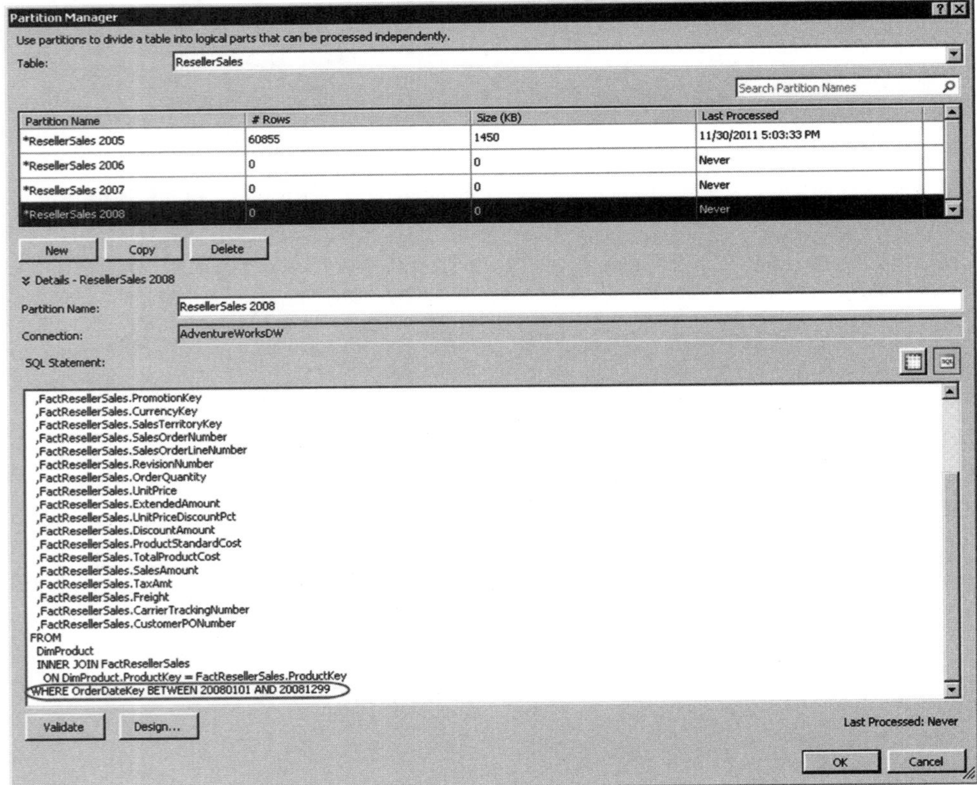


**Figure 11.5** The ResellerSales 2008 partition loads data for year 2008.

9. Follow similar steps to partition the InternetSales table by year.

### *Processing partitions*

Next, you'll process the partitions to load them with data.

1. Switch to the ResellerSales table.
2. Expand the Process Partitions drop-down menu on the Analysis Services toolbar, and then click Process Table.

   SSDT opens the Data Processing dialog box that shows the status of the process operation. If all is well, you should see a successful message that 60,855 rows were transferred. This is the total number of rows in the ResellerSales table that is now split into four partitions.
3. Click the Partitions toolbar button to open Partition Manager again, as shown in **Figure 11.6**. Notice that Partition Manager shows the number of rows and size next to each partition. This confirms that the partitions are loaded with data. Close the Partition Manager.

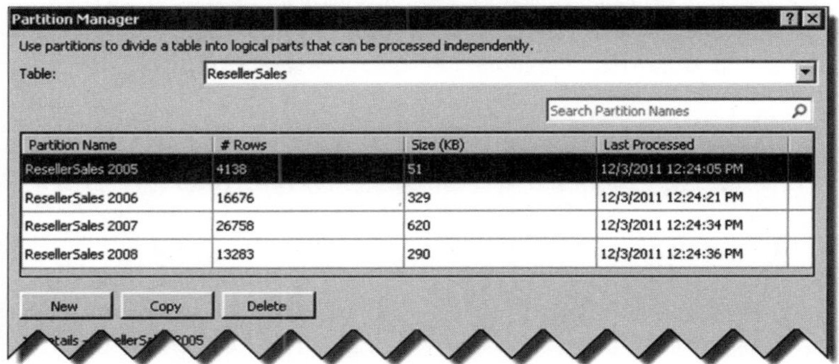


**Figure 11.6** Once partitions are processed, Partition Manager shows the number of rows loaded and the partition size.

4. Expand the Table menu, and then click Table Properties. Notice that the Table Properties dialog box shows the following message:

   This table has partitions. If you make changes to the set of columns in the table using this dialog, you must use Partition Manager to update the partition definitions to match. Do not set row filters in this dialog. Use Partition Manager to update the set of rows in the table instead.

   This message is displayed because the table uses a custom query to load data. As I explained, if you change the table definition, you must update the partition queries as well.

**TIP** Setting up many partitions manually is a tedious and error-prone process. I wrote the "Partition Generator for Multidimensional Cubes" code sample (http://bit.ly/partitiongenerator) to automate the process for Multidimensional. You can build a similar utility to auto-generate partitions for tabular models if you find that you have to do this often.

## 11.2 Designing DirectQuery Storage

The default VertiPaq in-memory store is the preferred storage mode when the model fits into memory because it's optimized for fast data retrieval and aggregation. However, it has also the following drawbacks:

- Data latency – Once you take a data "snapshot" by processing the model, the data becomes stale until you reprocess again. How much data latency is acceptable will depend on your operational requirements. In some cases, your end-users might mandate up-to-date (even real-time) information.
- Not enough memory – As you know by now, VertiPaq works best when all data resides in memory because performance degrades when data is paged to disk.

- Startup delay – When you restart the Analysis Services server, VertiPaq must load the model from disk and this operation can be time-consuming.

To address these challenges, Analysis Services Tabular supports another storage mode called DirectQuery, which I'll discuss next.

**NOTE** Readers familiar with Multidimensional might recall that it supports a mechanism called proactive caching to implement low-latency OLAP cubes. Proactive caching isn't supported with Tabular and you can't configure a Tabular model to monitor data changes and synchronize the VertiPaq cache automatically.

## 11.2.1 Understanding DirectQuery

As its name suggests, DirectQuery generates and passes queries directly to the data source. As a result, DirectQuery is to Tabular as what Relational OLAP (ROLAP) is to Multidimensional. It avoids processing the model and allows users to see the latest changes in the data source.

***VertiPaq and DirectQuery***

To understand how DirectQuery works, it might make sense to compare it with VertiPaq. **Figure 11.7** shows the high-level flow for each mode. When the model is configured for VertiPaq, clients can send DAX or MDX queries. The Analysis Services Formula Engine parses the query and then sends requests to the VertiPaq in-memory store to retrieve the data. By contrast, DirectQuery supports DAX queries only. When the server receives a DAX query sent to a model that's configured for DirectQuery, it translates the query to one or more SQL SELECT statements. The server than passes these statements to the data store (only SQL Server is supported at this time) to retrieve the data in real time and to send the results back to the client.

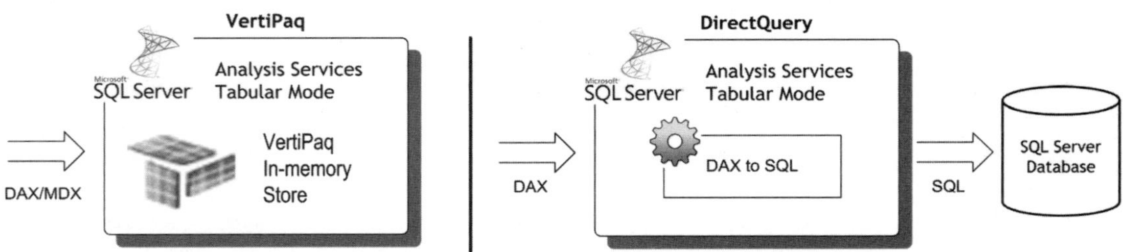


**Figure 11.7** This figure compares the VertiPaq and DirectQuery storage modes.

***When to use DirectQuery***

The primary scenario for using DirectQuery is to implement BI solutions for real-time data access. One approach to reduce data latency for a VertiPaq model is to process it more frequently. However, some scenarios might require reducing the data latency even further. For example, the Adventure Works business users might prefer to analyze the call-center activity in real time as customers place new calls to determine if the current call volume requires adding more customer service representatives.

Another scenario that might benefit from DirectQuery is analyzing large volumes of data that might not fit in the server memory. For example, you might have a data warehouse with billions of rows that you need to report on and you might not have enough memory on the server to load all the data. Even if there is enough memory to accommodate the VertiPaq cache, you might want to avoid processing such large datasets. While DirectQuery might look like a great solution to overcome these challenges, you must keep an eye on performance. For example, ad-hoc reporting typically precludes any type of preemptive database optimization and indexing because end users can request any column on the report. Since DirectQuery generates and passes through SQL queries to the database, the report performance could degrade when the query aggregates millions of rows.

**TIP** SQL Server 2012 introduces an impressive query acceleration feature that's based on a new type of indexes, called columnstore indexes. Behind the scenes, columnstore indexes use the same VertiPaq technology that powers Tabular. Columnstore indexes and DirectQuery make a great combination that can provide near-instantaneous response time for massive queries, which otherwise could take minutes to execute. For more information about columnstore indexes, read the "Columnstore Indexes for Fast Data Warehouse Query Processing in SQL Server 11" whitepaper at http://bit.ly/columnstore, and watch the "Columnstore Indexes Unveiled" presentation at http://bit.ly/columnstoreteched, both by Eric Hanson, Microsoft SQL Server Program Manager.

### *Understanding DirectQuery limitations*

In this first release, DirectQuery is an experimental feature that's subject to the following limitations:

- DAX queries only – A model configured for DirectQuery supports only DAX queries. As you know, among the Microsoft-provided reporting tools, only Power View generates DAX queries. Therefore, only Power View can use a Tabular model configured for DirectQuery.
- SQL Server only – A model configured for DirectQuery can have only one data source and that data source must be SQL Server (2005 or above).
- No calculated columns – The model can't have calculated columns, although it can have calculated measures.
- Unsupported DAX functions – Not all DAX functions are supported in DirectQuery mode. The most important subset of DAX functions unsupported in DirectQuery mode is time intelligence functions. Some Excel functions have restrictions on types or values of arguments. A small subset of Excel functions, which are impossible to translate to SQL, is not supported. For more information about the DAX support for DirectQuery, review the "Formula Compatibility in Direct Query Mode" Books Online topic at http://bit.ly/DirectQueryDAX.
- No mixed mode within the model – DirectQuery must be enabled for the entire model. You can't configure a subset of the model in DirectQuery, such as selected tables or partitions, while leaving the rest in VertiPaq. Don't confuse this with the hybrid modes that I'll discuss in a moment, which allow a report client to switch between VertiPaq and DirectQuery.
- No data security – DirectQuery doesn't support row-level security (this is discussed in Section 11.3). Instead, you need to rely on SQL Server security to protect sensitive data. As a result, the database administrator must decide how to handle data security, such as by creating SQL Server logins with the required rights or by enabling Windows security. For more information about designing data security, read the whitepaper, "Implementing Row- and Cell-Level Security in Classified Databases", by Art Rask at http://bit.ly/sqldatasecurity.
- No caching – Analysis Services doesn't perform any additional caching on the server, such as caching the query results from the generated SQL SELECT statements. In other words, even identical DAX queries result in SQL queries to the data source.

Now that I've introduced you to DirectQuery and its limitations, let's see how to enable it.

### *Enabling DirectQuery*

As a prerequisite for using DirectQuery, you must first tell SQL Server Data Tools (SSDT) that you intend to use it. You do this by changing the DirectQuery Mode model-level property from Off to On, as shown in **Figure 11.8**.

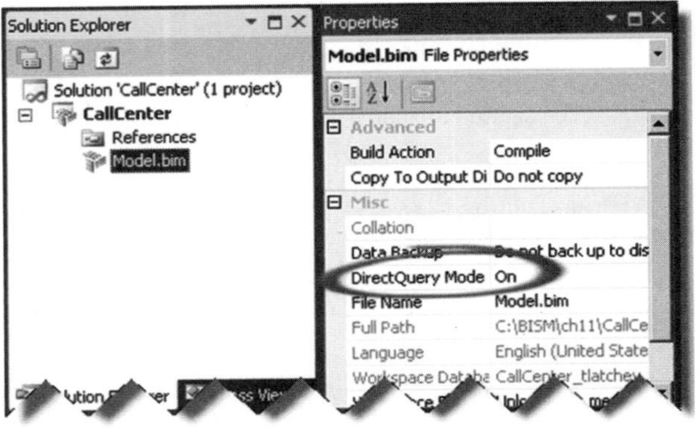


**Figure 11.8** Change the DirectQuery property to On to switch the model storage mode to DirectQuery.

This change causes SSDT to validate all the DirectQuery restrictions in order to verify that the model is DirectQuery-compliant. If changing the DirectQuery Mode property fails, review the errors in the Error List window and the limitations I've just discussed, in order to understand why DirectQuery can't be enabled.

**NOTE** It's important to understand that although you've changed the model storage to DirectQuery, the Data View in the tabular designer still shows data from the VertiPaq cache. That's because the workspace database can't talk directly to the data source. To see the effect of turning DirectQuery on, you must deploy the model to the server and Power View or SSMS to query the model.

### *Deploying the model*

As a prerequisite for deploying the model in DirectQuery mode, you must set an appropriate Query Mode deployment option in the project properties, as shown in **Figure 11.9**.

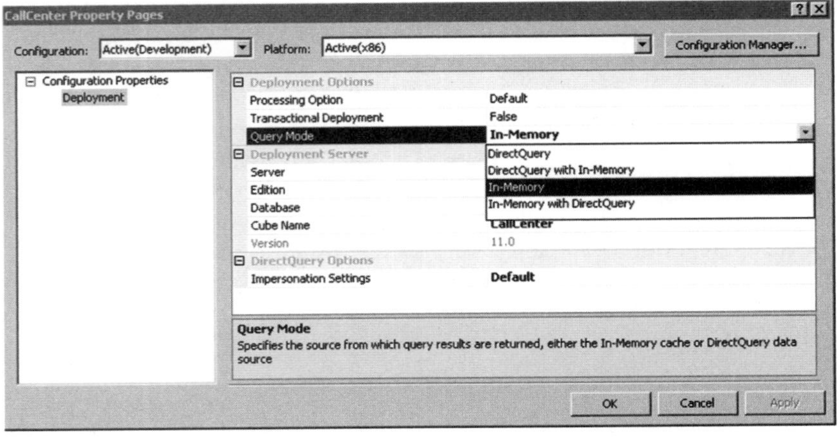


**Figure 11.9** Use the Query Mode property to switch between VertiPaq and DirectQuery storage modes, or to select a hybrid mode.

The Query Mode setting tells the deployment server which storage mode you want to use for the database. The default In-Memory setting will load data in the VertiPaq cache *irrespective* of the fact that you turned on the DirectQuery Mode model setting (again, the DirectQuery Mode setting is just for design-time validation). As you might have guessed, the Query Mode=DirectQuery setting will configure the database in a DirectQuery mode.

Tabular also supports two hybrid modes – "DirectQuery with In-Memory" and "In-Memory with DirectQuery". These hybrid modes set the default storage mode, but they allow clients to switch to the other. The difference between these two storage modes is the default place from which the data is retrieved. "DirectQuery with In-Memory" defaults to DirectQuery and passes through queries to the database, while "In-Memory with DirectQuery" uses the VertiPaq cache by default.

Remember that one of the DirectQuery limitations is that it allows only DAX queries. One advantage of using a hybrid mode is that you can support both OLAP clients that send MDX queries, such as Excel, and clients that send DAX queries (Power View) from the *same* model. On the downside, a hybrid mode requires you process the database in order to load the VertiPaq cache. This could be an issue with large data volumes because you might run out of memory.

Since DirectQuery is DAX-only, OLAP clients must always fetch results from the VertiPaq cache. Another limitation is that Power View doesn't allow you to switch back and forth between storage modes on the same model. Therefore, to support the "hybrid" scenario, you must use "DirectQuery with In-Memory" mode with this release of SQL Server.

**TIP** Assuming you've enabled a hybrid mode by configuring the database for "DirectQuery with In-Memory", an OLAP client can switch to VertiPaq by using a special connection setting called DirectQueryMode. This property supports the following settings (Default, DirectQuery, and InMemory). For example, Excel can use the following connection string to query a model configured for "DirectQuery with In-Memory":
Provider=MSOLAP.5;Integrated Security=SSPI;Persist Security Info=True;Data Source=<server>;
Initial Catalog=CallCenter; **DirectQueryMode=InMemory**;

***Configuring a DirectQuery-only partition***

Once you turn on the model DirectQuery property, you can optionally configure a DirectQuery-only partition. A DirectQuery-only partition is a partition that can never be processed. This could be useful in the following scenarios:

- DirectQuery-only model – Although the server allows you to process partitions in a DirectQuery-only model, it doesn't make sense to do so since the model will never use the cached data. You can configure the partition to be DirectQuery-only so the partition is never processed.
- Multiple partitions in a hybrid model – The partition definition for the DirectQuery partition would overlap with the partition definitions for the VertiPaq cache since DirectQuery requires a single partition bound to the full dataset. To avoid this, set the DirectQuery partition to never process.

**NOTE** The exact outcome of overlapping hybrid partitions depends on whether Tabular treats one of table columns as an internal unique column. A table has a unique column under one of the following conditions: it acts as a lookup table, one of its columns is marked as a Row Identifier, it uses custom sorting, or it's marked as a Date table. If there isn't a unique column, the process operation will succeed but that data will duplicate. If there isn't an unique column and you attempt to process overlapping hybrid partitions, you'll get an error on process.

**Figure 11.10** demonstrates the partition design for the second scenario, where you intend to support a hybrid mode by configuring the model in the "DirectQuery with VertiPaq" mode. Because I've changed the DirectQuery Mode model-level property to On, the first partition is automatically marked as a DirectQuery-only partition. The other two partitions are intended to be used in VertiPaq mode to support OLAP clients. In this case, the partitioning scheme is by year. Because the DirectQuery partition overlaps the VertiPaq partitions, you need to set its Processing

Option property to "Never Process this Partition". As a result, the first partition is configured as a DirectQuery-only partition. A table can have only one DirectQuery-only partition.

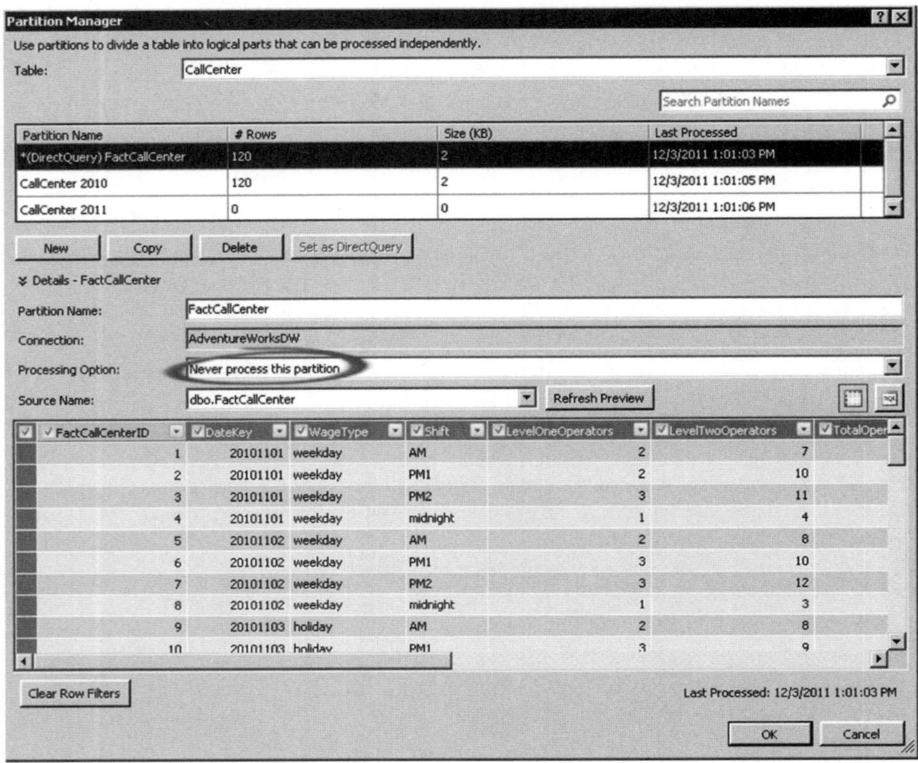

**Figure 11.10** Configure a DirectQuery-only partition if it won't be processed.

## 11.2.2 Implementing Low-Latency Models

Suppose that the Adventure Works call center data is ever changing. Due to the massive data volumes, processing and caching data is unacceptable. Next, you'll configure the CallCenter model for DirectQuery to support real-time analysis. As data changes are committed into the Adventure Works database, they can be analyzed instantaneously in Power View, without requiring explicit processing.

***Configuring DirectQuery***

Follow these steps to reconfigure the CallCenter model for DirectQuery:

1. In SSDT, open the CallCenter project with the changes from Chapter 10.
2. In Solution Explorer, select the Model.bim file. In the Properties window, change the DirectQuery Mode property to On. SSDT should successfully switch to DirectQuery because the CallCenter model doesn't violate any of the DirectQuery limitations.
3. In Solution Explorer, right-click the CallCenter project node (CallCenter.smproj), and then click Properties.

4. In the Property Pages dialog box, change the Query Mode property to DirectQuery. As a result, the CallCenter model will only support the DirectQuery mode, and it won't cache the data. If needed, change the Server property to point to your Analysis Services Tabular server where you want to deploy the model. Click OK.
5. In SSDT, click the CallCenter tab in the tabular designer, and then click the Partitions button in the Analysis Services toolbar. In Partition Manager, change the Processing Option of the first (default) partition to "Never process this partition". This configures the partition as a DirectQuery-only partition. Close Partition Manager.
6. (Optional) Change the partition design of the CallCenter to partition by year. For example, define two partitions, CallCenter2010 and CallCenter2011, to load data for years 2010 and 2011, respectively.
7. In Solution Explorer, right-click the CallCenter project file, and then click Deploy to deploy the project to the server.

   Deployment should be very fast because it deploys the metadata only and because it doesn't load the data.

***Testing DirectQuery***

Since DirectQuery works with DAX queries only, you'll use Power View to test it.

1. In SharePoint, create a BI Semantic Model Connection that points to the CallCenter model by following the steps in Section 10.3.2.
2. Hover your mouse cursor over the connection, expand the drop-down menu, and then click "Create Power View Report".
3. To observe the DirectQuery behavior, start the SQL Server Profiler from the Microsoft SQL Server 2012 ⇨ Performance Tools program group.
4. In SQL Server Profiler, click File ⇨ New Trace to start a new trace session. In the Connect to Server dialog box, expand the Server Type drop-down list, and then select Analysis Services. In the Server Name field, type in the name of the Analysis Services Tabular instance where you've deployed the CallCenter model to.
5. In the Trace Properties window, click the Event Selection tab, and then check the Show All Events checkbox. Check the "Direct Query Begin" and "Direct Query End" events.
6. In SQL Server Profiler, click File ⇨ New Trace again to start a Database Engine trace session. Connect to the SQL Server database engine that hosts the AdventureWorksDW2008R2 database. Accept the default event selection. Tile the two SQL Server Profiler windows vertically so that you can see the trace events from both servers.
7. In Power View, add a field from the CallCenter table to the report, and then watch the trace events.

   In the Analysis Services trace window, you should see a Query Begin event that Power View sends to Analysis Services, as shown in **Figure 11.11**. Immediately below that, you should see a Direct Query Begin event. The TextData section of this event shows the actual SQL SELECT statement that the Analysis Services server sends to SQL server. In the Database trace window, you should see a BatchStarting event that shows the same SELECT statement.

   To recap, PowerView sends a DAX query to the Analysis Service server. Analysis Services generates a SQL SELECT statement and sends it to the SQL Server. This test confirms that DirectQuery generates and sends queries to SQL Server instead of using the VertiPaq cache.

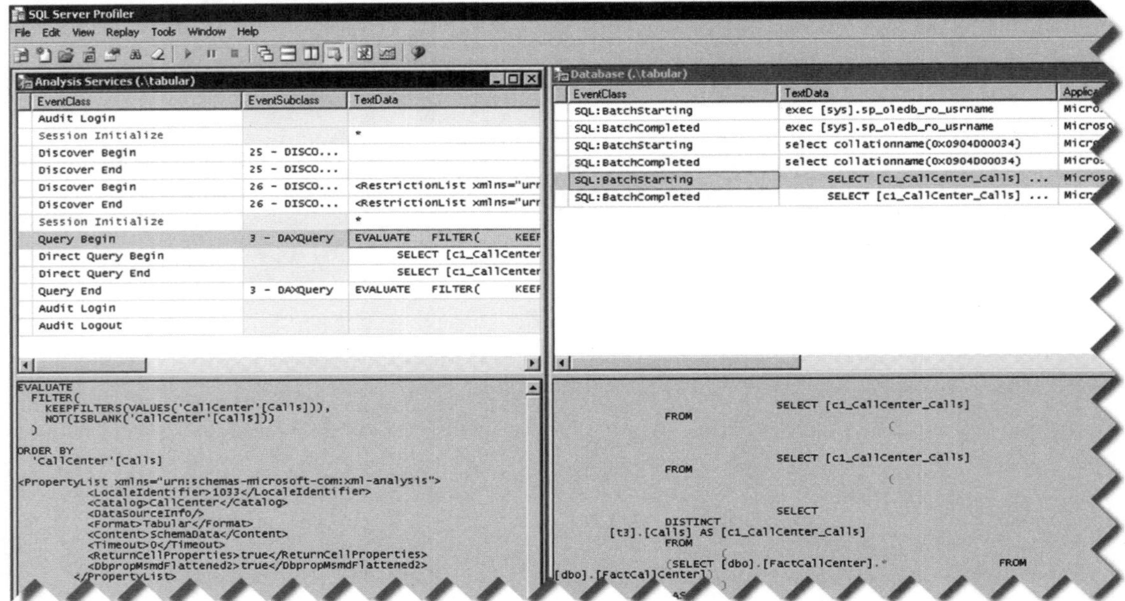


**Figure 11.11** DirectQuery generates and sends SQL SELECT statements to the data source.

8. In SSMS, connect to the Analysis Services Tabular instance.
9. Expand the CallCenter database, right-click the CallCenter table, and then click Partitions to open the Partitions dialog box, as shown in **Figure 11.12**.

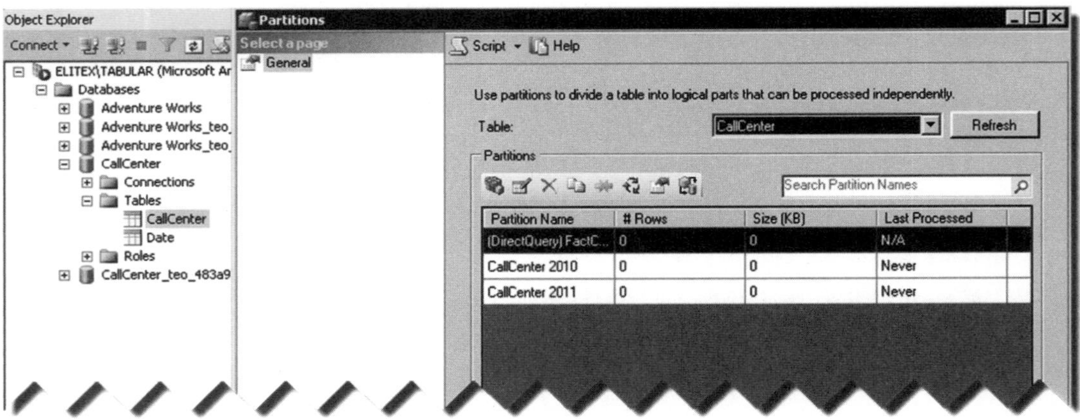


**Figure 11.12** A DirectQuery-only partition isn't processed, and it doesn't contain any rows.

Notice that the default partition of the CallCenter table doesn't have any rows (the "# Rows" column is zero). That's because, when you configured a partition as a DirectQuery-only partition, the server doesn't process that partition and the partition doesn't cache any data.

## 11.3 Designing Data Security

Besides configuring storage, another popular requirement for organizational BI solutions is data security, where end users can see only the data that they're authorized to access. Unlike PowerPivot, Analysis Services Tabular supports role-based security for restricting access to the model and to its data. Because the Analysis Services security model is layered on top of Windows, understanding security isn't easy, and explaining this topic in details is beyond the scope of this book. Therefore, I'll assume that you have a basic knowledge of how Windows authentication and authorization work.

**NOTE** As it stands, Analysis Services doesn't support custom security to replace the Windows-based security model. Analysis Services always authenticates and authorizes incoming requests using the Windows identity of the end user or the client application.

### 11.3.1 Understanding Roles

You'll probably find the Analysis Services role-based security similar to the security models of other Microsoft or home-grown solutions that you've come across. The implementation details are product-specific, but the underlying concepts are the same. In a nutshell, the user is authenticated, based on her Windows account, and then the user is authorized according to the security policies that the administrator has set up. In Analysis Services, the server enforces restricted access through roles. There are two types of roles in Analysis Services:

- Server role – A fixed role that provides server-wide access to an Analysis Services instance.
- Database roles – Custom roles to restrict access to the model and its data.

***Understanding the Server role***

The SQL Server setup program creates an implicit Server role and then assigns the individual users and groups you specify to that role. The Windows users and groups that you explicitly assign to the Server role become the server administrators and have unrestricted access to the server and all the databases. In addition, the setup sets the Security\BuiltinAdminsAreServerAdmins server property to True. Because of this, local Windows administrators gain unrestricted access as well. Follow these steps to add other users to the Server role:

1. In SQL Server Management Studio (SSMS), connect to the Analysis Services instance.
2. In the Object Explorer pane, right-click the server node, and then click Properties.
3. In the Analysis Services Properties dialog box, click the Security page to select it.
4. Click the Add button to open the "Select Users and Groups" dialog box, as shown in **Figure 11.13**.
5. Enter the Windows user name or group in the Domain\Login naming convention. Or, click Advanced, and then click Find Now to search Active Directory. Click the Check Names button to verify the account.
6. Click OK to add the Windows account to the Server role.

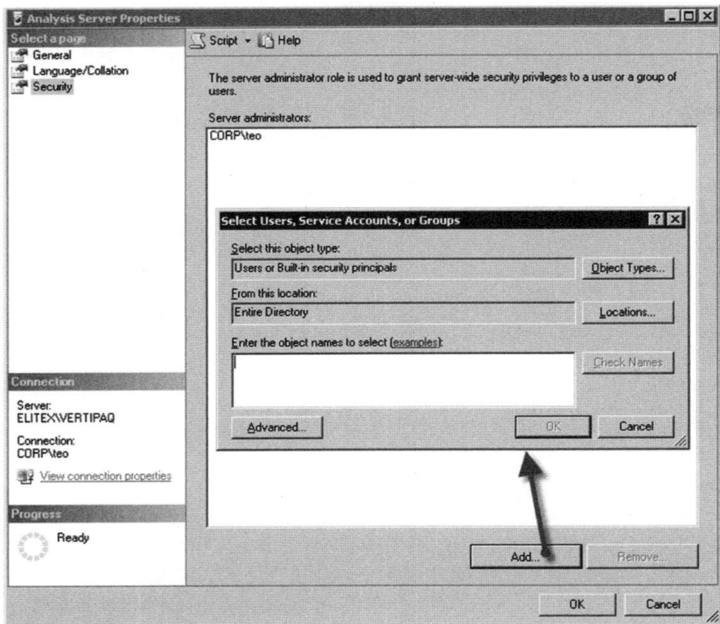


**Figure 11.13** Use the Security page in the Analysis Services Properties dialog box to grant other users administrator rights to the server.

**TIP** Suppose you need to prevent local Windows administrators from gaining automatically unrestricted access to the server after you've have assigned new members explicitly. In the Analysis Services Properties dialog box, select the General page in the left pane. Check "Show Advanced (All) Properties" to see the advanced properties. Change the Security\BuiltinAdminsAreServerAdmins property to False. You don't need to restart the server for this change to become effective. However, there is nothing stopping a local administrator from making system-wide changes, such as uninstalling the server, deleting the database folders, or editing the msmdsrv.ini file directly to change Security\BuiltinAdminsAreServerAdmins back to True.

### *Understanding database roles*

Database roles allow the modeler or the server administrator to grant other users restricted access to models and data. **Figure 11.14** is meant to help you visualize a database role.

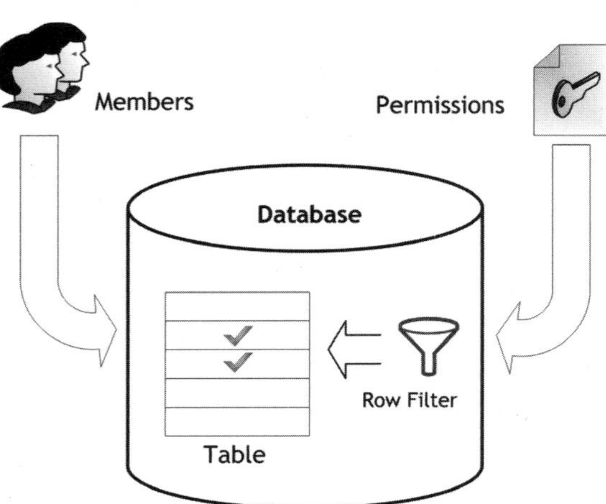


**Figure 11.14** A database role grants its members permissions to a database, and it optionally restricts access to table rows.

A database role grants its members specific permissions to a database. Members could be individual Windows users or Active Directory groups. A permission grants the user specific rights to the database. **Table 11.2** shows the permissions supported by Analysis Services Tabular.

**Table 11.2 Analysis Services Tabular supports the following permissions to grant access to databases.**

| Permission | Description | Row Filters |
|---|---|---|
| None | No access to the database schema and data. | |
| Read | Read access to data. Cannot change schema, refresh data, or read metadata, such as DAX formulas. | ✓ |
| Read and Process | Same as Read, plus the ability to process data. | ✓ |
| Process | Can process the database via automation only. Cannot view database schema. | |
| Administrator | Unrestricted access to the database. | |

By default, a new role is assigned the None permission, and its members have no access to the database. Therefore, you must use another database permission to assign the role selective rights.

***Creating roles***

At design time, you can use Role Manager (click the Roles button in the Analysis Services toolbar) to manage the database roles. Similar to designing storage, defining roles in SQL Server Data Tools (SSDT) is preferable because they become a part of the project and can be deployed with the model. **Figure 11.15** shows Role Manager. In this case, the model includes a single database role called Adventure Works. You can use the New, Copy, and Delete buttons to create, duplicate, and delete roles.

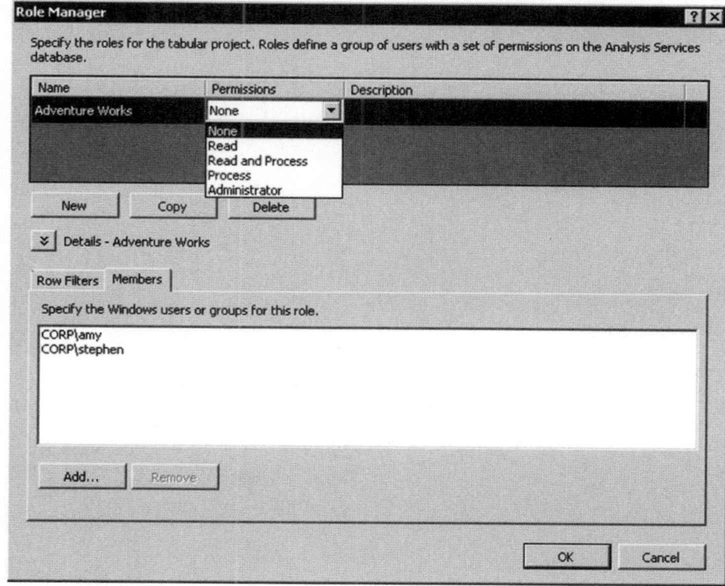


**Figure 11.15** Use Role Manager in SSDT to manage database roles and define row filters.

You can use the Members tab to add or remove Windows users or Active Directory groups to and from the role. As with partitions, it's preferable to include the role definitions in your project, so you can deploy them to the server when you deploy the project. If needed, the administrator can use SQL Server Management Studio (SSMS) to manage the roles outside the tabular project.

***Understanding role membership***

Roles are additive. If a user belongs to multiple roles, the user will get the superset of all the role permissions. For example, suppose Bob is a member of both the Sales Representative and the Administrator database roles. The Sales Representative role grants him Read rights, while the Administrator role grants him Process rights. Because roles are additive, Bob's effective rights are Read and Process.

If a user belongs to multiple roles, the user could elect to connect to the server with a specific role(s). This could be useful for testing security. Analysis Services supports a Roles connection string property, which the end-user or the application can use to specify a comma-delimited list of Roles that you want the server to evaluate. Here is an example connection string.

```
Provider=MSOLAP.5;Initial Catalog=Adventure Works;Persist Security Info=True; Data Source=<server>;Roles=Sales Representative
```

## 11.3.2 Understanding Row Filters

Many project requirements call for data (row-level) security, such as allowing a sales manager to see only the sales for her subordinates. You can implement data security by defining row filters on the tables you want to secure. Row filters can be defined only for roles with the Read and "Read and Process" permissions. You can define row filters in SSDT or SSMS.

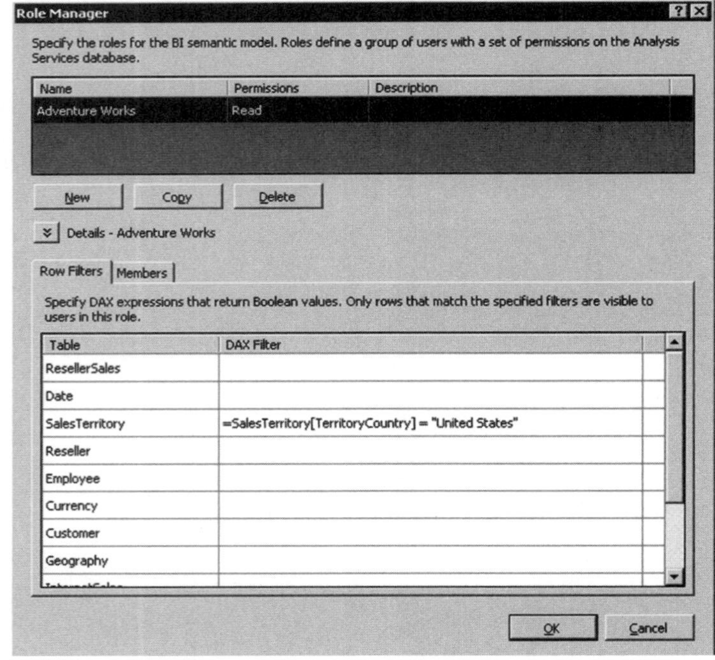


**Figure 11.16** This row filter allows members of the Adventure Works role to see only the United States row in the SalesTerritory table.

***Understanding row filter expressions***

As its name suggests, a row filter defines a filter expression that evaluates which rows the role is allowed to see. If a row filter isn't defined for a particular table, members of a role with Read or "Read and Process" permission can see all the rows in the table. To set up a row filter in Role

Manager, enter a DAX formula next to the table name. The DAX formula must evaluate to a Boolean condition that returns TRUE or FALSE. **Figure 11.16** shows a row filter applied to the Sales Territory table. This row filter has the following expression:

```
=SalesTerritory[TerritoryCountry] = "United States"
```

When the user connects to the model, the server applies the row filter expression to each row in the SalesTerritory table. If the row meets the criteria, the role is authorized to see that row.

**NOTE** Row filters are conceptually similar to allowed sets with dimension data security in Multidimensional because the net result is a set of rows that the user is allowed to see. The difference is that an allowed set expression uses MDX to return a set of allowed members, while a row filter defines a Boolean criterion for qualifying allowed rows. As it stands, Tabular doesn't differentiate between allowed and denied sets but a DAX expression can be used to disallow rows. For example, this row filter allows the role to see United States but not the Southeast region:
=SalesTerritory[TerritoryCountry] = "United States" && SalesTerritory[TerritoryRegion] <> "Southeast"
However, this isn't the same as a denied set because if the user is added to a second role, which allows access to the restricted rows, then it will overwrite the previously restricted rows (no strong deny is supported).

Although you can use Role Manager to enter an expression without prefixing it with an equal sign, entering an equal sign is preferable because you get Auto-complete while typing the formula (Auto-complete actively helps you fill out the formula). If the Role Manager detects a syntax issue with the expression, it displays a stop icon next to the expression. You can hover your mouse cursor over the icon to see the error text. If the expression is syntactically correct but it doesn't return a Boolean result, the Role Manager displays a warning icon, as shown in **Figure 11.17**.

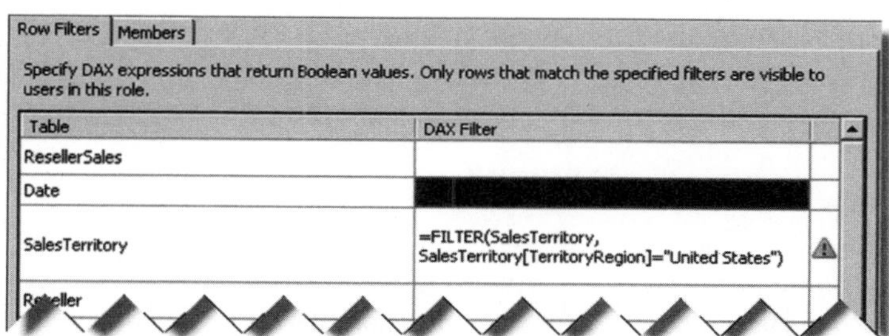


**Figure 11.17** If the expression doesn't return TRUE/FALSE, the Role Manager displays a warning.

Although the expression is syntactically valid in this case, it doesn't return a Boolean result. Role Manager does limited testing and it might not be able to catch all the errors. Test the security with a client tool to make sure that the row filters work.

**NOTE** Row filters can only use DAX formulas. Tabular doesn't support externalizing programming logic in Analysis Services stored procedures, such as to call a security service that evaluates some complex rules to determine the allowed rows. If external data is required to make security decisions, you could import the external data as a hidden table into the model so that it can be referenced in DAX row filter formulas. I demonstrate this approach in Section 11.3.5.

***How row filters affect data***

From an implementation perspective, the server applies some of the row filter restrictions at connect time when the client connects to the model and establishes a new session, and others at query time when the server queries the VertiPaq store. From an end-user perspective, rows the user isn't authorized to view and their related data simply don't exist in the model. Imagine that a global WHERE clause is applied to the model that selects only the data that's related to the allowed rows of all the secured tables. Given the example back in **Figure 11.16**, the user can't see any other sales territories in the SalesTerritory table except United States. Moreover, the user can't view data for these territories in the ResellerSales table or in any other tables that are directly or indirectly (via cascading relationships) related to the SalesTerritory table.

Suppose that you've applied a row filter to the SalesTerritory table to return only the Southeast region of United States. The server automatically applies this row filter to all the columns in the SalesTerritory table. For example, the role can see only United States in the TerritoryCountry column. Behind the scenes, the server applies a special behavior called Autoexists that cross-joins columns in the same table. Thanks to Autoexists, the server returns only the values that exist (intersect) in both columns.

Autoexists applies only to the secured table and to the tables that are related to that table and that are on the many side of the relationships. Autoexists doesn't work in the many-to-one direction. So if filter is set on a fact table, the lookup tables won't be filtered automatically. However, if row filter is set on a lookup table, the fact table will be filtered. Autoexists doesn't automatically apply to unrelated tables. For example, the role members will be able to browse all the resellers in the Reseller table instead of just the resellers in Southeast. However, because the SalesTerritory and Reseller table are related to the ResellerSales table, when the user browses the reseller sales, the user can view ResellerSales data for the resellers in the Southeast only.

**NOTE** Unlike Multidimensional, Tabular always applies Visual Totals and doesn't provide an option to disable it. Because of this, the report totals would reflect the contributions by the allowed members only. Personally, I like this behavior since based on my experience business users always prefer Visual Totals.

As it stands, Analysis Services (both Multidimensional and Tabular) doesn't support object security, such as to hide entire tables if the user isn't authorized to see them. Even if the row filter qualifies no rows, the table will show in the model metadata. The simplest way to disallow a role from viewing any rows in a table is to set up a row filter with a "=FALSE()" expression. If no row filter is applied to a table, "=TRUE()" is assumed and the user can see all data.

***Understanding dynamic data security***

The row filter examples that I've shown you so far return a fixed (static) set of allowed rows. This works well if you have a finite set of unique permissions, each of which corresponds to an Active Directory group. For example, if there are three regions, you can build three roles with three Active Directory groups as members. However, many real-life security requirements call for dynamic security. For example, suppose you must restrict managers to view only the sales data of the employees that are reporting directly or indirectly to them. If basic dimension data security were the only option, you'd have no choice except to set up a database role for each manager. This might lead to a huge number of roles and maintenance issues. Similar to Multidimensional, Tabular supports dynamic data security to address such security requirements.

The cornerstone of the Analysis Services dynamic security is the USERNAME function. This function returns the Windows identity of the user in the format Domain\Login. For example, if Stephen logs in to the adventure-works domain as stephen0, USERNAME would return the string "adventure-works\stephen0". Then, to apply security based on the organizational hierarchy, you need only a single database role with the following row filter applied to the Employee table:

```
=PATHCONTAINS(Employee[Path], LOOKUPVALUE(Employee[EmployeeKey], Employee[LoginID], USERNAME()))
```

This expression uses the DAX LOOKUPVALUE function to retrieve the value of the EmployeeKey column that's matching the user's Windows logon. Then, it uses the PATHCONTAINS function to parse the Path column in the Employee table in order to check if the parent-child path includes the employee key. If this is the case, the user is authorized to see that employee and the employee's related data because the user is the employee's direct or indirect manager.

**TIP** When USERNAME isn't enough, another option that's less frequently used for dynamic data security is to use the CustomData setting. A client can append a CustomData setting to the connection string in order to pass some custom text, such as CustomData=Partner to indicate that the user requesting the report belongs to a partner organization. Then, the row filter can use the CUSTOMDATA DAX function to obtain the identifier. This expression allows the user to see all rows when the CustomData setting is set to "Partner"

```
=IF(CUSTOMDATA()="Partner", TRUE, FALSE).
```

CustomData is typically used for roles with members which are service accounts used by external applications. Don't grant permissions based upon the CUSTOMDATA function in roles whose members are end users since this could open a security hole. The user could specify whatever CustomData property they want in the connection string.

## 11.3.3 Testing Database Roles

Once the database roles are in place, you can test them with Excel which you can launch by clicking the Analyze in Excel button in the SSDT Analysis Services toolbar. This brings you to the "Analyze in Excel" dialog box, as shown in **Figure 11.18**.

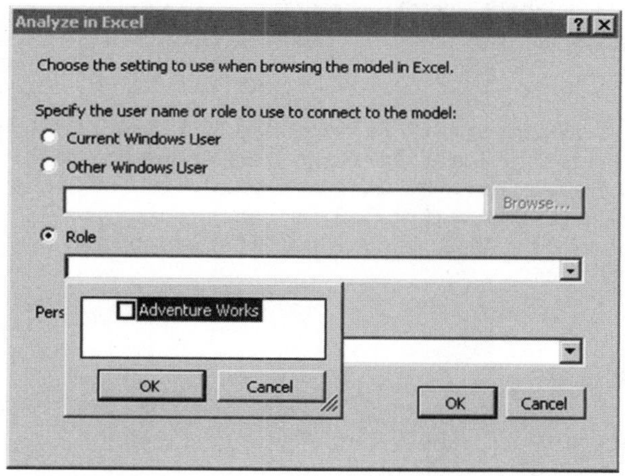


**Figure 11.18** Use the Analyze in Excel dialog box to test database roles by using a specific user or a role.

***Testing users***

The default selection is "Current Windows User" which doesn't modify the Excel connection string to impersonate a specific user or a role. As a result, Excel connects to the workspace server under your Windows identity. Use the "Other Windows User" option when you want to test a specific user who is a member of a database role. To do so, click the Browse button, and then enter the Windows account for that user in the format Domain\Login, such as prologika\teo. Behind the scenes, SSDT appends the EffectiveUserName setting to the Excel connection string, such as:

Provider=MSOLAP.5;Integrated Security=SSPI;Persist Security Info=True;Data Source=<server>; ... **EffectiveUserName=prologika\teo**;

As a result, if the role uses dynamic data security, the DAX USERNAME function will return that Windows login and row filters will be evaluated for that user. Using the "Other Windows User" option (EffectiveUserName) requires the following:

1. You must have administrator rights to the Analysis Services workspace server.

2. Your development machine and workspace server must belong to an Active Directory domain with a functional level of Windows Server 2003 or higher.
3. Proper Service Principle Names (SPNs) must be set up in Active Directory for the Analysis Services server. Even though no double hops are involved, this part of the Kerberos setup must be completed. Greg Galloway explains this in more detail in his blog post, "Using EffectiveUserName to Impersonate in SSAS" at http://bit.ly/effectiveusername.

**NOTE** If you use the SQL Server Profiler connected to the Analysis Services workspace server, you'll see all the requests still going under your identity when the "Other Windows User" option is used. This is by design because the "Other Windows User" option doesn't run Excel as another user (that will require that you know the password). Instead, it appends the EffectiveUserName setting to the connection string. However, EffectiveUserName can be seen in the XML properties that are listed at the bottom of the query in a Query Begin event.

***Testing roles***

The third option on the "Analyze in Excel" dialog box lets you select a specific role. As I previously explained, you must have administrator access to the workspace server. Consequently, even if you're a member of a database role that applies data security, you'll gain unrestricted access to all data because roles are additive. However, you can select the Role option and then specify a specific role that you want the server to evaluate.

Behind the scenes, when you use this option, SSDT appends the Roles setting to the connection string, as I explained in Section 11.3.1. If the database role(s) has row filters with the USERNAME function, make sure that the expression returns rows for your Windows login. Otherwise, you won't see any data.

**TIP** A simple way to test the row filter formula is to add a calculated column to the secured table. Since a calculated column can't use the Username function because the server stores the calculated values, you can hardcode the desired user name. For example, add a calculated column to the Employee column that uses this expression:
=PATHCONTAINS(Employee[Path], LOOKUPVALUE(Employee[EmployeeKey], Employee[LoginID], "<login>"))
Replace <login> with the Windows login of the user you want to test. The expression is evaluated for each row and returns TRUE or FALSE if the row meets the filter criterion.

## 11.3.4 Implementing Dynamic Data Security

Suppose that you're tasked to extend the Adventure Works tabular model with data security. Specifically, you need to allow the Adventure Works sales representatives to see only their data and the data associated with their subordinates. To meet these requirements, you'll implement an Adventure Works database role that will use dynamic data security to restrict access to the Employee table in the Adventure Works model.

***Setting up the test environment***

Ideally, you would have two domain Windows accounts for testing purposes. If this isn't an option, you can use your Windows login. In my case, I've created Windows accounts for Stephen Jiang and Amy Alberts to represent two Adventure Works fictitious users. Next, update the Employee source, and then replace the logins of these users to match your setup, as follows:

1. Open the Employees.txt file from the Ch03 folder in Notepad.
2. Find the row for Stephen Jiang (EmployeeKey = 272), and then change the value in the LoginID column from adventure-works\stephen0 to the login of your first test account, such as *corp\stephen*.

3. Find the row for Amy Alberts (EmployeeKey = 290), and then change the value in the LoginID column from adventure-works\amy0 to your second test account, such as *corp\amy*. Save the Empoloyees.txt file.

**NOTE** I included a copy of the Employees.txt file with the above changes in the Ch11 folder. If you decide to use it, change the Employees connection in the Existing Connection dialog box (Model ⇨ Existing Connections menu) to point to this file.

4. Open the Adventure Works project in SSDT. Select the Employee table to make it active.
5. Expand the Process Partitions drop-down button in the Analysis Services toolbar, and then click Process Table to reload the Employee table.

***Implementing a database role***

Next, you'll create a new database role and implement dynamic data security.

1. In SSDT, click the Roles button in the Analysis Services toolbar to open Role Manager.
2. In Role Manager, click the New button to create a new database role.
3. Change the role name to *Adventure Works*. Expand the Permissions drop-down list, and then select Read to grant the role rights to read data.
4. Select the Members tab, and then add the two test accounts as members of the role.
5. Select the Row Filters tab, and then set up a row filter for the Employee table that uses the following expression, which I explained in Section 11.3.2:

```
=PATHCONTAINS(Employee[Path], LOOKUPVALUE(Employee[EmployeeKey], Employee[LoginID], Username()))
```

6. Compare your role setup with **Figure 11.19**. Click OK to close Role Manager. SSDS applies the changes to the workspace database.

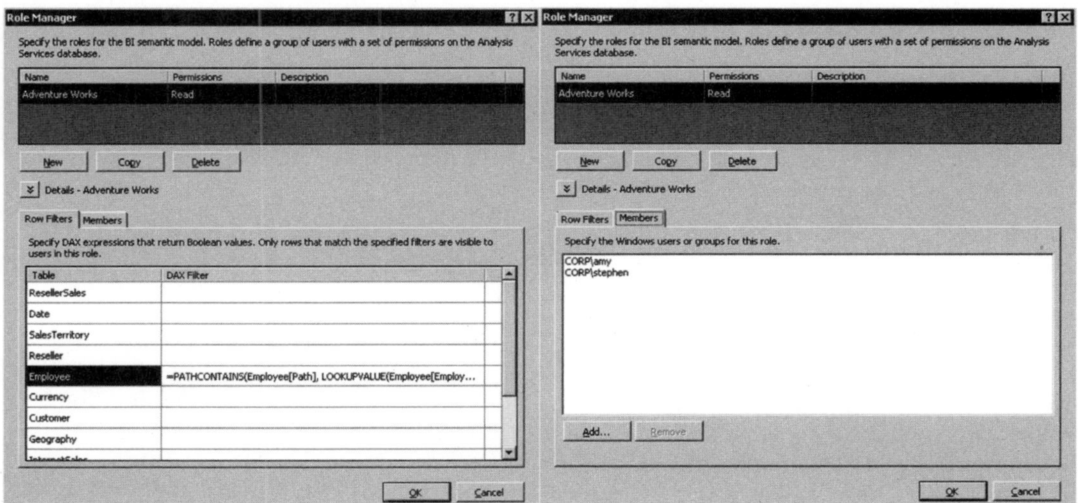

**Figure 11.19** This role has a row filter that uses dynamic data security to restrict data in the Employee table.

***Testing the Adventure Works role***

Now that the role is in place, let's use Excel to test it.

1. Click the "Analyze in Excel" button in the Analysis Services toolbar.

2. In the "Analyze in Excel" dialog box, select the "Other Windows User" option, and then click the Browse button. In the dialog box that follows, enter Stephen's Windows login in the Domain\Login format, such as *corp\stephen*, and then click OK. Click OK again to confirm the "Analyze in Excel" dialog box.
3. In Excel, create a pivot report with the Employees hierarchy (Employee table) in the Row Labels zone and with the ResellerSalesAmount field (ResellerSales table) in the Values zone, as shown in **Figure 11.20**.

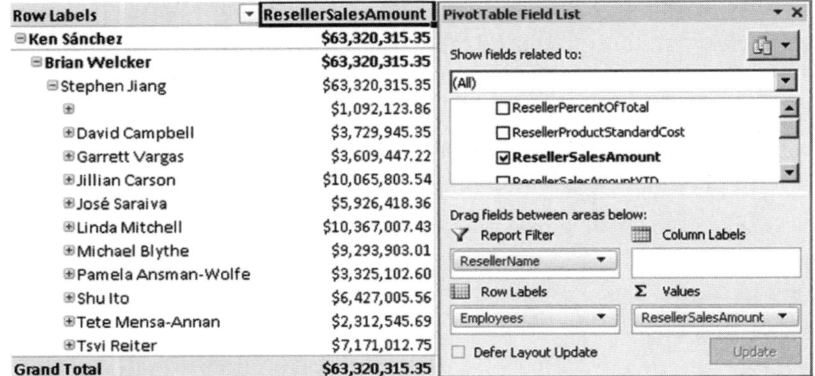

| Row Labels | ResellerSalesAmount |
|---|---|
| ⊟Ken Sánchez | $63,320,315.35 |
| ⊟Brian Welcker | $63,320,315.35 |
| ⊟Stephen Jiang | $63,320,315.35 |
| ⊞ | $1,092,123.86 |
| ⊞David Campbell | $3,729,945.35 |
| ⊞Garrett Vargas | $3,609,447.22 |
| ⊞Jillian Carson | $10,065,803.54 |
| ⊞José Saraiva | $5,926,418.36 |
| ⊞Linda Mitchell | $10,367,007.43 |
| ⊞Michael Blythe | $9,293,903.01 |
| ⊞Pamela Ansman-Wolfe | $3,325,102.60 |
| ⊞Shu Ito | $6,427,005.56 |
| ⊞Tete Mensa-Annan | $2,312,545.69 |
| ⊞Tsvi Reiter | $7,171,012.75 |
| Grand Total | $63,320,315.35 |



**Figure 11.20** This report shows that Stephen Jiang can view only the data for his subordinates.

Notice that dimension data security allows Stephen to navigate the Employee hierarchy in order to see his data and his subordinates' data only. Stephen can't see the sales for Amy, who's at the same organizational level as Stephen. To test security for Amy, you can open another "Analyze in Excel" session. However, a faster way is to simply change the connection string in the existing Excel session by following the next three steps.

4. In the Excel window, click the Data tab, and then click the Connections button.
5. In the Workbook Connection dialog box, click the Properties button. In the Connection Properties dialog box, click the Definition tab.
6. In the Connection String field, find the EffectiveUserName setting, and then replace Stephen's login with Amy's. Click OK, and then click Close. Accept the prompt that warns you that the connection definition won't be the same.

Excel refreshes the report. The report now shows Amy's data and she can't see Stephen's data.

## 11.3.5 Externalizing Security Policies

Suppose that Adventure Works uses a master data management application, such as Master Data Services (MDS), to associate a sales representative with a set of resellers that she oversees. Your task is to enforce a security role that restricts the user to see only her resellers. This would require importing a table that contains the employee-reseller associations.

**REAL LIFE** This approach builds upon the factless fact table implementation that I demonstrated in my "Protect UDM with Dimension Data Security, Part 2" article (http://bit.ly/protectudm). I've used this approach in many real-life projects because of its simplicity, performance, and ability to reuse the security filters across other applications, such as across operational reports that source data directly from the data warehouse.

*Implementing the security filter table*

A new table, SecurityResellerFilter, is required to store the authorized resellers for each employee, as **Figure 11.21** shows. This table is related to the Reseller and Employee tables. If an employee is authorized to view a reseller, a row is added to SecurityResellerFilter table. In real life, business users or IT pros will probably maintain the security associations. For the sake of simplicity, you'll use a static SQL SELECT statement to load the table.

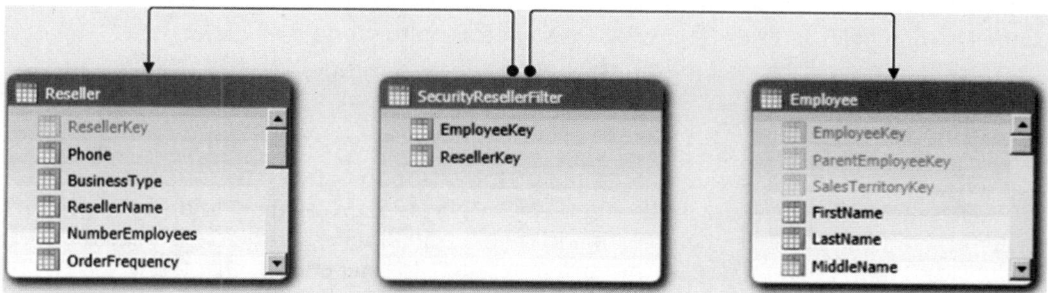


**Figure 11.21** The bridge table stores the authorized resellers for each employee.

Follow these steps to add the SecurityResellerFilter table to the model.

1. In SSDT, click the Existing Connection button in the Analysis Services toolbar.
2. In the Existing Connections dialog box, with the AdventureWorksDW connection selected, click the Open button to start the Table Import Wizard.
3. In the "Choose How to Import" step, select the "Write a Query to Specify the Data to Import" option, and then click Next.
4. In the "Specify a SQL Query" step, change the "Friendly Query Name" to *SecurityResellerFilter*, enter the following SQL SELECT statement, and then click Finish.

```
select 290 as EmployeeKey, 320 as ResellerKey
union
select 290 as EmployeeKey, 553 as ResellerKey
union
select 290 as EmployeeKey, 663 as ResellerKey
union
select 290 as EmployeeKey, 448 as ResellerKey
union
select 272 as EmployeeKey, 351 as ResellerKey
union
select 272 as EmployeeKey, 1 as ResellerKey
union
select 272 as EmployeeKey, 1 as ResellerKey
union
select 272 as EmployeeKey, 448 as ResellerKey
```

This statement associates selected resellers with Amy and Stephen.

5. Create a relationship between the SecurityResellerFilter [EmployeeKey] and Employee [EmployeeKey] tables, and a second relationship between the SecurityResellerFilter [ResellerKey] and Reseller [ResellerKey] tables.
6. To hide the SecurityResellerFilter table from users, right-click its tab, and then click "Hide from Client Tools".

**TIP** In addition to hiding the factless fact table, if it's not used as a lookup table (it doesn't have relationships to other tables), consider setting a =FALSE() row filter on it to hide its data.

***Implementing a row filter***

With the new table in place, change the Adventure Works database role as follows:

1. In the Analysis Services toolbar, click the Roles toolbar button to open Role Manager.
2. Next to the Reseller table, enter the following DAX expression to set up a row filter:

```
=CONTAINS(RELATEDTABLE(SecurityResellerFilter), SecurityResellerFilter[EmployeeKey], LOOKUPVALUE(Employee[EmployeeKey],
Employee[LoginID], USERNAME()))
```

Let's digest this expression one piece at a time. As you already know, the LOOKUPVALUE function is used to obtain the employee key associated with her Windows login. Because the row filter is set on the Reseller table, for each reseller, the CONTAINS function attempts to find a match for that reseller key and employee key combination in the SecurityResellerFilter table. Notice the use of the RELATEDTABLE function to pass the current reseller. The net effect is that the CONTAINS function returns TRUE if there is a row in the SecurityResellerFilter table that matches the ResellerKey and EmployeeKey combination.

***Testing security***

You can use again the "Analyze in Excel" feature to test the security changes. If you have an existing session already open, simply click the Refresh button in the Excel Data tab. The report should show fewer sales. Follow these steps to verify that that the user has access only to resellers the user is authorized to see:

1. Add the ResellerName field from the Reseller table in the Column Labels zone (**Figure 11.22**). The report columns should show only the resellers that are associated with that user in the SecurityResellerFilter table.

| Sum of SalesAmount | Column Labels | | | | |
|---|---|---|---|---|---|
| Row Labels | Accessories Network | Action Bicycle Specialists | Amalgamated Parts Shop | Capital Riding Supplies | Grand Total |
| ⊟Ken Sánchez | $2,165.79 | $71,774.18 | $197,327.59 | $5,404.20 | $276,671.76 |
| ⊟Brian Welcker | $2,165.79 | $71,774.18 | $197,327.59 | $5,404.20 | $276,671.76 |
| ⊟Amy Alberts | $2,165.79 | $71,774.18 | $197,327.59 | $5,404.20 | $276,671.76 |
| ⊞ | | $71,774.18 | | | $71,774.18 |
| ⊞Rachel Valdez | | | $197,327.59 | $5,404.20 | $202,731.79 |
| ⊞Ranjit Varkey Chudukatil | $2,165.79 | | | | $2,165.79 |
| Grand Total | $2,165.79 | $71,774.18 | $197,327.59 | $5,404.20 | $276,671.76 |

**Figure 11.22** The user can view only the resellers the user is authorized to see.

2. Expand the Column Labels drop-down list. Notice that it shows only the resellers that the user is authorized to view.
3. (Optional) Add a field from the Reseller table, such as Phone, to the Report Filter zone. When you expand the report filter drop-down list, you should see only values that intersect with the authorized resellers because of the Autoexists behavior. However, if you use a field from an unrelated table, such as SalesTerritory, you should see all the values because Autoexists doesn't automatically apply to other tables.

### 11.3.6 Advanced Security Scenarios

Analysis Services supports Windows security only, where the user is authenticated and authorized based on his or her Windows identity. This works great when users connect directly to the model, but it might present challenges with more complex deployments. Next, I'll discuss two common deployment scenarios that require additional planning and implementation efforts on your side in order to secure tabular models.

***Internet reporting considerations***

Windows security works great for intranet applications where the Analysis Services server and the end users are usually in the same domain or in a trusted domain, and you're using the Active Directory infrastructure that's already in place. However, Windows integrated security will almost never work with Internet-facing solutions because of firewall rules and other restrictions.

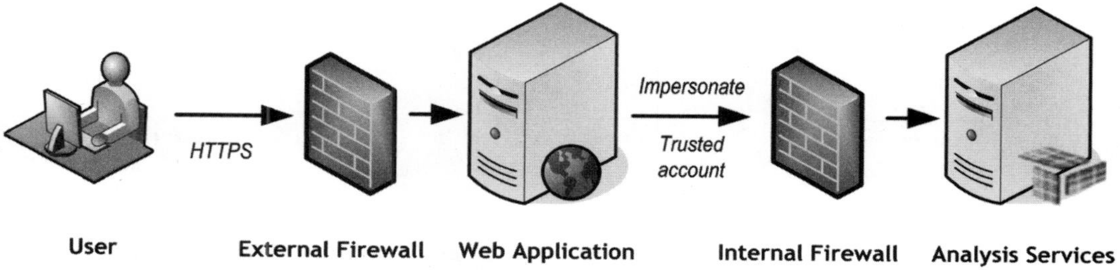


**Figure 11.23** The web application can impersonate the user or connect to the server using a trusted account.

Suppose, Adventure Works has an Internet-facing web application that needs to be enhanced so that Internet users can run operational reports from a tabular model. **Figure 11.23** shows one implementation option. In this case, the user connects to the web server via HTTPS. The web application uses a designated (trusted) account to connect to Analysis Services, such as by using the IIS application pool account. To filter report data, the web application can pass an identifier, such as the user's e-mail address, to a hidden report parameter.

This scenario is easy to implement, but Analysis Services won't be able to differentiate the users because all the requests are coming under the same Windows account. This presents an issue if the model uses dynamic data security. Consider the following options when you need to propagate the user identity to Analysis Services.

- Use the EffectiveUserName connection string setting – The application can append the EffectiveUserName setting to the Analysis Services connection string to pass the user identity. This can be a viable approach with custom applications because the application can change the connection string at run time. However, it could be problematic with Reporting Services operational reports because only embedded (report-specific) data sources can have expression-based connection strings.
- Impersonate the user – If the number of external users is relatively small, such as in the case of extranet reporting to external partners, consider creating Active Directory user accounts in a trusted domain. Then the web application can collect the user credentials and then impersonate the user or pass the credentials to the Reporting Services ReportViewer control, assuming that the user requests a Reporting Services report. This eliminates the double hop from the client to Analysis Services because the application authenticates the user.

What if you want to allow external users to use Microsoft Excel or another desktop client that requires direct connectivity to Analysis Services? You can configure Analysis Services for HTTP access by installing a special HTTP pump component on the IIS server, as explained in the "Configuring HTTP Access to SQL Server 2005 Analysis Services on Microsoft Windows Server 2003" technical article by Edward Melomed at http://bit.ly/ssasdatapump. For Intranet or extranet facing deployments, you should use Windows Basic authentication over the Secure Socket Layer (SSL) protocol, as I explained in my blog post, "Yet Another Post About Analysis Services HTTP Connectivity" at http://bit.ly/ssasdatapumpba.

***Multi-server deployment***

Multi-server deployment might require configuring Kerberos authentication when users are on the same domain or a trusted domain. Consider the deployment scenario shown in **Figure 11.24**.

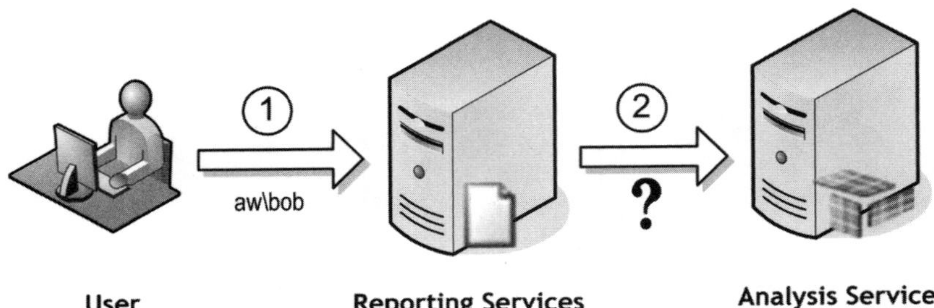


**Figure 11.24** Kerberos security is required to delegate the user identity beyond the first hop.

The user submits a report request to the report server which in turn needs to delegate the user identity to Analysis Services. This is a classic double-hop scenario, which Windows doesn't support by default. Since the report server doesn't have Bob's password, it can't delegate the call, and then the request fails. The issue manifests itself with this rather obscure error message when you view a Reporting Services report:

```
Cannot create a connection to data source '<data source name>'. (rsErrorOpeningConnection)
```

The solution to this predicament is to configure Kerberos security with delegation enabled. In fact, by default, the report server is configured to use Windows Negotiation, which attempts Kerberos first and then falls back on the NTLM protocol if the client doesn't support Kerberos. However, Kerberos necessitates additional steps for configuring the report server to delegate the call. These steps require some assistance from your Active Directory administrator, since you'll need domain administrator rights to make changes to Active Directory. The "Troubleshooting Kerberos Delegation" document (http://bit.ly/troubleshootingkerberos) is a great read to get you started with configuring and troubleshooting Kerberos security. Another good resource is the "Configure Kerberos authentication for SharePoint 2010 Products" whitepaper (http://bit.ly/spkerberos).

Kerberos works great but it's notoriously difficult to configure and troubleshoot. When Kerberos delegation isn't an option, consider the following workarounds. For operational reports and Power View reports that don't connect via BI Semantic Model connections, such as in the case when PowerPivot for SharePoint isn't installed, configure the Reporting Services data source, as shown in **Figure 11.25**. In this case, Reporting Services is configured for SharePoint integrated mode, but you can use the same technique if Reporting Services is installed in native mode.

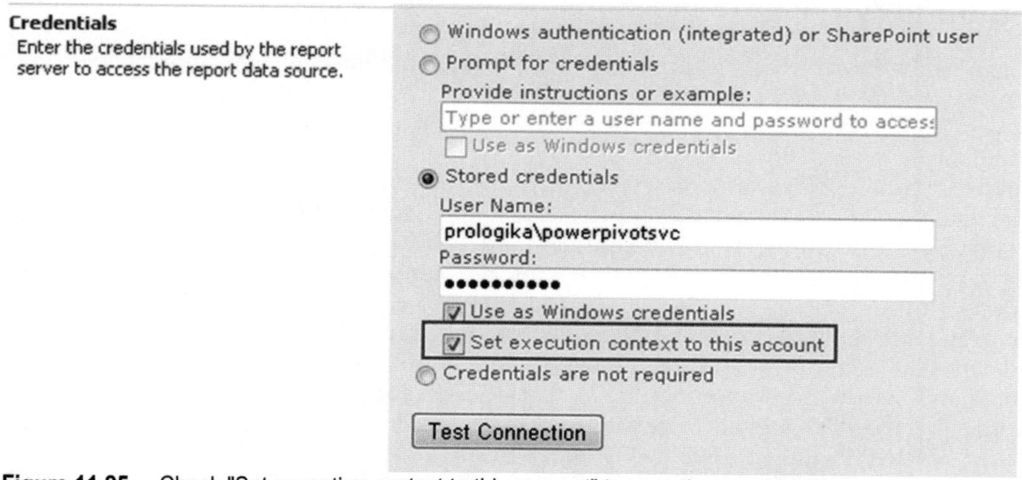

**Credentials**
Enter the credentials used by the report server to access the report data source.

Windows authentication (integrated) or SharePoint user
Prompt for credentials
Provide instructions or example:
Type or enter a user name and password to acces
Use as Windows credentials
Stored credentials
User Name:
prologika\powerpivotsvc
Password:
••••••••••
Use as Windows credentials
Set execution context to this account
Credentials are not required
Test Connection

**Figure 11.25** Check "Set execution context to this account" to pass the user identity.

When configuring the data source, select the "Stored credentials" option, and then specify a Windows account that has administrator rights to Analysis Services. Check the "Use as Windows credentials" checkbox. If you want to pass the user identity to the server, check the "Set execution context to this account" checkbox. As a result, the data provider appends the EffectiveUserName setting to the connection string and row filters that are using the Username function will be able obtain the user identity.

There is another option to bypass Kerberos. Microsoft has enhanced Reporting Services and ADOMD in SQL Server 2012 so that Kerberos is *not* a requirement when authoring Power View reports that are connected to a tabular model on a separate Analysis Services server. To use this option, you must do the following:

- Set the Reporting Services execution account to a Windows account that has administrator rights to the Analysis Services Tabular instance. To do so, in SharePoint Central Administration navigate to Manage Service Applications ⇨ <Your SSRS Service Application> ⇨ Execution Account. Check the "Specify an Execution Account" checkbox, and then enter the Windows credentials that you want to use.
- Create a BI Semantic Model Connection that connects to your tabular model, as I demonstrated in Section 10.3.

Assuming SharePoint is set up for Windows authentication (not Forms Based Authentication), the ADOMD.NET library will retry the failed connection attempt under the execution account, and then it will switch to the user account by using the EffectiveUserName connection setting. As it stands, this feature is limited to Power View and Tabular only, and it won't work when a multidimensional cube is used as a data source for operational reports.

**NOTE** The difference between using this approach over a Reporting Services data source with stored credentials is that the BI Semantic Model Connection first tries a direct connection. If Kerberos is configured, it will be used. However, if a direct connection fails and if the caller's thread principal is different than the process principal, then ADOMD will connect under the Reporting Services execution account and will add EffectiveUserName to the connection string. This is transparent to the calling application. In addition, EffectiveUserName is added to the query properties and can be viewed in SQL Server Profiler in order to discover the identity of the interactive user.

## 11.4 Summary

While retaining the PowerPivot elegance and simplicity, organizational tabular models add enterprise features for implementing scalable and secure models. The default storage mode is the in-memory VertiPaq cache. As data volumes increase, consider partitioning large tables to improve manageability.

Analysis Services Tabular supports several processing options to refresh data. Process Full is the easiest and cleanest way to reload all the data but it might take too long. When you're looking ways to shrink processing-time windows, consider more lightweight options, such as using Process Data to refresh specific tables or using Process Add to append only new rows.

Besides VertiPaq, Analysis Services Tabular supports a DirectQuery storage mode where the server generates and sends queries to a SQL Server database. Consider DirectQuery when you need real-time data access or when data doesn't fit in the VertiPaq cache.

Layered on top of Windows security, the Analysis Services role-based security allows you to secure data. You can use row filters to implement row-level security by using DAX formulas. You can use the USERNAME and CUSTOMDATA functions to implement dynamic data security based on the Windows identity of the interactive user.

Once your model is ready, it's time to deploy to a production server. The next chapter shows you how you can manage the model in order to keep it operational and performing well.

# Chapter 12

# Managing Tabular Models



As with any other software development lifecycle, it's unlikely that your Tabular journey will end when the model design is complete. In this chapter, you'll wear the administrator's hat and learn how you can manage deployed models. The good news is that if you've ever managed multidimensional cubes, you can seamlessly transfer most of your knowledge to managing Tabular.

As an administrator, you'll perform various tasks in different phases of the model lifecycle. This chapter starts by introducing you to Analysis Services management then and teaches you how to perform routine management jobs, such as backing up databases and scripting objects. Besides SQL Server Data Tools (SSDT) project deployment, you'll learn other options to deploy changes to the server. You'll also find out how to automate processing your models with scripting and with SQL Server Integration Services. Finally, I'll show you how to write .NET and PowerShell code in order to automate repetitive tasks.

## 12.1 Management Fundamentals

You might remember that Tabular and Multidimensional are components of Analysis Services and share the same management framework. As an administrator, you'll perform various day-to-day tasks, such as managing the server instance(s), deploying, backing up, restoring, and synchronizing databases. Analysis Services provides a comprehensive management framework to help you perform all of the above activities. Typically, you'll use SQL Server Management Studio (SSMS) to manage deployed tabular models.

### 12.1.1 Managing the Server

Besides introducing you to Analysis Services Tabular, I didn't discuss how Analysis Services server is implemented and, more importantly, how you can configure its settings. Let's fill this gap now so that you know how to check if Analysis Services is installed and how to connect to it in SSMS.

***Understanding the Analysis Services service***

The Analysis Services server is implemented as a Windows service called SQL Server Analysis Services as you can see by opening the Windows Services applet (see **Figure 12.1**). The physical name of the service executable is msmdsrv.exe. Knowing the service name is important for performance monitoring, such as to see how much memory is allocated to the Analysis Services process.

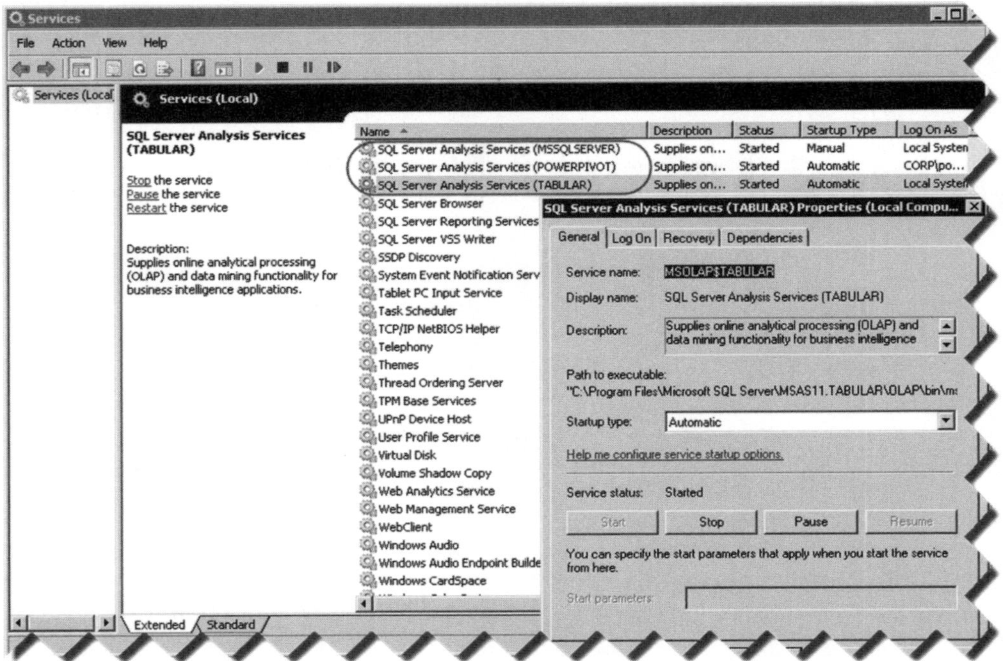


**Figure 12.1** Analysis Services is implemented as a Windows service.

In Chapter 10, I mentioned that you can install Analysis Services multiple times on the same machine by adding named instances. Each installation creates a new SQL Server Analysis Services service. In my case, I have three services of Analysis Services running side-by-side on this server – a default instance (MSSQLSERVER), a second instance named POWERPIVOT, which I've reserved for PowerPivot for SharePoint, and a third instance called TABULAR for Analysis Services running in Tabular mode.

| Name | State | Start Mode | Log On As | Process ID | Service Type |
|---|---|---|---|---|---|
| SQL Server Analysis Services (POWERPIVOT) | Running | Automatic | CORP\powerpivotsvc | 2220 | Analysis Server |
| SQL Server Analysis Services (TABULAR) | Running | Automatic | LocalSystem | 2272 | Analysis Server |
| SQL Full-text Filter Daemon Launcher (MSSQLSERVER) | Running | Manual | NT AUTHORITY\LOC... | 3764 | |
| SQL Server (MSSQLSERVER) | Running | Automatic | LocalSystem | 2336 | SQL Server |
| SQL Server Analysis Services (MSSQLSERVER) | Running | Manual | LocalSystem | 5456 | Analysis Server |
| SQL Server Reporting Services (MSSQLSERVER) | Running | Automatic | LocalSystem | 2964 | Report Server |
| SQL Server Browser | Running | Automatic | NT AUTHORITY\LOC... | 2596 | |
| SQL Server Agent (MSSQLSERVER) | Stopped | Manual | LocalSystem | 0 | SQL Agent |

**Figure 12.2** SQL Server Configuration Manager shows the SQL Server services.

Another tool that allows you to browse the installed SQL Server services is SQL Server Configuration Manager, which you can find in the Microsoft SQL Server 2012 ⇨ Configuration Tools program group (see **Figure 12.2**). SQL Server Configuration Manager reveals additional information that you can't find in the Windows Services applet. For example, use the Advanced tab of the service properties (double-click a service to open the Properties dialog box) to view the product version and service pack level.

You can use both the Windows Services applet and SQL Server Configuration Manager to start and stop the Analysis Services instances. However, you should use SQL Server Configuration Manager to change service accounts. That's because permissions on the service accounts are managed by group membership. When you change the service accounts in the Windows Services applet, you must manually remove the old accounts and then add the new accounts to the corresponding Windows local groups. By contrast, SQL Server Configuration Manager knows how to maintain the group membership.

***Managing the server configuration properties***

The server supports various configuration properties that are stored in the msmdsrv.ini configuration file. The default location of this file is the \Program Files\Microsoft SQL Server\MSAS11.<InstanceName>\OLAP\Config folder. In general, you should abstain from making changes directly to this file to avoid accidentally changing its structure and damaging the file. Instead, use SSMS to manage the server settings, as follows:

1. In SSMS, connect to the Analysis Services instance you want to manage. Notice that the Object Explorer pane shows a visual hint for you to know what configuration mode the Analysis Server instance is running under. A tabular instance is prefixed with a table icon, while a native instance has a cube icon.
2. In the Object Explorer pane, right-click the server, and then click Properties to open the Analysis Services Properties pane (see **Figure 12.3**).

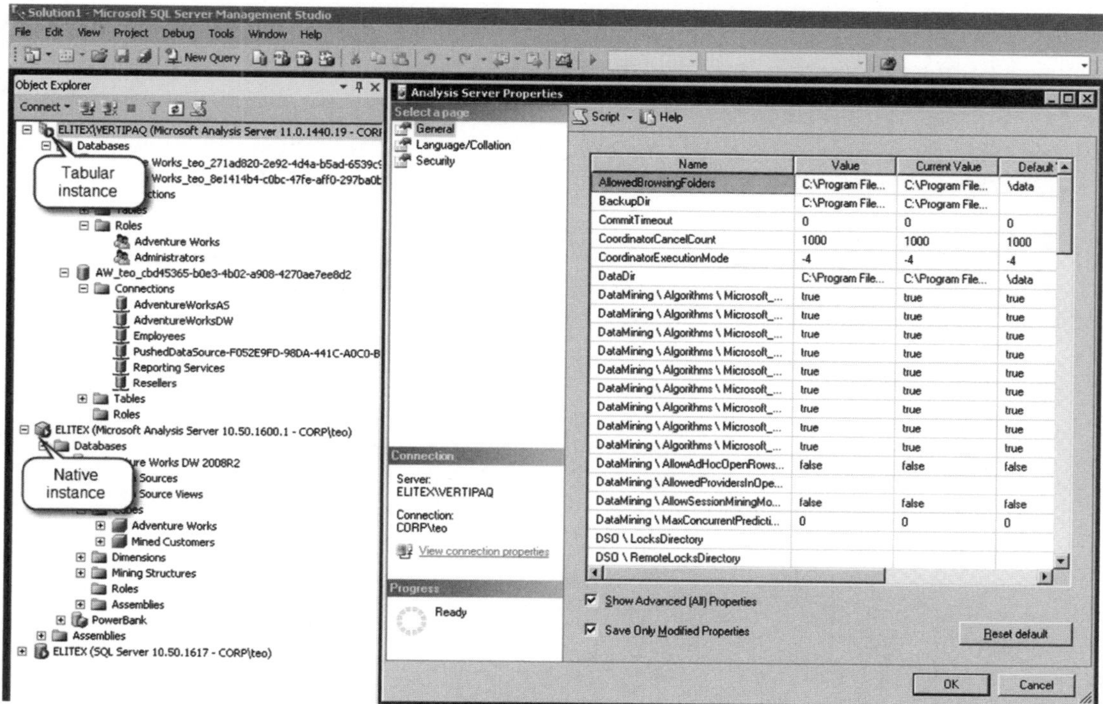


**Figure 12.3** Analysis Services supports various system-wide properties.

3. The Analysis Server Properties dialog box reads a subset of the configuration properties from the msmdsrv.ini configuration file and then displays them in the grid. To change a property, update the corresponding Value column of that property. By default, the dialog box doesn't show all the settings that you can change in SSMS. Click the "Shows Advanced (All) Properties" checkbox to see all the settings that are available in SSMS. The rest of the settings are only available in the msmdsrv.ini file.

   For example, one of the advanced properties is the Port number. The value of 0 specifies the default port on which the server listens (2383). If this is not desired, you can change the port number. Changing certain properties requires you to restart the Analysis Services service. The Restart column indicates if a server restart is required. For example, changing the AllowedBrowsing-Folders property, which restricts the folder navigation for backup and for data, doesn't require a server restart. However, changing the DataDir property, which points to the location where the server saves the processed data, requires restarting the server. For more information about the configuration properties, read the "Configure Server Properties in Analysis Services" topic in Books Online at http://bit.ly/ssasconfigprops.

**NOTE** Not all configuration properties are exposed in SSMS. One example is the DeploymentMode property. You can examine the DeploymentMode property in the msmdsrv.ini configuration file to understand the configuration mode of a given instance. The possible values are 0 (Multidimensional and Data Mining), 1 (PowerPivot for SharePoint), and 2 (Tabular). Unless you know what you are doing, don't change properties directly in msmdsrv.ini. For example, you shouldn't change the DeploymentMode property after setup.

***Managing dependent services***

Your Analysis Services instance might rely on other SQL Server services to function properly. For example, if you install two or more instances of Analysis Services on the same computer or if you change the port number on the default instance, then you also need to enable the SQL Browser service. This service listens for incoming requests and then redirects them to the port on which a given server instance listens. For example, suppose that you've installed Analysis Services Tabular on a named instance called TABULAR. If you need to connect to the TABULAR instance (Data Source=<SERVER>\TABULAR in the connection string), then the connection request will first reach the SQL Browser service, which will redirect it to the TABULAR instance.

**TIP** Use the netstat command line utility to find out which ports a given service listens on. This could be useful if you need to know which firewall ports to enable. The command netstat -a -b -n -o shows all the connections and listening ports in numeric format. Another way to find the port is to open the \Program Files (x86)\Microsoft SQL Server\90\Shared\ASConfig\msmdredir.ini file and examine the <Instances> XML node.

If you plan to automate management tasks on the Analysis Services server, the SQL Server Database Engine service and the SQL Server Agent service must be running. The SQL Server Agent service allows you to schedule jobs in order to run them in an unattended mode. If SQL Server Database Engine is installed on a separate server, then you can choose to run SQL Server Agent from that server and schedule jobs to manage Analysis Services remotely, such as to process a tabular database.

## 12.1.2 Managing Memory

Previously I explained in Chapter 11 that the default Tabular storage model is VertiPaq. VertiPaq is an in-memory store and performs best when the entire model fits in memory. When planning your Analysis Services Tabular deployment, you may wonder how to estimate memory.

***Estimating memory***

You can use the following crude formula to estimate the required memory for Analysis Services Tabular:

Estimated Memory = 2 x $M_t$ + $M_o$

$M_o$ represents the additional memory on the server that's needed for the operating system and for other applications running on the server. $M_t$ is the disk footprint for all the tabular databases on the server. You can get the disk footprint from the folder properties of the Analysis Services Data folder (\Program Files\Microsoft SQL Server\MSAS11.TABULAR\OLAP\Data by default).

As a rule of thumb, you should multiply the disk footprint at least twice. That's because depending on the nature of the data, the in-memory database footprint can be significantly larger than its disk counterpart. And, the server might need more memory during processing. For example, it might need to store a few million rows of uncompressed data during processing. Finally, additional memory might be required for complex queries and concurrent users.

***Understanding paging***

What happens if the model doesn't fit in memory? The server starts paging data out of memory to disk and the performance degrades. The exact paging behavior is controlled by the following server properties:

- VertiPaqPagingPolicy – If this property is set to 0, the VertiPaq memory utilization can't exceed the server's physical memory. If it does, you'll get an error that the server has run out of memory. If VertiPaqPagingPolicy is 1 or 2, then the server's total memory utilization can exceed the physical memory. When this happens and VertiPaqPagingPolicy is set to 1, the server uses the system page file exclusively, while VertiPaqPagingPolicy set to 2 uses memory-mapped files. The default setting is 1.
- VertiPaqMemoryLimit – This setting applies only to Analysis Services in Tabular and in SharePoint mode. If VertiPaqPagingPolicy is set to 0, it indicates the amount of memory as a percent of the total server memory that VertiPaq is allowed to use. With a paging policy of 1 or 2, its semantics are more complex because the server provides a way to prevent VertiPaq from interfering with the memory cleaning subsystem. In those modes, it causes the cleaner subsystem to ignore memory that's allocated for VertiPaq data beyond VertiPaqMemoryLimit when calculating the price of memory.
- HardMemoryLimit – This is the maximum memory that's allocated to the Analysis Services instance. If the server exceeds the hard memory limit, the system will aggressively kill active sessions to reduce memory usage. Sessions killed for this reason will receive an error about being cancelled due to memory pressure. In Analysis Services Tabular or Analysis Services in SharePoint integrated mode, when VertiPaqPagingPolicy is something other than 0, it's also the limit for the maximum working set of the process.
- TotalMemoryLimit – This is the high memory limit which is used to calculate the memory price for a normal cache eviction and memory cleaning. If the server exceeds TotalMemoryLimit, it will start evicting all the cached data that isn't currently in use. The TotalMemoryLimit setting must always be less than the HardMemoryLimit setting.

- LowMemoryLimit – Indicates the threshold above which the system will begin cleaning memory out of caches. As memory usage increases above the low memory limit, the server gets more aggressive about evicting cached data until it hits the total memory limit, at which point the server evicts everything that isn't pinned.

> **TIP** If the server is running Windows Server 2008 R2 with Service Pack 1 or later and if you expect the VertiPaq memory consumption to exceed the physical memory, then set the VertiPaqPagingPolicy property to 2 to let VertiPaq use memory-map files. Leave this property to its default setting of 1 for operating systems prior to Windows 2008 R2 SP1 because the server working set gets trimmed aggressively when memory-map files are used, resulting in poor performance even if the machine has plenty of physical memory available.

***Configuring memory settings***

You can configure the memory settings in SSMS as follows:

1. Open SSMS, and then connect to the Analysis Services instance that's configured for SharePoint integrated mode or for Tabular mode.
2. Right-click the server, and then click Properties.
3. In the Analysis Services Properties dialog box, check "Show Advanced (All) Properties".
4. Scroll down to the Memory section, as shown in **Figure 12.4**.

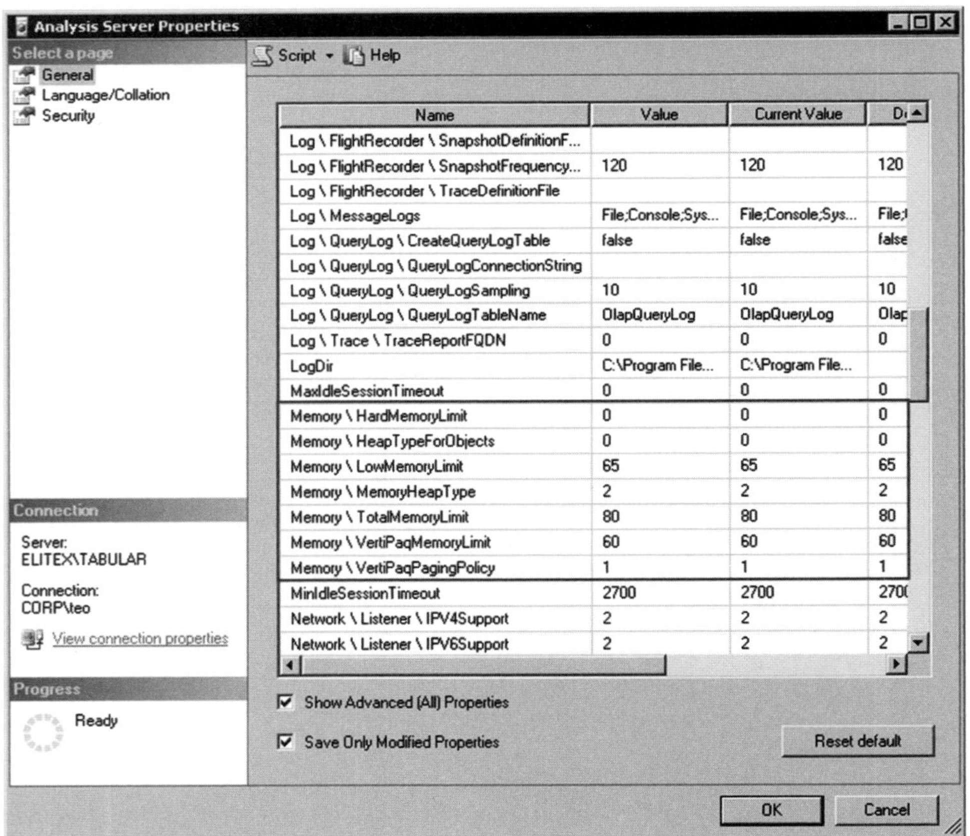


**Figure 12.4** Analysis Services supports several settings that control the server utilization.

## 12.1.3 Managing Databases

One ongoing activity that every administrator needs to master is database management. The database management tasks that I'll focus on in this section are configuring data sources, querying data, backing up, restoring, and attaching databases. I'll show you how SSMS can help you perform these database-related tasks. Note that you can't use SSMS to make design changes to your models, such as adding tables, columns, or relationships. You must use SSDT to change the model design. SSMS is limited to management tasks only.

**NOTE** Before you make changes in SSMS keep in mind that they might be overwritten when a developer deploys the model from SSDT. For example, if you add a user to a security role, that change will be overwritten upon the next deployment if the role is left unchanged in the project. So consider having the developers apply the changes in the project, or instruct them to use the Deployment Wizard, which I'll discuss in Section 12.2.1.

***Getting started with database management***

Immediately below the server node in the Object Explorer pane is the Databases folder. If you expand the Databases folder, you'll see a list of all the tabular databases deployed to the server. The list includes databases that are explicitly deployed to the server as well as workspace databases if the server is used as a workspace server.

1. Expand one of the database folders, such as Adventure Works. Notice that it has three folders: Connections, Tables, and Roles.

The Connections folder includes all the data sources that are defined in the model. As an administrator, you should verify that all the connection strings are valid after a new database is deployed to the server so that you can successfully process the database. The Tables folder shows the tables in the model. Typical table-level management tasks include processing a table or configuring partitions.

The Roles folder shows the database roles that are defined in the model. You can use SSMS to add or delete roles, change the role membership (add or remove members to a role), and change the row filters. You can right-click an object to see a list of management tasks that apply to this object. For example, you can right-click an object, and then click Properties to view and change the object's properties. Properties that appear grayed out are read-only and can't be changed.

2. Right-click the Adventure Works database, and then click Properties to open the Database Properties pane, as shown in **Figure 12.5**. Note that this pane shows the database estimated storage size and the last time it was processed. You can change the database DirectQuery mode if needed.

***Testing databases***

Once the database is deployed to the server, you should test the database to make sure that it's functional and available for reporting. You can use SSMS to browse the database data and to query it by writing custom MDX or DAX queries. To quickly test that the database is functional, right-click it in SSMS, and then click Browse. This action opens the familiar MDX query designer that's capable of auto-generating MDX queries as you drag objects from the Metadata pane to the Data pane. SSMS adds another toolbar (SSMS Toolbar) on top of the MDX query designer, as shown in **Figure 12.6**. You can use this toolbar to test security, reconnect to the database, refresh the metadata, change the language, or open Excel (if you prefer to analyze the model in Excel pivot reports).

**NOTE** You can't use the MDX query designer to test DirectQuery models because DirectQuery doesn't support MDX. You must use Power View or DAX queries in SSMS to test DirectQuery.

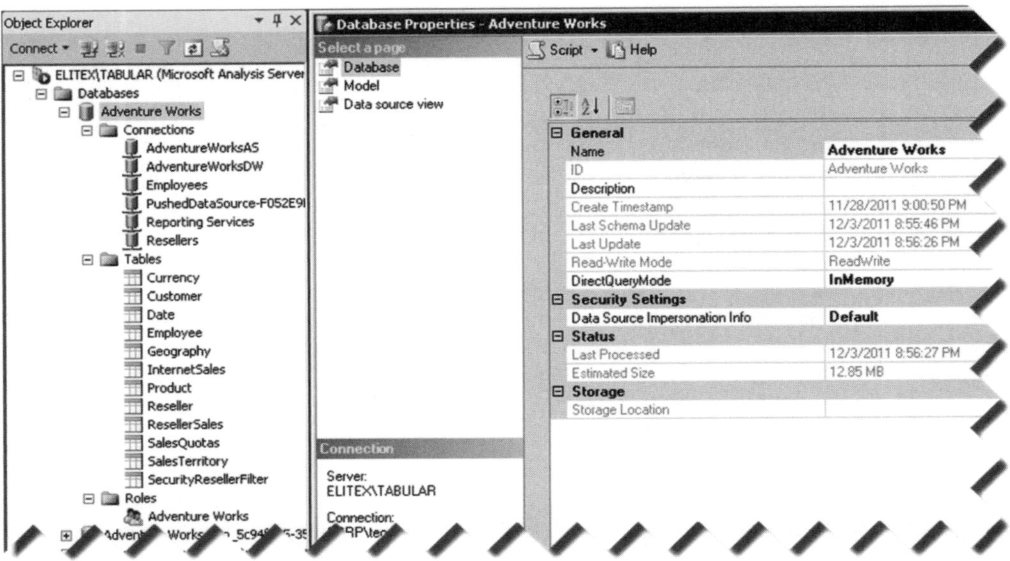

**Figure 12.5** Use SSMS to perform management tasks, such as changing the object properties.

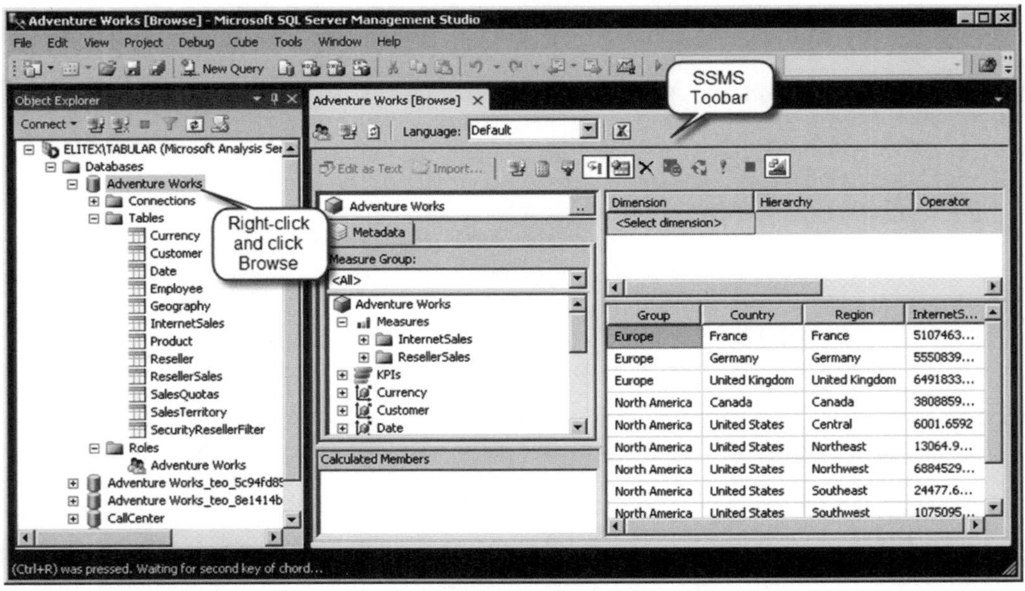


**Figure 12.6** Use the MDX query designer to browse tabular databases.

You can create and test custom queries in SSMS, as follows:

1. Right-click the database, and then click New Query ⇨ MDX.
2. Write a DAX query (see Chapter 10 for examples) or an MDX query. Click the Execute button (or Ctrl + E) to execute the query and see the results, as shown in **Figure 12.7**.

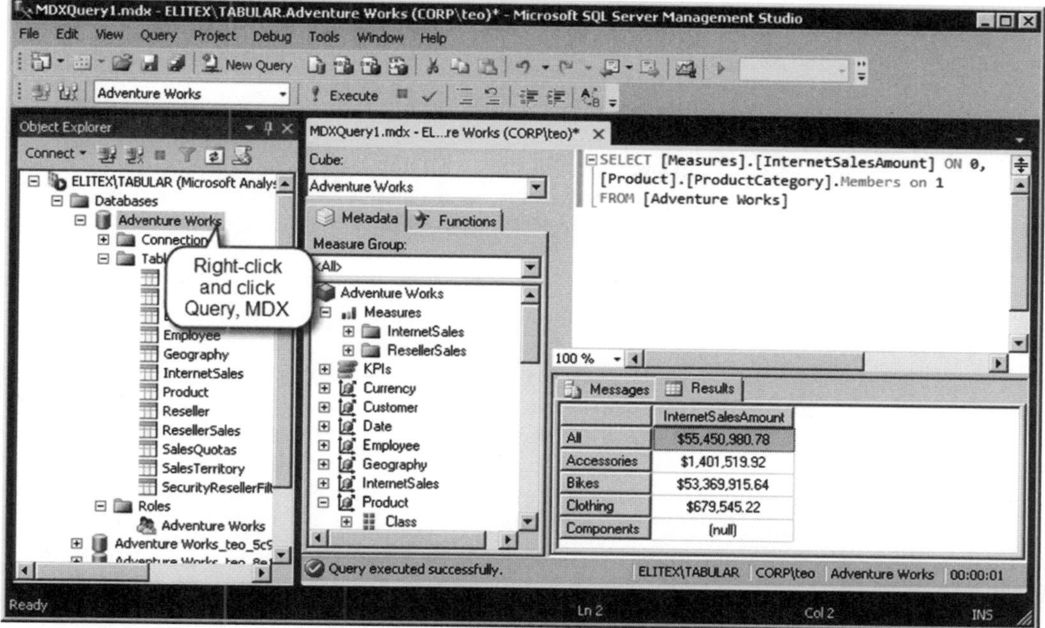


**Figure 12.7** You can execute custom MDX and DAX queries to query a tabular database.

When you query a Tabular model with MDX, you must use Multidimensional constructs, such as measures and members. In this case, the MDX query requests the InternetSalesAmount measure (InternetSalesAmount column in the InternetSales table), grouped by the members of the ProductCategory dimension (the unique values of the ProductCategory column in the Product table).

Unlike Multidimensional, the Language drop-down list in the MDX query designer isn't very useful for tabular models because Tabular doesn't support translations to localize metadata and data for international users. To be more accurate, Tabular doesn't support translating data, but it supports translating metadata, such as table and column names although it doesn't include user interface for the latter option.

**NOTE** A future version of the popular BIDS Helper add-in (http://bidshelper.codeplex.com) is expected to include user interface for configuring metadata translations. Changing the language in the Language drop-down list can help you see translated error messages and help you format dates and currencies based on your regional settings. For more information about language and collation settings, read the blog post, "Collation And Language Settings In Tabular Models" by Cathy Dumas at http://bit.ly/bismlanguage.

### *Backing up databases*

A routine maintenance task is backing up a tabular database on a regular basis. The backup process copies the entire database (both metadata and data) so that you can quickly restore the database when needed. The emphasis in the previous sentence is on quickly because you can always recreate an Analysis Service database by deploying the model and processing its data if a backup file isn't available. The backup operation isn't intrusive. This means that users can continue querying the model while the backup operation is running. Follow these steps to back up the Adventure Works database:

1. In SSMS, right-click the Adventure Works database, and then click Back Up to open the Backup Database dialog box.
2. Specify the location of the backup file.

**NOTE** Allowed backup folders are listed in the AllowedBrowsingFolders advanced server property. The default backup folder is \Program Files\Microsoft SQL Server\MSAS11.<INSTANCENAME>\OLAP\Backup, as specified by the BackupDir server property. If you want to save the backup file to a different folder, add that folder to the list of folders in the AllowedBrowsingFolders property. Use a semicolon as a delimiter. You can specify local folders and disk drives only.

If the Apply Compression option is selected, the server will compress the data in the backup file, but be aware that this will increase your backup time. Tabular data is already stored in a compressed format, so you won't gain that much storage if you select this option. Consider encrypting the backup file if the database contains sensitive information. To do so, leave the default "Encrypt Backup File" option selected, and then specify a password. Although the server doesn't enforce any password policies, you should follow best practices and use passwords that are difficult to guess. Save the password in a safe place because you'll need it in order to restore the database.

To restore a database from a backup file, right-click the database, and then click Restore (see **Figure 12.8**). As I demonstrated in Chapter 10, if a business user gives you an Excel workbook containing a PowerPivot model, you can restore it to the server by clicking the "Restore from PowerPivot" option. The Restore and "Restore from PowerPivot" actions bring you the same dialog box. The only difference is that "Restore from PowerPivot" doesn't ask for a password to decrypt the file because an Excel workbook can't be encrypted.

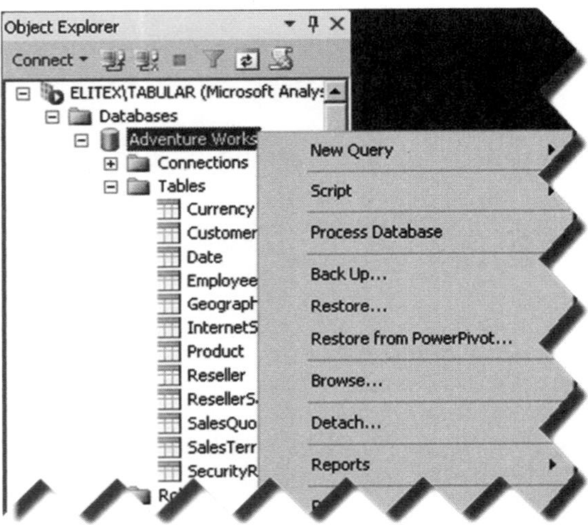


**Figure 12.8** You can restore a database from a backup file or from PowerPivot.

### *Attaching databases*

Suppose that you want to move all databases to a different folder. You can do so by detaching and attaching the databases, as follows:

1. In SSMS, right-click each database, and then click Detach.
2. In the Detach Database dialog box that follows, you can specify a password to encrypt certain files that might contain confidential information. Click OK to detach the database.

3. Use Windows Explorer or other means, such as Robocopy, to copy the database folders to the new location.
4. Right-click the server, and then click Properties. In Analysis Services Properties, change the DataDir property to the new location. Restart the Analysis Services service, and then reconnect.
5. In SSMS, right-click the Databases folder, and then click Attach.
6. In the Attach Database dialog box, click the ellipsis (…) button, and then navigate to the folder where you copied the database. Remember that the AllowedBrowsingFolders server property controls which folders you can browse.
7. If you've specified a password when detaching the database, enter the password in the Password field, and then click OK to attach the database.
8. Repeat steps 5-7 to attach the other databases.

Analysis Services allows you to attach a database in a read-only mode by checking the Read-Only checkbox in the Attach Database dialog box. When the database is in read-only mode, the server disallows certain management operations, such as processing and synchronizing the database. Attaching a read-only database could be useful to scale out Analysis Services when multiple servers connect to the same database on a shared SAN or DAS storage. For more information about this feature, read the "Scale-Out Querying for Analysis Services with Read-Only Databases" whitepaper by Denny Lee and Kay Unkroth at http://bit.ly/ssasreadonlydb.

## 12.2 Managing Deployment

Once the database is in production, you need to keep it up to date by deploying changes made in project mode. The two deployment options that I'll discuss in this section are the Deployment Wizard and synchronizing databases.

### 12.2.1 Working with the Deployment Wizard

As a best practice, your SQL Server Data Tools (SSDT) project should have all the database design changes, including storage and security settings. This approach ensures that the deployed database and its project counterpart are synchronized. However, sometimes you might need to apply changes directly to the deployed database. For example, you need to make role membership changes, such as to add users that belong to a domain that you don't have access to during the design lifecycle. Another example is when a provider wants to change the partition design once the model is deployed to the customer's premises to accommodate specific data loads.

This brings an interesting dilemma, though. How do you apply design changes in your project without overwriting the existing management settings on the server? Unfortunately, SSDT won't preserve the target server settings when you deploy the project and it will overwrite the entire database definition. Luckily, the Deployment Wizard is specifically designed to support incremental deployment to production servers. It uses a set of build files that SSDT generates when you build a project. The Deployment Wizard supports two deployment modes: interactive and command-line. In interactive mode, the wizard reads the build files and walks you through a series of steps. The wizard also supports command-line mode, which you can use to automate the wizard. For example, you can use the command-line method to call the wizard from MSBuild in order to automate deployment.

### *Understanding build files*

When you build an Analysis Services project, SSDT generates a deployment script and additional XML files in the project bin folder. The Deployment Wizard uses these XML files as a basis to deploy changes to the target database. **Table 12.1** describes these build files.

**Table 12.1 SSDT generates the following build files.**

| File | Description |
|---|---|
| Model.asdatabase | Contains the definition of all the objects in the project. |
| Model.deploymentoptions | Contains the deployment options from the project properties and additional user-configurable deployment settings, such as partition overwrite and role membership settings. |
| Model.deploymenttargets | Contains the names of the target deployment server and database. |

### *Understanding command-line mode*

In command-line mode, the Deployment Wizard execution can be controlled by various switches. For example, you can use the /a switch to make changes to configuration files that the wizard will use as a starting point the next time it's run. You can also automate the script generation by running the Deployment Wizard in command-line mode with the /o switch. To see a list of all the switches, open the command prompt, navigate to C:\Program Files (x86)\Microsoft SQL Server\110\Tools\Binn\ManagementStudio, and then type the following:

```
Microsoft.AnalysisServices.Deployment.exe /?
```

**REAL WORLD** One of my projects required an automated deployment of a few databases to several test servers with the Microsoft MsBuild system. We prepared a batch file that performed the deployment in several steps. First, the batch file would build the project to obtain the *.asdatabase file with the following command:

```
devenv.exe /Build projectfile
```

Next, the batch file would start the Deployment Wizard in command-line mode to produce a deployment script file:

```
"\Microsoft.AnalysisServices.Deployment.exe" <filename>.asdatabase /s /o:"<scriptfilename>.xmla"
```

Finally, the batch file would deploy the deployment script using the SSAS ascmd sample utility, as follows:

```
ascmd.exe -S <servername> -i <scriptfilename>.xmla
```

You can download the ascmd command-line utility from the Analysis Services 2008 samples page at http://msftasprodsamples.codeplex.com/. Cathy Dumas outlines another approach for automating tabular deployment in her blog post "Deploying Tabular Projects Using A Custom MSBuild Task" (http://bit.ly/tabularmsbuild).

### *Running the Deployment Wizard*

You can run the Deployment Wizard in interactive mode by clicking Deployment Wizard in the Microsoft SQL Server 2012 ⇨ Analysis Services program group. The Deployment Wizard walks you through the following pages:

1. In the "Specify Source Analysis Services Database" step, you specify the location of the Model.asdatabase deployment script file.
2. In the Installation Target step, you enter the names of the target server and the tabular database. If the database doesn't exist, the wizard creates it.

3. In the "Specify Options for Partitions and Roles" page (see **Figure 12.9**), you specify if you want to overwrite or retain the existing partition settings and security role settings on the target server.

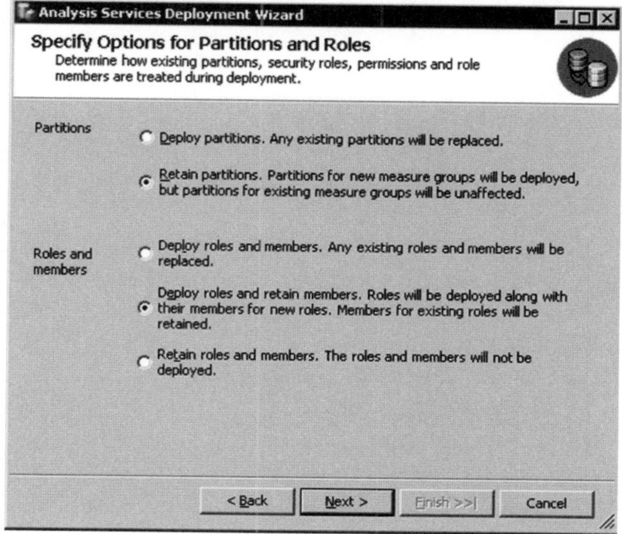


**Figure 12.9** Use the Deployment Wizard to retain partition and role settings on the target server.

4. In the "Specify Configuration Properties" page, you can optionally overwrite configuration, optimization, and impersonation settings, such as the connection string to the data source and impersonation information. The rest of the settings don't apply to Tabular (they apply only to Multidimensional), including the location of error log files, the storage locations at the cube, measure group, and remote partitions. If you don't plan to overwrite any of these settings, check the "Retain Configuration Settings for Existing Objects" and the "Retain Optimization Settings for Existing Objects" checkboxes.
5. In the "Select Processing Objects" step, select a processing option (Default, Full, or None). Select Default (Process Default) processing if you want the server to choose the appropriate processing mode for each object on its own. Select Full Processing (Process Full) to fully process all the objects, or select None to tell the server not to process the database and to deploy the metadata only. If you want processing tasks to happen within a transaction and to restore the database to its initial state if processing fails, then check the "Include All Processing within a Single Transaction" checkbox. For example, if you process two partitions and the first one succeeds but the second one fails, then processing them in a transaction will undo changes to the first partition.
6. In the Confirm Deployment page, shown in **Figure 12.10**, you can leave the Create Deployment Script check box empty to start the deployment process immediately after you click Next. Or, you can select the Create Deployment Script check box to save the deployment settings as a script file for later execution.

   If you decide to create a script, the Deployment Wizard generates an XMLA script file named <DatabaseName> script.xmla and then saves it in the specified location. To execute the script manually, simply open the script file in SSMS, connect to the target server when prompted, and then click the Exclamation toolbar button to run the script (or press CTRL+E). You can also schedule the script execution with the SQL Server Agent service, which is a component of SQL Server. SQL Server Agent supports an SQL Server Analysis Services Command task that's capable of executing any valid XMLA script.

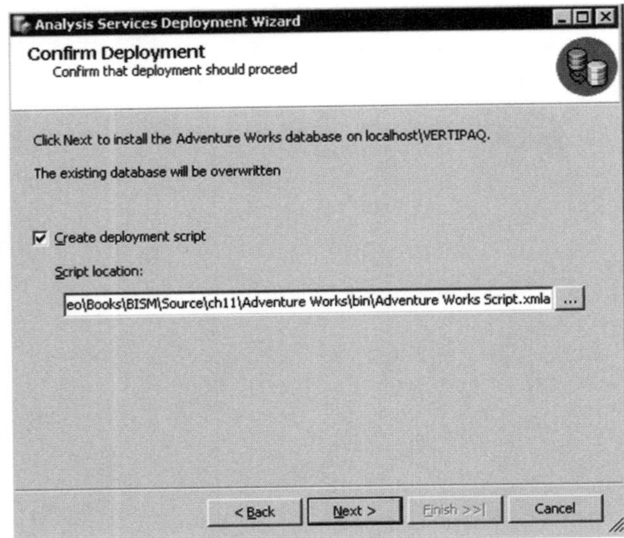


**Figure 12.10** You can save the deployment script as a file for later execution.

**NOTE** XML for Analysis (XML/A) is a specification that standardizes data access between OLAP clients and analytical data providers, such as Analysis Services. Since its debut in mid-2001, XMLA gained support with more than twenty vendors, including the three founding members -- Microsoft, Hyperion, and SAS. The XMLA specification is managed by the XMLA council (www.xmla.org). XMLA is the native protocol of Analysis Services. Irrespective of the communication protocol (TCP or HTTP), all commands to the Analysis Server follow the XMLA specification. SSMS uses XMLA as a scripting language. Many tasks, such as processing or partitioning, can be scripted as XMLA scripts and then executed immediately or at a later time, such as by scheduling them with SQL Server Agent.

## 12.2.2 Synchronizing Databases

Synchronizing two databases is a common management task. For example, you might need to process a model on a dedicated staging server and then deploy it to a farm of load-balanced production servers. Or, you might need to synchronize a corporate server with a remote server in a different geographical region. Analysis Services simplifies this task by providing the Synchronize Database Wizard.

***Understanding database synchronization***

The output of the Synchronize Database Wizard is a script that includes a single XMLA command called Synchronize. You need to send this command to the target server whose objects need to be updated. When the target server receives the Synchronize command, it forwards the command to the specified source server so that it can acquire a read lock on the source database. Next, the target server obtains a list of metadata and data files of the source database.

Having received the files, the target server releases the read lock on the source database because it can complete the remaining tasks on its own. The target server compares the source files against the state of the target database and then identifies the differences. Finally, the target server applies the metadata and data differences to the target database in order to make it identical to its source counterpart.

**NOTE** The important point here is that database synchronization is a file-based operation. It walks the internal object metadata tree and then goes to the file system, comparing file by file to detect which ones have changed. If the file on the source is a later date than the target, then it copies the entire file. It doesn't move internal records within the files. For example, even only one row within a partition has been updated, the server copies the entire partition file. The advantage of synchronizing databases (compared to reprocessing the database on the target server) is that the synchronization is much less processor-intensive and therefore doesn't slow down user queries as much as processing would.

Because copying the database metadata and the data is a privileged task, the Windows account under which the target server runs must have administrative rights to the source database. When you connect to the source server in SSMS, you connect under your identity. However, the target server executes the Synchronize command under its service account. If this is a local server account, the command fails. In order to avoid this, configure the target server to run under a domain service account, and then grant that account administrative rights to the source database.

***Using the Synchronize Database Wizard***

Use the following steps to synchronize two databases:

1. In SSMS, connect to the target server that you want to synchronize.
2. Right-click the Databases folder and click Synchronize to open the Synchronize Database Wizard.
3. In the "Select Database to Synchronize" page, enter the name of the source server in the Source Server drop-down list. Expand the Source Database list, and then select the source database.
4. In the "Specify Locations for Local Partitions" page, review the list of partitions that will be synchronized, and then click Next.
5. The wizard supports limited customization. You can use the Synchronization Options page to preserve the security settings on the target server by selecting the "Skip membership" option, as shown in **Figure 12.11**. Partition files can be very large, so the Synchronize Database Wizard supports very efficient compression to send the data changes across the wire. Leave the "Use compression when synchronizing databases" checkbox selected to compress the data.

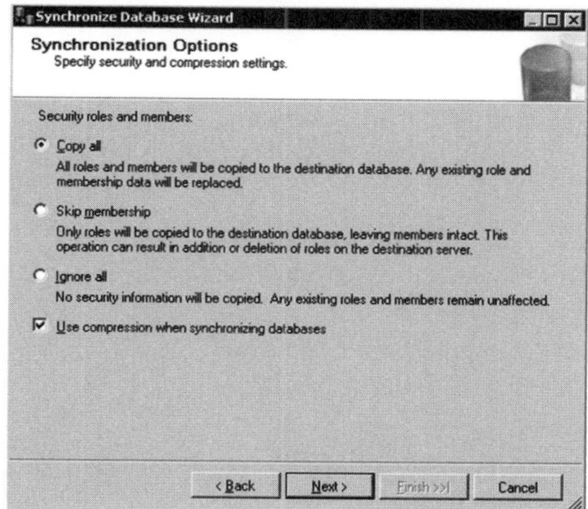


**Figure 12.11** Use the Synchronize Database Wizard to retain the security settings on the target server and to compress the synchronization files.

6. Use the "Select Synchronization Method" page to specify the deployment method. As with any deployment, you can start the synchronization process immediately, or you can generate a script and run it later.

# 12.3 Managing Processing

During the design lifecycle, SSDT shields you from the processing technicalities. You might remember that the default project-level processing option in SSDT is Process Default. As a result, when the project is deployed, SSDT identifies the changes that you've made and then applies the right processing option for you. However, once the model is deployed to production, you're responsible for processing it. For example, you'd probably want to automate the processing on a regular basis or to initiate it inside an ETL package. Another common requirement is to process objects incrementally in order to reduce the time it takes to process the model. The most popular options for automating processing jobs are scripting and using SQL Server Integration Services.

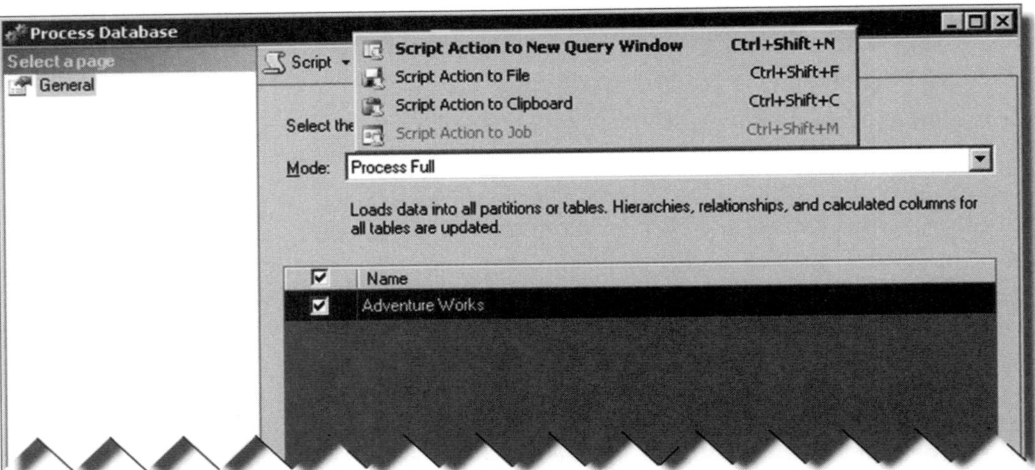


**Figure 12.12** Use the SSMS scripting support to obtain a processing script that fully processes a database.

## 12.3.1 Scripting Processing Jobs

The simplest way to automate Tabular processing is to generate an XMLA script and then schedule the script with the SQL Server Agent. When configuring the job, you can use SQL Server Analysis Services Command to execute the XMLA script.

***Scripting processing tasks***

Suppose you want to fully process the Adventure Works database on a predefined schedule. As a prerequisite, use SSMS to generate a processing script as follows:

1. In SSMS, right-click the Adventure Works database, and then click Process. In my case, SQL Server Agent runs on the same server where Analysis Services Tabular is installed.
2. In the Process Database dialog box, change the processing option to Process Full.
3. Expand the Script drop-down list, and then click Script Action to New Query Window, as shown in **Figure 12.12**. SSMS should generate the following processing script:

```
<Process xmlns="http://schemas.microsoft.com/analysisservices/2003/engine">
  <Type>ProcessFull</Type>
  <Object>
    <DatabaseID>Adventure Works</DatabaseID>
  </Object>
</Process>
```

4. Select the entire script, and then press Ctrl+C to copy it to the Windows Clipboard.

***Scheduling processing with SQL Server Agent***

SQL Server Agent is a component of the SQL Server Database Engine. It executes scheduled administrative tasks, which are called jobs. Follow these steps to schedule the processing script:

1. In SSMS, connect to the Database Engine instance that will run the script.
2. If the SQL Server Agent service isn't running, right-click it in the Object Explorer pane, and then click Start.
3. In Object Explorer, expand the SQL Server Agent folder. Right-click the Jobs folder, and then click New Job.
4. In the New Job dialog box, enter *Process Adventure Works* in the Name field (General tab).
5. A job can have one or more steps. In this case, you need only one step. Click the Steps page, and then click the New button to open the New Job Step dialog box (see **Figure 12.13**).

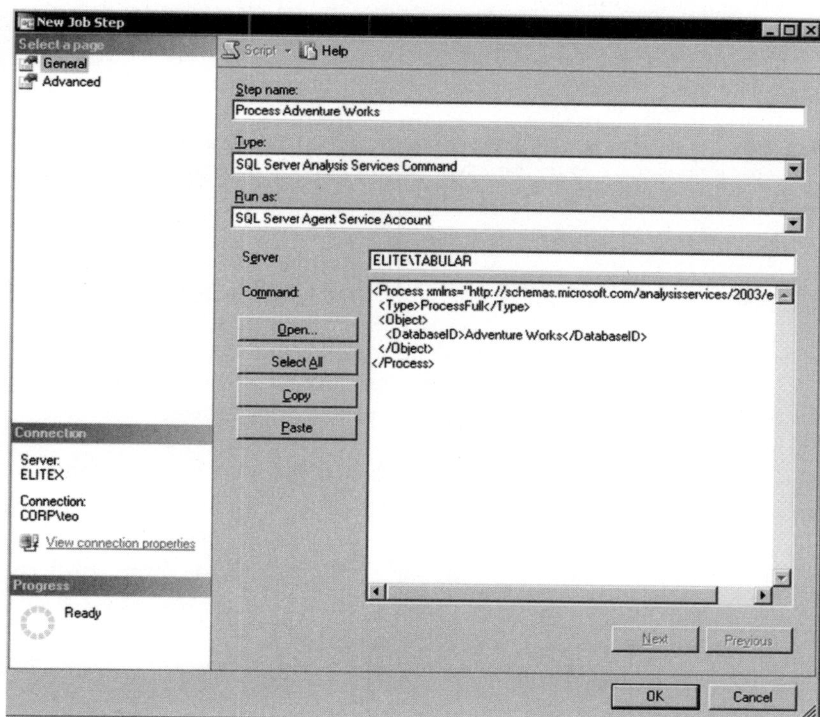


**Figure 12.13** Use the SQL Server Analysis Services Command job type to run an XMLA script.

6. In the Name field, enter *Process Adventure Works*. Expand the Type drop-down list, and then select "SQL Server Analysis Services Command".

**NOTE** By default, SQL Server Agent will connect to Analysis Services using its service account. Therefore, make sure that this service account belongs to an Analysis Services database role that grants it Refresh rights to the Adventure Works database. If Analysis Services Tabular is installed on another server, configure SQL Server Agent to run under a domain service account. Or, you can run the job under a proxy account. For more information about how to create a proxy account, read the "Create SQL Server Agent Proxies" topic in Books Online at http://bit.ly/sqlagentproxy.

7. In the Server field, enter the Analysis Services Tabular instance name.
8. In the Command field, paste the processing script, and then click OK to return to the New Job dialog box.
9. (Optional) Click the Schedules page, and then set up a new schedule to start the job. Click OK.
10. To run the job manually, right-click it in Object Explorer, and then click "Start Job at Step..."

    You should see a Start Jobs dialog box that shows the progress of the job execution.

### 12.3.2 Automating Processing with Integration Services

Another common scenario is initiating processing tasks inside a SQL Server Integration Services (SSIS) package. SSIS includes two tasks for automating processing jobs. The Analysis Services Processing Task is very easy to use, and it's a good choice for implementing basic processing where you explicitly select the objects that you want to process and then specify a processing option. More advanced processing scenarios, such as processing a partition incrementally, would require the Analysis Services Execute DDL Task that's capable of executing an XMLA script. The SSIS project included in the Ch12 folder of the book source demonstrates both approaches.

**NOTE** Readers familiar with Multidimensional might have used push-mode processing inside an SSIS package to push data directly into a multidimensional cube (by using the Partition Processing Task). This task isn't supported by Tabular.

***Processing changed data***

Suppose that to minimize the processing time, you decide to refresh only the latest Reseller Sales partition and its related dimensions at the end of your ETL process. As I discussed in the last chapter, the minimum processing tasks required to accomplish this objective is processing the partition with Process Data, followed by processing the database with Process Recalc. The Processing Update.dtsx package demonstrates how you can implement this. The package uses the Analysis Services Processing Task and Analysis Services Execute DDL Task (see **Figure 12.14**). Follow these steps to configure the Analysis Services Processing Task if you start from scratch:

1. In SSDT, click File ⇨ New ⇨ Project. In the New Project dialog box, click the Integration Services node in the Installed Templates pane, and then click the Integration Services Project template in the right pane. Enter the project name and location, and then click OK to create a project.
2. Drag the Analysis Services Processing Task from the SSIS Toolbox (Common category), and then drop it on the Control Flow tab of the Package.dtsx package. Rename the task to *Process Data*.
3. Double-click the Process Data task to open the "Analysis Services Processing Task Editor" dialog box.
4. If you haven't set up a connection manager yet, click the New button to set up a connection to the Adventure Works tabular database.
5. Click the Add button. In the "Add Analysis Services Object" dialog box, expand the Dimensions node, and then check the Date, Sales Territory, Reseller, Employee, Currency, Geography, and Product dimensions.
6. Expand the Cubes ⇨ Adventure Works ⇨ Reseller Sales node, and then check the Reseller Sales 2008 partition. Click OK. For the sake of simplicity, in this exercise you select a specific partition. In Section 12.5, I'll show you how to programmatically determine the latest partition, using Analysis Management Objects (AMO).

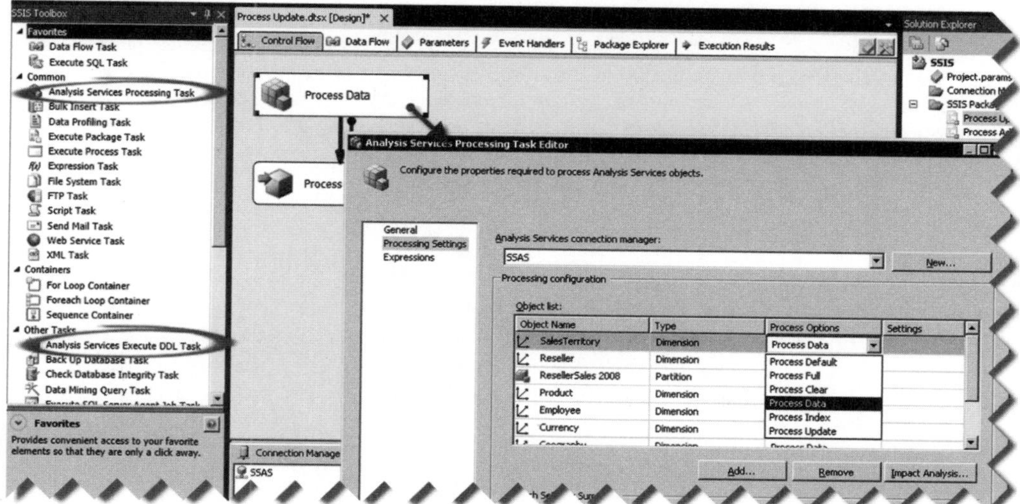


**Figure 12.14** Use the Analysis Services Processing Task to process tabular objects.

7. Change the processing option of all objects to Process Data.
8. Because the Analysis Services Processing Task doesn't support the Process Recalc option, you need to use the Analysis Services DDL Task. Start by generating a script. In SSMS, right-click the Adventure Works database in the Object Explorer pane, and then click Process Database. In the Process Database dialog box, change the Mode drop-down menu to Process Recalc. Expand the Script drop-down menu, and then click "Script Action to New Query Window" (or press Ctrl+Shift+N). SSMS should generate the following script:

```
<Process xmlns="http://schemas.microsoft.com/analysisservices/2003/engine">
  <Type>ProcessRecalc</Type>
  <Object>
    <DatabaseID>Adventure Works</DatabaseID>
  </Object>
</Process>
```

9. Select the entire script, and then press Ctrl+C to copy it.
10. Back in SSDT, drag the Analysis Services DDL Task from the Toolbox to the Control Flow tab of your SSIS package. Rename it to *Process Database*. Click the Process Data task, drag its green connector, and then drop it on the Process Database task to connect the two tasks together.
11. Double-click the Process Database task. In the "Analysis Services Execute DDL Task Editor", select the DDL page. Expand the Connection drop-down list, and then select the Connection Manager that points to the Adventure Works database. Paste the processing script in the SourceDirect property. Click OK.
12. Press F5 to run the package. The package should execute successfully.

**NOTE** Microsoft hasn't updated the Analysis Services Processing Task to support tabular models natively. As a result, the tabular metadata is mapped to multidimensional artifacts, such as dimensions and measure groups. Moreover, the default processing option for dimensions is Process Update, which isn't supported by Tabular. Tabular-specific processing options, such as Process Defrag and Process Recalc, must always be called from the Analysis Services Execute DDL Task. Also be aware that the Analysis Services Execute DDL Task hardcodes the database ID in the XMLA script for the processing task. As a result, changing the connection string in the connection manager has no effect (you must change the Source property of the task).

### *Processing new data*

Now, suppose that only new data is added to the ResellerSales table. The most efficient processing option then will be Process Add. The Process Add package demonstrates how you can incrementally process the Reseller Sales 2008 partition. It uses two Analysis Services Execute DDL tasks. Because the Analysis Services Processing Task doesn't support the Process Add option, the first Analysis Services Execute DDL task executes the following processing script:

```
<Batch xmlns="http://schemas.microsoft.com/analysisservices/2003/engine">
	<Parallel>
		<Process>
				<Object>
						<DatabaseID>Adventure Works</DatabaseID>
						<CubeID>Model</CubeID>
						<MeasureGroupID>0df53bfe-d65a-41d7-a66d-9d82dc7ffcc2</MeasureGroupID>
						<PartitionID>ResellerSales_648262c9-c9a6-467e-89c2-84ac26766a56</PartitionID>
				</Object>
				<Type>ProcessAdd</Type>
				<WriteBackTableCreation>UseExisting</WriteBackTableCreation>
		</Process>
	</Parallel>
	<Bindings>
		<Binding>
				<DatabaseID>Adventure Works</DatabaseID>
				<CubeID>Model</CubeID>
				<MeasureGroupID>0df53bfe-d65a-41d7-a66d-9d82dc7ffcc2</MeasureGroupID>
				<PartitionID>ResellerSales_648262c9-c9a6-467e-89c2-84ac26766a56</PartitionID>
				<Source>
				 <DataSourceID>928bbd64-0711-433c-afad-1fe0c76ac5a9</DataSourceID>
				<QueryDefinition>
						SELECT	DimProduct.ProductAlternateKey
							,FactResellerSales.ProductKey
							...
							FROM
							DimProduct
							INNER JOIN FactResellerSales
							ON DimProduct.ProductKey = FactResellerSales.ProductKey
							WHERE OrderDateKey >= 20110101
				 </QueryDefinition>
				</Source>
		</Binding>
	</Bindings>
</Batch>
```

The Process element instructs the server to process the Reseller Sales 2008 partition in the Reseller Sales measure group. The measure group is the "Model" cube, which is in the Adventure Works database. Notice that the script uses object identifiers and not names. For example, although you've changed the Cube Name project deployment property to "Adventure Works", its system identifier is "Model". You can obtain the object identifiers by scripting the entire database (right-click the database in SSMS, and then click Script ⇨ Script Database As ⇨ CREATE To).

Next, the script includes a Bindings element that specifies out-of-line binding in the form of a SELECT statement that retrieves the new rows. The SELECT statement schema must match the Reseller Sales table schema. Finally, similar to the Process Update package, the package uses a second Analysis Services Execute DDL Task to process the database with Process Recalc.

**TIP** You can connect to a multidimensional cube to generate a script that will process a partition incrementally to load only the new rows added to a table. In SSMS, right-click a partition, and then click Process. In the Process Partitions dialog box, change the partition option to Process Add, and then click the Configure link in the Settings column. This opens the Incremental Update dialog box that you can use to specify the table, the SQL view, or a SELECT statement that returns the new rows.

## 12.4 Monitoring the Server

An important management task is monitoring the server availability and performance. In real life, users might occasionally report errors or degradation of the server performance. By monitoring the server, you can ensure that it functions correctly and that's performing optimally. Analysis Services supports various options to help you track the health and utilization of the server, including tracing, performance counters, and dynamic management views (DMVs).

### 12.4.1 Tracing With SQL Server Profiler

SQL Server Profiler allows you to understand what's going on under the "hood" of the server. You would typically use SQL Server Profiler to monitor the server activity, such as the queries that are sent to the server and their execution times. SQL Server Profiler supports tracing both the SQL Server Database Engine events and the Analysis Services (Tabular and Multidimensional) events.

A trace is an Analysis Services object that exists on the server. As part of creating the trace, you specify which events you want to monitor. Once configured, the trace object outputs the selected events. Behind the scenes, the events are raised using the WMI (Windows Management Instrumentation) infrastructure that's baked into the Windows operating system. A WMI-aware application, such as SQL Server Profiler, can intercept these events and then display them for monitoring purposes.

***Starting an Analysis Services trace***

Let's see how we can leverage the SQL Server Profiler to monitor an Analysis Services server.

1. Start SQL Server Profiler from the Microsoft SQL Server 2012 ⇨ Performance Tools program group.
2. Choose File ⇨ New Trace. In the "Connect To Server" dialog box, select Analysis Services as a server type, and then enter the name of the server that you want to monitor. Click Connect to connect to the server.
3. In the Trace Properties window (General tab), name the trace *SSAS*. Note that you can save the trace to a file (with the extension .trc) or in a SQL Server table. Capturing the trace output to a file is useful if you want to replay the trace later.
4. Switch to the Events Selection tab, and then check the "Show all events" checkbox, as shown in **Figure 12.15**. Analysis Services provides many events that are grouped in event categories. A brief description of the event categories is in order.

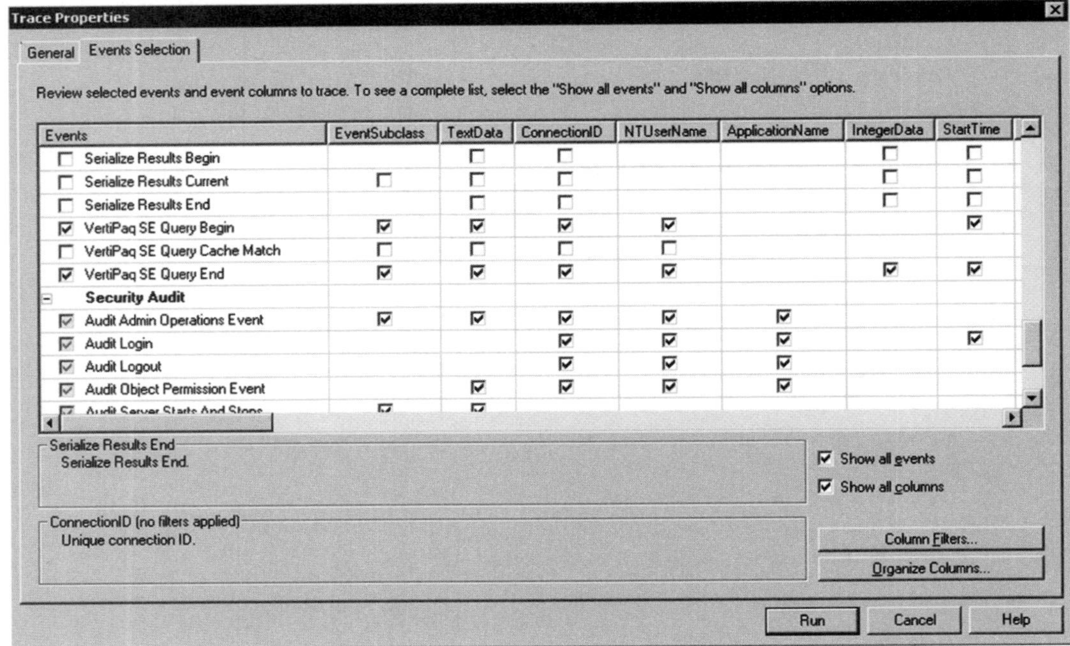


**Figure 12.15** Use the Event Selection tab to filter the events that you want to monitor.

***Understanding event categories***

Command events are raised when action-oriented statements are sent to the server. Examples of such statements are the scripting tasks that we performed in this chapter, including deploying, synchronizing, backing up, and restoring databases. Discover events are generated when you query the model metadata, such as to obtain a list of the tables in the model. Discover Server State events are a subset of the Discover events, which are raised as a result of querying the server state, such as to find the number of the currently open connections.

As the name suggests, the "Errors and Warnings" category contains events that the server raises when it encounters an error condition. For example, if you send a syntactically incorrect DAX query to the server, you'll get an error event. This is the most important category that you would want to monitor in order to troubleshoot failed queries. Every now and then, the server raises Notification events when it performs tasks that are triggered by internal events, such as when the Flight Recorder starts a new capture. The Progress events inform the client about the progress of a given task, such as when processing a database.

The Query events output the MDX and DAX queries that are sent to the server. As a first stop for trouble-shooting query performance issues, I recommend you trace the query that's sent to the server, and then find out how long it took to execute by examining the Duration column in the Query End event. The Query Processing event category includes events that reveal more information about how the server processes the query. There are also tabular-specific events – Direct Query, DAX Query Plan, and VertiPaq SE events. As I mentioned in Chapter 11, the server generates Direct Query events when the database is configured for Direct Query mode.

The DAX Query Plan events contain logical and physical plans generated when executing a DAX query. You can use these advanced events to troubleshoot performance issues. Jeffrey Wang, Principal Software Development Lead with the Analysis Services team, explains the DAX Query

Plan events in more details in his blog post, "DAX Query Plan, Part 1, Introduction" at (http://bit.ly/daxqueryplan).

Finally, the VertiPaq SE events help you understand how much time the storage engine spends when retrieving data from the VertiPaq store. Once the formula engine has parsed the DAX query it formulates internal requests to the storage engine that resemble SQL SELECT statements, which are exposed as VertiPaq SE events. **Figure 12.16** shows a DAX query and some of its associated VertiPaq SE events.

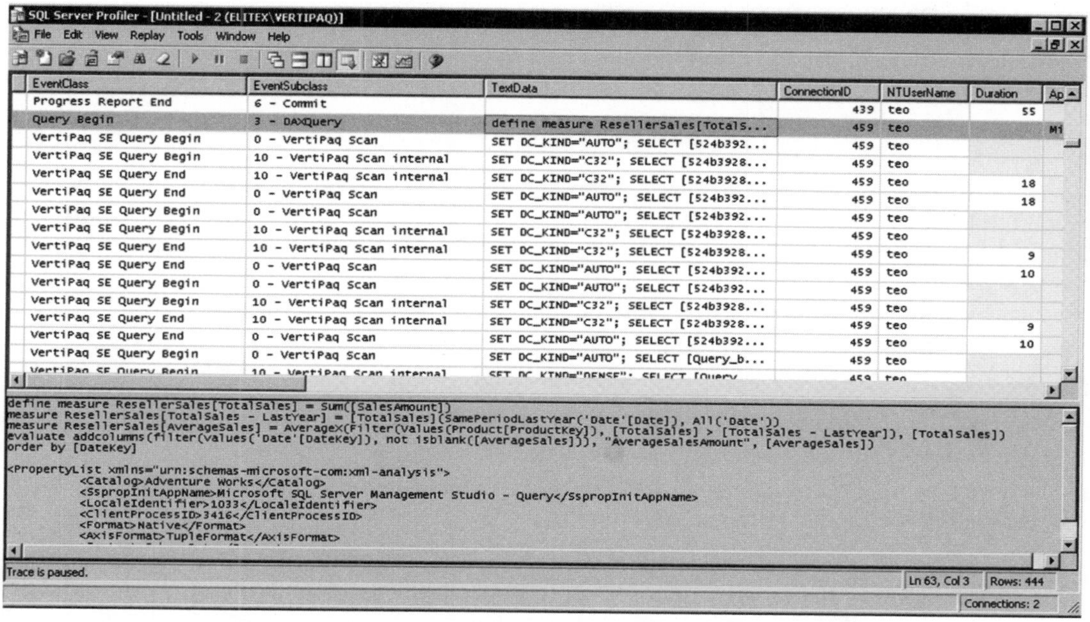

**Figure 12.16** Watch the VertiPaq SE events to monitor the requests to the storage engine.

More complex MDX queries might result in many repeating VertiPaq SE queries, which are very fast but they might add up to the overall query execution time. The server maintains a VertiPaq-level cache to resolve such repeating queries more efficiently. Cache hits are exposed as "VertiPaq SE Query Cache Match" events. You can monitor Security Audit events to find out who has logged in or out of the server. The Session Events category tells when a session starts or ends.

**NOTE** Most requests to the server work in the context of a session – a session encapsulates the server "state", such as the current catalog, and other stateful properties, as well as the state of calculations in each database that the session has accessed. Since sessions can be expensive, the server has a mechanism for expiring old sessions – the typical timeout is one hour with no activity. This timeout can be changed by setting the MaxIdleSessionTimeout server property.

The default trace output can be overwhelming. You can use the Column Filter button to filter the trace output if needed, such as to filter only queries that are sent to a specific database (DatabaseName column) or by a specific user (NTUserName column). Once you've made your selections, click Run to start the trace, and then watch the events in real time.

***Understanding the Flight Recorder***

Sometimes you might need to investigate the server state after it has taken place. For example, suppose that a user reports performance degradation when they ran a report 15 minutes ago. Every administrator knows that one of the most frustrating aspects of troubleshooting issues isn't being able to reproduce them. The Analysis Services Flight Recorder could help you diagnose server issues by allowing administrators to replay failure conditions. Similar to an airplane "black box", the Flight Recorder captures the server activity during runtime. The Flight Recorder is enabled by default. It captures all the events from the past hour and then stores them in a trace file. You can configure the Flight Recorder settings from the Analysis Server Properties dialog box:

1. In SSMS, right-click the server, and then click Properties.
2. In the Analysis Services Properties dialog box, check "Show Advanced (All) Properties".
3. Scroll down the property list to the Log\FlightRecorder category.

By default, the Flight Recorder saves its trace file (FileRecorderCurrent.trc) in the \Program Files\Microsoft SQL Server\MSAS11.<InstanceName>\OLAP\Log folder. Each time the capture duration is exceeded (controlled by the LogDurationSec property) or the server is restarted, a new trace file is generated, and the old file is renamed as a FlightRecorderBack.trc file. Not only can you examine the server events in the file, but you can also replay the activity as follows:

4. Open the trace file in SQL Server Profiler by double-clicking it.
5. Click the Start Replay toolbar button, or press F5.
6. You'll be asked to connect to the target server. Enter the server name and login credentials in the "Connect To Server" dialog box.
7. Use the Replay Configuration dialog box that follows in order to configure the server replay, such as to replay only the events within a given timeframe.

Once you confirm the Replay Configuration dialog box, SQL Server Profiler starts executing the captured events against the server. Moreover, SQL Server Profiler simulates the server state and load as closely as possible. For example, the server will create the same number of open connections and sessions as what had existed during the time of the capture.

## 12.4.2 Monitoring Performance Counters

Consider Windows performance counters when you need to track the server utilization over time. As a part of the setup process, SQL Server installs various performance counters that cover essential server statistics, including caching, connection management, memory utilization, query coverage, processing, and more. The Windows operating systems has its own counters that track the server utilization, including CPU, memory, and disk metrics. You can use the Windows Performance Monitor to track these statistics for local or remote servers. This can be especially useful for load testing, determining the maximum server throughput and identifying performance bottlenecks.

***Selecting performance counters***

Suppose you want to track the server utilization to understand the impact of processing the Adventure Works database. The following steps assume that you use Windows Server 2008 or Windows 7 operating system.

1. Start the Windows Performance Monitor from the Administrative Tools program group. Or, you can launch it from SQL Server Profiler (Tools ⇨ Performance Monitor). If you use Windows XP, go the Administrative Tools program group, and then click Performance.

2. Once the Performance Monitor opens up, in the left navigation pane, expand the Monitoring Tools group, and then click Performance Monitor. Notice that Performance Monitor is configured by default to track the "% Process Time" performance counter of the local machine.
3. Click the Add toolbar button (or press Ctrl+N) to open the Add Counters dialog box.
4. In the "Select Counters from Computer" drop-down list, type in the name of the Analysis Services Tabular server, and then press Enter.
5. Expand the Processor category, select the "% Processor Time" counter, and then click the Add button to add it to the Added Counters pane. You can check the Show Description checkbox to see a description of the selected counter.
6. Also, add the following performance counters: Avg. Disk Queue Length (LogicalDisk category), Available MBytes (Memory category), and "Rows read/sec" (MSOLAP$<InstanceName>\Processing category). Compare your results with **Figure 12.17**. Click OK.

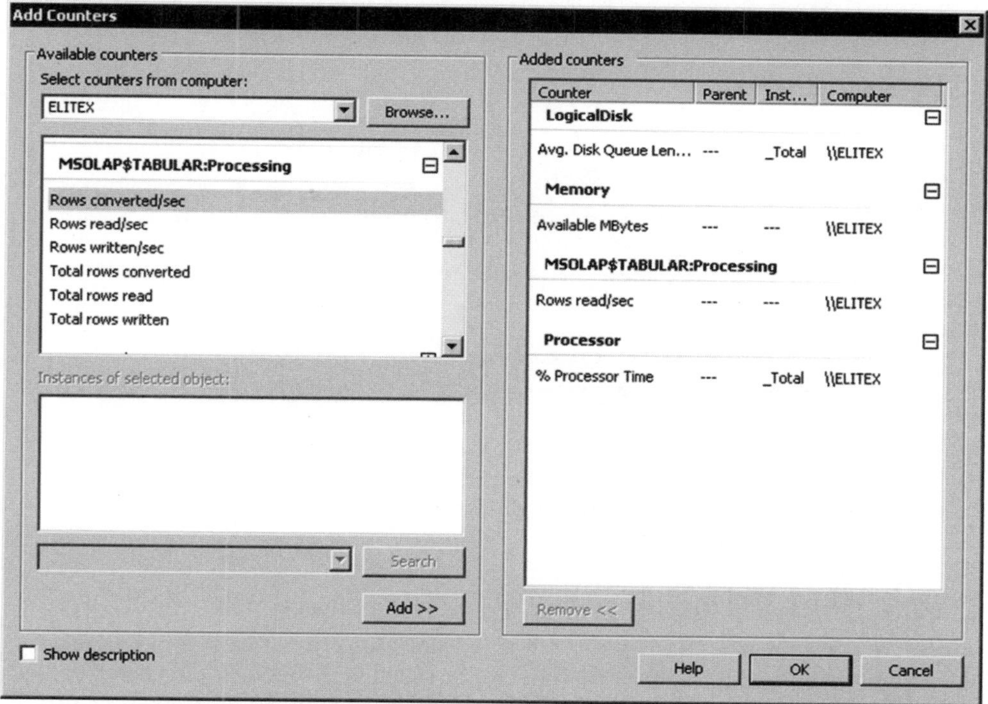


**Figure 12.17** Add performance counters to monitor the CPU, memory, and disk utilization.

***Monitoring performance counters***

To monitor the "Rows read/sec" performance counter:

1. Open SSMS, and then fully process the Adventure Works database.
2. While the server is processing the cube, switch to the Performance Monitor, and then watch the graphs. You should see a spike in the "Rows read\sec" performance counter as the server starts reading and processing rows from the data sources.

In my case, the server maximum throughput was 125,724 rows per second (see **Figure 12.18**). The processing task didn't put much pressure on the memory or CPU utilization. However, the disk queue is an area of concern during processing (disk I/O shouldn't be a concern when users query the model because VertiPaq keeps data in memory unless the data doesn't fit in memory, and then the server pages the data out to disk). Of course, your results will vary depending on the model size, hardware configuration, and other factors.

> **TIP** As noted, performance counters are very useful for load testing the server and for identifying performance bottlenecks. My presentation, "Can Your BI Solution Scale?" (http://bit.ly/scaleBI), outlines a methodology for load testing Analysis Services and Reporting Services. I harvested this methodology from real-life projects.

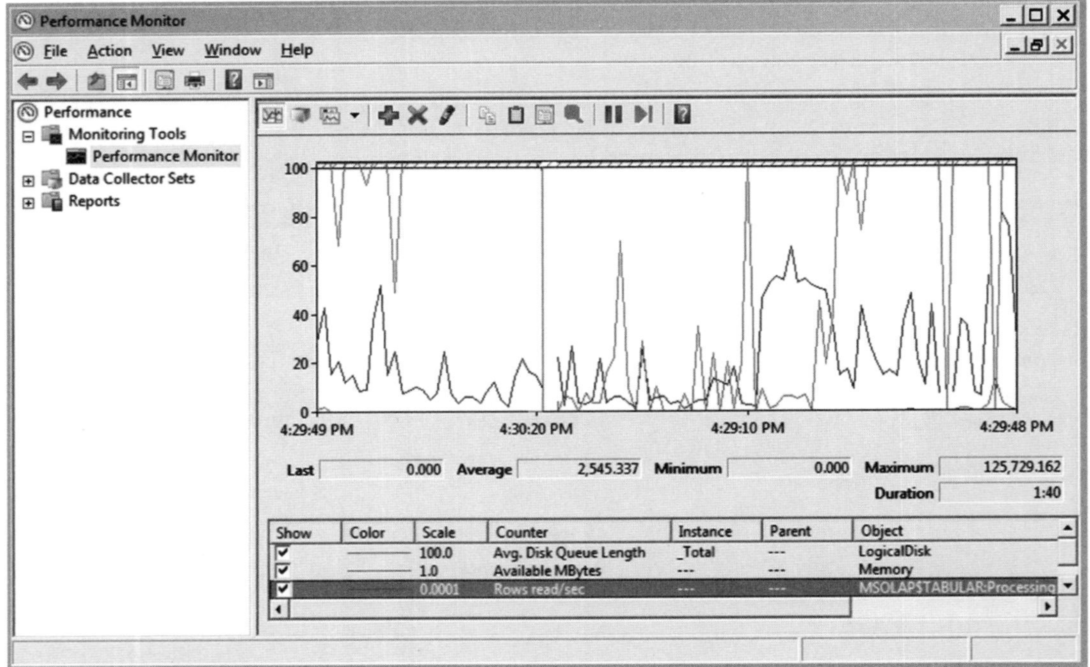


**Figure 12.18** Use Performance Monitor to watch the performance counters.

## 12.4.3 Using Dynamic Management Views

Analysis Services provides dynamic management views (DMVs) to help administrators monitor the health of a server instance, to diagnose problems, and to tune performance. You can use SQL-like SELECT statements to query these views just like you can query a SQL Server relational table.

***Understanding dynamic managements views***

**Table 12.2** lists Analysis Services schema rowsets that you might find particularly interesting. For a full list of the schema rowsets, see the SQL Server 2012 Books Online topic "XML for Analysis Schema Rowsets", at http://bit.ly/ssasrowsets, or execute the following XMLA query:

```
<Discover xmlns="urn:schemas-microsoft-com:xml-analysis">
    <RequestType>DISCOVER_SCHEMA_ROWSETS</RequestType>
    <Restrictions></Restrictions><Properties></Properties>
</Discover>
```

**Table 12.2 The most popular Analysis Services schema rowsets**

| Schema Rowset | Description |
|---|---|
| DISCOVER_COMMANDS | Provides resource usage and activity information about the currently executing or last executed commands in the opened connections on the server. |
| DISCOVER_COMMAND_OBJECTS | Provides resource usage and activity information about the objects in use. |
| DISCOVER_CONNECTIONS | Provides resource usage and activity information about the opened connections on the server. |
| DISCOVER_OBJECT_ACTIVITY | Provides resource usage per object since the start of the service. |
| DISCOVER_OBJECT_MEMORY_USAGE | Provides information about memory resources used by objects. |
| DISCOVER_SESSIONS | Provides resource usage and activity information about the currently opened sessions on the server. |

What is interesting about DMVs is that they maintain statistics since the start of the service. For example, the DISCOVER_CONNECTIONS rowset can tell you how long a given connection has been idle, how many bytes were received or sent through the connection, and when the last statement was sent.

***Querying DMV rowsets***

Follow these steps to query the DISCOVER_CONNECTIONS schema rowsets in order to find what connections a given user has made:

1. In SSMS, connect to the Analysis Services tabular instance.
2. Right-click the server node, and then click New Query ⇨ MDX.
3. Enter the following SELECT statement that queries the rowset. Notice that you must prefix the rowset with "$SYSTEM".

```
SELECT * FROM $SYSTEM.DISCOVER_CONNECTIONS
WHERE CONNECTION_USER_NAME = '<domain login>'
```

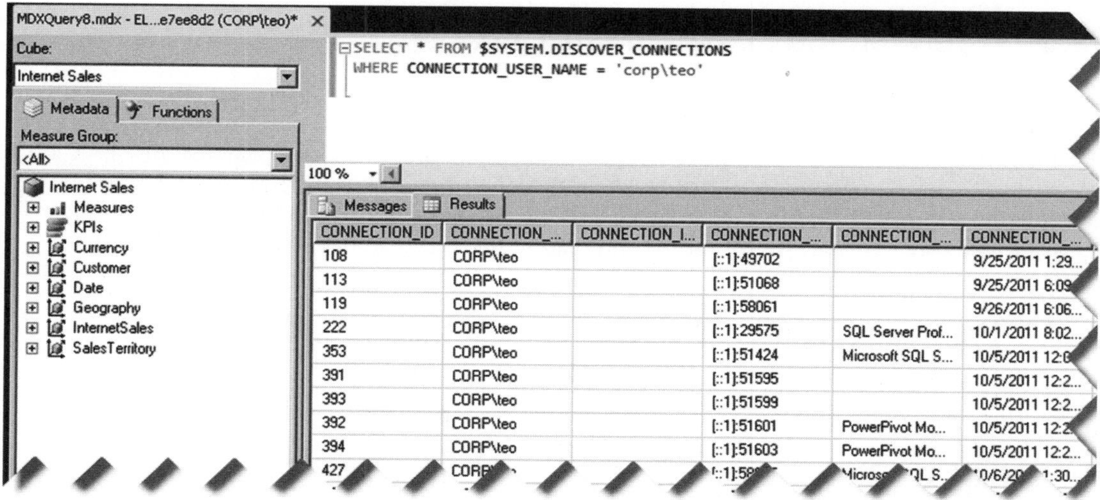


**Figure 12.19** Use the DISCOVER_CONNECTIONS schema rowset to obtain connection statistics.

4. Click the Execute button on the toolbar, or press Ctrl+E. The server shows all the connections that were open since the service was started (see **Figure 12.19**).

### 12.4.4 Error Logging and Reporting

Besides the Flight Recorder capture and replay features, Analysis Services supports other options for troubleshooting error conditions. They range from comprehensive error logging to preparing and sending crash dumps of the server state.

***Error logging***
As a first stop for troubleshooting server error conditions, I suggest you inspect the Windows Event log using the Event Viewer console (found under the Administrators program group). When things go sour, the server outputs various informational messages and error messages to the Application section of the Windows event log. Analysis Services also supports a system-wide error log file (msmdsrv.log) whose default path is \Program Files\Microsoft SQL Server\ MSAS11.<InstanceName>\OLAP\Log (it can be changed in the server properties).

***Dr. Watson crash dumps***
You can help the Microsoft Product Support team investigate server issues by using Dr. Watson minidumps. A minidump captures stack traces of the server process (msmdsrv.exe) and could help Microsoft Product Support to investigate the internal state of the server. One example of when a minidump would be desired is a problem report of a server hang or a server crash.

The Dr. Watson minidump feature is turned on by default. It can be controlled by the Log\Exception\CreateAndSendCrashReports property in the msmdsrv.ini file, which has three possible values – 0 (minidump isn't generated), 1 (create a minidump) and 2 (create and automatically send the minidump file to Microsoft Product Support). Once this property is enabled, the server will automatically generate minidumps when a critical (STOP) server error is encountered. The minidump files (*mdmp) are sequentially numbered and are generated by default in the C:\Program Files\Microsoft SQL Server\ MSAS11.<InstanceName>\OLAP\Log folder. This location is configurable by changing the CrashReportsFolder setting.

## 12.5 Programming Management Tasks

Sometimes (very rarely, indeed!) the Analysis Services management tools and scripting support might not be enough to meet more advanced management needs. For example, you might need to automate the process for creating new partitions, or you might need to write a custom application for processing objects. SSAS provides the Analysis Management Objects (AMO) programming for developers to write .NET code for managing Tabular. In addition, Microsoft provides Analysis Services PowerShell scripting support for automating repetitive tasks with PowerShell scripts.

### 12.5.1 Programming with Analysis Services Management Objects

AMO is a .NET library for programmatically accessing and managing Multidimensional and Tabular models. AMO is implemented as a .NET wrapper on top of XMLA and it's intended to be used by .NET managed clients, such as Visual Basic or C# applications. In fact, SQL Server Management Studio and SQL Server Data Tools, which are .NET-based applications, use AMO behind the scenes for all Analysis Services management tasks.

**NOTE** Be aware that not all AMO features might be supported with Tabular models. As of the time of this writing, Microsoft hasn't made an official announcement about AMO support for Tabular yet. For example, AMO modification tasks, such as generating or altering Tabular models, might not be officially supported.

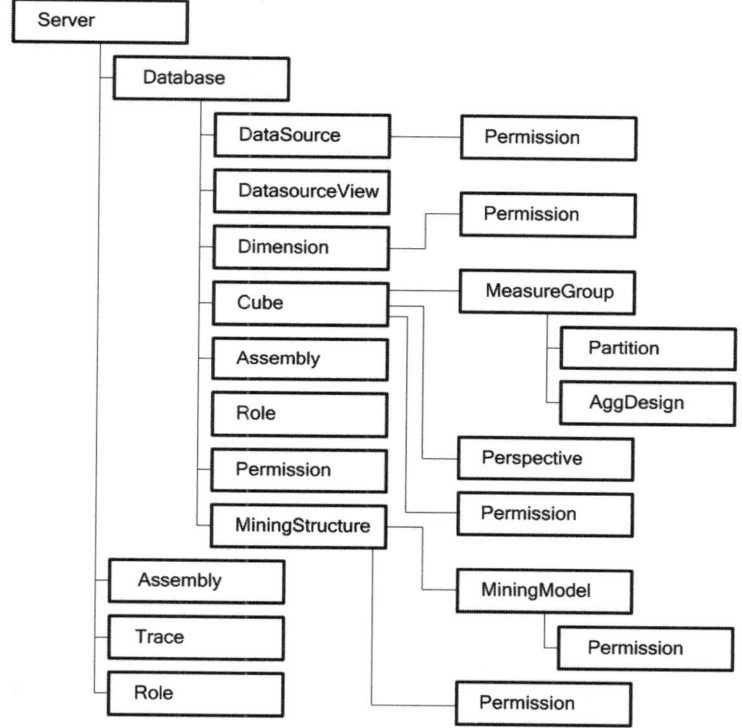


**Figure 12.20** AMO expresses tabular metadata as multidimensional artifacts.

***Understanding the AMO object library***

Although Tabular is a new model, internally Analysis Services expresses the tabular metadata in multidimensional elements, such as dimensions, attributes, attribute hierarchies, and attribute relationships. While this isn't intuitive, it allows you to use AMO to manage both Multidimensional and Tabular models using the same objects. **Figure 12.20** shows the AMO objects. Some objects, such as Assembly, MiningStructure, and AggDesign, apply only to Multidimensional because Tabular doesn't support this functionality.

As you can see, AMO organizes objects in hierarchies to reflect their logical relationships and to facilitate writing .NET code. For example, backing up an Analysis Services database with AMO takes four lines of code (the sample code is included in the Backup C# console application project in the Ch12 folder):

```
Server server = new Server();
server.Connect(@"Data Source=elitex\tabular");
DatabaseCollection databases = server.Databases;
databases.GetByName("Adventure Works").Backup(@"C:\Temp\Adventure Works.abf", true);
```

The Server object represents an instance of a running Analysis Services server. Once connected to the server, you can retrieve all the databases as a DatabaseCollection object. Each object exposes properties you can use to set the object state and methods in order to perform management tasks. For example, use the Backup method of the Database object to back up a database programmatically. If the code changes an object, call the object's Update method to propagate the changes to the server.

### *AMO vs. ADOMD.NET*

Microsoft provides another .NET-based library called ADOMD.NET for integrating .NET applications with Analysis Services. You'll undoubtedly find many similarities between the ADOMD.NET and AMO object models and might wonder how they differ. The ADOMD.NET object is optimized for querying the server metadata and data in a read-only mode. You can't use ADOMD.NET to make changes to the server metadata, such as to change a table name.

By contrast, AMO is optimized for making metadata changes. The AMO Server object supports an Execute method for sending data definition language (DDL) statements to the server, such as to create a database. AMO doesn't support result-based Multidimensional Expressions (MDX), Data Analysis Expressions (DAX), or Data Mining Extensions (DMX) queries.

**TIP** Use the AMO library when your main goal is automating management tasks. Use ADOMD.NET in .NET applications for sending queries to the model and retrieving the results from these queries.

### *Using AMO in Integration Services packages*

In Section 12.3.2, I showed you how to automate partition processing with SQL Server Integration Services. As useful as it is, the Process Update package has left room for improvement. As it stands, the Analysis Services Processing Task processes a specific partition that you chose at design time. However, a more useful package could dynamically determine the latest partition based on the current date. This is where AMO can help. The "Process Update with AMO" package builds upon the Process Update package. Its control flow is shown in **Figure 12.21**.

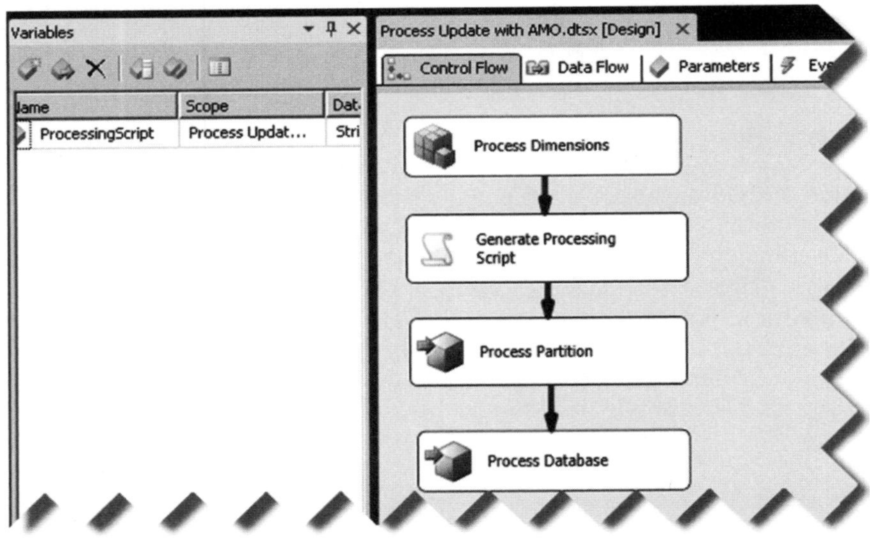


**Figure 12.21** The Generate Processing Script task uses AMO to query the server metadata.

As its predecessor, the first task (Process Dimensions) is an Analysis Services Processing Task although now it refreshes dimensions only. The "Generate Processing Script" task is an instance of the Script Task. Coded in C#, the "Generate Processing Script" task is responsible for preparing a script that refreshes the latest partition in the ResellerSales table and for saving the script in the ProcessingScript variable. **Figure 12.22** shows the code I've written to make this happen. The code has a reference to the AMO library (Microsoft.AnalysisServices.dll) and imports the Microsoft.AnalysisServices namespace with the following statement (line 5):

```
using Microsoft.AnalysisServices;
```

**NOTE** It is unfortunate that Microsoft chose not to install the Analysis Management Object library in such a way that it's enumerable in Visual Studio 2010. As a result, you won't see it in the Visual Studio Add References dialog box. Instead, search the \Program Files\Microsoft SQL Server\110\Tools folder and its subfolders for Microsoft.AnalysisServices.DLL to reference it during development. You don't have to distribute this assembly to other machines if it's installed in .NET Global Assembly Cache (GAC) already.

```
1  using System;
2  using System.Data;
3  using Microsoft.SqlServer.Dts.Runtime;
4  using System.Windows.Forms;
5  using Microsoft.AnalysisServices;
6
7  namespace ST_0cf1e2b1887a4046be9b321101cca63f
8  {
9      [Microsoft.SqlServer.Dts.Tasks.ScriptTask.SSISScriptTaskEntryPointAttribute]
10     public partial class ScriptMain : Microsoft.SqlServer.Dts.Tasks.ScriptTask.VSTARTScriptObjectMod
11     {
12         VSTA generated code
19
20         public void Main()
21         {
22             Server server = new Server();
23             ConnectionManager conn = Dts.Connections["SSAS"];
24             // connect to server
25             server.Connect("Data Source=" + conn.Properties["ServerName"].GetValue(conn).ToString())
26             // reference Adventure Works database from connection string
27             Database db = server.Databases[conn.Properties["InitialCatalog"].GetValue(conn).ToString
28             // cube reference
29             Cube cube = db.Cubes["Model"];
30             // referernce ResellerSales measure group by name
31             MeasureGroup mg = cube.MeasureGroups.GetByName("ResellerSales");
32             // obtain the latest partition for the current year assuming partitioning by year
33             //Partition p = mg.Partitions.GetByName(mg.Name + " " + DateTime.Now.Year);
34             // Since we use the Adventure Works database, hardcode the year to 2008
35             Partition p = mg.Partitions[mg.Partitions.Count-1];
36             // store processing script in ProcessingScript variable
37             Dts.Variables["ProcessingScript"].Value = GenerateProcessingScript(db.ID, cube.ID, mg.ID
38             Dts.TaskResult = (int)ScriptResults.Success;
39         }
40
41         private string GenerateProcessingScript (string dID, string cID, string mgID, string pID )
42         {
43             return String.Format(@"<Process xmlns='http://schemas.microsoft.com/analysisservices/2003/engine'>
44                                 <Type>ProcessData</Type>
45                                 <Object>
46                                   <DatabaseID>{0}</DatabaseID>
47                                   <CubeID>{1}</CubeID>
48                                   <MeasureGroupID>{2}</MeasureGroupID>
49                                   <PartitionID>{3}</PartitionID>
50                                 </Object>
51                               </Process>"
52                 , dID, cID, mgID, pID);
53         }
54     }
55 }
```



**Figure 12.22** The code of the Generate Processing Script task.

The Main function instantiates a Server object. The ConnectionManager variable references the SSAS connection manager to obtain the server name and the initial catalog from its properties. On line 25, I connect to the Analysis Services server. Next, I obtain a reference to the Adventure Works database (line 27). As I pointed out, tabular metadata is defined as multidimensional artifacts. The metadata defines a single cube that encapsulates all measure groups (tables). Its identifier is "Model". Line 29 obtains a reference to the cube. Then, I reference the ResellerSales measure group by its name. Each measure group in the cube corresponds to a table in the tabular model and the name of the measure group matches the table name.

Since I used a naming convention when setting up the table partitions in the format <TableName> <Year>, I can reference the latest partition by name by concatenating the name of its parent measure group and the current year. However, since the Adventure Works database includes data until the year 2008 only, I use the last partition (line 35).

Then, I call the GenerateProcessingScript helper function which returns the actual processing script. This function uses the String.Format .NET function to replace the placeholders that are defined in curly brackets. The {0} placeholder is replaced with the database identifier, the {1} placeholder with the cube identifier, the {3} placeholder is replaced with the measure group identifier, and the {4} placeholder is replaced with the partition identifier. Finally, the Main function stores the script in the ProcessingScript variable (line 37).

The actual partition processing happens in the Process Partition task. This task is an instance of the Analysis Services Execute DDL Task. I configured it to obtain the script from the ProcessingScript variable, as shown in **Figure 12.23**. As with the Process Update package, the control flow uses the Process Database task (another Analysis Services Execute DDL Task) to process the database with Process Recalc in order to update the database-level objects, which get invalidated after you use Process Data.

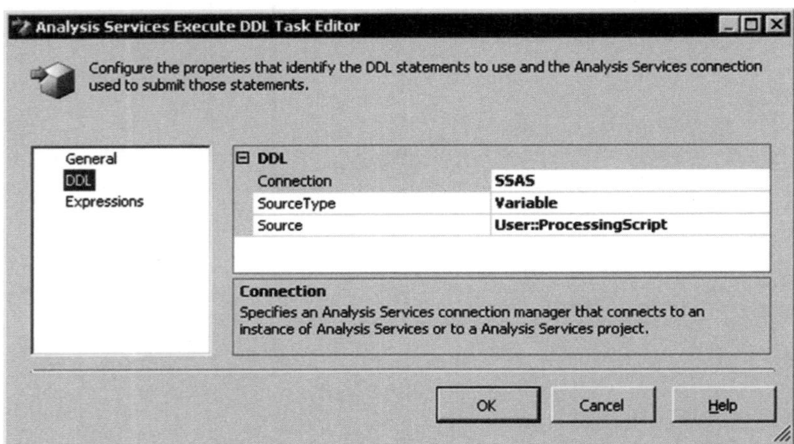


**Figure 12.23** The Process Partition task is configured to obtain the scrip from the ProcessingScript variable.

If you're looking for additional resources for AMO programming, the Adventure Works for SQL Server 2012 samples include an AMO2Tabular project that demonstrates how to create a tabular model with AMO. You can download the Adventure Works for SQL Server 2012 samples from http://bit.ly/2012aw.

## 12.5.2 Scripting with PowerShell

Windows PowerShell is a task automation framework, consisting of a command-line shell and an associated scripting language that's integrated with the .NET Framework. Like other shells, Windows PowerShell gives you access to the file system on the computer. In addition, Windows PowerShell providers enable you to access other data stores, such as the Windows registry. The PowerShell provider for AMO allows administrators to write scripts for managing Multidimensional and Tabular models. For more information about PowerShell for AMO, refer to the "PowerShell Reference for Analysis Management Objects" topic in Books Online at http://bit.ly/AMOpowershell.

### *Getting started with PowerShell management*

In PowerShell, administrative tasks are performed by executing cmdlets (pronounced "command-lets"). A cmdlet is a specialized .NET class that implements a particular operation. The AMO PowerShell cmdlets work for both multidimensional and tabular models. Similar to AMO, the cmdlets express tabular metadata in multidimensional artifacts, such as cubes, dimensions, and measure groups. There are two ways to get started with PowerShell management for Analysis Services:

- The sqlps snap-in – Navigate to the \Program Files (x86)\Microsoft SQL Server \110\Tools\Binn folder, right-click the sqlps.exe file, and then click Run as Administrator.
- Windows PowerShell – Start Windows PowerShell from the Administrative Tools program group, and then import the Analysis Services cmdlets by entering the following command, and then pressing Enter:

```
Import-Module 'C:\Program Files (x86)\Microsoft SQL Server\110\Tools\PowerShell\Modules\SQLASCMDLETS'
```

**NOTE** You need to have SQL Server Management Studio (SSMS) installed to get the AMO PowerShell cmdlets. If you're on a different machine than the server you want to manage, you'll need to navigate to the appropriate server. To do this, issue the following command (see **Figure 12.24**):
cd sqlas\<Machine Name>\<Instance Name>

```
Administrator: C:\Program Files (x86)\Microsoft SQL Server\110\Tools\Binn\SQLPS.exe
Microsoft SQL Server PowerShell
Version 11.0.1750.32
Microsoft Corp. All rights reserved.

PS SQLSERVER:\> cd sqlas\elitex\tabular
PS SQLSERVER:\sqlas\elitex\tabular> dir

Collections
-----------
Assemblies
Databases
Roles
Traces


PS SQLSERVER:\sqlas\elitex\tabular> _
```

**Figure 12.24** Navigate to the Analysis Services instance before you execute the cmdlets.

Once you've navigated to the server, you can start calling cmdlets either interactively or by supplying all the parameters in a single line. If you're unsure what parameters a given cmdlet takes, use the help command to see the cmdlet syntax, such as the following:

```
help Backup-ASDatabase
```

### *Backing up databases*

You can use the Backup-ASDatabase and Restore-ASDatabase cmdlets to back up and restore Analysis Services databases. The following example backs up the Adventure Works database to the default backup folder by calling the Backup-ASDatabase cmdlet interactively:

```
PS SQLSERVER:\sqlas\elitex\tabular>Backup-ASDatabase
cmdlet Backup-ASDatabase at command pipeline position 1
Supply values for the following parameters:
BackupFile: Adventure Works.abf
Name: Adventure Works
The database backup operation completed successfully.
```

Notice that unlike AMO, the cmdlets take object names as parameters and not object identifiers. This example supplies all parameters in a single line, including a password to encrypt the backup:

```
Backup-ASDatabase "C:\Temp\Adventure Works.abf" "Adventure Works" -ApplyCompression -FilePassword $P@ssword
```

And, the following command can be used to restore the database from the backup file:

```
Restore-ASDatabase "C:\temp\Adventure Works.abf" "Adventure Works" -AllowOverwrite -Password $P@ssword
```

### *Processing objects*

PowerShell for AMO includes Invoke-ProcessDimension and Invoke-ProcessPartition cmdlets for processing dimensions and partitions respectively. The following command processes the ResellerSales 2008 partition in the Reseller Sales measure group with the ProcessData processing option.

```
Invoke-ProcessPartition -CubeName "Adventure Works" -MeasureGroupName "ResellerSales" -Name "ResellerSales 2008" -Database
"Adventure Works" -ProcessType ProcessData
```

Since there isn't a cmdlet for processing the entire database, you need to use the Invoke-ASCmd cmdlet to execute the required XMLA processing script, as I'll demonstrate in a moment.

**NOTE** PowerShell for AMO includes an Invoke-ProcessCube cmdlet. However, this cmdlet is for Multidimensional and it's not supported for Tabular models.

### *Managing roles*

You can use the Add-RoleMember and Remove-RoleMember cmdlets to add and remove members to and from an Analysis Services security role. The following example adds a user, whose Windows login is prologika\bob, to the Adventure Works role in the Adventure Works database:

```
Add-RoleMember -MemberName prologika\bob -Database "Adventure Works" -RoleName "Adventure Works"
```

### *Sending XMLA scripts*

When the provided cmdlets are not enough, you can use the Invoke-ASCmd to send any XMLA script to the server. The following example processes the Adventure Works database with the Process Recalc processing option:

```
$processRecalcScript = "<Process xmlns='http://schemas.microsoft.com/analysisservices/2003/engine'>
<Type>ProcessRecalc</Type><Object><DatabaseID>Adventure Works</DatabaseID></Object></Process>"

Invoke-ASCmd -Query $processRecalcScript
```

First, I load the XMLA script in the processRecalcScript variable. Then, I call the Invoke-ASCmd cmdlet to send the XMLA script. Invoke-ASCmd also takes –Server and –Credentials parameters if you need to connect to the server. If you want to read the XMLA script from a file, substitute the –InputFile parameter for the –Query parameter.

## 12.6 Summary

As an administrator, you need to ensure that the server functions correctly and performs optimally. In this chapter, I covered essential management techniques that will help you meet this goal. The tool that you rely on most to carry out various management tasks is SQL Server Management Studio (SSMS). Use the server properties dialog to configure the server settings. Use the scripting functionality of Management Studio to script and automate tasks.

Analysis Services provides different options for database deployment. The Deployment Wizard allows you to deploy the database definition while preserving the storage and security settings of the target server. Use database synchronization to synchronize two databases. Add backup and restore database tasks to your management plan in case you must quickly restore a database. Consider attaching and detaching when you want to copy the database to another location or when you scale out Analysis Services.

Analysis Services provides various options for monitoring the server. Use SQL Server Profiler to watch the server activity in real time or to replay a captured activity. Consider the Windows Performance Monitor to track performance counters when you need to load test a server. Inspect the server logs to troubleshoot server errors. Query dynamic management views (DMVs) to review the server utilization.

Finally, when scripting and management tools are not enough, you can write code to automate management tasks. SQL Server Integration Services (SSIS) and .NET-based management clients can integrate with the Analysis Management Objects (AMO) library to manage programmatically all the aspects of a deployed tabular model. Finally, Analysis Services provides prepackaged PowerShell cmdlets to script common management tasks.

With this chapter we've reached the last stop of our Tabular journey. I sincerely hope that this book has helped you understand how Analysis Services and Tabular can be a powerful platform for delivering pervasive BI. As you've seen, you can use Tabular to implement a wide range of BI solutions for personal, team, and organizational BI on a single platform – Analysis Services.

- Personal BI (or self-service BI) – If you are a business user, you can build BI models for self-service data exploration with the tool that you probably use the most – Microsoft Excel. With a few clicks you can import the data into PowerPivot for Excel, build pivot reports, and gain valuable insights.
- Team BI – Once your PowerPivot model is ready, you can share the reports and dashboards you've implemented with other coworkers by deploying the PowerPivot model to SharePoint. Not only can your teammates view the reports that are included in the workbook, but they can also author their own operational and ad hoc reports that connect to your model.
- Organizational BI (or corporate BI) – If you're a BI pro, you can enhance the tabular models developed by your business users and deploy them to a dedicated server for added performance and security. Or, if you are starting new projects, you might find Tabular appealing because of its low learning curve for the rapid implementation of simple analytical models.

Don't forget to download the source code and watch the online video tutorials for the exercises that are marked with a play icon (▶) next to the section title. You can find this material at this book's companion web page (http://bit.ly/thebismbook). Happy data analyzing with Tabular!

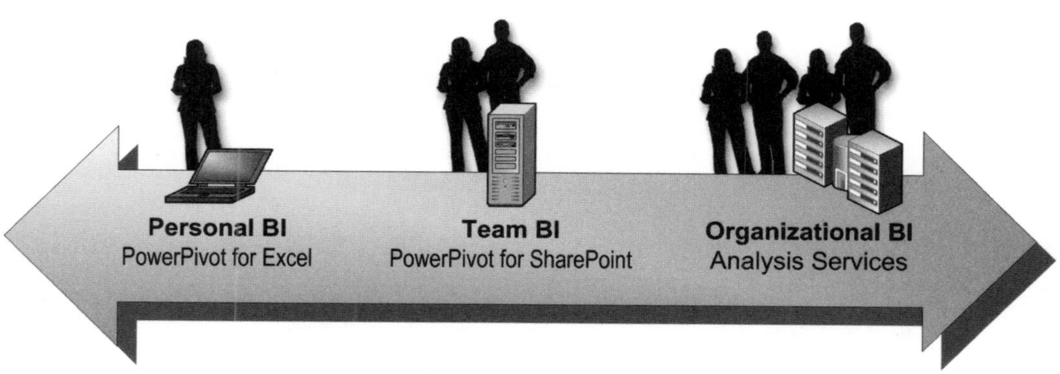

# *Appendix A*

# Glossary of Terms

The following table lists the most common BI-related terms and acronyms used in this book.

| Term | Acronym | Description |
|---|---|---|
| Analysis Services Tabular | | An instance of SQL Server 2012 Analysis Services that's configured in Tabular mode and is capable of hosting tabular models for organizational use. |
| Azure Marketplace | | The Windows Azure Marketplace is an online market buying, and selling finished software as a Service (SaaS) applications and premium datasets. |
| Business Intelligence Semantic Model | BISM | A unifying name that includes both multidimensional (OLAP) and tabular (relational) features of Microsoft SQL Server 2012 Analysis Services. |
| Corporate BI | | Same as Organizational BI. |
| Cube | | An OLAP structure organized in a way that facilitates data aggregation, such as to answer queries for historical and trend analysis. |
| Data Analysis Expressions | DAX | An Excel-like formula language for defining custom calculations and for querying tabular models. |
| DirectQuery | | An alternative storage mode for organizational tabular models, where the server generates and sends queries to the data source without caching the data. |
| Dimension (lookup) table | | A table that represents a business subject area and provides contextual information to each row in a fact table, such as Product, Customer, and Date. |
| Extraction, transformation, loading | ETL | Processes extract from data sources, clean the data, and load the data into a target database, such as data warehouse. |
| Fact table | | A table that keeps a historical record of numeric measurements (facts), such as the ResellerSales in the Adventure Works model. |
| Key Performance Indicator | KPI | A key performance indicator (KPI) is a quantifiable measure that is used to measure the company performance, such as Profit or Return On Investment (ROI). |
| Measure | | A numeric fact that is stored and aggregated in an OLAP cube, such as SalesAmount, Tax, OrderQuantity. |
| Multidimensional | | The OLAP path of BISM that allows BI professionals to implement multidimensional cubes. |
| Multidimensional Expressions | MDX | A query language for Multidimensional for defining custom calculations and querying OLAP cubes. |
| Multidimensional OLAP | MOLAP | A cube storage mode where the data and aggregations are stored in the OLAP server. |
| Online Analytical Processing | OLAP | A system that is designed to quickly answer multidimensional analytical queries in order to facilitate data exploration and data mining. |

| Term | Acronym | Description |
|---|---|---|
| Online Transactional Processing | OLTP | A system that stores data from a transaction-oriented application, such as Point of Sale (POS) applications. |
| Perspective | | A logical view that exposes a subset of the model metadata (dictionary) to reduce the perceived complexity of the model. |
| Personal BI | | Targets business users and provides tools for implementing BI solutions for personal use, such as PowerPivot models, by importing and analyzing data without requiring specialized skills. |
| Power View | | A SharePoint-based reporting tool that allows business users to author interactive reports from PowerPivot models and from organizational tabular models. |
| PowerPivot for Excel | | A free add-in that extends the Excel capabilities to allow business users to implement personal BI models. |
| PowerPivot for SharePoint | | Included in SQL Server 2012, PowerPivot for SharePoint extends the SharePoint capabilities to support PowerPivot models. |
| Report Builder client | | Included in SQL Server 2008 and above, Report Builder allows power users to author paper-oriented, ad hoc reports from a variety of data sources, including multidimensional cubes and tabular models. |
| Relational OLAP | ROLAP | A cube storage mode where data and aggregations are stored in the relational database. |
| Self-service BI | | Same as Personal BI. |
| SharePoint Products and Technologies | SharePoint | A server-based platform for document management and collaboration that includes BI capabilities, such as hosting and managing PowerPivot models, reports, and dashboards. |
| SQL Server Analysis Services | SSAS | A SQL Server add-on, Analysis Services provides analytical and data mining services. The Business Intelligence Semantic Model represents the analytical services. |
| SQL Server Data Tools | SSDT | Succeeding Business Intelligence Development Studio (BIDS), SQL Server Data Tools is an integrated environment for database and BI developers to implement SQL Server projects within the Visual Studio IDE. |
| SQL Server Integration Services | SSIS | A SQL Server add-on, Integration Services is a platform for implementing extraction, transformation, and loading (ETL) processes. |
| SQL Server Management Studio | SSMS | A management tool that's bundled with SQL Server that allows administrators to manage Database Engine, Analysis Services, Reporting Services and Integration Services instances. |
| SQL Server Reporting Services | SSRS | A SQL Server add-on, Reporting Services is a server-based reporting platform for the creation, management, and delivery of standard and ad hoc reports. |
| Snowflake schema | | Unlike a star schema, a snowflake schema has some dimension tables that relate to other dimension tables and not directly to the fact table. |
| Star schema | | A model schema where a fact table is surrounded by dimension tables and these dimension tables reference directly the fact table. |
| Tabular | | Tabular is the relational side of BISM that allows business users and BI professionals to implement relational-like (tabular) models. |
| Team BI | | Provides tools to allow business users to share BI solutions that they create with co-workers, such as by deploying PowerPivot models to SharePoint. |
| VertiPaq | | The storage engine of Tabular, VertiPaq compresses and stores data in memory. |

# index

## A



## B



## C

## F



## G



## H



## I



## J



## K



## L

## Q



## R

## S



## T

## U



## V



## W



## X

## Y

# *Also by Teo Lachev*

## Applied Microsoft SQL Server 2008 Reporting Services

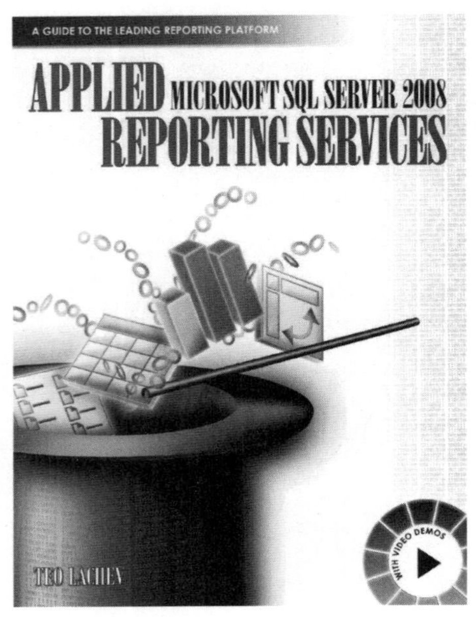


ISBN 978-0976635314
**Publisher website:** http://bit.ly/ssrs2008
**Amazon:** http://amzn.to/ssrs2008a
**B&N:** http://bit.ly/ssrs2008b

Supplying much-needed technological information to workers, administrators, and developers, this book shows you how to apply Reporting Services in real life to build innovative Business Intelligence solutions that drive decisions. Information workers will learn how to design feature-rich standard and ad hoc reports. The book gives administrators the necessary background to install, upgrade, and manage the report environment. It teaches developers ways to extend Reporting Services and to integrate it with a wide range of applications.

The book doesn't assume any prior experience with Microsoft Reporting Services. It is designed as an easy-to-follow guide for safely navigating the most intricate aspects of the technology. New concepts are introduced with step-by-step instructions and hands-on lessons. Video presentations help the reader stay on track when a picture is worth more than a thousand words.

*The book is available in bookstores worldwide. Prices and availability may be subject to change.*

Also, check out our online and onsite BI training classes at http://prologika.com/training/training.aspx

- ✓ Analysis Services
- ✓ Reporting Services
- ✓ PowerPivot